Along the Road

Along the Road

Aspects of Causewayed Enclosures in South Scandinavia and Beyond

Lutz Klassen

East Jutland Museum

Moesgaard Museum

Aarhus University Press

Along the Road

Aspects of Causewayed Enclosures in South Scandinavia and Beyond

By Lutz Klassen
East Jutland Museum Publications vol. 2
© Museum Østjylland and Aarhus University Press 2014

Graphic design: Jørgen Sparre
Typesetting: Ea Rasmussen
Cover illustration: Photo by Gitte Lauritsen
Printed at Narayana Press, Denmark

ISBN 978 87 7124 449 6

AARHUS UNIVERSITY PRESS
Langelandsgade 177
DK-8200 Aarhus N
www.unipress.dk

Gazelle Book Services Ltd.
White Cross Mills, Hightown
Lancaster LA1 4XS, England
www.gazellebooks.com

ISD
70 Enterprise Drive
Bristol, CT 06010
USA
www.isdistribution.com

Published with the financial support of

Carlsberg Foundation
Farumgaard-Fonden
Dronning Margrethe II's Arkæologiske Fond

Contents

· ·

285   # Part II

Geophysical survey of potential Neolithic enclosure sites in Djursland

By Lutz Klassen & Christina Klein

Preface

· ·

This book is the outcome of a research project conducted both at Moesgård Museum in 2011-2012 and East Jutland Museum in 2013-2014. The project was made possible by generous grants from the Carlsberg Foundation, the Danish Agency for Culture (Kulturstyrelsen) and Dronning Margrethe II's Arkæologiske Fond. I wish to express my thanks to all contributors for giving me the chance to deal with the fascinating topic of causewayed enclosures.

The Carlsberg Foundation, Farumgaard-Fonden and Dronning Margrethe II's Arkæologiske Fond have graciously provided the means necessary for the printing of this volume.

A tremendous number of colleagues have contributed to the study with invaluable help covering everything from providing unpublished information, helping with the GIS, helping to identify finds from field walking to securing grants and, not least, participation and contributions in many fruitful discussions. In no particular order, this is true for Jens Andresen, Bo Madsen, Niels H. Andersen, Jan Skamby Madsen, Jacob Kveiborg, Tobias Danborg Torfing, Søren H. Andersen, Uffe Rasmussen, Henrik Skousen, Peter Moe Astrup, Steffen Terp Laursen, Niels N. Johannsen, Michael Vinter Jensen and Peter Jensen (all from Moesgård), Johannes Müller, Martin Furholt, Jan-Piet Brozio, Hauke Dibbern, Franziska Hage and Wiebke Kierleis (all from Kiel), Stina Troldtoft Jensen (Varde), Jytte Nielsen, Jens-Henrik Bech (both Thisted), Samuel van Willingen (Zurich), Torsten Madsen (Galten), Pierre Pétrequin (Gray), Serge Cassen (Nantes), Daniel Nösler (Wilhelmshaven), Anders Ödman (Lund), Jonas Beran (Langenweißbach), Esben Aarsleff (Hillerød), Inge Kjær Kristensen (Struer), Signe Lützau Pedersen, Lennart Madsen and Frauke Witte (all Haderslev), Lis Helles Olesen (Holstebro), Günther Wetzel, Joachim Henning (Frankfurt), Christian Jeunesse (Strasbourg), Duncan Garrow (Liverpool), Knut Rassmann (Frankfurt), Poul Otto Nielsen (Copenhagen), Alasdair Whittle (Cardiff), Peder Gammeltoft (Aarhus), Doris Mischka (Erlangen), Miroslav Dobeš (Prague), Irenäus Matuschik (Freiburg), Niels Hartmann (Kalundborg), Magnus Artursson, Magnus Andersson and Björn Wallebom (all from Lund). My apologies to any I may have forgotten to mention here.

Special thanks to Niels-Axel Boas, Esben Kannegaard and Lisbeth Wincentz for providing a wealth of unpublished information regarding the causewayed enclosures of Djursland, to Benedikt Knoche for inspiring discussions on prehistoric roads and enclosures, to Ea Rasmussen for the graphical production of this book, to Jens Møller Simonsen for his hospitality, to Christina Klein for managing the geophysical field campaign under challenging conditions, to Samantha Reiter and Jens Damm for correcting the English language of the text and to Sanne Lind Hansen and Aarhus University Press for the fine cooperation regarding the publication of this book.

Randers, May 2014

..

Part I

Along the Road

Aspects of Causewayed Enclosures in South Scandinavia and Beyond

By Lutz Klassen

1 Introduction

In 1968, the first causewayed enclosure was found in the northern TRB distribution area in Büdelsdorf in Schleswig-Holstein (Hingst 1971a; 1971b; 1973; 1974). This discovery was followed shortly thereafter by others in Sarup, Denmark (Andersen, N.H. 1974; 1975a; 1975b). Since that time, an average of one such site has been found in the region every year. To date, the total number of confirmed enclosures nears 40. Given that a considerable number of probable or possible enclosures have yet to be assessed, it is very likely that several hundred of these perplexing sites where in use during the Neolithic in Southern Scandinavia.

The discovery of this new type of site and the concomitant development of new theoretical approaches had a marked impact both on settlement studies and the development of new models for the understanding of social and economical change in TRB society. This is true both in a local and in a regional perspective. The local perspective is best exemplified by the efforts of N.H. Andersen both with the Sarup enclosures as well as their surroundings (see a selection of N.H. Andersen's numerous publications in the reference list). For the regional perspective, by contrast, one should look to T. Madsen's work in eastern Jutland (1982; 1988) as well as a number of national and supranational surveys (i.e. Nielsen, P.O. 1993; 2004; Andersen, N.H. 1997; Klatt 2009; Larsson, L. 2012).

In the early days of archaeological investigation into causewayed enclosures, the best-favoured interpretation of their function revolved around the useage as fortifications (see the above-mentioned papers about Büdelsdorf and Sarup). However, doubts concerning this initial interpretation emerged rather quickly (Madsen, T. 1978b). Since the 1980s (Andersen, N.H. 1981; Madsen, T. 1982; 1988), causewayed enclosures in northern Germany, Denmark and southern Sweden have generally been viewed as sites for the assembly of larger groups of people in the broadest sense of the word. Just as in the first years of enclosure research, this interpretation is often reflected in the terminology used in site descriptions (Andersen, N.H. 1993).

In his recent study of the enclosures, Klatt (2009, 75ff.) gives a detailed summary of the various interpretations discussed over the course of the last four decades. His final conclusion epitomizes the current state of research on the subject, namely that causewayed enclosures were likely to have been assembly places where larger groups of people met to engage in ritual activities (such as those relating to death and burial) as well as secular social engagements and various other activities related to barter and exchange. Among the more recent debate contributions, it is only Haßmann (2000, 111, 119 and 175) who diverges from this widely held view of enclosures as assembly places. Due to the finds of large numbers of arrowheads at Büdelsdorf, he leans towards a more traditional interpretation of fortified settlements, at least as regards the site at Büdelsdorf.

The important role played by causewayed enclosures in settlement studies is due in no small part to their functional interpretation, as mentioned above. If one follows an interpretation of the sites as assembly places for people from a larger region, this allows for theoretical inferences in terms of group and territory sizes. This last is especially true when all certain or suspected enclosure sites are mapped within a region, as was done for eastern Jutland by T. Madsen (1988)(Fig. 1). Furthermore, as described by the same author (1982; 1988), many enclosure sites developed into huge settlements over the course of Middle Neolithic A, and therefore naturally flow into the course of settlement research. In fact, a considerable proportion of what we now know as enclosures were known as settlement sites long before they were recognized as causewayed enclosures. A classic example of this phenomenon is from the site of Trelleborg on Zealand. Trelleborg was first excavated in the 1930s (Mathiassen 1944), but was not recognized as an enclosure until 1982 (Andersen, N.H. 1982). It should be noted, however, that there appear to be regional differences in the post-constructional use of the enclosures. Increasingly larger settlement sites in the later parts of the TRB are absent from northern Germany (see Hinz et al. 2012), southern Sweden (Larsson, L. 2012) and northern Jutland.

Until recently, the accepted chronology of enclosure construction in South Scandinavia involved a short period of intense building activity in the late Early and early Middle Neolithic (EN II and MN A I, ca. 3500-3200/3100 BC). Recently, however, a certain amount of evidence has emerged to support the start of enclosure construction in the 37th or possibly even the 38th century BC. On the opposite end of the time scale, the evidence from the site of Kainsbakke possibly leads to a further blurring of an erstwhile clear picture of a short causewayed enclosure construction horizon in South Scandinavia (see the detailed discussion in chapters 3 and 10.3.1).

Settlement archaeological studies have yet to be adapted to these new insights into enclosure construction chronology. They emphasize the role of these sites during a phase of intensive change generally associated with the late Early and initial Middle

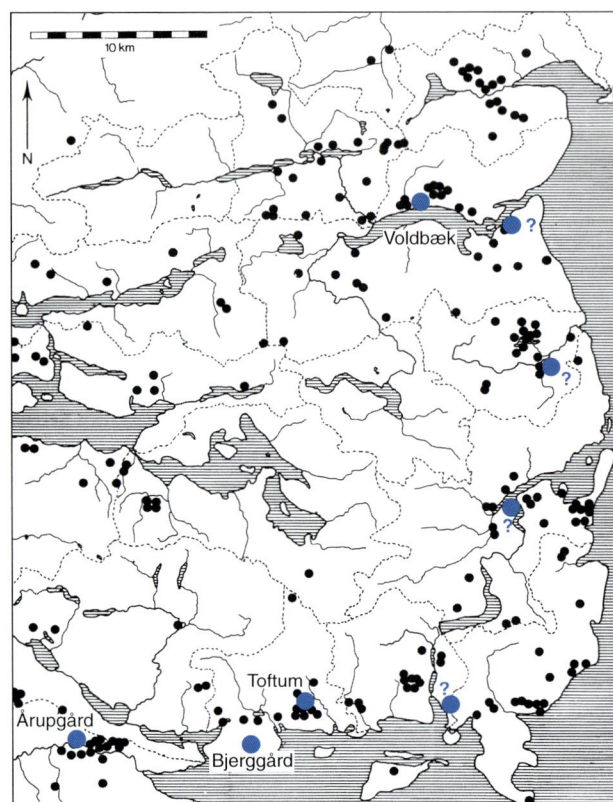

Fig. 1 | *The results of T. Madsen's east Jutland study in the 1980s had a profound influence not only on the interpretation of the origins of causewayed enclosures in the TRB Culture of South Scandinavia, but also on the interpretation of the regional organisation of TRB settlements around those enclosures. Indeed, his fingerprints are still felt within this area of research. On this map, large dots with site names refer to certain causewayed enclosures, large dots with question marks depict suspected causewayed enclosures and small dots mark the locations of megalithic graves (from Madsen 1988).*

Neolithic during which social organisation, material culture, burial customs and economy were in flux. However, it can be argued that the changes that have thus far exclusively been associated with the late Early Neolithic (EN II) started in the later phases of EN I (see Furholt 2011b). Therefore, it is possible that the models which deal with the interrelation of enclosures and ordinary settlements, graves etc. possibly only need minor modifications.

The study conducted here takes a new look at causewayed enclosures in South Scandinavia based on a research area restricted to the Djursland Peninsula in eastern Jutland. Given that the awareness of as many enclosures as possible is necessary in any attempt to evaluate their significance for Neolithic societies within a given area, a major part of this work is devoted to the development of predictive modelling for the detection of enclosures in the landscape. It is only in relation to this step that it is possible to engage with such questions as the reasons for which certain locations were chosen as enclosure sites and how these relate to the history of Neolithic settlement within the wider region. The results can then be compared to T. Madsen's work in eastern Jutland. The latter is at the heart of practically all settlement archaeological studies of the period under consideration in South Scandinavia. However, (at least with regard to causewayed enclosures), it has never been critically reviewed nor tested by comparisons with the results from other regions.

An important but never discussed part of Madsen's study is devoted to the role that enclosure building groups in neighbouring parts of Europe played in the process of introducing causewayed enclosures in the northern TRB Group. As will become apparent over the course of the arguments presented within this study, this European background is of much greater importance for the understanding of local processes related to causewayed enclosures than has hitherto been assumed. This is also true for the focal area of this study: the Djursland Peninsula. Therefore, a separate section is devoted to examining the European dimension of the Scandinavian enclosures in closer detail.

2 The area of investigation

The Djursland Peninsula in eastern Jutland was selected as region of concentration for several reasons (Fig. 2). The first is of a logistical nature and simply relates to travelling distances to and from the museum at which the research was conducted. Relative proximity ensured easy access on a daily basis without the need to establish a permanent base elsewhere in the research area itself. While the region around Århus would have been even better suited in this regard, it was disregarded due to the vast extent of modern day settlement around the city (with its extended suburbs, Århus is the second largest city in Denmark). The modern settlement boundaries cover a vast area, particularly along the coast, which would have been of particular interest to Neolithic peoples for the construction of causewayed enclosures. In fact, at least one causewayed enclosure (the Voldbæk site) has been located within the city limits of what is now an Århusian suburb. Another, more central location (Langenæs) has also been put forward as a potential enclosure site (Madsen, T. 1988).While it would thus have been possible to point out potential locations for enclosures in the area around Århus, controlling the prediction would have been problematic, due to the vast extent of modern settlement in the area.

A second important argument for the choice of Djursland as research area is the richness of the region in terms of megalithic graves and burial mounds, especially given that these kinds of sites play an important role in the predictive modelling approach (see below). Furthermore, a large number of Neolithic sites are already known from Djursland. Moreover, for part of the area, a thorough study of the relations between surviving monuments and known Neolithic sites on one side and the once present number of these sites/monuments has already been carried out (Vedsted 1986). Djursland therefore has excellent potential for conducting and contextualising the present research.

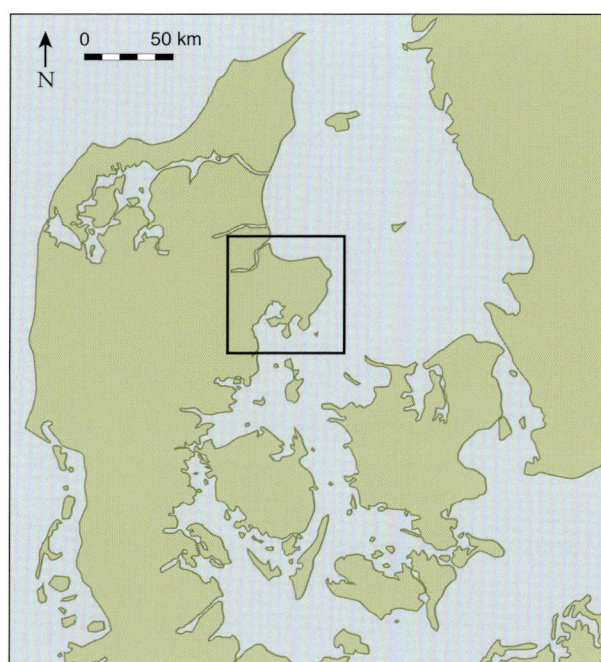

Fig. 2 | *Djursland is a peninsula which juts out into the Kattegat from the east coast of Jutland, Denmark.*

Finally, thanks to the efforts of N. A. Boas, Djursland is the region with the largest number by far of known Neolithic enclosures within the northern TRB Group distribution area (Boas 2001; see also the catalogue in Klatt 2009, from which a number of unpublished sites are missing). When all arguments are combined, the region therefore offered the best opportunities for the establishment of a model for the search of as-yet undiscovered sites on the basis of a comparatively large body of regional data.

The Djursland Peninsula juts out from the east coast of Jutland, between the present towns of Århus in the south and Randers in the north. There is no generally agreed-upon western border for the area. For this study, a border has been arbitrarily established running north to south between the villages of Uggelhuse (at the bottom of Randers Fjord) and Lisbjerg (at the bottom of the fossil Egå Fjord). The resulting area has a maximum east to west extent of ca. 48 km and a maximum north to south extent of ca. 50 km.

Some parts of Djursland have been excluded from the research area, either in order to reduce the area to be covered, or because these sub-regions lacked characteristics or data crucial to the predictive modelling employed here (burial mounds, well-defined watercourses)(Fig. 3). Due to these reasons, the former island of Rougsø in the northwestern part of Djursland as well as the southern part of Mols Peninsula in the southwest, Ebeltoft Peninsula in the southeast as well as an area measuring ca. 8 x 9 km in the central southern parts of Djursland were not included in this analysis (for a detailed description of the problems relating to the latter sub-region see chapter 7.1.4). The actual area under investigation thus measures ca. 48 km from east to west and 39 km from north

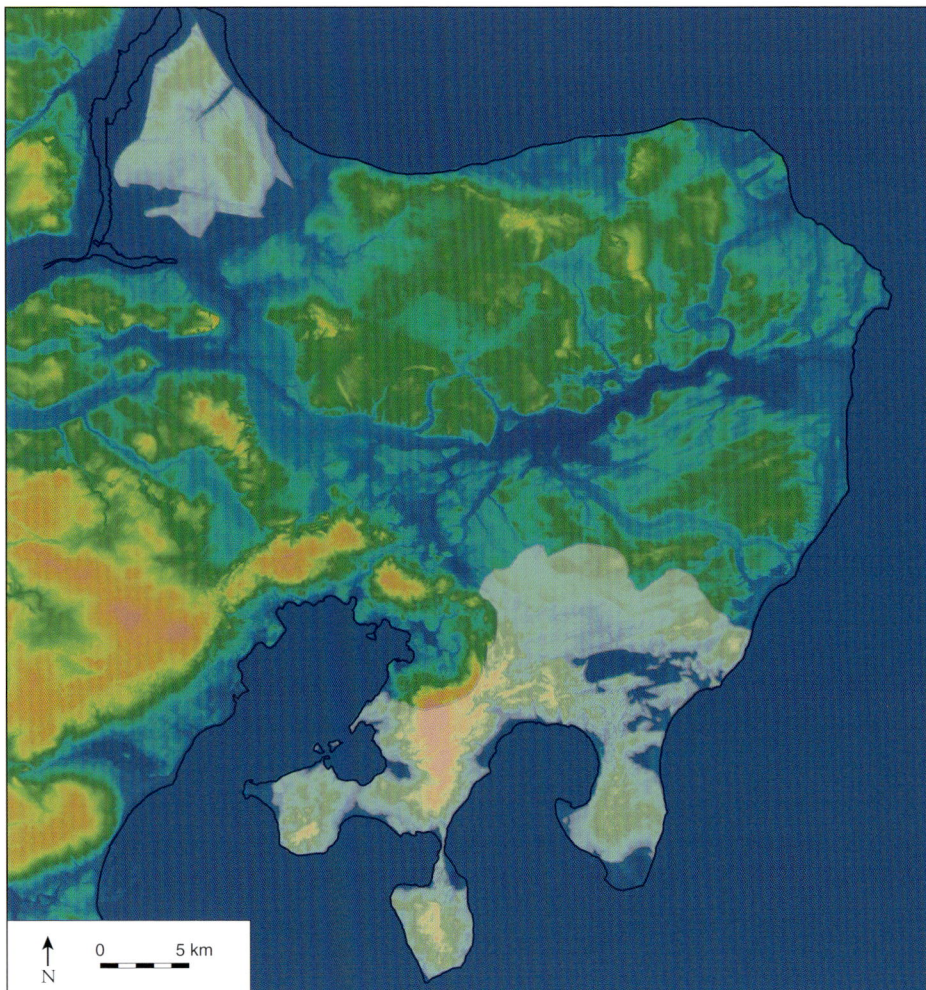

Fig. 3 | *Digital elevation model of the study area indicating disregarded sub-regions (light shading). The borders of the excluded sub-regions were partially determined by the location of the Neolithic coastline, as this diverged from that of the present day (see Fig. 4).*

to south. Comparatively large parts of this area are made up of firths and bays. The Neolithic land surface area covered by the present investigation measures ca. 1045 km².

Since the end of the last Ice Age, Djursland (as was the case with all of South Scandinavia) underwent dramatic changes with regard to its terrestrial-maritime relationship (see chapter 7.1.1). In the early Subboreal (approximately at the time of enclosure construction), a number of smaller (and one very large) fjords stretched far into areas which are currently used as agricultural land (Fig. 4). Kolindsund, the largest of these, split the peninsula into a number of islands. This fjord was ca. two km wide and approximately 10 m deep. It later turned into a freshwater lake due to isostatic land

rise and the development of beach ridges which closed its entries. In the narrow western parts, intensive growth of peat gradually transformed the lake into a bog. The wider and deeper eastern part remained a lake (Denmark's largest) until the later parts of the 19th century, when it was finally drained in the interest of increased agricultural production.

Northern Djursland formed the largest of the Neolithic islands and included almost all land north of the fjord. It measured ca. 35 km east to west and 15 km north to south. Northern Djursland is a moraine plateau with smooth, rolling hills situated between ca. 40 and 60 m above sea level. Several large peat bogs (which might have been lakes in the Early Neolithic, at least in part) are found in this area. The predominant type of soil is

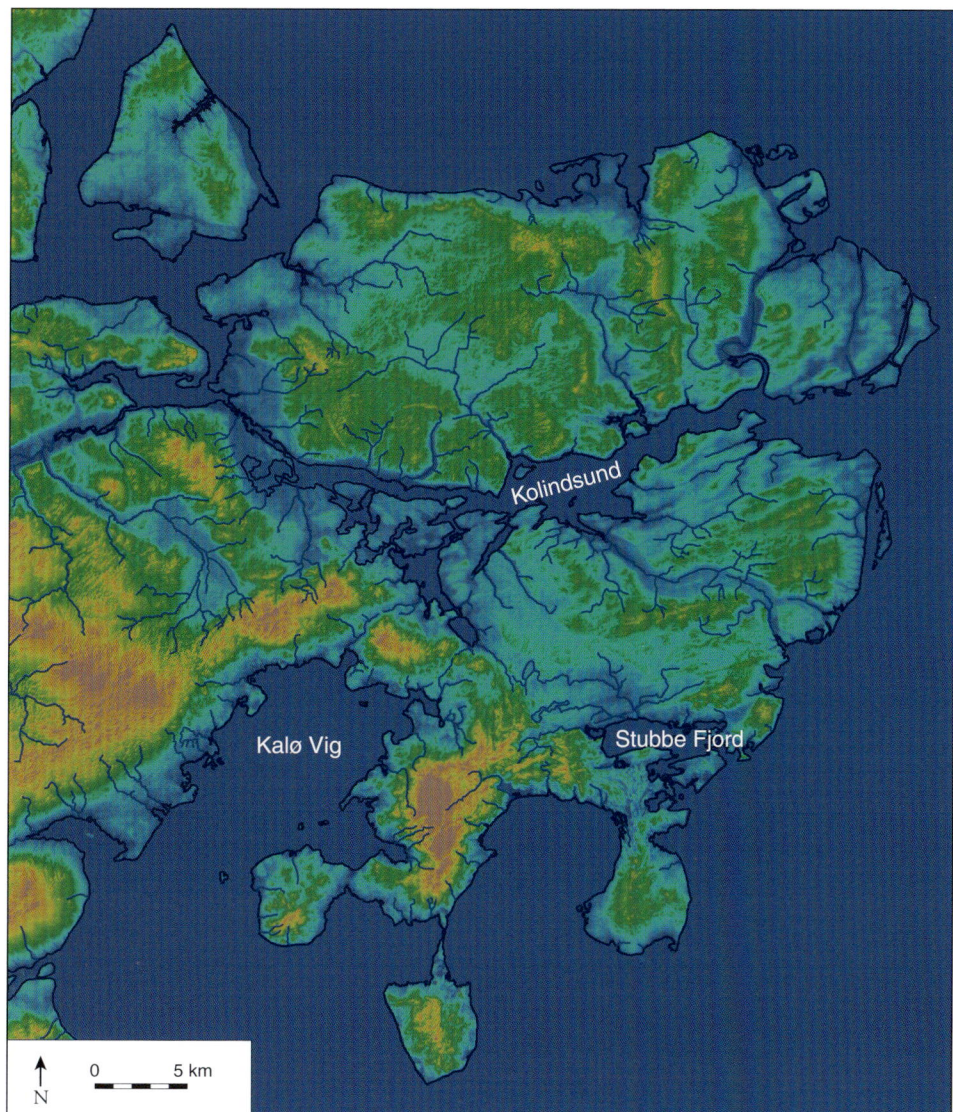

Fig. 4 | *Digital elevation model of Djursland, reconstructed for the early Subboreal (early 4th millennium BC). This model shows the approximate land-to-sea relationship at the time of causewayed enclosure construction. For details regarding the reconstruction, see chapter 7.1.1.*

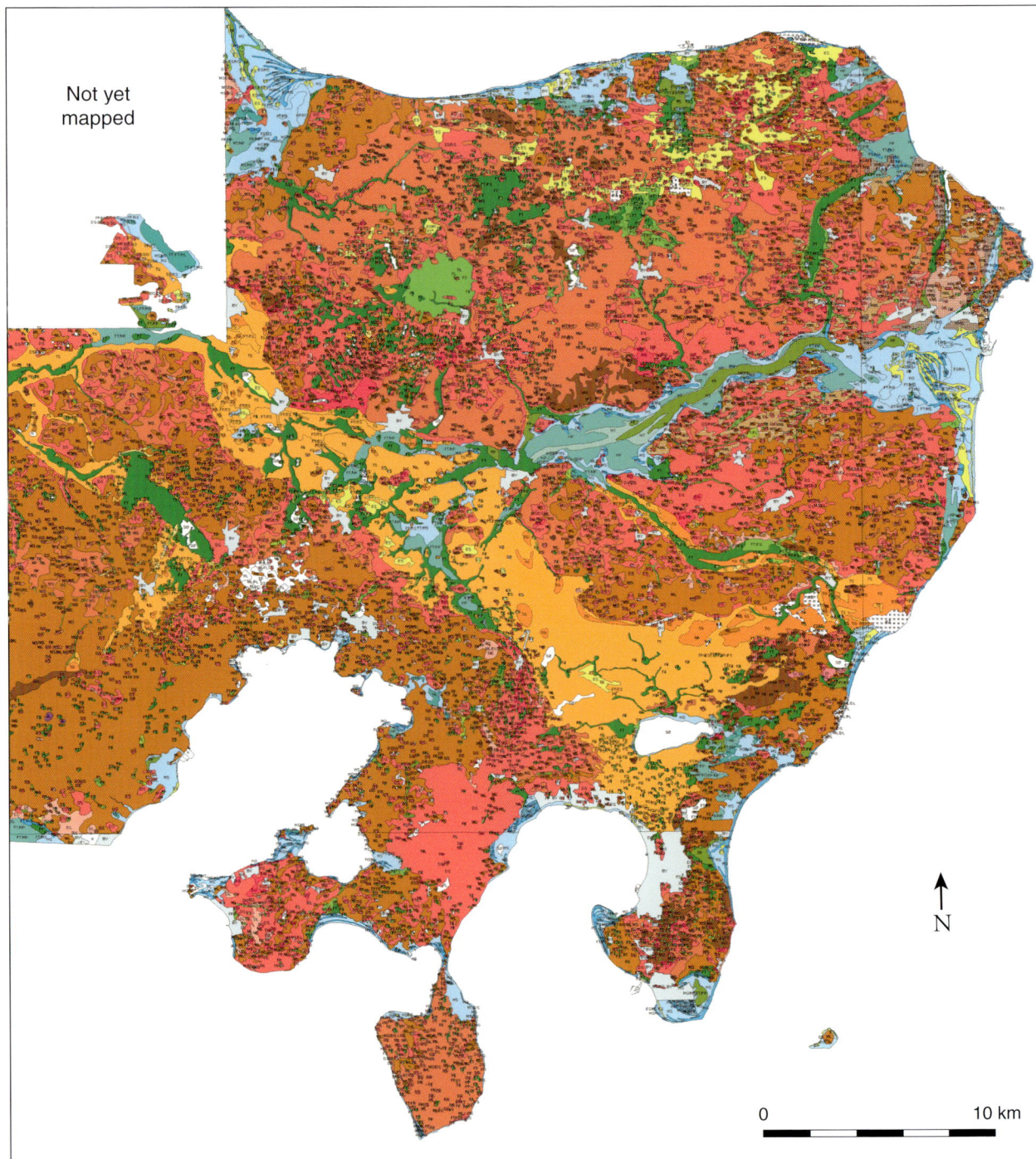

Fig. 5 | *Soil type map for Djursland (from Schack Pedersen/Strand Petersen 1997). Part of the area has not yet been mapped. Blue signatures: marine deposits, green signatures: freshwater deposits, yellow signatures: aeolian sand deposits, orange signatures: meltwater sand and gravel, brown signature: moraine clay, red and reddish brown signature: moraine and meltwater sand.*

sand, although more clayey soils are found in the northwest and northeast (Fig. 5). This kind of landscape is also found south of Kolindsund Fjord in the eastern part of Djursland. Due to the presence of some minor fjords and inlets which penetrated up to ca. 4 km inland, the northern and northeastern coasts of Djursland were much more irregular in shape than they are today.

From the central part of Djursland, a branch of Kolindsund penetrated up to eight km to the south. In its northern parts, this body of water was up to nine km wide and was filled with a number of large and small islands characterised by a complex coastline with low elevations.

In the western part of Djursland, a sandy, flat area called Tirstrup Hedeslette (2-5 km wide) follows the southern shores of Kolindsund Fjord. In Djursland's eastern parts, these meltwater deposits from the end of the last Ice Age follow the southern edge of the moraine plateau immediately south of Kolindsund. The area is characterized by very poor, sandy and gravelly soils.

Finally, south of Tirstrup Hedeslette, the peninsulas of Mols and (to a lesser degree) Ebeltoft are characterised by undulated moraine terrain. The coastal areas around Kalø Vig Bay as well as the eastern parts of Ebeltoft Peninsula are covered by clayey soil. The remainder is characterised by better-drained soil. The hills of the Mols Peninsula (which reach a maximum height of 137 m above sea level) are the highest in Djursland. They were pushed up by the last advance of glaciers in the last Ice Age, which also carved out the comparatively greater depths of Kalø Vig Bay near to the coast.

A detailed description of the landscape and its history was completed by Schack Pedersen and Strand Petersen (1997). A detailed description of the procedure employed here for the reconstruction of the Early Neolithic coastline is provided in a subsequent part of this text (see chapter 7.1.1).

3 Causewayed enclosures and related sites in Djursland

Within South Scandinavia, Djursland is the region with both the highest number and concentration of known causewayed enclosures (Fig. 6). This fact has gone largely unnoticed in the literature, certainly due to the fact that almost all of these sites remain practically unpublished, and – contrary to what was the case in eastern Jutland as investigated by T. Madsen – no further study of these enclosures' possible function etc. has been undertaken.

A short survey of published material is presented below, supplemented by a variety of unpublished information. I am grateful to N.A. Boas and L. Wincentz Rasmussen (the discoverers and excavators of most of these sites) as well as to E. Kannegaard Nielsen for the provision of valuable unpublished information.

Store Brokhøj, Vivild Parish

The Store Brokhøj enclosure is situated in the northwestern part of Djursland on a hummocky plateau overlooking the Kattegat (which lies less than 1000 m to the north) and Kolindsund Fjord (itself approximately equidistant to the west). Store Brokhøj is one of very few causewayed enclosures in South Scandinavia that is situated on a hilltop, the others being Bjerggård (Madsen, T. 1988, 309ff.) north of Horsens Fjord in eastern Jutland and Skævinge Boldbaner in the northern part of Zealand (Andersen, A.H. 1987). Because of a preliminary report (Madsen, B./Fiedel 1988),

it remains the best published of all Djursland's enclosures (Fig. 7).

The site was explored by rescue excavations in 1985 and 1986 after its discovery in some old gravel pits. Only a very small part of the enclosure (which consisted of a single ditch circuit) has been excavated. Its former size is unknown, and no sections through the ditches (ca. 1 m deep) have been published. Parts of what might have been a palisade trench with posts (up to 1.5 m deep) were observed, but the excavated parts of this feature formed no recognizable pattern. The most remarkable discovery on the site was that of a pottery kiln which still held the remains of ca. 15 misfired pots. Furthermore, large depositions of more than 70 pots were discovered in two excavated ditch segments. Madsen and Fiedel (1988, 84ff.) believe these large amounts of pottery were dumps of misfired vessels. However, as has recently been argued by Torfing (2011, 36f.), they more likely represent regular, ritual depositions of large amounts of pottery which had been produced on site.

The pottery from Store Brokhøj has been attributed to the late Early Neolithic (EN II) by Madsen and Fiedel (1988) as well as Ebbesen (1994, 78f.). Torfing's (2011; 2013) thorough analysis, however, argues that it most probably represents a local variant of the earliest Middle Neolithic (MN A Ia), which Torfing dubbed 'Blakbjerg-Brokhøj style'.

Due to the lack of any published profiles and stratigraphical information, it is not possible to

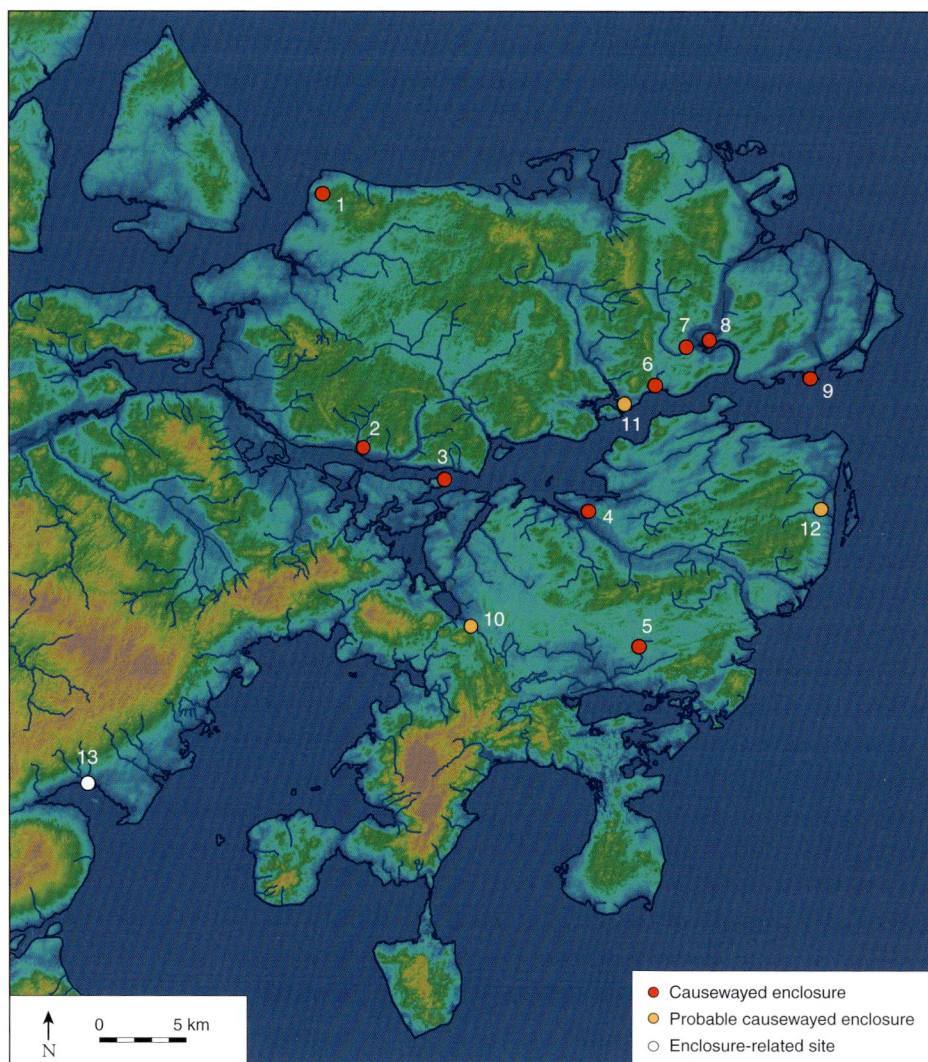

Fig. 6 | *The distribution of certain and probable causewayed enclosures as well as a single enclosure related site in Djursland. 1 Store Brokhøj, 2 Blakbjerg, 3 Ballegård, 4 Galgebakken, 5 Fuglslev, 6 Ginnerup, 7 Skærvad, 8 Kainsbakke, 9 Grenå, 10 Taastrup Kolindvej, 11 Fannerup, 12 Rævebakken, 13 Lystrup Kildevang I.*

● Causewayed enclosure
● Probable causewayed enclosure
○ Enclosure-related site

determine whether the Store Brokhøj enclosure was constructed in the MN A Ia, or whether it might have had an older phase. Unfortunately, no ^{14}C-dates have yet been taken. However, suitable samples for such dating may be available, as some bones were preserved, due to the deposition of marine shells in the ditch segments.

Blakbjerg, Marie Magdalene Parish

The Blakbjerg enclosure is situated on a moraine plateau just west of the town of Ryomgård. The site is bordered by water on three sides. To the south, a steep incline traces the 20 m elevation differential between the plateau on which the site is located and the former shores of Kolindsund. The deeply incised valleys of two minor rivers constitute the western and eastern borders of the site from which there is a magnificent view over Kolindsund to the south.

The site was discovered by schoolteacher and amateur archaeologist S. Andersen in 1917. However, it was first suspected to be a causewayed enclosure by Ebbesen some sixty years thereafter (Ebbesen 1979, 74). This suspicion was finally confirmed by the recent excavation of minor areas in 1991-92 (Boas 2001) as well as in 2004-2005 (unpublished). The material excavated by Andersen has been referred to in the literature on several occasions under different names ("Såbydal": Ebbesen 1979, 74; "Ryomgård": Madsen, T./Petersen 1984; Ebbesen 1994, 79, note 4). More recently, Torfing (2011; 2013) engaged intensively with the ceramics from the latest excavations.

Fig. 7 | *The Store Brok-høj enclosure in north-western Djursland is one of the rare hilltop enclosure sites in South Scandinavia. Over the course of a rescue ex-cavation, the remains of at least three ditch segments were discov-ered in a single circuit. A) Modern sand pit, B) Pottery kiln, C-E) Ditch segments (from Madsen/ Fiedel 1988).*

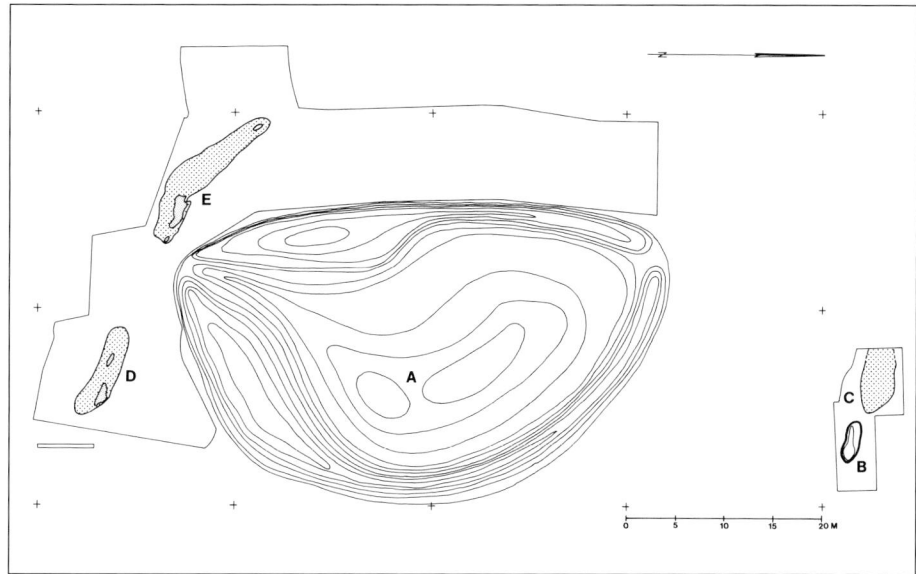

In the course of the earlier excavations, a single circuit of segmented ditches was demonstrated to exist along the eastern, northern and western sides of the plateau. However, whether there were ditch segments along the southern side of the pla-teau remains unknown. The outline of the site is almost rectangular. The latest excavations proved that the enclosure consisted (at least partially) of two circuits of ditches. The size of the enclosed area is approximately 9 ha. The excavator collected more than a thousand scrapers from the surface on a single day (Boas 2001).

Inside the ditch segments (up to 2.3 m deep and 4.5 m wide with a v-shaped cross-section), shifting layers of consciously deposited marine shells and sand were observed. Both animal and human bones (a mandi-ble) are preserved in situ where they are in contact with the shells. The observation of this stratigraphy and the finds contained in the different layers allowed Torfing (2011; 2013) to define three separate phases of use. These included one original excavation at the time of construction and two episodes of recutting. Torfing dated the three phases to the EN I/EN II tran-sition, EN II and MN A Ia, respectively. The sequence is topped by a cultural layer containing mixed finds dating to the EN II – MN A II period. The finds from the third phase as well as those from the Store Bro-khøj enclosure represent the local Blakbjerg-Brokhøj style at the start of the Middle Neolithic.

Three ^{14}C-dates on cattle bones (one from each of the three shell layers defining the three phases) were made in the course of this study. All three point to the third millennium BC, and thus to a phase from which no artefacts are known from the site. Fur-thermore, the results do not follow any stratigraphic order. It is obvious that these dates (listed in Tab. 12 together with those from other enclosures), are affected by some kind of yet-to-be identified error, and have therefore been disregarded.

Ballegård, Skarresø Parish

Five km southeast of Blakbjerg on the tip of an island in the central parts of Kolindsund lies the Ballegård enclosure. The site has a very low elevation and the ditch segments (which were present in two circuits) were partly flooded by the fjord, as evidenced by washed-in marine snails etc. (Boas 2001, 8).

As is the case for all causewayed enclosures in Djursland, excavations (1988 and 1993) only un-covered very small parts of the enclosure. This was probably the largest in the region with an estimat-ed size of more than 20 ha (N.A. Boas, personal communication; judgment based on faint, possible traces of segmented ditches on historical aerial photographs). Available information is restricted to very short excavation reports and comments (Hou-gaard Rasmussen 1989; Wincentz Rasmussen 1994 and Boas 2001, 8). Inside the segmented ditches (which ranged from 0.6 to 2.0 m deep), were found stratified layers with finds dating to the TRB, Late Single Grave Culture, early and late phases of the Late Neolithic (including Bell Beaker ceramics) and the Early and Late Bronze Age. The lowest (TRB) layers contained human bones. According to Hougaard Rasmussen (1989), the comparatively few TRB shards date to MN A I. Nevertheless, it is not clear whether these finds represent the time period during which the enclosure was constructed.

Galgebakken, Albøge Parish

The Galgebakken enclosure is situated on a promontory delimited by two small creeks which flow into Kolindsund Fjord a few hundred meters away. The only information available about the site comes from a very short description of the small-scale excavations which took place there in 2002 (Wincentz Rasmussen/Harder 2003) in which two ditch circuits (spaced 10 m apart) were recorded. The individual ditch segments were 3-8 m long and 2-4 m wide. Marine shells were deposited inside the ditches, which resulted in the preservation of bone as well as pottery and flint. The excavators dated all finds to the early Middle Neolithic (MN A I).

Ginnerup, Ginnerup Parish

The Ginnerup enclosure is situated on a high moraine plateau whose southern edge borders Kolindsund Fjord. The eastern side of the plateau is delimited by a steeply incised creek valley. Small-scale excavations in 2001 revealed two ditch segments in a single row. They were respectively 11 and 25 m long and ranged between 5-6 m wide. The two ditch segments were filled with marine shells and cultural layers dating to the Middle Neolithic Pitted Ware Culture (PWC)(Wincentz Rasmussen 2002). A single shard of the TRB Culture indicates, nevertheless, that the enclosure was constructed in TRB times (N.A. Boas, oral communication). Renewed excavations in 2003 uncovered a further 5-7 ditch segments lying in a row on three sides of the plateau and confirmed the presence of pre-

PWC layers at the bottom of the ditch segments (L. Wincentz Rasmussen, oral communication). Due to the lack of characteristic find material, these layers cannot be precisely dated.

Skærvad, Ginnerup Parish

This site contains an unpublished causewayed enclosure consisting of a single circuit of segmented ditches. Skærvad is situated on a well-defined promontory delineated by two minor rivers which flow into a northern branch of Kolindsund Fjord. The enclosure is known only from surface registration of the segmented ditches from which some PWC finds were noted (N. A. Boas, personal communication). As yet, no proper excavation has taken place.

Kainsbakke, Ginnerup Parish

Kainsbakke numbers as the third enclosure site within Ginnerup Parish. It is situated on a shallow oval elevation inside a river meander and is bordered on its southern side by a tributary of Kolindsund Fjord. Archaeological investigations of the site took place between 1979 and 1982, and then again in 1999 and 2001.

Early excavations concentrated on the investigation of half of a large pit (A47) which contained the largest closed assemblage of PWC finds that has been recovered in Denmark to date as well as skeletal remains from brown bear, elk and humans. Several other features on the site were also investigated. The results of the initial excavations were published, both in preliminary reports as well as a monograph (Wincentz Rasmussen/Boas 1982; Wincentz Rasmussen 1984; 2000; Richter, J. 1987a; 1987b; 1989; Wincentz Rasmussen/Richter1991).

Pit A 47 contained large amounts of marine shells as well as cultural debris, all of which belonged to the PWC. Several ^{14}C-dates from the shell-bearing layers (1 and 3) point to c. 2900-2800 BC, and thusly are in accordance with their cultural context. According to Wincentz Rasmussen/Richter (1991, 14), the earliest phase of the pit (layer 5) is actually located below the shell layers and their Pitted Ware material, demonstrating that the latter represent only a second stage of use. Due to a lack of characteristic finds and ^{14}C-dates, it was not possible to date layer 5 (and thereby the initial pit cut). While the pit may belong to the PWC, it could also be older.

This question is of great importance, particularly as later excavations (Østergård Sørensen/Boas 2002) demonstrated that the large feature (A47) was part of a row of a further four pits, one of which appears to have been fenced off. Furthermore, parts of a possible palisade were discovered as well. The site seems to represent an enclosure (or possibly an enclosure-related site, see chapter 4). Such constructions are unknown from PWC contexts. While it is possible that the pits in question were originally dug in TRB times, no TRB finds have been made there, leaving the actual age of this enclosure/enclosure-related site still undecided.

Grenå, Grenå Parish

This enclosure is also unpublished. It was situated on what was once a minor island a mere 150 m off the northern coast of Kolindsund Fjord. Today, this area is covered by the town centre of Grenå, the largest town in Djursland. During construction work close to the church, a single profile showing a v-shaped ditch containing a scatter of TRB pottery remains was recorded (N.A. Boas, oral communication). As is the case with the Taastrup Kolindvej site (see below), very little is known about this enclosure. While an alternative interpretation of the ditch as part of a grave construction is possible, apart from the TRB pottery, the overall geographical position of this site is much more in line with what is known from other TRB enclosures in Djursland and the remainder of South Scandinavia than with what one would expect for a funerary context in this region.

Fuglslev, Fuglslev Parish

Fuglslev is an unpublished site in the southern part of Djursland and is located on a promontory in a river meander. With a distance of ca. 2.7 km to what once was Stubbe Fjord (today Stubbe Lake),

Fuglslev is the only known causewayed enclosure in Djursland that was not situated on the coast.

The first excavations at this site took place some four decades ago. However, it is only more recently that Fuglslev has been recognized as a probable enclosure. This allocation was made by N.A. Boas in the course of renewed small-scale excavations in 1980 (Boas 2001, 8). The initial excavation report describes the presence of large stones on top of a ditch (N.A. Boas, oral communication) and is thereby reminiscent of the situation present at the possible enclosure at Taastrup Kolindvej (see below). A number of pottery shards from a pit uncovered there were dated to MN A I.

One additional site must be discussed in addition to the enclosures described above. While this last site cannot be classified as a classical causewayed enclosure, it closely resembles many known sites of this type in terms of its topography and setting as well as the presence of pits with traces of recutting and ritual depositions. For these reasons, it has been included in the present list.

Lystrup Kildevang I, Egå Parish

This site was fully excavated few years ago in the course of the motorway construction work by which it was subsequently destroyed. It is situated on a shallow south-facing promontory located on the northern shore of what was once Egå Fjord, and lies at the mouth of a minor stream which emptied into the latter body of water (Fig. 8). In contrast to a great many of the sites previously discussed, the excavation results from Lystrup Kildevang I were published in a number of papers (Ravn 2005; 2011; Skousen 2008, 156ff.).

On the edge of the promontory (and partly surrounding it) are a number of ritual pits with deliberately broken artefacts. The pits show clear traces of recutting. ^{14}C-dates suggest a use-window between the 38th and 37th centuries BC. Study of the ceramics suggests that the site can be allocated to the EN I Volling Group, a regional group of the Early TRB Culture.

In almost all respects, the Kildevang site shows strong resemblances to causewayed enclosures

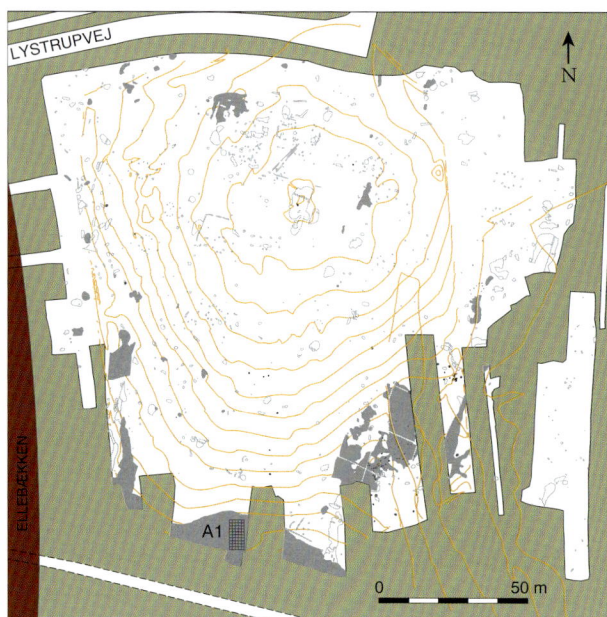

Fig. 8 | *Lystrup Kildevang I is not what one might consider a proper causewayed enclosure; it is rather what one might call an enclosure-related site. A row of pits was found on the western perimeter of a shallow promontory. These pits demonstrated traces of re-cutting. Select, sometimes deliberately broken artefacts were deposited in the pits (from Skousen 2008).*

and was consequently referred to as an assembly place by Skousen (2008). Its topographical situation on a promontory at the coast of a fjord next to a river mouth, the presence of ritual features showing recuttings and the deliberate deposition (and possibly also destruction) of selected artefacts at the edge of the promontory are conditions virtually identical to those observable at classical causewayed enclosure sites. The only difference appears to be the fact that its ritual features were comparatively small pits rather than oblong ditches. It should be noted that one of these ritual pits (A283) turned out to have originally consisted of three separate pits, which were combined into a single, larger version upon later recutting. Exactly the same process of amalgamation has been documented at both Danish (Sarup: Andersen, N.H. 1997, 46 Fig. 46) and Central European enclosures (Jeunesse 2011). These observations further buttress potential

links between the site of Kildevang I and standard causewayed enclosures. If one considers the possibility that construction came to a halt and was never continued, this site might represent the very first attempt to construct a causewayed enclosure in Scandinavia. Alternatively, it could represent the first reaction of a local TRB community to the ideas of enclosure construction that were spreading through Europe at this point in time (see chapter 10.3.2.3).

Apart from the nine regular enclosures and the single enclosure-related site listed above, there are three other sites in Djursland which are likely to be causewayed enclosures. Unfortunately, at present, these sites offer insufficient information for any categorical determination of their natures. One of these sites is Fannerup in Ginnerup Parish. Several decades ago, workers observed features in the ground that could probably have been identifiable as the segmented ditches of an enclosure. Due to the destruction of the site, unfortunately, this information can no longer be verified. The Ørum Aa kitchen midden is located on the tip of the promontory on which the enclosure possibly was located (Neergaard 1900, 135). The finds made during the small scale excavation of this site in the late 19th century comprise no less than three Middle Neolithic battle axes, what appears to have been a deposition of two flint axes and one greenstone axe and isolated human bones with cutting marks (Neergaard 1900, 138ff.). The character of this material is very unusual for an ordinary kitchen midden, but corresponds very well with what is known from causewayed enclosures, e.g. Sarup (Andersen, N.H. 1997). Also in terms of its location, Fannerup appears to be a good candidate for causewayed enclosure status: it is located on the southern coast of northern Djursland and borders Kolindsund Fjord at a river mouth, just as is the case for many of the other enclosures in Djursland.

No further information is available for the site of Rævebakken in Ålsø Parish. Rævebakken is located close to the east coast of Djursland and lies south of Kolindsund Fjord. Excavations of an Iron Age settlement were carried out on this location in the 1970s. In the course of said work, features that might well have represented segmented enclosure ditches where encountered (N.A. Boas, oral communication). The topography of the site is very typical for South Scandinavian causewayed enclosures; it is situated on a well-defined promontory at the confluence of two minor rivers and lies some 700 metres to the west of the Kattegat coast.

A potential enclosure was recently discovered (2010) during road construction at Taastrup Kolindvej in Feldballe Parish (unpublished). Although a single ditch profile (ca. 1 m deep) was observed, it was not recorded, due to profile collapse. On the bottom of the ditch, fragments of a thin-butted flint axe were discovered. A large stone was found in the uppermost part of the ditch (information kindly provided by the excavator, E. Kannegaard Nielsen). Through geophysical survey, it was possible to follow the ditch over a distance of approximately 16 m, revealing that the stones present appear to have been placed along the top of the ditch for almost its entire length (Klassen/ Klein, this volume).

The evidence available for this enclosure is sparse. Moreover, the observations that do exist could also possibly be interpreted as representing other kinds of constructions, even from entirely different periods of (pre-) history. However, according to N.A. Boas (who has excavated many of the enclosures known from Djursland), the type of the ditch fill which was present there was identical to that observed in many of the other enclosures and was decidedly "Neolithic" in character (personal communication). Furthermore, the site is situated at a place in which a minor river flows into Korup Sø, the southernmost part of what used to be Kolindsund Fjord. This setting is identical to that of most other enclosures in Djursland as well as the entire northern TRB distribution area. Therefore, this site is accepted here (with some reservations) as a probable TRB Culture enclosure, although final confirmation of this assertion is necessary through excavation on a somewhat larger scale. Such an excavation would also clarify whether the ditch might represent a yet-unknown variant of ditches previously observed on the sides of both earthen and megalithic long barrows. Several such barrows are known from the region, including the famous Barkær monuments (Glob 1949; Liversage 1992), which lay only 600 m removed to the northwest. Ditches resembling those typical for causewayed enclosures have been found on the side of a barrow in at least one instance in Djursland (barrow Sb. 44 in Hørning Parish – Fiedel 2006, 45ff. Figs. 22-23).

The distribution map of the certain and probable causewayed enclosures and related constructions described above shows a very clear picture (Fig. 6). Almost all known sites are distributed evenly along the shores of Kolindsund Fjord, spaced out like beads on a necklace. This is true for both cer-

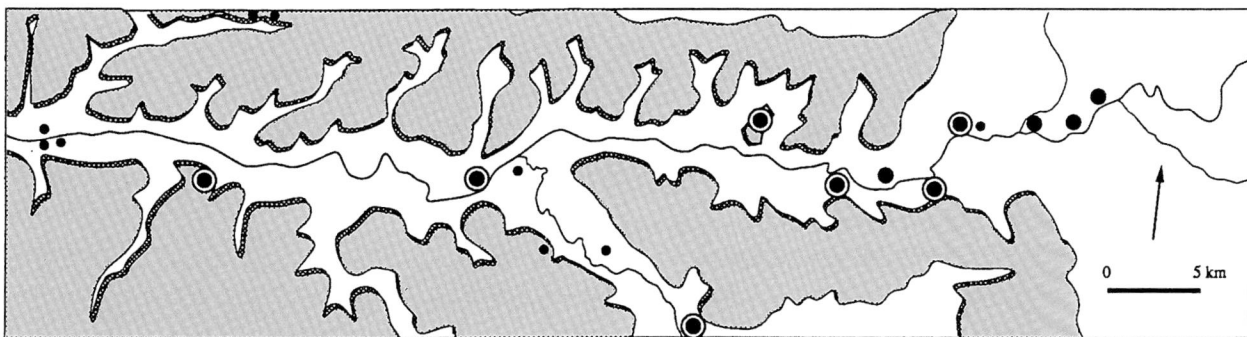

Fig. 9 | *Causewayed enclosures have been discovered in several parts of Europe with similar, approximately equidistant spacing along the course of rivers. The distributional pattern closely resembles that observed for enclosures along the shores of Kolindsund Fjord in Djursland. This illustration shows the older Michelsberg enclosures in the Aisne river valley in northern France as an example of this trend (encircled big dots)(from Dubouloz et al. 1991).*

tain and probable enclosures. Only three of the 13 mapped locations are found outside the Kolind-sund Fjord area. However, two of these are located either close to the shoreline of another fjord or in a near-coastal setting comparable to that of the site of Store Brokhøj. Only the Fuglslev enclosure deviates from this pattern (inland location).

This specific distribution pattern along Kolind-sund Fjord immediately recalls that of the river valley enclosures in northern France (Blanchet/ Martinez 1988; Dubouloz et al. 1988; 1991; Delor et al. 1988; Mordant/Mordant 1988) and hints at the potential presence of factors which might have had superregional importance (Fig. 9). This question will be taken up again later (chapters 10.4 and 11).

Another aspect of the distribution map that requires attention is the coastal or near-coastal situation of all causewayed enclosures (save one). The deviant site of Fuglslev immediately raises the outlier question, although one must also wonder whether a larger number of presently-undetected enclosures remain to be found in inland Djursland. This question is obviously of central importance if any reconstruction of settlement systems and social organisation shall be undertaken for the region and thus forms an extra incentive for further investigations.

4 Causewayed enclosures and related sites in the TRB North Group distribution area

A number of surveys of the causewayed enclosures known from the distribution area of the northern TRB Group have been published over the last three decades (i.e. Madsen, T. 1988; Andersen, N.H. 1997, Nielsen, P.O. 2004; Klatt 2009; Larsson, L. 2012). The area in question is comprised of Denmark, the southern and central parts of Sweden, parts of southern Norway and northern Germany. No causewayed enclosures have yet been published from the northernmost parts of this area (Norway, central Sweden). These regions are therefore disregarded here. Unfortunately, no single geographical term is sufficient to describe the remaining areas. In order to avoid lengthy descriptions, in the following, 'South Scandinavia' is employed in reference to this area (with the inclusion of northern German Schleswig-Holstein and Mecklenburg-Vorpommern, although those regions are not traditionally covered by that term).

A comparison between the different published lists of enclosures reveals some disagreements with regards to those sites that have been accepted as enclosures and those which have not. As this question is relevant with regard to the following studies, a few remarks are necessary here.

In general, only the sites with proven ditch segments in full or partial circuits which actually delimit a given area are counted as causewayed enclosures within this study. An exception to this rule is Vilsund in northern Jutland (Nielsen, J./Bech 1989 and see chapter 10.2.7). The site of Vilsund has an area enclosed by a turf wall held in place by a construction based on rows of posts on either side rather than by circuits of segmented ditches. However, a few pits or ditch segments have been found following the turf wall, and the topography of the site is completely in line with that typical for Danish causewayed enclosures on promontories. The site is dated to the late Early Neolithic and has thus nothing to do with the palisade enclosures known from the MN A-MN B transition in the eastern parts of South Scandinavia (Svensson 2002).

On a number of sites with ditch segments, only very small areas have been excavated. Several of these have been accepted as causewayed enclosures, even though we do not know at present whether the ditches of which we are aware form parts of full- or partial circuits. These sites were accepted on the basis of their topography, which in all cases was identical to that of causewayed enclosures on promontories.

The catalogue recently published by Klatt (2009) includes the vast majority of relevant sites with brief descriptions and references to original publications. The reader is referred to this publication for a general overview of published site plans and other information. However, a few unpublished or newly published enclosures have yet to be added. These include the sites of Starup Langelandsvej in southern Jutland (Lützau Pedersen 2010; Lützau Pedersen/Witte 2012), Bad Segeberg in Schleswig-Holstein (Guldin 2011), Fuglslev, Grenå and Skær-

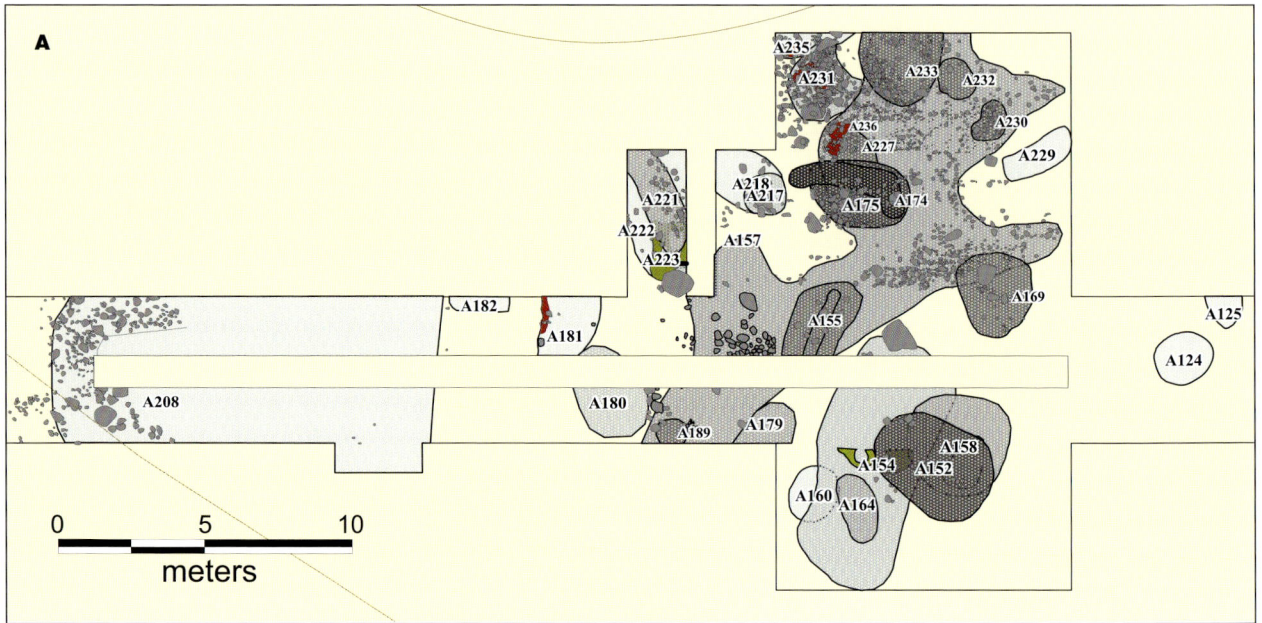

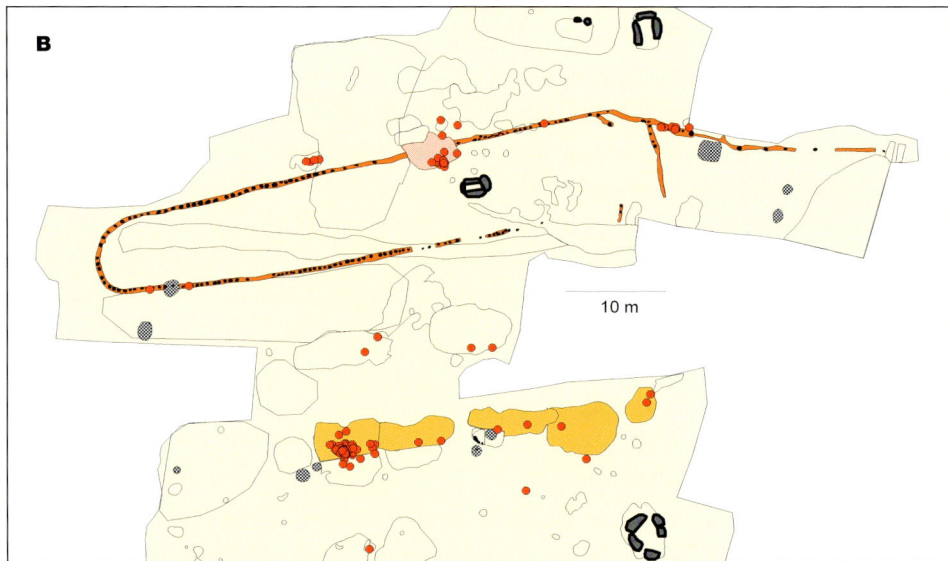

Fig. 10 | *Sites from Denmark and northern Germany that are related to causewayed enclosures. A) Aalestrup (from Madsen 2009), B) Sarup Gamle Skole (from Andersen 2009), C) Triwalk (from Müller/Staude 2012).*

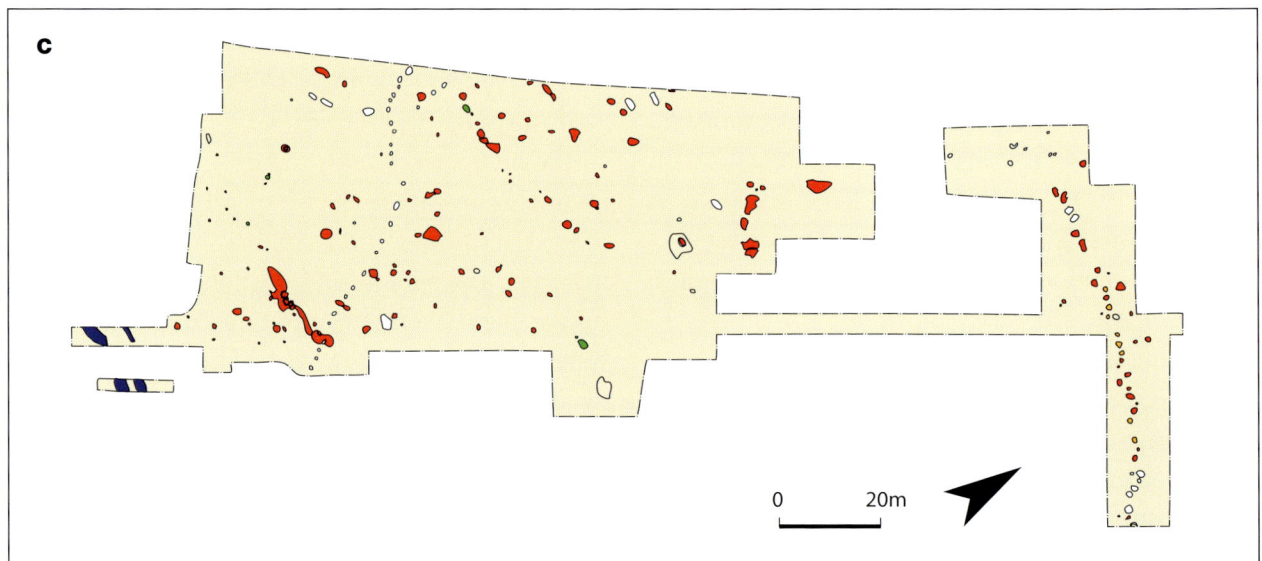

vad in Djursland (Boas 2001, 8 Fig. 10; see above), Mølbjerg II in northwestern Jutland (unpublished, information kindly provided by L. Helles Olesen, Holstebro Museum) and Gammeltoft Odde in western Jutland (Troldtoft Andresen 2013).

A few sites in Denmark and northern Germany are clearly related to causewayed enclosures (as defined above) and make up a second category of sites relevant to this discussion (Fig. 10). These include the Aalstrup site at Horsens Fjord (Madsen, T. 2009 and see chapter 10.1.3.1), the single row of ditch segments at Sarup Gamle Skole on the island of Funen (which might or might not be part of a true enclosure)(Andersen, N.H. 2009) and the Lystrup Kildevang I site in eastern Jutland (Ravn 2005; 2011; Skousen 2008, 158ff.; see above). The Troldebjerg site on the island of Langeland has furthermore been included in this category. Troldebjerg has been classified as an enclosure on several occasions (i.e. Madsen, T. 1988, 318; Nielsen, P.O. 2004, 31f.). However, only parts of a palisade have been excavated at the site and all attempts to prove the existence of ditch segments have failed (Skaarup 1985, 346 note 426). A fifth site (Triwalk in Mecklenburg-Vorpommern) can also be added to this category (Jantzen 2005; Müller, J./Staude 2012). Here, a long row of pits showing signs of deliberate recutting and refilling were excavated. The pit arrangement clearly deviates from what is found at ordinary settlement sites and is reminiscent of a row of ditch segments.

Recently, the Norwegian site of Hamremoen has been cited as a possible example of an enclosure (Glørstad/Sundström in press). Whether or not these claims are justified is difficult to judge, because the structures excavated at this site diverge from those of classical causewayed enclosures. Although it can possibly be classified as an enclosure-related site, Hamremoen is not taken into further consideration in the following.

In some cases, it is difficult to separate these latter sites from those on which pits with traces of recutting have been proven. While long barrows with accompanying side ditches (see Beck 2013; Fiedel 2006) can be differentiated from those sites related to causewayed enclosures as listed above

quite easily, the matter is sometimes more complicated, such as at Skejby (Rasmussen/Skousen 2012) or Lystrup Kildevang II, pit A250 (Skousen 2008, 172ff.). In the present study, only sites with more than one pit with traces of recutting have been registered as related to causewayed enclosures. Therefore, the single pits from Skejby and Lystrup Kildevang II referred to above have not been included in this category, although this definition may well turn out to be entirely artificial in future research.

Two sites that have been accepted here as true causewayed enclosures include Markildegård (Østergård Sørensen 1995a; 1995b) and Kainsbakke (Wincentz Rasmussen 1984; Wincentz Rasmussen/ Richter 1991; unpublished). These are characterised by long, almost straight rows of very short ditch segments or pits. In the proper sense of the word these cannot be considered to be enclosures, as the course of the ditches/pits does not enclose anything. However, those features which were detected might be part of very large ditch/pit circuits. In both cases, certain or possible palisades have been observed running parallel to the straight rows of pits/ditches approximately 20 m away (information on Kainsbakke kindly provided by L. Wincentz Rasmussen). Markildegård and Kainsbakke thus diverge in both the very short length of the pit-like ditch segments as well as the very large distance between palisades and ditches/pits from the enclosures proper. The long, straight course of the rows of pits on the other hand is reminiscent of the features observed at the site of Triwalk (described above), although the latter lacks a palisade.

As is apparent from the descriptions above, it is not always easy to differentiate between classic causewayed enclosures and sites that, while clearly related, diverge in one (or several) aspects. The latter class of sites is still very poorly understood and is in need of further research. While this group may contain several distinct sets of monuments, it could also represent sites that vary within the parameters of a certain theme.

Several sites which have been included in the catalogue of enclosures by Klatt (2009) are excluded from the following discussion unless specifically stated otherwise. Omissions include the site of Bækbølling I in central Jutland (Knudsen/Hertz 1993). Bækbølling was excluded because the chronological position of the supposed ditch segments is not verifiable by datable finds. The enclosures of Plate 3, Plate 14, Ruthen and Zietlitz (all in Mecklenburg-Vorpommern) have also been omitted. Their exclusion is effected on the grounds of insufficient information. Moreover, they appear to be situated in topographical settings generally different from those of all other enclosures (with the possible exception of Liselund in northern Jutland). Their construction, furthermore, seems to differ from that of the TRB enclosures in Denmark, southern Sweden and Schleswig-Holstein in that it lacks the frequent breaks in the ditch circuits.

Constructional differences from the South Scandinavian sites also are evident in a group of TRB enclosures in Brandenburg to the southeast. These were not listed in Klatt's catalogue and have only been recently recognized. Of the total of five sites discussed as certain or possible TRB enclosures in the literature (Wetzel 2000; Ungerath/Cziesla 2007; Beran/Hensel 2004; Beran/Hensel 2007; Beran 2010; Lehmphul 2009; Lück et al. 1999), only two (both from Potsdam) have been accepted as such here. The remaining three from Rathsdorf, Berge and Dyrotz have not been dated properly. In all three cases, there are indications of early Medieval activity. At Berge, ^{14}C-dates from two of the three ditches indicate such a young date (unpublished data obtained by J. Henning, who kindly allowed this information to be included in this study). No such dates are available for Dyrotz. However, Slav finds have been collected from the surface. There are also some TRB finds, but these date to Walternienburg-Bernburg (information kindly supplied by G. Wetzel, to whom I am grateful for a fruitful discussion on this matter). Even if the TRB finds were to provide a date for the enclosure, this would be somewhat younger than all other known northern TRB enclosures. Therefore Dyrotz is disregarded here, as is the last site (Rathsdorf) which probably dates to the Slavic period (J. Beran, personal comment).

5 Predicting the location of causewayed enclosures in South Scandinavia: Previous approaches

5.1 T. Madsen's work (1979-1988)

The first causewayed enclosure within the northern TRB distribution area was only identified in 1968 (Hingst 1971a; 1971b). Its discovery at Büdelsdorf (northern Germany) came as a surprise. At that time, Neolithic causewayed camps had been known in comparatively large numbers for decades, albeit in areas further south. Given the long archaeological tradition in South Scandinavia, it was expected that such sites would have been identified much earlier than was actually the case.

The fast accumulation of new discoveries after this first identification had already been anticipated in 1979, at which time a grand total of five enclosures were known in South Scandinavia (Madsen, T. 1979, 302). Based only on these five examples, Madsen identified specific positions in the landscape (i.e. promontories surrounded by watercourses/wet areas on two or three sides) as typical for the causewayed enclosure phenomenon. He knew that a large number of settlement sites with just such a position were already known, and (rightly) predicted that more causewayed enclosures would be identified in the following years. The fact that all five enclosures known at that point in time had previously been registered as (ordinary) settlements certainly leant strength to his argument.

Madsen's paper (referred to above) can be counted as the first attempt to predict the location of enclosures in the northern distribution area

of the TRB, although he made no specific claims for the location of new sites. His approach was based on the identification of three crucial positioning factors: 1) specific topography (position on promontories), 2) proximity to water (watercourses and wet areas) and 3) abundant Neolithic (surface) finds. Although his criteria can be refined (and new criteria added), Madsen's original characterization of causewayed enclosures still stands. The fundamentals of predicting the position of causewayed enclosures in the landscape were thus established more than 30 years ago and this was done on the basis of a mere handful of known sites.

A few years later, Madsen (1982) published his influential study of TRB settlement systems in eastern Jutland, in which he elaborated further on this causewayed enclosure positioning concept. This elaboration included both a more detailed presentation of parameters (topography, proximity to water, find material from the sites) already identified in his paper from 1979 as well as the addition of new parameters (soil type, relation to megalithic graves, size and date of sites) and the first proper and specific prediction of enclosure locations.

Madsen modified earlier statements regarding the topographical position of causewayed enclosures due to the discovery of the site at Bjerggård (published in Madsen, T. 1988). Bjerggård is situated on a hilltop high above the surrounding landscape rather than on a low promontory as were all other sites known at the time. He furthermore refined his description of the position of causewayed camps in relation to water by stating that the sites (with the exception of Bjerggård) were situated on promontories stretching out into narrow fjords, lakes and boggy areas, or at the confluence of two watercourses. With regard to the find material from the sites in question, emphasis now was laid on abundance and character; causewayed enclosure finds were often made up of complete pots as well as select beautiful stone objects.

New to the discussion were Madsen's observations regarding TRB preferences for well-drained soil types (sand, gravel) for the construction of the causewayed camps. He also pinpointed the timing of said construction. In today's terms, this phase is made up of the late Early Neolithic (EN II) and earliest Middle Neolithic (MN A Ia/b). These periods had a combined duration of approximately 300-400 calendar years. Madsen supplemented this information by observing that many of these sites served as ordinary settlements in subsequent phases of the MN A, which, over the course of time, reached impressive sizes in their apogee in the MN A V. Of equal utility in terms of detection is Madsen's association between the construction and position of megalithic graves and their proximity to causewayed enclosures.

It can be concluded, therefore, that 30 years ago Madsen had already identified the most crucial factors in the localization of causewayed enclosures, albeit with the notable exception of these sites' relation to ancient tracks or roads and, especially, river crossings (see chapter 6.3.2). In 1982, he himself used these factors to identify the sites of Langenæs, Beder, Aalstrup and Årupgård as probable causewayed enclosures. This list was enlarged by the addition of Studshoved in a later paper (Madsen, T. 1988; see Fig. 1). Madsen was most certain of Årupgård, which he published as a contour map with the location of nearby megalithic graves (Madsen, T. 1982, 209 Fig. 8). He justified this opinion by citing comparative finds from the Sarup enclosures (Andersen, N.H. 1997). While Madsen provided no specific details concerning this material, his remark

certainly brings to mind the Årupgård ceramic vessel hoard which contained amber beads and copper trinkets (Sylvest/Sylvest 1960; Klassen 2000, 81). Unfortunately, the Årupgård site has been destroyed by gravel extraction and can no longer be verified as a causewayed enclosure. Such verification was possible (at least in part) for one of the remaining four postulated sites. Madsen found a series of ditch segments at Aalstrup (Fig. 10 A)(Madsen, T. 2009). These segments did not enclose any particular area and are seemingly placed at random. While Aalstrup was doubtless closely related to the monuments of interest, it is not counted as a true causewayed enclosure here.

As to the remaining two (three) predicted locations, no data at all were given by Madsen in his various publications, nor were they mentioned again in the literature.

The criteria Madsen identified as crucial for pinpointing causewayed enclosure sites (i.e. topography, relation to water, proximity to megalithic graves, the potential continuation of such sites as Neolithic settlements and the prevalence of specific kinds of finds) are widely recognized in the literature and have been employed by several other studies' attempts to predict causewayed enclosure locations.

Unfortunately, most of these predictions have been published in only extremely abbreviated forms which are without much detail. With the exception of the site of Aalstrup (described above), no attempts have been made to verify these predictions (or, if they have, they have not been published). This applies to Skaarup's remarks on the Blandebjerg site (Skaarup 1985, 346 note 426) as well as Arnold's (1993, 11) comments regarding five sites in Schleswig-Holstein (northern Germany), one of which was identified by name in a later paper (Arnold 1994, 53). Further examples include Jørgensen's claims concerning three sites in southern Jutland (Jørgensen, E. 2000, 104) and Sparrevohn's proposition regarding a single, specific site on Zealand (Sparrevohn 2009, 50f.). The latter is the only one for which a somewhat detailed argument has been provided.

5.2 Klatt's study (2009)

The recently published study by Klatt (2009, 79f.) represents the most thorough attempt to predict the location of causewayed enclosures. It also differs from all earlier attempts insomuch as it applies GIS to the problem for the first time (Fig. 11). While all of the other authors referred to above took their point of departure in single, specific, previously known, 'suspicious' locations, Klatt investigated an entire region (the Baltic island of Rügen off the coast of Mecklenburg-Vorpommern) without any prejudices for or against certain locations. His approach resulted in the selection of a number of micro-regions which were likely to contain the type of prehistoric monument being sought. Unfortunately, he did not develop any acceptable means of testing his hypotheses, and bolstered his calculations only by means of Google Earth images.

Given that Klatt's approach was completely new from a methodological point of view (and is related to the one used in this study), it will be discussed in more detail below. Klatt classified known enclosures with regard to their positions in the landscape (Klatt 2009, 26ff.). This approach resulted in the specification of no less than 13 different types of location (including a category which encompassed the palisade enclosures from the MN A - MN B transition). With regards to late Early/ early Middle Neolithic causewayed enclosures, there was also a further classification. Besides examining mere topographical situation, this took into account other factors such as size, distance to megalithic graves and water and resulted in the definition of three different site types (page 65ff.). With regard to topography, these can be roughly defined as those situated on promontories (type 1a), on hilltops (type 1b) or on flat plateaus (type 1c). Because type 1a shows other specific traits (i.e. proximity to water and megalithic graves) and the two others appear to be less clearly defined with regard to these criteria, Klatt choose type 1a in his approach to predictive modelling.

Klatt's first step was to define the criteria used for analysis. These criteria include distance to water (rivers, lakes, fjords and wet areas), distance to megalithic graves, the density of megalithic graves and the topography type. Just as with any GIS calculation, it was necessary to quantify these criteria. To effect this, Klatt measured the distances of known causewayed enclosures to water and megalithic graves as well as the density of megalithic graves within a given distance to the enclosures. With the help of histograms, he defined several classes for each of the criteria for which he assigned values between 0 and 10. For each criterion, a grid was created, the cells of which contained these values. In the "distance to water"

Fig. 11 | *Predictive modelling of the location of causewayed enclosures using a GIS-approach whose parameters include the proximity to water, proximity to megalithic graves, density of megalithic graves within a given distance and promontory-type topography as applied by Klatt (from Klatt 2009).*

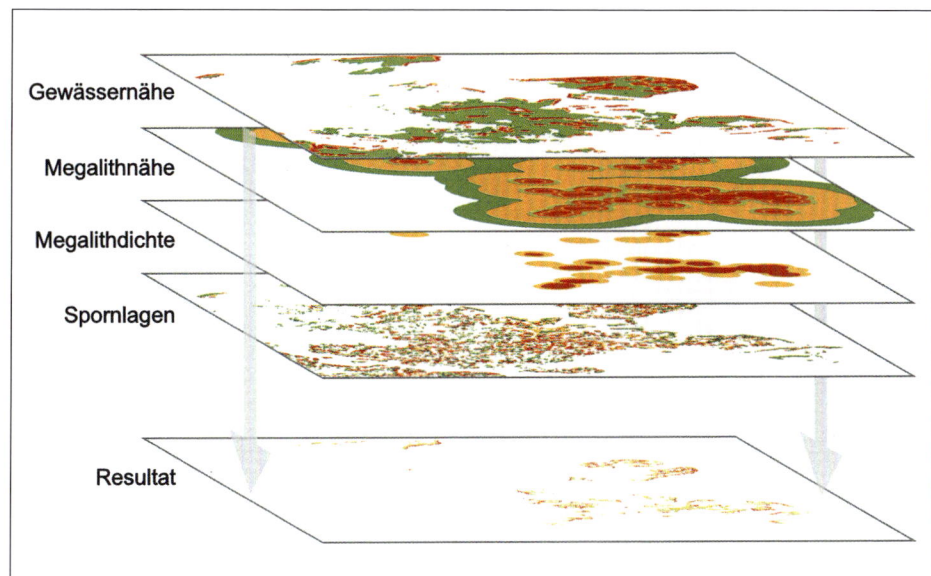

criterion, for example, all sites that were situated less than 250 m away from water were assigned the value of '10' in that area. In like fashion, places situated between 250 and 500 m away from water were given three points, locations lying between 500 and 2000 m to water were allocated one point and so on. Using this procedure, grids were calculated which contained information about the distance to water, the distance to megalithic graves and the density of megalithic graves for each point in the landscape.

In terms of the topographical approach, however, the procedure is somewhat different, especially given that a promontory is a complex structure not easily definable in GIS. To combat this problem, Klatt's first step was to calculate the average elevation of a 300 m-wide area around each spot. He then divided these values from the actual elevation grid. The resulting grids measure the elevation of each cell in relation to its surroundings (300 m radius circle). As the landscape around promontories is somewhat lower than the promontories themselves, the latter would be expected to have high relative elevation values. As points at steep slopes also show relative high values, only positions with moderate relative elevations were assigned high scores (up to 10m : 10 points, more than 60 m : 0 points).

In the final step, the four calculated values for distance to water, distance to megalithic graves, density of megalithic graves and topography were multiplied with each other. The values of the resulting grid were then classified into one of several categories and were projected onto a digital elevation model of the area under investigation. To finish, a control examination of the regions assigned the highest probability was undertaken (Fig. 12). This last resulted in the selection of several promising locations. To reiterate, Klatt unfortunately did not have a means of controlling his predictions other than the inclusion of Google Earth images. In the eyes of the present author, the reliability of this control is suspect. Nonetheless, Klatt's approach (2009) to predicting the location of causewayed enclosures is promising, as the use of GIS allows a large area to be searched on the basis of precisely-defined criteria.

The procedures described here are discussed below in greater detail with the intent of identifying their strengths and weaknesses. As Klatt explained (2009, 80), his methodology and area of investigation were guided in part by the availability of the necessary digital datasets. These limitations forced him to work within the boundaries of Mecklenburg-Vorpommern, in which no causewayed enclosures on promontories are presently known (although other types of enclosures are). It is therefore debatable whether searching for exactly this type of causewayed enclosure (type 1a) was either promising or relevant approach. Klatt chose type 1a enclosures because of the fact that said sites demonstrate characteristics which can be precisely defined for their inclusion in GIS searches. This is not the case for the other two types (1b on hilltops, 1c on plateaus). While this is certainly at least partly true with regard to his analytical parameters, one could argue that a comparable approach could be equally successful for 1b (and possibly also 1c) sites, should different parameters be employed.

5.2.1 The different criteria and calculations used by Klatt

Water

Klatt's first criterion (2009) in predictive modelling evaluated the distance to water. From his list on page 80, it is apparent that he did not include the open sea (Baltic, Kattegat, Skagerrak, and North Sea) within the calculations for this category. Although at first glance it is perhaps counterintuitive, this is without a doubt the correct approach, as is made apparent by Tab. 1, (which lists the distance of known causewayed enclosures to rivers, protected parts of the sea and the open sea). As can be seen, there is a distinct relationship between enclosures and rivers and enclosures and protected parts of the sea. Distances to the open sea, on the other hand, show much more diverse values. In the case of Søby Møllegård, these distances reach ca. 50 km (the precise distance is a matter of definition, as the area to the north of the site was an archipelago in Atlantic and early Subboreal periods). This figure

Fig. 12 | *Digital elevation model of parts of the Baltic island of Rügen. Areas with middle (yellow) or high (red) probability for the presence of causewayed enclosures are marked. Particularly promising sites (as identified by visual control) are marked by red circles (from Klatt 2009). Megalithic graves are indicated as well (black dots).*

approaches the greatest distances possible from Denmark to the open sea. Perhaps most important is the fact that none of the sites known at present directly border the open sea.

Lakes were also listed by Klatt as relevant bodies of water with regard to causewayed enclosure site choice. However, it is uncertain whether any of the causewayed enclosures presently known were actually bordered by lakes in the Neolithic. Although this might well have been the case at Gammeltoft Odde in western Jutland (Troldtoft Andresen 2013), the precise geological conditions of the surroundings of this site at the time in which

it was in use are not well understood. Other sites were bordered by wetlands (such as Toftum), and may have witnessed lake-like conditions in their immediate surroundings during periods of heavy rainfall. The Voldbæk site in Århus is situated today along a lakeside. However, in the Neolithic, this lake was part of a fjord.

On the other hand, wet areas do seem to have been important for the choice of location, even though it must be mentioned that there were several instances in which small rivers passed through these wet areas. The inclusion of wet areas in a GIS-approach is somewhat problematic, never-

Enclosure	Distance to freshwater stream	Distance to firth/bay	Distance to open sea	Topography type
Skævinge Boldbaner	ca. 1,4 km	ca. 1,4 km	ca. 16 km	(Hilltop)
Store Brokhøj	ca. 1,3 km	800 m	ca. 1,2 km	Hilltop
Bjerggård	ca. 250m	1000 m	ca. 11 km	Hilltop
Sigersted III	<100 m	ca. 25 km	ca. 25 km	Promontory
Trelleborg	<100 m	ca. 2 km (?)	ca. 3 km	Promontory
Vasagård øst	<100 m	/	ca. 2,5 km	Promontory
Vasagård vest	<100 m	/	ca. 2,5 km	Promontory
Sarup I	<100 m	600 m	2,7 km	Promontory
Sarup II	<100 m	600 m	2,7 km	Promontory
Hygind	<100 m	<100 m	ca. 1,5 km	Promontory
Åsum Enggård	<100 m	ca. 3,5 km	ca. 15 km	Promontory
Vilsund	ca. 200 m	<100 m	ca. 12.5 km	Promontory
Lokes Hede	<100 m	<100 m	ca. 37 km	Promontory
Ginnerup	<100 m	<100 m	ca.10 km	Promontory
Blakbjerg	<100 m	<100 m	ca. 14 km	Promontory
Ballegård	<100 m	<100 m	ca. 16 km	Promontory
Galgebakke	<100 m	300 m	ca. 11,5 km	Promontory
Kainsbakke	<100 m	<100 m	ca. 8,5 km	Promontory
Skærvad	<100 m	<100 m	ca. 9,5 km	Promontory
Fuglslev	<100 m	ca. 2,7 km	ca. 8,5 km	Promontory
Voldbæk	<100 m	<100m	ca. 7,5 km	Promontory
Toftum	ca. 300 m	1,5 km	ca. 13 km	Promontory
Mølbjerg I	<100 m	<100 m	ca. 25 km	Promontory
Mølbjerg II	<100 m	<100 m	ca. 25 km	Promontory
Søby Møllegård	<100 m	600 m	ca. 50 km	Promontory
Lønt	<100 m	<100 m	ca. 6 km	Promontory
Bundsø	<100 m	<100 m	ca. 5.5 km	Promontory
Starup Langelandsvej	<100 m	<100 m	ca. 6 km	Promontory
Stävie	<100 m	<100 m	6 km	Promontory
Büdelsdorf	<100 m	ca. 18 km	ca. 30 km	Promontory
Albersdorf Dieksknöll	<100 m	/	ca. 15 km	Promontory
Rastorf	<100 m	ca. 10 km	ca. 16 km	Promontory
Esesfeld	ca. 300 m	/	ca. 35 km	Promontory
Bad Segeberg	<100 m	/	ca. 30 km	Promontory
Liselund	<100 m	ca. 3.2 km	ca. 7,5 km	unclassified
Grenå	<300 m	<100 m	ca. 2,5 km	unclassified
Gammeltoft Odde	no data	no data	no data	unclassified
Markildegård	<200 m	ca. 4 km	ca. 11 km	unclassified
Related sites				
Sarup Gamle Skole	<100 m	250 m	2,5 km	Hillside
Aalstrup	ca. 300 m	250 m	ca. 5.5 km	Hillside
Lystrup Kildevang I	<100 m	<100 m	ca. 3,8 km	Promontory
Troldebjerg	ca. 300 m	/	900 m	Hilltop
Triwalk	no data	ca. 4 km	ca. 6 km	Hilltop

Tab. 1 | *The distance of known causewayed enclosures and sites related to causewayed enclosures from South Scandinavia to the nearest freshwater stream, fjord or bay and the open sea. All measurements are based on reconstructions of the coastline at the time of enclosure construction. The sites have been ordered according to topographical type. In one case (Gammeltoft Odde), measurements are somewhat uncertain due to the complicated geology along the west coast of Jutland.*

theless, as this type of landscape was extremely common in the overall causewayed enclosure distribution area at the time of their construction. Therefore, no separate measurements of the distance of the enclosures to the nearest wetland have been provided.

In summary, it can be concluded that proximity to water (excepting the open sea) was certainly an important factor which guided the choice of construction sites for causewayed enclosures in South Scandinavia. It is important, therefore, to include proximity to water in any GIS-approach to predict the location of causewayed enclosures, just as did Klatt. Nonetheless, some precautions should be taken regarding the inclusion of lakes and wet areas in this category.

Megalithic graves

Two of the four layers Klatt used in his GIS-approach contain data concerning the presence of megalithic graves. One holds information regarding the distance to the nearest stone-built chamber, while the second acts as a measure of the density of megalithic graves within an area with a radius of 1500 m around known sites. Contrary to the data in the distance to water grid (which can be defined precisely and with high certainty), those related to the two megalithic grave grids are dependent on a number of human-imposed factors. Because of this, they are in need of thorough and source critical evaluation. Unfortunately, such an evaluation is missing from Klatt's study, which renders its outcome doubtful.

In historic periods, megalithic graves were subject to severe destruction when the large stones they contained were used for construction work (churches, roads etc.). Furthermore, a detailed analysis of a part of the Djursland Peninsula conclusively demonstrated that the quality of the soil and the dependant intensity of modern agriculture were important factors in the survival of megalithic graves (Vedsted 1986). Unfortunately, these megalithic graves were often removed, as farmers viewed them as obstructing their work in the fields.

The estimated number of megalithic graves present in Denmark ranges from ca. 25,000 to 40,000 (Ebbesen 1985; Midgley 2008, 29). It is sad to say that less than 10% of this number remains today. Moreover, less than one third of this figure has been registered (Skaarup 1993, 104). The detailed regional study undertaken by N.H. Andersen in the Sarup area leaves us with serious doubts as to whether even these figures remain too optimistic. Four megalithic graves were registered within a 12 km² area surrounding the Sarup enclosures before the onset of field walking. Two of these graves are protected; the other two were destroyed by ploughing. Through field walking and geophysical survey, an additional 130 graves have been registered in recent years (personal comm. N.H. Andersen). This would mean that only three percent of all megalithic graves in the area had previously been registered. These figures make it obvious that any measure of the density of registered megalithic graves in a given area risks yielding erroneous results without intensive long term research. This has only been carried out in very few areas of restricted size.

Another problem in using the density measures of megalithic graves around known causewayed enclosures in predictive modelling is the uneven distribution of these tombs. Despite huge problems in assessing the real numbers of megaliths that were once present, there is no doubt that some regions in South Scandinavia once had much higher densities of these graves than others (see maps in Aner 1963, Skaarup 1993, Fritsch et al. 2010, Abb. 1 and Furholt 2011a, Abb. p. 30). None of these maps can be taken at face value; one must engage in detailed discussion of factors influencing the preservation of the tombs. What could be considered a high density of megalithic graves in one region could be a rather low density in another. Therefore, measures for the density of megalithic graves calculated on the basis of the survey of a given area around these sites are destined to yield misleading results when used in an approach such as Klatt's. This is a problem which clearly endangers super-regional approaches and may well also be present in studies of minor regions (like the island of Rügen used by Klatt) as well. It must be concluded, therefore, that the density of megalithic graves should not be used in the predictive modelling of the location of causewayed enclosures.

The potential relation between causewayed enclosures and megalithic tombs has long been postulated (Madsen, T. 1982; 1988). The find of a miniature dolmen inside a ditch segment at the site of Sarup Gamle Skole (Andersen, N.H. 2009, 29f.) is a good illustration of this connection, even though the site cannot yet be categorized as a true causewayed enclosure (see above).

The data presented in Tab. 2 underscore these conclusions. Megalithic graves are in fact present within the range of a few hundred meters from the majority of known causewayed enclosures. However, due to the reasons described above (unknown degree of destruction and varying amounts of megalithic graves built in different regions), the assignation of fixed values for GIS calculations to certain distances is problematic even without taking these factors into account. Unfortunately, this was not done by Klatt.

Promontories

The last factor taken into consideration in Klatt's predictive model is topography. Type 1a enclosures are situated on promontories. As described by Klatt, this type of topography is a complex construct which was not easily modelled in GIS. As is described above, he chose, therefore, to detect such topographies by looking for all sites that were (on average) slightly higher than their surroundings. According to the present author, this approach is problematic, although Klatt did address some of the problems thereby engendered. Such calculations automatically select not only promontories, but also other types of topography as well. Therefore, a manual control is necessary to sort out suitable locations from unsuitable ones. Furthermore, calculations of this type are rather sensitive to the gridsize of the digital elevation model (DEM) employed. Klatt's calculations are based on a cell size of 25 m, equalling the use of only 12 cells for calculation in each direction from the central calculation cell. In sharply undulating terrain with frequent slopes (as is often present in the distribution area

of the causewayed enclosures in South Scandinavia), this resolution may frequently result in the retrieval of sites with topographies different from that being sought after. Furthermore, if a promontory is faced by rising terrain on one side (as is the case with the Vasagård site on Bornholm – Kaul et al. 2002) or the Fuglslev site on Djursland (unpublished), the location might not be retrieved at all by the calculations as performed using Klatt's parameters.

It is not easy to reach a final conclusion regarding this step of Klatt's approach, as it is impossible to accurately evaluate his outcome based on the documentation in his publication. There is no doubt, nevertheless, that modelling a promontory via GIS is a very complicated task with many pitfalls. Since some locations that cannot be characterized as promontories are retrieved by his method, while at least some promontories are not, at the very least, the usefulness of this approach can be questioned. It may (with manual control) be suitable for the detection of the sites of some causewayed enclosures, but it is hardly suited to attempts to find as many of such sites as possible within a given region.

5.2.2. *Grid combination and calculation*

After creating grids holding information regarding the proximity to water and megalithic graves, the density of megalithic graves and topography, Klatt multiplied these scores which each other. This action resulted in 0 values for all cells that have a 0 value in any of the four grids. The resulting grid was classified in zones with very high scores and medium scores. At the same time, all regions with cells with low values were discarded.

This procedure is not without issues, considered the problems described above, especially when the calculation of the density of and distance to megalithic graves has been taken into account. Many regions are in danger of not being considered potential locations for causewayed enclosures because no megalithic graves have been registered nearby. As argued above, such a situation is a far cry from being one in which no megalithic graves were present.

Enclosure	Distance to nærest megalithic grave	Remark	Topography type
Skævinge Boldbaner	750 m		(Hilltop)
Store Brokhøj	2750 m	Many round barrows very close to the site	Hilltop
Bjerggård	900 m		Hilltop
Sigersted III	500 m		Promontory
Trelleborg	900 m		Promontory
Vasagård øst	200 m		Promontory
Vasagård vest	150 m		Promontory
Sarup I	150 m		Promontory
Sarup II	150 m		Promontory
Hygind	2000 m	Round barrow at a distance of 900 m	Promontory
Åsum Enggård	1200 m		Promontory
Vilsund	100 m		Promontory
Lokes Hede	200 m		Promontory
Ginnerup	600 m		Promontory
Blakbjerg	300 m		Promontory
Ballegård	600 m		Promontory
Galgebakke	400 m		Promontory
Kainsbakke	150 m		Promontory
Skærvad	150 m		Promontory
Fuglslev	1400 m		Promontory
Voldbæk	300 m		Promontory
Toftum	300 m		Promontory
Mølbjerg I	250 m		Promontory
Mølbjerg II	350 m		Promontory
Søby Møllegård	600 m		Promontory
Lønt	100 m		Promontory
Bundsø	500 m		Promontory
Starup Langelandsvej	500 m		Promontory
Stävie	no data		Promontory
Büdelsdorf	400 m		Promontory
Albersdorf Dieksknöll	1000 m		Promontory
Rastorf	700 m		Promontory
Esesfeld	2000 m		Promontory
Bad Segeberg	no data		Promontory
Liselund	800 m	Many round barrows at distances of c. 200 m to the site	unclassified
Grenå	5500 m		unclassified
Gammeltoft Odde	3100 m		unclassified
Markildegård	250 m		unclassified
Related sites			
Sarup Gamle Skole	0 m		Hillside
Aalstrup	50 m		Hillside
Troldeberg	1100 m		Hilltop
Lystrup Kildevang I	1800 m		Promotory
Triwalk	no data		Hilltop

Tab. 2 | *The distance of known causewayed enclosures and sites related to causewayed enclosures from South Scandinavia to the nearest registered megalithic grave. In a few cases, no data were available.*

A second problem is that the values assigned to the "distance to the nearest megalithic grave" and the "density of megalithic graves within a radius of 1500 m" grids are contradictory when both grids are multiplied with each other. In the case of the "distance to the nearest megalithic grave" grid, the value 'o' was assigned to all cells more than 7500 m away from graves. In the instance of the "density of megalithic graves" grid, the value 'o' was assigned to cells when the density of megalithic graves per square kilometre was o within a surrounding area with a radius of 1500 m. All cells with a distance greater than 1500 m from any megalithic grave were given the value 'o' in this grid, while five times this distance was allowed in the "nearest megalithic grave" grid. As a result, only locations at a maximum distance of less than 1500 m from megalithic graves were flagged as potential locations for causewayed enclosures. Nevertheless, several of the known South Scandinavian enclosures are located in areas which are even further from known megaliths (Tab. 2).

5.2.3 Conclusion

It is impossible to conclusively evaluate the consequences of the methodological shortfalls described above. Although some causewayed enclosures may well be detected within the regions indicated by Klatt (2009) via his method, many questions and uncertainties remain. Some of these can only be answered via individual, manual controls of the locations predicted; the others bring the value of the entire procedure into question. As has been indicated above, it is hardly a well-suited attempt for the detection of the maximum number of causewayed enclosures within a given region.

6 Predicting the location of causewayed enclosures in South Scandinavia: A new approach

Despite problems with the prediction-related parameters described above (especially those concerned with the "density of megalithic graves in the vicinity"), there is a general agreement with regards to the criteria that can be used to predict the location of causewayed enclosures. These parameters relate to both the natural environment (topography, proximity to water, type of subsoil) as well as to man-made features like megalithic graves and artefacts. As a geographical information system is well suited to handling both types of information, it is used here in the creation of a tool for the location prediction of causewayed enclosures. However, as was apparent from the earlier discussion of Klatt's (2009) GIS-approach, a detailed, source-critical evaluation of these individual criteria (as well as the mode by which said parameters are combined) is essential. Furthermore, the important topography-parameter is very difficult to implement in a GIS-approach and an improvement of the approach taken by Klatt is a precondition for successful predictions. Finally, a selection of new predictive criteria shall be introduced here.

6.1 Classification of known enclosures

Before engaging in a detailed discussion of individual predictive parameters, it is necessary to begin with a few comments regarding the classification of known causewayed enclosures into types. This

is necessary due to the fact that the various types have different topographical settings which in turn require different selections of criteria within predictive modelling.

Klatt (2009, 65 ff.) classified the causewayed enclosures of the EN II/MN A I by combining different categories of evidence: topographical settings, construction, size, and the nearby presence of megalithic graves. This resulted in three different types of causewayed enclosures, the two first of which only differ in terms of their topographical setting. Type 1a enclosures were constructed on promontories, while type 1b enclosures were situated on the tops or side of hills. The last type (1c), on the other hand, is characterized not only by a different topographical setting (on comparatively flat ground), but also by its monumental size. This typology is generally convincing, despite the fact that the classifications of a handful of enclosures should be changed. Toftum counts among this number. The site was classified as a 1b site. However, it may be better placed in group 1a, as the hill on which it is situated is comparatively low and the surrounding wet areas lend it a promontory-like aspect. This categorization is obvious when Toftum is compared with the topographical situation of the nearby enclosure at Bjerggård, which is a true hilltop site.

Liselund, which Klatt assigned to group 1c, should also be reclassified. The only similarity between Liselund and other 1c sites is its construction on level ground. However, the site at Liselund demonstrates an asymmetric ("egg-shaped") form when contrasted to the normal, rounder shape of the other 1c enclosures (which are exclusively located in Mecklenburg-Vorpommern, northern Germany). It also differs in terms of its architecture. Liselund has segmented ditches instead of the uninterrupted ditches which characterize type 1c enclosures in northern Germany. These deviations of shape and ditch segmentation find parallels in ordinary 1a enclosures, suggesting that Liselund should not be classified with the distant sites in Mecklenburg. Contrary to Klatt's suggestion, it is unlikely that a size greater than 10 ha should be considered an exclusive trait of 1c enclosures. There are a number of Danish sites for which very large sizes have been postulated: Lokes Hede, for example, is a typical type 1a enclosure with an estimated size ranging between 12 and 20 ha. Ballegård (probably a 1a site according to Klatt) was recorded with a possible size of up to 27 ha. Additionally, Galgebakke's 20 ha (which Klatt did not classify) should be cited.

Due to the reasons cited above, neither the distance to the nearest megalithic grave nor the density of said tombs should be used for the classification of enclosures, as was done by Klatt. In the current case, the ca. 800 m distance to the nearest megalithic grave for the Liselund site is still much shorter than that between the 1c sites in Mecklenburg and the respective closest stone built tombs. Therefore, even if this parameter were employed, it would not warrant an association between Liselund and 1c type enclosures. Furthermore, distances to the nearest megalith in (sometimes extreme) excess of 800 m are registered for a number of 1a and 1b enclosures. To bring the Liselund argument to a close, it must be remarked that, in spite of its comparatively level position, Liselund was constructed at the confluence of two small rivers. This trait has been encountered at many enclosures on promontories, and thus sets Liselund close to the 1a enclosure category.

To reiterate, it can be concluded that while the Liselund site differs from ordinary 1a enclosures due to its topographical setting, it is similar to enclosures in that category with regard to many other parameters, and clearly differs from the 1c enclosures in Mecklenburg. However, in this study, the Liselund site remains unclassified.

Besides Liselund, there are a few other enclosures that do not fit the definition of either promontory or hilltop location. One of these is the newly-discovered site at Gammeltoft Odde (Troldtoft Andresen 2013) which was constructed at a very low elevation inside either a lake or a fjord. The elevation is so low that the site might well have been periodically flooded. The same observation has been made for the Ballegård enclosure which lies on an island in Kolindsund Fjord (see chapter 3). Nevertheless, the Ballegård elevation is still somewhat higher than that at the Gammeltoft Odde construction site. Moreover, it is also better delimited. Therefore, Gammeltoft Odde has not been attributed to the promontory category. Instead, it remains unclassified. Also equally unclassified is the Grenå enclosure, which was apparently located on a comparatively small island in Kolindsund Fjord. In this regard, it resembles the Gammeltoft Odde site. The last unclassified site is that of Markildegård on Zealand (see discussion above, chapter 4).

Tab. 1 shows the general classification of South Scandinavian causewayed enclosures with regards to their topographical settings. With 31 of a total of 38 known sites, enclosures constructed on promontories are the dominant group by far. Apart from the four sites that have not been grouped into any topographical class, three sites are classified as hilltop enclosures (Bjerggård, Store Brokhøj and Skævinge Boldbaner).

The geographical distribution of the various topographical types is difficult to interpret due to the low numbers of non-promontory enclosures (Fig. 13). The following comments are thus only meant to describe possible trends which should be further examined at a later date. It is noteworthy that two of the enclosures close to the west coast of Jutland could not be assigned to any topographical class. This number is high when compared to the grand total of five known enclosures in this region, just as it is high when

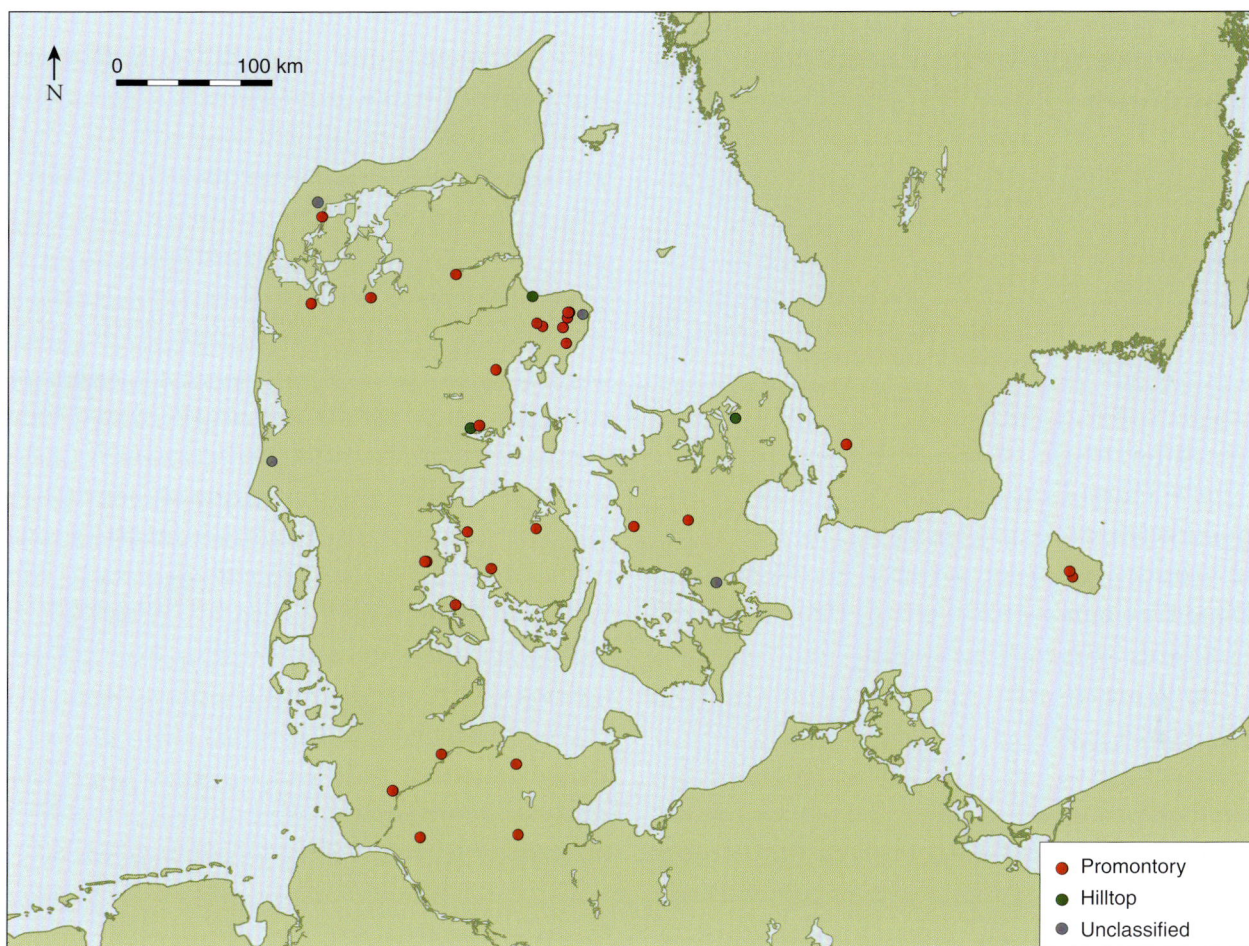

Fig. 13 | *The geographical distribution of causewayed enclosures in South Scandinavia according to the topography of their construction sites.*

viewed in light of the fact that four sites remain unclassified. Unfortunately, the numbers are too low to be statistically significant. For the same reasons it is not yet possible to tell whether the presence of two out of the three known hilltop locations in eastern Jutland indicates a real trend. Furthermore it is impossible to know whether or not the absence of hilltop and unclassified sites from the southern parts of South Scandinavia (Funen, southern Jutland and northern Germany) is a true reflection of prehistoric reality. It must finally be mentioned here that only half of all enclosures known from Zealand belong to the otherwise dominant promontory site class.

A total of five sites can be considered to be related – albeit not identical – to causewayed enclosures. It may or may not be coincidental that

only one of these (Lystrup Kildevang I) can be classified as a member of the promontory class. Hilltop sites appear to be overrepresented. Furthermore, two of the five sites remain unclassified. Both of these unclassified sites seem to have been constructed on the side of hills. Both have evidence for proper ditch segments. It may well be that these two sites represent another topographical class that has not yet been properly identified due to the low quantity of enclosures known overall. Both sites are also noteworthy because of the fact that megalithic graves were found directly on them. In the case of Sarup Gamle Skole, a megalithic grave was located inside a ditch segment. This observation sets them apart from all proper enclosures and deserves further attention at a later date.

6.2 Evaluation of the parameters hitherto employed in predictive modelling

6.2.1 Relation to water

The spatial relation of causewayed enclosures to water is one of the most important modelling parameters in this study. Three different types of water are differentiated as follows:

Freshwater streams

As described above, proximity to freshwater streams in particular played a decisive role in the choice of construction sites for causewayed enclosures. None of the causewayed enclosures on promontories are further than 300 m from this type of water source (Tab. 1). In fact, 28 of 31 promontory sites directly border a river (registered as <100 m in the table). The remaining sites are bordered by wet areas through which rivers pass at distances of not more than 300 m. Direct proximity to freshwater streams is thus a crucial predictive factor for causewayed enclosures on promontories.

However, the same does not apply for causewayed enclosures situated on hilltops. In this category, distances to freshwater streams range between 250 m and 1.4 km. Furthermore, these freshwater streams do not border enclosures, but rather naturally flow away from them. The "distance to freshwater stream" parameter, therefore, is unsuitable for searching for hilltop enclosures.

The sites which remain unclassified seem more in line with those on promontories in terms of their distances from freshwater streams. However, they do seem to have a potential tendency towards being slightly more distant from freshwater streams. It was not possible to obtain precise data for the Gammeltoft Odde site, due to uncertainties regarding its geological setting at the time it was in use. This enclosure may well have been located at quite a distance from the nearest river.

In summary, it can be concluded that the "proximity to freshwater stream" parameter appears to be well suited to predicting the location of ca. 90% of all causewayed enclosures (if the sites known at present are representative for the entire population). Nevertheless, due to the statistically low numbers of enclosures known overall, this figure should be taken with a grain of salt. There is little doubt, however, that the overwhelming majority of sites were placed very close to rivers. It should be added that the size of these rivers did not seem to play a particularly decisive role, as examples are known in proximity to both very large (on a South Scandinavian scale) and very small freshwater streams. One need look no further than to Büdelsdorf on the Eider river (the latter being one of the largest rivers in the area of interest) and Ginnerup in Djursland (situated at the mouth of creek which measures a scant 2.5 km in length) for examples of the variety within this category.

The sites which are related to enclosures also show comparatively low distances to freshwater streams. Unfortunately, no data were available in this regard from the hilltop location at Triwalk.

Fjords or sheltered bays

As is apparent from Tab. 1, the majority of all promontory type enclosures are situated very closely to either a fjord or a sheltered bay. While this appears to be especially true in the area under investigation, it is possible that this is more a reflection of the research strategies applied thus far than past Neolithic reality. The Fuglslev site in Djursland supports this proposition. Fuglslev lies 2.7 km from the nearest fjord. The Sigersted III site on Zealand, the Åsum Enggård site on Funen and the north German enclosures all demonstrate that immediate proximity to a fjord or sheltered bay was no definite precondition for the construction of enclosures on promontories.

It can be concluded, therefore, that promontory type enclosures were very often situated within a short distance from fjords or sheltered bays. Approximately half of all known sites of this type directly border a fjord. However, there are no strict rules by which this phenomenon can be defined, meaning, therefore, that the 'distance to fjord or sheltered bay' parameter can only be used in predictive modelling to find the potential location of a subset of promontory type enclosures. It is obvious that there is a great amount of regional variation with regard to this parameter, probably due to local topographies. This is illustrated by a juxtaposition of the situations in Horsens and Kolindsund Fjords. In the Horsens Fjord area, the Toftum and Bjerggård enclosures are situated between 1000 and 1500 m away from the coastline. By contrast, a distinct relation to the shore is evident in the Kolindsund area.

Hilltop enclosures, of course, have distance values to fjords/sheltered bays that are (on average) larger than those for the promontory type, although there is a considerable range in the data. The parameters therefore have a limited value in the predictive modelling for these types of enclosures. The same appears to be true for sites that are related to enclosures, even though three of these five sites have been found at distances of less than 300 m from the shore.

Distance to the open sea
Regardless of their topographical type, none of the known causewayed enclosures directly face the open sea. In the case of the unclassified Grenå enclosure, this is a matter of how one defines the 'open sea'. The island on which the site was situated is located very close to the coast and is sheltered by the latter on three sides. The fourth (southern) side faces the mouth of Kolindsund Fjord, which was ca. 3 km wide at the time of enclosure construction. The Kattegat is ca. 2.5 km to the southeast. Consequently, this latter value has been provided as that for the distance to the open sea in Tab. 1.

The lowest value for this measure is 1.2 km at the site of Store Brokhøj. Although modern environmental protection of the coastline (ban of house construction, etc.) may have hindered the discovery of enclosures closer to the open sea, it appears that this parameter can cautiously be used to exclude some near-coastal areas from the search. Sites related to causewayed enclosures clearly follow the same pattern, even though Troldebjerg (900 m from the Baltic) shows the lowest value of all registered sites.

6.2.2 Distance to megalithic graves

As has already been intimated above, almost all known causewayed enclosures have a distinct relation to nearby megalithic graves. Tab. 2 shows the distances from the enclosures to the nearest dolmen or passage grave as ordered by topographical type.

On average, the distance from hilltop sites to the nearest megalithic grave appears to be somewhat larger than that for promontory enclosures, even though several of the latter have much larger absolute values. Due to the low number of sites and the unknown degree of destroyed and unregistered stone chambers, it is not possible to draw any conclusions from this observation. It is possible, however, that this state of affairs might reflect prehistoric reality. In general, megalithic graves (in contrast to Bronze Age barrows) were not constructed on prominent hilltops. As a result of the source critical problems related to megalithic graves, it is not possible to accurately evaluate the fact that the two largest distances recorded were measured for unclassified enclosures. Vedsted's (1986) investigation clearly demonstrates that the 5500 m distance between the Grenå enclosure and the nearest grave (the largest value recorded) does not reflect the actual situation as it was in the Neolithic, given that many graves must have been destroyed in this region in historic times, due to the favourable properties of the soil for agriculture.

Despite these source critical issues, the data presented in Tab. 2 indicate that the distance to the nearest megalithic grave is a parameter that can be used to predict the location of causewayed enclosures, at least for promontory sites. The presence of nearby dolmens and/or passage graves is characteristic for these types of sites. Hilltop sites, on the other hand, may be characterised by the absence of (very) close megaliths. However, as this observation might be the result of a low sample size, it should be treated with caution. In any case, is it important to note that, while the nearby presence of a megalithic grave might indicate the location of a causewayed enclosure, the absence of such a grave does not prove the absence of an enclosure. This

Enclosure	Soil type	Topography type
Skævinge Boldbaner	no data	(Hilltop)
Store Brokhøj	Sand/Gravel	Hilltop
Bjerggård	Sand	Hilltop
Sigersted III	Sand	Promontory
Trelleborg	Clay	Promontory
Vasagård øst	Clay	Promontory
Vasagård vest	no data	Promontory
Sarup I	Sand	Promontory
Sarup II	Sand	Promontory
Hygind	Clay	Promontory
Åsum Enggård	Sand	Promontory
Vilsund	no data	Promontory
Lokes Hede	Sand	Promontory
Ginnerup	Sand	Promontory
Blakbjerg	Sand	Promontory
Ballegård	Sand	Promontory
Galgebakke	Sand	Promontory
Kainsbakke	Sand	Promontory
Skærvad	Gravel	Promontory
Fuglslev	Sand	Promontory
Voldbæk	Sand	Promontory
Toftum	Sand	Promontory
Mølbjerg I	Sand	Promontory
Mølbjerg II	Sand	Promontory
Søby Møllegård	no data	Promontory
Lønt	Sand	Promontory
Bundsø	Sand/Gravel	Promontory
Starup Langelandsvej	Sand/Gravel	Promontory
Stävie	Sand	Promontory
Büdelsdorf	Sand	Promontory
Albersdorf Dieksknöll	Gravel/Sand	Promontory
Rastorf	Sand/Gravel	Promontory
Esesfeld	Sand	Promontory
Bad Segeberg	Sand/Gravel	Promontory
Liselund	Clay	unclassified
Grenå	Sand/Gravel	unclassified
Gammeltoft Odde	Sand	unclassified
Markildegård	Sand	unclassified
Related sites		
Sarup Gamle Skole	Sand	Hillside
Aalstrup	Sand	Hillside
Lystrup Kildevang I	Clay	Promontory
Troldebjerg	Clay	Hilltop
Triwalk	no data	Hilltop

Tab. 3 | *Soil types for causewayed enclosures and related sites from South Scandinavia ordered by topographical type.*

statement stands, unless a thorough investigation of historical maps and comprehensive field survey can convincingly exclude the possibility that still unknown megalithic tombs had once been present in a particular area. As this condition is practically unfulfilled in South Scandinavia, nothing can be concluded from the absence of nearby megalithic graves with regard to the potential presence of causewayed enclosures. The distance to the nearest megalithic grave therefore is a parameter with restricted value in predictive modelling.

6.2.3 Soil type

Well-drained soils (such as sand or gravel) were generally preferred by the TRB Culture for settlements (Madsen, T. 1982). More recent investigations show a more varied picture, at least on Zealand (Madsen, M. 2010, 10) and in northern Jutland (I. Kjær Kristensen, personal communication). Causewayed enclosures demonstrate these same general preferences, as is apparent from Tab. 3. In a total of 34 cases, information about the character of the subsoil of the enclosures was available. In 30 cases, these were located on sandy or gravelly soils, while only four appear to have been constructed on clay or clayey soils. Ca. 80% are thus located on well-drained soils with 10% on less well-drained soil. For the remaining 10% of enclosures, this information is unavailable. With regard to the sites related to causewayed enclosures, the high frequency of clay soils (two out of five sites) is noteworthy, but should not be given too much weight, due to the very small size of the sample.

All enclosures on clay are found in regions which are largely dominated by said soil type. It is possible, therefore, that sandy patches of the size required for a causewayed enclosure may not have been available. It can, therefore, be concluded that soil type is a parameter which can be used in predictive modelling, although some caution is necessary in its employment and regional characteristics should be taken into account. Furthermore, in regions dominated by sandy soils (such as is the case within Djursland), this parameter may be of limited value.

6.2.4 Neolithic finds

In terms of surface finds recovered from enclosure sites, it is necessary to differentiate between finds contemporary with enclosure construction and those belonging to later Neolithic phases.

Surface finds contemporary with the construction of the causewayed enclosures are either rare or (apparently) absent. (It is possible that this is due to difficulties in the recognition of these finds, as typical elements, such as thin-butted flint axes or pottery decorated with vertical fringes cannot be precisely dated, especially when found in a fragmentary state). This absence at the surface is mirrored by the paucity of finds from the construction phase in the ditch segments themselves. The massive deposition of material typically only began with secondary use-phases of the ditches (i.e. recuttings). Observations from completely or near-completely excavated enclosure sites (Sarup I and II, Starup Langelandsvej) leave us with a very diverse picture. The near-complete excavations at the site of Starup Langelandsvej yielded only ca. 600 shards. Of these, the overwhelming majority were discovered at the end of the ditch segments, with almost nothing on the surface (Lützau Pedersen 2010; Lützau Pedersen/Witte 2012). At Sarup on the other hand, surface finds from the construction phase were abundant, but were also difficult to identify, due to the factors explained above. In earlier papers, the excavator only acknowledged the presence of very few (ritual) features at the site contemporary with the construction of the first enclosure (Andersen, N.H. 2000). However, as described in a more recent paper (Andersen, N.H. 2011) as well as the complete published documentation (Andersen, N.H. 1999a; 1999b), Andersen mentions construction-era finds in no less than 93 small pits. It is very possible that these finds are the remnants of an earlier cultural layer that were deposited in the small pits secondarily, as was proposed by N.H. Andersen (2011). In all cases, such finds were comparatively abundant over a rather large area. The two examples discussed here show that surface finds from the time of any one enclosure's con-

struction may or may not be present at the surface. The absence of such finds certainly cannot exclude the presence of an enclosure.

As previously described, many enclosure sites developed into regular settlements that grew in size over the course of the TRB Culture and reached their apogee in the latest TRB phase (MN A V). In Djursland, PWC complexes took the place of the late TRB ones, as was the case at Ginnerup, Skærvad and Kainsbakke. It should also be noted that Neolithic finds which postdate the TRB and PWC cultures are often encountered on enclosure sites. For example, in the investigation area, Single Grave, Bell Beaker and other Danish Late Neolithic and Bronze Age finds were recovered from the Ballegård enclosure.

In general, it can thus be said that, in the vast majority of cases, surface finds from different parts of the Neolithic are abundant on causewayed enclosure sites (Tab. 4). However, a few sites have rendered no (or only very few) artefacts as surface finds.

Another important aspect of finds from causewayed enclosures involves the deposition of entire pots or selected stone objects (e.g. Andersen, N.H. 1997; 2000). While depositions of these types of objects are common in wetlands (e.g. Becker 1947; Koch, E. 1998), they are comparatively rare in dry ground. Finds from the latter type of environment may therefore be indicative of the presence of a causewayed enclosure. As described above, this reasoning has previously been used in causewayed enclosure location predictions. This is true for the Årupgård example as well as that from Ellerødgård I (Nielsen, H. 1988; Andersen, N.H. 1993).

It can be concluded that the presence of TRB (or PWC and later Neolithic cultures') settlement materials, depositions and special objects are parameters that can be taken into account via a predictive modelling approach. These find categories may (with the exception of special objects) also be present on ordinary settlement sites. However, a lack of finds cannot be taken as proof of the lack of enclosures. In fact, enclosure sites with few finds on the surface as well as in the (excavated) features may be substantially underrepresented in the record as it stands at present.

Enclosure	Surface finds	Topography type
Skævinge Boldbaner	no data	(Hilltop)
Store Brokhøj	present	Hilltop
Bjerggård	abundant	Hilltop
Sigersted III	abundant	Promontory
Trelleborg	abundant	Promontory
Vasagård øst	abundant	Promontory
Vasagård vest	no data	Promontory
Sarup I	abundant	Promontory
Sarup II	abundant	Promontory
Hygind	abundant	Promontory
Åsum Enggård	abundant	Promontory
Vilsund	no data	Promontory
Lokes Hede	abundant	Promontory
Ginnerup	abundant	Promontory
Blakbjerg	abundant	Promontory
Ballegård	abundant	Promontory
Galgebakke	few	Promontory
Kainsbakke	abundant	Promontory
Skærvad	abundant	Promontory
Fuglslev	abundant	Promontory
Voldbæk	abundant	Promontory
Toftum	abundant	Promontory
Mølbjerg I	abundant	Promontory
Mølbjerg II	no data	Promontory
Søby Møllegård	abundant	Promontory
Lønt	abundant	Promontory
Bundsø	abundant	Promontory
Starup Langelandsvej	few	Promontory
Stävie	abundant	Promontory
Büdelsdorf	abundant	Promontory
Albersdorf Dieksknöll	present	Promontory
Rastorf	no data	Promontory
Esesfeld	no data	Promontory
Bad Segeberg	abundant	Promontory
Liselund	abundant	unclassified
Grenå	no data	unclassified
Gammeltoft Odde	few	unclassified
Markildegård	abundant	unclassified
Related sites		
Sarup Gamle Skole	present	Hillside
Aalstrup	abundant	Hillside
Lystrup Kildevang I	present	Promontory
Troldebjerg	abundant	Hilltop
Triwalk	present	Hilltop

Tab. 4 | *The presence of surface finds dating from the period of construction and later settlement usage of causewayed enclosures and related sites from South Scandinavia ordered by topographical type.*

6.2.5 Topography

6.2.5.1 Promontory type enclosures

Topography is an important factor in the classification of different types of enclosures and obviously also has a place within a predictive modelling approach. However (as discussed above), topography is not an easy parameter to use within a GIS-based approach. Not only is it difficult to define a promontory in GIS, but variations in the shape, orientation and size observed in enclosure promontories make the development of suitable search criteria extremely problematic.

How, then, is it possible to use topography as parameter for a GIS-based search for promontory type enclosure locations? In fact, there is a rather simple solution to this problem; rather than searching for promontories themselves, one must merely search for the elements that delimit promontories. The latter are much easier to define than the former. As is apparent from the discussion above, water in the form of freshwater streams, fjords and wet areas play a key role in this area. From Tab. 5 it appears that five different types of water-defined boundaries can be identified for promontory enclosures in South Scandinavia (Fig. 14).

The most frequent situation is one in which a promontory with causewayed enclosure was situated near to where a (small) river flowed into a fjord. This situation can be observed in 14 or 45,2% of all cases. Causewayed enclosures on promontories situated between two confluent rivers have been observed in 10 cases (32, 3%), while the number of enclosures on promontories in river loops or meanders is four (12,9%) and that of enclosures on promontories surrounded by wetland is two (6,5%). There also are two sites on peninsulas which projected into a fjord (6,5%). Only one known enclosure on a promontory – Mølbjerg II – was not delimited by any of the factors described above. Instead, this site merely sat beside a river. Its location was clearly related to that of the neighbouring Mølbjerg I site, which, however, was itself situated at a river mouth.

It should be noted that the evaluation of the character of the water-based delimitation of enclosure promontories was always based on reconstructions of the sea level at ca. 3500 BC rather than on current sea levels. The grand total of cases described above (33) is larger than the number of sites considered (31) because in two instances (Trelleborg and Hygum), enclosures were registered as being situated between confluent rivers and at river mouths at the same time. Which of the two possibilities is correct is dependent upon the particularities of sea level reconstruction at the time of construction. In these two cases, a few decimetres' difference in sea level had a dramatic effect on the shoreline. Thus, the possibility remains that at low tide, both sites were situated between confluent rivers at a considerable distance to the coast. At high tide, by contrast, these sites were situated directly on the coast itself. The same may have also been true for Søby Møllegård.

From the above counts it is apparent that 22 or 71% of the known 31 enclosures on promontories were either found between confluent rivers or at points at which rivers flowed into fjords or sheltered bays. Both river confluences and river mouths can be easily retrieved and defined by a GIS approach as well as by hand. Unfortunately, the same cannot be said for instances involving peninsulas, wetlands and/or river loops. Topographical

Enclosure	River confluence	River outlet	River loop	Wet areas	Peninsula
Sigersted III	X				
Trelleborg	X	X			
Vasagård øst	X				
Vasagård vest			X		
Sarup I	X				
Sarup II	X				
Hygind	X	X			
Åsum Enggård			X		
Vilsund					X
Lokes Hede		X			
Mølbjerg I		X			
Mølbjerg II					
Søby Møllegård	X				
Ginnerup		X			
Blakbjerg		X			
Ballegård					X
Galgebakke		X			
Kainsbakke		X			
Fuglslev			X		
Skærvad		X			
Voldbæk		X			
Toftum				X	
Lønt		X			
Bundsø		X			
Starup Langelandsvej		X			
Stävie		X			
Büdelsdorf			X		
Albersdorf Diecksknöll	X				
Rastorf	X				
Esesfeld				X	
Bad Segeberg	X				
	10	14	4	2	2

Tab. 5 | *Types of water-defined boundaries for promontory-type enclosures in South Scandinavia.*

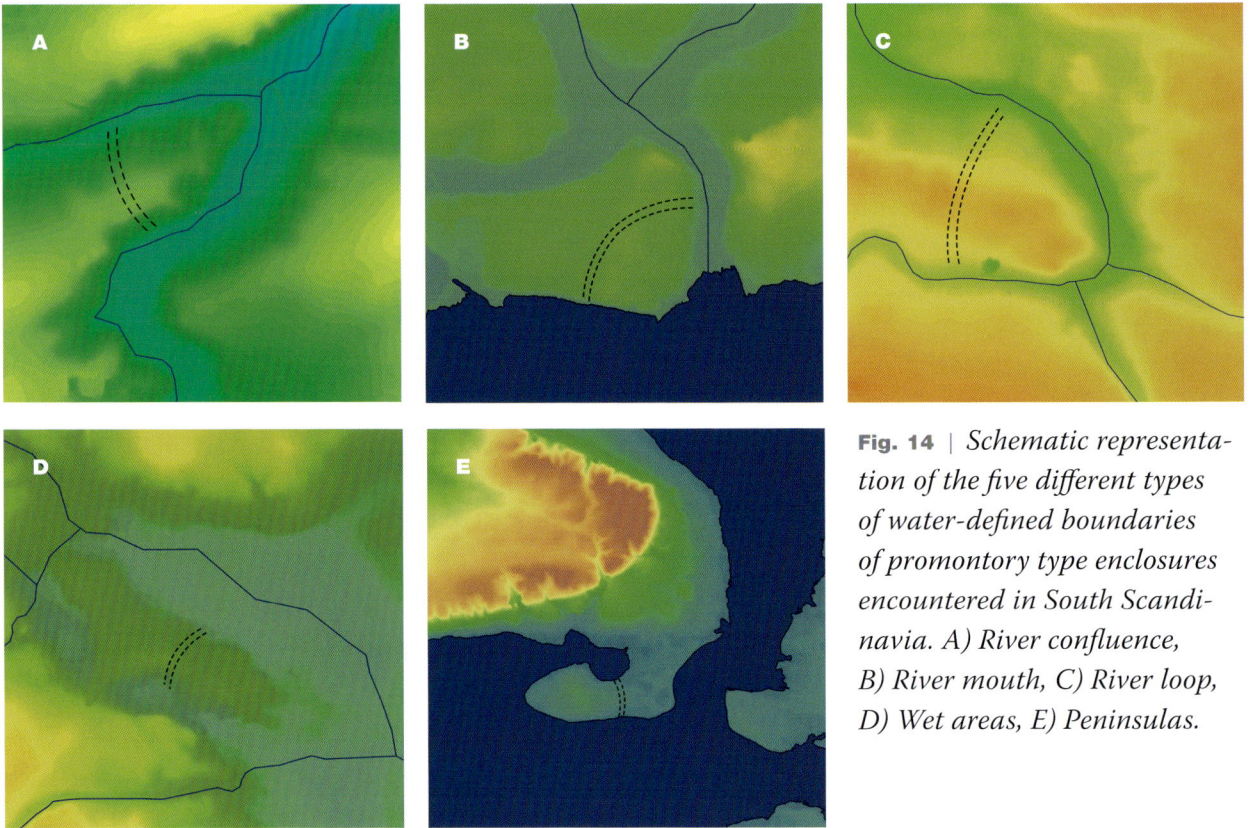

Fig. 14 | *Schematic representation of the five different types of water-defined boundaries of promontory type enclosures encountered in South Scandinavia. A) River confluence, B) River mouth, C) River loop, D) Wet areas, E) Peninsulas.*

parameters, therefore, are not well suited to finding potential promontory enclosure sites in these kinds of landscape settings. Nonetheless, the sites that are comparatively easily found by a GIS approach using the bypassed topography parameters constitute almost 58% (22 of 38) and thus cover a considerable portion of all types of the enclosures known at present.

The orientation of the promontories with known enclosures is listed in Tab. 6. It appears that promontories which faced directly south or west were

chosen more frequently than those which faced north or east, although a considerable number of sites are actually oriented to the northwest or northeast. Nevertheless, it is doubtful whether this observation is of any real use in predictive modelling. In many regions, there were not enough suitable locations for people to have a large selection of sites on which to situate their causewayed enclosures. This assumption is supported by the appearance of "double" enclosure sites in which two enclosures faced each other while being oriented in divergent or opposing directions (Mølbjerg I and II, Vasagård east and west, Lønt and Starup Langelandsvej)(Fig. 15). These sites clearly demonstrate that orientation was not of utmost importance in choosing a construction site. Therefore, orientation of promontories will not be used as parameter in predictive modelling.

6.2.5.2 Hilltop type enclosures

A GIS is well suited to locating hilltops. As it is possible to eliminate scale-related problems by specifying the size of the area in which the re-

Orientation of promontory	Number of sites
N	1
O	3
S	8
W	5
NW/NO	7
SW/SO	7

Tab. 6 | *The orientation of the promontories on which causewayed enclosures have been found.*

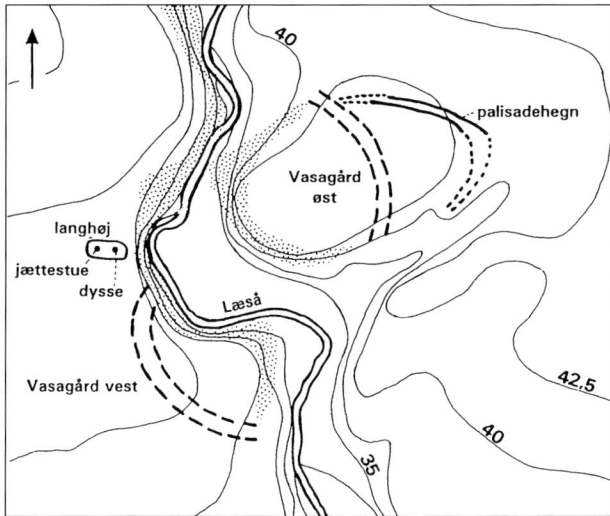

Fig. 15 | *Vasagård West and Vasagård East on the island of Bornholm are two neighbouring enclosures with opposite orientations (from Kaul et al. 2002).*

trieved cell of the DEM is the highest, in principle, this approach suffices as a means of pointing out potential enclosure locations. However, only a select few actual hilltop enclosures are known, and these present highly divergent topographical settings. At present, therefore, it is not possible to specify meaningful criteria for the search for hilltop locations. Without these specifications, any potential search for hilltop sites would result in an amount of potential locations so large as to be practically useless. Therefore, despite being well suited from a theoretical point of view, a GIS-based search for hilltop-type enclosures is not promising.

6.2.5.3 Conclusion

In summary, it can be concluded that many potential enclosure locations on promontories can be meaningfully and successfully sought via GIS. If the restricted number of known enclosures provides an approximate picture of the frequency in which enclosures appeared in different topographical situations, then the use of the "bypassed topography parameter" in a GIS-based predictive modelling approach should be able to point out the locations of approximately 60% of all yet-undetected sites. On the other hand, the remaining 40% (enclosures

on hilltops, atypical topographical situations and promontories in river loops, on peninsulas and in wetlands) are ill-suited for detection via topographical parameters with a GIS.

6.3 New parameters for predictive modelling

6.3.1. Inter-enclosure spacing

As mentioned in the introduction, Djursland is the region with the highest density of registered causewayed enclosures and related sites within South Scandinavia. The enclosures along Kolindsund are almost as evenly spaced as beads on a necklace. None is farther than 7.5 km away from its nearest neighbour. If the Fannerup site (one of two possible enclosures in this area) is included in these calculations, the maximum distance between these sites is reduced to 6.8 km. The sites of Skærvad and Kainsbakke (which are the two enclosures situated closest to each other) are only 1.2 km apart. On average, one enclosure is present every 4 km between the Grenå site in the east and the Blakbjerg enclosure in the west. Madsen's research in the Horsens Fjord area has demonstrated a comparable inter-enclosure distance of 3.5 km for the Toftum and Bjerggård sites (Madsen, T. 1988). Thus, it appears that enclosures can generally be expected to be spaced at a few kilometres' distance from each other. It is therefore of interest to note that practically identical inter-enclosure distances (ca. 4-5 km) have been found in other parts of Europe (Fig. 16), such as southern Britain (Oswald et al. 2001, 112), northern France (Dubouloz et al. 1988; see Fig. 9), northern central Germany (Fig. 16; Geschwinde/Raetzel-Fabian 2009, 244 Abb. 168) and the German Rhineland (Amtmann/Schwellnus 1989, 37).

Observations in the Kolindsund and Horsens Fjord areas as well as those known from abroad suggest that an inter-enclosure spacing of a few kilometres is to be expected, at least in the present investigation area as well as other regions with comparable natural environments and Neolithic settlement densities. While it remains impossible

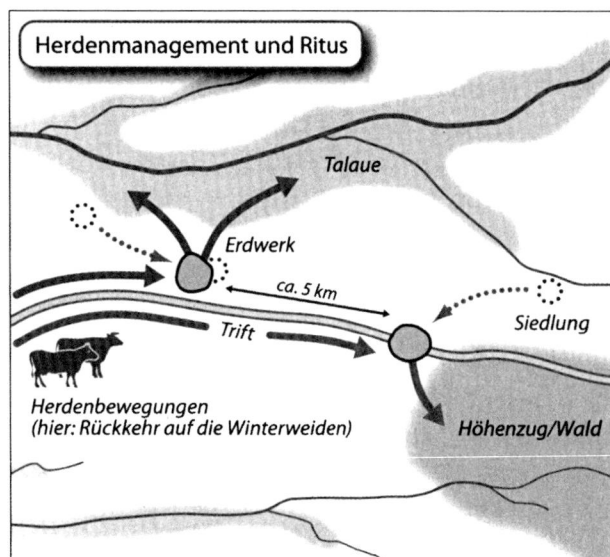

Fig. 16 | *An example of inter-enclosure distances comparable to those encountered in Djursland/ South Scandinavia from Northern central Europe (Germany)(from Geschwinde/Raetzel-Fabian 2009). Note that the illustration represents an idealized model based on information from a large number of registered enclosures and compare Fig. 9 for examples from another region.*

to identify a specific measure of the distance to the next enclosure (even though distances of 4-5 km appear rather frequently), large distances (more than 7-10 km) between known sites probably indicate the presence of intervening enclosures which have yet to be detected. Inter enclosure spacing can therefore be employed as a parameter in the predictive modelling conducted here. Although it cannot be used to pinpoint exact locations, it appears to be well suited to indicate minor regions with the potential for unknown sites.

6.3.2 Enclosures in relation to communication infrastructure

Climate warming following the end of the last Ice Age led to the spread of dense, primeval forests in South Scandinavia. While the various tree species by which these forests were comprised changed over the different climatic phases, they all had a limiting effect on transport and com-

munication. Water-based travel, therefore, was of utmost importance, not least in an area with the complex coastlines encountered in South Scandinavia. For example, the coastline of the comparatively small country Denmark has a length of no less than 7000 km. Settlement predominantly occurred near the coast or was bound to inland freshwater systems at the time in which causewayed enclosure construction began (see chapter 9.3 for a more detailed account). At this time (around the middle of the fourth millennium), the interior of the country started to be settled and communication lines on land became identifiable (see below). Whether these communication routes should be called roads or paths is a matter of definition. Paths can be considered routes that only were traversed by foot, while roads witnessed foot traffic as well as that of wagons or carts. The oldest traces of wagons or carts in South Scandinavia at present can be dated back to EN II and thus come from approximately the same period in which causewayed enclosures were built (Mischka 2011; Burmeister 2011). Clear indications of wagon- or cart-based travel on roads are available from MN A II (ca. 3100 BC) onwards (Johannsen/Laursen 2010). In the time of interest here (late EN I - MN A I), inland communication routes may thus have been travelled by carts and/or wagons. However, this cannot be demonstrated with certainty as yet. Therefore, the terms road and path are used interchangeably for the routes in question.

In Central European research, considerations regarding spatial relations between Neolithic enclosures and ancient roads and paths have been made for decades (e.g. Uenze 1981, 31ff.; Behrends 1998a, 1998b). This is true both in relation to Neolithic roads (e.g. Behrends 1998a, 1998b; Raetzel-Fabian 1999, 97ff; Raetzel-Fabian 2000, 89ff.) as well as to roads (mostly of Medieval age) known from historical sources (e.g. Hock 1989, 120f.; Raetzel-Fabian 1999, 97ff.; Wallbrecht 2000, 246; Raetzel-Fabian 2002; Knoche 2003, 25f.; Bakker/Knoche 2003, 24; Knoche 2008, 115 (with note 496), 139; Geschwinde/Raetzel-Fabian 2009, 225ff.; Gronenborn 2010, 243; Kellner-Depner 2011; Vaquer 2011,

234). In this context, the work of D. Raetzel-Fabian and M. Geschwinde and the recent study by Knoche (2013) should be emphasized. Raetzel-Fabian/Raetzel-Fabian and Geschwinde were the first to systematically investigate this relationship (Raetzel-Fabian 1999, 97ff.; 2000, 89ff.; 2002; Geschwinde/Raetzel-Fabian 2009, 225ff.). Knoche's (2013) extensive study was only available shortly before the completion of this manuscript. However, his work does take the discussion of the relationship between enclosures and ancient routes to a new level via both its intellectual depth and geographic scale.

With regard to South Scandinavia, the earliest comments regarding a possible connection between a causewayed enclosure (the Büdelsdorf site) and ancient roads were made by J.A. Bakker in 1976 (Bakker 1976, 83). Since then, several comparable comments have followed, but (with a single exception), they took only single sites into consideration. Only Steffens (2009, 88) considered more than one enclosure, but his list of three sites with relation to roads (Büdelsdorf, Rastorf and Markildegård) is far from complete. Furthermore, an in-depth discussion of his observations is missing. Therefore, a survey based on previously published information and an investigation of Danish enclosures is provided below.

The Büdelsdorf enclosure is situated on a promontory in a loop of the river Eider close to the place where the hærvej or Ochsenweg crosses the river. This ancient road is one of the most important long-distance routes in South Scandinavia. While it is well known from written sources from the Middle Ages onwards (Willroth 1986, 12), it can almost certainly can be traced back into prehistoric times, as suggested by the lines of burial mounds which trace its route (see the map of burial mounds in Jutland in Johansen et al. 2004, 37 Fig. 2 and compare with historic maps – e.g. Willroth 1986).

Steffens (2009, 88) mentioned the possible relationship between the position of the Rastorf enclosure and nearby roads. The situation of the Esesfeld site is also particularly interesting in this regard. The latter enclosure was discovered on the

site of a Carolingian stronghold. This is noteworthy because the site for the Carolingian castle was chosen due to its strategic position at the meeting point of two important long-distance roads as well as the fact that an important river crossing could be controlled from the site (Kühn 1989).

With regard to the two remaining north German causewayed enclosures of Albersdorf Dieksknöll and Bad Segeberg, no relations to ancient roads have yet been discussed in the literature. As is apparent from the "Topographisch Militärische Charte des Herzogtums Holstein" or Varendorfsche Karte, a map drawn between 1789 and 1796, the Dieksknöll enclosure is situated at the place at which a road crosses a river (Gietzelt 2000, Beilage). Bad Segeberg held a considerable strategic importance and is situated along a known road of historical importance (Beranek 2007, 51).

It can be concluded, therefore, that all five Neolithic causewayed enclosures known from Schleswig-Holstein in northern Germany had distinct relations to ancient roads as known from historical sources.

Comparable observations are almost completely lacking for the much more numerous Danish enclosures. Here, relations to ancient roads have only been noted for three of the 32 known sites. But, in contrast to the north German cases, none of these were roads known from Medieval or younger sources, but were rather reconstructed (and in one case also partly excavated) prehistoric roads or paths.

Close to the Markildegård enclosure in south Zealand, a prehistoric road was excavated (Fig. 17), which can (in part) be dated back to the Neolithic (Østergård Sørensen 1995a, 33; 1995b, 32f.). This road crosses a river close to the enclosure. Comparable observations have been made near the two Mølbjerg enclosures (Olesen 1994, 20) as well as for the Lokes Hede site (Birkedahl 1995, 31).

As no information regarding any possible relation between the vast majority of Danish (and thus South Scandinavian) enclosures and ancient roads (both those reconstructed from prehistory as well as historic) was available, the matter was investigated more closely.

Fig. 17 | *Parts of the Risby road/path excavated close to the causewayed enclosure of Markilde-gård on the island of Zealand, Denmark (from Schou Jørgensen 1977). This road dates to the Viking Age. However, earlier, more primitively constructed phases of the same road/path can be dated as far back as the Late Mesolithic. It is likely, therefore, that it was in active use at the same time as the nearby enclosure.*

6.3.2.1 Danish enclosures and reconstructed prehistoric roads/paths

The basics for the reconstruction of prehistoric roads/paths were established by S. Müller more than a hundred years ago by means of his thorough studies of barrow lines in northwestern and central Jutland (Müller, S. 1897, 331f.; 1904; see Johansen et al. 2004, 34 ff. and Johannsen/Laursen 2010, 38ff. for an up to date assessment of the discussion of Müller's hypothesis). By investigating the course of these barrow lines topographically while paying special attention to wet areas and fords across rivers, Müller convincingly argued for the existence of prehistoric roads. These roads were not necessarily always situated exactly where the barrows were (even though this was the case demonstrably often), but were always nearby. Slight deviations can especially be observed for Bronze Age barrows, which were often erected on the top of hills, while the actual roads must have been at the foot of these hills in well suited topographical positions. Nonetheless, even in instances in which there were deviations, these cases rarely surpassed a few hundred meters' distance. Therefore, in general, the course of prehistoric roads and paths can be reconstructed on the basis of barrow lines.

Müller investigated numerous examples in northwestern and central Jutland in which megalithic graves were rare. His reconstructions were therefore almost exclusively based on barrows of the Single Grave Culture and on those from the Bronze Age. Several of these barrow lines also contain long barrows, which possibly date from the TRB Culture. However, this problem was not specifically investigated by Müller, and it can only be concluded at present that Müller demonstrated the possibility of reconstructing roads and paths from the later parts of the Neolithic and the Bronze Age, but not for the TRB Culture period.

The possibility of reconstructing older (TRB) roads and paths based on lines of megalithic graves has been cautiously approached on several occasions (Brøndsted 1962, Kartenbeilage) and has even been directly denied (Hoika 1986, 201 and 205). However, Hoika's argument was mainly based on postulates rather than on demonstrated facts. His main point concerned the lack of megalithic graves and especially the potentially road-indicative lines of such graves in several regions in which he suspected Neolithic roads to have been present. At the same time, he did not recognize rather clear examples of Neolithic roads indicated by rows of megalithic graves in his own study region (eastern Holstein), the West Group of the TRB in northwest Germany and the Netherlands (Schlicht 1962; Schlicht 1968, 11 Abb. 1; Bakker 1976, 70 Abb. 7) and in the TRB North Group in the Falbygden dis-

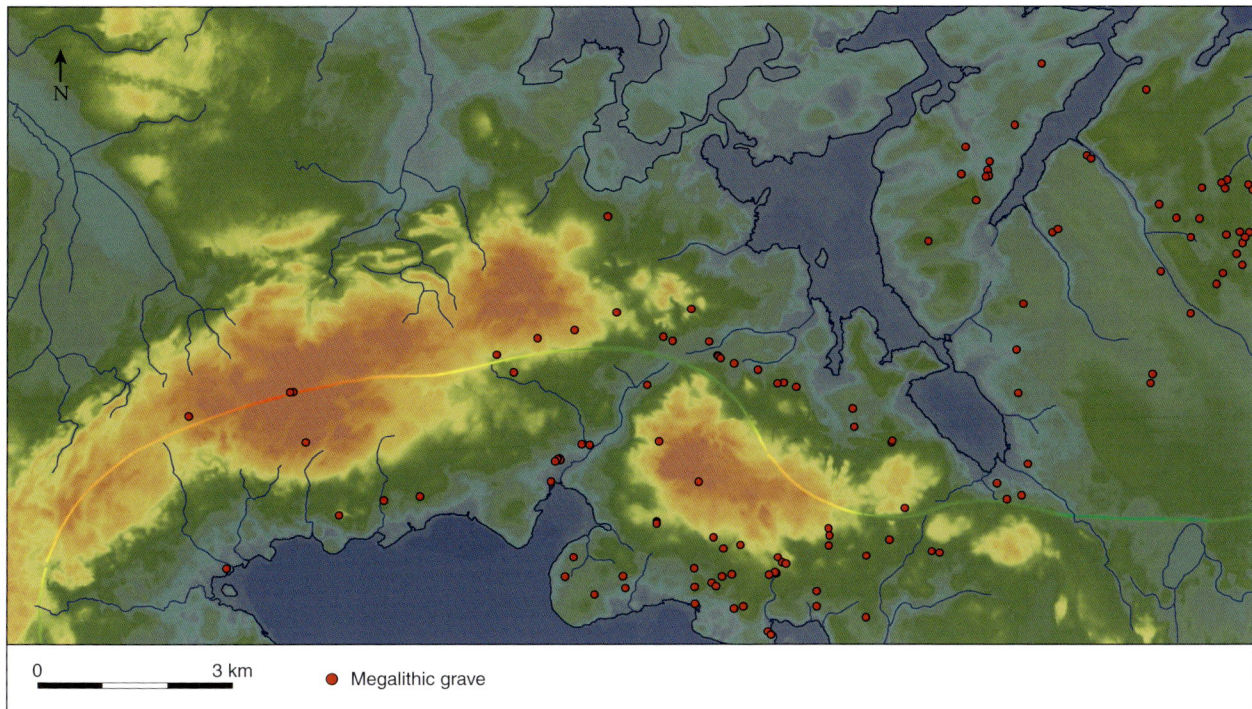

Fig. 18 | *Linear arrangements of megalithic graves in Djursland clearly represent Neolithic roads or paths, as they do in other parts of South Scandinavia. Several alignments of megaliths are visible in this example from the Kalø Vig Bay area. Note how similar the course of one of the barrow lines is to the course of a present day road, which is visible as a faint line in the illustration.*

trict of Sweden (Sahlström 1935, 27ff. Fig. 9), despite the fact that he cited these examples himself. Furthermore, Hoika's study unfortunately suffers from a surfeit of confidence in the reliability of modern megalithic grave mapping, even though he made great efforts to use historical information about graves that were destroyed in the past. Irrespective of the efforts one may take to go through historic archives, the example from the Sarup region (discussed above) clearly demonstrates that the modern mapping of megalithic tombs cannot be taken to be representative of the prehistoric conditions without great pains being taken on the ground to locate potential destroyed tombs.

The examples from Sweden, northwest Germany, the Netherlands and eastern Holstein referred to above leave little doubt that lines of TRB megalithic graves indicate contemporary roads or paths, just as did later lines of barrows (Fig. 18). Thus far, the best demonstrations of this relationship were recently provided by Johannsen & Laursen (2010, 46f.) for

a Danish case and possibly Andersson & Nilsson (2009a; 2009b) for a south Swedish case.

What was initially conceived as a TRB road at the Döserygg site in Scania was delimited by palisades alone on one side and by palisades and standing stones together on the opposite side. It could be followed for more than 700 m and likely continues outside the excavated area (Fig. 19B). Numerous dolmens were found on both sides of this road. The excavators recently altered their interpretation of the site, as new excavations demonstrated that the course of the palisades turns and crosses a ridge (Andersson/Wallebom 2013a; 2013b). The most recent interpretation suggests that it represents some kind of Neolithic enclosure related to classical causewayed enclosures. This interpretation might be contradicted by the presence of large numbers of dolmens both inside and outside of what would be the enclosed area. Future research is necessary to conclusively identify the nature of this remarkable site. Independent of these results, it is important to note that the site is situated along an important ancient route along which megalithic graves were built.

As shown by Johannsen & Laursen (2010), megalithic graves and mortuary houses of the TRB (EN II and MN I) are in several cases part of lines of stone heap graves from the later parts of the TRB as well as lines of barrows from the Single Grave Culture and Bronze Age in northwest Jutland (Fig. 19A). These last most certainly indicate the course of roads, given the numerous lines of evidence in their favour. Other recent and convincing Danish examples of the relationship between megalithic graves and roads have been provided by Sparrevohn (2009, 53f.) and Schülke (2009, 81f.).

It can, therefore, be concluded that lines of megalithic graves can be used to reconstruct the roads or paths which existed in the period during which causewayed enclosures were built. There are severe problems bound to this approach, nevertheless, as a large and – most importantly – unknown and unevenly distributed number of graves has been destroyed. This might lead to the false notion of the absence of roads in certain areas, or to incorrect reconstructions of roads based on the association of widely-spaced graves. It is necessary, therefore, to supplement information regarding the course of roads given by the distribution of megalithic graves with additional information. One part of this information, of course, is the topography and nature of the soil (avoidance of steep climbs and wet areas). Any reconstruction of prehistoric roads must take its point of departure in these factors, as was already stressed and demonstrated by Müller more than a hundred years ago.

Still, many roads may be missed completely and others may be reconstructed incorrectly. This situation can be improved drastically by the inclusion of barrows from later prehistoric periods (later Neolithic and Bronze Age) as well as especially the numerous barrows for which no precise dates can be given. In the Djursland area, the number of these barrows is more than five times as large as that of megalithic graves (3152 later or undated barrows as opposed to 585 megalithic graves). This relation illustrates how important the contribution of this data source is for the current purpose.

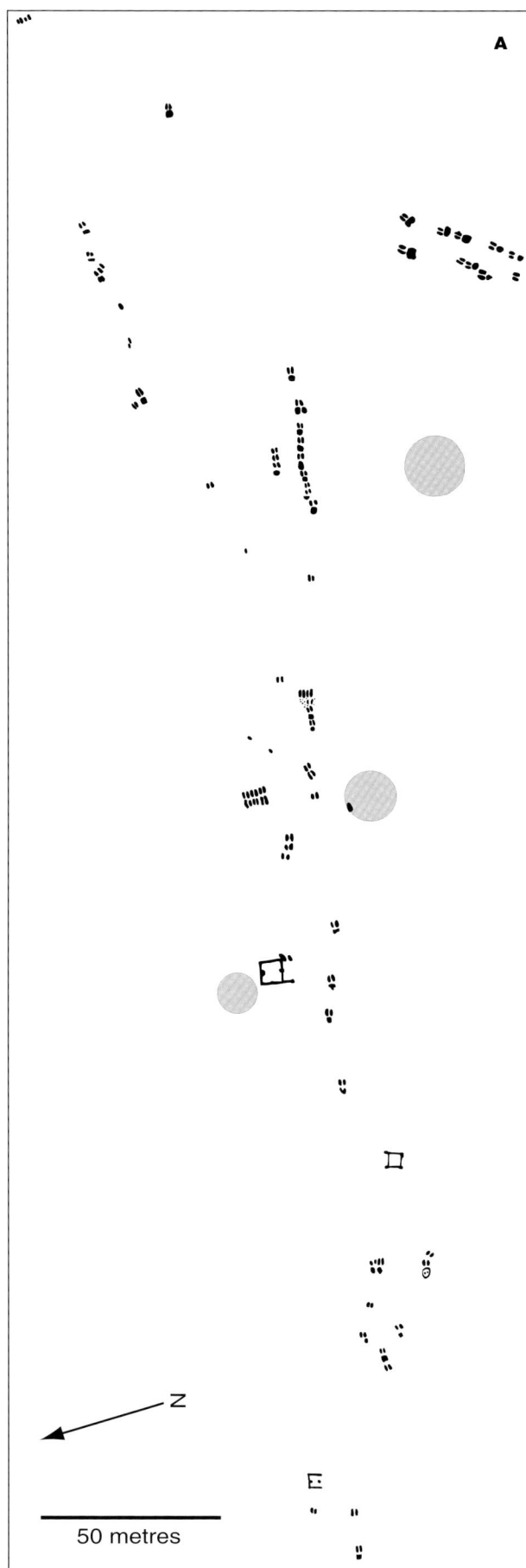

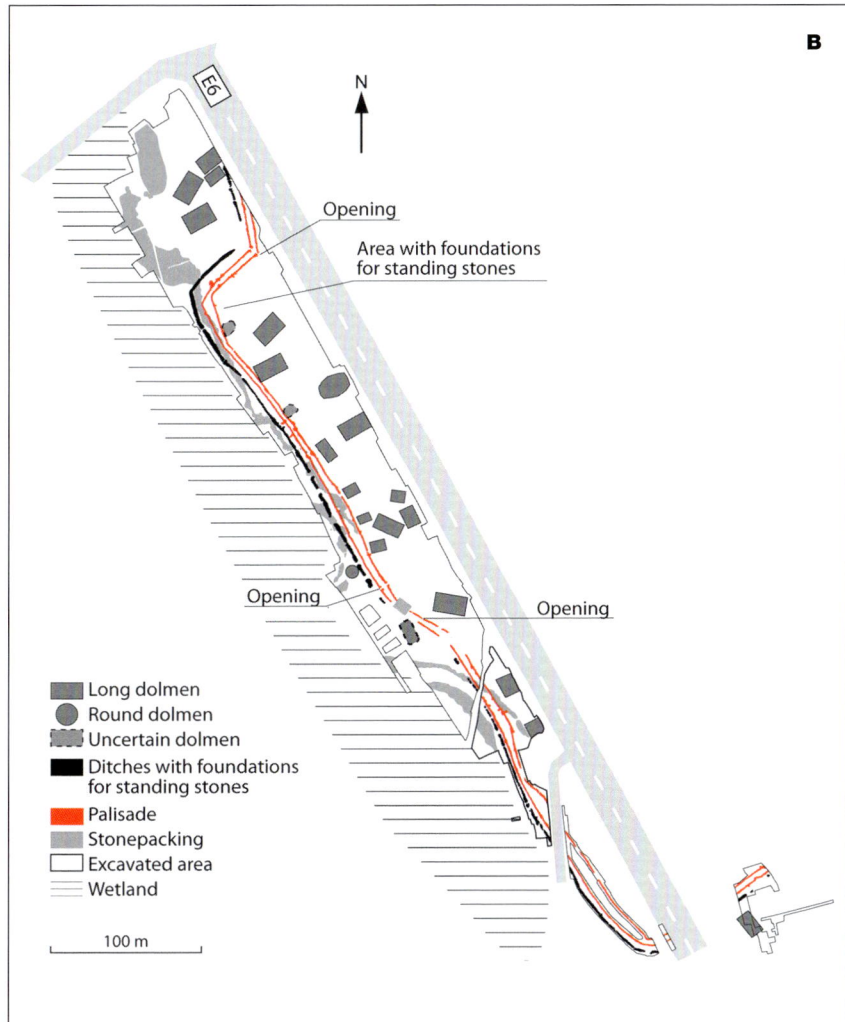

Fig. 19 | *A)(opposite page) Neolithic road at Vroue Hede in northwest Jutland, Denmark, as indicated by a row of stone packing graves form the later parts of the TRB as well as long- and round barrows holding megalithic chambers from the late Early/ early Middle Neolithic (from Johansen/Laursen 2010). B) Neolithic road/path at Haslöv in southwest Scania, Sweden. At the Döserygg site (literally the "ridge of the dolmens"), a TRB road delimited by palisades and standing stones was excavated which ran over more than 700 m. The palisaded road/path may have been much longer, or it may have been part of a palisade enclosure situated along an ancient route. Illustration by Henrik Pihl: Riksantikvarieämbetet UV Syd.*

A precondition for the inclusion of the later or undated barrows is of course supporting evidence for the underlying assumption that the course of the roads/paths remained largely unchanged throughout the Neolithic and the Bronze Age. In fact, it is possible to demonstrate that this assumption is correct (at least in many cases) via several distinct lines of evidence. Not only has it been demonstrated by recent studies that the recognizable barrow lines generally owe their existence to a process of accumulation of long duration (Holst et al. 2001), but it is also possible to illustrate this by a number of different examples. Some of these have already been referred to above (Johannsen/Laursen 2010, 46f.). Another extremely well investigated example is that of a 4 km long barrow line at Flintbek in northern Germany (Fig. 20), practically all monuments of which have been investigated archaeologically (Zich

1993). These excavations show that this line was comprised of a vast array of barrows constructed from Early Neolithic II through the Bronze Age, and that the line had thus formed over the course of approximately two millennia.

The examples given above clearly demonstrate that the same lines of communication and transport have been used throughout the Neolithic and the Bronze Age. Only with the advent of improved agricultural techniques in the Iron Age did this situation change, as these techniques enabled the cultivation of the heavy clay soils (where available) which had heretofore been avoided. This in turn led to a change in settlement and communication patterns (Willroth 1986, 12 with further literature). As very few Iron Age barrows were constructed, it is practically the totality of registered barrows that can be used to reconstruct Neolithic

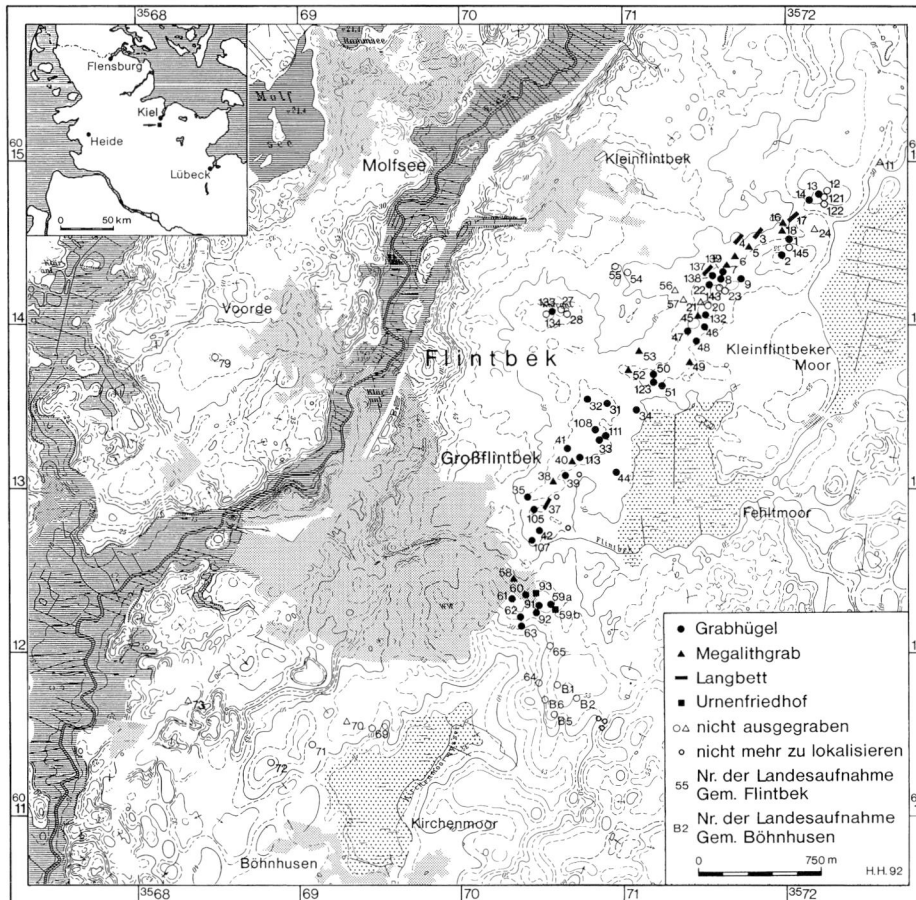

Fig. 20 | *At Flintbek, lines of prehistoric barrows of widely diverging age demonstrate the stability of the course of a prehistoric road/path throughout the Neolithic and Bronze Age (from Zich 1993).*

and Bronze Age roads/paths. As demonstrated by the examples cited above, these roads were established at the latest in the EN II and became more and more visible in the landscape through the accumulation of barrows over the course of the following two millennia.

The end of EN I and EN II probably mark a pioneering stadium in the creation of a widespread inland road/path network, as earlier settlements were bound tightly to the coastlines. As has already been mentioned, these coastal settlements were widely abandoned at the end of the first part of the Early Neolithic (EN I) around 3600 BC (Andersen, S.H. 2008, 71) when the interior of the country started to be settled. This is visible not least in pollen analyses, which demonstrate a marked landnam in this phase (Madsen, T. 1990, 29 with references to older literature and individual pollen diagrams. For more recent palynological investigations confirming the older results see e.g. Lütjens/Wiethold 1999, 45 and Dörfler et al. 2012).

In the following, an example from the present investigation area – the Store Brokhøj enclosure – is used to illustrate the importance of the inclusion of undated barrows in the reconstruction of roads/paths from the time of the construction of causewayed enclosures.

The Store Brokhøj enclosure is one of the very rare hilltop enclosures of the TRB, and its discovery was totally unexpected. Due to its position on a hilltop, it is neither delimited by rivers, lakes nor bogs. Only a few very short freshwater streams are found close to the site (Fig. 21A). All of these naturally lead directly away from it rather than surrounding the enclosure. The nearest bog (which might have been a minor lake in the Neolithic) is recorded 700 m to the south. While close to a fjord in the west (distance ca. 800 m), the distance is still considerable and the fjord by no means delimits the enclosure. The nearest recorded megalithic grave is also found at a considerable distance. With the caveat of the local conditions of the Djursland Pen-

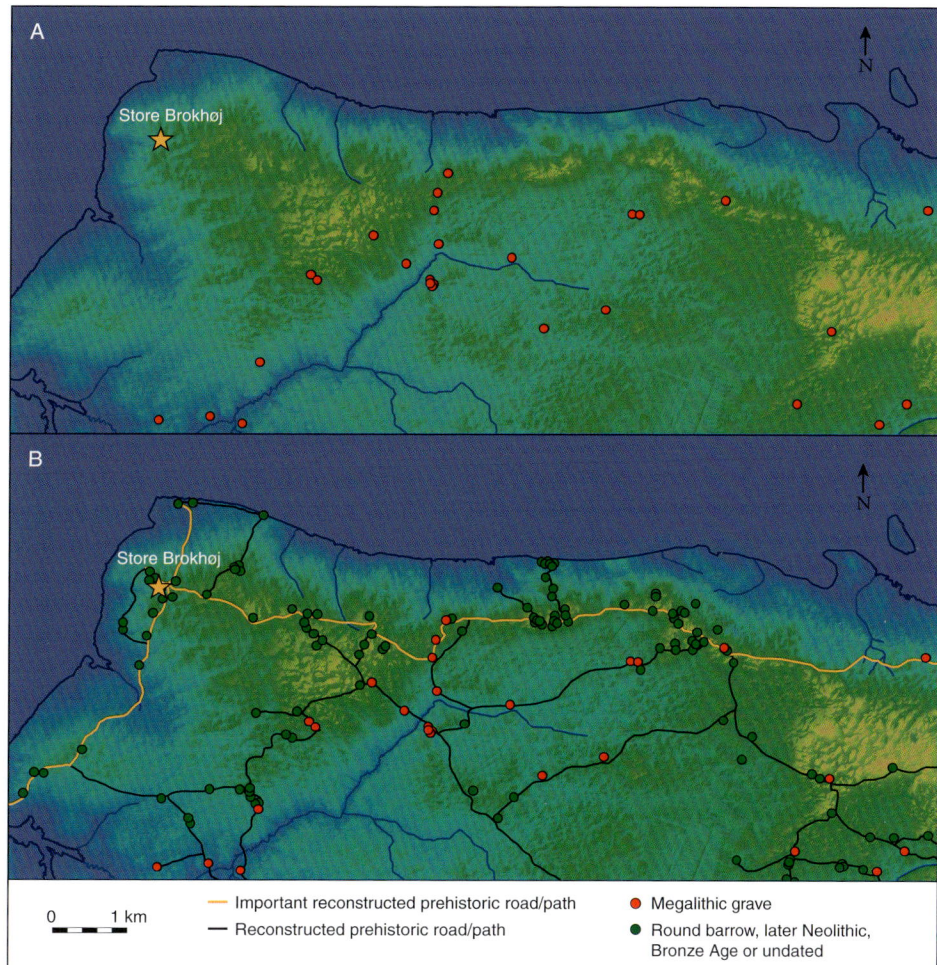

Fig. 21 | *The surroundings of the Store Brokhøj enclosure in the northwestern part of Djursland. A) Only megalithic tombs were mapped, B) All registered barrows were mapped irrespective of their age. They were then used to reconstruct the course of prehistoric roads or tracks. It appears that the enclosure was constructed at the juncture of the two most important roads/tracks.*

0   1 km

— Important reconstructed prehistoric road/path ● Megalithic grave
— Reconstructed prehistoric road/path ● Round barrow, later Neolithic,
    Bronze Age or undated

insula and its large number of megalithic tombs, the location of this grave 2800 m to the southeast is comparatively vast. In summary, with the parameters commonly used to locate causewayed enclosures, this site would have been virtually impossible to detect. The situation changes completely when all barrows from the wider surroundings of the site are included in the analysis. These barrows allow for the reconstruction of a number of roads in the area, the most important (i.e. longest) of which ran approximately parallel to the north coast of Djursland at a distance of ca. 1000 m while another followed the coast of the former fjord to the west at a distance of ca. 750 m (Fig. 21B). The Store Brokhøj enclosure is situated at the conjuncture of these two long-distance routes as well as the confluence of several other, shorter roads or paths. Therefore, this example illustrates the importance of roads/paths for the choice of location for the construction of causewayed enclosures as

well as the necessity of the inclusion of barrows of unknown age into analysis. It can be added that the construction of Neolithic causewayed enclosures at crossroads has also been demonstrated in Central Europe (Raetzel-Fabian 1999, 100; Knoche 2013, 163ff.). This is indicative of the fact that these hot spots of transport and communication are relevant points in the search for enclosures. The importance of such points in the Bronze Age has been demonstrated by Johansen et al. (2004) and the potential ritual importance of crossroads has been pointed out by Rudebeck (2002).

All barrows forming the roads or paths leading to the Store Brokhøj enclosure are undated. While not particularly likely, it is possible that all of these mounds cover megalithic tombs and thus do not postdate the enclosure. Therefore, a second example shall be included which should illustrate not only the potential usefulness but also the necessity of including barrows younger than the construc-

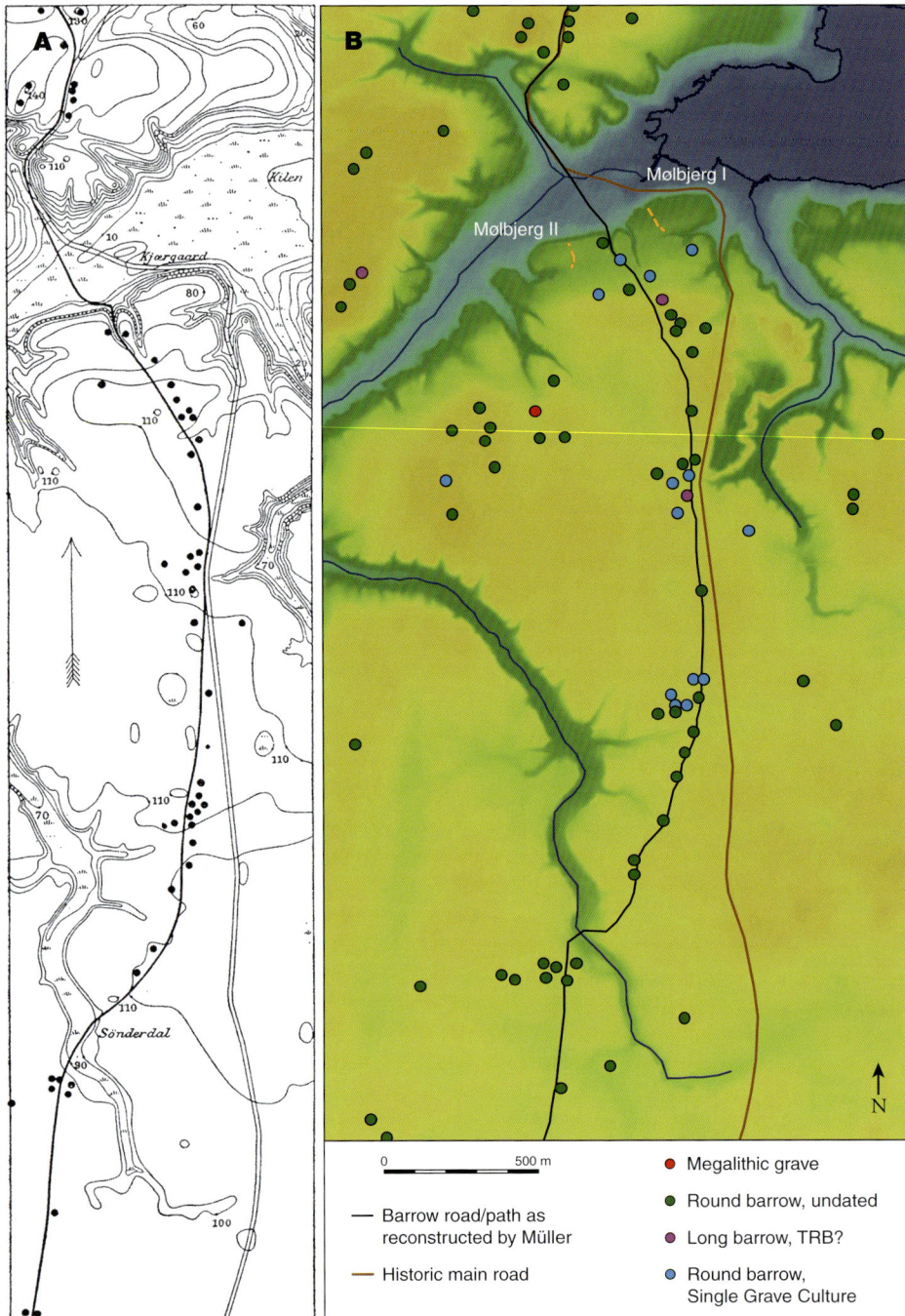

Fig. 22 | *Barrow roads near Fousing in north-western Jutland. A) The course of the road as reconstructed by S. Müller in his classic study of the relation between barrow lines and roads (from Müller 1904), B) The course of the Fousing road and its relation to barrows of different ages. Very few of these barrows can be dated to the TRB; most of them are significantly younger. The two Mølbjerg enclosures as well as the course of a historic main road have also been indicated. The sites are typical examples for the location of causewayed enclosures in South Scandinavia insofar as they are located on (at least partly) water-delimited promontories close to the point where a prehistoric road crosses a river and said river flows into a fjord.*

tion phase of the TRB enclosures in any predictive modelling aimed at the detection of unknown enclosures by means of including information derived from road/path systems.

One of the classic examples of barrow roads is a ca. 3.5 km long line of round barrows in Fousing Parish in northwest Jutland (Fig. 22 A). It was pointed out by S. Müller in 1904 (25ff., Fig. 17) as an example of a barrow line marking a road across less than ideal terrain at the least obstruc-

tive point. In the present case, this is the point at which the minor river of Bredkær Bæk runs through a widened valley with soft, wet ground immediately before flowing into Kilen (a side arm of Limfjorden Fjord). In the Neolithic, the barrow road/path would have crossed the river almost exactly at the point where it flowed into the fjord, as the water has withdrawn since then due to isostatic movement. What today (or in Müller's times) is a widened, wet meadow would then have been part of the fjord. In 1993, L.H. Olesen discovered a causewayed enclosure on a well-defined promontory on the southern shore of the fjord-arm by aerial survey – the Mølbjerg I enclosure (Olesen 1994, 20 ff.; Eriksen/Olesen 2002). The barrow-road identified by Müller runs only 150 m to the west of the ditch segments that cut off the promontory, a fact upon which Olesen also remarked. Furthermore, in the summer of 2010, she detected a second causewayed enclosure on another promontory on the southern shore of Bredkær Bæk, just opposite the first and immediately to the west of the barrow road. The two Mølbjerg enclosures are thus perfect examples of the typical position of causewayed enclosures in the North Group of the TRB: they are situated on well defined, water-surrounded promontories where a river flowed into a fjord and are near to a ford in the river (Fig. 22 B). It should furthermore be noted that these twin enclosures are not the only examples of their kind neither in South Scandinavia nor abroad. The other Scandinavian examples (Vasagård west and east; Lønt and Starup Langelandsvej) have already been mentioned above. Knoche (2013, 218f.) recently pointed out a number of examples from Central and Western Europe and convincingly argued for a special ritual significance associated with the twin enclosure phenomenon.

With regard to the barrow road leading from the south towards the two enclosures and the river crossing at Mølbjerg, it is interesting to note the age of the tombs. Those that constitute the road or path described by Müller have been dated to the Single Grave Culture in a number of cases. This is true for practically all excavated barrows. Furthermore, the barrow line contains two long-barrows. Although these have not been excavated, they should possibly be dated to the TRB (even though in two instances the old descriptions mention the possibility that the barrows originally may have been pairs of round barrows that 'grew' together over time). In fact, these few long barrows are the only monuments in the barrow line that possibly belong to the TRB – the remainder (the majority) is of unknown age. Nevertheless, most of these

undated mounds almost certainly belong to the Single Grave Culture due to their shape and size. A single passage grave is known ca. 500 m south of the Mølbjerg II enclosure. It represents the only certain megalithic grave within a 2.5 km radius around the two enclosures.

The Fousing barrow road/path leading to the two Mølbjerg enclosures thus not only illustrates the typical location of TRB enclosures, but also the relevance and necessity of including younger Neolithic, Bronze Age and undated barrows in the reconstruction of the roads or paths in predicting the location of causewayed enclosures. In the current case, the route could not have been reconstructed on the basis of certain or possible megalithic graves, as these are very rare in that area.

The Mølbjerg and Store Brokhøj enclosures described above as examples for the methodology of the reconstruction of prehistoric roads or paths clearly indicate the potential for an investigation of the communication infrastructure to point out potential enclosure sites. This applies for both promontory and hilltop sites.

Besides the Mølbjerg enclosures, the Markildegård and Lokes Hede sites have already been related to prehistoric roads within the literature. As apparent from Figs. 23 and 24, there is good reason for this association. While the destruction of the Markildegård site by modern road construction (visible in the digital elevation model used as basis of the illustration) renders this case less impressive, the Lokes Hede example is highly illustrative. It shows a very well defined barrow road/path passing immediately beside (or possibly even across) the Neolithic enclosure at the bottom of Mariager Fjord. This fjord with a length (in the Neolithic) of ca. 46 km stretched almost 40 kilometres inland from the east coast of Jutland. The enclosure site at the bottom of the fjord is therefore the first point on a 40 km stretch that allowed for land based travel along a north-south axis. Consequently, the site must have been a very important focal point for transport and communication. It was certainly the same reasons that guided the construction of one of the famous Viking ring fortresses – Fyrkat – just 2 km to the northeast of Lokes Hede on a peninsula on the southern shore of

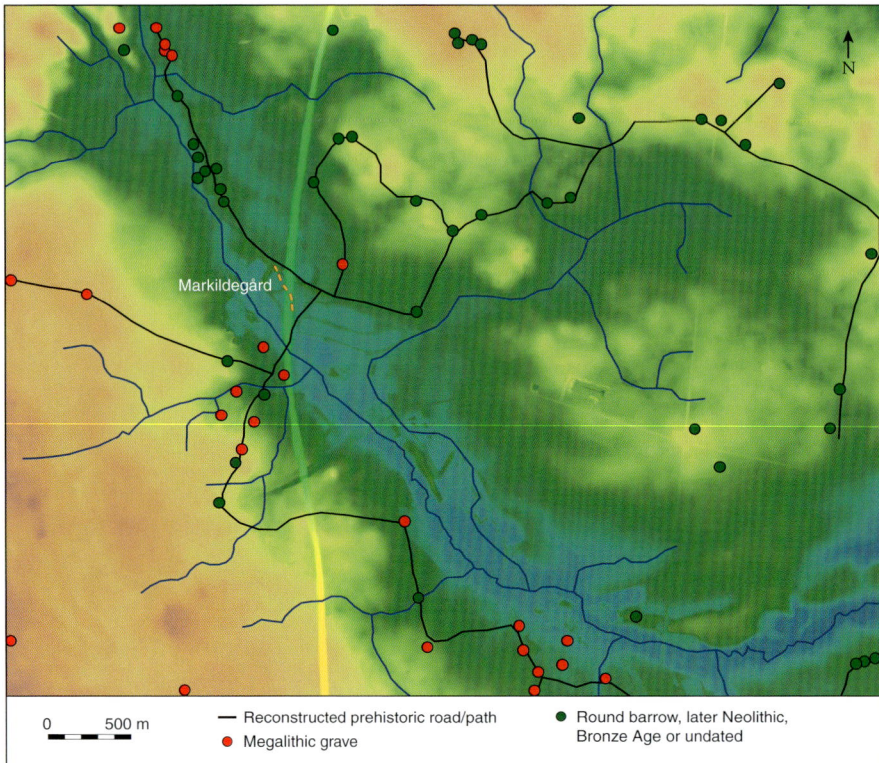

Fig. 23 | *The enclosure at Markildegård and its relation to barrow roads/ paths. The site was largely destroyed by recent road construction. (This is readily apparent in the digital elevation model). The fact that the modern road crosses the river at the same place as did the prehistoric road indicates the strategic importance of the location of the Markildegård enclosure with regard to prehistoric communication infrastructures. The approximate location of the row of ditches is indicated schematically in this illustration.*

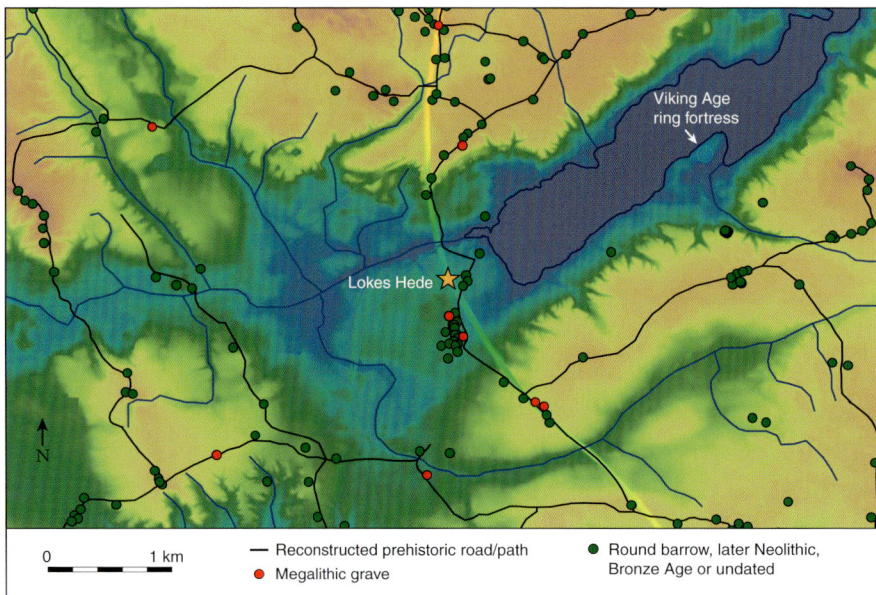

Fig. 24 | *The Lokes Hede enclosure and its relation to barrow roads/ paths. Just like at the Markildegård site, this enclosure was found during motorway construction near to a river crossing, which underlines the strategic importance of the site to this day. This enclosure was built in a position almost identical to that of the Mølbjerg enclosures: on a promontory near to the place at which a prehistoric road crosses a river near to its mouth. Note the Viking Age Fyrkat ring fortress on the southern bank of the fjord. No information regarding the course of the ditches has been published.*

Fig. 25 | *The location of the Liselund enclosure in northern Jutland in relation to prehistoric roads/paths as reconstructed from barrow lines. The approximate course of the two ditch circuits is indicated schematically in this illustration.*

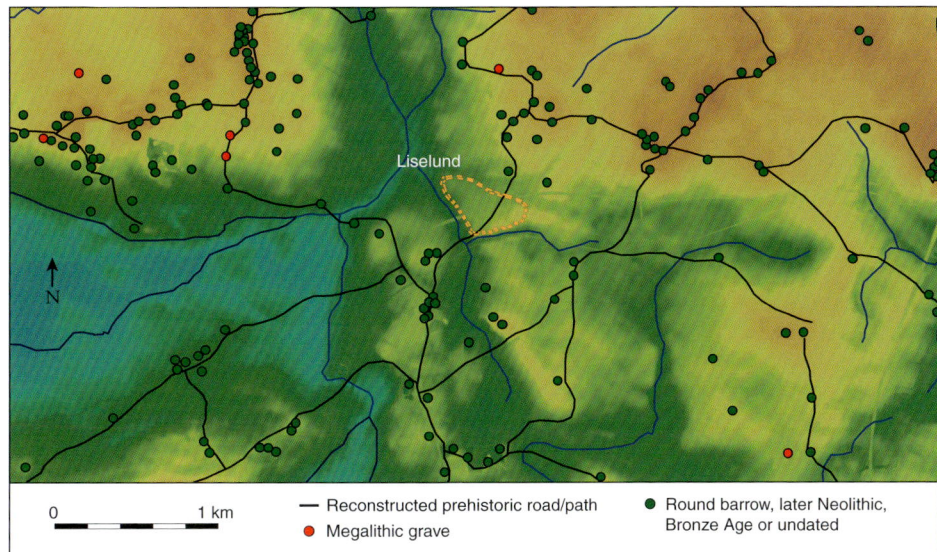

Liselund

0   1 km

— Reconstructed prehistoric road/path
● Megalithic grave
● Round barrow, later Neolithic, Bronze Age or undated

Fig. 26 | *The location of the Søby Møllegård enclosure in northern Jutland in relation to prehistoric roads/paths as reconstructed from barrow lines. No information regarding the course of the ditches has been published.*

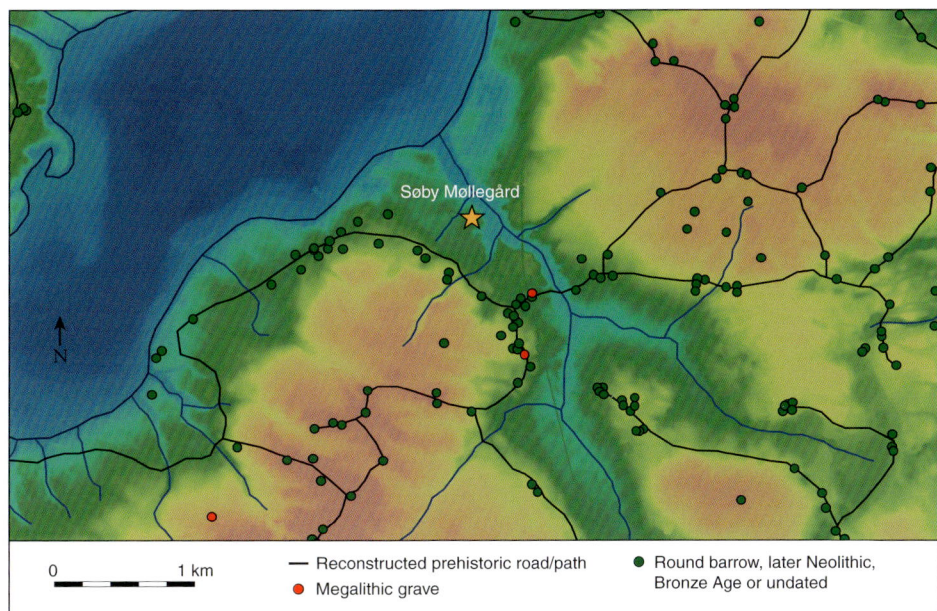

Søby Møllegård

0   1 km

— Reconstructed prehistoric road/path
● Megalithic grave
● Round barrow, later Neolithic, Bronze Age or undated

Mariager Fjord (Fig. 24; Olsen/Schmidt 1977, 37ff.). Even today, the most important north-south highway in Jutland passes the Neolithic enclosure which was actually discovered during its construction (visible in Fig. 24). It is therefore also worthwhile to consider a relation between the assumed large size of the enclosure (estimated to be between 12 and 20 ha – Birkedahl 1995) and its strategic position.

A look at the remaining Danish enclosures and barrow roads/paths shows that, in almost all cases, distinct relations do exist. This is true for the enclosures at Liselund (Fig. 25) and Søby Møllegård (Fig. 26) in northern Jutland as well as for the last known site in this part of Denmark: the Vilsund enclosure (Fig. 27). The latter is of special interest, as it is situated on a peninsula to which a barrow road or path leads. Another barrow road/path leads to the beach on the opposite side of the narrow sound (Vilsund), indicating that the enclosure site constituted an important juncture between land- and sea-based transport and communication.

The only other enclosure known from the top end of a peninsula is the Ballegård site in Djursland (Fig. 28). In that case as well, a barrow road or path appears to have led to the site which projected out into Kolindsund Fjord. Due to the low number of barrows in the area, the situation is less clear than at Vilsund, nevertheless. There is noth-

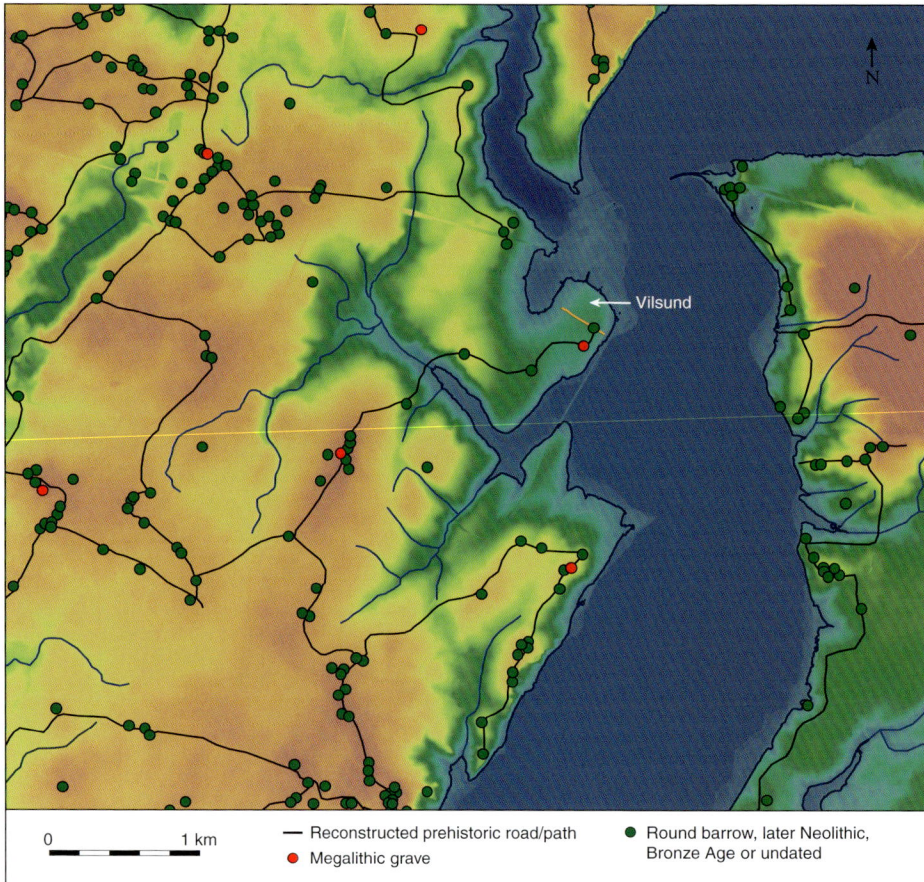

Fig. 27 | *The location of the Vilsund enclosure in northern Jutland in relation to prehistoric roads/paths as reconstructed from barrow lines. The approximate course of the turf wall with supporting rows of posts is indicated schematically in this illustration.*

0 1 km	── Reconstructed prehistoric road/path ● Round barrow, later Neolithic, ● Megalithic grave Bronze Age or undated

ing to indicate that an important crossover to the northern shore of Kolindsund was situated at the Ballegård enclosure. Still, the location appears to be extremely well chosen with regard to communication, as it marks the mouth of a side arm of Kolindsund which penetrates almost 10 km into the peninsula to the south. The possible enclosure of Taastrup Kolindvej is located at the very bottom of this branch of Kolindsund. The Ballegård site, therefore, indicates that land- as well as water-based communication routes played an important role in the choice of enclosure location.

Approximately 5 km to the west of Ballegård is a second entrance to a sailing channel leading to the Taastrup Kolindvej enclosure. Just opposite to this entrance (and on the northern banks of Kolindsund) lies the Blakbjerg enclosure. The site is located on a plateau with steep edges on three sides and a magnificent view over Kolindsund Fjord (Fig. 28). Two barrow roads/paths pass by the Blakbjerg enclosure on its western and southern side, further enhancing the enclosures' strategic position.

Three other enclosures are known with certainty from the northern shore of Kolindsund, all found in the eastern part of the fjord within a few kilometres' distance of each other. As apparent from Fig. 29, all are situated directly beside (or at least rather close to) the same road/path which ran parallel to the shore of the fjord. This is the same road/path that leads to the Blakbjerg enclosure further west. The strategic position of the Kainsbakke and Skærvad enclosures is immediately apparent. These sites were constructed close to an important passage to the north of a side arm of the fjord.

A few kilometres to the east, the Grenå enclosure is situated on a small island just off the northern coast of Kolindsund (Fig. 29). This is one of few Danish enclosures for which a relation to important land-based communication routes is not immediately apparent, as very few grave mounds survived the growth of what is today Djursland's largest town (Vedsted 1986). The fact that this town developed exactly here nevertheless hints at the

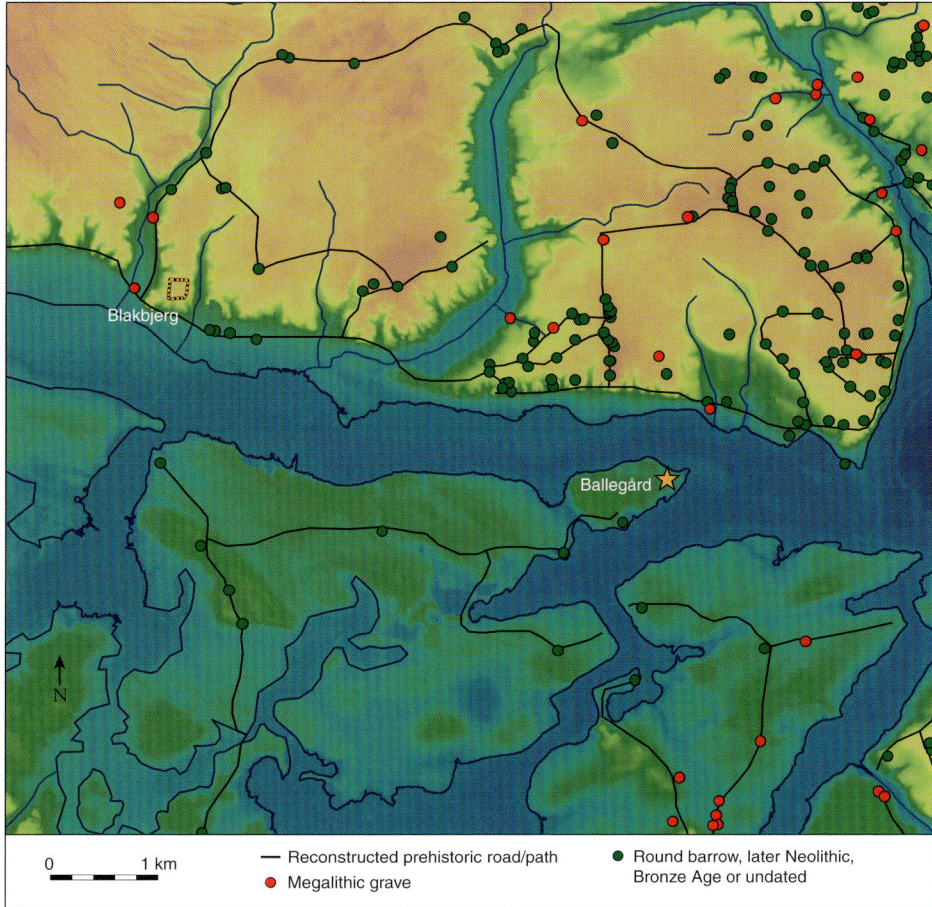

Fig. 28 | *The location of the Blakbjerg and Ballegård enclosures in Djursland and their relation to prehistoric roads/paths as reconstructed from barrow lines. No information regarding the course of the ditches at Ballegård is available at present. However, the approximate course of the two ditch circuits at Blakbjerg is indicated schematically in this illustration.*

Blakbjerg

Ballegård

0   1 km

—— Reconstructed prehistoric road/path
● Megalithic grave
● Round barrow, later Neolithic, Bronze Age or undated

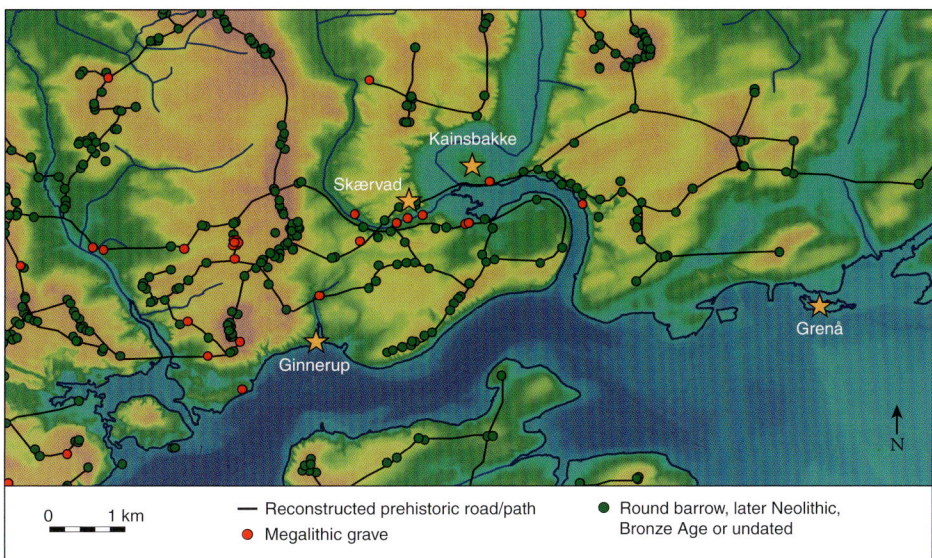

Fig. 29 | *The location of the Kainsbakke, Skærvad, Ginnerup and Grenå enclosures in Djursland and their relation to prehistoric roads/paths as reconstructed from barrow lines. No information regarding the course of the ditches at these sites has yet been published.*

Kainsbakke

Skærvad

Ginnerup

Grenå

0   1 km

—— Reconstructed prehistoric road/path
● Megalithic grave
● Round barrow, later Neolithic, Bronze Age or undated

strategic importance of its location at the point at which Kolindsund opens into the sea (Kattegat). Furthermore, a narrow sailing channel to the northeast meets Kolindsund here. With regards to transport and communication, the Grenå enclosure thus resembles the Ballegården site.

The Galgebakken enclosure, which is somewhat removed from the southern shore of Kolindsund, is comparable to the enclosure sites found on peninsulas, because several barrow roads lead to it (Fig. 30). It is possible that one of these roads crossed the Skodå River just south of the site, but it is not

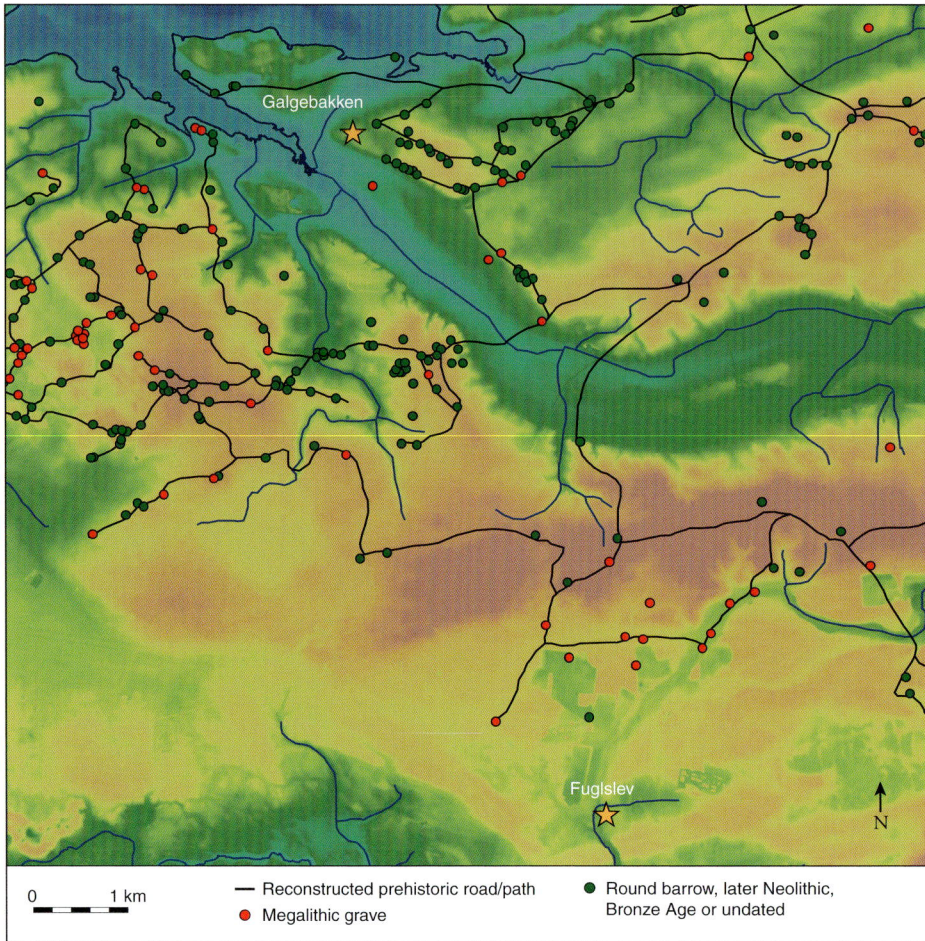

Fig. 30 | *The location of the Galgebakke and Fuglslev enclosures in Djursland and their relation to prehistoric roads/paths as reconstructed from barrow lines. No information regarding the course of the ditches at these two enclosures has yet been published.*

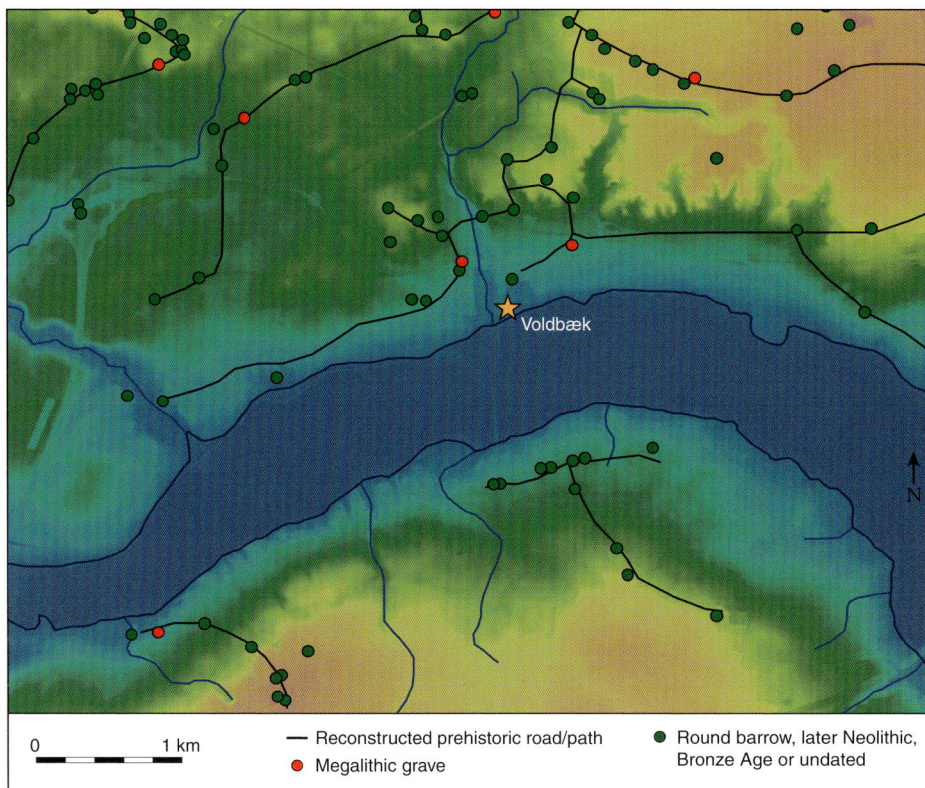

Fig. 31 | *The location of the Voldbæk enclosure in eastern Jutland in relation to prehistoric roads/paths as reconstructed from barrow lines. No precise information regarding the course of the ditches of this destroyed site has yet been published.*

possible to reconstruct such a river crossing with certainty, due to a lack of barrows. It may therefore well be that it is was not land-based travel, but rather the sailing channel leading into the important Skodå River that was responsible for the construction of the enclosure.

The Fuglslev enclosure (the last site from Djursland to be discussed) is situated in a region completely devoid of any grave mounds (Fig. 30). It appears, though, that several barrow roads from the north may lead to the site, which is situated on the upper end of a river leading to a fjord away to the south. The Fuglslev site may, therefore, also have had strategic importance as a crossing point between land- and water-based travels.

The Voldbæk site further south in Jutland is totally destroyed today and is situated in a suburb of the city of Århus. It is found on the northern shores of the Stone Age fjord of Brabrand which is currently a lake (Fig. 31). Approximately 500 m to the north, it is bypassed by an important barrow road/path

following the northern shore of the fjord. The choice of location for the construction of this enclosure thereby strongly resembles that of the enclosures on the northern shore of Kolindsund.

In the Horsens Fjord area further to the south, the situation appears to be slightly different with the two certain enclosures of Toftum and Bjerggård (as well as the enclosure-related site at Aalstrup) (Fig. 32) insofar as the enclosures/enclosure-related sites are not placed as close to the shoreline as in the cases discussed above. The choice of location is of strategic importance with regard to land-based transport and communication, just as was the case for many other enclosures. Bjerggård and Toftum (as well as Aalstrup) are clearly related to the barrow road or path that follows the northern shore of Horsens Fjord. A parallel road is seen north of the one nearest to the coast. However, this parallel road is interrupted approximately between the Toftum enclosure in the east and the Bjerggård enclosure in the west. All travel on the interrupted northern road/

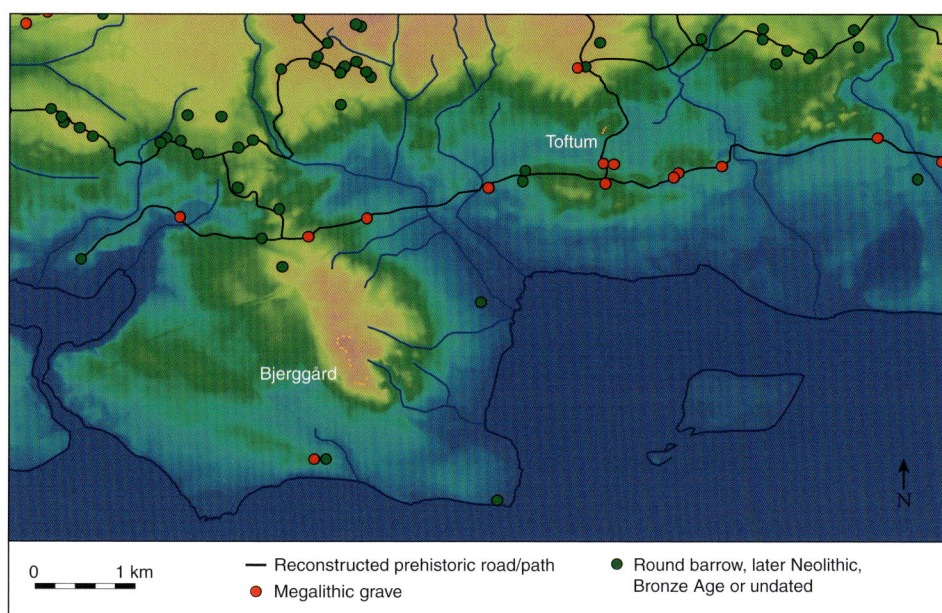

Fig. 32 | *The location of the Bjerggård and Toftum enclosures in eastern Jutland and their relation to prehistoric roads/paths as reconstructed from barrow lines. The approximate course of the ditches at the two sites is indicated schematically in this illustration. Seven and a half km to the east of Toftum, the enclosure-related site of Aalstrup is located near to where the same road/path to which Toftum and Bjerggård relate (along the northern shore of Horsens Fjord) crosses a river.*

path, therefore, ran over the southern road via north-south paths. The Toftum site is in direct association with the easternmost of these north-south stretches. The promontory on which it was constructed is situated immediately north of a very narrow dry passage through an extensive wet area to the east and west. This narrow passage is the only area through which the road/path could lead. The Toftum enclosure, therefore, is in a very strategic position (Fig. 33).

The situation is almost the same further to the south in Jutland on the southern shore of Haderslev Fjord where the Lønt and Starup Langelandsvej enclosures are separated from each other by a distance of only 700 m (Fig. 34). Both are clearly associated with a barrow road/path following the fjord on its southern side. Furthermore, a second barrow road coming from the southeast meets the first road between the two enclosures, emphasizing their strategic position.

The position of the Bundsø enclosure at the bottom of a long and narrow fjord (see Hoika 1987, 135ff.) is comparable to that of the Lokes Hede site. A whole range of well-defined barrow roads pass in close proximity to the Bundsø enclosure (Fig. 35).

The scarcity of barrows makes it difficult to analyse the relation of the Hygind site on Funen to land-based travel and communication (Fig. 36). The enclosure is situated on top of a promontory which might have become a peninsula in the bottom of a narrow bay at high tide.

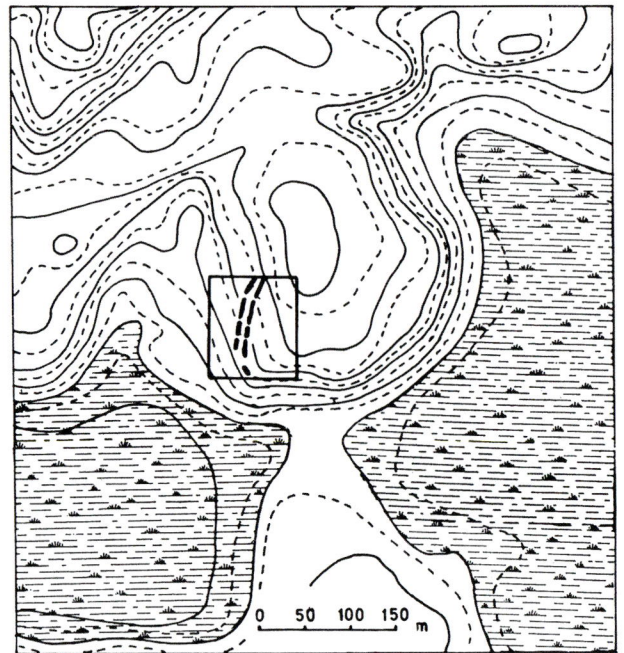

Fig. 33 | *The Toftum enclosure is located at a narrow and strategically important passage across an area of extensive wetlands (from Madsen 1978b).*

Despite the modest number of barrows in the vicinity of Åsum Enggård (another enclosure on Funen), it is possible to identify the strategic position of the site close to the juncture of an east-west and a north-south going road/path (Fig. 37).

The last of the known sites on Funen, the Sarup I and II enclosures as well as the enclosure-related

Fig. 34 | *The location of the Lønt and Starup Langelandsvej enclosures in southern Jutland and their relation to prehistoric roads/ paths as reconstructed from barrow lines. The approximate course of the ditches at the two sites is indicated schematically in this illustration.*

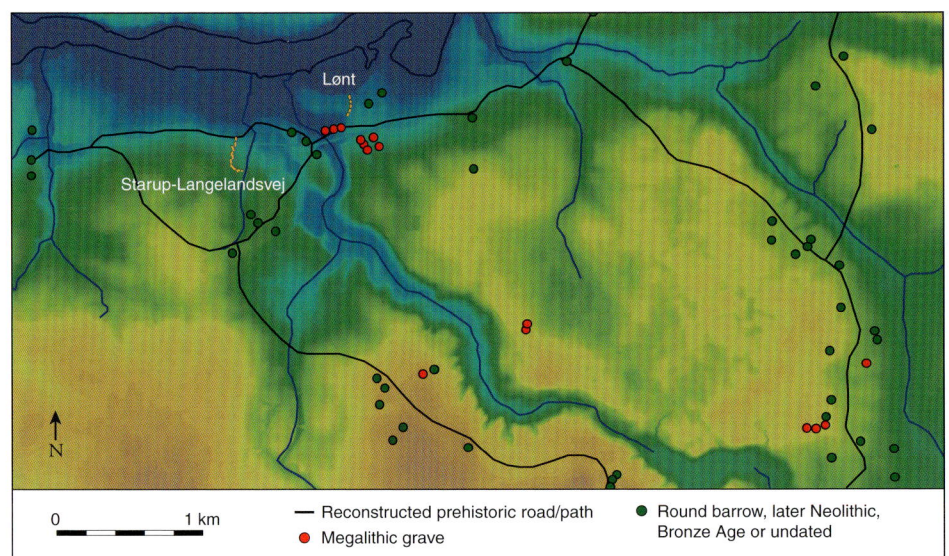

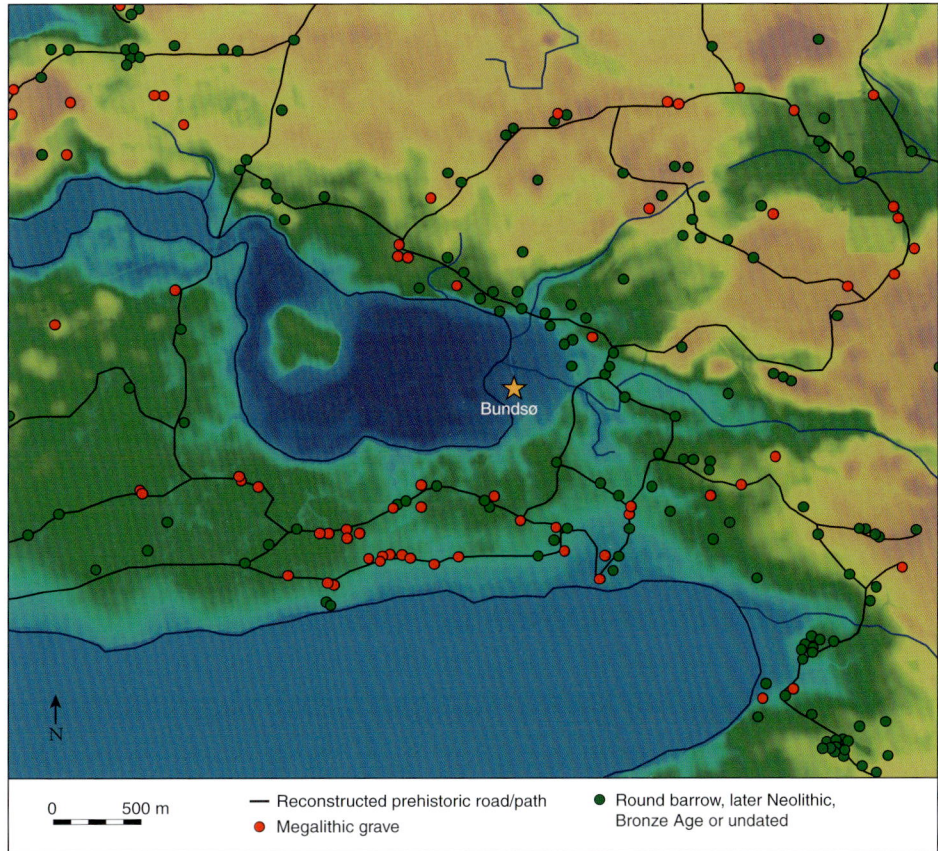

Fig. 35 | *The location of the Bundsø enclosure in southern Jutland in relation to prehistoric roads/paths as reconstructed from barrow lines. No information regarding the course of the ditches at this site has yet been published.*

Bundsø

0   500 m

— Reconstructed prehistoric road/path
● Megalithic grave
● Round barrow, later Neolithic, Bronze Age or undated

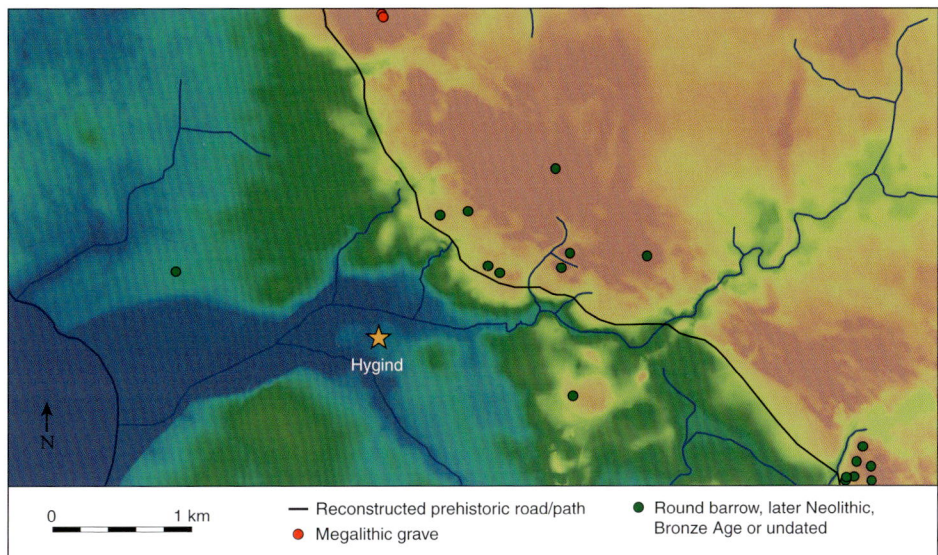

Fig. 36 | *The location of the Hygind enclosure on the island of Funen in relation to prehistoric roads/paths as reconstructed from barrow lines. No information regarding the course of the ditches at this has yet been published.*

Hygind

0   1 km

— Reconstructed prehistoric road/path
● Megalithic grave
● Round barrow, later Neolithic, Bronze Age or undated

site of Sarup Gamle Skole all show clear relations to an important barrow road that follows the southern shore of the island (Fig. 38). This is, in fact, the same road that passes by the Hygind enclosure further to the northwest.

Like the Hygind site, the Trelleborg enclosure on Zealand sits on top of a promontory that might have been a peninsula at high water (Fig. 39). A barrow road/path (not well defined due to its low number of barrows) passes by in the immediate vicinity. The strategic position of this enclosure is underlined by the fact that another Viking ring fortress (Trelleborg) was erected on exactly the same place. With Fyrkat, this is thus the second

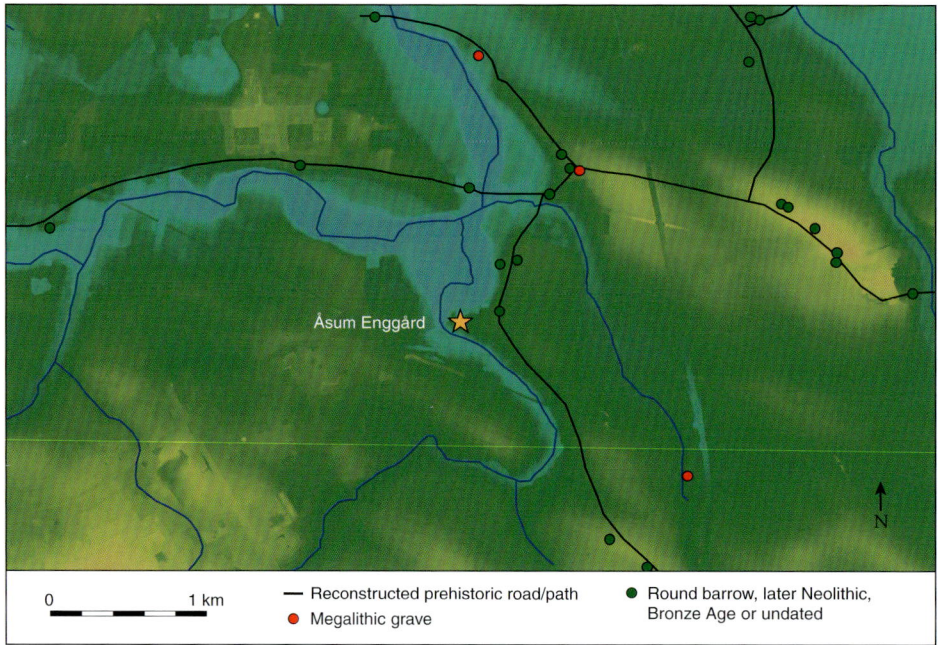

Fig. 37 | *The location of the Åsum Enggård enclosure on the island of Funen in relation to prehistoric roads/paths as reconstructed from barrow lines. No information regarding the course of the ditches at this site has yet been published.*

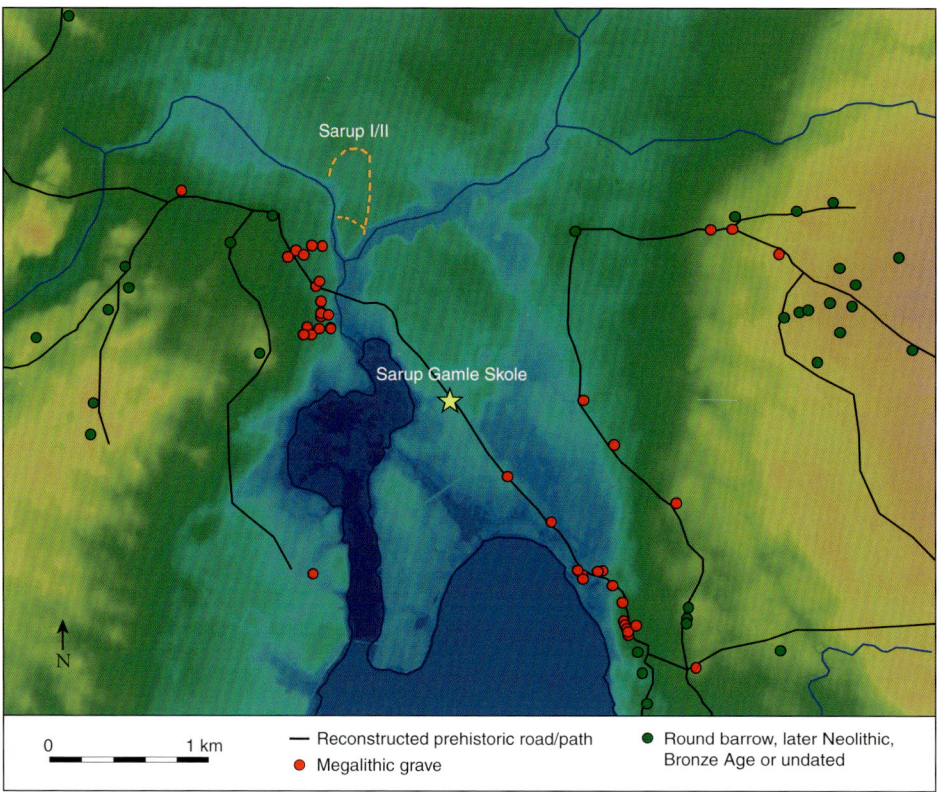

Fig. 38 | *The location of the Sarup I and II enclosures as well as the enclosure-related site of Sarup Gamle Skole on the island of Funen in relation to prehistoric roads/paths as reconstructed from barrow lines. The approximate course of the ditches of Sarup I and II is indicated schematically in this illustration.*

Viking Age fortress that shows a spatial relation to a Neolithic enclosure. This certainly is not due to chance and reflects a comparable way of reading the strategic potential of the landscape. It is further commented upon below.

The relation of the Skævinge Boldbaner enclosure to lines of communication is hard to judge due to the comparatively low number of barrows in the surroundings (Fig. 40). It appears that a prehistoric road may have passed south of the site at a distance of a few hundred metres.

The situation of the last Zealandic enclosure at Sigersted III (Fig. 41) is much clearer. The site sits on a promontory jutting out into the very sharply

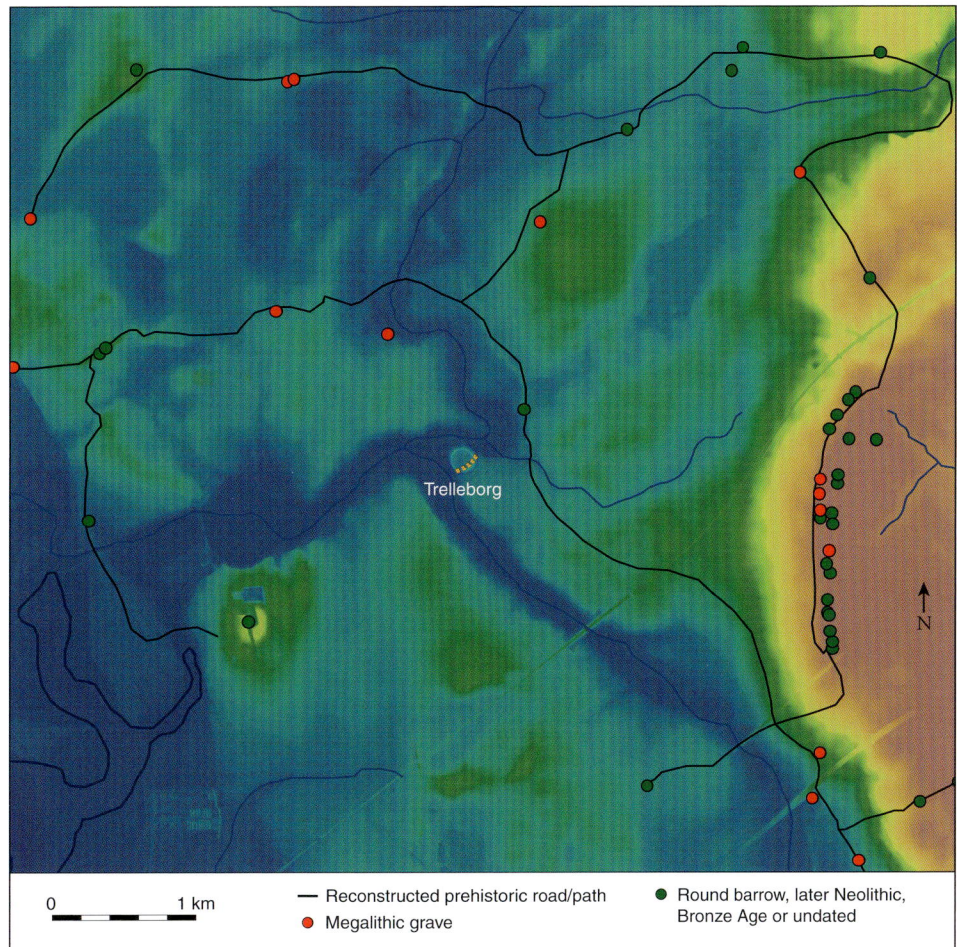

Fig. 39 | *The location of the Trelleborg enclosure on the island of Zealand and its relation to prehistoric roads/paths as reconstructed from barrow lines. The approximate course of the ditches is indicated schematically in this illustration.*

Trelleborg

— Reconstructed prehistoric road/path	● Round barrow, later Neolithic, Bronze Age or undated
● Megalithic grave	

0   1 km

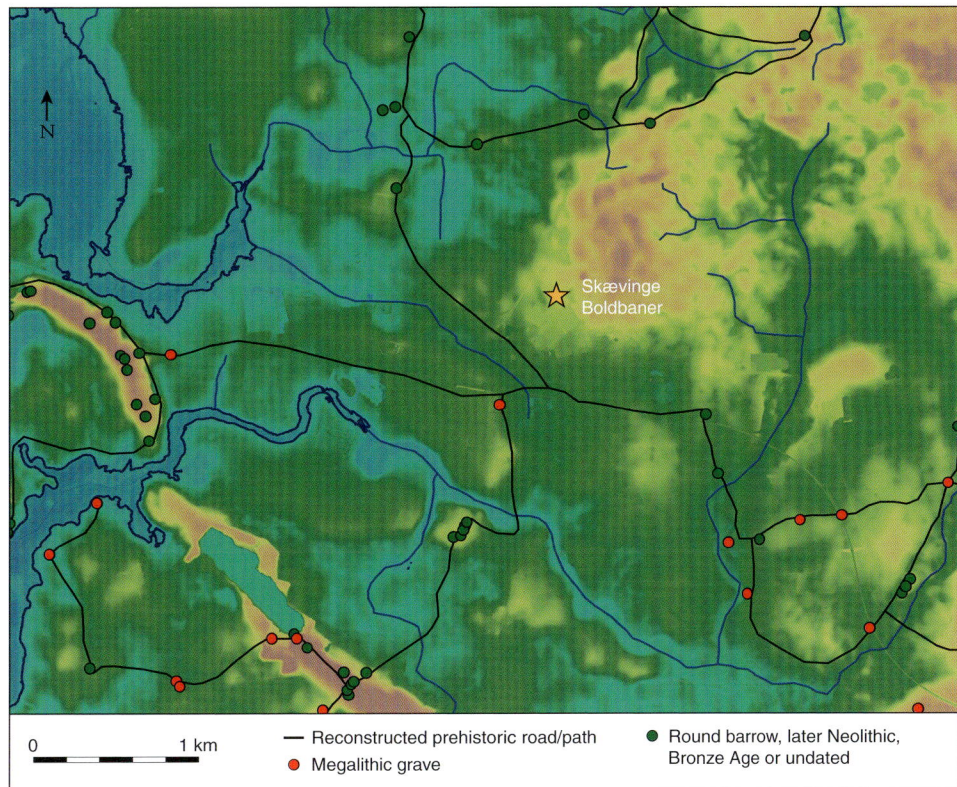

Fig. 40 | *The location of the Skævinge Bold- baner enclosure on the island of Zealand in relation to prehis- toric roads/paths as reconstructed from barrow lines. No information regard- ing the course of the ditches at this site has yet been published.*

Skævinge
Boldbaner

— Reconstructed prehistoric road/path	● Round barrow, later Neolithic, Bronze Age or undated
● Megalithic grave	

0   1 km

delimited valley of the Suså River, one of the largest freshwater streams on the island. The river valley is followed by a well-defined barrow road on its northern side, and it is to this barrow road that the enclosure clearly relates.

Finally, the two Vasagård enclosures on Bornholm have to be mentioned (Fig. 42). While the number of barrows in the vicinity is low, it appears that these two enclosures can be associated with nearby river fords.

In summary, it can be stated that almost all Danish enclosures appear to be clearly related to barrow roads or paths as far as can be told at present. Furthermore, it appears that this relation very often concerns roads of superregional importance (i.e. roads which follow the shores of a fjord or a river valley over many kilometres). Some sites clearly appear to be related to water-based travel. In many cases, the enclosure sites appear to be strategically well chosen with regard to communication lines. It can be concluded that the relation to barrow roads is clearly a parameter of great importance for the prediction of potential enclosure sites.

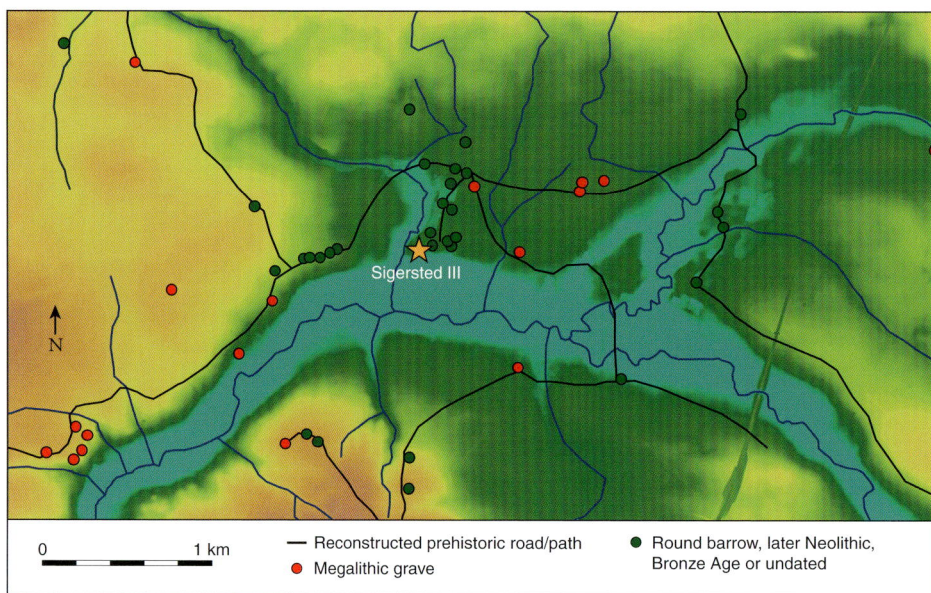

Fig. 41 | *The location of the Sigersted III enclosure on the island of Zealand in relation to prehistoric roads/paths as reconstructed from barrow lines. No information regarding the course of the ditches at this site has yet been published.*

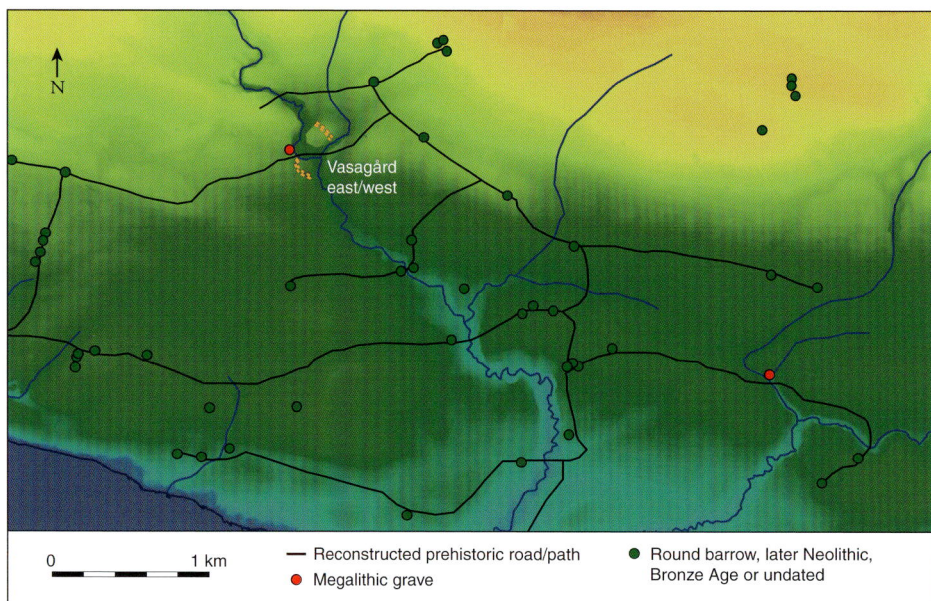

Fig. 42 | *The location of the two enclosures at Vasagård on the island of Bornholm in relation to prehistoric roads/paths as reconstructed from barrow lines. The approximate course of the ditches is indicated schematically in this illustration.*

6.3.2.2 Danish Neolithic enclosures and historic roads

While it was thus possible to demonstrate a potential relation between prehistoric (Neolithic) roads/paths and the location of Neolithic enclosures in Denmark, their relation to roads known from historical sources (Medieval and younger) remains unaddressed. This question is of interest because such a relation has already been demonstrated for the enclosures in Schleswig-Holstein. Moreover, if confirmed, the inclusion of information regarding the course of such roads could be a helpful tool in predicting enclosure locations.

A GIS-study of the relation between Danish causewayed enclosures and the precise course of Medieval roads is a very laborious task beyond the scope of this study. This is due to the fact that no dataset of these roads exists. The comparatively large uncertainties regarding the precise course of these roads resulting from the shifting quality of Medieval maps and descriptions is another problem. Due to these issues, a somewhat younger map of higher precision has been used in the following study. This map, the so-called Videnskabernes Selskabs Kort (Map of the Society of Sciences), was published at a scale of 1:120.000 between 1760 and 1820. However, the cartographers' concept maps completed at a scale of 1:20.000 are preserved and represent a well- suited data source. Church towers were used as triangulation points in the creation of these maps, and the concept maps even include indications of sight lines. The modern coordinates of these church towers can be taken from modern maps or extant databases comparatively easily and precisely, which allows for rather precise georeferencing. For the Djursland region, the course of roads has been digitized from these maps, while a pre-existing dataset of the roads has been used for the remainder of Denmark. This dataset was created by P. Dam, P.S. Nielsen, C. Dam and J. Bill. It can be downloaded from HisKIS.dk. For increased precision, this dataset was corrected in those cases where a main road passed by a known enclosure site at a distance of 1500 m or less.

A rather simple investigation of the spatial relation between Danish causewayed enclosures and historical roads as indicated on the Videnskabernes Selskabs Kort has been conducted for this study. Before this is described in detail, it is necessary to shortly discuss the different types of roads that are depicted on the map. There are two different signatures, one indicating ordinary, small roads and the other indicating landeveje – main roads of superregional importance (Fig. 43). The majority of these can be expected to date from distant time periods. The small roads, on the other hand, certainly mainly reflect the settlement pattern of the 18th century. The network of these small roads is so dense as to be useless to the current investigation. Therefore, only the main roads were used in the following analysis.

In a first step, the distance to the nearest main road on the Videnskabernes Selskabs Kort was measured for all known Danish causewayed enclosures. The sites related to enclosures were not taken into consideration in the investigation because their number is presently too low to allow for any statistically significant statements. As is apparent in Tab. 7, the distances measured range widely (between 0 m-15 km). In the case of the Büdelsdorf enclosure (Bakker 1976) as well as the numerous enclosures in the Braunschweig area in Germany (Geschwinde/Raetzel-Fabian 2009), distances of 1-2 km have been noted between Medieval roads and Neolithic enclosures. Examples from Westphalia cited by Knoche (2013) reside in approximately the same order of magnitude, albeit with a tendency towards shorter distances. As the data quality regarding the roads is much better in the current, Danish case (in addition to the fact that the number of recorded roads is much higher), the investigation was restricted to somewhat shorter distances (i.e. 500-1000 m). These smaller intervals were also a precondition for any potentially meaningful employment in predictive modelling, especially when taking into account the typical inter-enclosure distance of 4-5 km.

The data in Tab. 7 and Fig. 44 show that nine of the 32 Danish enclosures are located within 500 m from a historic main road, while the number of sites within 1000 m to these roads is 13. To test the significance of these counts, a simple chi-squared

Fig. 43 | *An example of a concept map from the production of Videnskabernes Selskabs Kort (ca. 1800). Two different signatures for roads of diverging importance have been used. For the present study, only the main roads are relevant.*

test was conducted. For this test, the size of the area covered by 500 and 1000 m-wide buffers around the main roads was calculated and compared to the size of the entirety of Denmark. The 500 m-buffer thus comprises 13.1% of the area of Denmark, while 28.1% of the known enclosure sites are located within it. For the 1000 m-buffer, the values are 24.66% of the area and 40.6% of the enclosures. From these numbers, it appears that the known Neolithic enclosures are overrepresented in the vicinity (up to 1000 m) of main roads in the late 18th century. The chi-square test confirms this observation, as the 0 hypothesis of an even distribution is rejected at the 0.025 significance level (500 m buffer) as well as at the 0.05 significance level (1000 m).

Several issues related to this simple investigation have to be discussed before the outcome can

be properly evaluated. One set of issues relates to the source of the road-related data, a rather recent 18th century map. Many of the main roads from the Videnskabernes Selskabs Kort certainly reflect very old transport and communication routes, which go back (at least partly) into prehistory. With regard to the Roman Iron Age, this has been convincingly demonstrated by Andresen et al. (2008). The course of these routes is determined to a high degree by the presence of well-suited paths through the landscape which avoided both steep climbs and wet areas. Furthermore, before the onset of intensive bridge building, the course of many roads would have been determined by the presence of fords at river crossings. Bridge building in Denmark started in the Viking Age at the latest, but was very restricted before the mid 19th century. As the map employed here predates the main bridge building period and early bridges (especially in the case of the most important roads) would have been built at or close to sites where obstacles (rivers) would earlier have been forded, the course of main roads will reflect roads that are relevant to this study to a high degree.

However, at the same time, the map must be expected to contain a number of rather recent roads among the main roads. Some of them are known to have been built in post Medieval times at the king's behest (Danish kongeveje). The inclusion of such comparatively modern roads is also apparent from the many roads that lead to important Medieval towns (forming star-like shapes). At the same time, not all roads of prehistoric significance would have held the same importance in Medieval and post-Medieval times, and thus have been included in the 18th century map. Therefore, this contains roads which were not relevant to prehistory and lacks information about roads which are likely to have been significant. Another problem is the fact that the density of the net of main roads as depicted on the map varies widely from region to region. This problem has already been addressed by Andresen et al. (2008).

Furthermore, the calculation of area had to be based on the area of present day Denmark. Due to isostatic and eustatic movement since the time of Neolithic enclosure construction, land has been gained in the northeastern parts of Denmark while it has been lost in the southwest. This also affects the area covered by the buffer around the 18th century main roads, several of which are situated on raised seabeds. But as the deviations between the historic and prehistoric situation affect calculations in both directions, the outcome would almost certainly be very much like the actual result, provided that calculations could be based on the situation at 3500 BC.

Finally, modern day building activity is more likely to be concentrated close to the main roads of the map than in areas removed from them. In turn, this means that one would have a higher probability of discovering enclosures close to the roads which would thus skew statistical tests. However, a closer

Enclosure	Distance to main road (m)
Starup Langelandsvej	0
Mølbjerg I	0
Markildegård	0
Grenå	0
Lønt	120
Sarup I	150
Sarup II	150
Mølbjerg II	250
Galgebakken	460
Åsum Enggård	640
Vilsund	650
Skærvad	770
Lokes Hede	900
Kainsbakke	1430
Hygind	1470
Ginnerup	1820
Fuglslev	1830
Sigersted III	2260
Trelleborg	2470
Søby Møllegård	2510
Bundsø	2640
Vasagård Øst	2780
Vasagård Vest	2780
Liselund	3500
Voldbæk	3840
Blakbjerg	3890
Skævinge Boldbaner	3900
Bjerggårde	3990
Ballegård	4000
Toftum	4370
St. Brokhøj	8400
Gammeltoft Odde	15000

Tab. 7 | *The distance of the known Danish enclosures to main roads as depicted on the Videnskabernes Selskabs Kort.*

look at the circumstance of discovery of the known enclosure sites (not least those that are situated close to the roads in question) demonstrates that many of these have not been discovered through rescue excavation caused by construction work and building activity, but were rather uncovered due to research (excavation) and aerial surveying.

It was not possible to correct for the numerous source critical problems mentioned above within this project. Such a study would be very time con-

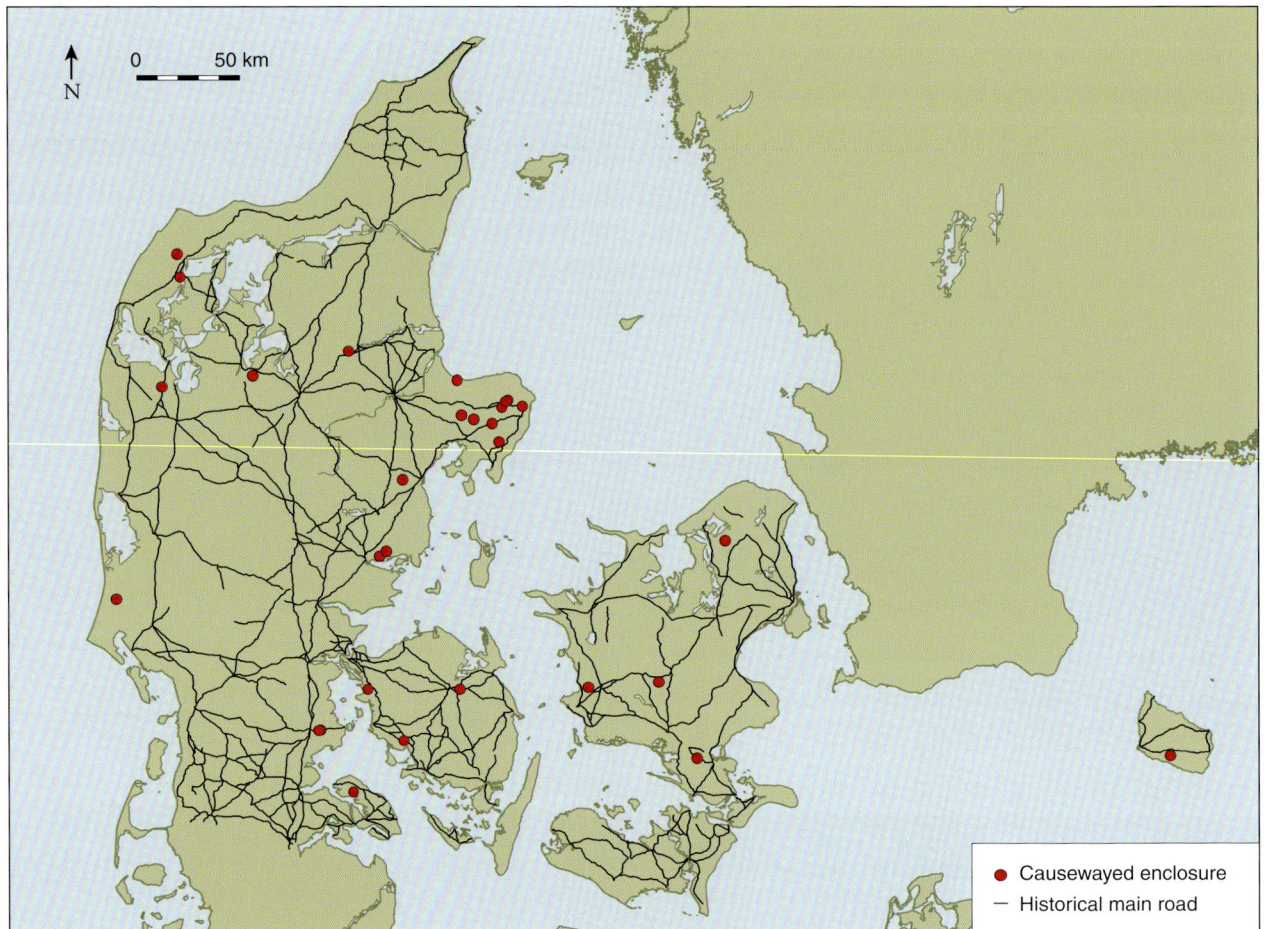

Fig. 44 | *The relation between known causewayed enclosures in Denmark and main roads as depicted on the* Videnskabernes Selskabs Kort *(late 18th century). A close relation between causewayed enclosures and roads is clearly apparent, although some notable exceptions do exist. In the present study area of Djursland, many enclosures were clearly related to a waterway (e.g. Kolindsund Fjord) rather than to land-based routes.*

suming and would require assistance from historians. But despite the shortfalls mentioned (whose influence on the outcome of the simple statistical test is diametrically opposed) Andresen et al.'s (2008) study demonstrates the general applicability of the Videnskabernes Selskabs Kort for work relating to prehistoric topics. Therefore, the results of the simple investigation can cautiously be used in predictive modelling, although more sophisticated and time demanding statistical analyses (like those conducted by Andresen et al.) should be tested with more advanced road datasets in the future.

It can be concluded, therefore, that not only the vicinity to reconstructed prehistoric roads, but also the vicinity to main roads from the late 18th century

Videnskabernes Selskabs Kort are factors that can be employed in attempts to predict the location of Neolithic enclosures. The vicinity to a main road increases the likelihood that a given location will house a Neolithic enclosure. At the same time, the absence of such a spatial relationship does not itself allow for any conclusions to be drawn.

6.3.3 River crossings

As was already apparent from the discussion above, not only is there an apparent relationship between prehistoric roads/paths and enclosures, but also (more specifically) between enclosures and the points at which said roads/paths cross a river. This observation is of great importance for any attempt to predict the location of unknown enclosures, as river crossings are distinct points in the landscape that allow for the selection of possible locations with much higher precision than would be possible for roads alone. Contrary to the relationship between roads and enclosures, the relationship between river crossings and enclosures has until recently only been briefly commented upon in the literature (Raetzel-Fabian (1999, 97ff.; Geschwinde/ Raetzel-Fabian 2009, 225ff.; Knoche 2008, 139). However, Knoche's (2013, 163ff., 210, 248) recent study leaves no doubt that river crossings also were of utmost importance for the choice of enclosure construction sites in Central Europe.

A relation between fords/river crossings and causewayed enclosures appears to be common in South Scandinavia. With few exceptions, all promontory type enclosures were situated within 700-800 m of river crossings by barrow roads (where they could be reconstructed via a sufficient number of barrows). The exceptions are those sites that were situated at the top ends of peninsulas or on islands, such as Vilsund, Grenå and Ballegård. In the case of Vilsund, at least, it can be argued that a road crossed the narrow sound close to the enclosure. In the case of Toftum, it is an area of extended boggy wetland that was crossed, not a river. But the principle, however, appears to be the same.

The location of sites where prehistoric roads/ paths crossed rivers (and, to a minor degree, narrow sounds and wetlands) therefore seems to be a powerful tool for predictive modelling. This is only true for promontory enclosures. Hilltop sites, obviously, cannot be predicted by means of this parameter.

6.3.4 Enclosures and Viking Age/Medieval military installations

Two known causewayed enclosures – Trelleborg on Zealand (Andersen, N.H. 1982) and Esesfeld in northern Germany (Lornsen 1987; Kühn 1989) – were discovered during the planned excavation of a completely different type of site: that of Viking Age/ Medieval fortresses (Fig. 45). This observation is striking and (seen from a statistical point of view)

hardly coincidental, even though the low total number of observations has to be taken into account in any evaluation. A survey of the surroundings of other known causewayed enclosures adds a number of cases with comparable spatial relations.

The vicinity of the Lokes Hede enclosure to another of the four Danish ring fortresses of the Viking Age – the Fyrkat site – has already been mentioned (Fig. 24). The distance between the two is ca. 2 km, but it may well be that at least part of this distance can be explained by the geological development of Mariager Fjord. In the Neolithic, the fjord would have been somewhat longer, making it possible to reach Lokes Hede by boat. Accessibility by ship almost certainly was an important factor for the choice of the location for the Fyrkat fortress as well (Dobat 2013, 236, 245). Due to the uplift of the land, the innermost part of Mariager Fjord (and thus the Lokes Hede location) could no longer be reached by boat (at least not by a Viking longship) in the Viking Age. Fyrkat probably was built further to the northeast for this reason. Both the Lokes Hede and Fyrkat sites may well have marked the very end of Mariager Fjord at their respective times of construction.

A distinct relation to causewayed enclosures can also be demonstrated for a third of the total of five known Viking Age ring fortresses of the Trelleborg type. The only known causewayed enclosure in Scania, southern Sweden is at Stävie (Larsson, L. 1982), and can be found a scant 1000 m from Borgeby, which also happens to be the only known Scanian ring fortress (Ödman 2002). The strategic importance of this location is further emphasized by the fact that a Medieval castle was later built on the same spot.

As three of the five known Viking Age ring fortresses are situated either directly on top or close to Neolithic causewayed enclosures, it is important to briefly review the two remaining ring fortresses. The Nonnebakken ring fortress is located in the centre of the present town of Odense on Funen. The closest known Neolithic causewayed enclosure, the Åsum Enggård site (Jensen/Nikolaisen 1989; 1990) is situated ca. 5 km to the east. This distance is in the order of the typical inter-enclosure distance and the presence of a yet unknown

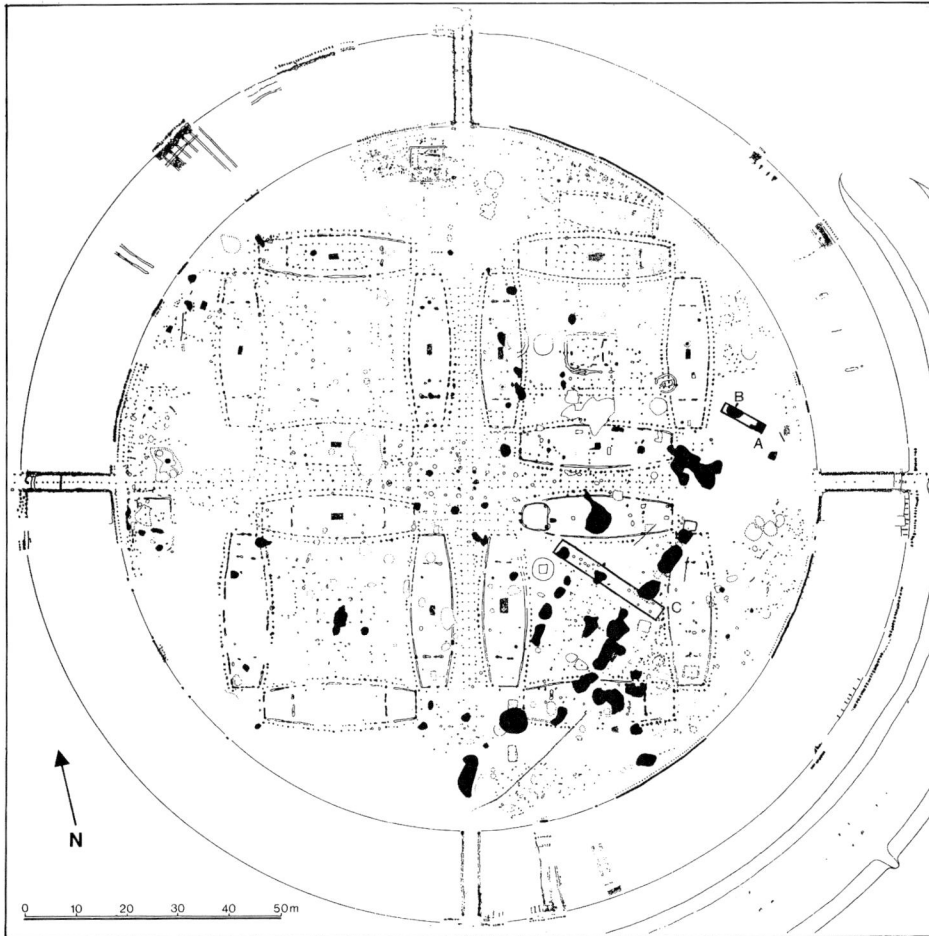

Fig. 45 | *The rows of Neolithic pits that were found beneath Viking Age Trelleborg ring fortress were first recognized as the remains of a causewayed enclosure by N.H. Andersen some decades after the excavation had taken place (from Andersen 1982).*

enclosure below or close to Nonnebakken would thus make perfect sense. However, due to its location in the town centre, a potential enclosure at or near to the Nonnebakken site might have been completely destroyed by later building activity, or would be difficult to identify in the small trenches that could potentially be opened up in this densely developed region. As demonstrated by the example of Soest in Westphalia (Knoche 2008; 2013), such detection remains a possibility.

With regard to the last Viking Age ring fortress (that at Aggersborg in northern Jutland), it is of interest to note that a TRB settlement with finds from EN II and MN A I was discovered under the site (Andersen, S.H. 1986, 35ff. with Fig. 6). However, no enclosure ditches were found there.

The Büdelsdorf enclosure was built close to the point where an important long-distance road crossed the Eider River. At around 1100 A.D., a

first fortification of the strategically important river crossing has constructed on an island in the river. This has later given name to the present town of Rendsburg (…'burg' is the German word for 'castle'). The distance between this early Medieval fortress and the Büdelsdorf enclosure is around 1500 m.

By searching the surroundings of other known Neolithic enclosures, potential relations to fortifications from historical times can be demonstrated for a number of sites. At Sarup, no less than two fortifications are known 850 m northwest and 700 m east of the enclosures of Sarup I and II (Fig. 46). The eastern rampart is situated directly at a ford of the Hårby Å River. Another important river crossing is found respectively 1000 m and 900 m to the south of the two military installations. This latter ford is situated exactly where the enclosure-related site of Sarup Gamle Skole is located.

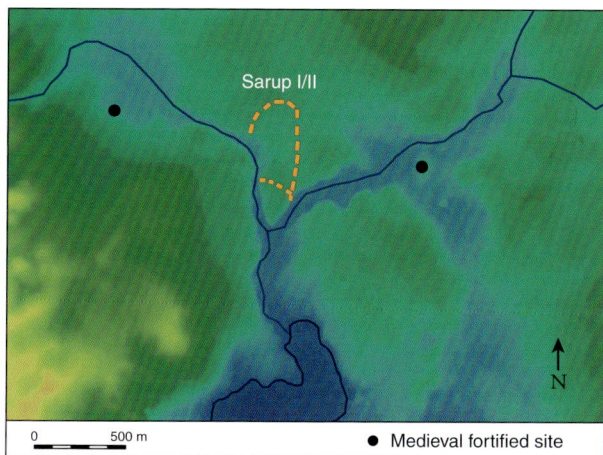

Fig. 46 | *The enclosures of Sarup I and II and their spatial relation to fortified medieval sites to the east and west. The approximate course of the enclosure ditches is indicated schematically in this illustration.*

Further examples of possible relations between Neolithic enclosures and military installations from early historic times include the Liselund site (a fortification 1200 m to the southwest), the Søby Møllegård site (a fortification 1500 m to the southeast), the Skærvad site (a fortification 1000 m to the west), the Toftum site (a fortification 800 m to the west), the Bjerggård site (a fortification 800 m to the south), the Lønt site (a fortification 600 m to the south), and the Starup Langelandsvej site with a fortification 700 m to the south-southwest.

This list of sites is based on Viking age and Medieval fortresses, castles and ramparts as recorded in the digital central register of the Danish Agency for Culture (KUS). Given that this register may be incomplete, a close spatial relation of fortifications from historical sites to Neolithic enclosures may be more common than is apparent at present.

The choice of location for the construction of fortifications in early historical times was certainly guided by the intention to control points of strategic interest with regard to transport and communication as well as borders. The fact that at least some river crossings represented such points is clearly illustrated by the historically well illustrated cases of Büdelsdorf and Esesfeld. The fact that many Neolithic enclosures are situated close to fortifications from early historical times is therefore hardly coincidental and reflects the general importance of river crossings as well as the fact that the location of many roads had the potential to remain stable over long periods of time. In many cases, rivers also functioned as borders.

It is important to note that the observed proximity between Neolithic enclosures and Viking Age/Medieval fortifications cannot be read as an indication of any military function of the Neolithic monuments, but instead points to the fact that areas of importance for transport and communication held an important role in both Neolithic and early historical societies. While the nature of this importance is immediately evident in historical times, the situation is more difficult to define with regard to the Neolithic. This question will be discussed in more detail in chapter 9.3.5.6.

A relation between Neolithic causewayed enclosures and Iron Age/Medieval fortifications is by no means a trait specific to South Scandinavia. The same relationship is observable in numerous instances in other regions as well, such as the southern parts of Britain. In this region, Iron Age hillforts are often located on top of causewayed enclosures (Oswald et al 2001, 34, 137ff). The same is true in northern central Germany, where numerous enclosures are situated close to Medieval castles (Geschwinde/Raetzel-Fabian 2009, 29ff., 236 Abb. 166.). In one case at least an enclosure was discovered below such a fortification (at Ahlen-Dolberg in Westphalia: Grünewald 2013; Knoche 2013, 173).

It can be concluded that the presence of Viking Age/Medieval fortifications can be indicative of the existence of a Neolithic enclosure in the vicinity, suggesting that proximity to such sites can also be used as a parameter in predictive modelling.

7 Predicting enclosures in Djursland

7.1 Preparing required datasets

From the discussion above it appears that promontory type enclosures are by far the most frequent types of enclosures in South Scandinavia. At the same time, these enclosures are also the easiest ones to detect using a GIS-approach. Therefore, the search for potential enclosure sites will first be directed at promontory type enclosures. Hilltop sites can be examined in a second step, using the potential promontory enclosure sites previously retrieved and the inter-enclosure distance parameter as points of departure. The latter will also be the most important tool in detecting enclosures in deviating topographical settings like those encountered at a number of identified sites which remained unclassified in this study.

As was apparent from the detailed discussion of the different parameters that appear to be relevant for the location of promontory type enclosures, both proximity to water and the relation to ancient roads/paths and the river crossings by these roads/paths hold key positions within the present approach. The topography parameter is obviously also very important. However, as described above, the topography parameter is very difficult to define in a GIS-approach and has therefore been bypassed here using two specific types of water proximity situations: the confluence of fresh water streams as well as sites where rivers flow into fjords or sheltered bays. Such locations can be defined as

points. The advantage of using these points is that they indirectly combine the water proximity criterion with a topography criterion, as the majority of the promontories that house known causewayed enclosures are situated at exactly these types of points. Furthermore, the point dataset that results from this step is easily employed in subsequent calculations. Therefore, the first step in the predictive modelling approach as it is applied here is the retrieval of river confluences and sites where rivers flow into fjords/sheltered bays and the subsequent definition of these points in point datasets.

7.1.1 Reconstructing the coastline at 3500 BC

South Scandinavia and thus also Djursland witnessed considerable change between land and sea since the end of the last Ice Age (Jessen 1920). It is important to correct the present-day digital elevation model for this change in order to retrieve the coastline at the time of causewayed enclosure construction and to thus enable the detection of points where rivers flowed into fjords/ sheltered bays.

The observed change in the land-sea relationship is due to the combination of two factors: sea-level change proper (eustatic change, transgressions and regressions) as well as isostatic movements that led either to land-uplift or subsidence, dependant on its position relative to a so-called tilting line (Mertz 1924). This tilting line runs across Denmark

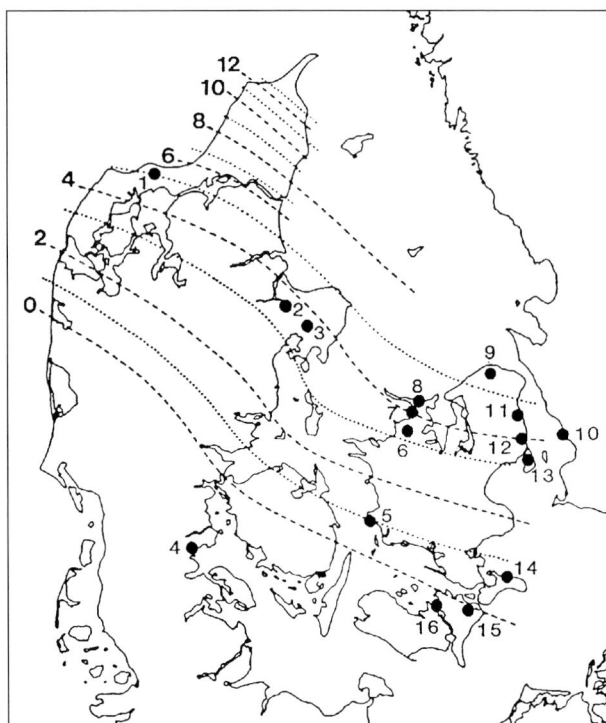

Fig. 47 | *Contours for the post-glacial sea level maximum in metres as defined by Mertz in 1924 (from Christensen 1995). It appears that the sea level maximum in the area of investigation (which was reached in the early Subboreal) was 3-5.3 m higher than that today.*

approximately between the towns of Ringkøbing on the west coast of Jutland and Køge on the east coast of Zealand (Fig. 47). The present investigation area of Djursland is situated north of the tilting line and thus has risen several metres since the end of the last Ice Age.

The precise relation between land and sea in Djursland during the Holocene has been investigated in detail at the classical Ertebølle site of Dyrholmen (Troels-Smith 1942). Based on his geological work at the site, Troels-Smith could differentiate between four different transgressions, the last of which reached the highest levels above present day sea level in the area under investigation here. This transgression appeared in the early Subboreal. This is of importance for the reconstruction of the land-sea relationship, as it means that the maximum extent of the sea is roughly contemporaneous with the construction of causewayed en-

closures. Therefore, the highest detectable former sea level in Djursland can be used for coastline reconstruction in this study. This remains true despite the fact that the sea level at the time of enclosure construction might have fallen a bit from its absolute maximum in the early Subboreal. The areas from which the sea potentially had receded would have been made up of wet areas which were periodically flooded. Just like fjords, such wet areas were also important spatial delimiters of causewayed enclosures.

The digital soil type map at a scale of 1:25.000 (Fig. 5) provided by the Geological Survey of Denmark and Greenland (GEUS) differentiates between a total of five different types of marine sediments: marine clay, gyttia, sand, gravel and peat. For the reconstruction of former sea levels, the extension of these deposits (Fig. 48) was projected on the digital elevation model and values for the present day elevation of marine deposits were thereby acquired. Marine gravel has been excluded from the selection, because most beach ridges consist of this type of sediment. The beach ridges formed under extreme weather conditions (high winds, exceptionally high tide) and are therefore not representative of the average water level in early Subboreal times.

The elevation values retrieved for marine sediments were subsequently submitted to a critical assessment. This took into account edge errors resulting from the overlay of the relatively imprecise soil-type map with the highly precise digital elevation model. To cope with this problem, a comparison with the general values for land-uplift as provided by Mertz (1924) was carried out. For a total of 21 points distributed over the entire investigation area, those values thought to be representative of actual sea-level change were chosen. These range between 2,85 m in the southwest and 5,30 m in northeastern Djursland. In a next step, elevation values for all other cells of the investigation area grid were calculated by interpolation with the Inverse Distance Weighted method. The resulting elevation grid was then subtracted from the present day digital elevation model and the 0 m contour line derived from the result of the calculation.

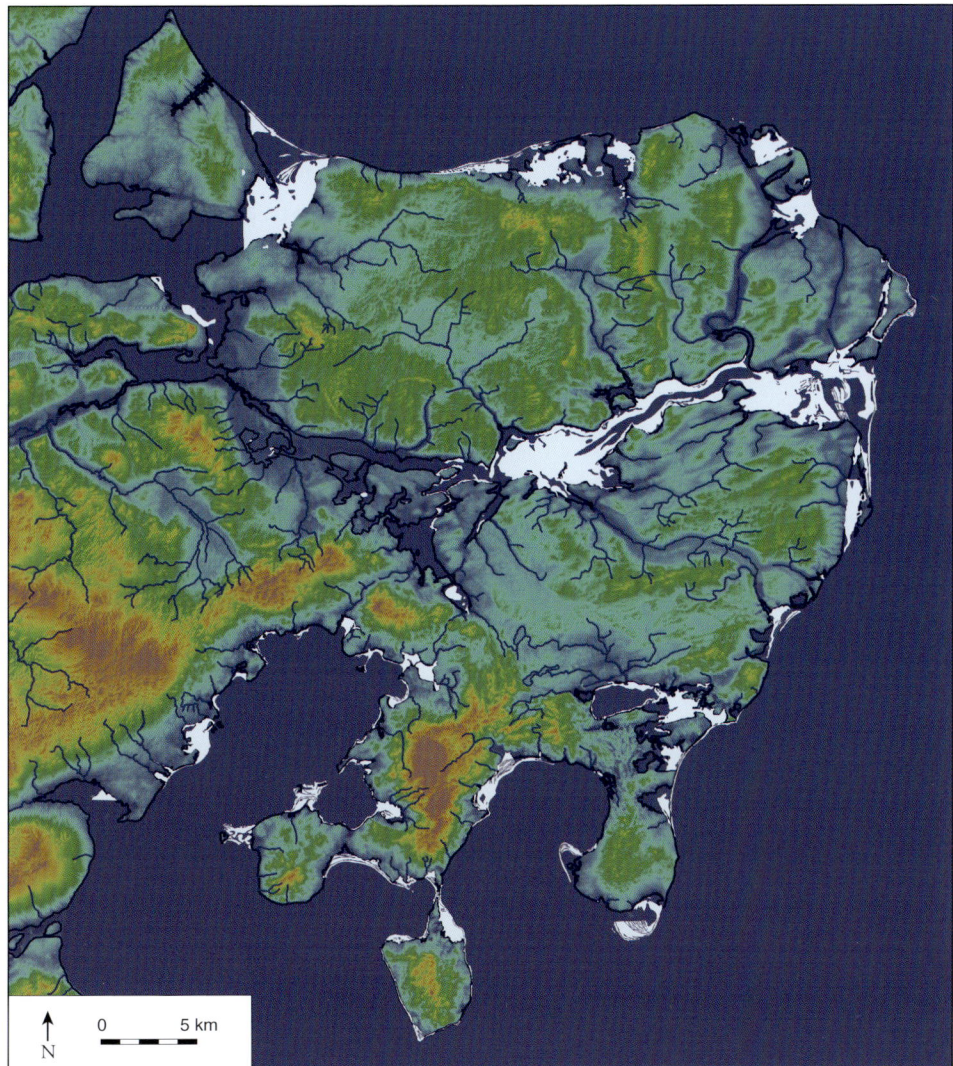

Fig. 48 | *The extent of marine deposits near the surface in Djursland. In the western parts of the former fjord of Kolindsund, these deposits were removed by erosion. In other parts, they are overlain by thick layers of freshwater peat (extracted from the digital version of map in Schack Pedersen/ Strand Petersen 1997).*

0   5 km

N

A second step corrected this coastline manually for various errors. One of these involved the removal of beach-ridges, not all of which could be eliminated by excluding marine gravel from the calculations. Another error was due to the presence of modern roads and bridges across low-lying areas, which (as described in the following sub-chapter) frequently appear as elevations and therefore affect the calculation of the former coastline. Finally, the coastline in parts of the western Kolindsund Fjord area was established based on the distribution of peat bogs. As described by geologists (Schack Pedersen/Strand Petersen 1997, 75), this part of the former fjord almost completely lacks marine deposits, due to the river which flows through the area today. It was not indicated as a fjord by the calculations carried out here. Nonetheless, isolated patches of marine de-

posits inside boggy areas indicate that the sea was present there at one time. Given that the calculated coastline in parts of this area follows the distribution of peat deposits exactly, the borders of such deposits were chosen for a hypothetical reconstruction of the former maximum sea extent. This reconstruction might include minor areas which were occasionally above water (such as in extreme weather situations). As already explained above, this potential error has no negative effect on the present investigation, as both wet areas and the fjord were factors relevant for the choice of location of causewayed enclosures.

The outcome of this coastline-reconstruction process gives a very good overall impression of the land-sea distribution around 3500 BC (Fig. 4). However, it should not be taken as a precise reflection of the course of the ancient coastline in its minor details. One important problem is the fact that the growth of peat bogs after the Subboreal transgression in many locations can have led to inaccuracies in coastline reconstruction. This was suggested by the observation of seashells present during excavations in the Skodå River valley at a site which (according to the present coastline reconstruction) was never flooded by the sea (information provided by E. Kannegaard Nielsen).

7.1.2 Defining freshwater paths and river confluences

The best way of preparing a digital dataset of the freshwater paths certainly would be a calculation by water flow analysis within GIS. Besides its precision, this method has the obvious advantage of rendering additional data such as the length of individual river segments or the relative amount of water passing through at any given point.

Unfortunately, the nature of the digital elevation model in the present case was unsuitable for the present purpose. The LIDAR-scans which are available (a cell size of only 1.6 m) have a resolution that was sufficient in many cases to show modern day infrastructure (see e.g. Figs. 23 and 24). While this was not too problematic with regard to modern settlement and industrial areas (apart from huge gravel pits), things look different with regard to modern day infrastructures like roads and railways. These are often constructed on slightly elevated damns – especially when crossing river valleys. In consequence, these dams appear as linear structures with elevated heights in the digital elevation model and stop the

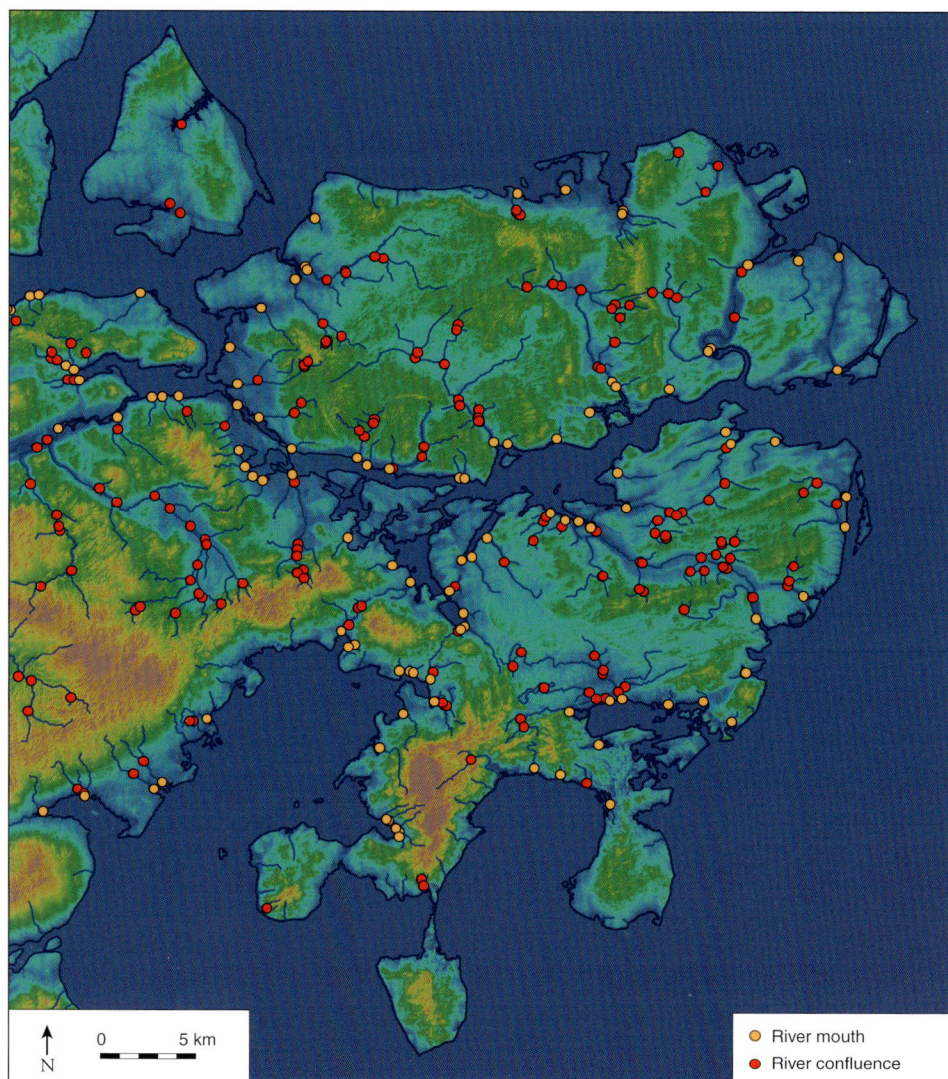

Fig. 49 | *Digital elevation model for the area under investigation with a reconstructed Early Neolithic coastline, freshwater paths, river confluences and river mouths (fjords and sheltered bays only).*

Legend:
- River mouth
- River confluence

0   5 km

N

virtual water flow in GIS calculations. While the computational removal of these modern structures from the digital elevation model may be possible, it was deemed too complex an operation for this study.

Therefore, the freshwater path dataset was created by digitizing watercourses as mapped in the Høje Målebordsblade from the second half of the 19th century. Modern topographical maps should not be used for the purpose, as a large number of especially minor rivers have disappeared entirely due to modern drainage or the lowering of the ground water table (with the resulting drying up of springs). Other water courses have been considerably altered by the use of pipelines. Therefore, it is important to use old maps for this purpose. The Høje Målebordsblade at a scale of 1.20.000 are in general well suited for this purpose, due to their accuracy and age. However, at the time in which these maps were created, many patches of land had already been drained and river courses altered. Therefore, the dataset containing rivers in their natural courses as digitized from the Høje Målebordsblade had to be supplemented by digitizing river valleys as visible in the digital elevation model. This was of course only necessary in the cases in which the Høje Målebordsblade did not show any rivers at all or rivers whose courses had clearly been altered. This step includes the risk of including glacial meltwater valleys that did not actually house freshwater streams in the Holocene. However, this risk was judged to be small in relation to the possible gains such method would provide to this study.

Based on the freshwater path dataset derived in the manner described above, river confluences could easily be defined both by GIS-calculations and manually (Fig. 49). The relevant information was stored as a point dataset counting 182 entries for the entirety of the region of Djursland (including those sub-regions that were later excluded from analysis).

7.1.3 Defining river mouths

The retrieval of points at which rivers flowed into fjords and sheltered bays at the time of causewayed enclosure construction around 3500 BC could be conducted both manually and by means of the sim-
ple multiplication of the coastline dataset (fjords and sheltered bays only) with the freshwater path dataset described above. The result (Fig. 49) was stored as a point dataset, counting a total of 105 entries for Djursland (excluding the former island of Rougsø, but including sub-regions that later were excluded from analysis).

7.1.4 Reconstructing Neolithic roads/paths and river crossings

The background for the reconstruction of prehistoric roads and paths based on the distribution of barrows has already been described above. In the current area of investigation, the coordinates of 585 megalithic graves and TRB long barrows as well as those of 3125 barrows from the later parts of the Neolithic and the Bronze Age and barrows of unknown age were downloaded from the central register of monuments managed by the Danish Agency for Culture (KUS). The count was based on the entire region of Djursland, excluding only Rougsø in the northwest.

The distribution of the total 3710 barrows within this area is very uneven, showing regions that had high densities of barrows (i.e. the central parts of Djursland adjacent to the former fjord of Kolindsund) while others were completely barrow-free (Fig. 50). An effort was made to evaluate the observations regarding the lack of barrows in some parts of the region, but it was not always possible to find adequate explanations. The most striking case remaining unexplained is that of an area measuring approximately 8 by 9 km in southeast Djursland, to the north and west of the Neolithic Stubbe Fjord. Neither the soil type, the extensive agriculture, a lack of research nor the distribution of forests at the time of the registration of most barrows in the central parish register (around the year 1900) can explain the lack of barrows in this area. The observation is even more striking, as settlements, depositions and even a causewayed enclosure (the Fuglslev site) from the TRB are known there. This part of Djursland was excluded from further study, as one of the two most important predictive parameters – the course of prehistoric roads/paths

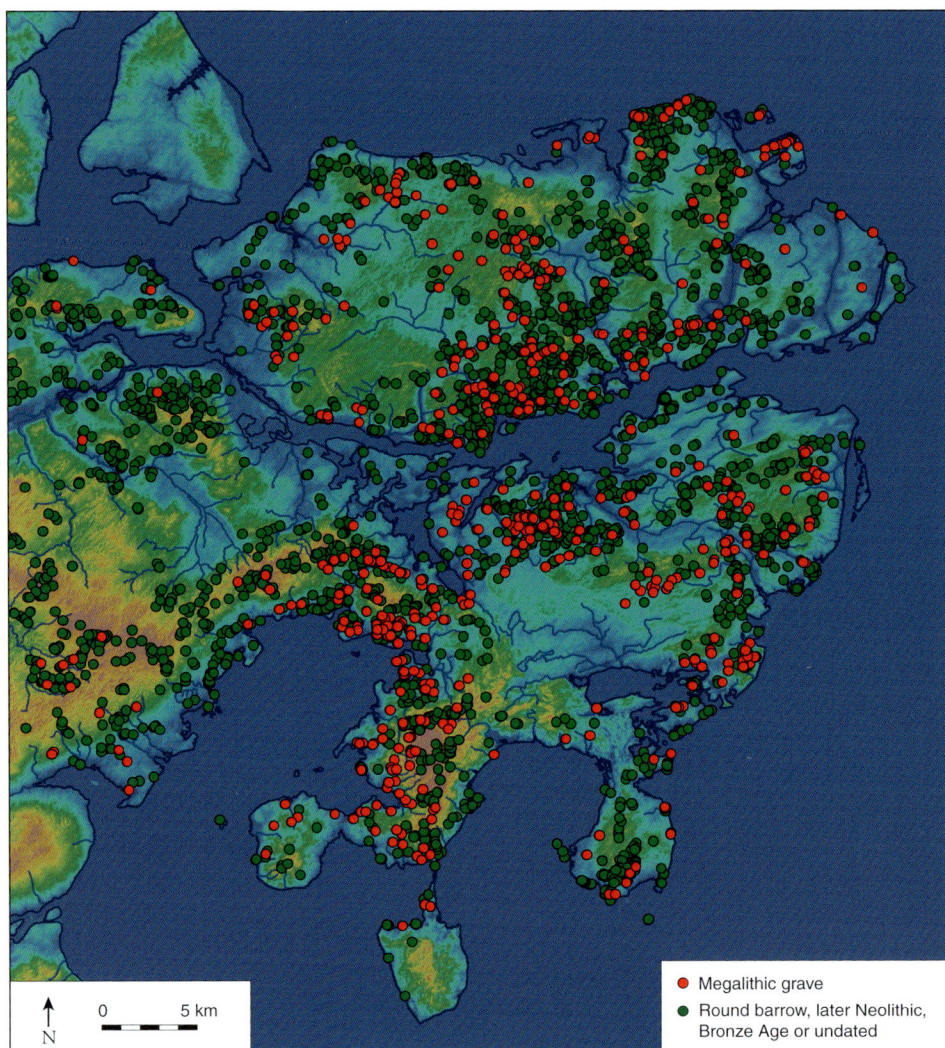

Fig. 50 | *The distribution of megalithic graves (n = 585) and round barrows from later parts of the Neolithic and the Bronze Age as well as undated barrows (n = 3125) in Djursland, excluding the island of Rougsø in the northwest.*

reconstructed on the basis of barrow distribution – was unavailable for study. Other parts of Djursland with no or very few barrows (e.g. the central parts of the largest Neolithic island north of Kolindsund Fjord) remained in the study, as the scarcity of barrows could here be explained (among other things) through the presence of vast stretches of bog. The registration of barrows in this area might nevertheless be influenced by the presence of large, old woodlands in the region.

In many minor areas of Djursland, obvious barrow lines are apparent when looking at the distribution map Fig. 50. The Kalø Bay region can serve as an example. In these cases, the reconstruction of the course of prehistoric roads/paths was rather straightforward. In other cases, things were more difficult, either due to the scarcity of barrows or to their very high density. The longer the distance

between two barrows, the more uncertain is the reconstruction of the route between them. The digital elevation model was used in all cases to find the topographically most likely route. In case of a high abundance of barrows, the digital elevation model was equally used to define the most likely course of the numerous possible roads/paths. The result of this reconstruction process was stored as a line-dataset. The combined length of all reconstructed Neolithic paths/roads for Djursland (excluding the Rougsø Island in the northwest) is 1186 kilometres (Fig. 51).

By combining the road/path dataset with that of the freshwater streams, the location of river crossings could be detected and stored as a point dataset (Fig. 51). This data set counts 189 entries for the entirety of Djursland (again, excluding Rougsø but including the sub-regions that were excluded

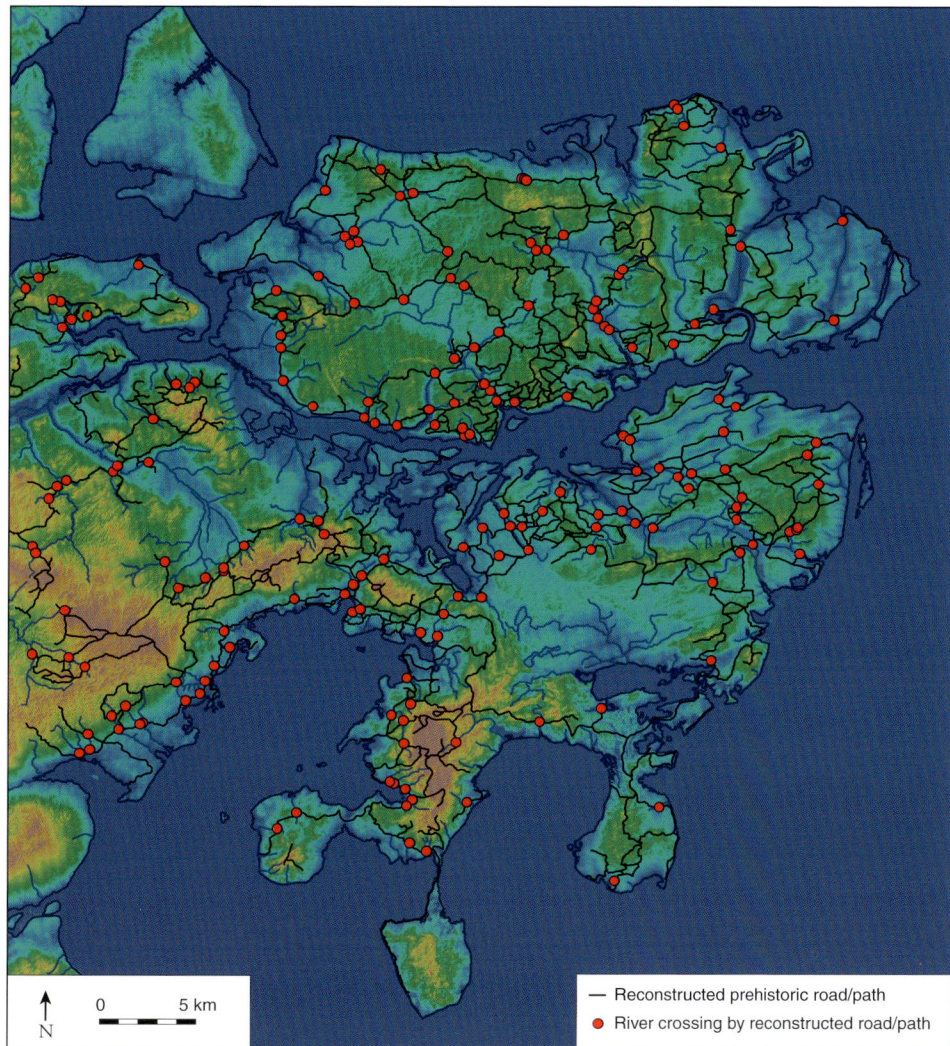

Fig. 51 | *Prehistoric roads and paths as reconstructed on the basis of the distribution of barrows in Djursland. Points mark river crossings by these reconstructed roads and paths. The island of Rougsø in the northwest was excluded from this study. The lack of reconstructed roads in other parts of the peninsula is due to a lack of registered barrows in these areas.*

— Reconstructed prehistoric road/path
● River crossing by reconstructed road/path

from further analysis as indicated in Fig. 3). In cases where well defined barrow roads/paths lead to the banks of a river from both sides, the precise location of the former river crossing was fairly obvious. In the cases where the barrow roads or paths were less well defined (due to a low number of barrows), information derived from historic maps on which the location of fords was indicated (the Høje Målebordsblade from the second half of the 19th century) was used (as far as was possible) to locate the most likely sites for river crossings.

7.1.5 Point datasets for Viking Age/Medieval fortifications and Neolithic finds

Coordinates for Viking Age or Medieval fortifications as well as those for Neolithic finds were downloaded from the Danish central register of

monuments (Fig. 52). The resulting point dataset for the fortifications has 31 entries. The data for Neolithic finds were divided into three different datasets: TRB settlements and single finds (200 entries), TRB depositions (16 entries) and finds of the PWC (32 entries). As the Neolithic finds registered in the database were far from complete, information regarding yet-unregistered settlements and artefacts was acquired in several cases from N. A. Boas and E. Kannegaard Nielsen, East Jutland Museum. However, these additional finds were not entered into the point dataset.

7.1.6 Soil type map

A digital soil type map at a scale of 1:25.000 was acquired from the Geological Survey of Denmark and Greenland (GEUS). The map covers the investigation area except for a minor area in the northwest for which no soil type information was available (Fig. 5).

7.1.7 Historic roads

The course of the main roads from the second half of the 18th century (Fig. 53) was digitized from the cartographers' concept maps of the Videnskabernes Selskabs Kort, as described above.

7.2 Pointing out potential enclosure locations

As is apparent from the preceding chapter, proximity to water, topography, proximity to prehistoric roads/paths and, last but not least, points where rivers or wetlands are crossed by these roads are the main parameters used in pointing out potential enclosure locations. Additional (secondary) parameters which can best be used for the further evaluation of potential enclosure locations include soil type, known Neolithic finds, the presence of Viking Age or Medieval fortifications in the vicinity, the presence of megalithic graves and inter-enclosure distance.

The distribution of known causewayed enclosures as well as that of sites suspected to house these monuments in Djursland shows a clear preference for being in proximity to fjords (Fig. 6). However, one site (Fuglslev) demonstrates that enclosures were also constructed farther inland. Because only a single inland site is known, it is not possible to evaluate whether the inter-enclosure distance of ca. 4-6 km apparent from the distributional analysis of the coastal and near-coastal sites in Denmark also

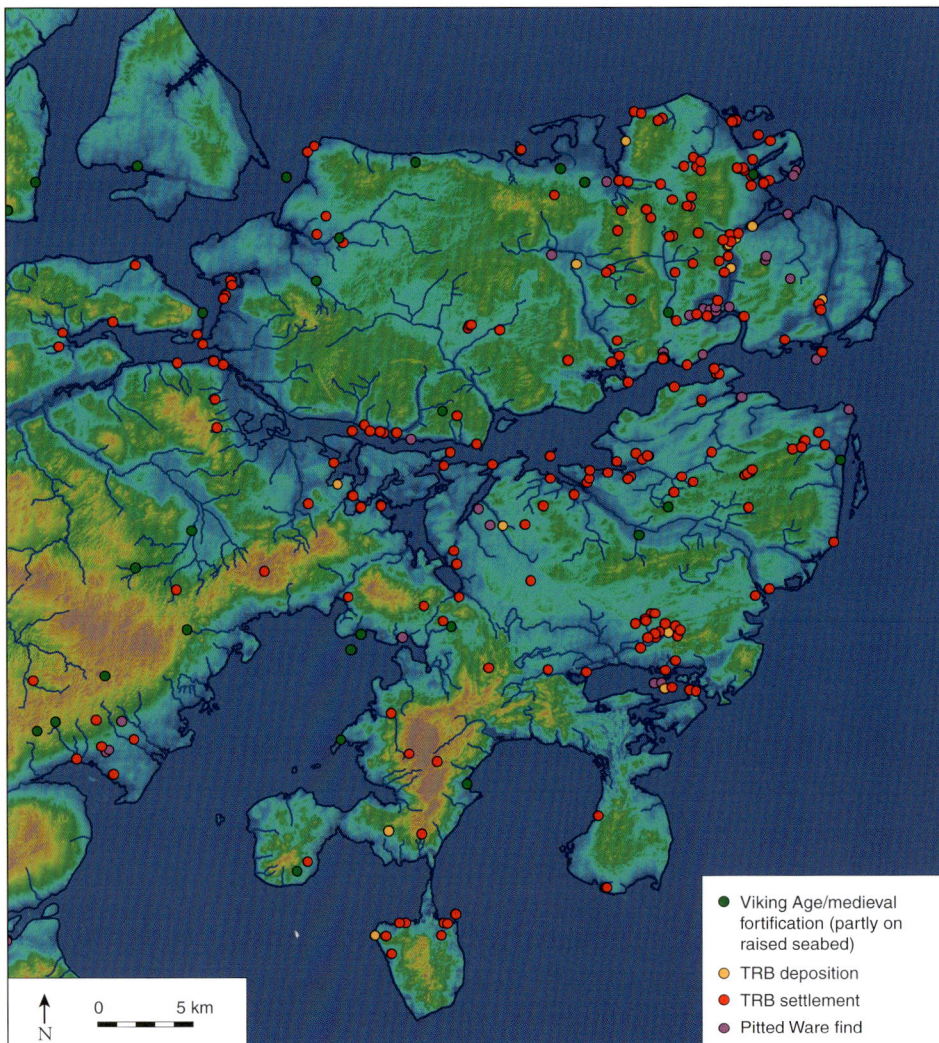

Fig. 52 | *The distribution of Viking Age and medieval fortifications, TRB settlement finds, TRB depositions as well as finds of the Pitted Ware Culture in the investigation area.*

Legend:
- Viking Age/medieval fortification (partly on raised seabed)
- TRB deposition
- TRB settlement
- Pitted Ware find

0   5 km

N

applies for enclosures in the hinterland. However, this has been used as a working hypothesis for the following analysis in order to make sure that no potential enclosure sites were excluded.

The analysis of the known Danish enclosures has shown that almost all promontory type sites were situated within 700-800 m of a river crossing. The overwhelming majority were constructed between two confluent rivers or at points where rivers flowed into a fjord or sheltered bay. The first step, therefore, was to calculate the distance between all river confluences, river mouths and the nearest river crossing. The resulting values for the 182 river confluences are spread between 18 and 9279 m, those for the 105 river mouths between 19 and 3900 m.

Within Djursland, 48 river mouths (fjords and sheltered bays only) and 89 river confluences have distances to the nearest river crossing of 800 m

or less. If only the restricted investigation area is considered (excluding some areas in the southern parts of Djursland), the numbers are 38 and 79 respectively. The combined number of these points of interest is 117. However, this is not the number of possible enclosure locations. While there is only one possible enclosure site in a river confluence, there may well be two (one on each side of the river) at river mouths. On the other hand, topography and soil conditions are far from being well suited to the construction of an enclosure at all retrieved points. The next step included an evaluation of the situation at every single site and was done by examining all available data (digital elevation models, historic maps, soil type maps) and by investigation on the ground. As a result, only sites at river confluences or river mouths with topographies and soil conditions comparable to those en-

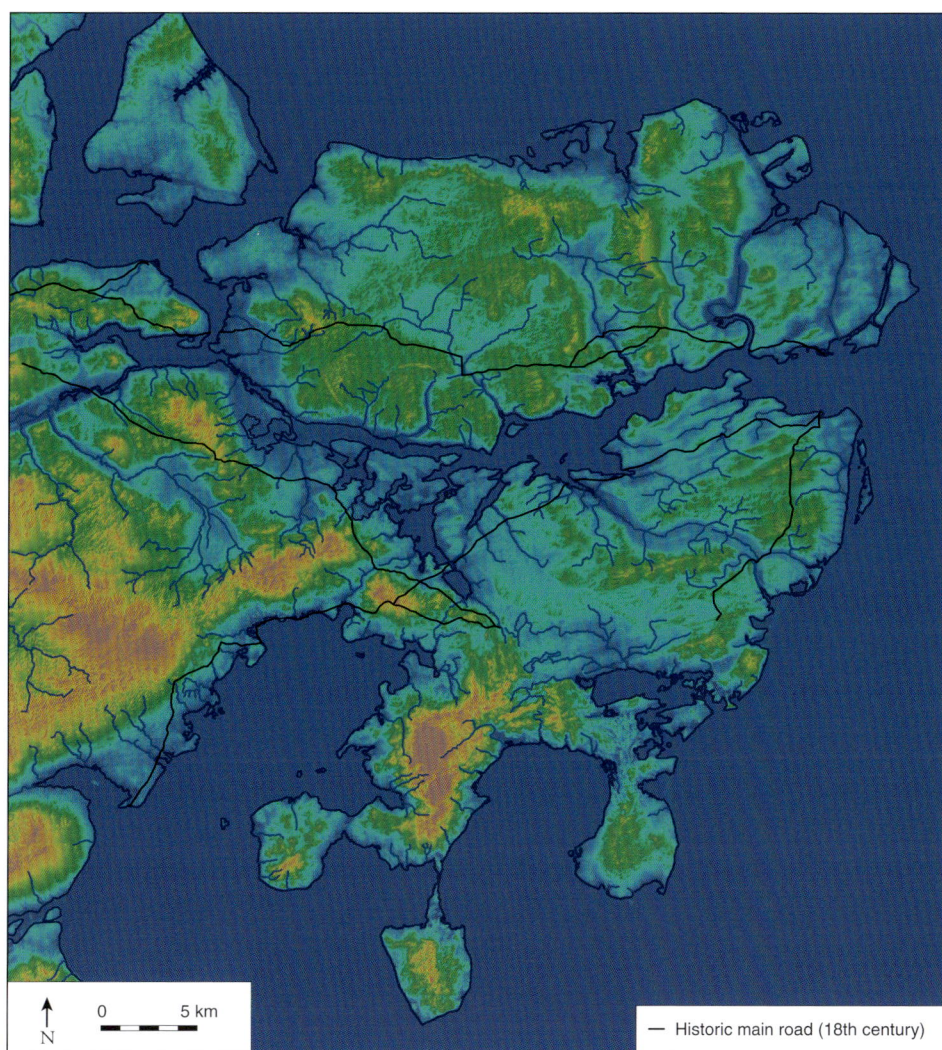

Fig. 53 | *The course of the main roads from the Videnskabernes Selskabs Kort in Djursland.*

0   5 km
N

— Historic main road (18th century)

countered at known enclosures were selected. The number of these sites, however, is still much too high. Many are situated very close to each other. To narrow down the search, the selection was evaluated by the secondary parameters (including inter-enclosure distance). The point of departure for the latter step was from previously known enclosures. However, in regions far from these (which are of a very restricted size due to the limited extent of the investigation area and the rather large number of already known enclosures), the least promising sites where removed from the selection in cases of close proximity.

As a result, a total of 103 potential sites were retrieved. This number is of course much higher than the number of possible, as-yet undetected enclosures. It results from the fact that several sites with equally suitable topography etc. were often present within a rather limited area. In the present case, the 103 possible enclosure locations are thought to represent 49 potential enclosures. This number still is very high and is the result of the underlying hypothesis that enclosures might have been present at inter-enclosure distances of ca. 4 km throughout the entire area, as was described above. The investigation area has a surface area of 1045 square km, which leaves room for approximately 80 enclosures when calculating with an inter-enclosure distance of ca. 4 km. The above-mentioned figure of 49 may thus (at least theoretically) not even encompass the entirety of causewayed enclosures in this region.

The (theoretically) lacking 30 sites can be explained by two different observations. In several parts of the investigation area, rather vast stretches of wetlands were unsuited for the construction of enclosures. These areas also lack barrows and, consequently, barrow roads are also absent. Therefore, no potential enclosure sites have been pointed out in these areas (e.g. in the western part of the large Neolithic island north of Kolindsund).

The second explanation for the presence of still undiscovered enclosure sites is the fact that the method employed above can only detect promontory sites in river confluences and at river mouths and will therefore exclude those that might be lo-

cated on peninsulas, river loops or other wet areas. Furthermore, hilltop sites have not even been considered yet. Therefore, regions still devoid of potential enclosure sites have been re-investigated with regard to the presence of well-suited sites in river loops close to river fords by barrow roads. The result of this search includes six sites in river loops (representing five potential enclosures), three sites on hilltops (representing two potential enclosures), three sites on promontories projecting into wetland (representing two potential enclosures) and finally five additional sites (representing four possible enclosures in divergent settings that were included mainly because of a marked promontory type topography in spite of the fact that these sites did not fulfil some of the criteria that otherwise have been regarded as mandatory, such as a nearby river crossing).

As final result, 121 locations representing a total of 59 potential enclosures were detected (Fig. 54 and Tab. 8). The number of potential enclosures is lower than the sum of potential enclosures when added up from the different categories, because in three cases, potential enclosures had multiple potential sites of different types (e.g. one in a river confluence and one in a neighbouring loop of the same river). The number in front of the name of the locations as listed in Tab. 8 indicates the number of the potential enclosure. As described above, there are up to five different locations sharing the same enclosure numbers. These range from 1 to 80 and not to 59 and include several missing numbers. These numbers are absent due to the removal of some regions from the working area subsequent to the start of numeration. In order to avoid confusion, this numeration was maintained despite these later adjustments.

7.3 Testing potential enclosure locations

There are various methods available for testing potential enclosure locations. These range from field and aerial surveying to trial excavation and geophysical prospection. For the present project, trial excavations were dismissed due to concerns with

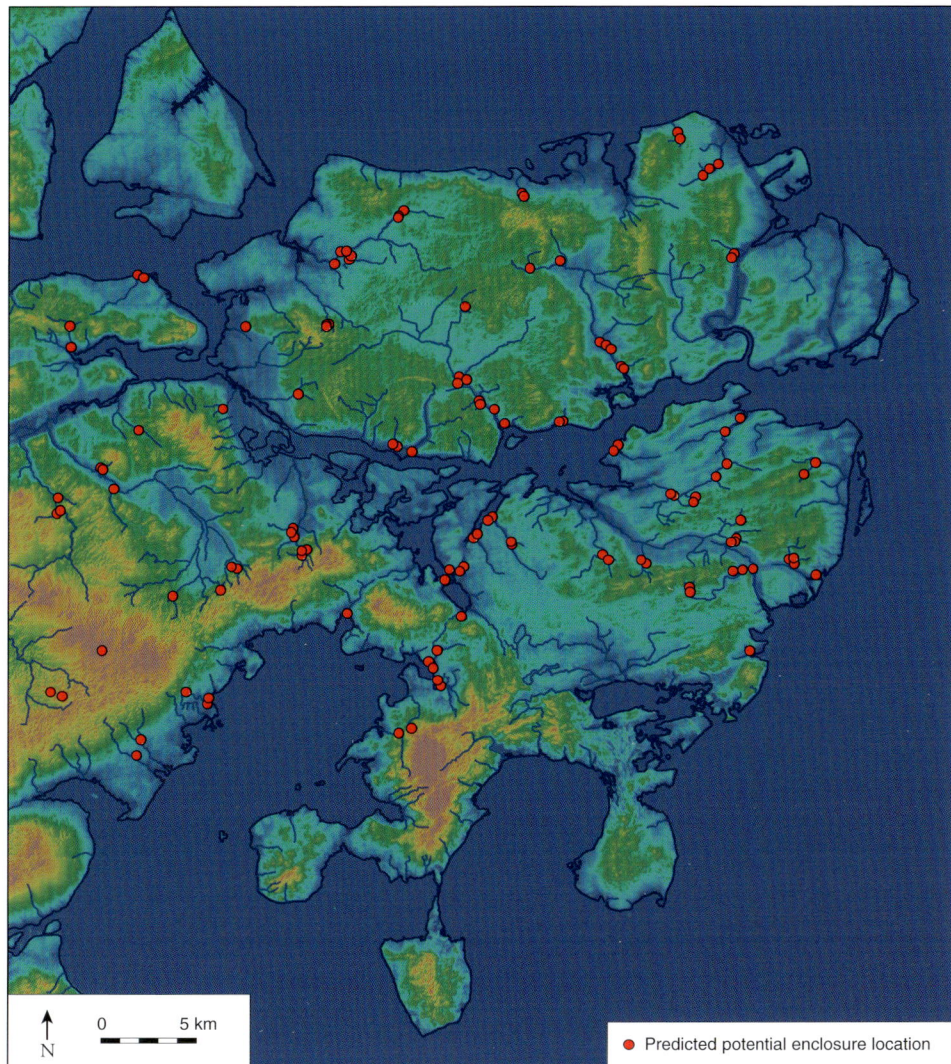

Fig. 54 | *As a result of the predictive process, at total of 121 individual sites thought to represent 59 potential enclosures were pointed out.*

cost and individual landowner digging permissions. As geophysical survey is also a costly affair, aerial survey (here the examination of extant photos) and field survey were employed; these results were then utilized for the selection of sites that were subsequently investigated by geophysical testing.

7.3.1 Aerial survey

In many parts of Europe, impressively large numbers of enclosures have been detected either by chance or via dedicated aerial survey (see e.g. Braasch 2002; Schwarz 2003; Geschwinde/Raetzel-Fabian 2009). Unfortunately, conditions for detection from the air are not good in South Scandinavia due to soil type and climate. Only comparatively few enclosures have been found by aerial survey:

the Mølbjerg I and II sites (Olesen 1994/unpublished), Vasagård Vest (Kaul et al. 2002), Sigersted III (Martens/Nielsen 1996), Albersdorf Dieksknöll (Arnold 1992; 1993; 1994; 1997; 2000) and Gammeltoft Odde (Troldtoft Andresen 2013). In a few other cases, crop marks caused by the presence of ditch segments were observed after the sites had been recognized as enclosures from the ground, e.g. Liselund (Westphal 2000), Markildegård (Østergård Sørensen 1995b) and Ballegård (B. Madsen, oral communication).

The comparatively large number of enclosures found by O. Braasch (an experienced aerial surveyor) in Mecklenburg-Vorpommern around the year 2000 (Plate 3, Plate 14, Ruthen and Zietlitz: Brandt 1998; Brandt 2000; Braasch 2002; Remmel 2002, Klatt 2009, 120) might indicate that

Potential enclosure	Site name	Mapsheet 1:25.000	Description	Coordinate X	Coordinate Y
1	Følle Vig	1315 II SV	promontory facing west at river mouth	590352	6240459
2	Kolkær	1315 II SV	promontory facing south close to river mouth	594630	6237898
2	Vesterskov	1315 II SV	promontory at river mouth	594859	6237546
2	Nymølle vml	1315 II SV	promontory between to confluent rivers	595056	6238480
3	Korup Sø	1315 II SV	site located at river mouth	596368	6240293
4	Næshøj	1315 II SV	peninsula in fjord	595487	6242258
4	Oldmose Gård	1315 II SV	promontory at river mouth	595727	6242801
4	Holmhøj	1315 II NV	promontory between confluent rivers close to river mouth	596493	6242942
4	Sølille Gårde	1315 II NV	promontory between confluent rivers close to river mouth	596307	6242698
5	Tarkjær Gårde	1315 II NV	promontory at river mouth	598003	6245647
5	Næhund	1315 II NV	promontory at river mouth	597744	6245440
6	Ryomgård I	1315 II NV	promontory between confluent rivers close to river mouth	592961	6249403
6	Ryomgård II	1315 II NV	promontory at river mouth	592728	6249537
6	Ryomgård III	1315 II NV	peninsula in fjord close to a river mouth	593744	6249099
7	Vejvad Bro	1315 II NV	promontory at river mouth	598619	6250607
7	Dybdalsgård	1315 II NV	promontory bordered by two rivers	598095	6251353
8	Pognæs I	1315 II NØ	promontory at river mouth	601752	6250721
8	Pognæs II	1315 II NØ	promontory at river mouth	601550	6250696
10	Søby I	1315 II NØ	promontory at river mouth	604705	6249470
10	Søby II	1315 II NØ	promontory at river mouth	604488	6249150
11	Revn I	1315 II NØ	promontory at river mouth	611240	6250897
11	Lillemølle	1315 II NØ	promontory between confluent rivers	610447	6250158
12	Studstrup I	1315 III SØ	promontory at river mouth	582935	6235626
12	Studstrup II	1315 III SØ	promontory at river mouth	582980	6235931
12	Bøgehøj	1315 III SØ	promontory in river loop	581787	6236236
13	Hovmosegård N	1315 II SV	promontory at river mouth	595286	6236577
13	Ovst Bro	1315 II SV	promontory at river mouth	595079	6236869
14	Elkjær	1315 II SV	promontory in river loop	593074	6234080
14	Tornholm	1315 II SV	elevation bordered by wetlands and a river	593743	6234318
18	Katholm Skov Syd	1415 III SV	promontory at river mouth	615318	6242516
19	Grund V	1315 IV SØ	promontory at river mouth	579190	6258550
19	Grund Ø	1315 IV SØ	promontory at river mouth	579509	6258405
24	Todbjerg Møllebakke	1315 III SØ	hilltop	575212	6236022
24	Todbjerg Bakke vest	1315 III SØ	hilltop	574610	6236256
26	Krogsbæk Kirke	1315 III NØ	promontory between confluent rivers	577943	6247137
26	Marbæk N	1315 III NØ	promontory between confluent rivers	577230	6248251
26	Marbæk S	1315 III NØ	promontory between confluent rivers	577353	6248153
27	Ringgård N	1315 III NØ	promontory between confluent rivers	583737	6251402
28	Næsdrup Høj	1315 II NØ	promontory in river loop	603886	6243593
28	Drammelstrup NV	1315 II NØ	promontory between confluent rivers	604186	6243301
29	Østerballe I	1415 III NV	promontory between confluent rivers	613908	6243327
29	Østerballe II	1415 III NV	promontory between confluent rivers	614179	6243074
29	Østerballe III	1415 III NV	promontory between confluent rivers	614161	6243403
30	Balle 1	1315 II SØ	promontory between confluent rivers	611978	6242820
30	Balle 2	1315 II SØ	promontory in river loop	611400	6242748
30	Lysballe Høj	1315 II SØ	promontory in river loop	610881	6242698
31	Nielstrup I	1315 I SV	promontory between confluent rivers	590429	6259424
31	Nielstrup II	1315 I SV	promontory between confluent rivers	590506	6259622
31	Nielstrup III	1315 I SV	promontory bordered by wet areas	589963	6259829
31	Nielstrup IV	1315 I SV	promontory bordered by rivers and wet areas	590283	6259873
31	Nielstrup V	1315 I SV	promontory between confluent rivers	589659	6259165
33	Brunmose	1315 II NV	promontory between confluent rivers	587743	6252205
34	Nimtofte Nord	1315 II NV	promontory between confluent rivers	596228	6253138
34	Svenstrup	1315 II NV	promontory between confluent rivers	596143	6252789
34	Krogården	1315 II NV	promontory between confluent rivers	596644	6252974
35	Ørbæk I	1315 I SØ	promontory between confluent rivers	603739	6254958
35	Ørbæk II	1315 I SØ	promontory between confluent rivers	604063	6254795
35	Ørbæk III	1315 I SØ	promontory between confluent rivers	604322	6254589
36	Stenvadgård	1315 I SØ	promontory between confluent rivers	599976	6258928
37	Brønninggård	1315 I SØ	promontory between confluent rivers	601580	6259330

38	Horsballund Bakke	1315 I SØ	promontory between confluent rivers	610904	6259711
39	Albæk	1315 I SØ	promontory between confluent rivers	609258	6263890
39	Korrishøj	1315 I SØ	promontory between confluent rivers	609618	6264230
39	Brunbakke Syd	1315 I SØ	promontory in wet river valley	610070	6264472
40	Auning N	1315 I SV	promontory in wet river valley	584953	6255829
41	Tustrup I	1315 I SV	promontory in river loop	593294	6262020
41	Tustrup II	1315 I SV	promontory bordered by wet areas	593036	6261732
41	Tustrup III	1315 I SV	promontory between confluent rivers	593004	6261634
42	Ramten Skov	1315 I SV	promontory bordered by river	596554	6256857
46	Virup Skov	1315 III SØ	promontory between confluent rivers	579375	6233710
46	Virup Skovgård	1315 III SØ	promontory between confluent rivers	579168	6232853
47	Ballehøj	1315 III SØ	hilltop	577316	6238503
50	Ørup	1315 II SØ	promontory between confluent rivers	608570	6241841
50	Ørup S	1315 II SØ	promontory in river loop	608595	6241587
51	Ladegårdsbakke Ø	1315 II NØ	promontory bordered by river	606223	6243119
51	Ladegårdsbakke V	1315 II NØ	promontory bordered by river	605966	6243293
53	Trustrup I	1315 II NØ	promontory between confluent rivers	608873	6246671
53	Trustrup II	1315 II NØ	hilltop, surrounded by wetlands	608771	6246384
53	Obdrup Bro	1315 II NØ	promontory between confluent rivers	607725	6246751
53	Nygård Ø	1315 II NØ	promontory between confluent rivers	607559	6246834
55	Fladstrup S	1315 II NØ	promontory between confluent rivers	610567	6248460
55	Lundskovgård	1315 II NØ	promontory between confluent rivers	609983	6247762
57	Holstens Bjerg	1315 II NV	promontory between confluent rivers	587542	6244560
57	Bolbakke	1315 II NV	promontory between confluent rivers	587480	6245032
57	Falkjær Gårde	1315 II NV	promontory between confluent rivers	587372	6244827
58	Assenbakke	1315 III SØ	promontory between confluent rivers	583613	6241701
59	Mørke SV I	1315 III NØ	promontory bordered by wet areas	584513	6242847
59	Mørke SV II	1315 III NØ	ridge bordered by wet areas	584222	6242946
60	Løvenholm Østerskov I	1315 I SV	promontory between confluent rivers	589372	6255933
60	Løvenholm Østerskov II	1315 I SV	promontory between confluent rivers	589230	6255917
60	Løvenholm Østerskov III	1315 I SV	promontory between confluent rivers	589239	6255814
61	Skeldal N	1315 II NØ	promontory at river mouth	604861	6253674
61	Skeldal S	1315 II NØ	promontory at river mouth	605005	6253536
62	Lykkeshom V I	1315 II NØ	promontory between confluent rivers	611045	6244467
62	Lykkesholm S	1315 II NØ	promontory between confluent rivers	610987	6244273
62	Lykkesholm V II	1315 II NØ	promontory between confluent rivers	610780	6244244
63	Birkehøj	1415 III NV	promontory between confluent rivers	614680	6247896
63	Høbjerg V	1415 III NV	promontory between confluent rivers	615284	6248509
64	Drageshøj N	1315 I SØ	hill bordered by wet areas and rivers	599528	6262925
64	Drageshøj S	1315 I SØ	promontory between confluent rivers	599621	6262783
65	Rugård S	1315 II SØ	promontory at river mouth	611781	6238473
66	Grimsbjerg V	1315 II NV	hill bordered by wet areas and rivers	587964	6243563
66	Fårup V	1315 II NV	hilltop, bordering river on one side	588209	6243866
66	Lundbæk Bakke	1315 II NV	hilltop, bordering river on one side	587964	6243799
70	Skader N	1315 III NØ	promontory between confluent rivers	574995	6246636
70	Skader SV	1315 III NØ	promontory between confluent rivers	574929	6245832
70	Skader SØ	1315 III NØ	promontory between confluent rivers	575121	6245973
71	Svejdal Næs	1315 IV SØ	promontory between confluent rivers	575584	6255831
71	Ammelhede Næs	1315 IV SØ	promontory at river mouth	575651	6254715
72	Sønderskov V Nord	1315 II NV	promontory between confluent rivers	597262	6251819
72	Sønderskov V Syd	1315 II NV	promontory between confluent rivers	597330	6251627
74	Storebavle	1315 I NØ	promontory in river loop	607892	6266192
74	Storebavle S	1315 I NØ	promontory between confluent rivers	608034	6265847
76	Esbensminde	1315 III NØ	ridge between to river valleys	579269	6250236
77	Tendrup	1315 III SØ	promontory between confluent rivers	581090	6241386
78	Stenhøj S	1315 II NØ	promontory between confluent rivers	611276	6245437
79	Mårup S	1315 II NV/NØ	promontory between confluent rivers	599013	6244106
79	Mårup N	1315 II NV	promontory between confluent rivers	598987	6244266
80	Mårup Skovgård S	1315 II NV	promontory at river mouth	596987	6244492
80	Mårup Skovgård N	1315 II NV	promontory at river mouth	597218	6244727

Tab. 8 | *The 121 potential enclosure sites representing 59 potential enclosures. Coordinates refer to the approximate centre of the potential enclosure area and refer to the projected WGS84 (UTM-zone 32N) coordinate system.*

Fig. 55 | *An aerial photo from 1979 of the potential enclosure site 3 Korup Sø which shows a circular structure approximately 300 m in diameter which consists of a number of large, diffuse dark and light patches (possibly pits). Aerial photo copyright COWI.*

the potential of air survey has not yet been fully exploited in South Scandinavia. It might also be due to differing soil/climate conditions. Another factor at play regarding these specific enclosures in Mecklenburg-Vorpommern may be their construction, which clearly differs from that of the other enclosures within the TRB North Group distribution area. This type of construction may facilitate their detection from the air.

Unfortunately, it was not possible to obtain the necessary grants for an aerial enclosure survey directly targeted towards Djursland. Instead, online archives of historic and more recent aerial pictures were examined. The likelihood of detecting enclosures from within the confines of the extant archives were judged to be low, given that they were not taken with archaeological objectives in mind. Approximately 10 sets of pictures of sufficient resolution from different years were available. Of these, practically only those from 1974 and 1979 proved to be of any value, as they were taken during the summer and (possibly) under draught conditions.

An initial step controlled the location of all known enclosures and related sites in the research area. However, not a single of these sites could be

recognized in the existing pictures. In a second step, aerial photographs of all predicted sites in Djursland were studied. Unfortunately, once again, no causewayed enclosure of the typical TRB type could be detected from these pictures. Although this negative result was not unexpected given the results from the search for aerial indications of known enclosures, this second step did result in the detection of other features which are, nevertheless, of interest with regards to this study.

The first of these includes a completely circular structure with an outer diameter of ca. 300 m at the site of 3 Korup Sø (Fig. 55). This feature is visible as diffuse dark patches separated by lighter areas. No parallels are known, but the almost perfect symmetry of the feature renders a human origin at least possible. Two potential pits are suggested by the presence of a pair of dark maculae close to the centre of the structure. They are situated on a slight elevation, which proved in later survey to be particularly rich in flint surface finds. A wet area (potentially a spring) is apparent in the northeastern part of the potential enclosure. The presence of a spring inside the circular feature is of special interest, as springs and wells were often focal points of ritual activities in the TRB (Nilsson/Nilsson 2003; Brozio 2011; Rasmussen/Skousen 2012). Furthermore, the palisade enclosure of Helgeshøj on Zealand which dates from ca. 2800 BC has a spring in its enclosed area (Giersing 2004). Nevertheless, due to the very diffuse nature of the dark spots defining the circle observed at site 3 Korup Sø, there are some severe doubts regarding the assumed nature of the entire structure.

The second feature detected in historical aerial photos is that of a circular structure ca. 120 m in outer diameter at site 10 Søby I (Fig. 56). The southwestern part of this structure is not visible due to a road and some other (very dark) feature. The remainder shows itself as a very weak and diffuse ring-shaped feature. This potential ring-ditch does not show any clear interruptions or entrances. Field survey at the site produced a handful of flakes. However, neither tools nor anything that could indicate the age of the structure

Fig. 56 | *Aerial photo from 1979 of the potential enclosure site 10 Søby I, showing a diffuse, ring-shaped feature ca. 120 m in diameter. Aerial photo copyright COWI.*

Fig. 57 | *Aerial photo from 1979 of the potential enclosure site 11 Revn I, showing a group of dark spots south of the hedge (possibly pits of prehistoric age). Aerial photo copyright COWI.*

was recovered. No comparable features are known from the South Scandinavian Neolithic or other prehistoric periods. It is too large to represent a destroyed grave mound, and the feature is also too regular to represent the remains of an old gravel pit. Moreover, according to the farmer who owns the land on which this site is located, no drainage or other modern features have been dug there. Possible explanations of this feature were sought by surveying Neolithic structures from areas south of Denmark. In this area, there is one type that partially matches the observations at site 10 Søby I with regard to architecture and the scarcity

of finds. The 'Kreisgrabenanlage' Belleben type (known from the eastern central parts of Germany) seems to match the features observed at 10 Søby I quite precisely with regards to size, the uninterrupted single ditch (excepting one narrow entrance) and round shape. Furthermore, the well investigated site of Belleben I could be dated to the period 3600-3400 BC by means of ^{14}C analysis (Rück 2012). Finds made at the excavation belong to the Baalberg Group of the TRB. As the Belleben site belongs to a culturally related group a few hundred kilometres south of Djursland and was constructed at a time when numerous enclosures were built in South Scandinavia, it is at least a possibility that the structure observed at 10 Søby I represents an enclosure of comparable type. The topographical situation at 10 Søby I is very different from that of the Belleben enclosure as well as those of other sites with related enclosure types known from Central Europe. The diffuse ring visible in the photo encircles a depression and points to a possible geological origin. The interpretation of the somewhat smeared nature of the ring structure (in comparison to Belleben) also warrants caution.

The last feature of interest was detected in an aerial photo of site 11 Revn I (Fig. 57). Close to the hedge in the northern part of the area were a large number of clearly visible dark spots. These were present in the subsoil, which appears particularly light in this part of the potential site. These spots (or at least a portion of them) might well represent prehistoric features. This latter suspicion is supported by the high density of Neolithic surface finds in the area; see below. However, there is no direct indication of the presence of an enclosure.

In summary, it must be concluded that the survey of existing aerial photographs in the present case was not well suited to testing the outcome of the predictive modelling process. Future research should examine whether this result was caused only by the fact that the available pictures were taken at random times or whether causewayed enclosures in Djursland are generally invisible from the air, even under optimal survey conditions.

7.3.2 Field survey

As described above, the overwhelming majority of all causewayed enclosures known in Scandinavia have delivered abundant surface finds. However, said surface finds do not necessarily date from the time of enclosure construction, but rather from the later use phases of the sites. The interiors had often turned into regular settlements by that point, and therefore produced a certain amount of specific domestic rubbish and normal object loss.

Whether or not this result is representative for all TRB enclosures is debateable, as sites poor in (or almost devoid of) surface finds are likely to be underrepresented. Still, there is a large number of enclosures with high (or very high) surface find densities. Therefore, a large proportion of these sites were known long before they were identified as enclosures by excavation or by the more recent re-evaluation of old excavation reports. Due to the abundance of surface finds on many sites, a field survey of the potential locations of causewayed enclosures on Djursland was a logical step in testing the results of the theoretical predictions. Of the total 121 predicted enclosure locations, only 48 (roughly 40%) were accessible for field survey. The remaining sites could not be surveyed for many different reasons. Many are situated in forests or are covered by grass. While these sites have been visited, a survey of those situated in forests was only possible in one case: site 64 Drageshøj S. At this site, older trees had recently been felled and new ones planted following a deep ploughing of the soil. While almost the entire surface of the site was covered by scrub, small trees and deadfall, a number of flakes attesting to the production of flint axes were collected. Although it was not possible to date these finds with any certainty, they most probably belong to the TRB.

In case of the potential enclosure locations covered by grass, the only possibility of retrieving finds was by examining molehills. This procedure led to the detection of finds in two cases (1 Følle Vig and 58 Assenbakke), one of which included the only pieces of TRB pottery from the entire survey campaign (two thumbnail-sized undecorated wall shards from site 58 Assenbakke which probably can be allocated to a late Early or early Middle Neolithic phase of the TRB due to the fabric).

Other sites could not be surveyed because they had been destroyed by gravel digging or building activities. Moreover, in a number of cases, the landowners did not permit their fields to be examined. Finally, several sites could not be surveyed due to scheduling glitches and the pressures of a single field-walking season. In these cases, many fields had already been re-sown with fast growing crops like rapeseed. The search of cornfields also proved to be problematic because the heavy equipment (and broad tires) used in harvesting this crop tended to press all flint items deep into the mud, thereby rendering them invisible to the naked eye.

Due to the large number of sites that had to be surveyed and because survey had to be completed in a single season (late summer/autumn of 2011), it was not possible to wait for optimum survey conditions for all sites. In consequence, some fields had to be surveyed after harvest, but before ploughing. This was no easy task, especially in those cases in which a secondary crop had already been sown. These fields turned green again almost immediately following harvest. While some others had been ploughed, they had not received the amount of rainfall required to wash away the overturned earth from the flints.

In cases where field survey was possible, a systematic approach was employed. As far as accessible, the entire potential enclosure area (as judged by topography) was surveyed by walking in lines at approximately 3 m intervals. Depending on the density of finds, this distance was altered over the course of the survey. Given that very large (and finds-rich) structures were sought after, even the maximum inter-line distance (ca. 8 m) would certainly have resulted in the retrieval of finds, should they have been present. The survey design thus did not aim at the collection of the entirety of find material present, but rather the first detection of potential find scatters over a large expanse. The latter can be expected to have been present on most causeways enclosures either due to finds throughout or ranging across large parts of the enclosures or even in the area of the ditch segments alone. Field conditions, soil type and weather conditions were noted in all cases. These factors are crucial to appropriately gauging the amount of material recovered. Sunshine (especially from a low autumn sun), vegetation and the amount of rainfall after ploughing all heavily influence the outcome of a survey (see e.g. Jacobsen 1984).

The chosen survey method turned out to be very effective, allowing for the search of all but two sites within no more than four hours apiece. In cases in which there was a total lack of finds, the entire potential enclosure area could typically be surveyed in one or two hours, after which the survey was consequently abandoned. The amount of finds as well as the size of the find areas on the respective sites were recorded, as both are important criteria that can be used (at least theoretically) to differentiate between an ordinary settlement and an enclosure site (see discussion below).

In order to best gauge find amounts, they were classified into four categories. These groups were labelled no finds (category 0), few finds (category 1), medium amount of finds (category 2) and abundant finds (category 3). Before placing a site in any of these classes, the actual number of collected finds was evaluated in light of field and weather conditions, as described above. The categories, therefore, do not represent an absolute but rather a relative classification system. While this procedure is of course subjective, it was necessary to enable any direct comparison between individual sites as surveyed under different conditions. In a few cases (excavation or survey by third parties) a classification within this four class system was impossible, due to the lack of adequate information.

The size of the find scatter on the surveyed field was also classified into four categories, ranging from no finds (0) through to small (1), medium (2) and large (3). In some cases, it was impossible to make a judgement due those same reasons listed above. The small, medium and large categories were defined according to typical site sizes as

known from systematic survey. As argued by T. Madsen (1982), in general, TRB settlement sites can be divided into catching sites, residential sites and "centres". The latter term describes enclosure sites. TRB catching sites are almost exclusively known from the Early Neolithic. They were typically placed directly on former shorelines (Madsen, T. 1982, 203ff.). Due to the topographical type of sites chosen for the current survey, the detection of catching sites is unlikely. This assumption was apparently confirmed by the outcome of this survey, as only a single transverse arrowhead was found. Of course, this might also be due to the fact that they were overlooked due to their small size. However, given that other items of similar size were regularly collected as well as the fact that the author has previously found transverse arrowheads while on field survey, this outcome is probably fairly accurate.

Residential sites from the TRB in eastern Jutland show a marked development in size, as was described by T. Madsen (1982, 205ff.). While those of the Early Neolithic rarely surpass 700 m², sizes reached at least 4000 m² in the early parts of Middle Neolithic A (MNA I-II) and as much as 20-30,000 m² in late Middle Neolithic A (MN A III-V). The latter sites are often identical to causewayed enclosures. They can reach sizes of at least 150,000 m², although finds are not necessarily spread throughout the entire area. Based on these observations, the size classes used here were defined as follows. Sites were classified as 'small' when the find surface scatter was under 1000 m² (size category 1). Corresponding values for medium and large sites are 1000-5000 m² (size category 2) and over 5000 m² (size category 3), respectively. The largest detected sites (3 Korup Sø, 11 Revn I and 53 Trustrup II) ranged between 50,000 and circa 100,000 m², although they had uneven find densities within these huge areas. It should be noted that this classification was irrespective of chronological information. The number of finds that could be precisely dated were insufficient for differentiating between find scatters produced from a small settlement which was continuously relocated over time and a single site of large extent from a single phase. Therefore, it is not possible to identify the type of site or its precise chronology by means of find scatter size alone. Tab. 9 gives an overview of the sites included in (and the results produced from) this survey.

7.3.2.1 Results of the survey
Of the total 121 sites predicted representing 59 different potential enclosures, only 48 (39.7%) could be surveyed. The remaining 73 sites (60.3%) were inaccessible for the variety of different reasons

Site name	TRB finds	Amount of finds	Size of find bearing area	Early and late finds	Axe production
3 Korup Sø	yes	1	3	no	yes
8 Pognæs I	yes	1	1	no	yes
11 Revn I	yes	3	3	yes	yes
13 Ovst Bro	yes	1	1	no	yes
19 Grund V	yes	1	1	no	no
19 Grund Ø	yes	unknown	2	no	unknown
24 Todbjerg Møllebakke	yes	2	2	no	possibly
28 Drammelstrup NV	yes	1	1	no	yes
31 Nielstrup I	yes	unknown	2	no	possibly
36 Stenvadgård	yes	2	1	no	yes
39 Albæk	yes	3	2	no	unknown
46 Virup Skovgård	yes	3		no	unknown
53 Trustrup I	yes	2	1	no	unknown
53 Trustrup II	yes	3	3	yes	yes
55 Fladstrup S	yes	3	3	no	yes
58 Assenbakke	yes	unknown	unknown	no	possibly
62 Lykkesholm S	yes	2	2	no	yes
63 Birkehøj	yes	2	2	no	yes
63 Høbjerg V	yes	2	2	no	yes
70 Skader SØ	yes	1	3	yes	yes
78 Stenhøj S	yes	1	1	no	yes
79 Mårup N	yes	3	3	yes	yes
6 Ryomgård III	no	0	0	no	no
10 Søby II	no	0	0	no	no
11 Lillemølle	no	1	0	no	no
13 Hovmosegård N	no	0	0	no	no
14 Tornholm	no	1	1	no	yes
Todbjerg Bakke west	no	1	3	no	possibly
26 Marbæk N	no	0	0	no	no
26 Marbæk S	no	0	0	no	no
27 Ringgård N	no	0	0	no	no
34 Svenstrup	no	0	0	no	no
47 Ballehøj	no	0	0	no	no
59 Mørke SV II	no	1	2	no	no
61 Skeldal N	no	2	2	no	yes
62 Lykkesholm V II	no	0	0	no	no
70 Skader SV	no	1	2	no	yes
72 Sønderskov V Syd	no	0	0	no	no
1 Følle Vig	possibly	unknown	unknown	no	no
2 Vesterskov	possibly	1	3	no	possibly
10 Søby I	possibly	1	1	no	no
26 Krogsbæk Kirke	possibly	1	0	no	no
50 Ørup	possibly	unknown	unknown	no	unknown
50 Ørup S	possibly	unknown	unknown	no	unknown
64 Drageshøj S	possibly	unknown	unknown	no	yes
70 Skader N	possibly	2	2	no	yes
77 Tendrup	possibly	1	1	no	yes

Tab. 9 | *Overview of the results of 48 sites examined by field survey. The codes used for the "Amount of finds" and "Size of find-bearing area" categories are explained in the text. "Early and late finds" refers to the presence of finds from the time of the thin-butted axe (EN I - MN AII) and the time of the thick-butted axe (MN AIII - MN AV) on the same site.*

detailed above. These 48 surveyed sites must be further subdivided. Actual field walking was completed on 36 of their number, while information from recent third party excavations or surveys was utilized for the remaining twelve.

Of the 48 surveyed sites, 23 (47.9%) yielded finds which could be allocated to the TRB with certainty, while a further nine sites (18.8%) produced finds that probably or possibly belong to this culture. In these latter cases, the uncertainty derived from the fact that only some of the collected artefacts (axes and chisels, different types of flint knives, some cores and daggers) could be clearly attributed to specific Neolithic cultures. The most common artefact type on Neolithic sites as well as in this survey (scrapers) was more difficult to handle in this regard. The same situation applied to drills. Based on the fact that finds from other Neolithic/Bronze Age periods were rather scarce (artefacts attributable to the Single Grave Culture, the Late Neolithic or Early Bronze Age from eight sites, or 16.7% of all sites surveyed) and those from the Mesolithic were almost absent, most of the scrapers/other finds from the sites in question are most likely TRB.

7.3.2.2 The finds

A selection of characteristic finds from the field survey is depicted in Fig. 58. A short description for the individual collected types is provided below.

A total of 12 flint axes were collected from nine different sites. There are seven neck fragments and one fragment of a cutting edge. The latter (from a thin-butted axe) was deliberately destroyed by fire, a practice that is known from the TRB both from ordinary settlement finds as well as special sites (where large amounts of axes and chisels were sacrificed – Larsson, L. 1989; Andersen, N.H. 2009, 27ff). Furthermore, burned axes and chisels were regularly deposited at megalithic graves in the later part of the TRB (Andersen, N.H. 2000).

Three axes are represented by flakes with scant remains of polished surfaces only. One blade with a significant amount of gloss struck from the cutting edge of a thin-butted TRB axe was also found.

The clear dominance of neck fragments compared to cutting edge fragments differs from the picture observed for the intensely surveyed Sarup region (Andersen, N.H. 2009, 28). Whether this reflects any real difference is doubtful, as the material from the present survey is not large enough for any statistically valid comparison. In general, axe neck finds can be expected to outnumber those of axe edges in settlements, as necks were taken back to the settlement for replacement, insofar as they were still hafted to an axe handle. Edges, by contrast, were destroyed by heavy work and were discarded at the work site if they were unsuited to secondary use (e.g. as a core).

From a chronological point of view, two of the collected axes are identifiable as B-axes from the Single Grave Culture or possibly also the Late Neolithic. A third axe, which is only represented by a flake, should probably also be dated to this later part of the Neolithic because of the nature of its polish. It is very smooth and lacks the striae that are typical of the polish on TRB axes (Madsen, B. 1984; B. Madsen, oral comm.). The remaining finds are either certainly (or are likely to be) TRB. All are fragments of thick-bladed axes. Four belong to thin-butted and four to thick-butted types, representing early (EN I-MN A II) and late (MN A III-V) phases of the TRB, respectively.

The latest TRB phase (Store Valby, MN A V) is not known from Djursland, where it appears to have been replaced by the PWC. Some of the thick-butted axe finds may thus belong to the latter culture. No attempts to place the thick-butted axes more closely within one of the phases of the late MN A have been made, as they are either roughly hewn or show traces of secondary use. This last is the case for one piece which was transformed into a core from which blades were struck in opposite directions (a bi-polar core).

The two chisels represent one very carefully made, fully polished fragment of a Middle Neolithic TRB artefact and a very crude (unpolished) but completely preserved item that possibly dates to the later TRB. Nevertheless, a somewhat younger age for this obviously unfinished item cannot be excluded.

A total of nine drills were collected from five different sites. Of these, four were from a single site

Fig. 58 (opposite page) | *A selection of artefacts found during the field survey of 36 potential enclosure sites. Photos: Moesgård Museum, Department of Photo and Media, Rikke Grøn Larsson. 1: 11 Revn I; 2,10,11,12,15,17,18: 53 Trustrup II; 3,5,7: 79 Mårup N; 4: 70 Skader N; 6,14,16: 55 Fladstrup S; 8,9: 58 Assenbakke; 13,19: 70 Skader SØ.*

(3 Korup Sø), while isolated pieces were collected from a further four sites. The artefacts show considerable variation in size. Particularly the smaller versions also demonstrate clear use wear. While it is not possible to date these items to any specific period of the Neolithic, it can be stated that all collected types are known from TRB sites.

Scrapers are the most frequent tools recovered from Neolithic settlements. They also dominate the finds from the current field survey with a total of 90 pieces from 16 different sites. The number of pieces per site ranges from 1 to 20. While scrapers on more or less round flakes (often waste flakes from axe-production) were typical for the TRB, other shapes (especially more oblong ones) are also known from that culture. Comparable scrapers appear in later Neolithic as well as Mesolithic or Early Bronze Age cultures, making it difficult to assign single finds to a specific culture with certainty. Only one scraper (made from a very strong and long blade) can be clearly identified as not belonging to the TRB Culture. This find from site 24 Todbjerg Møllebakke must date from the Younger Bronze Age.

No less than 84 of the 90 scrapers from the current survey were collected on 13 sites that also yielded finds that were clearly attributable to the TRB. A further four come from two sites that did not deliver any culturally specific finds. Only two are from a single site (61 Skeldal N) that also yielded a fragment of a flat-flaked sickle of Late Neolithic/Early Bronze date but no TRB finds. This scraper deviates due to its regularity and thin profile. Even though five of the 13 TRB sites with finds of scrapers also delivered finds that can be dated to the Late Neolithic or Early Bronze Age, the majority of the scrapers from these sites (as well as from those that only delivered TRB finds) can probably be identified as TRB artefacts. The same conclusion can be reached by a simple quantification of the

total number of finds (see above). Therefore, sites that did not deliver any culturally-specific tools but yielded finds of scrapers have been classified as possible TRB sites.

As was mentioned above, only two small and undecorated shards of TRB-pottery were found in the entire survey (both from site 58 Assenbakke). No later Neolithic or Bronze Age pottery was retrieved (and Iron Age and Medieval finds have been disregarded here).

The entirety of the field-survey only resulted in five arrowhead finds from five different sites. Four are of the same type (Late Neolithic/Early Bronze Age) and represent either semi-finished, flat-flaked triangular arrowheads or (more likely) finished, primitive items. All are made of thin, more or less triangular flakes that show signs of pressure-flaking along the edges. A single transverse TRB-type arrowhead was collected from site 11 Revn I.

The 22 blade finds from ten different sites are very difficult to judge from a chronological point of view. The majority of these items (16) were collected from sites that had nonetheless also yielded certain TRB-finds. One very regular piece may have been aimed at the production of transverse arrowheads or was intended for use as a sickle (no gloss). One small fragment was burned, while four pieces from four different sites were recovered with a strong, white patina. None of these latter sites yielded up clear TRB-finds. Therefore, it is possible that these blades may date from the Mesolithic. However, no certain Mesolithic finds where made on these four sites, so they may represent items that were either re-deposited or, in fact, were from the Neolithic.

From site 53 Trustrup II came the only flint dagger found: a fragment of a flat-flaked Late Neolithic item of very high quality.

Four different types of sickles were collected in a total of nine pieces from four different locations.

The long and narrow blade with intensive gloss that was struck from the edge part of a polished thin-butted TRB axe from site 70 Skader SØ has already been mentioned. In addition to this piece, a further four blade sections from site 11 Revn I are likely identifiable as TRB sickle blades. However, they demonstrate no clear traces of gloss. The remaining pieces belong to the Late Neolithic or Bronze Age. Two of them are small fragments of flat-flaked sickles which cannot be precisely dated to either of these two possible periods. However, two thick blade sections from site 53 (Trustrup II) probably date from the Bronze Age.

Nine knives of different types have been collected from six sites. Most of these are of the type which is called 'buekniv' in Danish. These artefacts often have a convex edge that was retouched to be used as handle opposite a sharp, straight edge used for cutting. They generally date from the TRB Culture. The second type ('skivekniv' in Danish) is characterised by a retouched edge, approximately one cm of which was left to form the cutting edge. Only one of the nine pieces belongs to this category (find from site 62 Lykkesholm S), which appears to be present only on TRB sites dated to MN A I (Eriksen/Madsen 1984).

Eleven cores were collected from four sites. Eight were small, rather primitive flake blocks that could not be dated to any specific phase of the Neolithic and may just as well have been Mesolithic in age (although this is rather unlikely, given the general absence of Mesolithic finds in the survey as a whole). Of said cores, five come from two sites that delivered abundant TRB material, (53 Trustrup II and 55 Fladstrup S), making it likely that these cores were deposited in the TRB period. A single core (from site 24 Todbjerg Møllebakke) may well have been used for the production of microliths in the early Mesolithic. The remaining two cores are bipolar blade cores. Although it was damaged, one is still roughly cylindrical (from site 70 Skader SØ), while the other is a re-used thick-butted axe from which blades were struck from one face (from 55 Fladstrup S). Both cores can probably be dated to the PWC or the very late TRB Culture, ca. 2900-2500 BC.

The thousands of collected flakes were examined to identify those reflecting the production of flint axes, as axe production is a characteristic activity very often identifiable at the causewayed enclosures that have been investigated to date. However, it also is known from ordinary settlements and specialised production sites. No less than 20 sites delivered characteristic axe-production debris. A further six sites yielded the possible remains of axe production activities.

On 12 locations, more or less recent excavations or field surveying by third parties took place. None of these excavations/surveys resulted in the discovery of ditch segments characteristic of an enclosure. However, this does not necessarily mean that no enclosures were present at these sites, given that the excavations which took place were often spatially-restricted in nature and could potentially have missed the ditch segments.

In five cases, TRB finds were excavated or were known from survey, while in five others no TRB finds were made. The last site (77 Tendrup) yielded only an isolated pit filled with axe production debris. While this could well date to TRB times, this is not necessarily the case.

Of the sites that yielded TRB finds, two were excavated by N. A. Boas (53 Trustrup I (Wincentz Rasmussen 2011) and 39 Albæk). Both could be classified as ordinary settlements. The size of the excavation in at least one of these cases (39 Albæk) makes it possible to eliminate the possibility that an enclosure was present. However, the same cannot be said for the remaining three sites possessed of TRB finds. One (46 Virup Skovgård) is known only from a farmer's collection, while the other two (19 Grund Ø and 31 Nielstrup I) were partly excavated by O.A. Schmidt from the Kulturhistorisk Museum Randers in the late 1980s. In both cases, the surface was cleared of topsoil in a restricted area, revealing the presence of a number of cooking pits/fireplaces, few of which were investigated in any greater detail (Kulturhistorisk Museum Randers, journal nr. 72/88 and 161/71). The excavator dated the pits to the TRB due to flint artefact finds as well as rare pottery shards. The latter indicate a date at the transition point between the Early and Middle Neolithic (EN II/MN AI), at least for the Nielstrup I site. However, the Neolithic date assigned to these structures should be viewed with caution, as the TRB finds made in them could have been deposited there secondarily due to later prehistoric activity. Pits like the ones encountered at the two sites in question are very common in the Younger Bronze Age as well as the first part of the Iron Age (see e.g. Kristensen 2009), where they often appear in huge groups or long rows. However, they are also known from the TRB, where they do not belong to the features normally observed on ordinary settlements. On the contrary, their appearance here appears to have been exclusively bound to causewayed enclosures or sites that can be related to causewayed enclosures. In Denmark, this is true for the enclosure-related Lystrup Kildevang I site (see e.g. Skousen 2008, 167 Fig. 128). Nonetheless, the best example is the Büdelsdorf enclosure in northern Germany, where no less than 134 of these pits were excavated in the enclosure's interior (Hage in press and F. Hage, personal communication).

Pits of this kind have also been observed on a second site which can be classified as being related to causewayed enclosures – the Aalstrup site at Horsens Fjord (Madsen, T. 2009, 111). Contrary to what is the case at Lystrup Kildevang I, it was not possible to date the pits here to the TRB with any degree of certainty. These pits may thus very well be younger.

Pits with fire-cracked stones from another Danish TRB site dated to EN II – MN A II have already been mentioned in the literature (Røsnæs-Kongstrup: Schülke 2009, 127). The field report concerning the excavation of this site (kindly provided by N. Hartmann from Kalundborg Museum) leaves severe doubts regarding the age of these fireplaces. They contained no finds and have a ^{14}C-date which points to the early Middle Ages.

The recently published site of Sievern close to the mouth of the Elbe River in northwest Germany contains a row of double fireplaces with fire-cracked stones whose layout is highly reminiscent of causewayed enclosures (Fig. 59). By means of ^{14}C-analysis as well as a few finds, those fireplaces have been dated to the EN I, ca. 3900 BC (Nösler et al. 2011, 31 Abb. 4 and D. Nösler, personal communication).

Finally, it can be remarked that pits filled with fire-cracked stones (the remains of feasts of some kind) also are known from the interior of causewayed enclosures elsewhere (Cerny enclosure of Balloy in northern France – Mordant 1997).

It can be concluded that pits filled with fire-cracked stones or fireplaces with heat-affected stones appear on several sites with a clear affinity to causewayed enclosures in both Denmark and northern Germany in the first part of the Neolithic (EN I). Furthermore, in at least one case (the Büdelsdorf enclosure) they were excavated in the interior of a proven causewayed enclosure. There

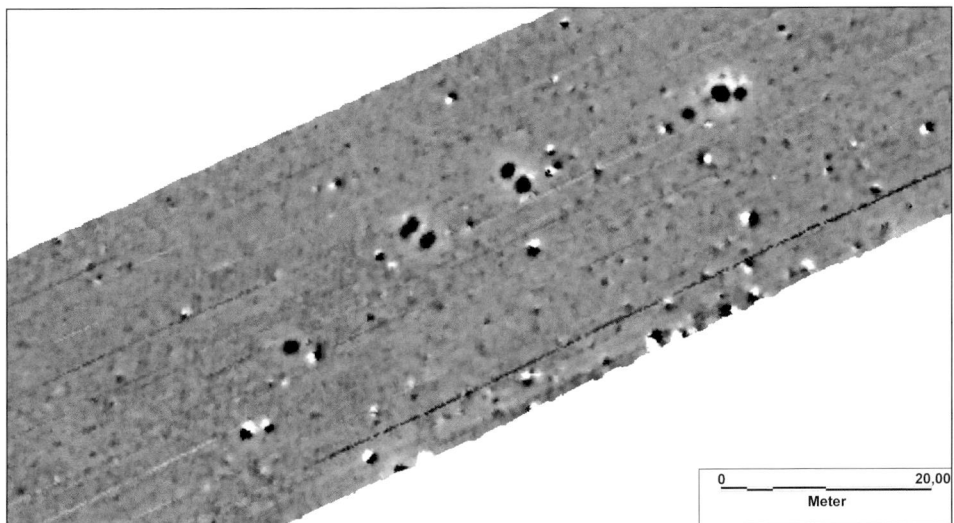

Fig. 59 | *Curved row of pits filled with fire-cracked stones which date from the very early TRB Culture (from Nösler et al. 2011; © Niedersächsisches Institut für historische Küstenforschung).*

may be even more such examples, as "ovens" were mentioned at the Lokes Hede enclosure in Denmark (Birkedahl 1995). Even though it bears repeating that the dating evidence for the two sites in Djursland which was discussed here (19 Grund Ø and 31 Nielstrup I) is insufficient and a TRB association cannot be established with any certainty based on the presence of the artefacts observed alone, these sites are of special interest in the present context.

7.3.2.3 Discussion

Forty-eight percent of predicted sites on which field survey was feasible or previous excavation or survey had taken place were positively identified to contain TRB finds. A further 19% yielded finds that could possibly be identified to the TRB Culture. The number of sites from which finds were recovered exceeded even the most optimistic estimate of undiscovered enclosures. There must be a rather high number of 'ordinary' settlements among the sites detected. This conclusion has been corroborated by excavation on some of these sites. Despite sufficiently large areas of investigation, these excavations did not produce any evidence for the presence of segmented ditches. An initial conclusion to be drawn from the present work is, thus, that the method employed here appears to be well suited to the detection of TRB settlement sites.

When confronted with the task of selecting the most likely enclosure sites among those that delivered certain or possible TRB finds, several criteria should be employed. These criteria can almost all be derived from T. Madsen's (1982) settlement study, as described above. Find scatters on enclosures are often much larger than those on ordinary settlements. A total of eight surveyed sites were classified as belonging to size category 3 (Tab. 9). In all cases, the actual area observed with finds was very large, reaching ca. 100.000m² in one case (11 Revn 1).

The second criterion is that of the amount of finds. A total of six sites were classified as belonging to category 3 with abundant artefact material on the surface. Of these, four were also very large

sites (category 3), while the size of the find areas was unknown for the remaining two.

The next criterion is that of the chronological distribution of the finds. Sites which included finds from both the enclosure construction phase (EN II/MN A I) and the later Middle Neolithic TRB phases are of special interest when trying to point out potential enclosure sites (due to the later development of many enclosures into settlements, as described above). Furthermore, finds of the Single Grave Culture/the Late Neolithic are known from a number of enclosures (e.g. Sarup: Andersen, N.H. 2000; Ballegård: Hougaard Rasmussen 1989; Wincentz Rasmussen 1994; Büdelsdorf: Haßmann 2000 and Albersdorf Dieksknöll: Dibbern/Hage 2010; Dibbern 2011; 2012), while they are otherwise only rarely found together with TRB-material.

As was already mentioned, the survey could only be carried out in one season and hence had a very restricted amount of time per site. This resulted in a rather limited number of finds which could be dated with enough precision to differentiate between the two periods in question. These two eras can roughly be equated with the use periods of thin-butted and thick-butted flint axes (both A- and B-types). Therefore, this criterion is of restricted use in the current case. Nonetheless, four sites delivered finds from both periods and are, therefore, of special interest (70 Skader SØ, 11 Revn I, 79 Mårup N and 53 Trustrup II).

As apparent from Tab. 9, three sites (11 Revn I, 53 Trustrup II and 79 Mårup N) found during the survey fulfil all three criteria discussed above (large size, high amount of finds, finds from different periods). Furthermore, axe production is attested to at all of them. Two sites (55 Fladstrup S and 70 Skader SØ) fulfil two of the criteria (and show evidence of axe production), while five others only fulfil one. Of the latter, one delivered finds that could belong to the TRB (2 Vesterskov), while another delivered no TRB finds at all (24 Todbjerg Bakke V). For two others (46 Virup Skovgård and 39 Albæk), only restricted information was available. These sites were not surveyed. Therefore, both may actually fulfil more than one of the criteria.

It can be concluded that, when judged from field survey alone, sites 11 Revn I, 53 Trustrup II and 79 Mårup N must be considered the most likely enclosure location candidates, followed by 55 Fladstrup S and 70 Skader SØ.

7.3.3 Geophysical survey

The following section presents the reasoning behind the selection of a total of 20 locations for geophysical survey. A short summary of the most important survey results is given. A more detailed account of the survey itself can be found in Klassen/Klein (this volume).

7.3.3.1 Selection of locations

In an ideal world, the totality of the more than 100 potential enclosure sites in the investigation area would have been subjected to geophysical survey. However, this was obviously an impossible task. Nevertheless, resources kindly made available by the Danish Agency for Culture for measurement were sufficient to cover the considerable number of 20 sites. The selection of these 20 sites was guided by a number of factors which were themselves related to a number of different research problems. The first of these concerns the distribution of certain or probable causewayed enclosure locations in Djursland, as described in chapter 3. One must wonder whether the only enclosure known at present that was not situated in the immediate vicinity of the Neolithic coastline was an outlier, or whether a network of enclosures existed throughout the entire area with inter-enclosure spacing comparable to that observed for the enclosures on the coast of Kolindsund Fjord. This question is obviously of great importance for the general reconstruction of enclosure distributions not only in Djursland but also in the entire distribution area of the TRB North Group. Therefore, the selection of sites for geophysical survey was purposefully directed towards sites situated at some distance from the coastline.

The second research question related to the distribution of causewayed enclosures focuses on the evenly-spaced distribution observable in the area

around Kolindsund (Fig. 6). On the northern coast of the fjord, there is a considerable gap between the probable site of Fannerup in the east and the Blakbjerg enclosure in the west, even if the site of Ballegård (on an island in the middle of the fjord) is included. To the west and north of Blakbjerg is an even more obvious gap in the known distribution (i.e. between the enclosures at Blakbjerg and Store Brokhøj). As the distribution of sites presently known in the Kolindsund area suggests that several yet-undetected enclosures should be located in these gaps, two locations were chosen that could potentially connect these places. The chosen gap is the one located between Blakbjerg and Fannerup, as all potential enclosure sites between Blakbjerg and Store Brokhøj selected by this study were situated inland. An investigation of these sites could, therefore, not answer whether a continuous 'coastal string' of causewayed enclosures existed close to the shores of the fjord.

The two locations chosen for geophysical survey as a result of the research problem outlined above are 7 Vejvad Bro and 8 Pognæs I, both of which were situated at river mouths between Blakbjerg and Fannerup on the northern shore of Kolindsund Fjord. This is the typical location of the enclosures which are already known in the area. Furthermore, both sites fit into the observed pattern of inter-enclosure distances. Fieldwalking on site 8 Pognæs I produced TRB finds (including a flake from a thin-butted axe), albeit in modest quantities and over an area of restricted size. The geophysical investigation of this site, therefore, could also answer the question as to whether this surface find pattern – generally assumed to be typical of a minor TRB settlement – could also indicate the presence of a causewayed enclosure. The second site, 7 Vejvad Bro, could not be surveyed because it was covered by high grass at the time of field survey. The topography and the location of this site are particularly striking at the mouth of Nimtofte Å, one of the largest rivers flowing into Kolindsund. The place name of this location was taken from the Høje Måleborsblade map and contains the Danish terms for road ('vej'), bridge ('bro') and ford ('vadested') at the same time. The site obviously holds a strategically important position and would fit the pattern hitherto observed for enclosures in the area very well.

The second set of research problems which guided the selection of sites for geophysical survey relates to the factors that were weighted in predictive modelling (e.g. surface finds, relationship to historic roads, inter-enclosure distance or proximity to historic fortifications). It was important to evaluate the predictive power of these criteria due to the fact that improved insight into their relevance to causewayed enclosure locations would obviously allow for increased accuracy in predictive modelling. Therefore, a number of survey sites were selected with specific predictive factors in mind.

The results of the field survey were used to select five sites for geophysical survey. These five were the sites that were pointed out above as likely candidates due to the abundance, spread and chronological distribution of the finds collected during field survey: 11 Revn I, 53 Trustrup II, 79 Mårup N, 55 Fladstrup S and 70 Skader SØ.

Fifty-one predicted locations (representing 25 potential enclosures) were situated within 1500 m from a main road marked on the 18th century Videnskabernes Selskabs Kort map. For the 1000 m distance, 37 locations represent 20 potential enclosures. Three of these sites were already selected for geophysical survey due to their surface find patterns (79 Mårup N, 55 Fladstrup S and 11 Revn I) and were situated between 500 and 1000 m from an important historical road. One additional site, 1 Følle Vig, was selected as well because of its particular relevance to this parameter. This location was not only very close to the route of the historic road (within 100 m distance), but was also in proximity to one of the best-defined barrow roads which followed the coast of Kalø Vig Bay. Furthermore, two Medieval fortifications (including the royal castle of Kalø Slot) were situated less than 3 km away and hint at the general strategic importance of the region. Indeed, the setting of site 1 Følle Vig is particularly remarkable due to its position at the bottom of a minor protected bay, making it an ideal crossing point between water-

and land-based transport and communication. The site is covered by grass and, therefore, could not be properly surveyed. However, examination of a few molehills produced several flakes indicative of Stone Age occupation.

The potential enclosure sites at Nielstrup are situated almost precisely 4 km from the known enclosure at Store Brokhøj. It is, therefore, particularly interesting that a further three potential enclosure sites are situated at Tustrup at the same distance from both Store Brokhøj and Nielstrup. As is the case at Nielstrup, the presence of river crossings is particularly striking there. Furthermore, a well-known concentration of megalithic graves and a mortuary house is located at Tustrup just a few hundred meters away from two of the potential enclosure locations predicted in that area (Kjærum 1955; Kjærum 1957; Kjærum 1967). The third is situated immediately beside those graves. Because of these observations, all three potential enclosure sites at Tustrup (Tustrup I, II and III) as well as one of the five Nielstrup sites (Nielstrup I) were selected for geophysical survey. Unfortunately, sites II-V at Nielstrup (which were in the immediate vicinity) were not accessible, either due to vegetation or because the landowners' refusal of access. The chosen site of Nielstrup I was of particular interest, not only because of its distance to the Store Brokhøj enclosure, but also because a Medieval fortress/rampart can be found a scant 250 m away. Furthermore, as described in detail above, a number of pits filled with fire-cracked stones (which might indicate the presence of an enclosure or an enclosure-related site) are known from this location. The second site possessed of known TRB fireplaces/pits with pot boilers (also located directly alongside an 18th century main road at 19 Grund Ø), unfortunately could not be surveyed due to the landowner's refusal of access.

Site 55 (Fladstrup S) had already been selected for geophysical survey due to its surface find pattern. Interestingly, Fladstrup S is situated between two other chosen locations: 53 Trustrup II and 11 Revn I. It is at a distance of ca. 3 km from both of these. The site is therefore well suited to the investigation of enclosure distribution in non-coastal areas. Finally, site 63 Høbjerg V was chosen due to its distance (ca. 4.5 km) to two other selected locations.

Two neighbouring sites – 70 Skader SØ and 70 Skader N – were chosen as a means of testing whether enclosures could be proven to exist at a distance from any known megalithic grave (ca. 3 km) in a region from which very few TRB sites have been registered. Finds from the field survey as well as obvious topographic settings indicate two possible locations north and south of Skader village, one of which (70 Skader SØ), had already been chosen for inclusion, due to its surface find pattern. An important ford across the Skader Å River further piques interest in this location, as the Skader Å is deeply incised in the landscape and must thus have been difficult to cross for a considerable distance in either direction.

As described above, three potential enclosure sites showed features of interest in existing aerial photos – possible ditches/pits in two cases (3 Korup Sø, 10 Søby I) and large numbers of possible pits in one case (11 Revn I). Site 11 Revn I had already been chosen for survey due to the richness of its TRB surface finds. For site 3 Korup Sø, additional arguments for selection include its immediate proximity to a historic main road as well as the large size of its surface find scatter.

In the westernmost part of the investigation area, site 24 Todbjerg Møllebakke was selected for geophysical prospection because it differed from all other predicted enclosure locations in a variety of ways. The site is situated at a marked elevation and offered a magnificent view over both the surroundings and large parts of the Århus and Kalø bays. The surroundings of this site are characterised by a landscape formed by *Toteis*. The gently undulating terrain includes numerous small kettle-holes, but very few well-defined freshwater streams. The elongated hill on top of which 24 Todbjerg Møllebakke was situated constitutes a very prominent topographical feature in this landscape and offers a rather dramatic topography (particularly within Denmark) with steep drops to both north and south. The site also differs from the others with regards to its soil type. Large parts of the hill (including the site itself) are made up of clay. Field survey produced a fragment of a thick-butted axe, possibly of TRB-date, among other things. Many barrows of unknown age as well as a few megalithic graves are known to have existed on the hill. Large stone-built chambers may once have played a more prominent role in the landscape than is currently suggested by the few megalithic graves which are registered today. The site is also located at a typical inter-enclosure distance (4.5 km) from the Lystrup Kildevang I site, which was classified as being one of a number of sites related to causewayed enclosures.

Dramatic landscape settings certainly played a role in the choice of location for the construction of causewayed enclosures in Djursland, as is demonstrated by the Blakbjerg and Ginnerup sites' beautiful views over large parts of Kolindsund (Fig. 60). Besides 24 Todbjerg Møllebakke, two other

Fig. 60 | *View from the Blakbjerg enclosure site towards the south across the former fjord of Kolindsund. Photo Lutz Klassen.*

Site	Linear distribution pattern	Surface Finds	Proximity to historic road	Inter enclosure distance	Pits with fire cracked stones	Fortification from historic times	Paucity of megaliths	Aerial survey	Hillptop/ dramatic landscape setting	Distance to coast
7 Vejvad Bro	X			X						
8 Pognæs I	X			X						
11 Revn I		X	X					X		
53 Trustrup II		X								X
79 Mårup N		X	X							X
55 Fladstrup S		X	X	X						X
70 Skader SØ		X					X			X
1 Følle Vig		X				X				
41 Tustrup I				X						X
41 Tustrup II				X						X
41 Tustrup III				X						X
31 Nielstrup I				X	X	X				X
70 Skader N							X			X
10 Søby I								X		
3 Korup Sø		X						X		
24 Todbjerg Møllebakke				X					X	X
58 Assenbakke									X	X
28 Næsdrup Høj				X					X	X
63 Høbjerg V				X						X

Tab. 10 | *The 19 potential enclosure sites on which geophysical survey was conducted and the criteria employed in the process by which they were selected.*

sites were chosen for geophysical survey because of their comparatively dramatic landscape settings. Although none could be surveyed properly by field walking due to grass coverage, at 58 Assenbakke, two TRB-shards and an axe-production flake were picked up from a molehill. This site is located on a prominent, steep-sided ridge at the confluence of two minor rivers. At around 65 m above sea level, it offers a magnificent view over the surrounding landscape (Fig. 63).

Finally, site 28 Næsdrup Høj is situated on a prominent promontory in a river meander and was surrounded by a great many grave mounds of unknown age as well as a few certain megalithic graves. It is also situated between 3 and 5 km from the known enclosure of Galgebakken as well as other sites selected for geophysical survey.

An overview of the criteria used to select the 19 sites for geophysical survey is given in Tab. 10. It

was additionally decided that initial geophysical measurements should be conducted on one known potential enclosure site in order to test the abilities of the geophysical equipment to produce results within the spectrum of local soil conditions. The probable enclosure at Taastrup Kolindvej was selected for this purpose, because it was only known from a single profile observed during road construction work. In addition to testing the equipment, measurements on this site could therefore also serve to enlarge the general knowledge of this potential enclosure.

Fig. 61 shows the geographical distribution of the 20 sites that were chosen for geophysical survey. Of these, seven were located on the coast, while the remaining 13 were situated further inland. As described above, this distribution (which was skewed in relation to the enclosures presently known in Djursland) was obtained with

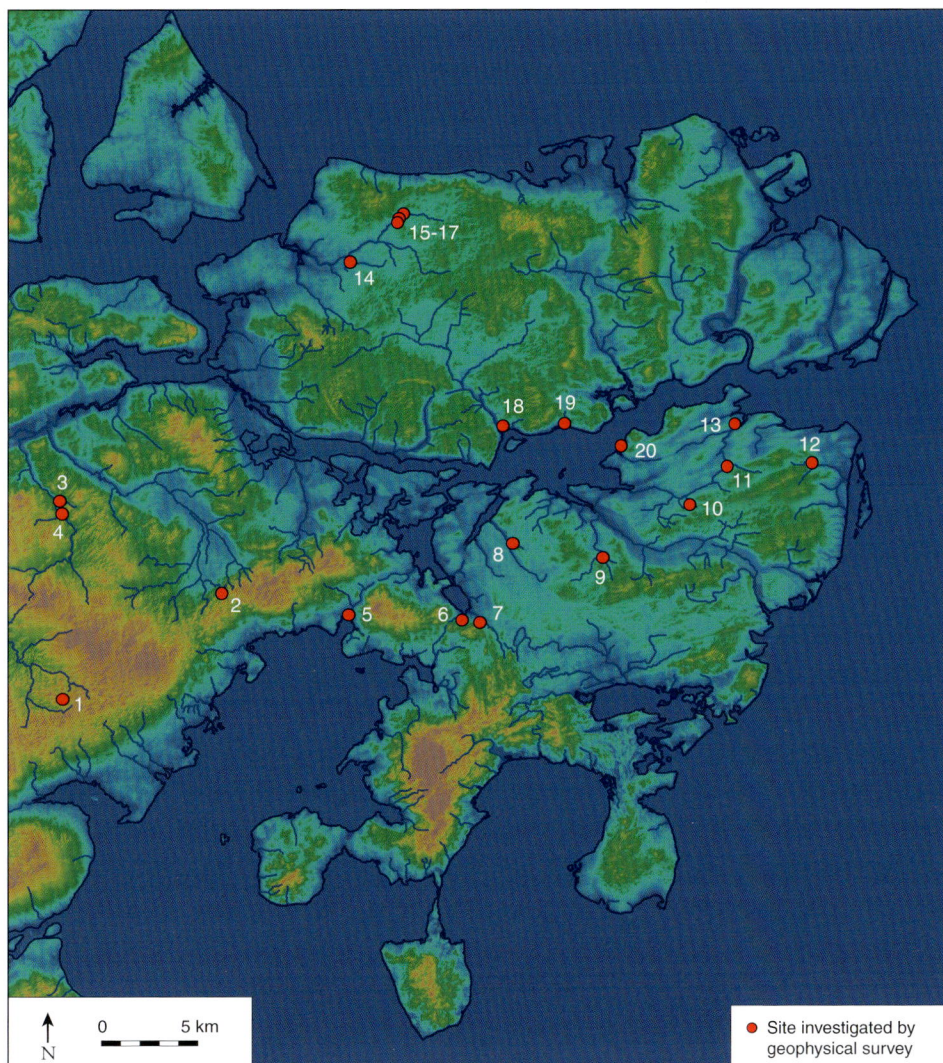

Fig. 61 | *The geographical distribution of the 20 sites on which geophysical survey was carried out. 1: 24 Todbjerg Møllebakke; 2: 58 Assenbakke; 3: 70 Skader N; 4: 70 Skader SØ; 5: 1 Følle Vig; 6: 3 Korup Sø; 7: Taastrup Kolindvej; 8: 79 Mårup N; 9: 28 Næsdrup Høj; 10: 53 Trustrup II; 11: 55 Fladstrup S; 12: 63 Højbjerg V; 13: 11 Revn I; 14: 31 Nielstrup I; 15: 41 Tustrup I; 16: 41 Tustrup II; 17: 41 Tustrup III; 18: 7 Vejvad Bro; 19: 8 Pognæs I; 20: 10 Søby I.*

a specific goal in mind: testing whether or not enclosures were regularly built at inland locations. The known enclosures in the Kolindsund Fjord area show a clear predominance on the northern shore. By contrast, the sites selected for geophysical survey were predominantly located on the southern shore (four sites as compared to two on the northern shore). Therefore, geophysical investigation of the sites selected could possibly indicate whether or not the distribution of causewayed enclosures as known at present is truly representative of Neolithic reality or whether it is an artefact of present research.

There is a clear predominance of sites south of the Kolindsund Fjord (14) in comparison to those located north of the fjord (6). The main reason for this imbalance is the relative abundance of large forests and plantations in northern Djursland. Many otherwise promising sites (as judged by their relation to watercourses, Neolithic and historic roads as well as their topography) are concealed within these woods and, therefore, were accessible neither for field survey nor any meaningful geophysical prospection.

Finally, with the exception of Lystrup Kildevang I, all known enclosures or related sites are distributed in areas with a clear predominance of light, poor soils. Among the sites selected for geophysical survey, a total of four (24 Todbjerg Møllebakke, 70 Skader SØ, 70 Skader N and 3 Korup SØ) are located in areas with heavier soil types. Three of these are in the western part of the investigation area, while one (3 Korup Sø) is found in a region with abundant sandy soils. The

Site	Area surveyed by ground penetrating radar (ha)	Area surveyed by geomagnetics (ha)
1 Følle Vig	0.9	3.63
3 Korup Sø	0.8	6.01
7 Vejvad Bro	1.5	
8 Pognæs I	0.6	
10 Søby I	0.3	1.82
11 Revn I	1.2	2.51
24 Todbjerg Bakke	0.4	
28 Næsdrup	1.2	
31 Nielstrup I	0.24	2.2
41 Tustrup I	0.48	0.36
41 Tustrup II	0.06	0.88
41 Tustrup III	1.15	
53 Trustrup II	1.3	
55 Fladstrup S	0.23	1.5
58 Assenbakke	0.2	0.75
63 Høbjerg V	0.5	
70 Skader N	0.2	
70 Skader SØ		2.24
79 Mårup N	0.5	
Taastrup Kolindvej	0.2	0.98

Tab. 11 | *Type of geophysical measurement and surveyed area for the 20 sites investigated.*

geophysical investigation could, therefore, also potentially shed light on the question of whether or not sandy soil was of great importance in choosing enclosure location.

In summary, the 20 sites that were chosen for geophysical investigation were selected specifically to answer as many questions as possible regarding the choice of enclosure location in the Neolithic. Tab. 11 lists the types of geophysical measurements (as well as the size of the areas surveyed) for these 20 sites.

7.3.3.2 Results

Geophysical survey resulted in the discovery of one certain (58 Assenbakke), one probable (55 Fladstrup S) and two possible (79 Mårup N, 53 Trustrup II) causewayed enclosures. Furthermore, a range of unusual structures – some of which may well be related to causewayed enclosures – were discovered (or known in advance but not recognized as such) from at least four other locations (41 Tustrup

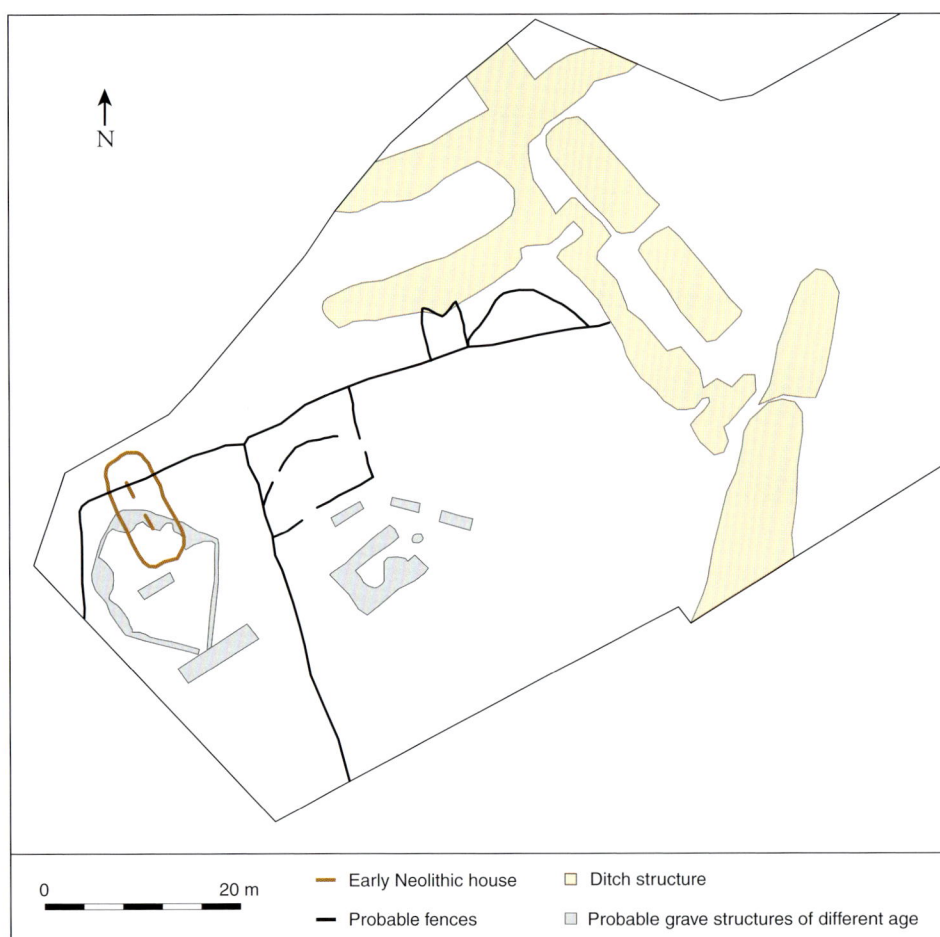

0   20 m

— Early Neolithic house   ☐ Ditch structure

— Probable fences   ☐ Probable grave structures of different age

Fig. 62 | *Interpretation of the results of the geophysical survey at site 58 Assenbakke. A detailed account for the individual features is found in Klassen/ Klein, this volume.*

II, 31 Nielstrup I, 1 Følle Vig and 11 Revn I). Before evaluating the predictive model, these discoveries will be briefly described.

Certain or possible causewayed enclosures

58 Assenbakke

A causewayed enclosure was detected on a melt-water ridge at the confluence of two minor rivers. It was made apparent by the presence of what was either two rows of parallel ditches or one ditch and one parallel row of large pits or ovens. These last seem similar in position to those known from Büdelsdorf (Hage in press)(Fig. 62). Several of the ditch segments (pits) of the innermost row appear to have been fenced. Furthermore, a row of loosely-spaced posts may have been present in this area. These posts may have served as supports for horizontal timbers which held an earthen bank in place. The individual ditch segments (pits) appear to be 4-6 m wide at the top and have a depth of ca. 1 m. They have an apparent V-shaped cross-section. Powerful magnetic anomalies indicate the deposition of material with magnetic properties. This could consist of large amounts of organic material, pottery or burned wattle and daub. The outer ditch (of comparable dimensions) demonstrated no interruptions (which is unusual). It may, however, represent a row of ditch segments that were united through re-cutting into one, continuous ditch.

A number of unusual features were detected in front of the enclosure and just outside these linear features. An area of ca. 60 x 40 m appears to have been fenced. This area was further divided into several compartments. One compartment contained the probable remains of a round barrow. Oriented towards the enclosure, this barrow contained a rectangular, U-shaped structure with a large stone in front of the opening. This feature resembles the mortuary house at Tustrup. Rectangular anomalies (oriented tangentially around the central part of the barrow) probably represent secondary inhumation graves. Another fenced compartment contains a structure of unknown type which appears to be partly aligned to the U-shaped structure inside the supposed round barrow. Therefore, it could also represent some kind of mortuary construction.

The fence composing the compartments appears to have been overlain by a comparatively small, two-aisled long house, every post of which was visible in the magnetometer survey. Due to its characteristic dimensions and shape (e.g. rounded gables), this house can probably be dated to the Early Neolithic or earliest Middle Neolithic.

Very few features could be discerned in the enclosure's interior, probably due to the presence of a cultural layer preventing geophysical detection. Nevertheless, the presence of some pits as well as one possible very large stone can be recognized.

The hill on which the Assenbakke enclosure is located is characterized by a remarkable topography, as it is very long and narrow in shape and has very steep sides (Fig. 63). The distance from the tip of the promontory at the confluence of two minor rivers to the rows of ditches/pits (i.e. the length of the enclosed area) is 275 m. The width of the enclosure, however, counts less than 100 m (possibly only ca. 80 m) at its widest part (behind the segmented ditch/pits). This area measures much less nearer to the confluence of the two rivers. Today, the terrain is very uneven. This may at least be partially the result of modern sand digging. The enclosed area (more or less horizontal today) measures not more than 1 ha – very little when compared to the length of the site. However, one cannot exclude the possibility that the rows of ditches/pits do not represent the only enclosure on Assenbakke hill. It is possible that there is another row further to the west, inside an area which is covered by forest today. This potential enclosure would, then, have been much larger than the first.

The nearest known megalithic grave at Balskov (141106-36) is located precisely 1 km to the east of the Assenbakke enclosure (Fig. 64). Further to the east and south, several more megaliths are found, but already at the considerable distances (for Djursland) of 2.5 km or more. To the west and north, the closest graves of the type in question are no less than 7 and 10 km away, respectively. If round barrows of unknown age are included in the survey, a different picture emerges. One such monument is

Fig. 63 | *View from site 58 Assenbakke towards the north. From the site, the moraine plateau some 11 km away on the northern shore of Kolindsund Fjord is visible (this was the site on which a string of causewayed enclosures was constructed). The steep-sloped topography characteristic of Assenbakke Hill is apparent from this photo. Photo: Christina Klein.*

registered at a distance of only 160 m to the west of the rows of ditches/pits (141104-2), while another is found 240 m to the northeast of the confluence of the two rivers (141104-3). As was indicated by the discovery of what appears to be a fenced round barrow only 30 m from the segmented ditch, these two barrows may contain megalithic graves/other grave types datable to the TRB.

55 Fladstrup S

On a sandy promontory near the confluence of two rivers, what appears to be a trench for a palisade or loosely-spaced row of posts was detected alongside a segmented ditch or row of large pits 2-3 m in depth. The observed architectural features are in line with what is known from excavated causewayed enclosures and do not appear to

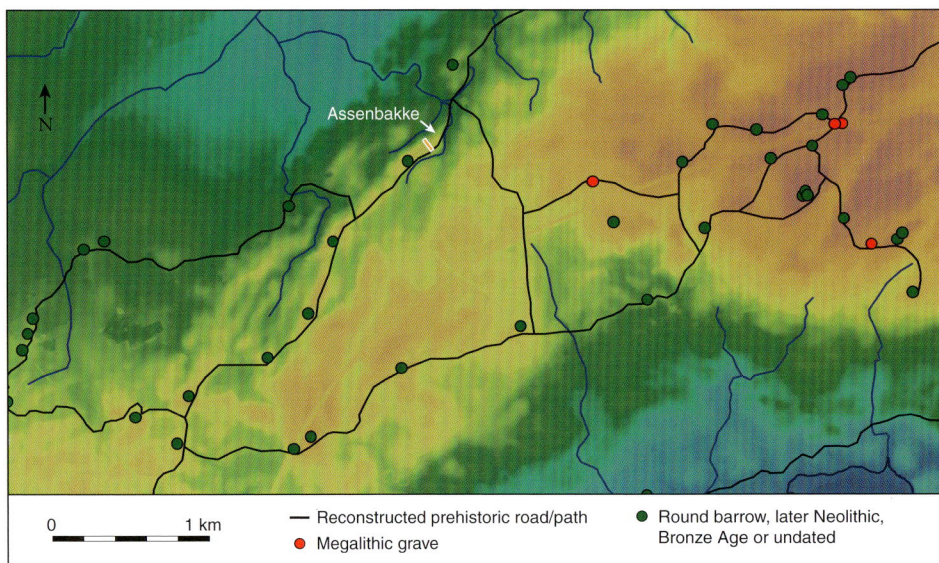

Fig. 64 | *The location of the causewayed enclosure detected by geophysical survey at site 58 Assenbakke in relation to prehistoric roads/paths as reconstructed from barrow lines. The approximate course of the enclosing elements is indicated schematically in this illustration.*

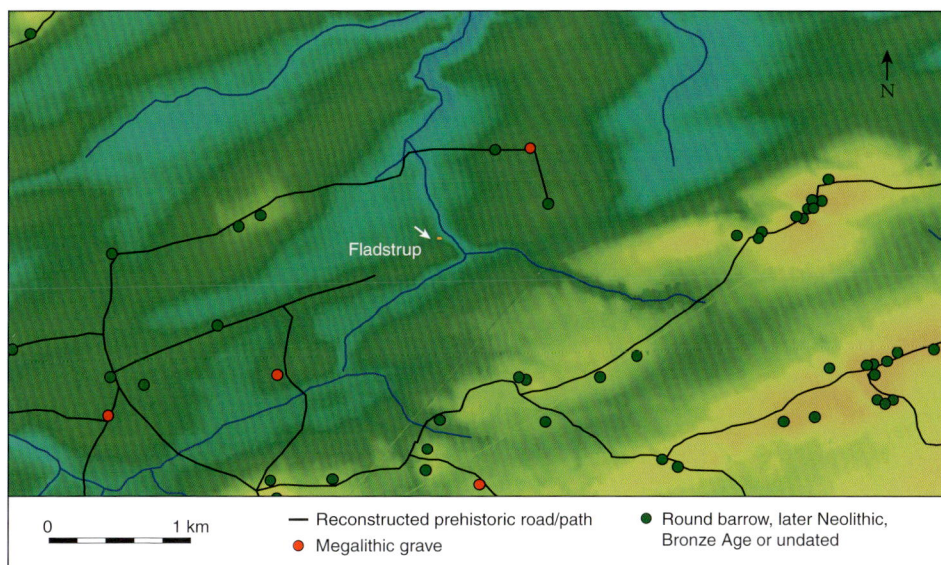

Fig. 65 | *The location of the probable causewayed enclosure detected by geophysical survey at site 55 Fladstrup S in relation to prehistoric roads/paths as reconstructed from barrow lines. The approximate course of the potential palisade and row of ditch segments was only detectable in an area of limited size due to the fact that the neighbouring field was not accessible for geophysical survey.*

be similar to constructions from other prehistoric periods. They could only be detected within an area approximately 20 m wide, due to the fact that the neighbouring field was inaccessible. Photographs taken by the local farmer immediately after ploughing show a linear feature marked by slightly differently coloured soil. It appears to be a prolongation of the anomalies described above. This linear feature can be followed for at least another 30-40 m. According to the course of the observed anomalies, the size of an enclosure at this site would range from 3-4 ha. However, trial excavation is needed to confirm this interpretation and to rule out other possibilities (e.g. geological features). At present, observations at site 55 Fladstrup S can therefore only be regarded as probable indications of a Neolithic causewayed enclosure. Field survey resulted in abundant artefacts dating from several different periods of the Middle Neolithic TRB Culture. Few megalithic graves have been recorded in the region around Fladstrup. The distance to the nearest of these is almost 1000 m (Fig. 65).

53 Trustrup II

Traces of what might be an enclosure ditch up to 7 m wide and ca. 1.75 m deep were recorded by GPR measurements comparatively high on a sandy hill surrounded by small watercourses and wet areas (Fig. 66). Nevertheless, the possibility that this feature represents a geological structure rather than a Neolithic ditch cannot be excluded at present. Trial excavation is needed to clarify this question. If confirmed as Neolithic ditch, according to its recorded course, the feature would probably constitute one of the rare hilltop enclosures, and could have spread over 2 ha. Abundant finds from the TRB and the Late Neolithic were collected during field survey on the hill. The distance to the nearest megalithic grave – which, generally speaking, are scarce around this site – is almost 1000 m.

79 Mårup N

As was the case at 53 Trustrup II, a possible single Neolithic ditch was recorded at 79 Mårup N. It cuts across a sandy promontory between two

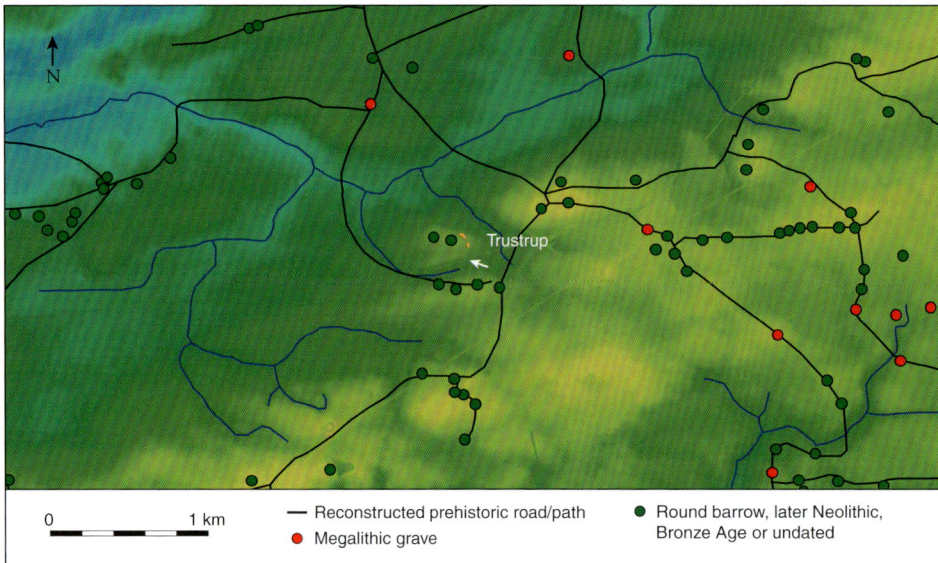

Fig. 66 | *The location of a possible section of an enclosure ditch detected by measurements with ground penetrating radar on site 53 Trustrup II and the relation of the site to prehistoric roads/paths as reconstructed from barrow lines.*

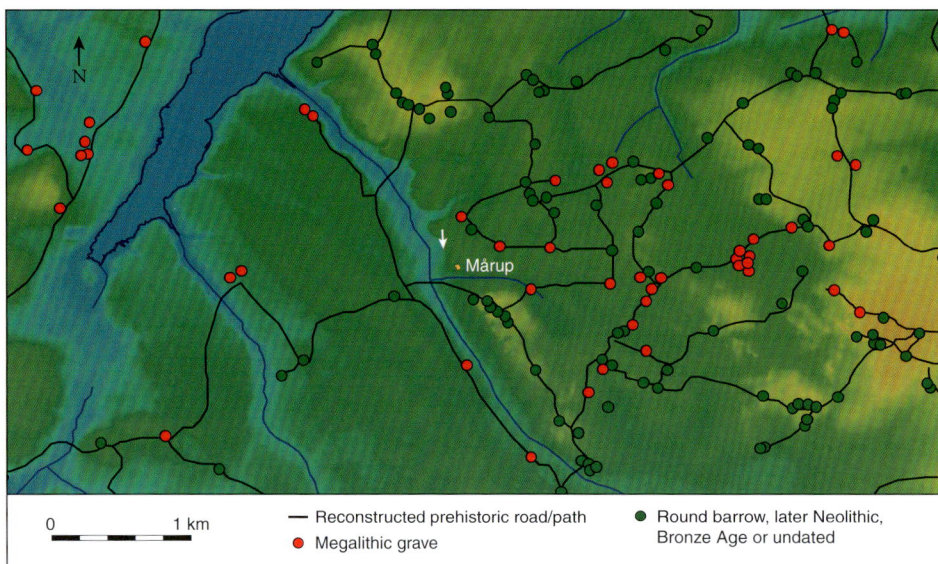

Fig. 67 | *The location of a possible section of an enclosure ditch detected by measurements with ground penetrating radar on site 79 Mårup N and the relation of the site to prehistoric roads/paths as reconstructed from barrow lines.*

confluent rivers and possibly delimits an area ca. 3-4 ha in size (Fig. 67). Finds from several periods of the TRB were collected during field survey. A deposit including three thin-butted flint axes is also known from the field in question. The distance to the nearest recorded megalithic grave is ca. 300 m, although a large concentration of these tombs can be found ca. 1000 m to the east.

However, the structure recorded at Mårup might be of geological rather than human origin. Until a trial excavation reveals the true nature of the feature, site 79 Mårup N must be regarded as a possible Neolithic enclosure.

Unusual structures possibly related to causewayed enclosures

31 Nielstrup I

Groups of pits filled with fire-cracked stones (probably representing fireplaces that were used to prepare food in feasts) were known at this site prior to geophysical survey. A number of strong positive, round anomalies recorded during the survey almost certainly represent these structures. As was already discussed above, these may well date to the TRB. Known examples of such pits which date to the TRB show a clear relation to causewayed enclosures as

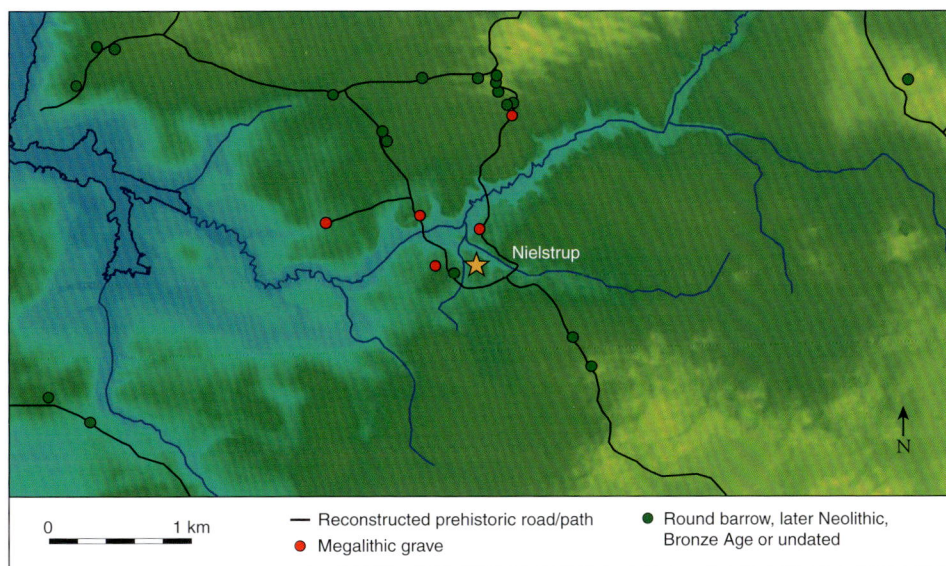

Fig. 68 | *The location of pits filled with fire-cracked stones on site 31 Nielstrup I as indicated by geomagnetic measurements and the relation of the site to prehistoric roads/paths as reconstructed from barrow lines. Previous excavation of a few of these pits rendered TRB finds. However, without ¹⁴C dating, it is impossible to know whether these dates represent a secondary, later admixture or if they are indeed indicative of the age of the pits.*

well as to sites related to them. 31 Nielstrup I (Fig. 68) may thus be a further example of such a site. Confirmation of the age of the fireplaces at Nielstrup is needed. At present, there is no way to determine whether the TRB artefacts found in some of these fireplaces or pits represent only secondary admixture from structures built in later parts of prehistory (Late Bronze Age/Early Iron Age).

41 Tustrup

No structures related to causewayed enclosures were detected in geophysical survey on any of the three sites investigated at Tustrup. Still, the location is remarkable, due to the presence of a cult house of singular, semi-megalithic construction which clearly differentiates it from ordinary TRB sites (Fig. 69). In the light of the discoveries at Nielstrup and Store Brokhøj – both located 4 km from Tustrup – this was most likely not a coincidence.

11 Revn I

At site 11 Revn I, what appears in some parts to be two long rows of pits were detected by geomag-

netic survey. Some of those are also visible in existing aerial photos (Figs. 57 and 70). With lengths of up to 200 m, these closely resemble structures like those excavated at the Triwalk site in Mecklenburg, which can be related to causewayed enclosures (see above chapter 4 and Fig. 10C). The pits at Revn

Fig. 69 | *The cult house at Tustrup is singular within the TRB Culture due to its semi-megalithic construction. Reconstruction at Moesgård Museum. Photo Rógvi Johansen.*

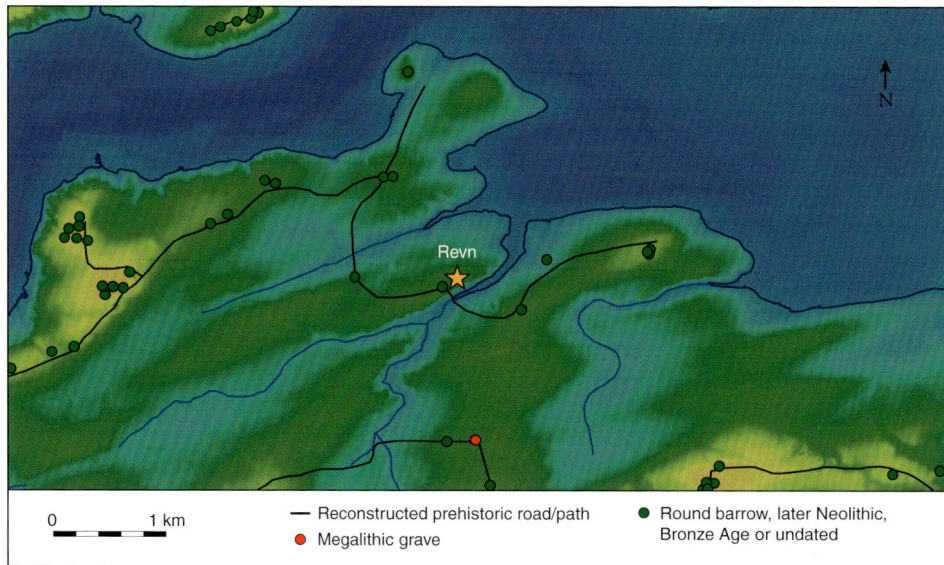

Fig. 70 | *The location of pits which probably date to the TRB Culture as detected by geophysical survey at site 11 Revn I and the relation of the site to prehistoric roads/ paths as reconstructed from barrow lines.*

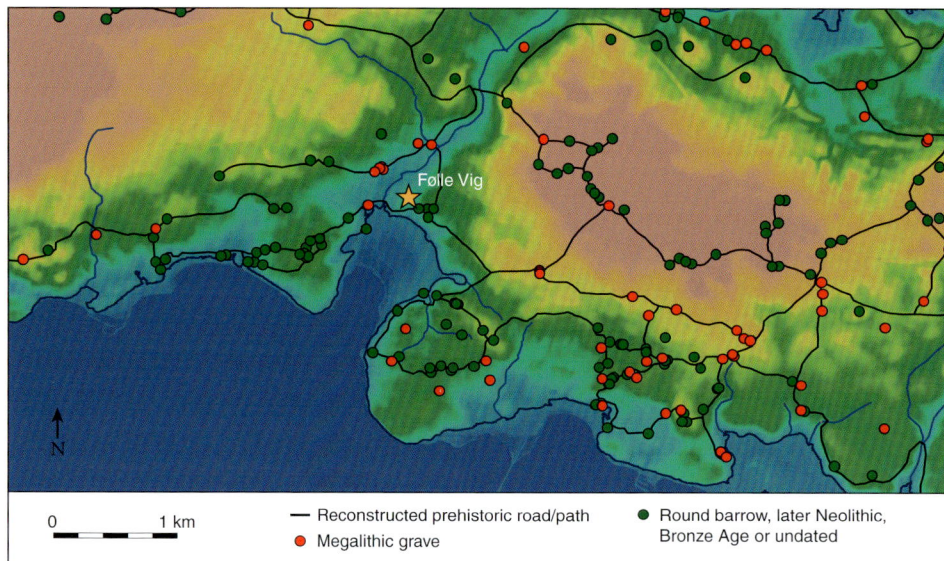

Fig. 71 | *The location of positive magnetic anomalies at site 1 Følle Vig and the relation of the site to prehistoric roads/ paths as reconstructed from barrow lines. The anomalies might represent postholes (not yet dated).*

have not been dated. Therefore, no certain conclusions can be drawn as to their nature. However, a very high density of TRB finds coming from the area in which the pits are found is indicative of a TRB date. The shape of some of the geomagnetic anomalies could indicate the presence of either fireplaces or pits filled with pot boilers.

1 Følle Vig

A very unusual structure was detected at site 1 Følle Vig (Fig. 71). It consisted of long rows of regularly- spaced positive magnetic anomalies, which might well represent the placement of wooden posts. This structure was comprised of a curved line almost 80 m long which ran into a rectangular area measuring 50 x 30 m. This last was delimited by the same type of regular features. The original size of this structure may well have been even larger still; it appears to have continued outside the surveyed area. No parallels could be found. In the absence of any dating material, the structure unfortunately cannot be securely linked to the TRB. Trial excavations are needed to establish its age.

8 The predictive model: evaluation of predictive parameters, test methods and results

Despite the fact that many of the sites listed in the preceding section are in need of further investigation before they can be accepted as causewayed enclosures (or even as sites related to causewayed enclosures), it can be stated that the general procedure employed here was successful. However, it is also very laborious and is, therefore, difficult to employ. In the following, both the predictive parameters employed in pointing out potential enclosure locations as well as the methods used to test the predictions made thereby will be critically assessed. The goal of this section is to refine the model, thereby rendering it more attractive for future research.

8.1 The predictive parameters

The decisive factor employed in predictive modelling employed here – the proximity to places where prehistoric roads crossed rivers – is a basic criterion with great potential. This is evident from the fact that no less than four sites with certain, probable or possible enclosures were detected. Moreover, the method uncovered a further four sites which can be characterized as being possibly related to enclosures. It is also evident from the fact that certain or possible TRB finds have been collected on two thirds of all surveyed locations. Proximity to river crossings is thus a factor of broad importance for studies of TRB settlement systems.

While the topography parameter was bypassed in computer modelling, topographically well-suited sites were selected on the ground as well as by means of the study of maps and digital elevation models. This process was crucial for the detection of enclosures. However, it cannot be automated. It is important to note at this point that there are apparent regional differences within South Scandinavia with regard to the kind of topography chosen for enclosures construction. While the selection of sites judged to be likely for causewayed enclosure construction remains a subjective process, where possible this process can and should be guided by an analysis of the topographic setting of known enclosure sites nearby. In light of this, it is of interest to note that the certain enclosure detected at site 58 Assenbakke and the probable enclosure at site 55 Fladstrup S are located in topographic settings which most closely resemble those known from other enclosures in Djursland; they are dramatic and/or are topographically well-distinguished from their surroundings.

The outcome of the present study is difficult to evaluate with regard to soil type, as the entire region under investigation is dominated by light soils. These soils seem generally to have been preferred for enclosure construction in the TRB. Among the eight sites listed above, five were located on well-drained, gravelly to sandy soils (79 Mårup N, 58 Assenbakke, 31 Nielstrup I, 41 Tustrup and 1 Følle Vig), while the remaining three (53 Trustrup II; 55

Fladstrup S and 11 Revn I) can be characterised by slightly heavier (but far from clayey) soils.

The proximity to water criterion was doubtless of great significance. Of the eight certain or possible enclosures or enclosure-related sites, four were situated at the confluence of two rivers, two at the outlet of rivers into fjords and one (41 Tustrup) either at a river turn/loop or the confluence of two rivers. One site (53 Trustrup II) was found on a hilltop, although the hill was rather low and was also almost completely surrounded by small rivers and wetland. Regional variation obviously applies to this criterion, especially in regions which lack fjords.

Problems relating to the parameter which measured proximity to megalithic graves have already been discussed in detail. It suffices to say, therefore, that the distance to the nearest stone-built tomb ranges between practically 0 (sites at location 41 Tustrup) to near 1500 m (11 Revn I). Half of the sites have distances of ca. 1000 m or more, including the certain enclosure 58 Assenbakke. Geophysical survey of the sites 70 Skader SØ and 70 Skader N – which had been deliberately chosen as a means of testing whether enclosures could be present at greater distances from known megalithic graves (ca. 3 km in both cases) – did not produce any evidence for such monuments. However, the most promising site (70 Skader SØ) could unfortunately only be investigated by geomagnetic survey. As a result, the presence of an otherwise undetectable enclosure could not be excluded. The survey of the distance to the nearest megalithic grave for all known TRB enclosures has shown that some of them were indeed of the same order of magnitude as the two sites at Skader. It must be concluded that the parameter regarding the nearby presence of megalithic graves was not well-suited to the search for causewayed enclosures, despite the fact that a concentration of such graves may have acted as an indicator of the presence of such a monument.

The last of the parameters identified in previous research as relevant for the prediction of enclosure locations includes the presence of surface finds. In this study, only finds which were previously known were used in the predictive process proper. Systematic field surveying was used only as a test method. However, the latter could just as well have been an integrated part of the predictive process and will, therefore, be shortly discussed below.

The field survey of a large range of potential enclosure locations resulted in the identification of a surprisingly high number of sites with certain or possible TRB finds. Given that not all of these could represent enclosure sites, trends in the material were examined by means of examining the amount of finds, their chronological composition and the size of the surface scatter. Based on these criteria, five of the 20 sites that were subsequently geophysically surveyed were selected. It is reassuring to find that four of these five sites (11 Revn I, 53 Trustrup II, 79 Mårup N and 55 Fladstrup S) are among the eight locations where certain or possible enclosures or enclosure-related structures were subsequently identified. The presence of an enclosure on the fifth site – 70 Skader SØ was neither demonstrable nor conclusively disproven. It must additionally be mentioned that none of the remaining three sites on which enclosures or enclosure-related structures were identified were available for proper field surveying due to the presence of various kinds of vegetation. It can be concluded, therefore, that simple field survey is a method well-suited to identifying relevant sites if the selection is based on the strict criteria described above. However, as a method, field survey is not well-suited to predict all enclosures within a region, given that there will always be locations that cannot be properly surveyed and because there are some enclosures which have very few finds. While the latter problem applies to the entire distribution area of the TRB North Group, it is of special importance in those areas where the enclosures did not develop into huge settlements in subsequent periods (such as was especially the case in northern Germany).

An additional aspect deserving of short discussion is the use of deposits of select artefacts as were observed in the interior as well as in the ditches of a number of known enclosures as a predictive parameter. In the present case, such a deposition (of 'three beautiful thin-butted axes') was known only from a single site: 79 Mårup N. The detection of a possible enclosure ditch at this site hints at the potential value of this parameter.

Besides the 'river crossing by reconstructed prehistoric road/path' parameter, three others have been introduced in this investigation: 1) proximity to historic roads, 2) proximity to fortifications from early historic times and 3) inter-enclosure distance. The evaluation of the latter can be skewed by a circular argument; the selection of potential enclosure sites pulled heavily upon their proximity to known enclosures. The newly discovered certain or possible enclosures and enclosure-related sites do indeed follow the inter-enclosure distance criterion, indicating that this is also a valuable tool. Nonetheless, it cannot be stated with the same degree of certainty that no enclosures were overlooked in the midst of those that had already been pointed out. Furthermore, it is of interest to note that none of the sites selected for geophysical survey exclusively based on the inter-enclosure distance parameter turned out to house an enclosure or related site, while the opposite was the case for several sites where other parameters applied. This suggests that, while it is useful as parameter for predictive modelling, inter-enclosure distance should not be used to point out potential enclosure sites in isolation. The inter-enclosure distances of all presently known enclosures and enclosure-related sites will be discussed in detail in a later section.

The 'proximity to historic fortifications' parameter is also somewhat difficult to evaluate, because the number of fortifications known within the area of investigation is comparatively low. Observed distances for the eight relevant sites (certain, probable or possible enclosures or enclosure-related sites) range between 250 m (31 Nielstrup I) to 6 km (11 Revn I; 79 Mårup N). Therefore, this parameter has only restricted usefulness. However, based on the investigation at present, there is no indication as to whether or not the close spatial relationship between one site (31 Nielstrup I) and a fortification is coincidental.

One of the eight sites (1 Følle Vig) was located directly at a main road indicated on the Videnskabernes Selskabs Kort map, while three others (55 Fladstrup S; 11 Revn I and 79 Mårup N) are between 500 and 1000 m distant from such roads. When compared to the total numbers from Denmark, sites in the immediate vicinity (500 m or less) to the roads in question, thus, appear to be underrepresented. However, those within 1000 m appear to be overrepresented. Due to low sample numbers, these values should be taken with a grain of salt. In general, it appears that proximity to an important historic road is indeed a relevant parameter for finding causewayed enclosures. This is underlined by an additional observation: the detected enclosure site 58 Assenbakke is located more than 3000 m from one of the Videnskabernes Selskabs Korts main roads, but is directly adjacent to an important Medieval road which later declined in importance (Svane 1984, 216 no. 2045[2]). It is entirely possible that comparable situations exist at the remaining three sites which appear to be distant from those historic roads registered in this study. However, no detailed investigation of this problem has been conducted. It can be concluded that the presence and proximity of important historic roads are indeed important predictive factors in search for Neolithic causewayed enclosures, just as proven in those regions of Central Europe which have been investigated in this regard.

In summary, it can be concluded from this short survey that, aside from the basic 'river-crossing-by-prehistoric-road/path' parameter, vicinity to an important historic road, specific topography, proximity to water (confluence of two rivers or river outlet), the presence of deposits of select artefacts, the typical inter-enclosure distance of approximately 4-5 km (in combination with other parameters) and a specific pattern of surface finds are the best suited criteria in a predictive modelling approach designed to find causewayed enclosures and related sites. On the other side of the spectrum is the vicinity to megalithic graves criterion, which did not prove effective at all. Proximity to fortifications from historic times cannot be dismissed as a relevant parameter. Nevertheless, it is not particularly well-suited to this purpose, as evidenced by the low numbers of such sites. A comparable problem applies to the soil type parameter, which is not helpful in regions dominated by well-drained soils. However, it could well be of importance in regions characterised by clayey soils. It must be emphasized that regional variation is also present, such as is visible with regards to surface find patterns, proximity to water and topography.

8.2 The test methods

8.2.1 Aerial photographs

The fact that several causewayed enclosures in South Scandinavia have indeed been discovered from the air clearly demonstrates that the study of existing photographs is a suitable method for controlling the outcome of the predictive process. However, as was also made apparent by the present case, the visibility of enclosures is dependent upon both local soil conditions as well as the weather at the time at which the photographs were taken. If the latter cannot be controlled, that is, if only pre-existing photos are at hand and no specific survey from the air can be conducted with optimum weather conditions, then the use of this test method is only of restricted value. Suitability will, of course, also vary from region to region, dependant on geological conditions. For example, the Mølbjerg I enclosure (which was, in fact, discovered from the air) is visible in a large range of existing aerial photographs taken at random times. However, the same series of pictures belie not a single of Djursland's many known enclosures.

Furthermore, the sometimes very heterogeneous Quarternary soils in South Scandinavia show a whole range of geological structures when seen from the air. These structures can easily be confused with man-made features. This was the case at two locations examined in the present study chosen for geophysical survey. In both cases, survey demonstrated that the observed features were likely of geological origin (3 Korup Sø and 10 Søby I).

8.2.2 Field surveying

The detection of a large surface scatter with an abundant amount of TRB finds from different periods proved very effective in locating causewayed enclosures or enclosure-related sites. This was true both for the present investigation and for many of the causewayed enclosures known in other parts of South Scandinavia. As a comparatively simple and cheap method, field surveying was, therefore, well-suited to this purpose. However, the sample size from this investigation was much too small to conclusively demonstrate that large amounts of finds of varying age in a large area always indicated the presence of causewayed enclosures or enclosure-related sites. In this study, such a correlation appears to have existed, although it must be noted at present that many of the sites detected only represent possible hits in need of confirmation. Furthermore, regional variation certainly applies, making field survey less well-suited in parts of the TRB North Group distribution area (particularly parts of northern Germany and southern Sweden). Finally, it is known that enclosures with low numbers of finds have also been found in areas where enclosures rich in material are present.

8.2.3 Geophysical survey

A detailed discussion of technical aspects of the geophysical survey conducted over the course of the present project can be found in Klassen/Klein (this volume). It suffices to say that, while it was possible to identify one enclosure with certainty and a further three with diverse degrees of probability by conducting geophysical measurements, the approach proved to be generally difficult. The fact that geomagnetics would be unreliable in the present context was anticipated. However, the unreliability of area renderings of GPR measurements was unexpected, given the good results obtained via that method at the Albersdorf Dieksknöll enclosure in northern Germany The reasons for the failure could not be identified with certainty. However, too wide profile spacing as well as adverse soil conditions are possible explanations. Nevertheless, the current project proved that potential Neolithic segmented ditches could be identified in GPR measurements by the close scrutiny of individual profiles. This is a complicated and time-consuming method which, however, does not exclude the possibility that relevant structures will be overlooked.

The likelihood of identifying an enclosure certainly increases in accordance with the size of the area geophysically surveyed as well as the availability of both geomagnetic and GPR measurements. Therefore, the survey design of potential future campaigns should be adjusted to routinely include multi-method measurements of all locations investigated thereby. However, it is more difficult to make precise statements regarding the size of the area to be surveyed, given that the scientific questions which initiate research as well as available resources have a major impact in that regard. Nonetheless, it might be more efficient to use comparatively small and narrow areas of investigation for GPR measurements (as was done here) at the subsequent cost of later trial excavations for the confirmation of uncertain results rather than making time-consuming and expensive large-scale GPR measurements right from the beginning.

At sites 53 Trustrup II, 55 Fladstrup S and 79 Mårup N, possible enclosures with single rows of segmented ditches have been found. At 58 Assenbakke, by contrast, two parallel rows (or one row of ditches and a parallel row of large pits) could be detected. Obviously, the presence of more than one ditch circuit renders the identification of causewayed enclosures easier. It also increases their credibility with regard to geophysical measurements. In the present case, it could be argued that the fact that only one ditch circuit appears to have been present in all three sites suspected to be enclosures could indicate that false conclusions were drawn concerning the nature of the sites and, therefore, that a geological explanation for the observed anomalies would be more plausible. The chance of confusion between a single row of segmented ditches and geological features or man-made ditches from other periods is certainly much higher than that for characteristic double ditch circuits.

Sites with single and double ditch circuits are almost equally represented among the 38 South Scandinavian enclosures that were known before this study; there are 17 cases of double ditches and 16 of single ditches. More than two ditch circuits are known from two sites, while insufficient information is available for three others. These figures support concerns regarding the credibility of the identification of possible enclosures with a single row of ditches via geophysical measurements alone at three sites in Djursland. However, a closer look at the region of Djursland alters this picture. Certain single circuit sites (5) in Djursland outnumber those with double circuits (3). In one case (Grenå), the number of circuits is unknown. The Taastrup Kolindvej site has not been included in these calculations, as the amount of information available for this site was insufficient prior to the taking of geophysical measurements. If this possible single ditch circuit enclosure should be included in the count however, the double ditch circuit enclosures in Djursland are outnumbered by single ditch sites two-to-one. Of course, these numbers are not statistically significant due to the low number of samples. Nevertheless, they do indicate that regional variation may well apply to this construction trait. The frequency of enclosures of either type does not, therefore, necessarily indicate a confusion of geological and man-made features in the interpretation of geophysical measurements in Djursland.

8.3 Archaeological results

The selection of sites for geophysical survey was guided by a number of specific research questions, among other things. The results of the survey will be discussed briefly below with regard to their impact on these research questions (8.3.1). Another short section will summarize the present knowledge regarding causewayed enclosures in Djursland (8.3.2) before this knowledge is then related to settlement patterns before and during the time of enclosure construction in the region (8.3.3). Finally, the results of this study will be compared to those obtained by T. Madsen's (1988) examination of neighbouring east Jutland (8.3.4).

8.3.1 Specific research questions

Chapter 7.3.3.1 described the selection of sites for geophysical survey as directed by various research questions. One of these dealt with the relevance of individual predictive parameters for the identification of enclosure locations and has already been examined above. The second portion encompassed two specific questions:

1) Were enclosures always located very close to the contemporary coastline (with the Fuglslev site as an outlier), or did a network of enclosures exist in the hinterland with inter-enclosure distances comparable to those encountered for coastal sites?

2) Did a line of enclosures placed at approximately equal distances exist along the northern shore of Kolindsund Fjord (including the area between the Blakbjerg enclosure and the probable Fannerup site, which demonstrates a distributional gap)?

Unfortunately, the latter query is difficult to answer in a straightforward manner. Neither certain nor possible enclosures were detected on the two sites selected for survey in order to examine this research problem. Aside from the possibility that the geophysical instruments may not have been able to detect ditch segments due to adverse local soil conditions, or even that the presence of enclosures was not recognizable within the complexities of the data that were recorded, several other factors may explain the lack of causewayed enclosure detection in these areas.

At site 8 Pognæs I, the length of the area investigated by GPR measured approximately 220 m. This investigation area was too small to detect an enclosure of very large size (more than ca. 8 ha in this case). Furthermore, on the opposite side of a deeply-incised river valley which defines the promontory on which 8 Pognæs I is located, lies another potential enclosure site: 8 Pognæs II. According to data from the landowner, many flint axes have been found in this area. Unfortunately, said landowner withheld permission for geophysical survey. It must be concluded at present that the presence of a Neolithic enclosure on one (or theoretically also two) side(s) of the river valley cannot be discounted. The absence of such an enclosure in the geophysical measurements, thus, cannot be equated to proof of the absence of an enclosure.

At site 7 Vejvad Bro, only a minor portion of a large plateau on which an enclosure may have been located could be surveyed. Therefore, the possibility remains that an enclosure remains on the parts of the plateau that were not available for investigation. Furthermore, the site was pointed out as a potential enclosure site due to its position at the mouth of Nimtofte Å River. The valley of this river is somewhat wider than that of those rivers north of Kolindsund at whose mouths enclosures have been detected. If a river crossing was a crucial factor in choosing an enclosure site, the Nimtofte Å mouth may have been disregarded as enclosure location. The enclosure may have been built further upstream, possibly where the town of Nimtofte is situated today. Nimtofte is found at the meeting point of several river valleys, making the place a communication crossroads. Several potential enclosure sites have been pointed out here, of which the most likely – 34 Nimtofte N – was unfortunately inaccessible due to forest cover.

Unfortunately, it is therefore impossible at present to give an unambiguous answer to the question posed above. Regardless, the two topographically best-suited locations have been investigated without the positive identification of a causewayed enclosure. It is interesting, therefore, to point to the previously known and identified enclosures of Ballegård and Galgebakken. The sites are situated on the southern shores of the fjord and on an island in the fjord and could, therefore, have acted as alternative "gap-fillers". If these two enclosures are included in the observations, a more or less continuous line of enclosures at comparatively equal distances to each other can be identified between the Blakbjerg site in the west and the Grenå enclosure in the east. Given its location in the middle of a fjord, the selection of the Ballegård site for an enclosure indicates that water cannot necessarily be considered as a dividing element. It should also be noted that the Galgebakken enclosure was located directly opposite to the potential enclosure site(s) at Pognæs on the northern shore of the fjord. Although the fjord was over 3 km wide at this point, Galgebakken may well have fulfilled the role of another "gap-filler", connecting the Fannerup/Ginnerup sites to the east to the Blakbjerg enclosure to the west. In the Neolithic, water probably provided better and easier ways of transport and communication than land. Therefore, it is likely that the fjord should be viewed as a feature of the landscape which was a force of connection rather than of division. This is probably also reflected in the choice of the location of the Ballegård enclosure, which was, as mentioned above, constructed on an island in the fjord. Furthermore, as was pointed out previously (chapter 4), rows of enclosures situated along linear watercourses (rivers) are also known from northern France. A closer look at the locations of the northern French sites (Fig. 9) quickly demonstrates that these were situated along alternating sides of the river. This also included rivers of considerable size, such as the Yonne and the Seine. With regards to their breadth, these bodies of water do not greatly differ from Kolindsund. While the present investigations thus do not allow for the exclusion of the presence of enclosures on the northern shores of Kolindsund, either at the sites investigated or in areas nearby, the European evidence lends credibility to the alternative proposed here. It appears likely, therefore, that the row of enclosures along the shores of Kolindsund predominantly includes sites on its northern shore as well as some sites on islands in the fjord as well as along its southern shore.

The second research question used to select sites for geophysical survey was that of the regular situation of enclosures at locations more than a few hundred metres distant from the contemporary coast. With the discovery of the Assenbakke enclosure (3.0 km) as well as the probable or possible sites at Fladstrup (2.2 km), Trustrup (3.3 km) and Mårup (1.8 km), this question can now be conclusively answered. It appears that the Fuglslev site was not an exception. Furthermore, the distances between newly discovered sites (if confirmed in three of the four cases) as well as known enclosure locations all fall within the typical inter-enclosure distance generally recorded for causewayed enclosures. It is, thus, entirely possible that a network of more or less equally-distributed enclosures existed along Kolindsund Fjord as well as its hinterland.

However, test diggings at the unconfirmed sites are necessary before any conclusions regarding the precise character of the enclosure distribution in the hinterland can be drawn. Nevertheless, one aspect has already emerged and will be discussed in depth in the following chapters: none of the certain or possible enclosures sites in Djursland is further than a few kilometres from the coast. It is unlikely, therefore, that a complete network of enclosures ever existed in the interior of the study area.

8.3.2 Causewayed enclosures and related sites in Djursland: State of research after predictive modelling

In chapter 3, nine certain and three probable causewayed enclosures as well as one site related to causewayed enclosures were listed for the region of Djursland. To this list, one certain enclosure (58 Assenbakke), one probable enclosure (55 Fladstrup S), two possible enclosures (79 Mårup N and 53 Trustrup II) and three possible enclosure-related sites (1 Følle Vig, 11 Revn I and 31 Nielstrup I) can be added based on the results of the geophysical survey. However, there is a group of a further five sites which will be included in the following discussion of the distribution of enclosures and related sites in the region. The sites in this group are certainly in need of verification before any far-reaching conclusions can be drawn. Their inclusion in the following discussion could be classified as speculative. However, both the results of this study as well as the personal experience of the discoverer of many of the known enclosures (N.A. Boas) are arguments in favour of the inclusion of these sites in the following debate. Whether or not these sites are themselves the location of causewayed enclosures or whether they represent merely the presence of sites related to these monuments has yet to be determined.

Three of the sites in question are identical to potential enclosure sites pointed out in this study. Locations 34 Nimtofte N, 19 Grund V/Ø and 38 Rousings Mark all closely resemble locations of enclosures known from Djursland as well as other parts of South Scandinavia. All of them would have been included in geophysical survey, if not for the presence of forest cover (38 Rousings Mark, 34 Nimtofte N) or the refusal of the landowner (19 Grund V/Ø).

One of the two possible sites in Grund has already been mentioned, due to the presence of pits with fire-cracked stones which apparently date to the TRB (chapter 7.3.2.2). They are assumed to comprise a possible enclosure location, not only because they are situated near to where a river flowed into a fjord, but also because a historic main road as well as a barrow road lay close by. Relevant surface finds are known from both locations.

The reasons for the selection of site 34 Nimtofte N have already been listed above. They are entirely centred on its intriguing strategic position at the crossroads of several river valleys and barrow roads as well as the potential lack of an enclosure site on the shores of Kolindsund Fjord a few kilometres to the south.

Site 38 Rousing Mark is very close to the point at which a river flowed into a fjord and is also near to the well-known sacrificial sites at Veggerslev Kær (Becker 1947, 53ff. nr. 135-138). TRB finds are also known from the site (Danish parish register 140114-57).

Abundant TRB finds or finds of special character are known from both of the remaining two sites that were included in the list due to information provided by N.A. Boas. To the northwest of Nørager in the northwestern part of Djursland, a well-defined promontory is found at the confluence of two rivers. From a topographical point of view, this site was certainly well-suited for an enclosure. The same is true with regard to transport and communication. The reason why this site was not pointed out as a potential enclosure location is the fact that no barrow roads cross any of the rivers that define the promontory. In fact, neither a single megalithic grave nor any Bronze Age or undated round barrow is known within 1000 m of the site (which is situated equidistant from Tustrup in the northeast and Nielstrup in the southwest, at which the nearest river fords are present). No enclosure was found at Tustrup or Nielstrup over the course of geophysical surveying. While an enclosure could be present at Nielstrup (only one of five potential locations could be investigated here), it is also entirely possible that an enclosure was constructed between these two locations. However, in light of the general trends present for all Danish enclosures, it appears rather unlikely that no barrow road was present close to the site if an enclosure actually was situated there. Therefore, it is feasible to suggest that many barrows may have been destroyed in the area around the promontory before the instigation of systematic registration at the end of the 19th century.

Sølebakkegård, the second site that was mapped as a result of N. A. Boas' work, is located in northern Djursland at Øster Tustrup. It is to be found on a hill that is bordered by small rivers on two sides. These rivers eventually flow into the former Bønnerup Fjord. This is a typical location for causewayed enclosures in Djursland (as well as other parts of Denmark). A pit was excavated on this site which contained a quernstone as well as the fragments of two vessels. The finds had the character of a deposition more than that of a typical settlement find. This is evident not least from the remains of a beautifully crafted bowl dating to MN A I of which only parts appear to have been deposited (Fig. 72). This type of pottery is generally known only from megalithic graves, cult houses, bog offerings and enclosures (Andersen, N.H. 2000, 32ff. Figs. 32-33).

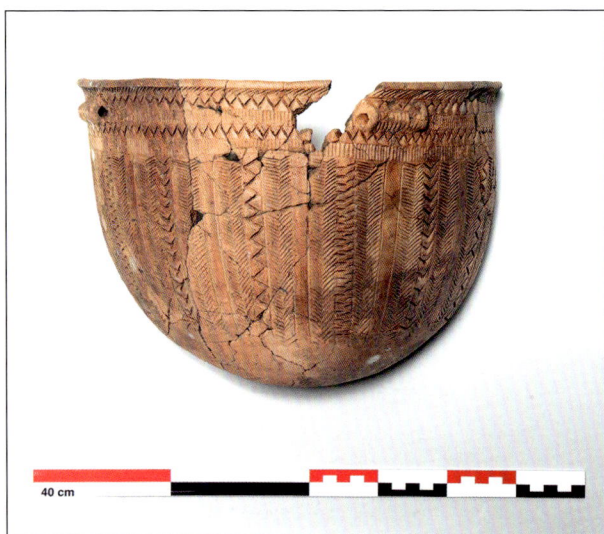

Fig. 72 | *Beautifully decorated bowl from a pit at Sølebakkegård. Photo Hans Grundsøe.*

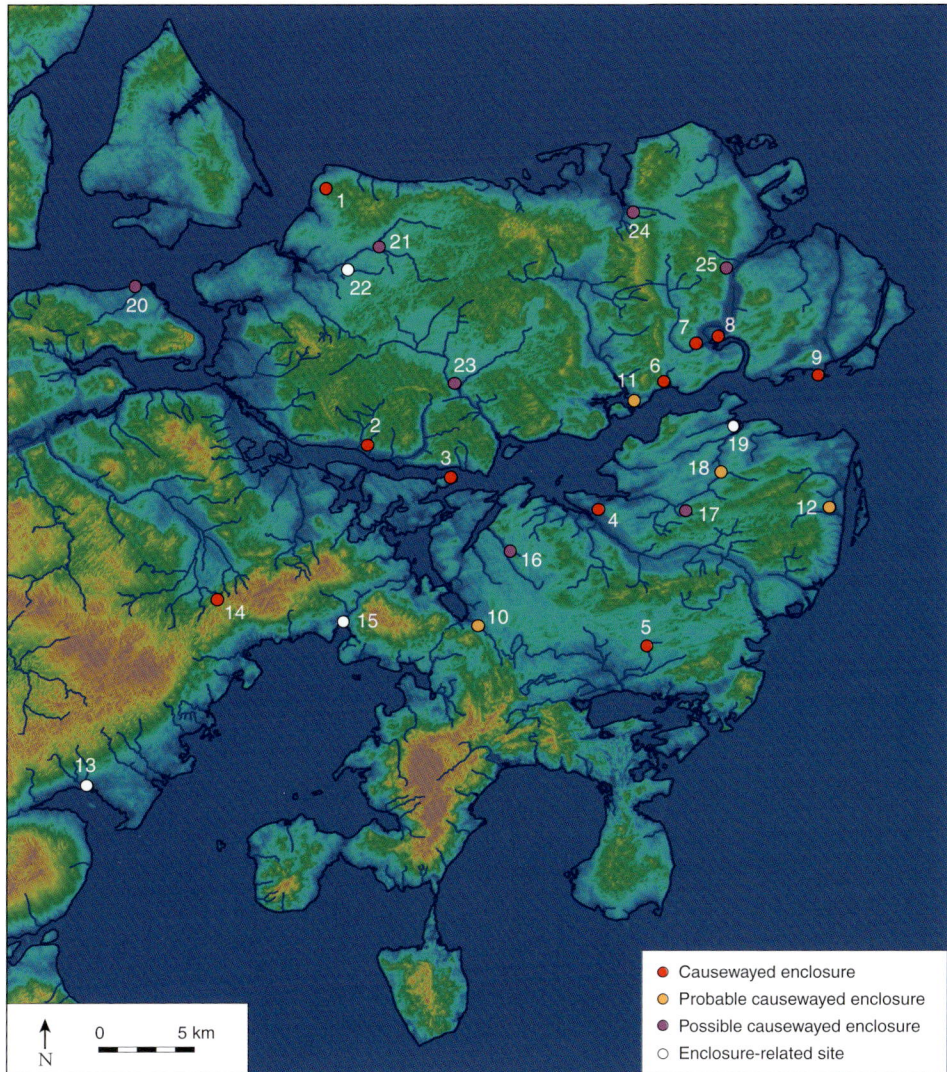

Fig. 73 | *The distribution of certain, probable and possible enclosures and enclosure-related sites in Djursland according to the state of research after predictive modelling. 1 Store Brokhøj, 2 Blakbjerg, 3 Ballegård, 4 Galgebakken, 5 Fuglslev, 6 Ginnerup, 7 Skærvad, 8 Kainsbakke, 9 Grenå, 10 Taastrup Kolindvej, 11 Fannerup, 12 Rævebakken, 13 Lystrup Kildevang I, 14 Assenbakke, 15 Følle Vig, 16 Mårup, 17 Trustrup, 18 Fladstrup, 19 Revn, 20 Grund, 21 Nørager, 22 Nielstrup, 23 Nimtofte, 24 Sølebakkegård, 25 Rousings Mark.*

As the Sølebakkegård location can be excluded as a representation of any of the first three site types mentioned, it likely represents an enclosure. The fact that only parts of the vessel appear to have been deposited in the pit also points in this direction, as the same phenomenon has been repeatedly observed at causewayed enclosures or sites related to causewayed enclosures (Lützau Pedersen 2010; Andersen, N.H. 2011).

The reason why the Sølebakkegård site has not been identified as a potential enclosure location in the predictive modelling approach is the same as that for the Nørager site described above: a relative scarcity of megaliths/barrows in the area around

the site resulted in the lack of a positive identification of a barrow road crossing one or several of the small rivers mentioned above. This aptly illustrates the vulnerability of the predictive model employed in this study, as the addition of very few barrows to the map would allow for the reconstruction of the 'missing' barrow road.

In summary, it can be stated that ten certain and four probable causewayed enclosures are known in Djursland. To this, seven possible enclosure sites have to be added (five of which may not house a proper enclosure, but rather an enclosure-related site). At present, there are four certain sites in this last category (Fig. 73).

9 Aspects of causewayed enclosures in South Scandinavia in light of the results of this study

In this chapter, some aspects of central importance for the general understanding of causewayed enclosures will be examined utilizing the results of this study as their point of departure. Due to the uncertainties bound to three of the sites derived from the geophysical survey in particular and the additional five locations from Djursland discussed above, it is difficult to reach sweeping conclusions based on the combined evidence from all sites. However, there are several aspects which bear further investigation here.

9.1 Causewayed enclosures and their relation to the contemporary coastline

As mentioned above, the results of the geophysical survey show that some enclosures were indeed located at some distance from the coast. It can be added that two of the possible sites introduced here (34 Nimtofte N and Nørager) belong to the group of sites found in the hinterland. Both are located 3.5 km from the coast. This distance from the coast is in the same range as that observed for the Assenbakke and Fuglslev enclosures as well as for the probable or possible enclosures at Fladstrup and Trustrup. Even though it is difficult to make definitive statements given that many sites have yet to be confirmed or dismissed as enclosures by excavation, the present evidence hints at a second line of enclosures ca. 3 km from the coast, at least in some

parts of Djursland. At present, the evidence for this second line mirroring the Kolindsund Fjord coastal line is particularly strong for the areas south of the fjord. It is entirely possible that these locations indicate the course of a Neolithic road/track which was of particular importance.

It is worth noting that no certain or suspected enclosure location is found more than 3.5 km from the coast. Even in Djursland with its centrally positioned Kolindsund Fjord, these distances are very modest. Sites situated in the central parts of land either north or south of the fjord appear to be absent. While the situation to the south of Kolindsund is difficult to evaluate (some regions in the area have been excluded from this study), there are no possible explanations for the absence of possible enclosure sites in the northern parts of Djursland and in the western part of the present investigation area. The widespread distribution of forests and large bogs in northern Djursland may be part of the reason why no possible enclosure sites have been pointed out there. However, this can hardly account for their complete absence from the area. It can, therefore, be cautiously concluded that there is some evidence that causewayed enclosures in Djursland were built only in coastal and near-coastal locations rather than inland.

Furthermore, this conclusion is much in line with what can be derived from the data for all known enclosures from the TRB North Group (which were rarely located more than 4 km from the coastline)

(Tab. 1). Indeed, of all the Danish and Swedish sites for which information was available (33 enclosures), only one – the Sigersted III enclosure – seems to deviate from this pattern. Larger distances regularly appear, albeit only in northern Germany. As was already pointed out above, northern Germany also appears to deviate from Denmark and southern Sweden in terms of other enclosure-related aspects. Regional variation is obviously at play here. It can be added that all five sites that were classified as being related to proper enclosures also follow the pattern observed; none is more than 4 km away from the sea, a fjord or a bay.

A diagram demonstrating the distance of all Danish enclosures (and the single Swedish site) to the sea demonstrates, furthermore, a slightly bimodal distribution (Fig. 74). Twenty-two (approximately two thirds) of all sites in a first group are located within 1000 m of the coast. The majority of these enclosures by far are located almost immediately along the shoreline. The remaining third (encompassing a second group) shows values between 1000 and 4000 m, with a slight preponderance in the 2500-3500 m range. The only exception (as mentioned above) is the Sigersted III enclosure which was constructed 25 km from the nearest coastline.

As demonstrated by a comparison of these figures with those calculated for certain, probable and possible enclosures in Djursland (Fig. 74), both distributions closely resemble each other. In the Djursland dataset, a dominant coastal/ near-coastal group of enclosures mostly found less than 500 m from the coast can be separated from a group with distances between 1000 and 3500 m. Within this latter group, values for distances of 3000-3500 m are slightly elevated. The Djursland dataset thus shows a slight tendency towards a relatively higher frequency of sites within 500 m from the coast as well as a general tendency for inland enclosures to be slightly closer to the coast than was the norm in Denmark. These differences may very well have occurred as a result of local topography and the presence of the expanse of Kolindsund Fjord. However, due to the uncertainties related to almost half of the entries for Djursland as well as the low total sample size, this observation is in need of further study before definitive conclusions can be drawn. The agreement between the two datasets with regards to a dominant near-coastal group, the total range of distance values and a slight dominance of enclosures around 3000 m from the coast among the non-coastal sites are nevertheless remarkable. Such correspondence within the data may indicate that the data for Djursland are not essentially skewed by the inclusion of many still unconfirmed sites, and that the data actually do reflect prehistoric reality.

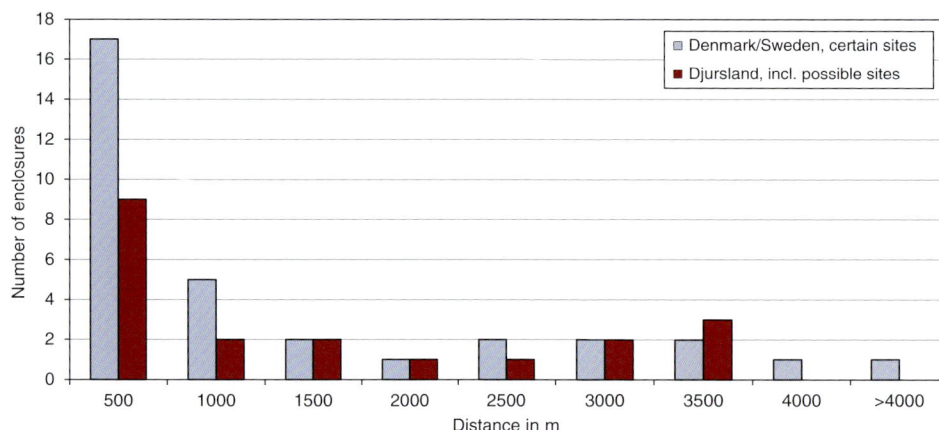

Fig. 74 | *The distance of all known causewayed enclosures in Denmark and Sweden to the nearest coast in comparison to values for certain, probable and possible enclosures in the Djursland region alone. All measurements are based on reconstructed Neolithic coastlines.*

9.2 Causewayed enclosures and inter-enclosure distances

The identification of a number of new certain, probable or possible enclosures (as well as enclosure-related sites) is of interest with regard to inter-enclosure distances. As stated earlier, the coastal sites at Kolindsund Fjord show inter-enclosure distance values between 1.2 and 7.5 km, with an average of ca. 4 km. The question is whether comparable distances can be found between the newly-identified inland sites on the one hand and between inland and coastal sites on the other. Due to the fact that only two certain inland enclosures are known in Djursland (and that approximately one half of all enclosure sites are suspected with varying degrees of probability), no certain answer to the question is immediately apparent. It can, however, be stated that the as-yet unconfirmed enclosure sites generally seem to fit a pattern of inter-enclosure distances with average values around 4 km. These values thus correspond quite exactly to those between confirmed coastal sites. At least, this pattern appears to be true between inland and coastal sites. The following values are worth noting: The distance from the possible inland enclosure site 79 Mårup N to the known enclosures Ballegård and Galgebakken as well as the probable enclosure at Taastrup Kolindvej is 4.5, 5 and 5 km respectively. Another of the suspected inland sites – 53 Trustrup II – is located 4.5 km from the Galgebakken enclosure. Other examples include the probable inland site 55 Fladstrup S, which lies at a distance of 5.5 km from the Ginnerup enclosure. At the opposite side of Kolindsund Fjord, the suspected inland site 34 Nimtofte N is found 5 km from Ballegården and 6 km from Blakbjerg. The last suspected inland site at Nørager is 4 km away from the enclosure at Store Brokhøj.

For distances between probable and possible inland sites, the 3 km between 55 Fladstrup S and 53 Trustrup II is worthy of note. All other inter-enclosure distances between certain or suspected inland sites are somewhat larger, reaching between 7.5 and 11 km. These comparatively large values possibly hint at the existence of yet-undetected

inland enclosures rather than real inland inter-enclosure distances. This last is illustrated by the fact that coastal and inland sites seem to be spaced at 4-6 km intervals on average. In other words, given that the existence of a coastal line of enclosures with low average inter-enclosure distances is known as is the fact that most of the certain coastal and suspected inland locations are also located at equally low distances to each other, it is likely that there was also an inland line of sites with the same approximate inter-enclosure distances. Unfortunately, the situation regarding the inland sites is still very uncertain. However, if future attempts to verify suspected inland sites are successful, it should be possible to point out the location of the "missing" inland sites quite precisely based on inter-enclosure distances in relation to previously identified potential enclosure sites. It can be added that the suspected near-coastal site of 38 Rousings Mark is located at a distance of 4.5 km from the coastal Kainsbakke enclosure as well as 5.5 km from another suspected coastal site (Sølebakkegård). These possible enclosures, therefore, dovetail perfectly with the known inter-enclosure distances for coastal enclosures.

In conclusion, the following working hypothesis can be formulated: In Djursland, coastal and near-coastal sites seem to be spaced at distances of an average of 4-5 km. At present, a line of enclosures can be demonstrated to exist in large parts of Kolindsund, but the Store Brokhøj enclosure as well as the suspected enclosure sites of Sølebakkegård and Rousing Mark may well indicate that a comparable line of enclosures existed along the northern Djursland coast. Isolated probable or possible coastal or near-coastal sites in other parts of Djursland may indicate further enclosure lines. The demonstrated (or suspected) linear nature of the distribution patterns probably reflects communication routes, either on the water or in the form of roads/tracks which closely followed the coastline. A comparable network of enclosures may well have existed (at least in part) in the hinterland. At the moment, this can best be demonstrated for the area south of Kolindsund Fjord and possibly also at Kalø Vig Bay. Due to the high number of yet-unconfirmed sites, this cannot be considered to be much more than a working hypothesis. If such a line of inland enclosures did, in fact, exist, it is very likely to have followed a contemporaneous road or track. It should be noted that – at least in some areas – the course of this road/track would have been closer to that which presumably followed the coast or sailing route in Kolindsund Fjord rather than the typical inter-enclosure distance, as the possible and probable inland sites are situated between 1.8 and 3.5 km south of Kolindsund Fjord.

9.3 Causewayed enclosures and TRB settlement in Djursland

The subsequent section is an attempt to relate causewayed enclosures to the development of settlement and society in Djursland between the Late Mesolithic and the early Middle Neolithic. This investigation will then provide the background for a comparison with the neighbouring region of east Jutland following the investigations of T. Madsen (1988).

The relation of causewayed enclosures to the contemporaneous settlement was explored early on in Scandinavian research history. The influential settlement models developed by T. Madsen (1982; 1988) in which enclosures are treated as centre sites can be referred to here as representative examples. The relation of the enclosures to the settlement pattern preceding them, by contrast, has not received nearly as much attention.

Naturally, a precondition for any discussion of this subject is knowledge of enclosure chronology. As was summarized in chapter 1 and is discussed more in detail in chapter 10.3.1, the construction of enclosures and enclosure-related sites in South Scandinavia started in the later parts of EN I (38th/37th century BC) and lasted approximately until 3200 BC, with a possible extension to the early third millennium. Unfortunately, almost nothing is known about the chronology of the enclosures in Djursland, as most of them remain unpublished and ^{14}C-dates remain the exception rather than the rule. Furthermore, the extent of excavation has been very modest in most cases.

The ^{14}C-dates from Lystrup Kildevang I indicate, nevertheless, that enclosure building may have also started early in this region. This suspicion is possibly confirmed by the pottery found in the construction layers of the Blakbjerg enclosure. As demonstrated by Torfing (2011; 2013), this pottery shows typological traits related to the late part of the EN I. It can, therefore, be concluded that there are at least some indications for the start of enclosure construction in Djursland which date back to the late EN I. At present, it is not possible to tell how many of the enclosures may have been built at this early time, or if there are any chronological differences between coastal and inland sites. From the rather regular inter-enclosure distances, it can only cautiously be deduced that most of the enclosures were functioning contemporaneously at some point in their use-history. According to the available information, this point in time may well have been as late as early MN A I, as finds from this period have been identified in a number of locations for which information is available (Store Brokhøj: Madsen, B./Fiedel 1987; Blakbjerg: Torfing 2011; 2013; Ballegård: Hougaard Rasmussen 1989; Galgebakken: Wincentz Rasmussen/Harder 2003; Fuglslev: unpublished, journal nr. DJM 1924, information kindly provided by N.A. Boas).

It is a characteristic trait not only of the Danish, but also of related causewayed enclosures in Germany (e.g. Geschwinde/Raetzel-Fabian 2009) and in Britain (Bayliss et al. 2001, 716), that the deepest layers in the ditches (which date to the time of enclosure construction) are often very poor in finds or only contain uncharacteristic artefacts. For Denmark in general, this phenomenon has been described for Sarup (Andersen, N.H. 1997, 49), Bjerggård (Madsen, T. 1988, 310) and Toftum (see below), to cite some prominent examples. For Djursland, Blakbjerg (Torfing 2011; 2013), Ginnerup (oral comm. N.A. Boas) and Kainsbakke (Wincentz Rasmussen 1984; Wincentz Rasmussen/Richter 1991) can also be referenced. This means that many enclosures believed to have been constructed in EN II or MN A I could well be older. This question can only be solved by systematic ^{14}C analysis.

As was argued by T. Madsen (1988, 321), the evidence for settlements found inside causewayed enclosures seems to generally postdate enclosure construction. This statement still holds true today. As a matter of fact, it is reinforced by the realisation that many enclosures had construction dates which were earlier than had hitherto been assumed (see above). In fact, it is only at Toftum (Madsen, T. 1978a; 1978b) that the settlement was apparently contemporaneous with enclosure construction. However, Toftum is among the enclosures that are unfortunately characterised by time-of-construction deposits which are poor in finds. Therefore, the construction of the Toftum enclosure could very well be older than the Fuchsberg settlement (EN II) found inside (Madsen, T. unpublished). At the end of the day, all that can be known for sure is the fact that, at some point in time, the ditches of Toftum functioned together with a settlement located inside the enclosure.

In summary, it can be concluded that there is an increasing amount of evidence for enclosure construction in late EN I. It seems as if these sites did not initially serve as settlements. As a consequence, finds from the later part of EN I – rather than those stemming exclusively from EN II and MN A I – must be taken into account for any discussion of the relationship between causewayed enclosures and contemporaneous settlements. For any comparison between enclosure distribution patterns and settlement patterns in preceding times, the Late Mesolithic and earliest Neolithic must be examined.

The data represented in the following maps have been downloaded from the digital central register of the Danish Agency for Culture (KUS). This register is not necessarily complete, as many single finds from Djursland alone have not yet been registered therein. With regard to the Late Mesolithic Ertebølle Culture and its extremely consistent settlement pattern, this presents no problem. The addition of further find spots would only lead to a higher density of sites rather than a substantially different distributional pattern. Data for the Early Neolithic I (3950-3500 BC) in the database are very sparse. Therefore, relevant finds have been regis-

tered for this study in the collections of the museums in Randers, Grenå and at Moesgård, while data for finds stored in the National Museum in Copenhagen were kindly supplied by L. Sørensen (National Museum of Denmark).

9.3.1 Late Mesolithic

Fig. 75 shows the settlement pattern characteristic of the Ertebølle Culture: Almost all known finds are entirely bound to the coastline, while very few find spots from the interior of the country are known. Only four of the 127 sites mapped here are inland locations, and of these, three represent somewhat doubtful single finds. Only one location (Rosenholm in the western part of the area) represents an inland settlement. This is situated within what is today a huge bog. In Ertebølle times, the same area must have been a lake. Comparable with the well-known site of Ringkloster in eastern Jutland (Andersen, S.H. 1975; 1998), Rosenholm almost certainly represents a seasonal, specialised hunting/gathering station in an environment dominated by a large freshwater system. As described by Johansen (2006), this station may well have been the seasonal settlement of a minor group and not a satellite camp to a larger coastal site. Inland sites may in general be underrepresented in the map, as they are often of restricted size.

The coastal sites in Djursland, like those found elsewhere, represent both kitchen middens and settlements without shellfish deposits. The famous kitchen midden of Mejlgaard in northern Djursland (Sehested 1884; Madsen, A.P. 1888; Andersen, H.H. 1961) and the equally important large Dyrholmen settlement without shell depositions in the northwestern part of the present investigation area (Mathiassen et al. 1942) can be cited here as examples. Another noteworthy site is Nederst (Mathiassen et al. 1942), from which several graves are known (Kannegaard Nielsen 1989; 1991; Kannegaard Nielsen/Brinch Petersen 1993).

Intense research into Ertebølle coastal sites in Djursland has been ongoing for many decades (Mathiassen et al. 1942; Andersen, S.H. in prepa-

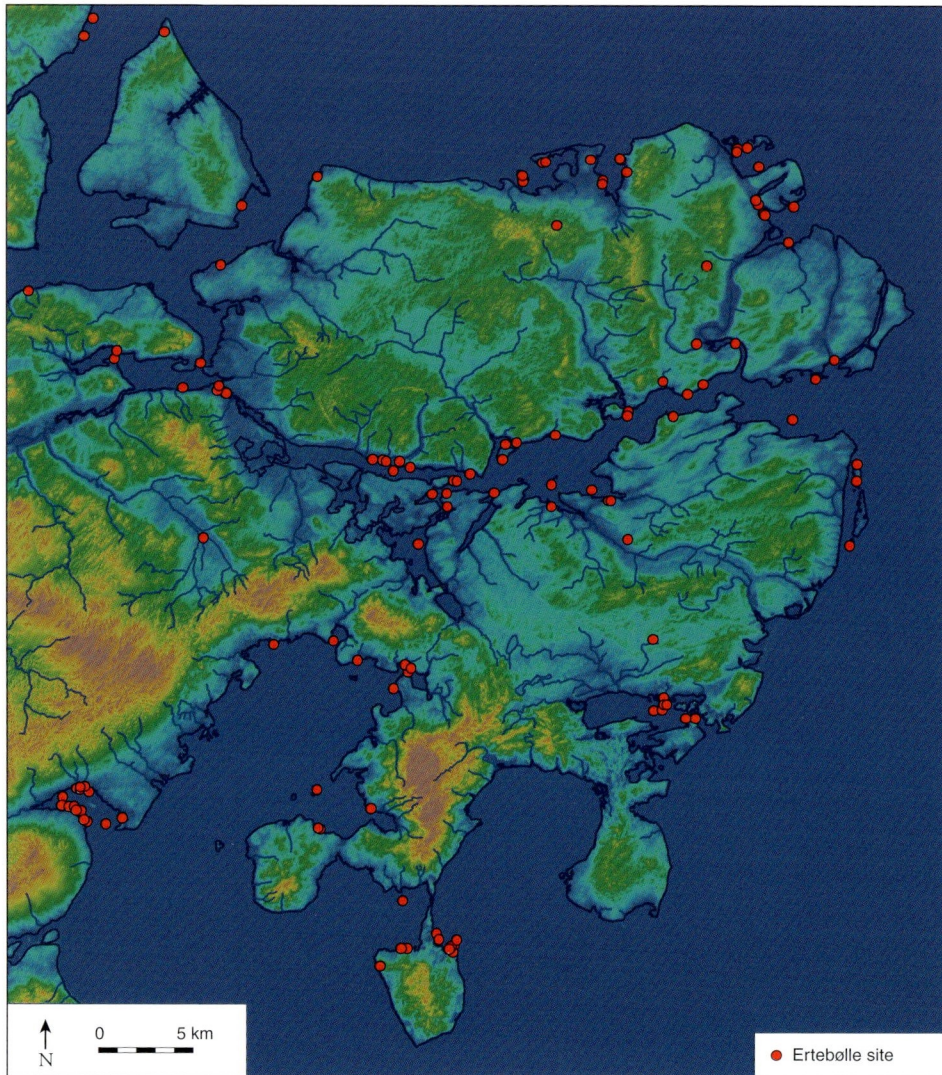

Fig. 75 | *The distribution of Ertebølle sites and finds (ca. 5400-3950 BC) in Djursland.*

ration). Although the results of newer investigations have not yet been published, there is little doubt that the Ertebølle settlement pattern in Djursland is comparable to that apparent from better-investigated areas. As was argued by Johansen (2006), this settlement system was probably characterised by comparatively small social units, possibly consisting of extended families which moved throughout a restricted territory during the year to several locations along the coast and inland. Some coastal locations with an abundant and stable supply of resources were probably visited over extended periods of time, thus leading to the creation of apparently huge settlements. Possible examples for such sites from Djursland are Dyrholmen and the Kolind kitchen midden (Mathiassen et al. 1942).

9.3.2 Early Neolithic (EN I)

With regard to the first part of the Early Neolithic, all finds from EN I (3950-3500 BC) were first mapped (Fig. 76). The later part of this period possibly overlapped with that of the construction period of the earliest causewayed enclosures in the region. This period has been included here because the evidence for enclosures in Djursland from this time is still very limited. Therefore, many of the sites mapped probably reflect the presence of pre-enclosure settlements. An attempt to separate an early part (ca. 3950-3800 BC) from a late part of EN I (ca. 3800-3500 BC) was nevertheless made in a secondary step.

In general, it is much more difficult to create a representative distribution map for Early Neolithic

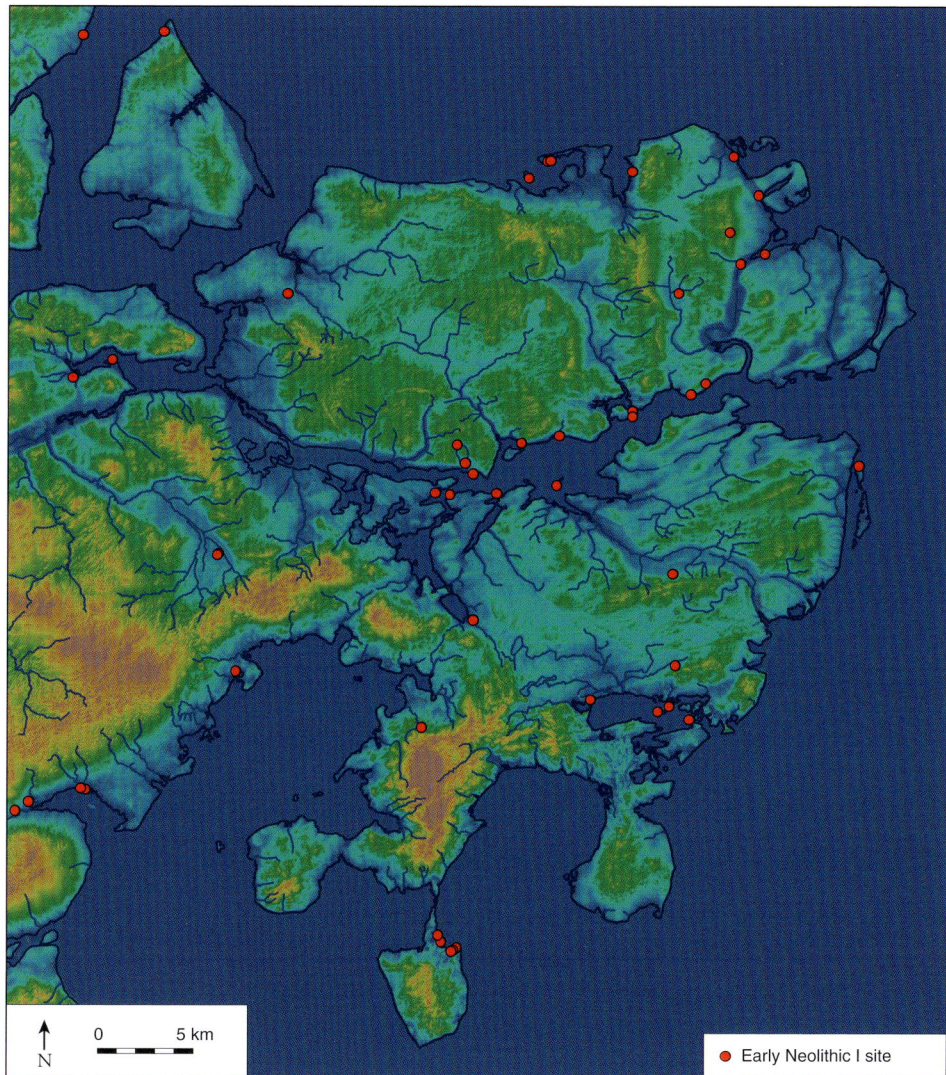

Fig. 76 | *The distribution of all known sites and finds from the Early Neolithic I (ca. 3950-3500 BC) in Djursland.*

0   5 km

N

● Early Neolithic I site

I than for the Late Mesolithic because the number of diagnostic artefacts that were in use only during the former period were far more restricted. Furthermore, while the majority of Ertebølle sites mapped in Fig. 75 represent settlements with precisely known locations, this is only true for a few of the earliest Neolithic sites. Many of these are made up of singly found flint axes with pointed butts (types 1-3 according to P.O. Nielsen (1977)), for which most often only very imprecise finds data are available (typically only the name of the parish in which the artefact was found).

Apart from very few Early Neolithic settlements and even fewer graves for which the precise find location is known, all Ertebølle kitchen middens were mapped according to their precise locations. However, the presence of Early Neolithic deposits has only been stated for a select few of these sites (Kolind and Nederst, Mathiassen et al. 1942). The problem with these layers is that they are much more exposed to destruction through natural erosion as well as modern agriculture than the Ertebølle layers which lie below them. Registration in well-investigated regions shows that ca. 80% of all Ertebølle kitchen middens still have the more or less well-preserved remains of Early Neolithic layers. Therefore, it can be assumed that probably all (or almost all) of these coastal sites once held such layers (S.H. Andersen, personal communication). For this reason, all registered Ertebølle kitchen middens were mapped here irrespective of the presence or absence of Early Neolithic layers, among the Early Neolithic sites whose locations have precise coordinates.

Finds with imprecisely known find spots were mapped approximately in the centre of their possible area of origin. Almost all dots on the map represent single finds of flint axes with pointed butts. However, one hammer axe of the early type (an F-axe, according to Zápotocký 1992) and two greenstone axes with pointed butts were also included.

Finds whose origins are known were chiefly centred along the coastline, as was the case in the preceding Ertebølle Culture. This is, of course, partly due to the mapping of the same sites (kitchen middens). However, Early Neolithic settlements without shell deposits also show the same distribution. Upon closer inspection, however, it becomes apparent that the latter sites were typically withdrawn from the coast by a few hundred meters. For example, the well-investigated settlement at

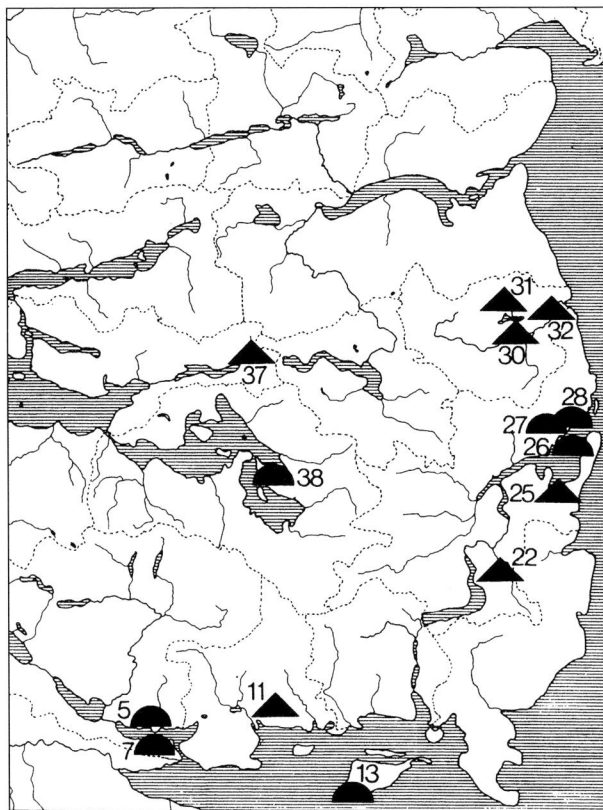

Lisbjerg Skole can be mentioned (Skousen 2008, 117ff.). Very few sites are located further than a few hundred meters' distance from the coastline. Among the exceptions is a find from Mørke Kær (a single flint axe with a pointed butt) in the western part of the investigation area. This axe was found in the same huge bog/lake area mentioned above (Ertebølle inland settlement). Thus, there was apparently continuity in the use of this inland wetland area from the Late Mesolithic to the Early Neolithic, just as was the case in the coastal areas.

The finds with imprecisely known find locations show a somewhat divergent distributional pattern. While some are from coastal or very near-coastal locations, others are found further inland, even though distances to the coast surpass 2-3 km only in a few, rare instances.

With regard to Early Neolithic I (between 3950 and 3500 BC), it can, therefore, be concluded that the overall settlement pattern was still comparatively coastal. However, apart from those sites located directly on the shoreline (as was the case in Ertebølle times), others are found somewhat removed (by a few hundred meters) as well as in a zone which stretched a few kilometres inland. Apart from the above-mentioned settlement showing continuity from the Ertebølle Culture, the inland sites of the early TRB probably represent agriculturally based settlements established by small social groups which were likely to have been occupied year-round. Coastal sites and the inland sites situated along large freshwater systems (generally the same as those occupied in Ertebølle times) probably represented satellite hunting sites for the short term exploitation of certain resources, such as fish (Johansen 2006). Agricultural sites removed from the coastline were only inhabited for shorter periods of time (several years) and were, therefore, smaller in size with restricted find densities. These sites are hard to locate and must, therefore, be expected to be underrepresented by the map as it stands at present. The restriction of these sites to a zone stretching only 2-3 km into the interior can be expected to be a reflection of the actual state of affairs in the Neolithic. This was demonstrated by the intensive regional study conducted in the neighbouring region of east Jutland, for which EN I settlements were found to have been restricted to a zone stretching ca. 3 km inland (Fig. 77; Johansen 2006, 209; Madsen, T. 1982, 213 Fig. 11; Madsen, T./Jensen 1982, 78). Nevertheless, other regions of South Scandinavia may well have deviated in this respect, as was described by Johansen (2006, 209).

An attempt was made to divide the period from 3950-3500 BC into an earlier (3950-3800 BC) and a later (3800-3500 BC) section. The purpose was to test whether any developments in settlement location over the course of the almost half a millennium-long EN I could be detected within the investigation area. However, the number of finds from each of the two sub-periods was very small, which restricted the possibility of obtaining reliable results. The division attempted was identical to that between the early phase of the Oxie Group (with beakers of type 0 according to E. Koch, 1998) and the Volling Group, as was observed in kitchen midden stratigraphies in eastern and northern Jutland (Andersen, S.H. 1991; 1993). ^{14}C-datings from the Lisbjerg Skole settlement indicate that the same division was probably also valid for Djursland. In this settlement, pits with finds from the early Oxie Group were dated to 3945-3805 BC, while finds of the Volling Group from the same site date after 3800 BC (Skousen 2008, 117ff.). This possibly indicates that the later phase of the Oxie Group (with type I beakers which, according to E. Koch (1998), are best known from eastern Denmark and Scania) was not represented in this area.

In Denmark, pointed-butt flint axes have only been found in Oxie Group contexts. According to P.O. Nielsen (1977), these axes can be subdivided into types 1-3. These types constitute a chronological sequence in which type 1 is the oldest and type 3 is the most recent. It could thus be argued that type 3 belongs to the younger part of the Oxie Group. As type 3 is well represented in Djursland according to the registrations completed for this study, it could be argued that the late Oxie Group was represented there, in direct contrast to what was stated above. However, a closer look at closed finds of pointed-butt axes and Oxie ceramics in South Scandinavia reveals that only axe types 1 and

2 are represented. Type 3 is not present. Furthermore, the latter type has been found in contexts associated with the Svenstorp Group in Scania, a regional parallel to Jutland's Volling Group (Larsson, M. 1984, 162). Additionally, type 3 axes have been found in hoards together with the earliest eastern types of thin-butted axes (Hernek 1988, 217). Therefore, it can be concluded that type 3 axes appeared around or after 3800 BC and probably belong to an early phase of the Volling Group, at least in Djursland. This is also possibly substantiated by a find (although it was, unfortunately, not closed) from Ørvadgård in the southwestern part of the current investigation area in which type 3 axes were discovered together with Volling pottery (Skousen 2008, 105 Fig. 79). It can be concluded that type 3 axes do not indicate the presence of the late part of the Oxie Group in Djursland. They have been mapped together with finds belonging to the Volling Group. In this way, the map covers the period from 3800-3500 BC.

The map in Fig. 78 represents the Early Neolithic between 3950 and 3800 BC and shows finds of settlements with (early) Oxie ceramics as well as pointed-butt flint and greenstone axes of types 1 and 2. Only four settlements with ceramics finds are presently known. The Lisbjerg Skole site was already mentioned above (Skousen 2008, 117ff.); the same is true for the Kolind kitchen midden (Mathiassen et al. 1942, 37ff.; Nielsen, P.O. 1985, nr. 38). The two remaining settlements were discovered beneath or besides well-known non-megalithic long barrows: at Barkær (Liversage 1992, 37) and Konens Høj (settlement unpublished, grave see Stürup 1965). The first three of these sites also have delivered flint axes of types 1 and 2. Further finds of axes of these types (as well as greenstone axes of the same shape) are known from the Nederst kitchen midden (Mathiassen et al. 1942, 59f.). The remaining axe finds lack precise provenience information.

Map Fig. 79 shows the distribution of finds in Djursland from a later part of Early Neolithic I between 3800 and 3500 BC. This map includes finds from settlements and graves as well as votive finds with Volling Group pottery as well as type

3 pointed-butt axes. An attempt has been made to exclude the finds that belong to the latest part of the Volling Group, which in northern Jutland and Djursland continues until the beginning of the Middle Neolithic (Madsen, T./Petersen 1984; Klassen 2000, 87ff.). However, the possibility that a few late Volling type finds were included in the map cannot be excluded, given that a clear division between early and late Volling pottery is difficult to establish at present. Unfortunately, it is not possible in Djursland to separate the earliest thin-butted axes (dating to between 3800 and 3500 BC) from later types, as, according to P.O. Nielsen (1977), type IV appears to have been present in the area (as well as Jutland as a whole) for a long period. Therefore, thin-butted flint axes could not be included on the map.

Volling settlements represented in the map include several recently excavated sites on the northern shores of the fossil fjord of Egå (Lisbjerg Skole, Lisbjerg Terp, Ørvadgård, Lystrup Kildevang I (Skousen 2008), Barkær (Liversage 1992), Kolind (Mathiassen et al. 1942, 37ff.) as well as a few unpublished sites. Furthermore, despite the lack of actual finds, known kitchen middens were also included in this map due to the fact that coastal settlements which had been in use since Ertebølle times were generally abandoned around 3600 BC in Denmark (Andersen, S.H. 2008, 71). Votive finds are known from Veggerslev and Emmelev Kær (Becker 1947) as well as Mørke Kær (unpublished), while graves from Langkastrup (Ebbesen 1994, 87), Sandmarken II (Fiedel/Berg Nielsen 1989) and Rimsø (Madsen, B./Nielsen 1977) are represented.

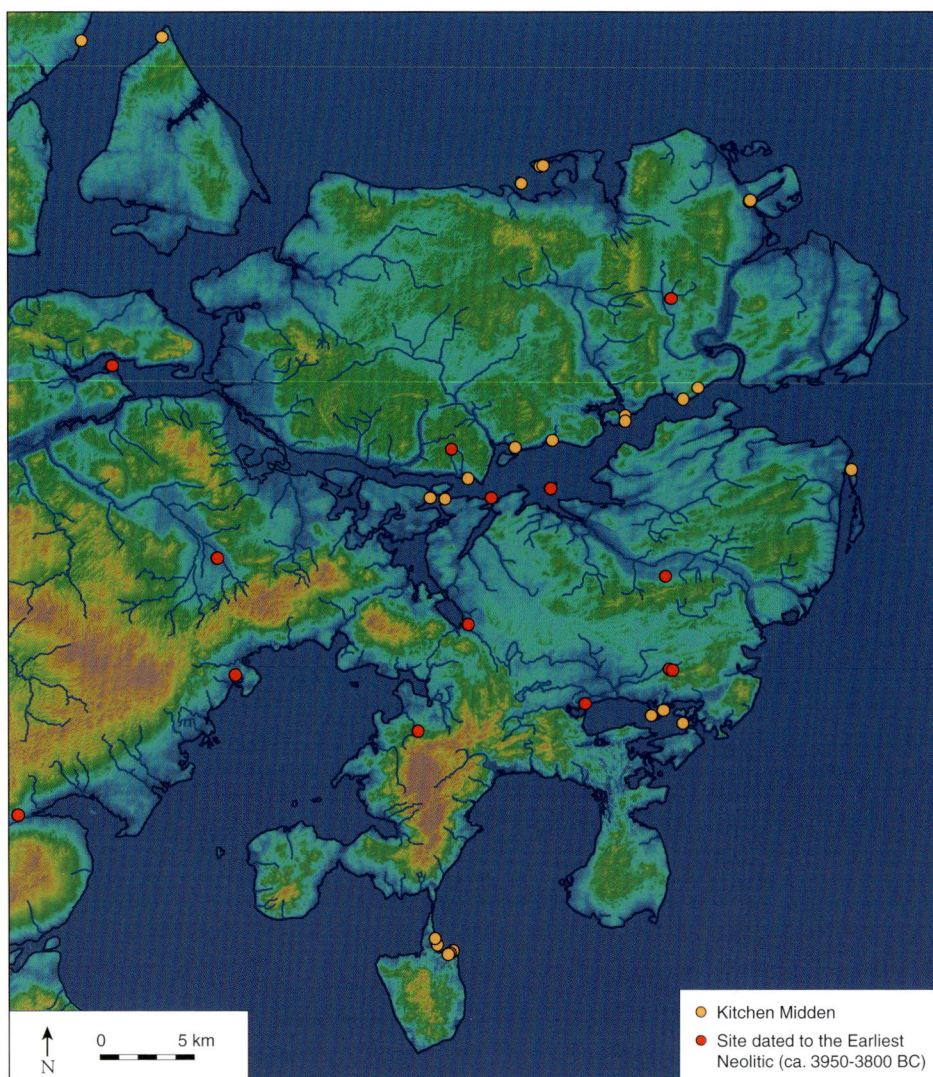

Fig. 78 | *The distribution of sites and finds from the very earliest Neolithic (ca. 3950-3800 BC) in Djursland.*

Even if kitchen midden sites without actual evidence for finds from one or both EN I sub-periods are disregarded, there appears to have been remarkable settlement stability between both phases. In fact, many of the settlement sites (Lisbjerg Skole, Barkær, Kolind, probably Dyrholmen) at or very near the coast show continuity between both phases. The same appears to be true for bog offerings in the large bog/lake area Mørke Kær as well as for several sites with imprecise information concerning their find location which yielded axe single finds – both from coastal and inland locations (e.g. Vosnæsgård on the western coast of Kalø Vig and Hyllested north of Stubbe Fjord). Obviously, no dramatic shifts in settlement pattern took place. Nevertheless, the possibility that settlement in the interior intensified in the later part of the

period cannot be excluded, although nothing on the maps is indicative of such a development. However, one cannot forget that no thin-butted axes have been mapped. There are still no indications of any settlement in the deeper interior beyond a few kilometres' distance from the coastline.

9.3.3 Late Early and early Middle Neolithic (EN II – MN A I)

In the late Early Neolithic (EN II) and early Middle Neolithic (MN A I) between ca. 3500 und 3200 BC, the situation as described for the preceding periods profoundly changed, at least in some sub-regions of Djursland. This is the time of use and, in many cases, was probably also the time during which causewayed enclosures were constructed. It is also

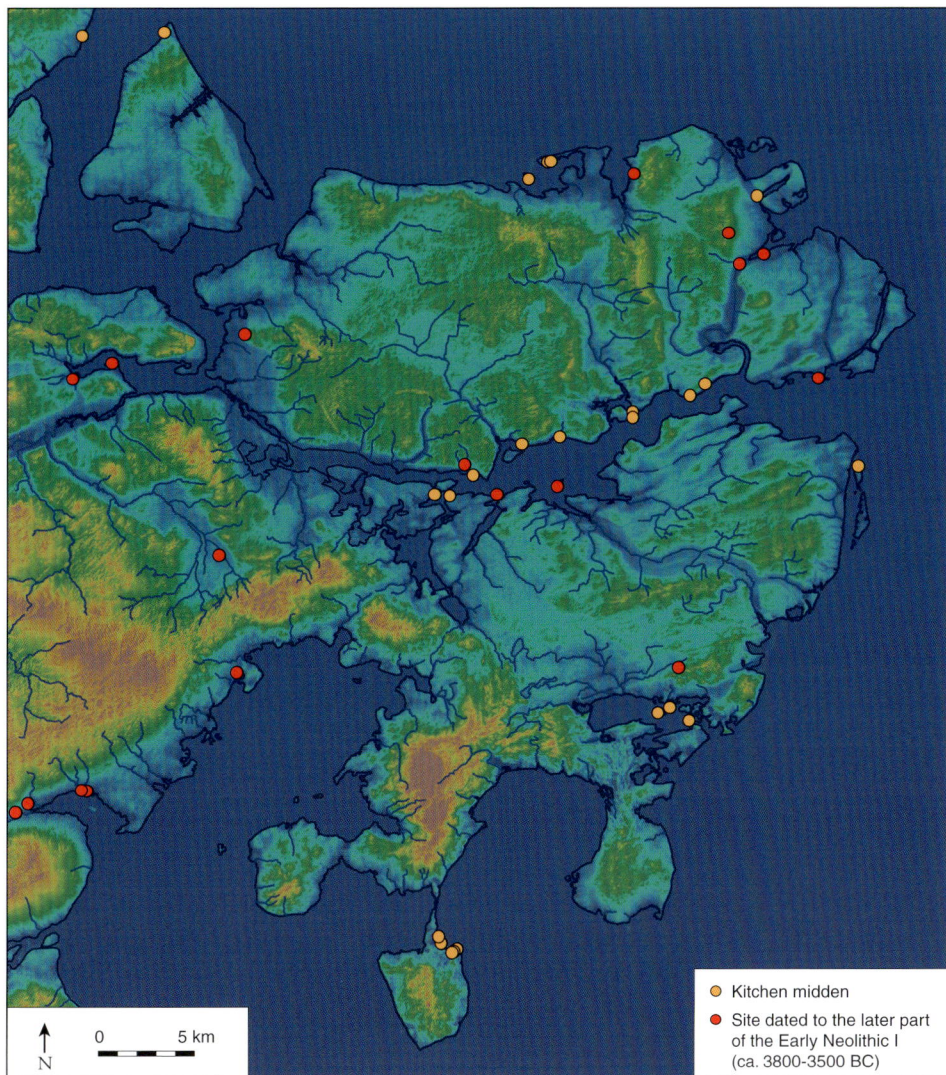

Fig. 79 | *The distribution of sites and finds from the later part of Early Neolithic I (ca. 3800-3500 BC) in Djursland.*

○ Kitchen midden

● Site dated to the later part of the Early Neolithic I (ca. 3800-3500 BC)

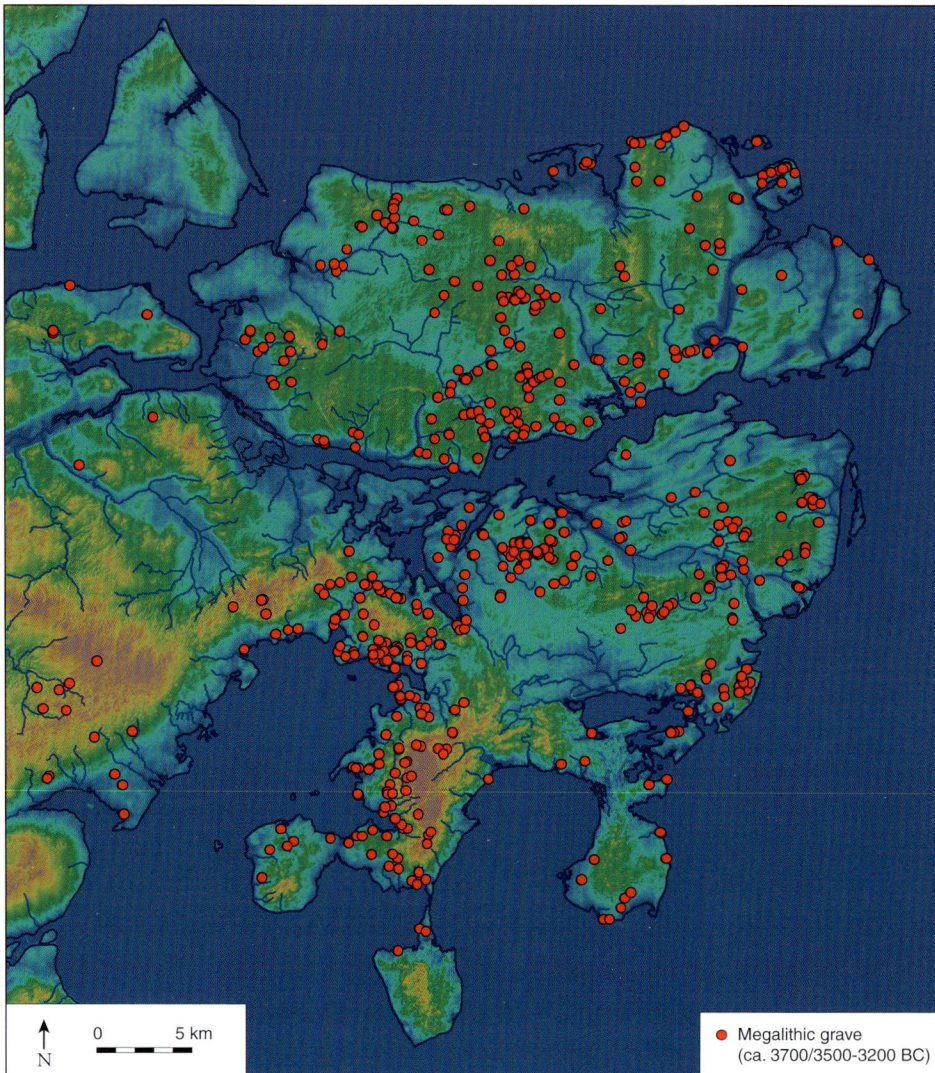

Fig. 80 | *The distribution of TRB Culture megalithic graves in Djursland as reflection of settlement in the late Early Neolithic (EN II) and earliest Middle Neolithic (MN A I), ca. 3500-3200 BC.*

the time of construction of megalithic graves, some of which might have been built in the later phase of the EN I, nevertheless. In Fig. 80, the distribution of megalithic graves was used to illustrate the general settlement pattern in EN II and MN A I, as the overwhelming majority of tombs were certainly constructed during this period. However, the distribution pattern that emerged must not be taken too literally, as the dolmens and passage graves have been subjected to various degrees of destruction in different parts of Djursland (Vedsted 1986). The absence of these types of graves from several regions cannot, therefore, be taken as a definite reflection of the absence of settlement from the time in question without an in-depth study of the areas in question. Unfortunately, this last is beyond the scope of this study. Nonetheless, the map demonstrates the fact

that the interior of the country (at least in some parts of Djursland) was settled in that particular part of prehistory. This is most obvious in the central parts of northern Djursland as well as in the south-eastern part of the Djursland Peninsula.

It is interesting to compare this distribution to that observed in eastern Jutland between the modern towns of Århus and Horsens (Fig. 81). With regard to the distribution of megalithic graves, this region appears to follow the same pattern as that which was present in Djursland. Apart from coastal locations, tombs are also known from the interior of the region, and in locations which were more than just a few kilometres from the coastline. Nevertheless, they were not scattered across the landscape. Just as was the case in Djursland, some large regions appear to be more or less devoid of megaliths. Even though it was demonstrated above that the lack of megalithic tombs in some regions of Djursland is more likely a reflection of a lack in registration than a lack of settlement in those areas, the general agreement between the observed patterns in Djursland and eastern Jutland can cautiously be interpreted as a reflection of a real pattern. Apparently, not all parts of the interior of Jutland were settled in EN II and MN AI.

9.3.4 Summary and conclusions

To sum up, the following development of settlement in Djursland from the Late Mesolithic to the early Middle Neolithic is recognizable: Apart from a few inland wetland sites (which might be underrepresented by the maps), Late Mesolithic settlements were entirely centred directly along the fjord shoreline as well as the Kattegat and different bays. The sites which are known probably reflect seasonally occupied settlements, some of which (through extended use) would eventually grow to a large size. Many of these sites continued to be used as satellite extraction camps for specialised purposes in the Early Neolithic (EN I). The main settlements of the EN I took the form of small, permanently inhabited sites located within 3 km from the coast. In some cases, these settlements might have been located directly along the coastline. However, they were often found to be located a few hundred metres removed from it. In the late Early and earliest Middle Neolithic, the area occupied was extended further inland. In some regions at least, the entire interior part of the area was settled. However, in other regions it was unfortunately not possible to decide whether the lack of evidence reflects a lack of settlement or the lack of settlement registration.

With the establishment of an approximate picture of settlement development throughout the Early Neolithic and the beginning of the Middle Neolithic in Djursland, it is then possible to relate that development to the location of the causewayed enclosures. As far as it is currently possible to state, enclosures in Djursland were built very closely to the coast (albeit not directly on the coastline) as well as in a 2-4 km-wide zone within the coastal

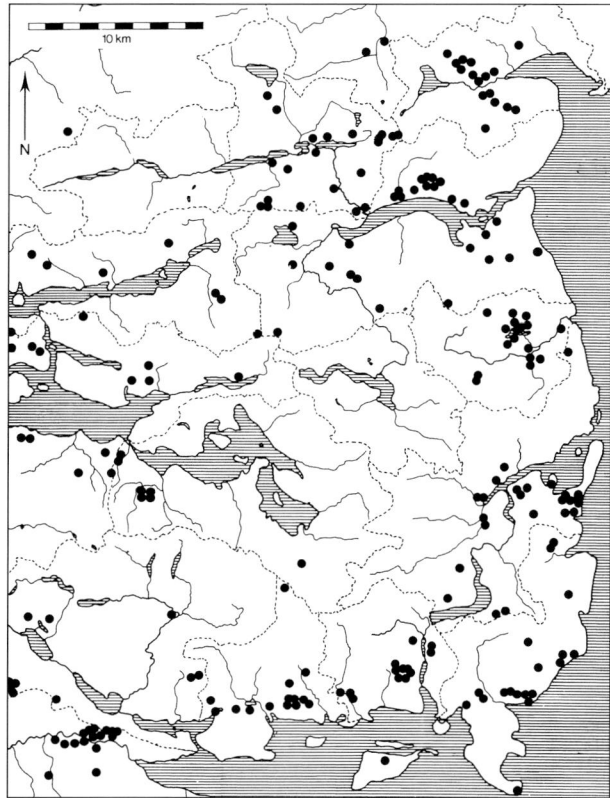

Fig. 81 | *The distribution of TRB Culture megalithic graves in eastern Jutland in the late Early Neolithic (EN II) and earliest Middle Neolithic (MN A I), ca. 3500-3200 BC (from Madsen 1982).*

region. Neither certain, probable nor suspected sites are known from the interior of the country beyond this 4 km coastal zone (Fig. 73). The distributional pattern of the enclosures obviously exactly matches that of settlements in Early Neolithic I (Fig. 76). However, it diverges from that of the late Early Neolithic and earliest Middle Neolithic (Fig. 80). This is especially remarkable because of the fact that the distributional pattern of enclosures matches that of the settlements in the period preceding enclosure construction and use rather than the distribution pattern of settlements when said enclosures were under construction/use. Three possible explanations for this phenomenon are discussed in the following:

1. The discrepancy observed in the distribution pattern possibly reflects the state of research into the distribution of causewayed enclosures rather than that which was present in the Neo-

lithic. Therefore, it could be argued that enclosures were indeed present in the interior, but have yet to be found.

This proposition cannot be disproved, as the presence of absence cannot be equated with the absence of presence. This is (and will always be) a possible explanation for the distribution patterns remarked upon above. However, as has already been discussed, the combined evidence of all known Danish enclosures seems to confirm the distributional pattern observed for causewayed enclosures in Djursland.

Only a single Danish enclosure – Sigersted III in the centre of Zealand (Martens/Nielsen 1996; Nielsen, P.O. 1998; 1999; 2000) – is located at a (considerably) greater distance from the coast. On the other hand, inland sites are common in north Germany. It appears, therefore, that regional differences may exist with regard to the location of enclosures. In this regard, it is of interest to note that regional differences also seem to exist with regard to the ordinary settlement patterns. For example, EN I settlements in Djursland as well as in east Jutland seem to be restricted to narrow zones along the coastline. However, this is the case in neither Scania (Johansen 2006, 209) nor Zealand (i.e. at Sigersted III). With regard to the region around Sigersted itself, this is easily demonstrated by the presence not only of a causewayed enclosure, but also of an Early Neolithic Oxie Group settlement (Nielsen, P.O. 1985). Therefore, it is clear that the Sigersted III enclosure was constructed in an area already settled in EN I rather than in an area to which settlement first extended in EN II/MN AI.

Other differences between EN I settlement in Zealand and contemporary settlement in (at least parts of) Jutland are also apparent. As was recently described by M. Madsen (2010), settlements (among others) were built on heavy clay soils in Zealand. Furthermore, as many as 19 house sites have been discovered in a single settlement (Ullerødgård: Rosenberg 2006). On the other hand, in the east Jutish area intensively studied by T. Madsen (1982), EN settlement was clearly restricted to very well-drained soils. Moreover, rare Early Neolithic

house sites in that area always seem to have been isolated. Finally, in Scania, numerous houses from the same settlement site (Dagstorp) are known, just as was the case in Zealand (Andersson 2003).

The existence of enclosures far from the coast in other regions of South Scandinavia may, therefore, very well be a reflection of regional differences in general settlement patterns. However, what all regions of South Scandinavia have in common is the fact that causewayed enclosures only appear to have been built in areas that were settled in previous (very early) phases of the Early Neolithic (EN I). The apparent lack of causewayed enclosures in the zone furthest away from the coast in Djursland, therefore, cannot be ascribed to a simple lack of the registration of such sites. Instead, it must be a reflection of Neolithic reality.

2. A second possible explanation for this particular distribution pattern is an insufficient state of research with regards to enclosure construction chronology in Djursland. Enclosure distribution may thus be indicative of construction in (a late part of) the EN I with a subsequent continuation of use in EN II/MN A I. This assumption would result in matching enclosure distribution patterns at the time of construction and contemporaneous settlement.

In like fashion, it must also be stated that the only two sites whose construction dates can be established with an acceptable degree of precision (the Blakbjerg enclosure and the enclosure-related site Lystrup Kildevang I) were both constructed in EN I or during the EN I- EN II transitional period. It is also true that many Danish enclosures dated to EN II or MN A I may, in fact, have been constructed earlier. In principle, it is, therefore, possible that all remaining enclosures in Djursland were constructed as early as EN I. However, there are several enclosures in Denmark which were most certainly constructed after EN I (see chapter 10.3.1 for a detailed discussion of enclosure chronology). At present, the number of South Scandinavian enclosures that can be dated to (late) EN I (2) is clearly outnumbered by the number of enclosures that were built in EN

II or MN A I (6). Therefore, it appears unlikely that enclosure construction in Djursland should have been restricted to the first 200 years of the (at least) half a millennium-long overall construction phase (at least from 3700 to 3200 BC). It follows, then, that enclosures in Djursland must have been built during periods in which settlement expanded inland from near-coastal areas. Therefore, the second possible explanation for the lack of enclosures in the Djurslandic interior should also be dismissed.

3. The last explanation for the distribution pattern of enclosures and settlements in Djursland assumes that enclosures were constructed in both the later part of EN I as well as EN II-MN A I (as discussed above). At the same time, they were also related to Early Neolithic societies before their expansion inland. Therefore, enclosure construction continued to be restricted to the near-coastal area settled in EN I, despite the enlargement of settled areas into the interior in EN II/MN A I. Groups that settled inland either did not construct and use enclosures, or they participated in one or both of these activities in areas which were located closer to the coast.

As the lack of causewayed enclosures in the interior of Djursland can apparently be explained neither by the lack of registration of sites nor by the hypothetical possibility that enclosures in Djursland might only have been constructed during the chronological horizon before the inland settlement expansion, enclosure location must reflect a special importance of the *Altsiedelgebiete*. At the same time, it appears that (for one reason or another) the newly settled regions of the interior were not suited to the construction of these monuments.

It is possible to refer to at least two closely related cases which seem to confirm the conclusions drawn here for the region of Djursland. In both cases, the construction of enclosures did not start until several hundred years after the region's first settlement by Neolithic farmers, in spite of the fact that those early farmers were doubtless aware of the enclosure concept. One of these examples even hails from South Scandinavia: the Neolithic appeared in this region

around 4000 BC, although the reasons behind the introduction of agriculture (as well as the circumstances surrounding its arrival in South Scandinavia) are much debated. However, the earliest Neolithic pottery of the region shows unmistakable links to the Michelsberg Culture, especially to regional groups in northern central Germany (Lower Saxony, Westphalia). Moreover, the import of artefacts from these regions can be demonstrated (Klassen 2004). In the author's opinion, it is likely that there was some migration of minor (?) groups from northern central Germany to South Scandinavia at this time (Klassen 2004; in press; Sørensen/Karg in press). But even if a neolithisation model is applied without migration, there cannot be much doubt that the earliest Neolithic population in Denmark was aware of the causewayed enclosures of the Michelsberg Culture in Lower Saxony and Westphalia (part of which date to Michelsberg phases II and III which corresponds exactly to the time around 4000 BC; see e.g. Siegmund 1993; Knoche 2008). Despite this knowledge, no enclosures were constructed in South Scandinavia at the time of neolithisation, nor for the two to three centuries thereafter.

The second example closely parallels the first. In the British Isles, large-scale neolithisation occurred approximately at the same time as in South Scandinavia (Bayliss et al. 2011). It is, of course, possible that earlier, more sporadic and more regionally-restricted neolithisation episodes may have occurred (see Sheridan 2010). The pottery of the earliest Neolithic societies in the south of Britain (Carinated Bowl Neolithic) shows clear typological relations to the Chasséen septentrional, Spiere Group and Michelsberg Culture present on the opposite side of the Channel. As was the case in South Scandinavia, the 'how' of neolithisation remains a much-debated topic. Nonetheless, regardless of whether or not migration took place, there can be no doubt that the earliest Neolithic population in the south of Britain was aware of the enclosures associated with the above-mentioned groups on the Continent. Still, just as in South Scandinavia, no enclosures were constructed in newly settled regions.

The two examples above demonstrate that – much like the enclosures themselves – this problem has a European dimension. Thus, it cannot be solved by a single regional investigation. Both regional and superregional aspects have to be taken into account. An in-depth study of the superregional dimension of TRB enclosures is found in chapter 10. The relevant local aspects are discussed below.

As mentioned above, the people who settled outside the area in which enclosures were constructed may have participated in building activities (as well as in the use) of those sites. In the European Neolithic, there are several examples from different times and regions in which populations from very large regions used – and even constructed or moved – enclosures and henge monuments. The most prominent of these is Stonehenge, which was probably disassembled, moved and then rebuilt at its present location in the early third millennium BC after a dislocation of ca. 250 km. Furthermore, Neolithic groups from large parts of the British Isles appear to have frequented the place (and possibly even taken part in its construction) to which end they covered distances of many hundreds of kilometres (Parker Pearson 2012). Another example of the superregional use of a site of ritual sig-

nificance comes from the Linear Pottery enclosure at Herxheim in Rhineland-Palatinate (Fig. 82), Germany, which may have been frequented by groups living up to 300-400 km away (Zeeb-Lanz 2010). The first results of isotopic investigations confirm the presence of foreign people at the site. However, it is not yet possible to determine whether those persons originated in the regions represented by "imported" pottery (Zeeb-Lanz 2012, 172).

In the light of these two examples, the idea that TRB groups from the interior of Djursland used or even constructed causewayed enclosures in the coastal zone is by no means far-fetched. In practice, it will be very difficult to determine whether or not this was the case. It might be possible to gain knowledge regarding this problem by means of a detailed stylistic analysis of large inventories of decorated pottery from both regions. However, such analyses are not available at present. Therefore, the following considerations will concentrate on an attempt to identify one or several aspects that might be able to explain why enclosures were only constructed in areas with a somewhat longer Neolithic settlement history. Over the course of this discussion, the model for the introduction and function of causewayed enclosures in South Scandinavia put forward by T. Madsen (1988) will be reviewed.

A natural point of departure would be in the observation that causewayed enclosures show a clear relation to Neolithic roads/tracks, both in South Scandinavia and abroad. It appears that not all roads or tracks were suited to having enclosures at their sides, but only a certain selection. When Neolithic settlement expanded into the interior of Djursland, for example, new roads/tracks were established. However, no enclosures were constructed along these roads, neither immediately in the pioneering phase of settlement expansion, nor in the centuries which followed. This cannot be explained by the fact that the enclosure concept might have fallen out of use at that time. As demonstrated by the construction in MN A Ib around 3200 BC (see chapter 10.3.1), enclosure construction in the coastal zone went on for at least 300 years after the initial expansion of settlement into the interior.

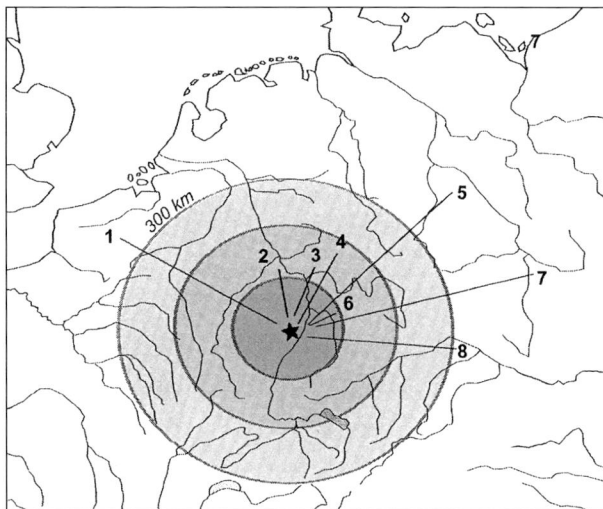

Fig. 82 | *Pottery was recovered from a number of distant regional groups at the Linear Pottery Culture enclosure at Herxheim in Germany. These finds possibly indicate the presence of people that had travelled up to 400 km to reach the site (from Zeeb-Lanz 2010). Numbers indicate the regions from which the exotic pottery originated.*

Geschwinde & Raetzel-Fabian (2009, 241ff.) and Knoche (2013) recently put forward a theory which applies to the relation of causewayed enclosures to long-distance routes in different parts of Germany. According to their research, these routes may have originated in the development of an economy with a strong emphasis on cattle, as has been observed for the Michelsberg Culture. The roads would, therefore, have served the seasonal movement of cattle herds. Accordingly, the function of the enclosures (or their immediate surroundings) in such an economic system would have been to house the herds upon their departure or return from distant grazing grounds during herd management activities. For these events, feasts and rituals would have been performed that would have led to the kinds of clearly ritual finds that are regularly encountered in the ditches and pits (i.e. the excavation and more or less immediate refilling of ditch segments as well as the manipulation of human bones).

While applicable in northern central Germany (but see below), the so-called "Braunschweig-model" is not a good fit for this type of site in South Scandinavia. Here, marginal regions well suited as grazing grounds were present in the central and western parts of Jutland. However, nothing indicates that these regions were used to that end in TRB times. Massive grazing activities seem to start rather suddenly there with the beginning of the Single Grave Culture around 2800 BC, as evidenced from pollen analysis (Odgaard 1985a; 1986; Odgaard/Rostholm 1987; Andersen, S. T. 1998). Cattle may of course have been moved along paths in coastal areas in South Scandinavia in TRB times. However, this hardly seems to have been a large-scale or seasonal activity. This was further underlined by isotopic studies which demonstrated the fact that Early Neolithic cattle grazed on widely-available, naturally grass-covered areas along the fjords which would thus have been in close proximity to enclosures and regular settlements (Noe-Nygaard et al. 2005). It should also be added that – contrary what can be observed in northern central Europe (Knoche 2013) – the growing of cereals was intensified during the period of enclosure construction in South Scandinavia. Depositions of cereals in causewayed enclo-

sures (e.g. at Sarup I: Jørgensen, G. 1977; 1982; at Liselund: Westphal 2000, 51) indicate that this part of the economy was of growing importance from a ritual perspective as well. There is, thus, nothing to suggest that the economy in South Scandinavia would have been based on mobile cattle herding to any degree at the time in question.

The idea of an (at least partially) mobile economic system with a main emphasis on cattle herding for the Central European Michelsberg Culture is plausible and forms an important contribution to creating an understanding of this peculiar archaeological phenomenon. However, it is doubtful whether causewayed enclosures played the role that Geschwinde & Raetzel-Fabian and Knoche suggested within this system. South Scandinavian and northern central European enclosures show numerous specific similarities (including general constructional traits as well traces of the same specific activities, relations to roads/paths and inter-enclosure distances). The arguments put forward against the cattle-management/ritual model for South Scandinavia also shed doubt on its applicability to northern central Europe. Two observations are worth noting in particular. The first is the inter-enclosure distance of 4-6 km which appears to be the same in many parts of Europe, (including South Scandinavia and northern central Europe). This observation has no reasonable explanation in the assumed function of the enclosures as sites of importance for cattle herding – neither in simple profane function, nor in the cattle-related ritual activities which certainly existed, as convincingly argued by Knoche (2013).

The second observation worth discussing is the position of many enclosures on alternating sides of waterways (see chapter 3; Fig. 9). This location clearly indicates a relationship between enclosures and water travel rather than to the roads or paths which ran parallel to them. Consequently, these enclosures can hardly have been related to the movements of cattle herds. Finally, it should be noted that there are no indications whatsoever either in the enclosures of northern central Germany or in enclosures from other relevant parts of Europe for seasonal ditch re-cutting. These events appear to have been much rarer, occurring on average on a

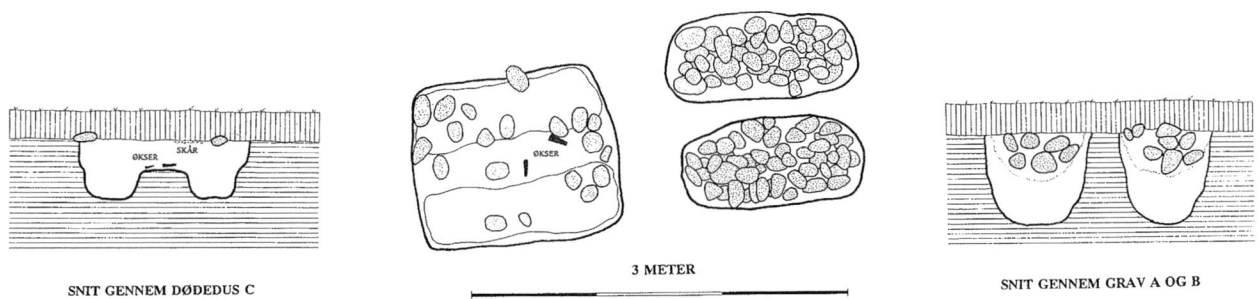

SNIT GENNEM DØDEDUS C   ØKSER   SKÅR   ØKSER   3 METER   SNIT GENNEM GRAV A OG B

Fig. 83 | *Typical stone heap grave consisting of two parallel bathtub-shaped pits and an associated rectangular feature representing the burial of a cart and a pair of draught cattle (from Jørgensen 1993).*

generational scale (or even less frequently). Seasonal, cattle-related ritual activities may thus be reflected in pits in the interior of enclosures or in the pits that made up enclosure-related sites (Knoche 2013, 149f.), but cannot be related to the construction and use of enclosure defining elements (ditches and palisades). It can be concluded that, while it is reasonable to assume that the creation and maintenance of long-distance roads/paths in Central Europe was related to a mobile economic system with emphasis on cattle herding, it is difficult to explain the creation of causewayed enclosures at regular intervals along these routes via a focus on cattle-related activity. Other, ritual aspects related to these routes obviously have to be taken into account.

With regard to Djursland, therefore, it can be concluded that the model proposed for northern central Germany by Geschwinde & Raetzel-Fabian (2009) and Knoche (2013) cannot explain the spatial distribution of causewayed enclosures. It can only be concluded that some roads or paths in Djursland might have had a different function than others, and that this difference was rooted in these routes' locations in regions with pre-enclosure settlements. The specific function of these roads/paths appears to have had some kind of ritual content. While this sounds odd, there is, in fact, ample evidence from the Neolithic of both South Scandinavia and many parts of Europe that points in this direction. Two intriguing examples from Denmark and Sweden – which were mentioned earlier (chapter 6.3.2.1) – will be discussed in the following, while the European evidence (which is

directly related to causewayed enclosures) will be discussed in a separate chapter dealing with European evidence in general (chapter 10).

In the northwestern parts of Jutland, a peculiar burial custom is known from the later parts of the TRB, ca. 3100-2800 BC. The so-called stone heap graves consist of two parallel, bathtub-shaped pits and a rather quadrangular feature with two parallel, somewhat deeper ditches within it (Fig. 83). Traditionally, the two pits have been interpreted as graves, while the quadrangular feature was believed to be some kind of mortuary house. The individual features were covered by stones, which led to the birth of the term 'stone heap graves'. In a recent study, Johannsen and Laursen (2010) convincingly re-interpreted these graves as being representative of the burial of a pair of draught-cattle (the two bathtub-like features) and a cart (the quadrangular feature). Stone heap graves have often been found arranged in long rows (Fig. 19A), one set of features immediately following the other. The authors referred to above could demonstrate that these lines of graves follow the course of (long-distance) routes through the landscape. What is of special interest in the current context is the fact that the graves that were found along the same route (on either one or even several separate graveyards) were always oriented in the same direction (Fig. 84). For example, all graves along routes in the western part of Jutland are oriented towards the north. This pattern was clearly guided by some kind of convention of orientation that was bound to specific routes.

The stone heap grave phenomenon underlines the fact that certain roads played a significant role in popular belief at the time, given that the dead were sometimes buried in cattle drawn vehicles along these routes. As was described by Johannsen and Laursen (2010), this custom was likely to reflect the journey of the deceased from the world of the living to the world of the dead. What precisely governed the direction of this travel (i.e. the orientation of the wagon graves along the route in different regions) remains unknown. However, this fascinating example clearly demonstrates that particular (long-distance) routes could have been connected to specific cosmological beliefs. While the graves demonstrate that this was true for a person's last journey, there is little doubt that specific beliefs regarding movement along these routes would have also impacted the living travelling along the road.

A further three aspects of the stone heap grave custom should also be mentioned. One is the fact that megalithic graves older than the stone heap graves are found aligned along the same routes, indicating that specific beliefs might have already been bound to these at the time of causewayed enclosure construction (chapter 6.3.2.1 and Fig. 19A). Therefore, despite their more recent age, the specific regional custom of burying the dead in carts along the roads can serve as an illustration of the possibility that certain roads and – more specifically – the movement along these roads was connected to particular beliefs at the time of interest.

The second aspect relates to the regional distribution of this specific grave custom. As demonstrated by Johannsen & Laursen (2010), north-western Jutland is only one of several provinces

Fig. 84 | *The general orientation of stone heap graves in the northwestern parts of Jutland follows a specific pattern that was clearly connected to conventions related to specific long-distance routes. On the map, each stone heap grave icon represents the orientation of a row/ longer lines of graves or, in some cases, that of individual graves. Graves for which no orientation information was available are represented by circles (from Johannsen/ Laursen 2010).*

in Europe in which comparable customs seem to have been practised. This implies that the idea of travel along some roads being connected to specific beliefs was likely present in large parts of Europe. It was potentially expressed actively in the specific form discussed here only in some (geographically isolated) regions.

The last point of importance for the question of causewayed enclosures and their relation to certain roads is the fact that the rows of stone heap graves seem to be linked to specific long-distance roads (as well as some minor roads connected to them which may have potentially come from settlements). This may well imply that only some roads were connected to specific beliefs, while others were not. This aspect will be taken up again later in connection with the discussion of wider European evidence. For now, it can be concluded that the restriction of causewayed enclosures to certain routes may be explained by the fact that specific ritual beliefs were bound to these routes as well as to travel on them. If this is the correct explanation, then the restriction of enclosure construction to routes passing through the primary area of Neolithic settlement may indicate that ancestor-related beliefs played an important role for those travelling these routes. Comparable assumptions have been made by Midgley (2008, 200) based on the distribution of megalithic graves along certain routes. This interpretation is strengthened by anthropological data; in many of the world's mythologies, the ancestors are often credited with having established roads (Helms 1988; 1993, 224f; Rudebeck 2002, 172ff.).

This latter aspect is certainly emphasized by the second example: the palisaded road or enclosure excavated at the site of Döserygg near Håslöv in southwestern Scania (Andersson/Nilsson 2009a; 2009b; Andersson/Wallebom 2013a; 2013b; see above chapter 6.3.2.1 with Fig. 19B), which was accompanied by standing stones and a large number of dolmens on both sides. According to the published ^{14}C-dates (Andersson/Wallebom 2013a; 2013b)(which should be treated with caution until the precise context and nature of the samples used has been published), construction of these dolmens could have started around 3700 BC (dolmens 5 and 13). In the excavation, the road or palisaded passage along an enclosure could be followed over a combined length of more than 700 m. However, it also continued on both sides of the areas opened during excavation. The topographic situation as well as the distribution of dolmens in the surroundings may indicate that this exceptional construction may have continued for several kilometres, if it was a road. However, according to Andersson and Wallebom (2013a; 2013b), the newest excavation results seem to suggest that the palisade construction may, in fact, have been an enclosure. The Döserygg site is located along an ancient communication route and it is, thus, remarkable that travel on this route would then have included passage through a palisaded corridor with dolmens and standing stones on both sides.

Regardless of which interpretation is correct (palisaded road or enclosure), the Döserygg site is one of the most extraordinary examples from South Scandinavia of a connection between roads, road travel and the ancestors. It is not possible to determine how common this kind of structure may have been. However, linear arrangements of megalithic graves are common throughout the area (and have been used in this study for the reconstruction of roads). As was the case for roads flanked by stone heap graves, it is evident that ancestor-related beliefs and road travel were intimately tied to each other at Döserygg.

Before entering into a discussion of the interpretational possibilities which emerge from this perspective, it seems wise to review current models for the function of causewayed enclosures in South Scandinavia. As was mentioned in the introduction to this book, scholars have reached a general agreement regarding their function as meeting places. These sites were used in several different contexts of social interaction and ritual practice, at least partially in relation to death and burial. Different older theories (like their use as fortified settlements, as corrals, or for astronomical purposes etc.) will not be described here. Critical discussions of these aspects can be found in N.H. Andersen (1997, 301f.) and Klatt (2009, 70ff.). Instead, the focus here is upon models that take into account larger regions with several enclosures as well those that deal with the role of the enclosures in relation to the development of (Early) Neolithic societies over time.

9.3.5 *The east Jutland model: A critical review*

The most comprehensive theory concerning the relation between causewayed enclosures and settlement in a larger region (east Jutland) was developed by T. Madsen in the early 1980s and was published in detail in a paper several years later (Madsen, T. 1982; 1988 and see Fig. 1). With regard to the understanding of larger regions with several enclosures as well as the interrelation between ordinary settlements, graves and enclosures and the social and economic development of early TRB societies, Madsen's model has remained largely unchallenged and has only been criticised to a moderate degree (e.g. Thorpe 1996, 138). In general, Madsen's ideas have been taken over by most Scandinavian scholars working with the topic (e.g. Nielsen, P.O. 1993) and have been supplemented either by more detailed interpretations of the function of individual sites within a micro region (Andersen, N.H. 1997, 311ff.; 1999a, 292ff.; 2011) or more detailed evaluations of individual aspects (e.g. Nielsen, P.O. 2004). In the following, the most central aspects of Madsen's model are summarised in order to provide a description of the current state of research into this matter, which can then be compared to the evidence from Djursland.

9.3.5.1 *Summary of the east Jutland model*

According to Madsen, prior to enclosure construction, small groups of farmers lived in short-term residential settlements near the coast (in the earliest part of the Neolithic (EN I)). Their economic basis was grounded in agriculture and husbandry and was supplemented by fishing, hunting and gathering. The latter activities (especially fishing) were carried out from specialised sites along the coast. Pollen diagrams reveal almost no traces of human intervention within the surrounding environment. Therefore, economic activities must have been primarily based upon the use of the natural forest environment. Pollen evidence as well as

animal bone finds suggest that pig husbandry was likely to have been the dominant activity, with slash and burn agriculture on small plots of land rounding out subsistence activities to a lesser degree.

Madsen argues that these economic activities used an extensive amount of land. In combination with a slowly growing population, huge demands for land would have led to increased tension between individual groups. Economic changes and an intensification of ritual activity were instigated as a means of resolving this conflict in the later part of EN I. With regard to subsistence activities, increasingly more stable husbandry systems were established by shifting from pigs to cattle as the dominant livestock. Grazing areas for cattle were established in forested areas by ringbarking trees. Nevertheless, all activities were land-hungry, meaning that intergroup stress was likely to have increased. This stress was relieved by means of increased amounts of ritual activities from EN II onwards. Among other things, this included the production of ever-larger amounts of elaborate pottery with decorative styles. Said items can no longer be interpreted as a possible large scale expression of ethnicity, as was perhaps the case in the first part of the Early Neolithic. The pottery styles of this period followed strict rules and may have served to secure the uniformity of hierarchical principles over large areas. Another aspect of increased ritual activity was demonstrated by the construction of megalithic tombs (in large numbers) as well as causewayed enclosures. These large sites were built and used by many small units within the same group, who negotiated rights to land/other disputed issues by participating in common rituals. Everything appears to have been carried out according to strict rules and obligations which regulated an individual's role in society. In this way, a Neolithic society maintained a flat social structure without a strong hierarchy.

Madsen mapped the distribution of megalithic tombs, certain as well as suspected enclosure sites and reconstructed group territories (Fig. 1). According to him, enclosures were located at the centre of these territories and were surrounded by clusters of graves. The latter served as territorial markers. Nevertheless, the extreme amount of investment in ritual activity reflected by the construction of megaliths and enclosures could not be maintained for very long. After a few hundred years, both activities ended (in MN A II). At the same time, pottery started to lose its elaborate and strict designs, settlements continued to grow in size and stability and the forests began to recover. This can be interpreted as the result of small groups moving in together on ever-larger settlements. In many cases, these settlements were located in areas where inter-group conflict had previously been solved by rituals involving many small settlement units: the enclosure sites. The more permanent presence of larger groups of people on the same site also necessitated the development of a more stable economy using fixed areas close to the settlement. This led to larger, permanent openings in the forests around the enclosure sites as well as to the recovery of the forest in other areas.

Madsen was aware of a possible major drawback to his explanatory model: the clear resemblances of both the construction and use of the Scandinavian enclosures with those of wide areas in Central and Western Europe. These resemblances were so close in many of their details that it is impossible that the Scandinavian sites were a local development. Madsen rejected the idea that the enclosure concept travelled from Central Europe to Denmark by means of diffusion. Both the large distributional gap between the Danish enclosures and their nearest parallels in Germany as well as the timing of the appearance of enclosures in Denmark contradict such a simple explanatory model. According to Madsen, given that the start of enclosure construction in Denmark was a consequence of specifically local requirements, it is highly unlikely that the enclosure idea should have reached Denmark by means of simple diffusion at that precise moment in time. Therefore, he assumed that the general enclosure concept had become widely known early on as it spread throughout Europe – even into South Scandinavia. However, knowledge of this concept was only translated into construction activity when local TRB societies had reached a certain point in their internal development. For this to be possible, Madsen assumed that the enclosure concept was

strong enough to retain its main elements despite being employed in a different context than was the norm in Central and Western Europe.

Madsen's explanatory model is elegant; its huge success in Scandinavian archaeology is also easily understandable, given that it does not view causewayed enclosures in isolation. On the contrary, it integrates these monuments into the long-term development of all aspects of TRB society. In the following, the validity of Madsen's model is tested by updating the data that were used in its formation and by adding further information. In an initial portion, this is completed with regard to local Scandinavian aspects, while the European perspective is dealt with in a subsequent chapter.

9.3.5.2 Chronological aspects

As mentioned earlier (and described in detail in chapter 10.3.1), the idea that all enclosures were built within a narrow chronological horizon between 3500 and 3200 BC is in need of revision, not least due to the earlier start of enclosure construction (38th/37th centuries BC) and its potential persistence into the early third millennium. However, this new developmental start date also applies to that of the construction of megalithic graves (see above) and, therefore, has no effect on the parts of Madsen's model that exclusively relate to the tombs. However, these changes impact several other aspects of the model, which are discussed below.

9.3.5.3 Economic aspects

In terms of the economic aspects of Madsen's model, no remarkable change occurred in the pollen evidence. According to him (Madsen, T. 1988, 329), a number of pollen diagrams showed the beginnings of change in forest composition ("Iversen's Landnam") which predate EN II. New evidence for this earlier start (which can be dated to around 3700 BC) has recently been produced for the north German TRB distribution area (Dörfler et al. 2012; Müller, J. 2011, 59ff.). This date coincides with that now established for the construction of the first causewayed enclosures as well as megalithic graves, and does not, therefore, conflict with Madsen's model.

A review of current Early Neolithic faunal assemblage evidence is more problematic with regard to this model. To begin with, it must be stated that the animal-oriented aspect had only a very weak foundation in Madsen's original study. The background data employed are not published in the 1988 paper on causewayed enclosures, but are part of earlier (Madsen, T. 1982) and later (Madsen, T. 1990) publications by the same author. From these data it appears that Madsen did not use a single inventory for EN I in the construction of his model, but rather one from EN II. Furthermore, the latter assemblage from the Toftum enclosure only consists of 97 bones. Thus, these 97 bones form the entire basis for what Madsen's postulated as a dominance of pigs among domesticates in the first 500 years of the Neolithic. This is problematic not only because of the low number of samples and sample size, but also because Toftum is a causewayed enclosure. Faunal remains from such a site cannot be taken to reflect the everyday economy of the period, but might rather be more representative of feasts or other forms of ritual practice. It must be concluded that this part of Madsen's model is rather hypothetical. He does not present any data that could sustain a gradual shift from pigs to cattle throughout the Early Neolithic, despite the fundamental importance of this aspect to the emergence of causewayed enclosures within his model.

While not overtly abundant due to the acidic soils prevailing in South Scandinavia, today there is a number of faunal assemblages which shed light on the relative importance of cattle versus pigs and sheep/goat in the Early Neolithic. Almost all of these assemblages are very small, but they all point in the same direction and can therefore be assumed to provide a true impression of Neolithic domesticate trends.

Two Volling Group faunal assemblages have recently been published from sites in the area presently under investigation (Lisbjerg Skole and Lindegård Mose: Skousen 2008, 135 and 155 Fig. 118). Both are small and, thus, should not be overemphasized. Still, it is remarkable that both point towards cattle rather than pigs as the most important domesticate. A whole series of data point in the same direction

from other parts of Denmark. Domesticated pigs are absent from several sites with small assemblages which do include cattle (see data in Noe-Nygaard 1995; Noe-Nygaard et al. 2005; Bødker Enghoff 2011; Fischer/Gotfredsen 2006). The same picture emerges from north German assemblages (Siggeneben-Süd and Wangels (Heinrich 1999; Nobis 1983)) in which cattle and pigs appear either to be of equal importance (Siggeneben-Süd), or to have a dominant cattle contingent (Wangels). In a number of cases from Scania (Malmer 2002, 19ff.), it was not possible to differentiate between aurochs and cattle or wild boar and pig.

It appears, therefore, that cattle and not pigs were the dominate livestock even in the earliest part of the Neolithic. Noe-Nygaard et al. (2005) conducted a study which demonstrated the fact that the cattle grazed on natural meadows close to the fjords and thus explained why it was not necessary to clear forest for grazing grounds. Madsen's model of increasing inter-group tension leading to the construction of causewayed enclosures, however, was based on the idea that there was a heavy reliance on pigs with only a gradual shift towards cattle. The data available today have proven this assumption to be wrong. It is not possible to identify the reason for which forest clearings began to appear around 3700 BC with any degree of certainty, as both increasing agriculture, a lack of space for growing cattle herds and general population growth could explain this phenomenon.

9.3.5.4 Pottery styles

The revised chronology regarding the start of enclosure construction in South Scandinavia impacts Madsen's model, especially due to the fact that the development of homogenous pottery styles in ever-widening regions no longer appear to have been synchronous with the construction of enclosures. However, the change in pottery styles may have been a gradual process and the intensity of enclosure building may have increased towards EN II/MN A I. However, this trend question is impossible to evaluate due to the present lack of ^{14}C-dates. Therefore, Madsen's correlation between the development of pottery decoration styles and enclosure construction activity remains applicable, although future confirmation through an increased number of precisely dated enclosures (as well as a better understanding of the chronological aspects of pottery style evolution) are necessary steps to winnowing out the exact manner in which this change took place.

9.3.5.5 Settlement

The most problematic portion of Madsen's model relates to settlement development. His observations regarding the size increase of residential sites over the course of the Early and Middle Neolithic phases of the TRB are still valid (even though they are only applicable in parts of South Scandinavia). The same is true of the fact that coastal catching sites were largely abandoned in the later parts of the Early Neolithic. However, one important change took place at the same time as the construction of megaliths and enclosures: an enormous enlargement of the area settled by Neolithic groups in the interior (chapter 9.3.3). At the same time as stone chambers and causewayed enclosures were being built, large parts of the interior were settled for the first time by farming peoples. This phenomenon is not apparent from the mapping of known settlement sites (Madsen, T. 1982, 203 Fig. 3b). However, the distribution of megalithic tombs stretched deeply inland and clearly indicates that the interior of east Jutland was settled at this time (Fig. 1). The lack of settlements must be due to a lack of recording and may, therefore, reflect types of settlement that differed from those present nearer to the coast (unless one subscribes to the argument that the interior was exclusively a landscape of the dead).

That fact that a clear enlargement of the settled area was seen at the time when megalithic graves (and enclosures) were built is of great importance. It raises serious doubts regarding the validity of Madsen's model (which explains the creation of enclosures as the stress-induced result of a lack of sufficient land). Obviously, if this stress existed, the settled area could just as well have been enlarged settling new, hitherto non-exploited parts of the landscape (at least in the Neolithic). As far as it is possible to tell, this is exactly what happened.

Seen from this perspective, Madsen's model cannot explain the reasons for which enclosures were built despite the fact that the potential stress was relieved by an extension of settled area. Furthermore, it cannot explain why these monuments were not constructed in the interior, despite the inland presence of megalithic graves. According to scholars' general understanding (which is largely based on the work of N.H. Andersen in the Sarup area in addition to Madsen's studies), megalithic graves should be closely connected to the ritual activities which were conducted at the enclosures.

9.3.5.6 Enclosures and territories

With regard to the reconstruction of territories and the location and function of the enclosures therein, Madsen's work (1988) is clearly inspired by a study conducted by Renfrew (1973) in Sussex, southern Britain. Both Renfrew and Madsen describe what they interpret as group territories defined by clusters of grave monuments and enclosures that probably served as a central site. This idea can be traced back in British archaeology to the 1930s (Curwen 1938, 37). A comparable case is the "Calden model" developed by Raetzel-Fabian (1999; 2000 and see Meyer/Raetzel-Fabian 2006, 28 and Geschwinde/Raetzel-Fabian 2009, 241ff. for a modern reassessment), in which settlements and not grave monuments were connected to a central enclosure.

An important aspect regarding reconstructed territories is the assumed location of the enclosure therein. In Britain (Renfrew 1973 and a number of other authors – see Oswald et al. 2001, 34), the term 'central site' was understood as being related to an enclosure's position – naturally in the centre of a reconstructed territory. This assumption was taken over by Madsen for east Jutland (Fig. 1), but not by Raetzel-Fabian for northern central Germany. Based on an analysis of the surrounding landscape, Raetzel-Fabian argued that enclosures were likely situated at the periphery of a group's territory. This peripheral enclosure location in relation to reconstructed territories has also been part of a renewed interpretation of the available evidence by British researchers since the 1980s (Oswald et al.

2001, 34 with references to individual studies). It is assumed today that remote locations were chosen for enclosure construction, at least in the case of the enclosures located on high ground. They are no longer seen as belonging to individual groups, but are rather thought to have been communal efforts situated in neutral borderlands which served as meeting places for different groups (e.g. Thomas 1991, 33, 36; Oswald et al. 2001, 119). In northern central Germany, Raetzel-Fabian (Meyer/Raetzel-Fabian 2006, 28; Geschwinde Raetzel-Fabian 2009, 242 ff.) and Knoche (2013) have entirely abandoned the idea of fixed territories surrounding central enclosures. As was already mentioned, these authors assume that enclosures served as herd management facilities or were the site of cattle-based ritual activities used by mobile groups in seasonal events.

As is apparent from this overview, the idea that Danish enclosures were constructed by individual groups in the centre of their respective territories is based on older interpretations of English evidence which have been since laid aside. Of course, this does not necessarily mean that the model proposed for east Jutland cannot be maintained; individual evaluation is necessary in order to determine whether that model still holds water. After all, the natural environment of southern England (and northern central Germany) differs greatly from that in eastern Jutland (and other parts of South Scandinavia as well). Although remote and largely unsettled areas did exist in some parts of South Scandinavia, in general there is no evidence supporting the use of these areas in TRB times (see above). In Denmark, southern Sweden and northern Germany, enclosures were apparently constructed within densely settled (coastal) areas (and only there). In this way, they differed from their British and German counterparts. It could, thus, be argued that an entirely different interpretation is needed for a Scandinavian enclosure context. This would conflict with the numerous general resonances between Scandinavian, British and northern central German enclosures as well as the choice of enclosure sites adjacent to (long-distance) routes in all regions. It is necessary, therefore, to look at the Scandinavian evidence with fresh eyes and to

investigate whether or not Scandinavian enclosures were constructed in the centre of individual territories (as was originally proposed by Madsen). An alternative explanation would involve the location of South Scandinavian enclosures in border situations between group territories, although these borders could not have been located along the periphery of densely settled areas, as was the case for upland enclosures in southern England. One must also consider whether the enclosures were directly related to group territories at all.

In the general absence of unpopulated, remote space between the (near-coastal) settlement areas which potentially belonged to specific, individual groups, it is necessary to seek out and investigate other aspects that might cast light on the location of the potential borders between these groups. Madsen used the distribution of megalithic graves to this end. However, there are two severe drawbacks to this approach. The first is the source-critical issue which has already been mentioned numerous times; the present distribution of megalithic graves can in no way be taken to reflect the prehistoric pattern. The second involves Madsen's reconstruction of potential enclosure sites. While his postulate was well argued, his suggested inter-site distance of 8-10 km is significantly greater than the 3.5 km measured between the Toftum und Bjerggård enclosures. This shorter distance matches closely with other distances recorded both in Djursland and abroad and, therefore, must be assumed to be an approximate measure for typical inter-enclosure distance (between 4-6 km on average). However, this means that many potential enclosures were not predicted by Madsen. If these sites are slotted in between the postulated ones, this results in an average (and appropriate) inter-enclosure distance of 4-5 km. Interestingly, the additional sites are situated exactly at the borders between the territories Madsen drew.

Rather than megalithic graves, two alternative observations will be utilized as a means of engaging with the relation between enclosure sites and potential group territories: the proximity to river crossings and the proximity to fortifications which date from historic times. The fact that the location of Neolithic sites coincides in many cases with that of military installations postdating those sites by 4500 years can only be understood as a reflection of similar 'readings' of the landscape (i.e. examinations regarding the course of topographically- and hydrologically-determined natural borders). These were often wet areas or rivers. The fact that a distinct relation between river crossings and causewayed enclosures existed (both in South Scandinavia and abroad) was, therefore, probably indicative of these monuments' construction in border situations rather than in central locations. The Sarup enclosure(s) serve as perfect examples of this scenario, as they are situated close to the place at which an important road/path (both prehistoric, as denoted by the presence of grave mounds and historic, as demonstrated by the Videnskabernes Selskabs Kort) crossed a river. Nearby Medieval fortifications relating to this border situation are found on both sides of the river (Fig. 46). Another classical example is that of the Lokes Hede enclosure which lies at the end of the very long Mariager Fjord. The Mariager Fjord naturally divides the area into a northern and southern territory. The enclosure is situated at the exact location where the road between these two parts crossed a river which constituted the natural inland prolongation of the fjord border (Fig. 24).

It can, thus, be concluded that, as was the case in southern Britain and northern central Germany, the sites chosen for enclosure construction in South Scandinavia were probably not located in the centre of areas claimed by specific groups, but were more likely located in border situations. In the densely populated coastal areas of South Scandinavia, this would in many cases have concerned locations directly bordered by settlements. However, just as in Britain and northern central Germany, some locations were probably more peripheral. This was especially applicable in terms of the (possibly occasionally flooded enclosures) at Gammeltoft Odde and Ballegård, both of which are located at very low elevations in fjords (or a lake in the case of Gammeltoft Odde). These locations were probably relatively remote from the core settlement area in their respective regions.

An additional argument in favour of the border location of enclosures (and, thus, the participation of different groups in their construction and use) is discussed in the following. The reduction in number of South Scandinavian regional ceramic groups (in MN A Ib, they coalesced into a single group) reflects not only the operation of very strict rules regarding shape and decoration of pottery (which could have had some symbolic meaning with regard to the regulation of relationships between groups, as postulated by Madsen), but also reflects the existence of a very effective communication system which stretched over hundreds of kilometres. This system was likely one in which each group participated in strictly regulated social interactions with several different groups on various sites along its borders. In the form proposed here, it certainly would have been very effective in creating a communicative network which stretched over large distances without necessitating that individuals or groups cross the borders of their own territories. In this way, enclosures would have served as the nodes along a communication network. The fact that the ovens which are known to have been used in the production of ceramics have all have been found in causewayed enclosures (Store Brokhøj: Madsen, B./ Fiedel 1988; Sarup: Andersen, N.H. 1976, 15f.; Stävie: Larsson, L. 1982, 68f., 88f.; possibly Lokes Hede: Birkedahl 1988 and Büdelsdorf: Bjørn/Hingst 1973; Hage in press; Haßmann 2000, 28) or sites related to causewayed enclosures (Triwalk in Mecklenburg: Jantzen 2005; Müller, J./Staude 2012) supports such an interpretation, as has already been noted by S. Nielsen (1999, 133).

Taking into consideration the short distances between enclosures (again, typically 4-5 km), it is necessary to reflect on the nature of the areas located in between. The use of the word 'territory' tends to favour an interpretation in which the space was claimed by a group which was genealogically and ethnically cohesive. Although this is very difficult to prove, comparison with better-illustrated examples from England and Germany as well as additional observations or evidence concerning the existence of an effective communication network would lend weight to this conclusion. According to the present state of knowledge, settlement in South Scandinavia at the time in question was characterised by single farms that were likely home to an extended family of ca. 10 persons (at least in the western parts of Denmark). The farms in question lasted only a short time (maybe 20 to 30 years). After their short use-life, instead of repairing or building a new house on the same site, people moved on to another place at which they built another (new) house. Just how many settlement units of this type existed at the same time in the 'territory' delimited by enclosures is unknown. The settlements are characterised by their small size and thin artefact scatters, which naturally also renders them difficult to identify.

The fact that the same inter-enclosure distances are present in different parts of Europe is a reason to doubt the simplistic equation of inter-enclosure space with group territory. If this association should prove to have been correct, then comparable group structures would have to be postulated for all areas involved. The existence of such comparable structures could be claimed for South Scandinavia and England, as both areas seem to have experienced comparable and contemporary neolithisation events. It could thus be postulated that comparable group structures formed in the two regions over time. However, such a hypothesis would ignore one important way in which these two regions differed: Scandinavian coastal areas probably exhibited comparatively high population density, whereas the population of England was likely to have been much more dispersed. Whether comparable group structures would have emerged in both regions is doubtful, even despite their related neolithisation history. Furthermore, history of Neolithic settlement in northern central Germany diverged greatly from those in England and South Scandinavia insofar as it emerged some 1500 years prior. Regardless of the start date of Neolithic settlement, the same inter-enclosure distances can be observed in all three regions.

The examples referred to above cannot exclude the possibility that the typical inter-enclosure distance related to a specific group structure within Neolithic society. However, at present no evidence supports this view. It is possible that the social organisation of Neolithic groups within the three geographic regions differed in spite of the fact that comparable enclosure spacing was present. This must be kept in mind when discussing causewayed enclosures. At present, it must be concluded that the space between two enclosures cannot be positively identified as the representation of a group's territory.

Geschwinde and Raetzel-Fabian (2009, 243) queried the source of the manpower necessary to construct monumental enclosures at 5 km distances from each other (said distance can be equated with an hour's walk). According to them, the population inhabiting an area of the size in question would not have been able to mobilise a sufficient labour force for such an endeavour. While this may be true, one should not underestimate the amount of resources mobilised by persons with religious motivations. The authors cited here themselves refer to Medieval gothic cathedrals. However, the context under discussion here might best be compared to 'simple' parish churches. In 12th century Denmark, there was a boom in the construction of such houses of worship. In many regions, the distances between such parish churches are not unlike those encountered between Neolithic causewayed enclosures. The tens of thousands of megalithic graves which were constructed during the same period as the enclosures give witness to a Neolithic population that was able to invest a great deal of time in non-subsistence activities.

In summary, it must be concluded that it is not possible at present to decide whether the population of an area that could be traversed in an hour would have been able to mobilise the workforce necessary to construct an enclosure in the Neolithic. Given that these monuments could have been located (at least theoretically) along the borderlines between social groups, they could have represented the communal efforts of two distinct, neighbouring social entities. However, as each group in such a scenario would have been involved in the construction of at least two enclosures, the labour force necessary for construction would have been the same as or larger than that necessary to construct an entire enclosure alone. Keeping in mind those examples of ritual sites in the European Neolithic which involved people from very large regions (see above) as well as the position of causewayed enclosures along (long-distance) routes, it is equally plausible to suggest that people from much larger areas participated in the construction of the individual sites. People settling along the roads (as well as those living at considerable distance to them) may have been involved. These observations also cast doubt on the idea of a direct relationship between enclosures and group territories.

In summary, therefore, it must be concluded that the equivalent distances observed between enclosures in different parts of Europe, the rather close spacing of the enclosures and the European evidence suggesting that groups from distant places participated in the construction and use of enclosures all cast doubt on the general identification of the space between individual enclosures as group territories. At present, however, the state of research is such that it is not possible to entirely rule out this possibility for South Scandinavia.

9.3.5.7 Conclusion

As was apparent from the discussion of its individual aspects, Madsen's model for the creation of causewayed enclosures in South Scandinavia no longer conforms to the state of research as it stands at present. Basic assumptions – especially regarding the importance of different species of domesticates which play a key role in Madsen's model – have recently been proven incorrect. Furthermore, Madsen's general assumption that the construction of enclosures was a means of resolving the stress caused by land scarcity is unconvincing. A considerable enlargement of the area settled by early farmers occurred at the same time in which enclosures where constructed. Finally, the idea that inter-enclosure space was a reflection of group territories must be questioned. Enclosures were almost certainly constructed in border situations rather than in the central parts of potential territories.

At this point, it is not yet possible to formulate an alternative to Madsen's theory which would encompass all of the aspects involved. What can

be stated, however, is the fact that enclosures were constructed at regular 5 km intervals along long-distance routes. These routes were exclusively located in areas that were settled by early farmers prior to the start of enclosure construction around 3700 BC. At least some of the routes probably held some specific ritual significance (possibly related to an ancestor cult). The frequent presence of human bones in the enclosures may be one aspect of this ancestor cult. The inter-enclosure distances observed equal approximately one hour's travel by foot and cannot be certainly correlated to group territories. Still, enclosures appear to have been built in naturally-defined border regions that (at least in some cases) may have represented the edges of social territories. The workforces that built the enclosures, however, could have emerged from a much larger area than just the one encompassing a swathe of territory which measured approximately 20 km². The production of pottery and flint axes in the enclosures probably at least partly reflected some aspects of ritual communication. However, not all activities at the sites were necessarily of ritual character. As was already mentioned, the use of the large Late Mesolithic and Early Neolithic coastal fishing sites discontinued after ca. 3600 BC (Andersen, S.H. 2008, 71). This was approximately at the same time when enclosure construction began. As described by Johansen (2006), these coastal sites may have witnessed large seasonal gatherings of social importance in the earliest parts of the Neolithic. Causewayed enclosures may thus have subsequently fulfilled some of the social functions previously bound to such large fishing sites. Such continuity could represent at least part of the explanation for the clear dominance of coastal and near-coastal enclosures.

While the above observations cast light on a number of different aspects of causewayed enclosures, they do not address the reasons for which these monuments first began to be built. This problem can only be addressed in a European context, as was indicated by the surprising and numerous parallels which exist between South Scandinavian enclosures and comparable monuments abroad.

10 Scandinavian enclosures from a European perspective

So far, an alternative to T. Madsen's (1988) model has been presented, albeit only with regards to enclosure location and function (and then only in part). However, one major aspect related to these monuments is obviously the question of why they were built in South Scandinavia in the first place. The present stage of research suggests that Madsen's explanation is unlikely and that alternatives must be sought. Causewayed enclosures are obviously not South Scandinavian inventions. Large numbers of closely-related and (in many cases) older sites of this type are known from large parts of Central and Western Europe. In a number of instances, specific similarities between Scandinavian, German, English and French enclosures have been briefly addressed above. These aspects of superregional significance are investigated in the following (among other subjects) in order to evaluate whether enclosure construction in South Scandinavia may have been initiated by developments from the outside.

As described above, Madsen recognized the European background of South Scandinavian enclosures, but explained their appearance in Scandinavia exclusively in terms of local economic and intergroup relational developments. According to his view, the enclosure concept was known by Early Neolithic societies in the region right from the start. However, it was only implemented when the need arose locally. This idea has clearly been influenced by the processual approach typical for some parts of Danish archaeological research in in the 1980s. Such approaches tended to favour factors inherent

to what were perceived to have been local cultural systems at the expense of external agencies. As a result, the role of Neolithic groups abroad in inter-Scandinavian cultural change was reduced to those of secondary characters who conveniently entered the stage only at the behest of local protagonists. Much the same situation is visible in the Scandinavian discussion of the Mesolithic-Neolithic transition from that period (Klassen 1999; 2004). The following text addresses the available evidence for and against this view with regard to causewayed enclosures. Additionally it presents an alternative view.

10.1 Parallels between Scandinavian and other European enclosures: An overview

Taking into account the abundant evidence for intense contact and interaction between South Scandinavia and Central and Western Europe in the Neolithic (especially in the Early Neolithic), arguments exclusively based on the assumption of local agencies as agents of change are difficult to sustain. This is true both with regard to the process of neolithisation as well as the introduction of causewayed enclosures. Therefore, a short overview of obvious parallels between enclosures in South Scandinavia and those in Western and Central Europe is included below. Only a short description is included for the cases that were discussed elsewhere in this text. However, some additional aspects are discussed in more detail. The main emphasis is placed on aspects of chronology and architecture, as these are best suited to uncovering the reasons for which enclosures were first built in South Scandinavia at a particular point in time. To this end, the following common traits can be identified:

Inter enclosure distance: As described earlier (chapter 6.3.1), causewayed enclosures in many parts of Europe appear to have been constructed at fairly regular 5 km intervals, a distance which corresponds on average to an hour's walk.

Relation to routes: As became apparent in chapter 6.3.2, causewayed enclosures in many parts of Europe were constructed along routes of which the majority were of superregional importance. These routes included both roads/tracks on land as well as rivers or fjords.

Alternating positions along watercourses: As was described in chapter 8.3.1, the enclosures that were built along watercourses in different regions of Europe can often be found on alternating sides. This probably indicates that they were related to water transport rather than to travel on the roads/ tracks which ran parallel to the watercourses.

Position at crossroads: As described in chapter 6.3.2.1, there are convincing indications that Neolithic causewayed enclosures were often constructed at or near to crossroads both in Central Europe and South Scandinavia.

Construction of twin enclosures: Chapter 6.3.2.1 includes examples of enclosures which were built directly opposite each other or within each other's line of sight. Examples of such sites are known from both South Scandinavia and Central Europe. As argued by Knoche (2013, 218f.), these spatial arrangements were likely related to specific ritual ideas.

Construction of causewayed enclosures in positions bordered by water: While the position of enclosures close to rivers in all parts of Western, Central and Northern Europe could have been

grounded in simple, practical reasons, this was certainly not the case for the sites that were periodically inundated, either by the sea or by rivers (see chapter 6.1 and below chapter 10.2.8). This is evidenced by the enclosures that were located on shallow elevations completely (or mostly) surrounded by water. Some of these locations (e.g. Gammeltoft Odde in western Jutland (Troldtoft Andresen 2013) and Lillemer in Brittany (Laporte et al. 2007)) are characterised by strikingly similar topographical settings that can hardly have been coincidental.

Relation to later fortifications: Chapter 6.3.4 described occasions in which South Scandinavian causewayed enclosures showed close spatial relations to sites upon which military fortifications were constructed several millennia later, i.e. in early historic times (Viking Age and Middle Ages). The same or comparable observations were made in both southern Britain and Germany.

Few artefacts in construction time layers: In South Scandinavia (see chapter 9.3 and discussion below), the lowest layers in enclosure ditches are very often either completely devoid of deposited material, or contained very few (often uncharacteristic) artefacts. Comparable observations are available from Britain (Bayliss et al. 2011, 716) and northern central Germany (Raetzel-Fabian 1999, 89).

Deposition of human remains: The deposition of human remains in causewayed enclosures is a much-discussed topic, especially in the distribution area of the Michelsberg Culture and the British Early Neolithic (e.g. Seidel 2008, 378ff.; Oswald et al. 2001, 126f.; Andersen, N.H. 1997, 190ff.). Disarticulated bones which often show signs of secondary manipulation are regularly discovered, entire skeletons are infrequent. Due to the acidic soils prevalent in South Scandinavia, skeletal evidence from this region is sparse. However, human remains have been described from at least nine different sites (Sarup I and II, Blakbjerg, Kainsbakke, Hygind, Ballegård, Sigersted III, Bundsø and Åsum Enggård). With a single exception, a few badly preserved and partly burnt bones have been recovered. However, bone preservation at Hygind is excellent. Part of a human skull with traces of secondary manipulation (cutting marks) was found there (Andersen, N.H. 1997, 273 with Fig. 287; 1987; 1988; 1989).

Deposition of animals: Due to the conditions of preservation, the same problems as those described for human remains apply to animal bones. However, at Hygind (Andersen, N.H. 1988), Bjerggård (Madsen, T. 1988, 310) and Kainsbakke (L. Wincentz Rasmussen, personal communication), collections of bones sorted by species have been documented. Comparable observations have been made at a number of British enclosures (Andersen, N.H. 1997, 255) as well as at Michelsberg sites (Andersen, N.H. 1997, 193).

Re-cutting and backfilling: Actions including the deliberate backfilling and re-cutting of enclosure ditches have been observed across the entire distribution area of causewayed enclosures. As a rule, there is little naturally deposited silt at the bottom of the ditches; therefore, it is often suggested that ditches must have been backfilled shortly after they were excavated. The number of detailed accounts regarding this specific trait is limited. The level of documentation necessary for such observations is not present at all excavations. As prominent examples for deliberate backfilling, the Sarup enclosures in Denmark (Andersen, N.H. 1997) and the Calden enclosure in northern central Germany (Raetzel-Fabian 2000) can be cited. Slower rates of (natural) infilling have also been observed in various regions, nevertheless (Seidel 2008, 377ff.; Bayliss et al. 2011, 706ff.).

Violence: A particularly striking observation concerns acts of violence at causewayed enclosures. Bayliss et al. (2011, 716f.) recently classified abundant British evidence into three classes: inter-personal violence (determined by trauma on human bones), collective violence (demonstrated

by large amounts of arrowheads indicating some kind of battle), and traces of extensive burning. Exactly these observations have also been made in different parts of Central Europe as well as in South Scandinavia. For example, extensive traces of destructive fires have been recorded at the Michelsberg site of Heilbronn-Klingenberg "Schlossberg" (Seidel 2008) in southwest Germany and at Albersdorf Dieksknöll in northern Germany (Dibbern 2011; 2012).

Huge amounts of arrowheads attesting to assaults by larger groups are known from the Altheim enclosure in Bavaria (Driehaus 1960) and from the Büdelsdorf enclosure in northern Germany (Haßmann 2000, 110ff., 175), among others. Trauma on human bones are frequently recorded for Michelsberg Culture enclosures (Seidel 2008, 379). Unfortunately, in South Scandinavia, this aspect cannot be properly evaluated, due to poor bone preservation and the possible lack of adequate investigation and publication for the remains which actually are present. However, two specific artefact types known from Scandinavian enclosures may well testify to inter-personal violence. Flint halberds are known from seven causewayed enclosures: Sarup I (Andersen, N.H. 1997), Toftum (Madsen, T. 1978a), Markildegård (Østergård Sørensen 1995b), Blakbjerg (Boas 2001), Rastorf (Steffens 2009), Bad Segeberg (Guldin 2011) and Büdelsdorf (Haßmann 2000). Such finds (Ebbesen 1994; Lübke 1999) are extremely rare on settlements. Ebbesen (1994) only lists two such finds from Barkær (Liversage 1992) and Fannerup (Eriksen 1984). As was earlier intimated, it is possible that the Fannerup site represents an enclosure (see chapter 3). Given the fact that many more settlements are known in the region than causewayed enclosures (and that investigations of enclosures often have been very restricted in size), this count is striking, as is the fact that the halberds from enclosures are almost all fragmented. Furthermore, fragments of stone maceheads were discovered in the enclosures of Sarup I (Andersen, N.H. 1997, 61 Fig. 72m), Toftum (Madsen, T. 1978a, 176f. Fig. 12b) and Blakbjerg (Boas 2001, 7 Fig. 9). Interestingly, at

Toftum, a single complete item was also recovered. This type of artefact is completely unknown from other contexts. Both artefact groups can be classified as weapons suited for close, personal combat and may thus well indicate the presence of inter-personal violence at causewayed enclosures. Their general scarcity may reflect (ritualised) one-on-one clubbing/stabbing as known from the Yanonamo in Brazil (see Whittle et al. 2011b, 896 with discussion and references).

The list of similarities in the construction and use as well as the perception of these sites by contemporary Neolithic communities, while certainly incomplete, is both long and (in some respects) also very specific. The means by which these striking similarities came to be needs further discussion. In this regard, T. Madsen's (1988) proposal that the enclosure concept was adapted to local South Scandinavian conditions by means of an exclusively locally-controlled process of enclosure introduction into Scandinavia is not immediately convincing. Therefore, specific aspects of enclosure architecture and chronology are investigated below on a European scale in order to re-evaluate the causes behind their introduction into Scandinavia as well as the feasibility of a functional adaption to local conditions. The modest state of research in South Scandinavia as well as the poor preservation conditions for organic material (especially bone) somewhat restricts these efforts. Nonetheless, as will be demonstrated, some aspects of interest and explanatory power can be addressed in a meaningful way.

10.2 Aspects of enclosure architecture

The causewayed enclosures of South Scandinavia have never been investigated with regards to their possible relations to enclosures in other parts of Europe. Although it took steps in that direction, N.H. Andersen's (1997, 267) work remains on a fairly general level, resulting in the recognition of TRB enclosures as belonging to an architectural tradition characterised by segmented ditches. This tradition, however, can be found in enclosure constructions

in large parts of Western and Central Europe. The comparison of the sites of the TRB North Group with those in Britain, France, Belgium and Germany, for example, is clearly hampered by the low number of complete site plans available from South Scandinavia. Therefore, it is hard to recognize those enclosure types characterised by a specific overall design, such as was done by Geschwinde & Raetzel-Fabian (2009, 212, Abb. 157) in Central Europe. Still, a few architectural traits from better-published sites are suitable for the present purpose and are, therefore, discussed below in detail. These traits comprise specific entrance constructions and the design and outlay of rows of segmented ditches.

The following uses approximately 400 comparable sites from Western, Central and Eastern Europe for comparison with TRB North Group enclosures. The selection of these sites was guided by chronology and enclosure type. In general, it comprises all sites built between ca. 4700 BC and 3200 BC in a region stretching from Ireland and western France to southeast Poland. Tor enclosures from southwest Britain were also included, due to their clear relation to causewayed enclosures. However, in terms of the earliest enclosures, only those belonging to the same general architectural tradition as TRB sites (i.e. with segmented ditches) were included. In like fashion, those of what Central European colleagues would call the Middle Neolithic were excluded (Grossgartach, Rössen, Oberlauterbach, Lengyel Culture proper). From the latter region, only enclosures from the late 5th millennium onwards (a broad definition of what one might call 'late Lengyel') were included in this study. At the opposite end of the time frame, none of the numerous enclosures built after the Central European Baalberge Group (the numerous enclosures of the Bernburg and Cham Cultures, among others) were taken into consideration, as they were constructed after TRB North Group enclosures. The only possible exception are a few Salzmünde enclosures, which might have been built around 3300 BC. However, the only of these enclosures that has been reliably dated (Salzmünde-Schiepzig: Meller/Schunke 2013, 352) postdates the timeframe relevant here. Therefore, all four certain or possible

Salzmünde enclosures have been omitted. Furthermore, the numerous enclosures of the Peu Richard and Taizé Groups in central western France (Néolithique récent II) have not been mapped because it is not possible at present to differentiate between those built before 3200 BC and those built between 3200 and 2900 BC (see Ard 2011 for a discussion of chronology). The appendix provides an overview of the sites selected.

10.2.1 Enclosures with three or more (partial) ditch circuits

Geschwinde & Raetzel-Fabian (2009, 245) have recognized a regionally restricted distribution of enclosures with three circuits of segmented ditches in northern central Germany. They interpreted this to be a reflection of a specific tradition, either of construction or cultic use, which differed from those of other enclosures with single or double ditch circuits. In the following, the South Scandinavian evidence is surveyed in order to investigate whether or not comparable conclusions can be reached.

Five cases of superimposed or directly neighbouring causewayed enclosures with two (partial) ditch circuits are presently known within Denmark. The Sarup I and II enclosures are placed on top of each other (Fig. 85), the Vasagård east and Vasagård west sites are situated directly opposite to each other on opposing riverbanks (Fig. 15), the Mølbjerg I and Mølbjerg II enclosures oppose each other on either side of a prehistoric road/path (see chapter 6.3.2.1 with Fig. 22) and the Starup Langelandsvej and Lønt enclosures (Lützau Pedersen/Witte 2012, 87) were constructed a scant 700 m from each other (Fig. 34). Finally, the Mølbjerg II enclosure appears to have had two separate, superimposed phases (unpublished; information kindly provided by L. Helles Olesen). Despite the fact that this can be demonstrated conclusively only at those enclosures that can be ordered via a vertical stratigraphic sequence (Sarup I/II and the two phases of Mølbjerg II), the five examples listed above could all reflect chronological construction sequences (see also Lützau Pedersen/Witte 2012, 87 for Starup Langelandsvej/Lønt). However, as discussed ear-

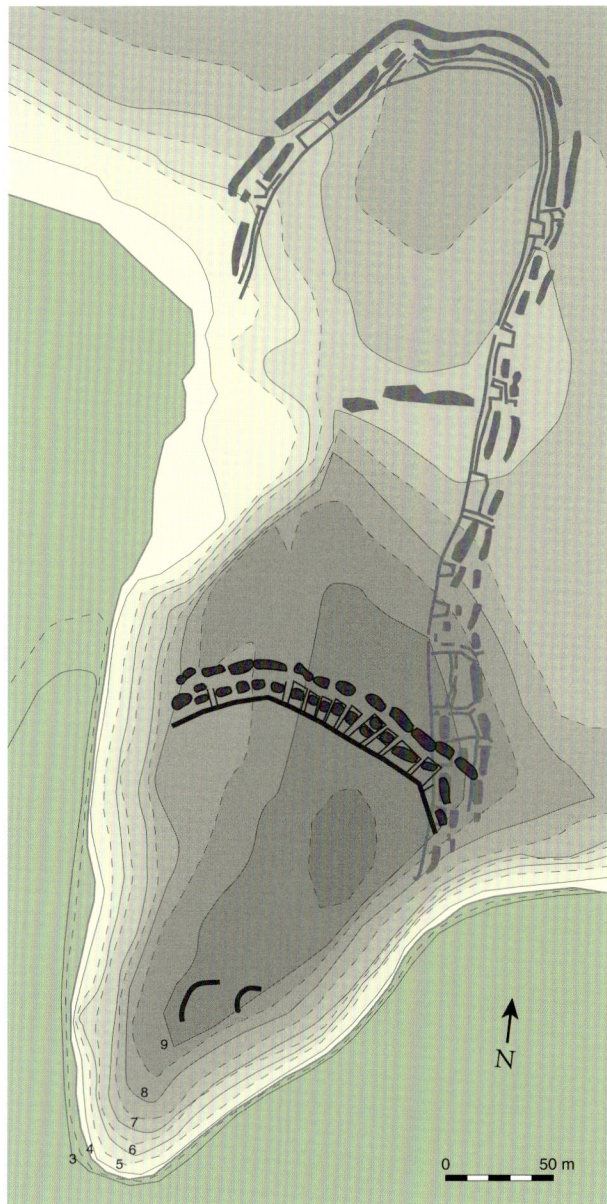

Fig. 85 | *Two enclosures were built on the same promontory at Sarup. The first, larger enclosure of Sarup I was constructed ca. 3400 BC. It is approximately 200 years older than the smaller enclosure of Sarup II. The latter partly overlaps the ditches, palisade and fences which belong to Sarup I (redrawn from Andersen 1997).*

lier, the twin aspect of these sites also signals partial contemporaneity. With regard to the present investigation, it is important to note that, in all cases, new enclosures were built in their entirety rather than appending an extra (third) ditch circuit to a pre-existing enclosure. The enclosures that consist

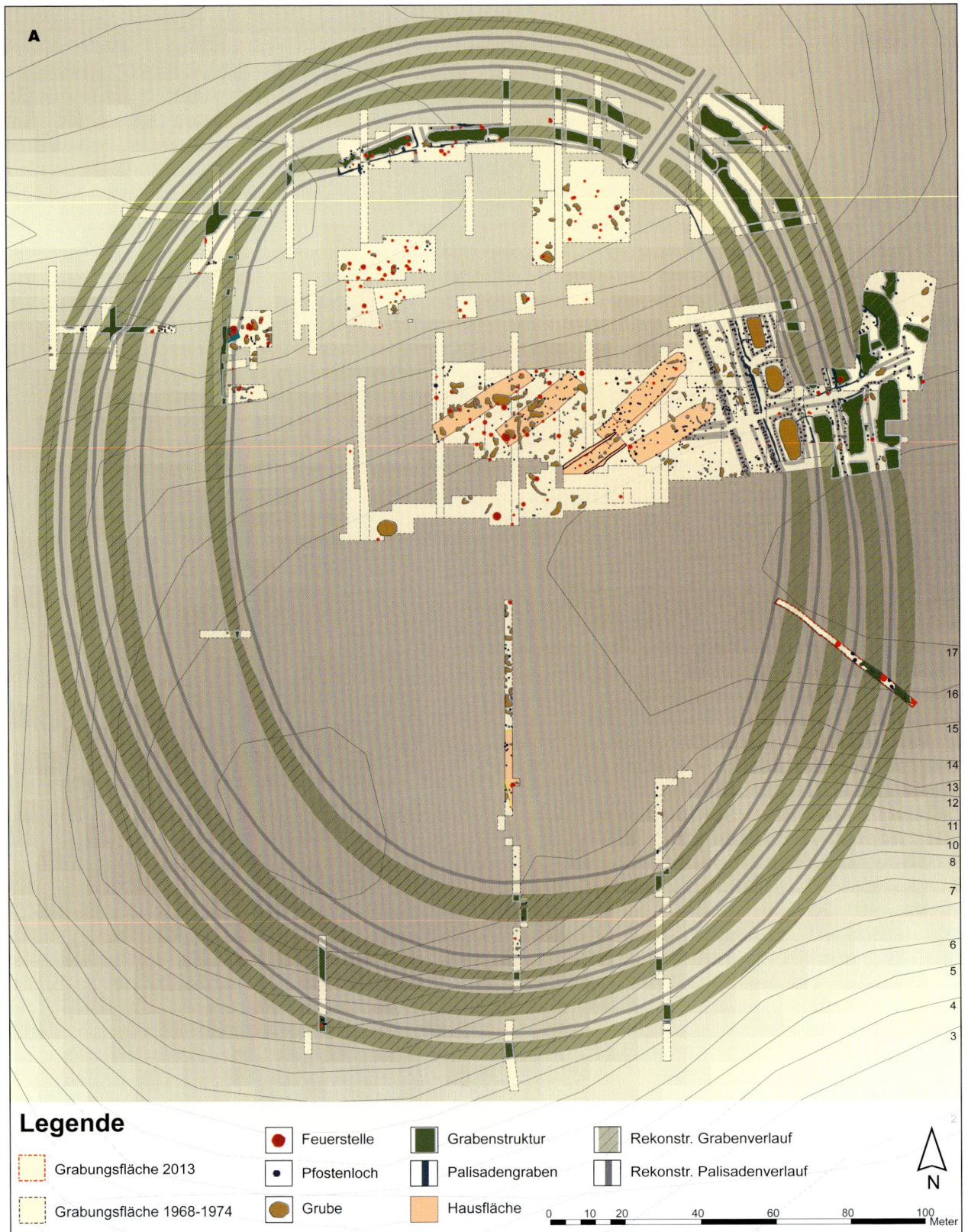

A

Legende

🔴 Feuerstelle	
• Pfostenloch	
🟤 Grube	

Grabungsfläche 2013

Grabungsfläche 1968-1974

🟢 Grabenstruktur	
▮ Palisadengraben	
🟧 Hausfläche	

Rekonstr. Grabenverlauf

Rekonstr. Palisadenverlauf

0   10   20   40   60   80   100
Meter

N

of three or even more ditch circuits, therefore, cannot be explained as the simple result of a longer use life in comparison to those that have only one or two. The examples discussed above indicate that the construction of a third ditch circuit was purposefully avoided. In other words, enclosures with more than two ditch circuits must reflect a specific choice and architectural tradition.

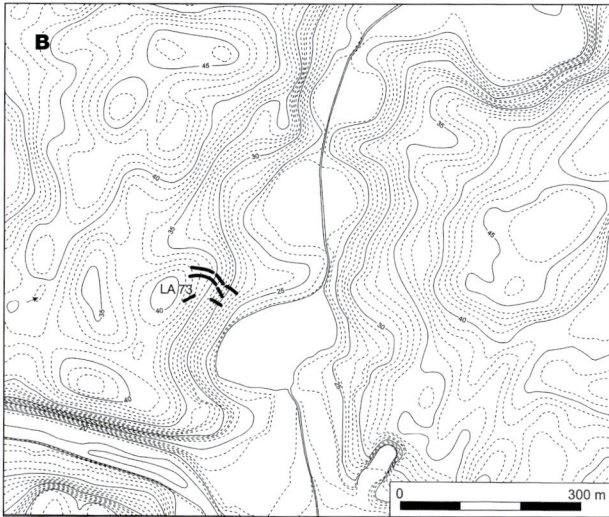

Fig. 86 | *Enclosures with more than two ditch circuits in South Scandinavia. A) (opposite page) Büdelsdorf (from Hage 2014, B) Rastorf (from Steffens 2009).*

In South Scandinavia, only two of the 39 (including the Assenbakke site) known enclosures have more than two ditch circuits: Büdelsdorf and Rastorf (Fig. 86). It could be argued that the size of the area excavated in a number of Danish cases was too small to exclude the presence of more than the recognized one or two ditch circuits. However, this was only rarely the case (less than five). The distribution of enclosures with three or more ditch circuits – which exclusively appear in the southern (i.e. north German) portion of the overall distribution area – likely reflects prehistoric reality rather than the state of research (Fig. 87). One must ask whether the exclusive presence of such sites near the southern periphery of the overall TRB North Group enclosure distribution area might reflect specific relations to neighbouring groups outside the latter zone. As demon-

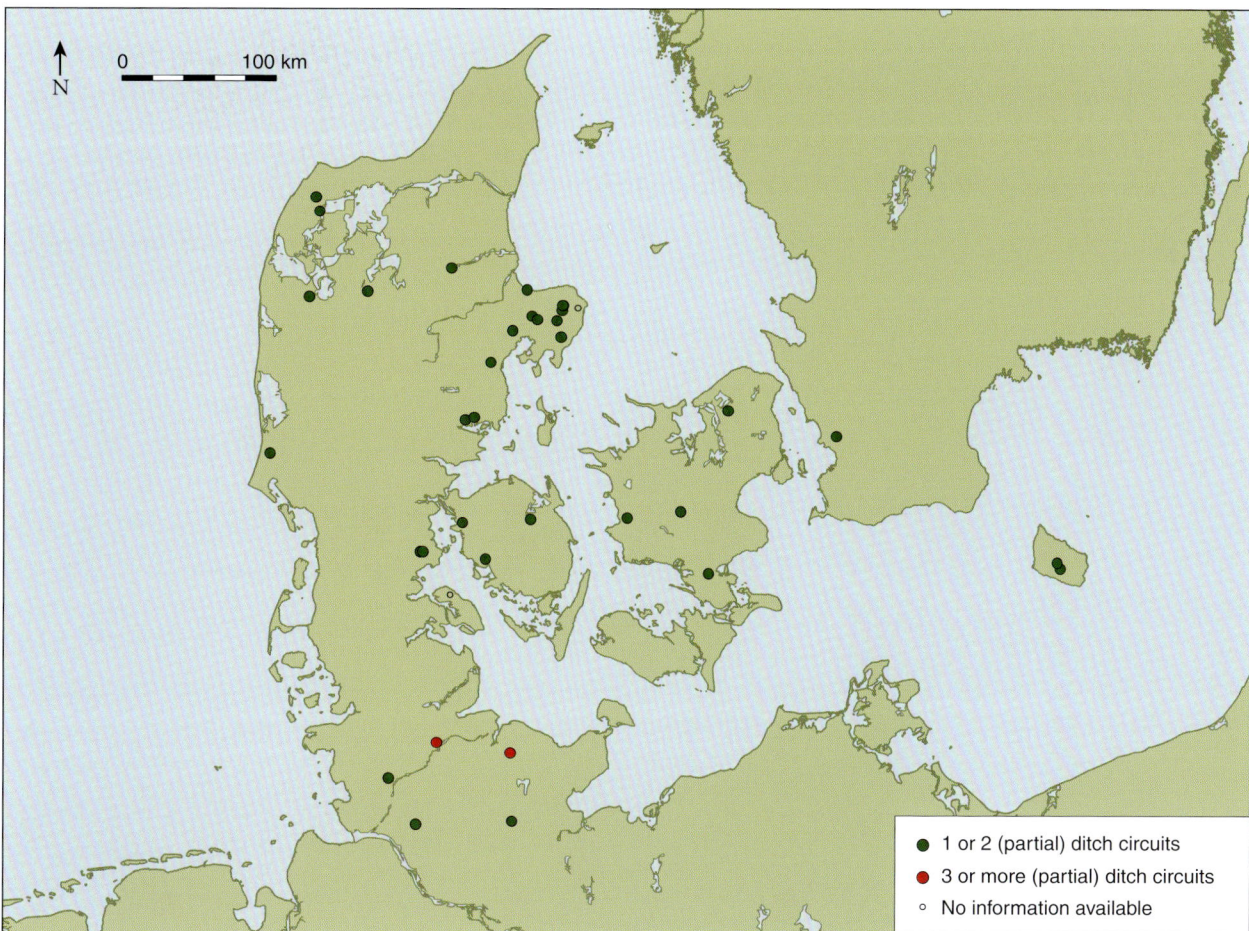

Fig. 87 | *The distribution of enclosures with one or two (partial) ditch circuits and of enclosures with three or more (partial) ditch circuits in South Scandinavia.*

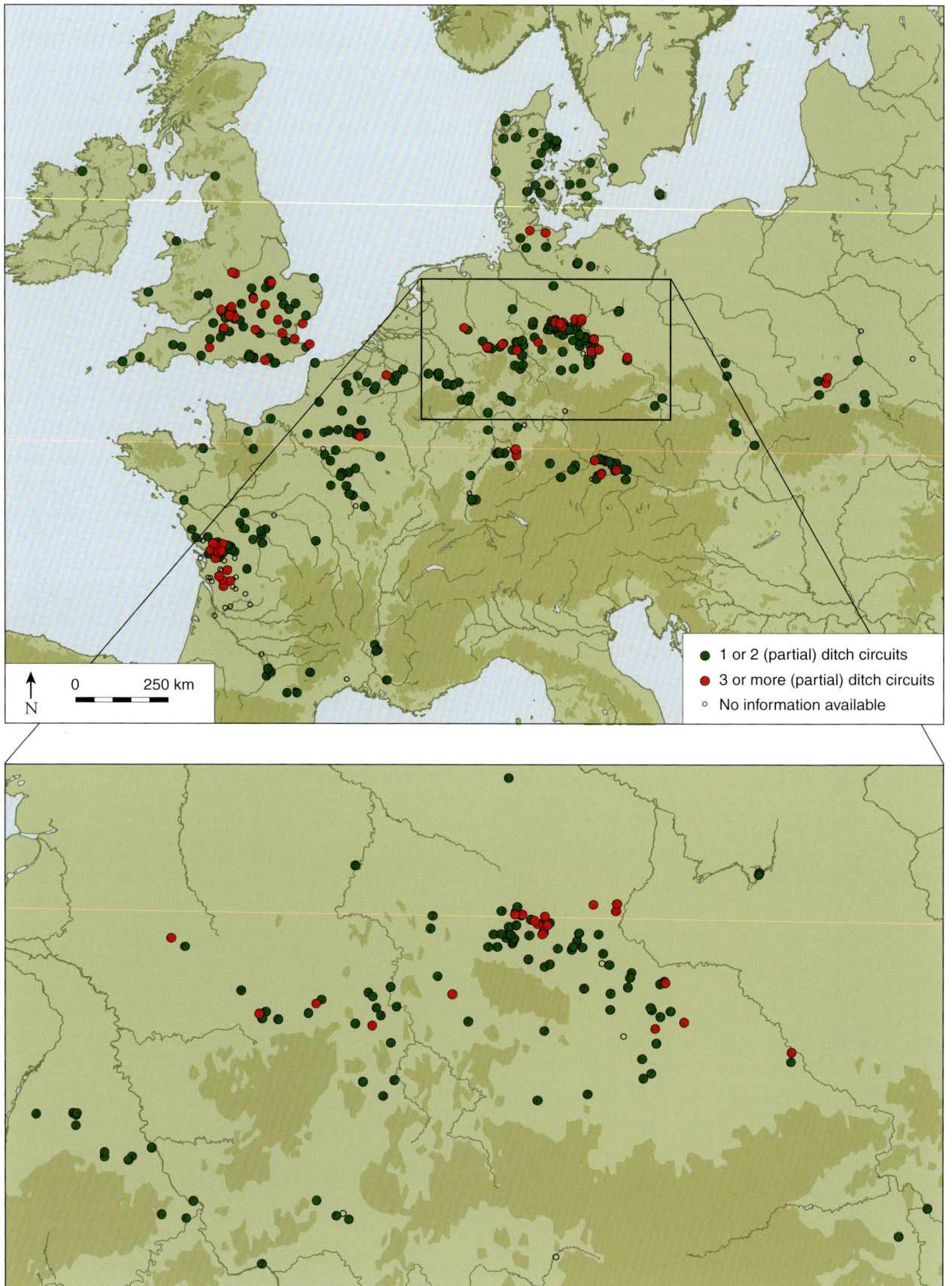

Fig. 88 | *The distribution of enclosures with one or two ditch circuits and of enclosures with three or more (partial) ditch circuits in Europe. Regarding the overall selection of mapped sites, see the text.*

strated by the European distribution map (Fig. 88), this is likely to have been the case.

The overwhelming majority of all European causewayed enclosures have either a single or double (partial) ditch circuits. Among the 457 enclosures contained in the study (including the TRB sites), 328 (71.8%) belong to this group. In 64 cases (14.0%), no information regarding the number of ditch circuits was available. Three or more circuits of ditches have been demonstrated for 65 (14.2%) of the sites. Mapping demonstrates that these were not evenly distributed. In many regions, enclosures of this type are exceptions rather than the rule. However, clear concentrations are present in central western France close to the Atlantic coast, in southern Britain and in northern central Germany. In Britain, a regional differentiation with a clear-cut border is visible between the east and west including Wales, Devon, Cornwall (including Tor enclosures) and Ireland. Such a border may also have been present in central western France. Enclosures with three or more circuits appeared regularly throughout the region, but those with only one or two circuits appear to be restricted to the northern parts. However, no information was available for a comparatively large number of sites in the south. Thus, the picture may change once this information becomes available.

The distribution of enclosures with different numbers of ditch circuits strengthens the conclusions made above. Enclosures with three or more circuits obviously constitute a distinct class of monument rather than the products of chance.

Neither those enclosures in western France nor in southern Britain can be related to the two sites at the southern periphery of the TRB North Group distribution area. However, this does appear to be possible for the enclosures which are presently known between Westphalia and the Elbe River, especially those north of the Harz Mountains in Lower Saxony. As Geschwinde & Raetzel-Fabian (2009) already recognized, these sites form a distinct cluster. This discovery is rather remarkable, as the area in question is the one closest to the TRB enclosures. It is also part of the area from which originated a large number of different items which had been exchanged with South Scandinavia since Ertebølle

times (Klassen 2004, 105ff.). Furthermore, it is either very close to (or part of) the region that played a key role in the neolithisation of South Scandinavia several hundred years before the start of enclosure construction. This is apparent from clear typological links between the Michelsberg ceramics found in the area and the earliest TRB ceramics in South Scandinavia (Klassen 2004, 148ff.). These multiple strings of evidence possibly indicate long-lasting contact between South Scandinavia and the region to the north and west of the Harz Mountains (potentially including areas further to the west, albeit to a minor degree). Therefore, there is reason to believe that the construction of causewayed enclosures with more than two ditch circuits in the southern part of the TRB North Group distribution area was due to contact with this specific region in north Germany. There is some evidence suggesting that migration from the southern parts of Lower Saxony and (possibly) eastern parts of Westphalia was a potential cause for South Scandinavian neolithisation (Klassen 2004, 318; Klassen in press; Sørensen/Karg in press). The construction of causewayed enclosures with three or more circuits of segmented ditches in Schleswig-Holstein could, therefore, have resulted from occasions in which the descendants of the first colonists maintained contact with their forebears' home areas, especially in the Harz region. According to Anthony (1990, 902ff.), this kind of contact is typical for long-distance migrations. However, as described above, even if no migration should have taken place at the time of neolithisation, close connections between the regions in question can be demonstrated (and could thus account for the appearance of causewayed enclosures with three or more ditch circuits at the southern periphery of the TRB North Group's distribution area).

These enclosures in northern central Germany can be dated to the late Michelsberg Culture (MK V) and Baalberg Group, i.e. ca. 3700-3500 BC (Geschwinde/Raetzel-Fabian 2009). Unfortunately, the time of construction is unknown for both the Büdelsdorf and the Rastorf enclosures. The datings referred to above for the counterparts with three or more ditch circuits from northern central Germany line up with those from the oldest known

A

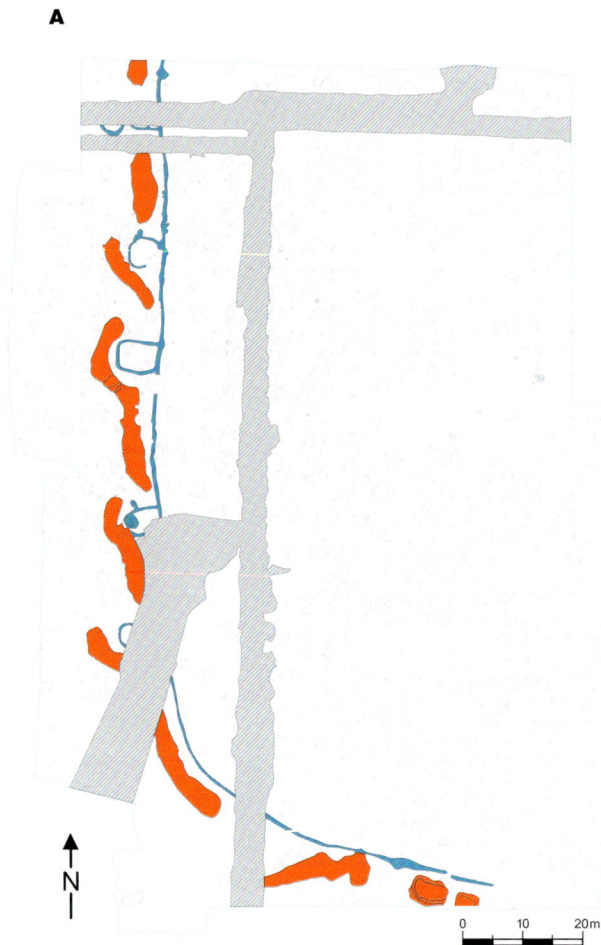

Scandinavian enclosures (Albersdorf Dieksknöll and Starup Langelandsvej). Büdelsdorf and Rastorf, therefore, can be assumed to be of the same age (or slightly younger) than the northern central European sites. However, this statement should be confirmed by new investigations at Büdelsdorf (the Rastorf site has been completely destroyed by gravel extraction).

10.2.2 Enclosures with clavicle-type ditch segments and rectangular palisade annexes

The Starup Langelandsvej site in southern Jutland is unique within the TRB North Group due to the peculiar design of its ditches (Fig. 89A). The enclosure is comprised of a palisade to which small rectangular fenced annexes were attached on the outer side (comparable to those known from Sarup I). A single

Fig. 89 | *European enclosures with clavicle-shaped ditch segments and rectangular palisade annexes. A) Starup Langelandsvej (from Lützau Pedersen/Witte 2012), B) Sandomierz (from Kowalewska-Marszalek 1990).*

B

SANDOMIERZ – WZGÓRZE ZAWICHOJSKIE

Gesamtplan der Fundstelle

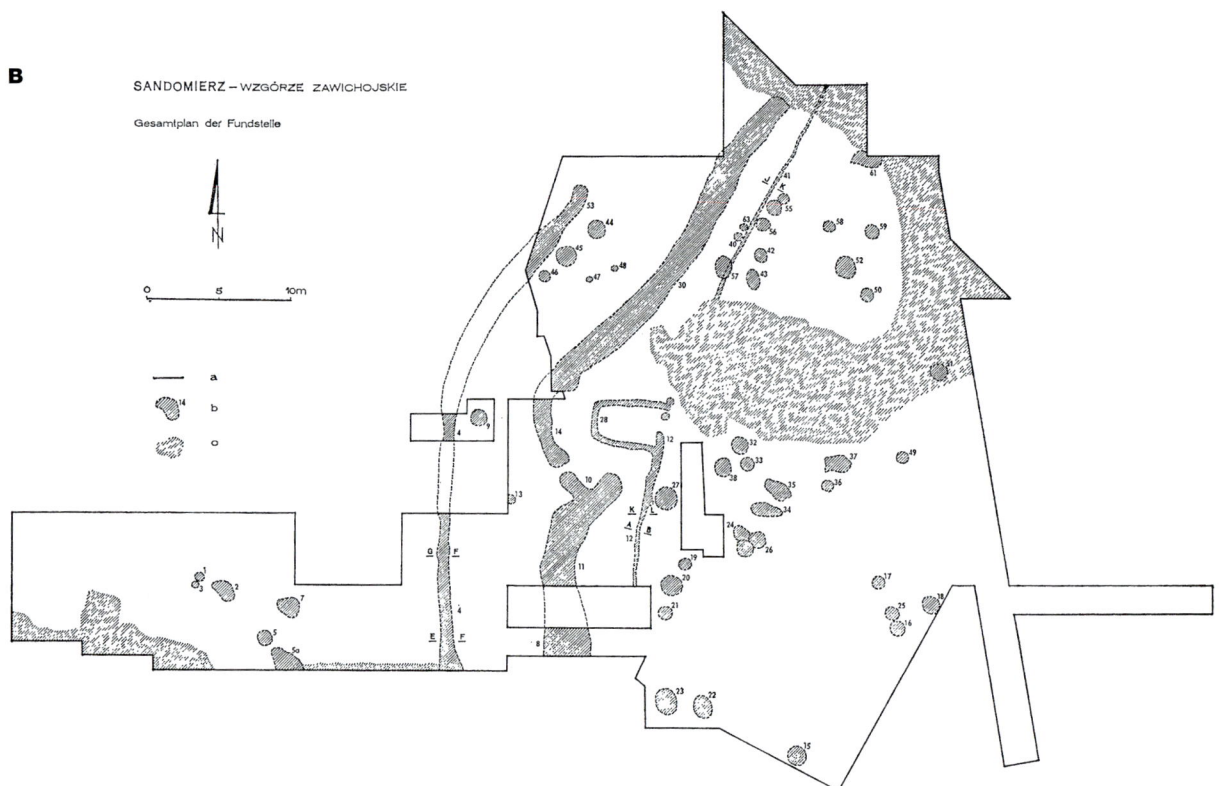

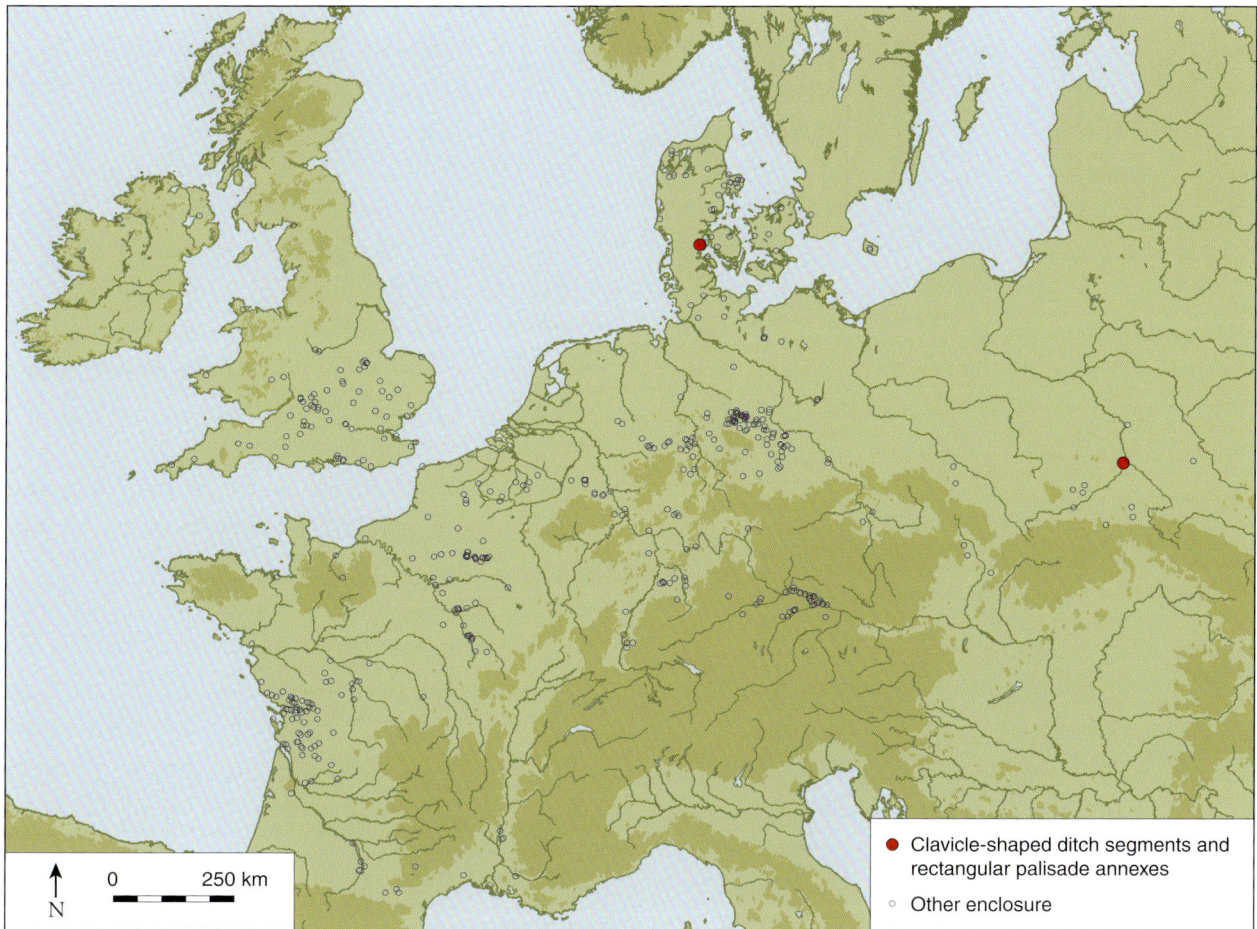

Fig. 90 | *The distribution of enclosures with clavicle-shaped ditch segments and rectangular palisade annexes across Europe.*

row of segmented ditches follows the palisade and curves around the fenced rectangular areas above which the ditches are interrupted. Thereby, individual ditch segments obtain a strange clavicle-like shape reminiscent of the profile of a spoon.

The design of the Starup Langelandsvej site is paralleled only in one other enclosure within the investigation area (Fig. 90). The enclosure of Sandomierz Wzgórze Zawichojskie (Kowalewska-Marszalek 1990; 2007) in Little Poland (950 km from Starup) has a palisade with a rectangular annex just like that at Starup Langelandsvej. Additionally it has a row of segmented ditches that follows the palisade and curves around the rectangular annex (Fig. 89B). Minor differences between the two monuments can be observed in the design of the interruption of the ditch; while an access through the palisade into the rectangular annex is present at Sandomierz, it

is absent at Starup. Sandomierz additionally has a second, outer ditch circuit which also does not appear at Starup. Still, the peculiar design of palisade, annexes and especially ditch segments clearly demonstrates that both enclosures belong to the same architectural tradition.

Possibly related (but not identical) structures are known from the Neolithic of eastern central Germany from the early 5th millennium onwards (Stroke Ornamented Pottery Culture: Schwarz 2003, 43 and Figs. 16-18; Baalberg Group: Schwarz 2003, 66 with Fig. 37). These sites suggest the possibility for enclosures whose construction was identical to those at Starup and Sandomierz in eastern central Germany. In any case, the association between such sites would close the peculiar distributional gap between the two sites which are presently known.

A number of ^{14}C-dates date the construction of the Starup Langelandsvej enclosure to around (or slightly before) 3600 BC (Lützau Pedersen/Witte 2012), while the Sandomierz Wzgórze Zawichojskie site belongs to the Lublin-Volhynian Culture. Seven ^{14}C-dates are available for the enclosure (Chmielewski 2008, 71 Fig. 10). These dates cover a comparatively large time span between 4300 and 3700 BC. According to Kowalewska-Marszalek (2007, 439ff.), the enclosure should date to the younger phase of the culture. Therefore, it is probably only slightly older than its Danish counterpart.

10.2.3 Enclosures with wide ditch circuit spacing

Causewayed enclosures with more than one (partial) circuit of segmented ditches make up quite precisely half of all known sites in South Scandinavia. From 18 sites, two (partial) circuits are known, in one of these cases (Mølbjerg II), there are two sets. As discussed above, more than two ditch circuits are known from Rastorf (three partial circuits have been observed, but four may have been present – Steffens 2009, 72ff.) as well as from Büdelsdorf.

Thus, in total, there are 21 sets of multiple ditch systems from 20 different sites. In three cases (Hygind, Åsum Enggård and Voldbæk), no further information regarding the spacing of the circuits was available, while the distance between the (partial) circuits in the remaining 18 cases is apparent from Fig. 91. With a single exception, all values cluster between 3 and 14 m. The exception is the Mølbjerg

I enclosure from northwestern Jutland, whose distance is considerably larger at 40 m (Fig. 92).

As in the case of enclosures with more than two ditch circuits, it is of interest to compare the data on circuit spacing for the TRB enclosures with measurements for enclosures from other parts of Europe (Fig. 93). The basic assumption in all cases is that individual circuits related to each other. This would obviously have been the case should they have been dug and used contemporaneously. However, such relationships would also have played a role should an older circuit still have been marked on the surface and was then, therefore, taken into consideration during the construction of later, additional circuits. Such relations would be expressed by ditch courses which are parallel or concentric.

In this study, measurements for enclosures from the British Isles (data from Oswald et al. 2001, 69 Fig. 4.19) as well as from Western and Central Europe (northern France, Belgium, the Netherlands and Germany) were used as a means of comparison. Data for the latter regions were obtained from the publications of Seidel (2008, 360f. Tab. 43), Geschwinde/Raetzel-Fabian (2009, 29ff.) and several other individual publications (Seidel 2009; Schreurs 2005). Most of the sites examined belonged to the Michelsberg Culture. Corrections of values published in Seidel's table were made for the Northeim-Kiessee site, for which Seidel listed distances of 16 and 38 m. However, according to Siegmund's (1993, 25 Abb. 4) original publication, those distances measured only six and 12 m, respectively. Circuit spacing at Boitsfort-Etangs in Belgium appears to be only ca. 13 m (Hubert 1971),

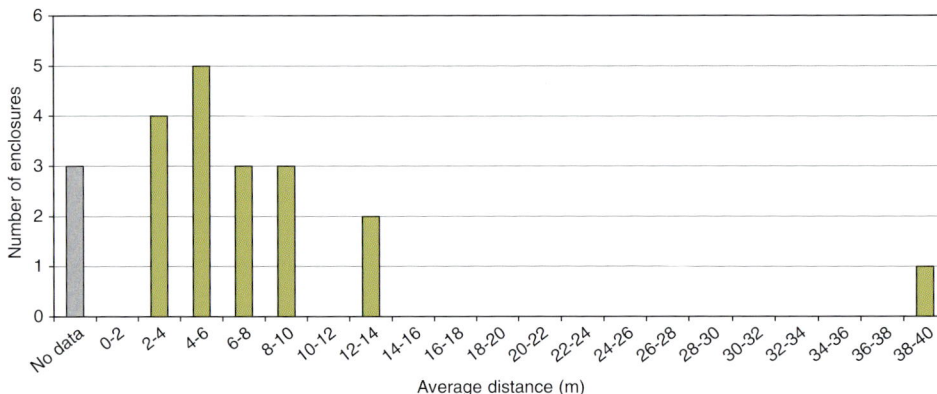

Fig. 91 | *The distance between (partial) ditch circuits for 18 enclosures from South Scandinavia.*

Fig. 92 | *Vertical aerial photo of the Mølbjerg I enclosure, showing the large distance between the two partial ditch circuits as well as clear differences in width (Photo: L. Helles Olesen).*

as is apparent from the illustration provided by Boelicke (1977, 107 Fig. 34.3) rather than the 20 m indicated by Seidel.

Enclosures from central western France could not be included in the diagram shown in Fig. 93 because no precise measurements were available. However, in some cases, published plans/aerial photographs clearly indicate wide circuit spacing which must have surpassed 20 m. Therefore, relevant sites have been included in mapping (Fig. 94).

For enclosures that had more than two (partial) circuits of segmented ditches, when all circuits showed even spacing, only one value was recorded. However, several values were noted in cases of uneven spacing, such as at the Northeim-Kiessee

enclosure referred to above. In cases where Seidel (2008) provided a range of values, the mean of these values was used. In total, the 18 available measurements for multiple ditch systems from the northern TRB could be compared to 62 British and 34 Central/Western European measurements. For comparison, the values have been divided into 5 m classes, as this was the format Oswald et al. (2001) used for British sites.

Fig. 93 reveals some obvious similarities and differences between the three regional groups of data. It appears that Central/Western European and TRB North Group sites were generally in agreement. In both regions, almost all values for ditch spacing are confined to the 5-15 m intervals within which they

Fig. 93 | *A comparison of the distances between (partial) ditch circuits in enclosures from South Scandinavia, southern Britain as well as Western and Central Europe.*

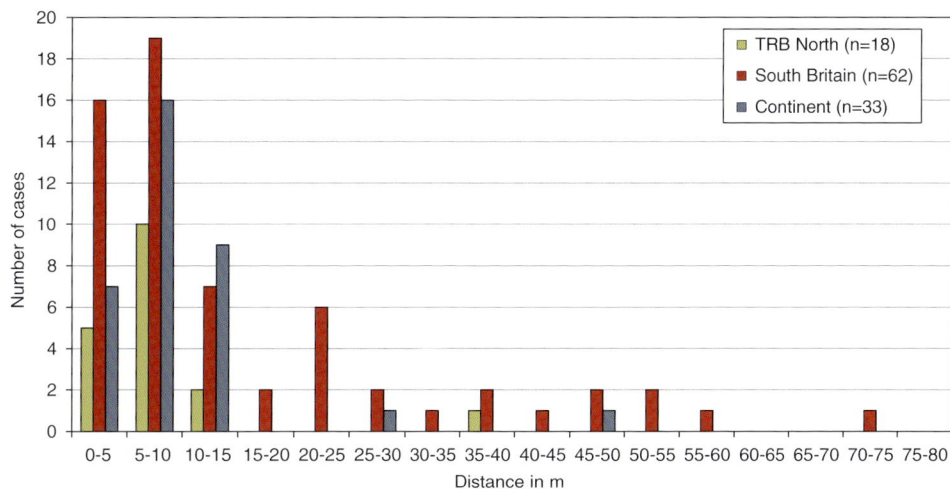

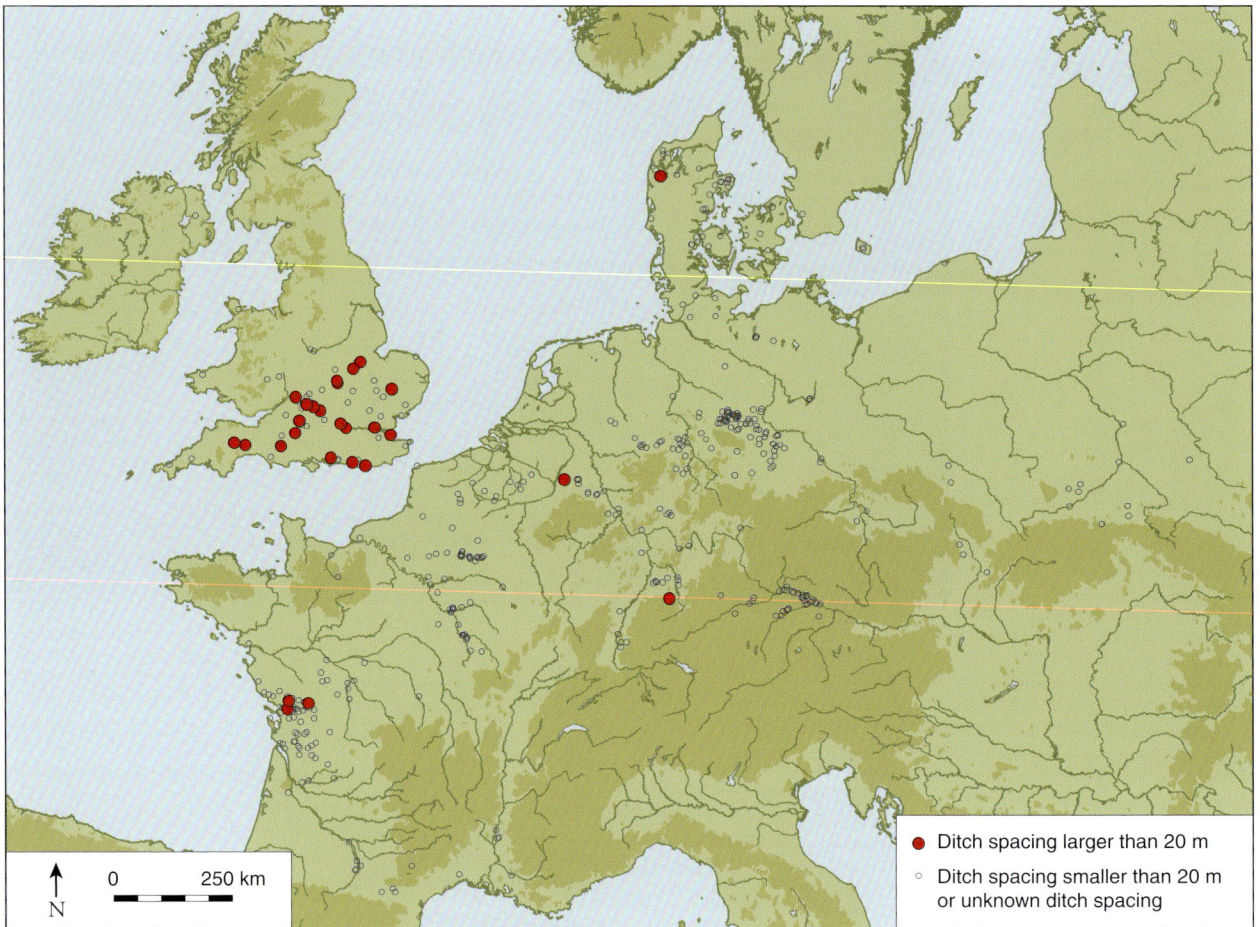

Fig. 94 | *The European distribution of enclosures with ditch circuit spacing larger than 20 m.*

show something resembling a normal distribution. Additionally, there are very few outliers. The Mølbjerg I site mentioned above is the only such case within the TRB North Group, while two exceptions can be noted for Central/Western European sites (for which approximately twice as many measurements are available): the Michelsberg enclosure of Heerlen Schelsberg in the Netherlands (Schreurs/Brounen 1998; Schreurs 2005, 311 Fig. 5f.) and the enclosure of Leonberg "Silberberg" in southwest Germany (Seidel 2009). The latter belongs to the late Munzingen Culture. Study of the site suggests that one of the two ditches might be significantly older than the other (Bischheim ?). The British enclosures, on the other hand, clearly diverge from those of the two other regional groups. While the majority of the monuments from Britain have a circuit spacing comparable to that of Continental and South Scandinavian sites, approximately one third

of the enclosures diverge by means of larger circuit spacing (reaching 75 m in one extreme case).

In terms of the current investigation, it is of interest to observe that the Mølbjerg I enclosure's ditch circuit spacing of ca. 40 m corresponds well to the data from Britain. A good parallel to Mølbjerg I with regard to the spacing of the partial circuits of segmented ditches as well as the position on a promontory is known from Abingdon in Oxfordshire (Fig. 95), where two partial circuits of segmented ditches at a distance of ca. 65 m from each other delimit a low promontory at the confluence of two rivers (Case 1956; Oswald et al. 2001, 24 Fig. 2.16). These observations are of interest due to the geographical position of the Mølbjerg I enclosure (Fig. 94). It was constructed close to the west coast of Jutland at the bottom of Kilen, a minor western side-arm of Limfjorden which lies close to the North Sea. This location is favourable with regards to western maritime contacts. Historical

Fig. 95 | *The causeway enclosure from Abingdon (Oxfordshire, southern Britain) is a good parallel for the Mølbjerg I enclosure in Jutland in terms of wide circuit spacing (from Oswald et al. 2001; © British Heritage).*

sources indicate that the Vikings used the western Limfjord as assembly and re-assembly place for the fleets that attacked England (Zeeberg 2000).

It is, thus, an obvious possibility that the wide ditch circuit spacing observed at Mølbjerg I was due to contact with Early Neolithic societies in southern Britain. Due to the resemblance of earthen long barrows in both regions (Madsen, T. 1979; Rassmann 2011), such relations have long been known to have existed. Causewayed enclosures thus appear to constitute the second (recognized) example of related Early Neolithic monuments on both sides of the North Sea. The North Sea makes for particularly difficult sailing. Therefore, contact between these regions must have taken place via a communication network strung up along the

fringes of the North Sea rather than by means of expeditions which ran directly across it.

The two Continental sites showing wide ditch circuit spacing cannot be directly related to the contact network at the fringes of the North Sea. Therefore, they cannot be associated with the Mølbjerg I enclosure. The two sites are discussed in more detail in a later section. The three enclosures with large ditch circuit spacing near the Atlantic coast of western France, however, deserve immediate mention within the context currently under discussion, as they may very well have been somehow related to both British and Jutish enclosure(s) through a possible maritime contact network stretching along the Atlantic fringes of Europe and through the Channel and the North Sea.

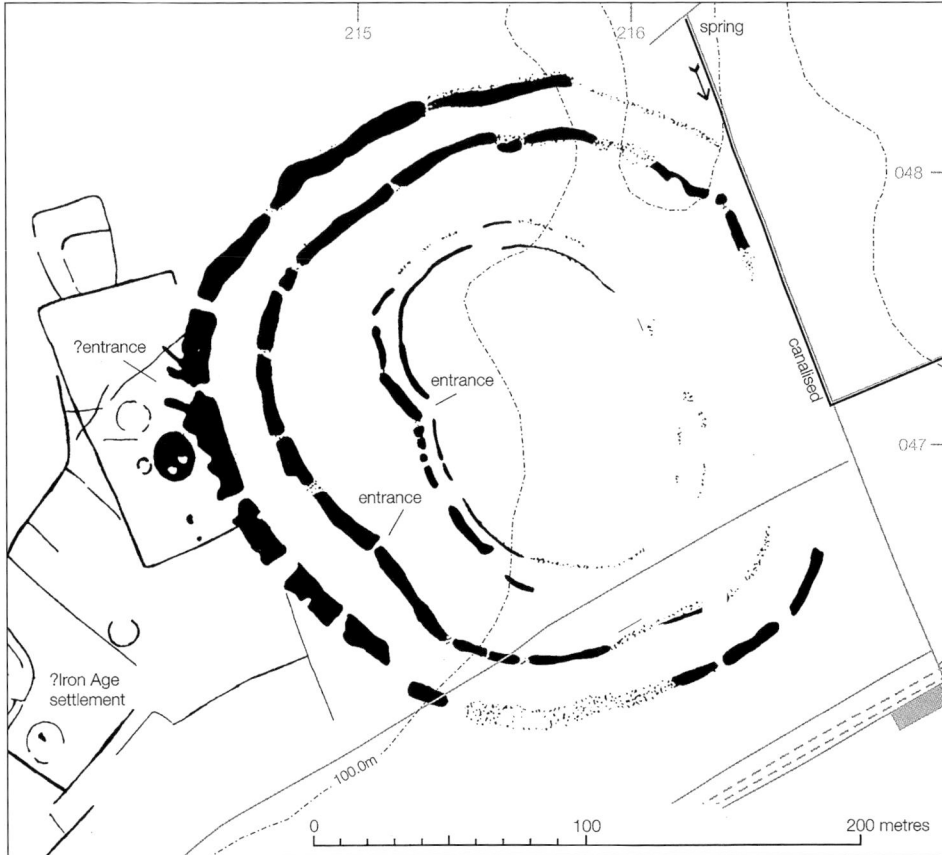

Fig. 96 | *The causewayed enclosure at Eastleach in Gloucestershire is a typical example of a British enclosure with individual circuits of differing width. Ditch width increases from the inside to the outside (from Oswald et al. 2001; © British Heritage).*

From a chronological point of view, it can be stated that British enclosures can generally be dated to the late 38th to early 36th century BC (Whittle et al. 2011a). The Dutch enclosure of Heerlen-Schelsberg belongs to the older part of the Michelsberg Culture (MK I/II) and thus the late 5th millennium BC (Schreurs/Brounen 1998, 26), while Leonberg "Silberberg" likely dates to the second quarter of the 4th millennium BC (Munzingen B: Seidel 2009). Of the three sites in central western France, one (Echiré "Les Loups" – Burnez 1996) counts among the oldest enclosures in the region having had the start of construction take place in what is locally referred to as Middle Neolithic (probably the first quarter of the 4th millennium BC, but possibly even older). Another belongs to the Néolithique récent (older part of Les Matignons) and thus dates to the second quarter of the 4th millennium BC ("La Mastine" in Nuaillé d'Aunis: Cassen/Scarre 1997; Cassen, personal communication). For the last, unfortunately, no date has been established ("Le Haut du Tertre" in Gué de Velluire: Cassen 1987, Fig. 106). While the Mølbjerg I

enclosure is itself not dated, it is important to note that all parallels listed appear to be older (or in some cases possibly contemporary) with the oldest known enclosures within the TRB North Group.

10.2.4 Enclosures with differing circuit widths

As is clearly apparent from the vertical aerial photograph of the Mølbjerg I enclosure (Fig. 92), the ditch segments of the outer partial ditch circuit are much wider than those of the inner partial ditch circuit. Within the TRB North Group, Mølbjerg I is the only known enclosure which shows this trait. However, a number of British sites were constructed according to the same architectural principle (Fig. 96; Oswald et al. 2001, 69f.). The overall distribution is thus the same as that observed for enclosures with the wide circuit spacing discussed above. In turns, this confirms the assumed relation between Mølbjerg I and Britain (Fig. 97).

Just as with the preceding case, an example of an enclosure with ditch circuits of different width

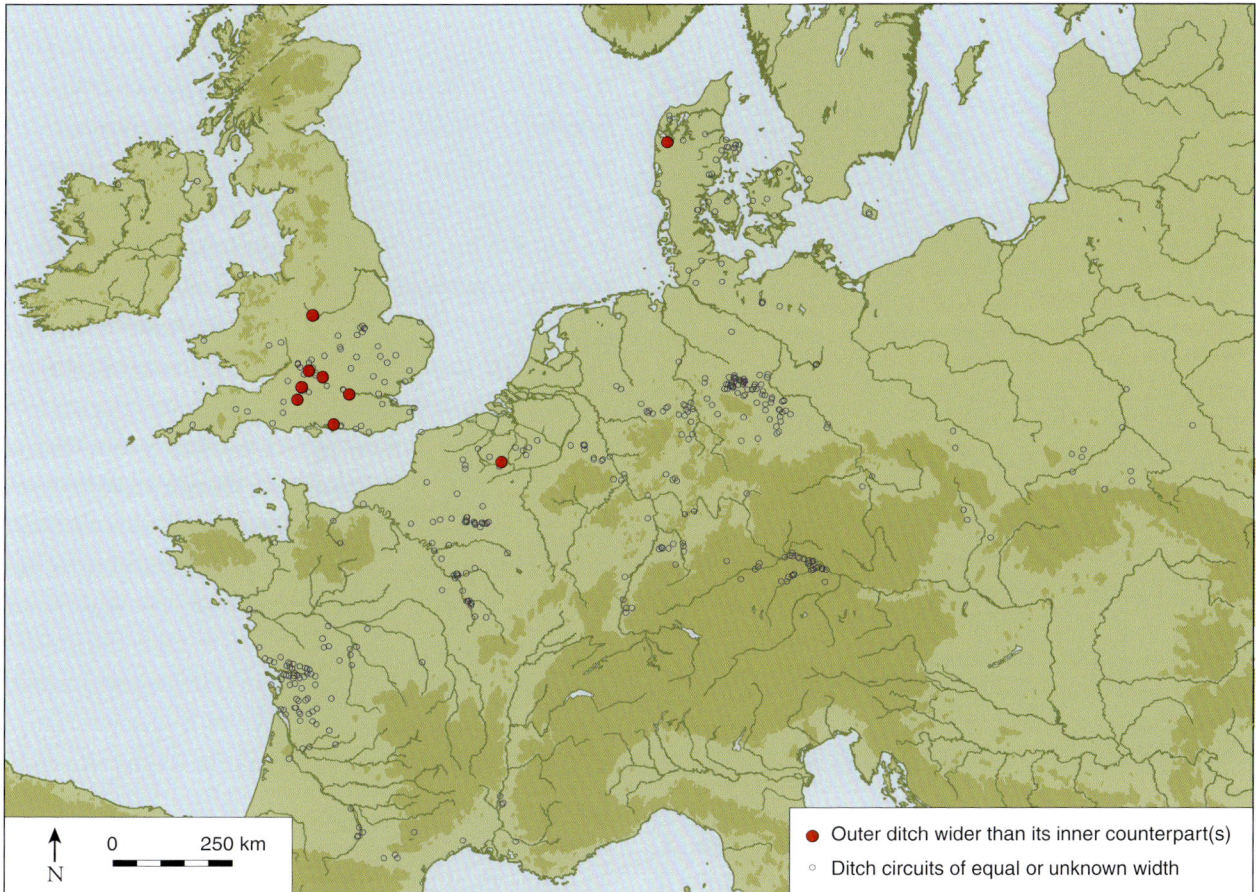

Fig. 97 | *The European distribution of enclosures with a (partial) outer ditch circuit which is wider than its (partial) inner counterpart(s).*

can also be found on the Continent. The Thieusies enclosure in Belgium (Vermeersch/Walter 1980), which shows this trait, is situated on the Continental side of the Channel (opposite the British sites) and thus may well be related to them.

In general, the British sites listed above can be dated to the south British enclosure building horizon (late 38th to early 36th century BC). However, the Thieusies enclosure ditches cannot be precisely dated within the Michelsberg Culture (Vermeersch/Walter 1980, 41). The finds from the site range from MK II to MK IV (ca. 4200-3700 BC). The foreign parallels are, therefore, probably older (or possibly contemporary) with the Mølbjerg I enclosure.

10.2.5 Enclosures with egg-shaped site plans

Among the few South Scandinavian enclosures for which a complete (or sufficiently complete)

site plan is available is Gammeltoft Odde close to the west coast of Jutland (Troldtoft Andresen 2013; Fig. 98). As far as it is possible to judge, this enclosure shows a clear "egg-shape" rarely seen in the TRB North Group distribution area. The only other probable examples include Liselund in Thy, northwestern Jutland (Westphal 2000) and Esesfeld in northern Germany (Lornsen 1987; Kühn 1989). Interestingly, both of these are close to the west cost of Jutland. At Liselund, only small parts of the course of the ditch circuits of the very large enclosure are known due to excavation and partial observation from the air. However, the sum of this information is combinable in such a way as to give evidence for an elongated, egg-shaped enclosure (Fig. 99A). At Esesfeld, approximately half of the enclosure was documented over the course of the excavation of a fortification from Carolingian times (Fig. 99B).

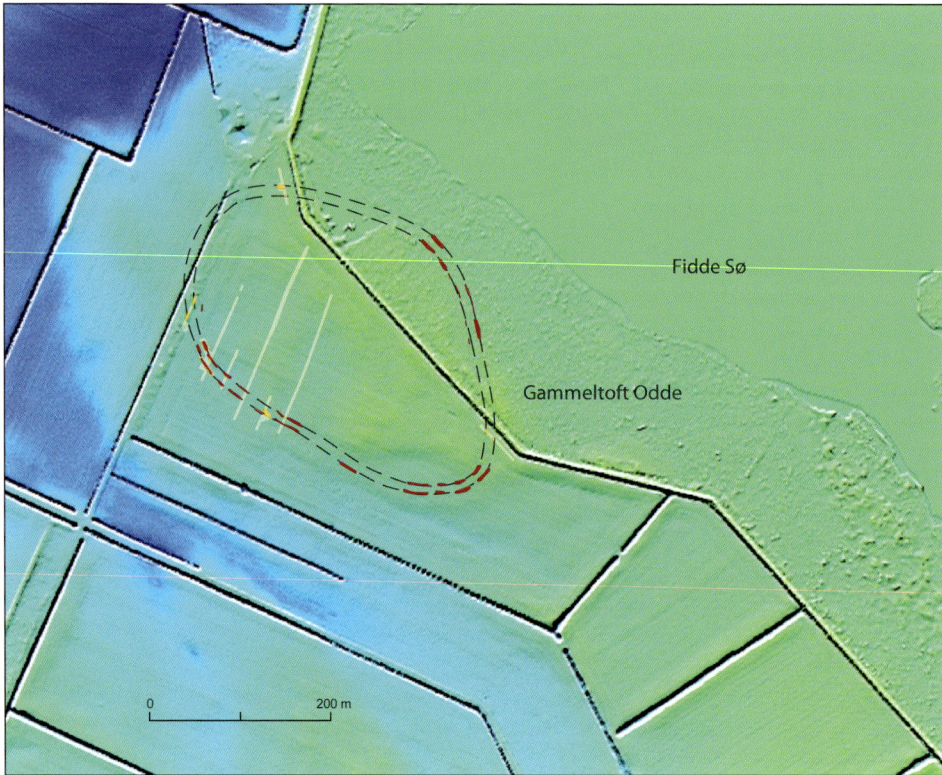

Fig. 98 | *The Gammel-toft Odde enclosure from western Jutland. The site plan was compiled from the results of trial excavations and an aerial photo from 1954 (from Trold-toft Andresen 2013).*

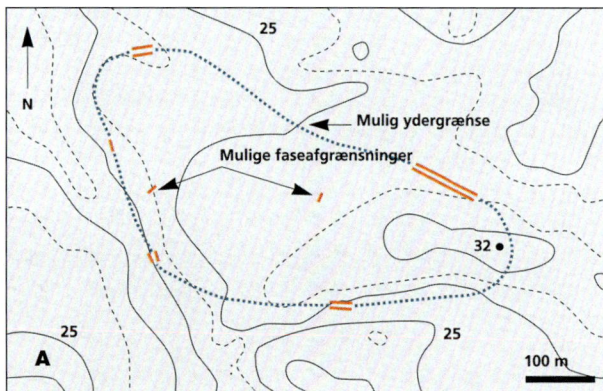

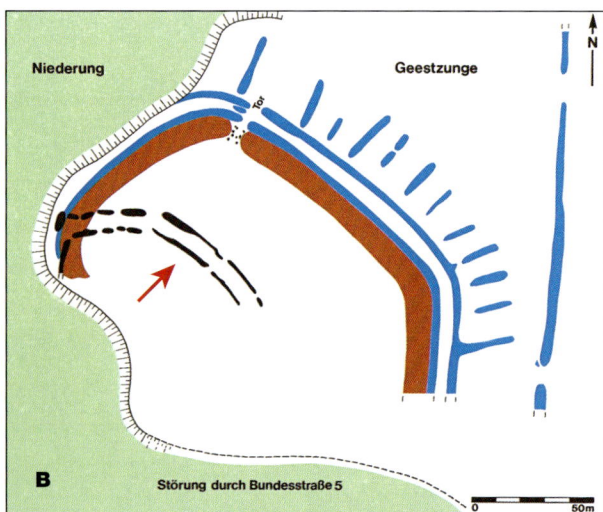

The Esesfeld enclosure diverges from those at Gammeltoft Odde and Liselund because of the angled course of the two ditch circuits. This is discussed further below.

Mapping egg-shaped enclosures results in a distributional pattern much related to that encountered for several previously investigated architectural traits (Fig. 100). Apart from the west coast of Jutland, egg-shaped enclosures are known from Britain (Oswald et al. 2001) and the Continent (Carvin "La Gare D'Eau": Monchablon et al. 2011). The location of the latter enclosure was near to the Channel. It appears, therefore, that the shape of the Danish enclosures at Gammeltoft Odde and (probably) at Liselund was due to contact with Neolithic groups which were part of a network along the fringes of the North Sea and the Channel. It is likely that there are several

Fig. 99 | *The enclosures from Liselund and Esesfeld both probably show egg-shaped site plans of different variants. A) Liselund (after Westphal 2000), B) Esesfeld (after Lornsen 1987, arrow added).*

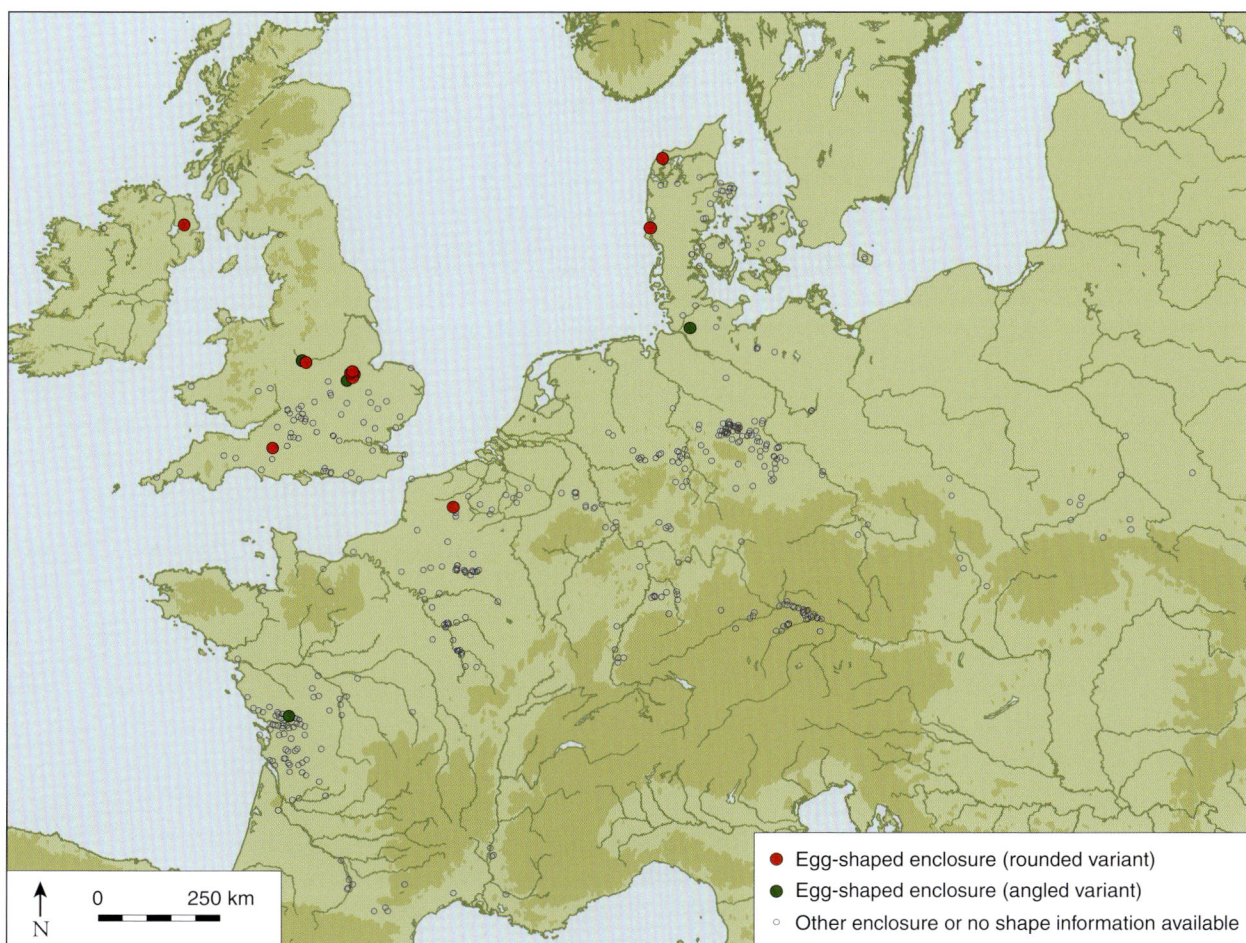

Fig. 100 | *The European distribution of egg-shaped enclosures with and without angled ditch circuits.*

other sites constructed according to this principle that have yet to be recognized as such (probably because the parts of the site plans that are known are too small). As is apparent from the mapping of a specific variant of the egg-shape with one angled side (see below), the overall distribution area of egg-shaped enclosures may well have also included central western France.

A few egg-shaped enclosures deviate from those discussed above by having one strongly-angled side close to a natural slope. These sites are peculiar because the slope could have been used as a natural border in the overall enclosure design (e.g. by allowing the course of the ditch circuit/s to end at the slope). Instead, the course of said ditches takes a sharp angle in front of the slope and then (at least partly) continues parallel to it. In Britain, the Mavesyn Ridware and Southwick enclosures follow this design principle

(Oswald et al. 2001), while the Champ-Durand site in central western France (e.g. Joussaume 1988) shows a design almost identical to that of Mavesyn Ridware (Fig. 101). Within the TRB North Group enclosures, the Esesfeld site (Fig. 99B) is the only example with an angled course comparable to that of the aforementioned British and French sites. Only approximately half of the Esesfeld enclosure site plan is known. Nonetheless, the design principle in question is so characteristic, that the site is very likely a member of the same sub-group of egg-shaped enclosures. Like the Liselund and Gammeltoft Odde sites, Esesfeld is situated close to the west coast of Jutland and thereby confirms the conclusions arrived at here (Fig. 100).

As in the case of the round egg-shaped enclosures, the mapping of those showing one angled side must be assumed to be incomplete. However,

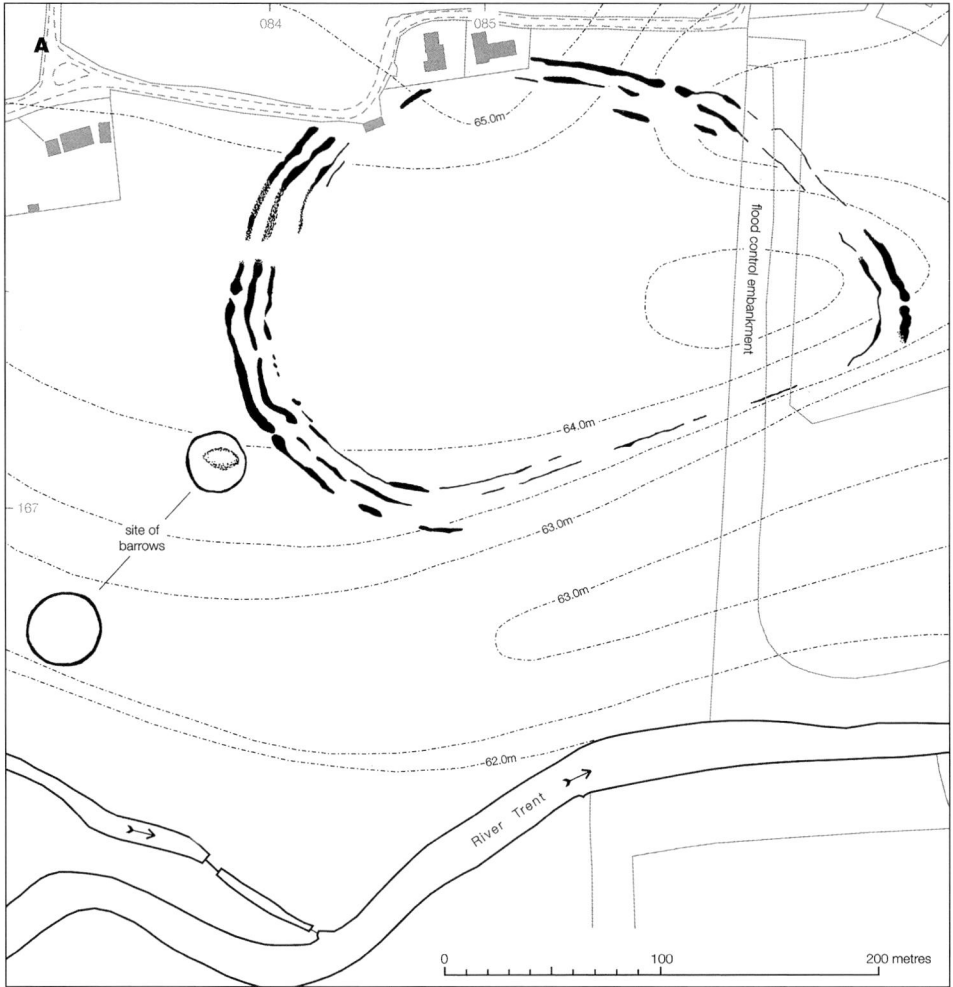

Fig. 101 | *A) Plan of the British Mavesyn Ridware enclosure (Oswald et al. 2001; © British Heritage), B) Plan of the Champ-Durand enclosure in central western France (Joussaume 1988). These two sites resemble each other closely and can probably be related to the Esesfeld enclosure in northern Germany (Fig. 99 B).*

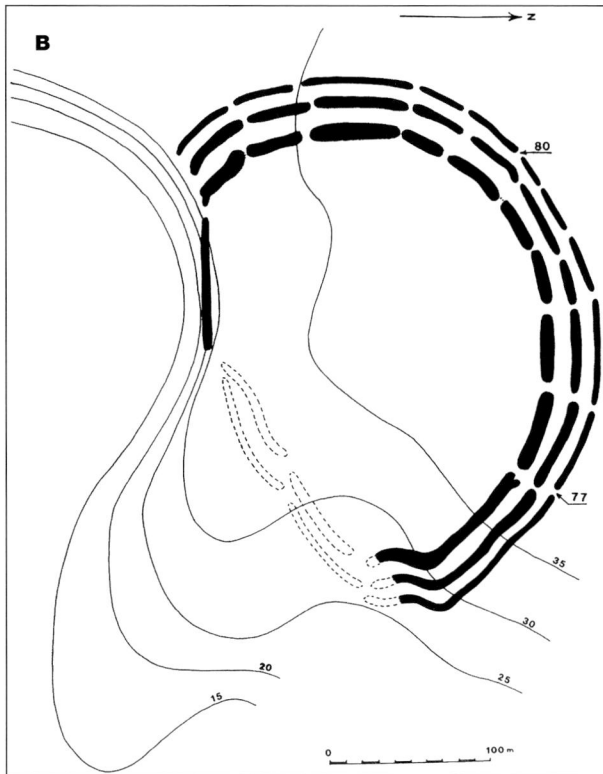

both variants share a characteristic distributional pattern that has been observed with regard to several other specific traits investigated here. It probably reflects a communication network which stretched along the Atlantic fringe and North Sea coasts.

British egg-shaped enclosures date to the late 38th to early 36th centuries BC (Whittle et al. 2011a) and the Champs-Durand enclosure to the second quarter of the 4th millennium BC (Les Matignons ancien – Ard 2011, 286 nr. 4). The northern French site of Carvin "La Gare D'Eau" belongs to the Spiere-Group and has consequently been attributed to the Néolithique Moyen II by Monchablon et al. (2011). This implies a date between the later 5th and early 4th millennium BC. None of the TRB sites have been dated properly. However, it should be noted that all parallels referred to above are either older than or possibly contemporary with the oldest known TRB enclosures.

10.2.6 Enclosures with double post entrance structures

Entrance structures consisting of two massive posts have been recognized at two South Scandinavian enclosures. At Gammeltoft Odde, these posts were located 1.5 m from each other on the middle of a causeway between two ditch segments, themselves on the inside of a pair of ditch circuits. The posts were aligned with the course of the ditch segments (Troldtoft Andresen 2013). These posts may once have held some kind of rather massive gate.

Comparable (but not identical) entrance structures have been found on a number of European sites. At the Michelsberg enclosure of Heerlen-Schelsberg in the Netherlands (Schreurs 2005, 311 Fig. 5f), three rather than two postholes (placed in a triangle formation) were found on a causeway. A similar formation was recorded at Gravon in northern France (Mordant/Mordant 1988, 237 Fig. 13.4). At this site, the three postholes were placed in a triangular arrangement, of which one post was located at an opening of the palisade while the other two were situated between the segmented ditch and the palisade. At Champ-Durand (Vendée, central western France; Fig. 101B), two sets of double posts were placed on a causeway (Joussaume 1988, 287 Fig. 16.7), while at Miel in the Rhineland, Germany, sets of double posts were placed on the inside and outside of a causeway between two ditch segments (Eckert 1990, 402 Abb. 4).

The best parallels to the entrance construction observed at the Gammeltoft Odde enclosure are known from southern Britain and central western France. Massive double posts were observed at the entrances to the enclosures at both Freston in Suffolk and Haddenham in Cambridgeshire. At Freston, the double post construction is not situated on the actual causeway between the ends of the ditch segments. Rather it lies just outside the course of the outer ditch (Oswald et al. 2001, 47 Fig. 3.14). The construction of the entrance at Haddenham, on the other hand, appears to be identical to that at Gammeltoft Odde (Fig. 102A). The same is true

for one of the entrance constructions from "La Coterelle" in Saint-Germain-de-Lusignan (Charente-Maritime) in western central France (Fig. 102B) (Cassen/Boujot 1990, 457 Abb. 2).

Before this survey of parallels can be concluded, however, it is necessary to mention the northern French enclosure of Goulet "Le Mont" (Ghesquière et al. 2011). At that location, two round pits were found on a causeway in a position identical to the pattern observed at Gammeltoft Odde. However, Ghesquière et al. do not consider these to be the remains of an entrance structure. Instead, they believe that the pits are the remains of the first phase of the enclosure (in which said enclosure was delimited exclusively by such round pits (Ghesquière et al. 2011, 192 Fig. 11). Therefore, these features are not considered further, although it is, of course, not possible to exclude the possibility that these pits actually were the postholes of an entrance structure.

The distribution of sites with entrance structures identical to that observed at Gammeltoft Odde appears to be just another supporting example of the presence of the above-mentioned communication structure bound to the Atlantic and North Sea coasts (Fig. 103). It can be added that the sites with related (but not identical) structures show a similar distribution pattern, with the single exception of the Miel enclosure in the German Rhineland.

Additionally, from a chronological point of view, the same pattern that was observed several times before appears once again. Parallels in Britain and France (both precise and less precise) are either older than (or at least as old as) the oldest known TRB enclosures. Based on a single ^{14}C-date from a sample close to the bottom of a ditch segment, the construction of the Gammeltoft Odde enclosure can only be dated to the late 37th-early 34th centuries BC (see chapter 10.3.1.1)

The second TRB enclosure at which an entrance structure consisting of two massive posts has been observed is Albersdorf Dieksknöll in northern Germany (Fig. 104). However, those posts do not appear to have been as isolated as those at the Gammeltoft Odde enclosure. Instead, they were

Fig. 102 | *Entrance constructions identical/nearly identical to those observed at the Gammeltoft Odde enclosure in western Jutland are known from Haddenham in southern Britain and from the enclosure of "La Coterelle" in Saint-Germain-de-Lusignan, central western France. A) Haddenham (from Oswald et al. 2001; © British Heritage), B) La Coterelle (from Cassen/Boujot 1990). Arrows indicating entrance constructions added.*

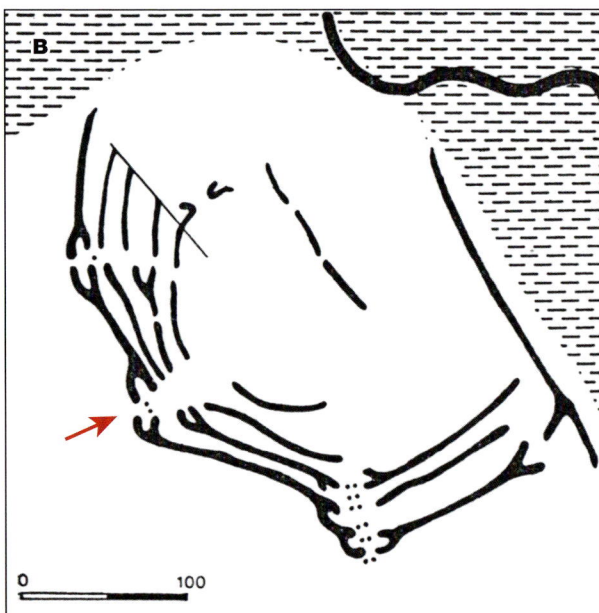

integrated into a transverse pit on a causeway. Contrary to what was the case at Gammeltoft Odde, these posts were not aligned with the course of the ditch circuit, but were rather oriented perpendicularly to it.

No parallels to the transverse pit/massive double post combination are apparent from other enclosures. However, this picture changes if pits and posts are examined independently. The evidence for transverse pits will be discussed below. With regard to transverse double posts, only one possible parallel could be identified among the hundreds of surveyed enclosures: the Michelsberg enclosure at Blicquy, Belgium (Demarez/Constantin 1986, 50 Fig. 2; Constantin et al. 2009, 157 Fig. 5). Several pits and individual postholes

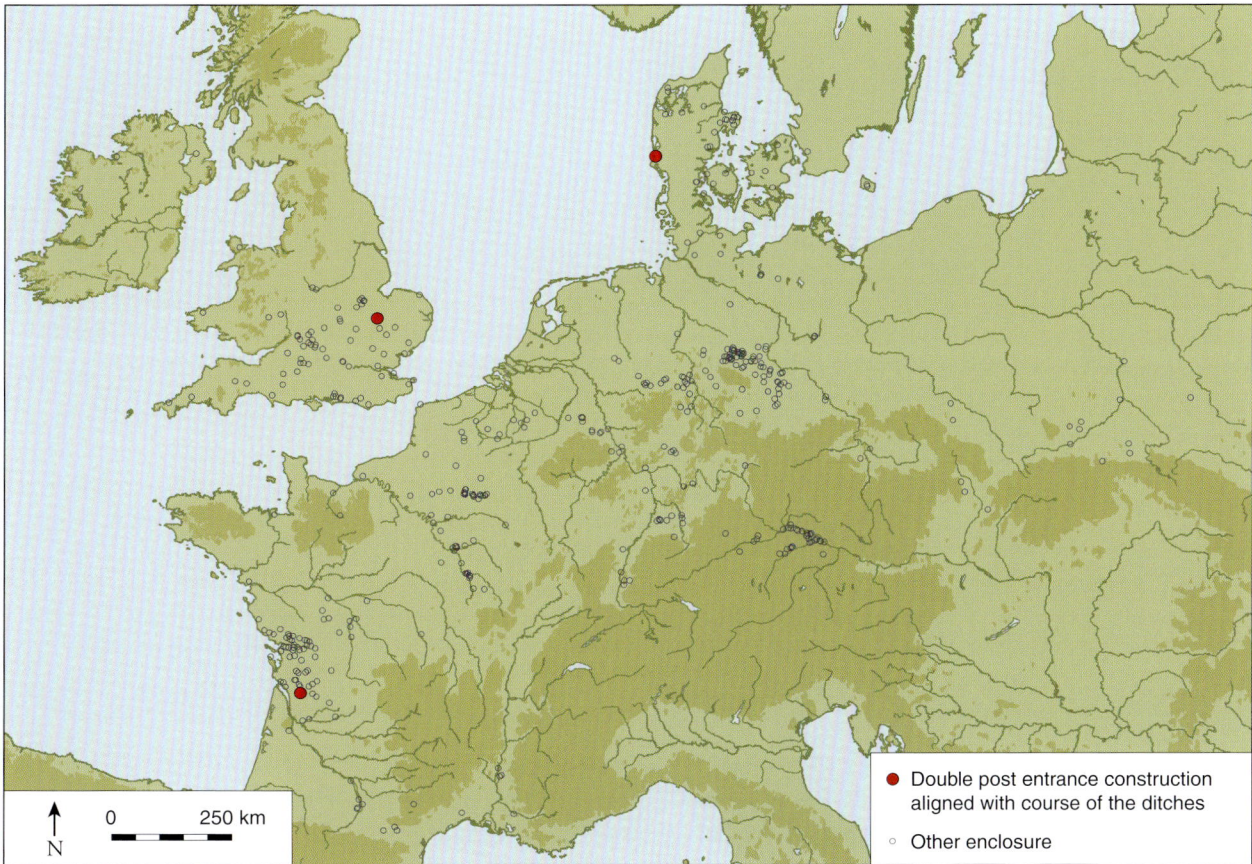

Fig. 103 | *The European distribution of enclosures with entrance structures consisting of a pair of massive posts placed in alignment with the course of the ditch circuit on a causeway between the ends of two ditch segments.*

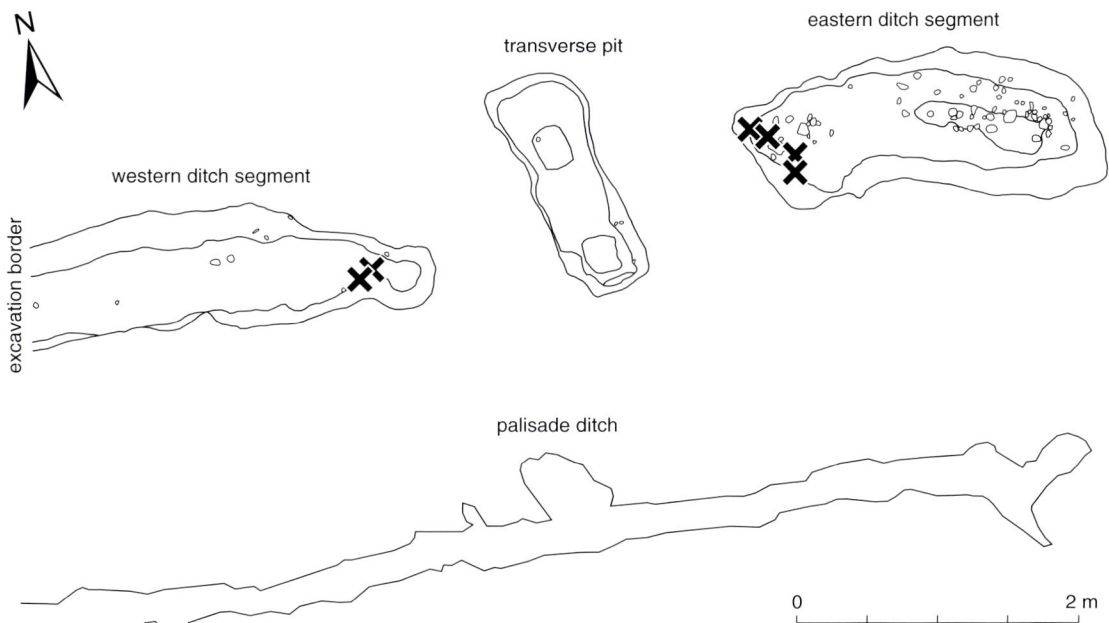

Fig. 104 | *Transverse pit with two massive posts inserted at right angles to the course of the ditch circuit at Albersdorf Dieksknöll, northern Germany (from Dibbern 2012).*

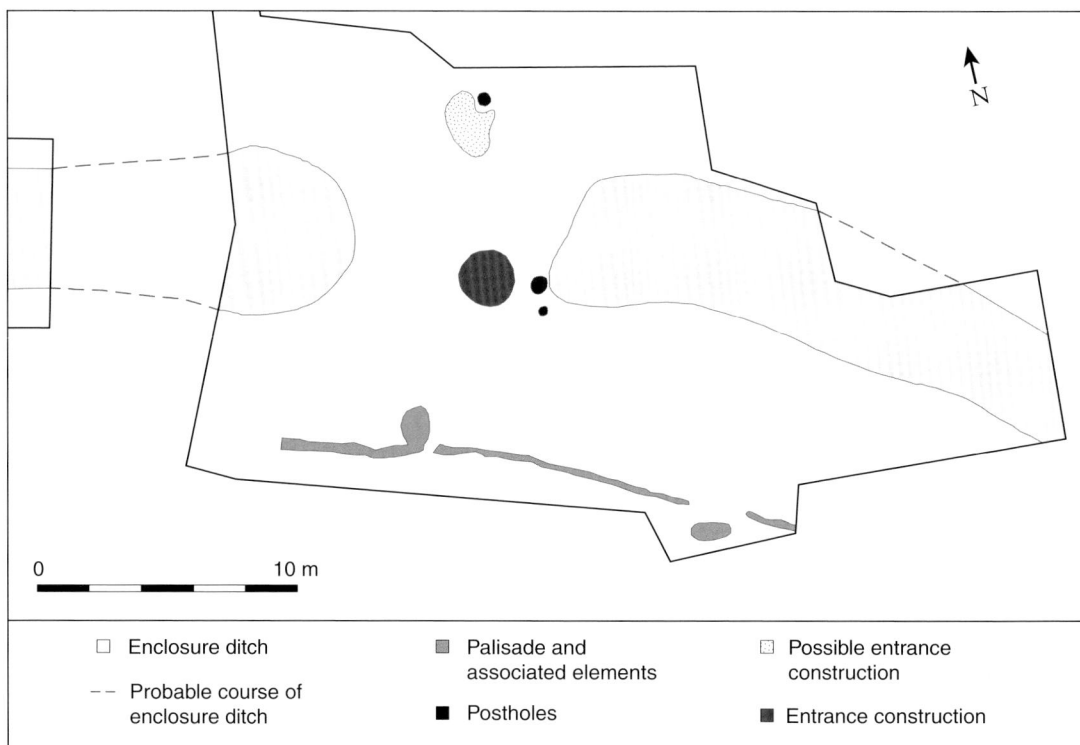

Fig. 105 | *The first interruption of the single ditch circuit forming the large Michelsberg enclosure at Blicquy in Belgium (redrawn from Constantin et al. 2009). Two features in the causeway or small postholes associated with them may represent parallels with the post setting at Albersdorf Dieksknöll. However, according to the excavator, the northern of the two features is much older than the enclosure and thus has nothing to do with it. In any case, the postholes may also be relevant in this context.*

were identified on a causeway which formed the first ditch interruption at Blicquy (Fig. 105). Unfortunately, the structures at the site are not easy to identify, and one of the features that could have been part of a transverse double post arrangement (which is, according to the excavator, similar to that at Albersdorf Dieksknöll) is much older than the enclosure itself. Regrettably, Constantin et al. (2009, 153 ff.) provide no further description. It must be concluded, therefore, that the post setting in the Blicquy enclosure entrance may be related to the one found at Albersdorf Dieksknöll. However, this cannot be confirmed at present. It can be added that if Blicquy should indeed be understood as a parallel to Albersdorf Dieksknöll, it would confirm previous observations regarding geographical distribution and the age of enclosures with architectural features related to the west coast of Jutland. The construction of the enclosure at Blicquy (and thus the

entrance structure) can be dated to the MK II phase in the late 5th millennium BC (Constantin et al. 2009). Thus, Blicquy is considerably older than the Albersdorf Dieksknöll enclosure. As Blicquy is located in Western Europe at not too great a distance from the Channel (Fig. 106), it could number among the constructions under discussion here as being related to the contact network at the fringes of the Channel, North Sea and Atlantic described above.

10.2.7 Enclosures with post framed banks and ditches on both sides of the bank: The Vilsund site

A unique Early Neolithic enclosure was excavated 25 years ago at Vilsund in northwestern Jutland. Unfortunately, only a small amount of information is available and comprises merely a few lines (Nielsen, J./Beck 1989). The author gratefully ac-

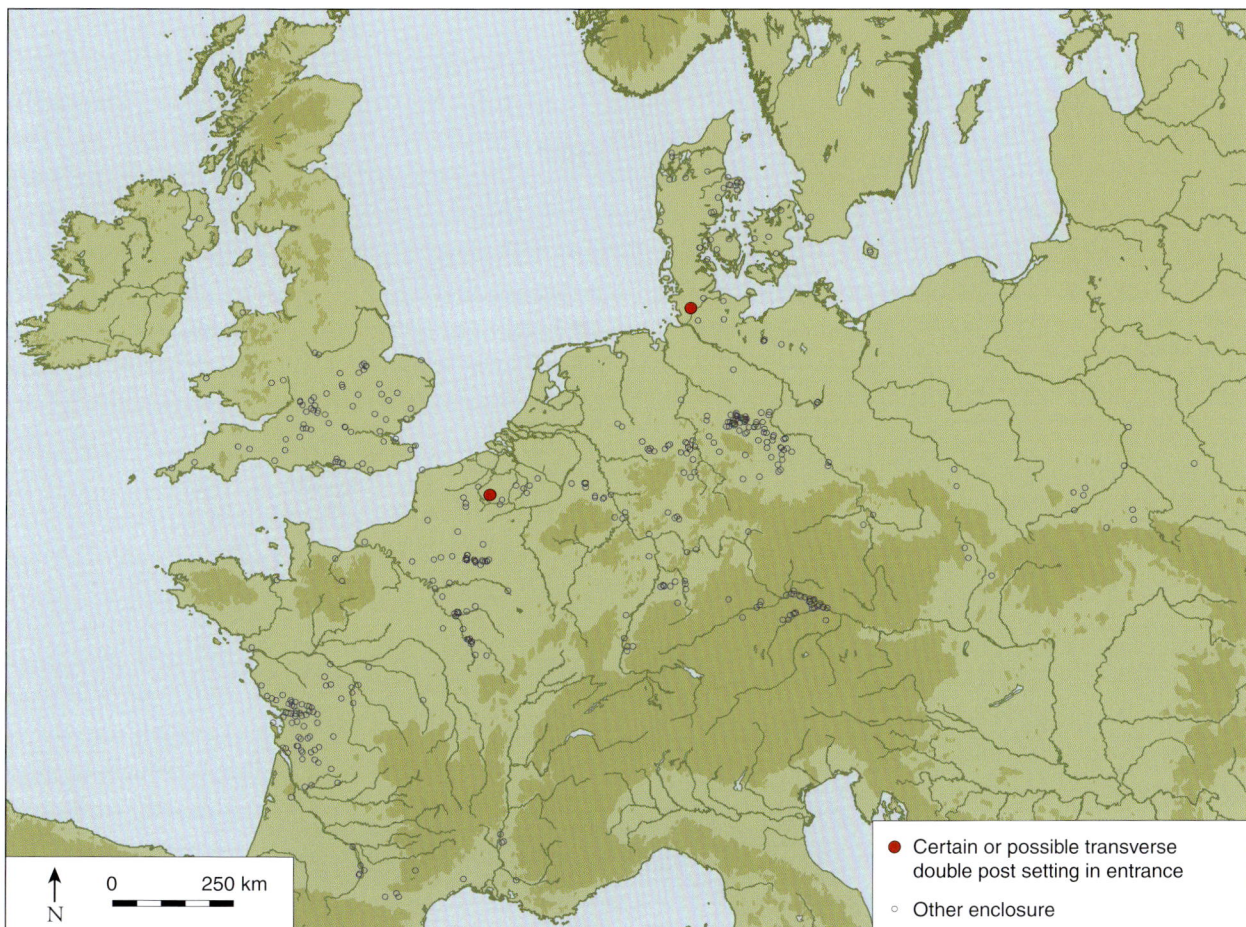

Fig. 106 | *The European distribution of certain and possible transverse double post settings in enclosure entrances.*

knowledges J. Nielsen and J.-H. Bech, (Thy and Vester Hanherred Museum) for their permission to publish this site in more detail here.

The enclosure is located on the Kappelhage Promontory, which juts out into Vilsund, a narrow sound separating the island of Mors from Thy, the northwest part of Jutland (Fig. 27). The enclosure is located very close to the narrowest point of the sound.

Excavation in January 1988 was precipitated by construction work in the northeastern part of the promontory (journal nr. THY 2369). In the spring and summer of the same year, excavators ran a NW-SE trench across the promontory at the highest and central parts accompanied by a number of narrow sondages running northwards from that transversal trench (THY 2346). In the eastern part of the NW-SE trench, two parallel rows of posts could be

followed for almost 150 m (Fig. 107). These rows were set 3-4 m apart. The individual posts were spaced between 1 and 1.5 m from each other. The diameter of the posts ranged from 0.20 to 0.25 m. They were only preserved for a few centimeters' depth. The double row of posts disappeared to the west, almost certainly due to erosion. In the westernmost part of the trench, postholes were discovered that could not be assigned to any specific structure. These postholes may very well have been part of the same double row of posts clearly recognizable to the east. At least this is what is suggested by the site topography. If the site is reconstructed to a length of ca. 250 m, the construction with the two rows of loosely spaced posts would cut straight across the promontory.

A burial mound was placed on top of the post construction on the highest point of the promontory. This burial mound had been largely destroyed

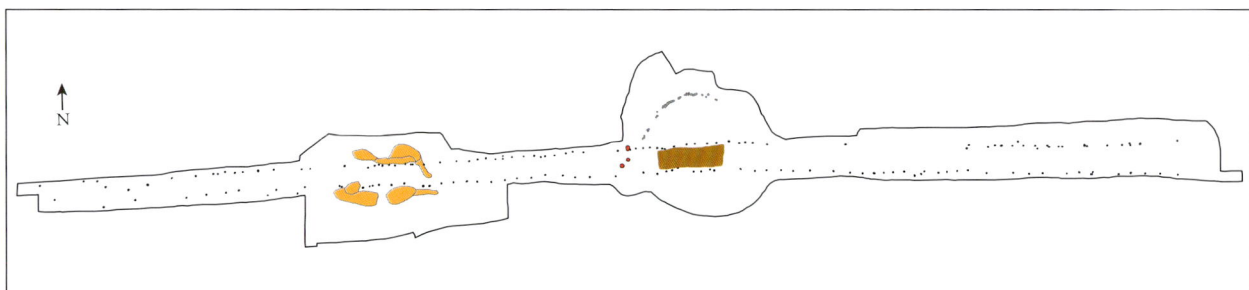

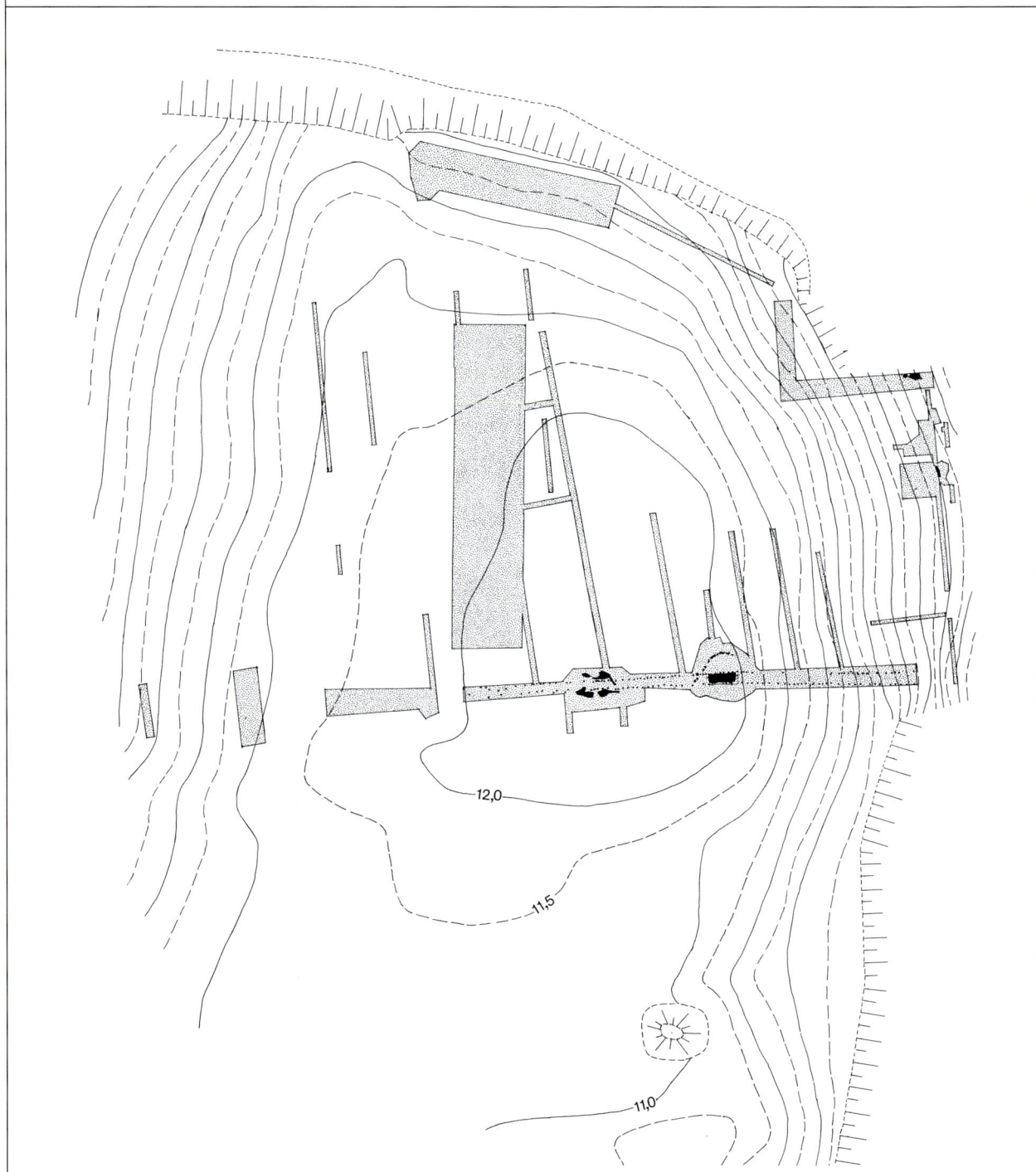

by agriculture and modern digging activity. Therefore, it could not be dated precisely. However, part of the mound fill was preserved. This fill had covered (and thereby preserved) a turf-built bank. The remains of this 3 m wide bank could be observed for over 8 m. The preserved thickness measured between 15 and 20 cm. Archaeologists documented a thin layer of grey sand with charcoal particles between this preserved layer and the natural underground. No finds suitable for dating were made in the preserved remains of the bank. However, this was clearly related to the two rows of posts on both sides and must, therefore, be assumed to be of the same age. It is not possible to conclusively determine whether the bank continued outside the area previously covered by the mound. However, this seems likely, as the preserved parts of the bank stop precisely at borders of the mound. Furthermore, the low preserved depth of the postholes indicates considerable erosion across the entire promontory. Thus, the original construction probably consisted of a ca. 3 m wide turf bank held in place by a construction in which posts were spaced at 1-1.5 m intervals along both sides. The posts must have served to support horizontal timbers or a wattle construction which held the turves in place. This reinforced turf bank cut right across the promontory in a completely straight course which ran ca. 250 m. It is not possible to estimate the previous height of this bank, nor is it possible to tell how many interruptions may have been in it.

Approximately 50 m to the west of the preserved remains of the bank lay four pits measuring up to 40-50 cm in depth. The size of these pits varied from 1.5 x 3.0 m to 1.9 x 6.7 m. They were placed two by two in opposition to each other along both sides of the rows of posts/bank (whose shape they clearly respected). They only contained a few uncharacteristic artefacts of general Neolithic character. Nonetheless, they can be dated to the same time as the bank/post structure due to the stratigraphic relationship described. A further two minor pits may belong to the same complex, but the precise stratigraphic relation of these smaller pits to the larger ones could not be established. The four large pits clearly resemble the ditch segments of an ordinary causewayed enclosure. They may be uncompleted features and would, therefore, indicate that the construction of the site was never finished.

The peculiar enclosure at Vilsund can be dated both by a vessel from one of the postholes and by stratigraphical observations. A few metres west of the preserved parts of the bank, a pit 60 x 80 cm in size and 10-15 cm in depth was found to be stratigraphically above one of the postholes which frame the bank. Characteristic pottery dating to the latest phase of the TRB (MN A V) was found in the pit, giving a terminus ante quem for the erection of the bank. The enclosure's probable construction date is indicated by a funnel beaker of which almost the entire profile was preserved (Fig. 108A). This beaker was found inside another of the postholes which delimit the bank. The vessel was probably originally placed at the bank/post and then later slid into the posthole when the post was pulled out or rotted away. The deposition of pots and other material at enclosure palisades is well documented at Sarup (Andersen, N.H. 1997, 34) as well as at the later palisade enclosures in Scania, eastern Zealand and Bornholm (Svensson 2002).

The vessel is a funnel beaker with a high, widely splayed neck separated from the belly by a pronounced, rounded shoulder. The height of the vessel is reconstructed to ca. 17 cm. Its rim is decorated by an incised herringbone-pattern followed by incised vertical fringes ca. 2 cm in length. Groups

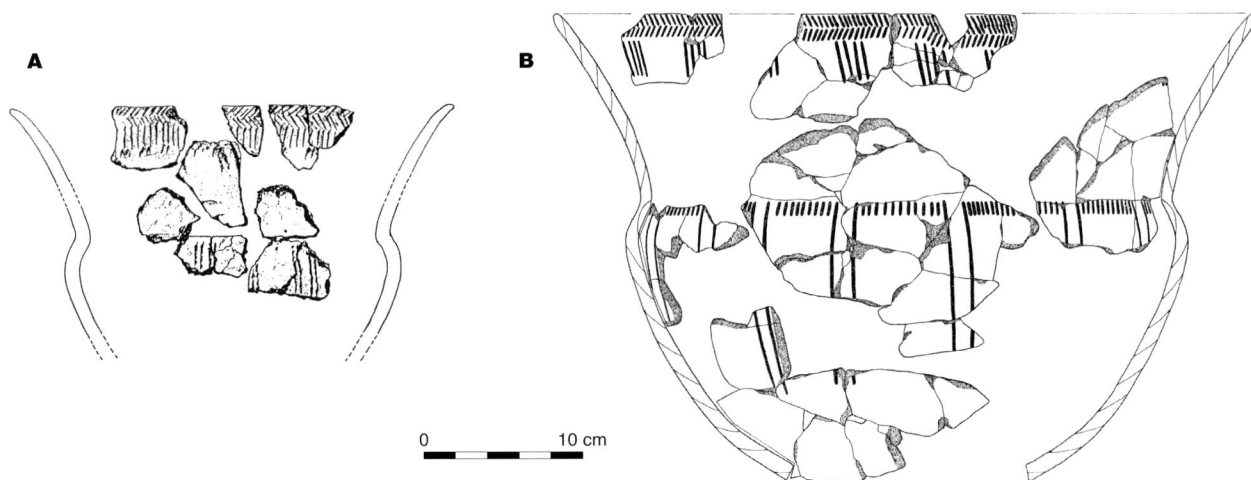

Fig. 108 | *Funnel beaker found in one of the postholes making up the enclosure at Vilsund A) and B) its parallel from Tolstrup III (from Madsen 1975). The vessels can be dated to the chronological period between 3500 and 3300 BC (EN II). A) Drawing Museet for Thy og Vester Hanherred.*

of short double stabs made by a pin at regular distances constitute the lower border of this decorative zone. After an undecorated area on the lower part of the neck, a new decorative zone appears on shoulder and belly of the vessel. It consists of vertical fringes executed via a stab and drag technique. These fringes seem to appear in groups of two double lines separated by undecorated zones.

Very close parallels to this vessel (in terms of both shape and decoration) are known from Tolstrup III in northern Jutland (Madsen, T. 1975, 129 Fig. 4.2-5 and 133 Fig. 6; Fig. 108B). Pottery of this type can be dated to the Late Volling Group in northern Jutland, which is contemporary with the Fuchsberg Group further south, and thus belongs to EN II between approximately 3500 and 3300 BC (Madsen, T. 1975; Klassen 2000, 88).

Thus, available evidence points to a construction date for the Vilsund enclosure in EN II. A slightly earlier date cannot be excluded, as it is not possible to demonstrate that the vessel described above was deposited at the bank immediately after construction. However, no traces of renewal of the posts and bank (which would certainly have started to collapse after comparatively few years) were observed during excavation. This indicates a comparatively short phase of use, which probably took place in EN II.

Traces of Neolithic occupation inside the enclosed area were discovered on the northeastern part of the promontory, where a cultural layer with a few, diffuse traces of pits was investigated. The finds suggest the presence of flint and amber working on site. The decoration of the pottery shards is closely paralleled by finds from Tolstrup III (see above) and indicates that this activity zone and the enclosure were approximately contemporary.

Of special interest, however, is a construction consisting of a 3.9 m long, 0.6-0.7 m wide and 1.1-1.2 m deep pit, inside which the traces of three posts made of cloven trees were observed (Fig. 109; Mikkelsen 1989). These posts (which were up to 60 cm wide and 20 cm thick) were spaced at distances of 65 and 80 cm from each other. They were dug a further 50 cm below the bottom of the pit and were held in place by a massive stone packing. The pit was oriented N-S and the flat sides of the split trees were oriented to the west. It appears that they were pulled up again at some point in time.

Three pots were found inside the pit. The best preserved (a 9 cm high lugged jar) was found inside one of the postholes, suggesting that it probably fell into the hole upon the removal of the post (Fig. 110A). The other two pots (both funnel beakers) were found beside each other, most likely in their

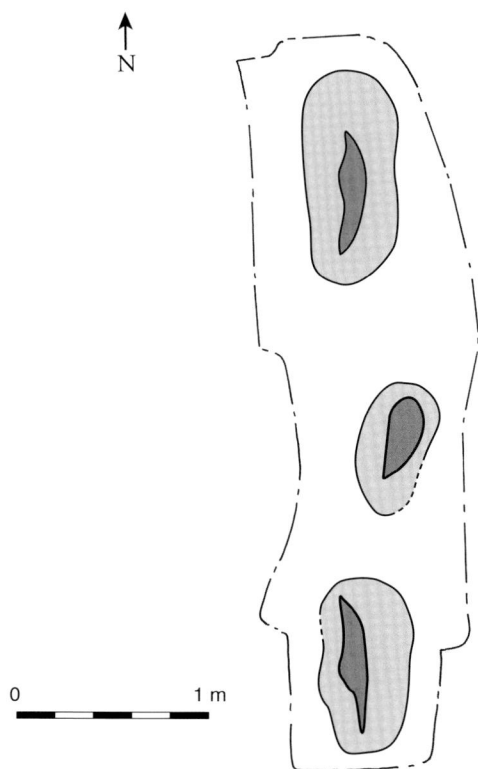

Fig. 109 | *Pit with remains of three massive posts found inside the enclosed area at Vilsund. Three pots had been deposited at the posts, which almost certainly represent the remains of a façade which likely delimited the eastern end of an earthen long barrow.*

places of original deposition. One stood upside down, while the second stood on its base. This last was the only (and very badly) preserved part of the latter. As far as it is possible to tell, both beakers were closely related in type.

The lugged jar is decorated with six rows of two-ply cord on the cylindrical neck, while the remainder of the vessel is covered by a stabbed zigzag pattern marked with a tool with a 0.8 cm wide edge. Four lugs are found at the transition between belly and base. This vessel can clearly be associated with the north Jutish Volling Group. However, in the absence of a detailed typo-chronological study of Volling ceramics, it is unfortunately impossible to date the vessel more precisely within this group. Indeed, the Volling Group was present in northern Jutland between ca. 3800 and 3300 BC, i.e. in both EN I and EN II. The decoration of the neck could

indicate an early date, while the decoration of the belly could be indicative of a later time period.

The second (and probably also third) vessel can be described as a c. 7 cm tall funnel beaker with a 3 cm high cylindrical neck (Fig. 110B). The diameter at the neck is 6 cm. The belly of the vessel is rounded, which was probably also true for the base, although this was unfortunately not preserved. Therefore, one cannot exclude the possibility that the vessel had lugs similar to those on the one described above. The neck of this vessel is decorated by three rows of two-ply cord impressions crossed by short oblique rows at regular intervals made in the same technique. The lower part of the neck, shoulder and belly are divided into vertical fields bordered by furrows probably incised via the stab-and-drag technique. The fields have differing widths (alternating broad and narrow). The narrow fields are undecorated, while the wide ones show large angles consisting of two impressions each.

The decoration of the neck of this vessel is also known from Tolstrup (Madsen, T. 1975, 137 Fig. 10.2). The decoration found on vessel bellies from this same site also appears to be closely related (Madsen, T. 1975, 139 Fig. 13.20). Shards showing the decorations described at Tolstrup were found in connection with construction (grave) III. Thus, it appears that the vessel(s) discussed here find their best parallels at Tolstrup III, as did the vessel from the palisade and the shards from the cultural layer. All three appear to be more or less contemporary and can be dated to EN II.

The N-S oriented pit with three massive posts inside and three deposited vessels can be identified as the eastern terminal structure of an Early Neolithic earthen long barrow. At a number of sites, identical (or nearly-identical) observations have been made regarding the size and orientation of pits, stone packing, the cleaving of posts/orientation of the flat side of the posts, the removal of posts and the deposition of vessels (see e.g. Madsen, T. 1979; Kaul 1988, 58ff.; Kristensen 1989, 80ff.; Liversage 1992, 85ff.; Woll 2003; Rassmann 2011). However, no traces of either grave or barrow were detected at Vilsund, even though the excavation field was enlarged to the west of the described feature specifically with the intent of

Fig. 110 | *A) Lugged jar of the Volling Group which was found inside the pit representing a façade of an earthen long barrow at Vilsund. The vessel belongs to the Volling Group but cannot be dated more precisely at present. In northern Jutland, the Volling Group period lasted from ca. 3800 BC to 3300 BC. B) Remains of a Volling Group funnel beaker or lugged beaker found inside Vilsund's façade pit. The vessel most likely dates to the EN II, therefore indicating that the earthen long barrow was probably more or less contemporaneous with the enclosure. Photos: Klaus Madsen.*

identifying potential remains. Therefore, while there can be no doubt that the pit with inserted posts and deposited vessels is an element that was usually associated with burials in earthen long barrows, it is impossible to determine whether such a grave was once present at Vilsund (but is no longer preserved) or whether the post-construction was erected in isolation. Loss due to heavy erosion appears to be the most likely explanation, all the same.

The topographic situation, relation to prehistoric roads (see chapter 6.3.2.1 and Fig. 27) and date of the enclosing structure at Vilsund match perfectly with ordinary TRB causewayed enclosures in Denmark. However, the site is characterised by a number of unique traits which will be discussed shortly below. These traits include the fact that the enclosing element is not made up of one (or

several) rows of segmented ditches, as is usually the case, but is rather comprised of a turf bank held in place by a construction of double-sided rows of posts. Moreover, the enclosing structure's course across the promontory is completely straight rather than the standard curve. Additionally, pits (which clearly resemble ditch segments) are found on both sides of the enclosing structure. Finally, a probable grave construction contemporary with the enclosure was found within the enclosed area.

1. Construction of the enclosing structure
While preserved remains of banks are known from some enclosures in Germany and Britain, for example, they always seem to occur in combination with segmented ditches of ordinary causewayed enclosures (see e.g. Tackenberg 1951 (Beusterburg),

Eckert 1990, 403 (Bonn-Venusberg), Oswald et al. 2001, 43 (examples from Britain) and Seidel (2008, 363ff.) for enclosures of the Michelsberg and related cultures in Central and Western Europe). Structures identical to the one found at Vilsund are not present elsewhere, although the existence of banks held in place by palisades and other constructions has been debated elsewhere (Seidel 2008, 363ff.).

Palisade enclosures without ditches are known from Western Europe (Belgium, France, possibly also the German Rhineland) from the second half of the 5th and the first half of the 4th millennia BC (e.g. in the northern Chasséen: Martinez/Blanchet 1988). However, contrary to Vilsund, these structures can be characterized as having true palisades with closely spaced posts. Therefore, they have a different character than the post structure excavated at Vilsund (which was not a proper palisade, but rather a supporting structure for a turf wall). The same difference also applies to the palisade enclosures known from the eastern parts of South Scandinavia (Zealand, Scania and Bornholm) from the early third millennium BC (Svensson 2002; Klatt 2009). At present, the Vilsund enclosure must, therefore, be considered a local variant of classical causewayed enclosures. It may be understood as a structural parallel to the situation in southwest Britain (Cornwall). In Cornwall, the so-called Tor enclosures have been identified as the stone-built counterparts of classical causewayed enclosures (Oswald et al. 2001, 85ff.).

2. Pits/ditch segments on both sides of the bank/turf wall

In one instance, ditch segments were observed on both sides of the palisade in a regular causewayed enclosure (Fig. 111). The monument in question is located at Freston, Suffolk in southeast England (Oswald et al. 2001, 47 Fig. 3.14). Taking into account the slightly deviant character of the pits on both sides of the Vilsund turf wall and the scarcity of parallels to the feature under discussion, the present evidence should not be overestimated. However, the geographical situation of the enclosures at Freston and Vilsund is striking, as both were built close to the North Sea coast. Given that other enclosures from the west coast of Jutland could

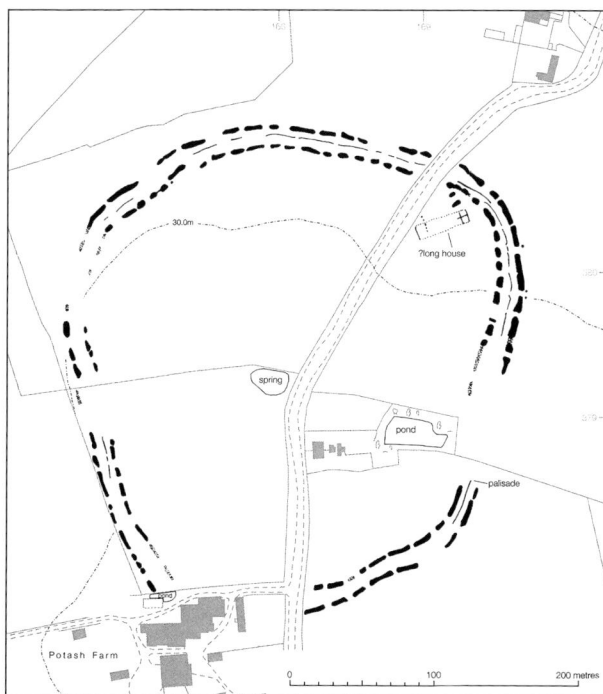

Fig. 111 | *The causewayed enclosure at Freston in Suffolk (southern Britain) is the only known classical causewayed enclosure with circuits of segmented ditches on both sides of a palisade (from Oswald et al. 2001; © British Heritage).*

clearly be related to the British enclosure tradition, it is likely that the construction of the enclosure at Vilsund was at least partly guided by ideas that were relayed through the communication network that existed along the North Sea fringe (Fig. 112).

Unfortunately, the enclosure at Freston is not among those dated by Whittle et al. (2011a). However, considering the rather narrow time horizon that has been established by the latter for the construction of a very large number of British enclosures (late 38th to early 36th centuries BC), it is likely that the Freston enclosure was also built in this time interval. It is probable, therefore, that Freston is somewhat older than the Vilsund enclosure (probably 35th or 34th century BC).

3. Utterly straight enclosing elements

Enclosures delimited by an enclosing element with a completely straight course are also very rare. The numerous enclosures known are normally made up of rows of segmented ditches with an outwardly-

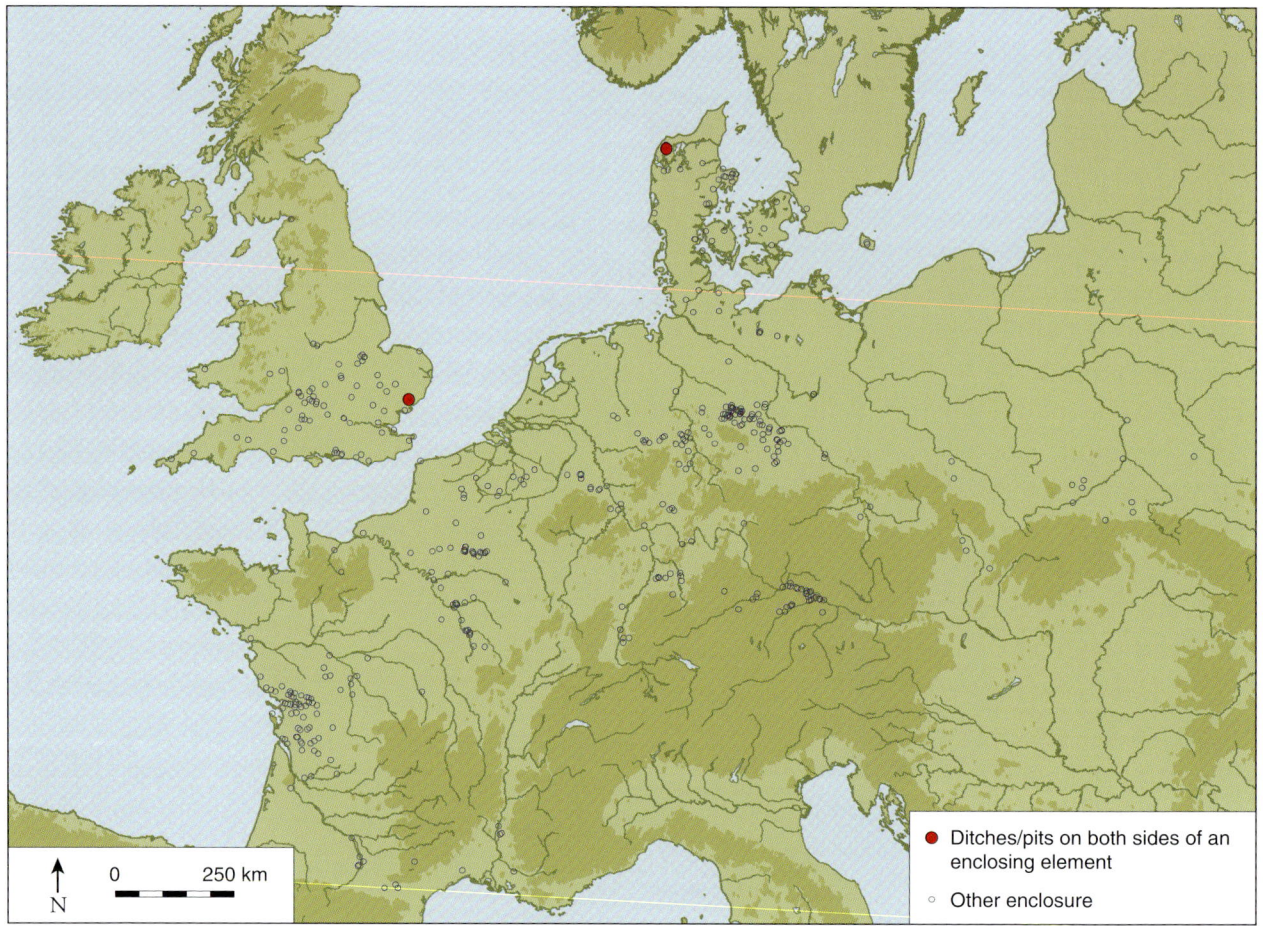

Fig. 112 | *The European distribution of enclosures with ditch segments/pits on both sides of a palisade or other enclosing element. The sites of Vilsund in Denmark and Freston in England can probably both be related to a contact network which stretched along the fringes of the North Sea.*

curving course. However, at least one (probably two) causewayed enclosures from the Michelsberg Culture in Westphalia, Germany have completely straight ditches (Fig. 113). At Nottuln-Uphoven, one straight ditch with a palisade dating to MK III (early 4th millennium BC) has been documented for over 250 m (Eckert 1987; Knoche 2008, 28ff.), while at Osterwick (a few km from Nottuln-Uphoven) four parallel, straight ditches ran for at least 85 m (Wilhelmi 1977, 10ff.; Willms 1982). However, these ditches were not immediately accepted as potential enclosure ditches because of their completely straight course. Until this discovery, such a formation had been completely unknown in a Michelsberg context. The discovery of the enclosure at Nottuln-Uphoven several years later indicates that the ditches from Osterwick may very

well be enclosure ditches (Knoche 2008, 150). As at Nottuln-Uphoven, find material from Osterwick points to MK III as time of construction.

As was the case with the ditches on both sides of the enclosing element, evidence for parallels to the completely straight courses of the enclosing structure is scanty (Fig. 114). Therefore, whether or not connections existed between the Vilsund enclosure and those of the Michelsberg Culture in Westphalia is difficult to evaluate. Nonetheless, the existence of such relations was certainly possible.

4. Regular funerary structure inside the enclosed area

This particularly striking element of the Vilsund enclosure has few known counterparts among European enclosures, provided that regularly-appearing depositions of humans or parts of humans in both the ditches and special pits in the interior of enclosures are disregarded and the survey is restricted to ordinary grave types regularly known from non-enclosure contexts. This is, obviously, a difficult exercise, especially with regards to the Michelsberg Culture (for which it is difficult to define an "ordinary" grave – Jeunesse 2010 with further literature). If this problem is disregarded, possibly only a single case can be referenced in which a grave was recorded inside an enclosure. At Warburg-Rimberg (Knoche 2003, 11f.), a so-called gallery grave is located inside a late Michelsberg Culture enclosure (Fig. 115). Until recently, this type of semi-megalithic grave has been regarded as belonging to the (early) Wartberg Culture of eastern Westphalia and Hessia in the last third of the 4th millennium BC (regarding Warburg-Rimberg see Knoche 2003, 19). However, Knoche's (2008, 193f.;

2013, 153f.) recent observation as well as new ^{14}C-datings from two gallery graves at Schmerlecke in Westphalia demonstrate that the construction of this type of grave may well have started as early as 3700 BC. If this was the case, it did indeed date from the late Michelsberg Culture (Schierhold et al. 2012). The Warburg-Rimberg enclosure is dated to the 37th century BC (Knoche 2003, 17). It is, therefore, at least possible that the site's enclosure and gallery grave were in use contemporaneously.

As has previously been the case, it is difficult to conclude too much from the scant evidence presented here. However, it is noteworthy that two of the four unique features encountered at Vilsund find parallels in Westphalia (although in different regions of Westphalia located more than 100 km from each other). Likewise, a third feature has a potential parallel on the east coast of England, a region with numerous other paral-

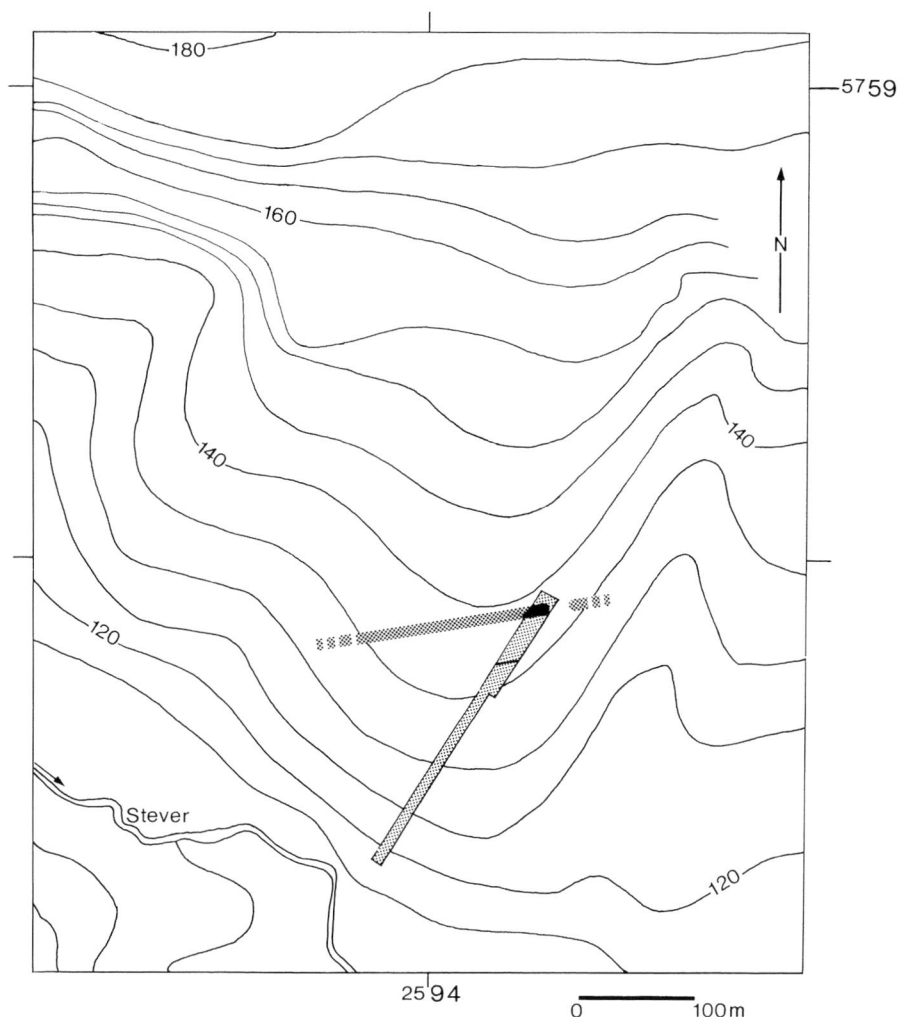

Fig. 113 | *Just as was the case at the Vilsund enclosure, the Michelsberg enclosure of Nottuln-Uphoven in Westphalia was delimited by a constructional element with an entirely straight course (from Eckert 1987).*

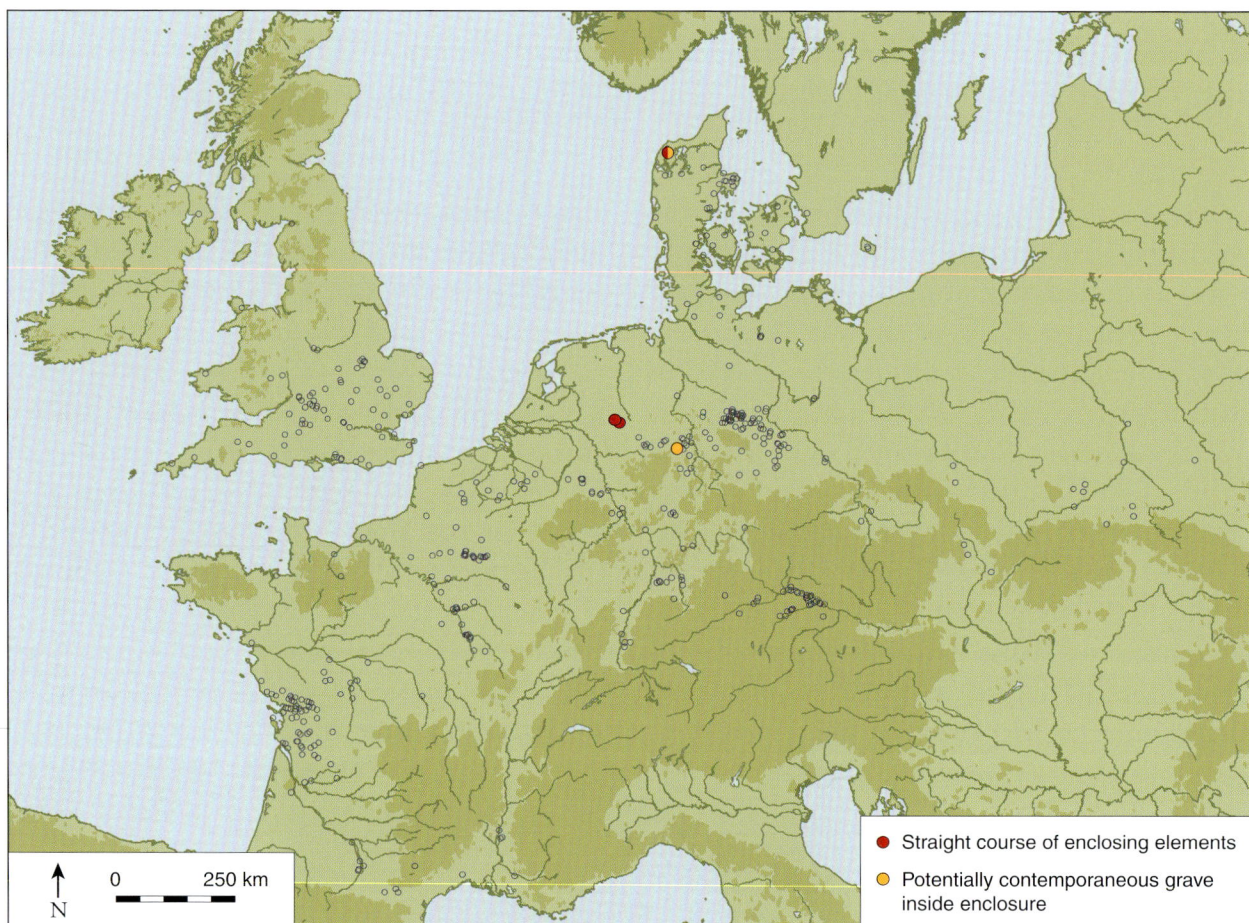

Fig. 114 | *The European distribution of enclosures showing some of the same elements as those encountered at Vilsund (i.e. straight course of enclosure construction and regular contemporaneous grave construction inside the enclosure).*

lels to enclosures along the west coast region of Jutland (where Vilsund is located). It is, thus, at least possible that a re-combination of individual elements derived from different sources in Western and Central Europe took place at Vilsund. A comparable process can possibly be observed at another TRB enclosure located close to the west coast of Jutland: the Albersdorf Dieksknöll site. At Albersdorf Dieksknöll, a double post setting in the entrance can potentially be related to the communication network operating in the near-coastal areas of the North Sea region (see above chapter 10.2.6) and a transverse pit on a causeway can certainly be related to the Michelsberg Culture in southwest Germany (see chapter 10.4.1.1 below). It is important to note that in both cases (Vilsund and Albersdorf Dieksknöll), elements derived from

Western Europe through the North Sea contact network were probably combined with elements derived from the south. Both enclosures in question are located close to the west coast of Jutland.

10.2.8 Additional observations

The vast majority of TRB enclosures were built on more or less pronounced promontories; a much smaller proportion were constructed on hilltops. The same general type of location (with some variation due to general topographic diversity between different parts of Europe) was used for a large number of enclosures in many parts of Central and Western Europe. The same is true for locations at river confluences, while locations at river outlets into fjords are naturally absent from most regions

Fig. 115 | *Enclosure of the late Michelsberg Culture at Warburg-Rimbeck with a potentially contemporaneous grave (marked by added arrow) inside the enclosed area (from Knoche 2003).*

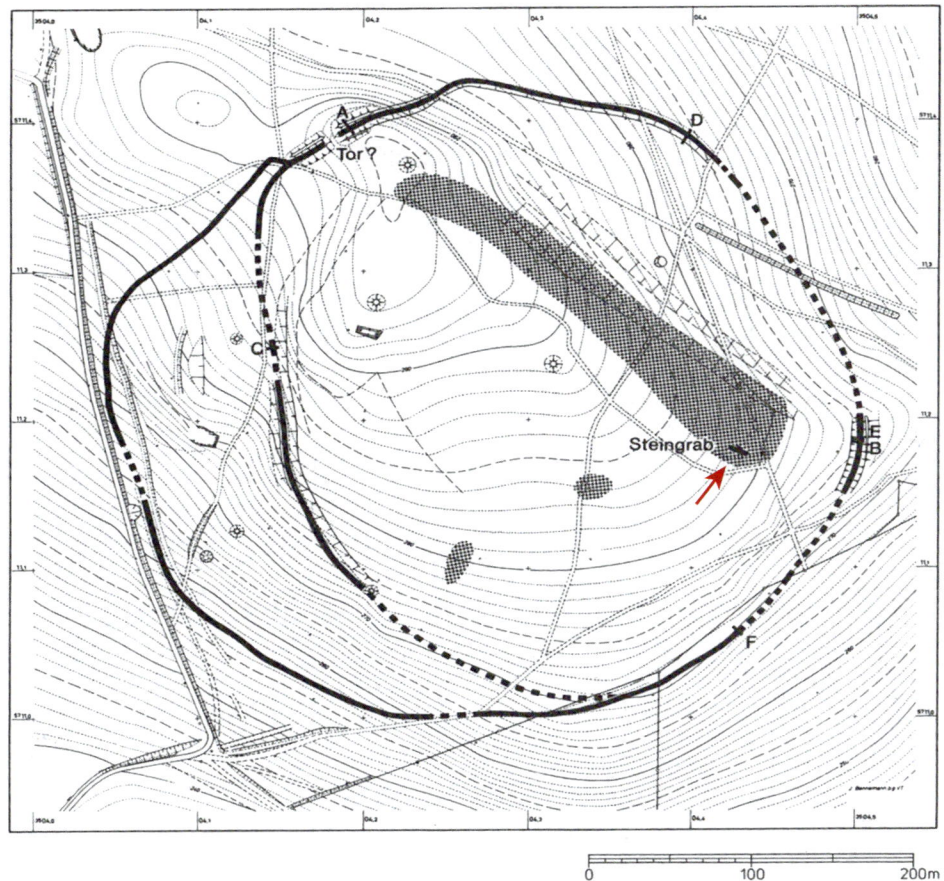

used for comparison. A detailed investigation of these parameters is, therefore, not likely to produce any significant evidence for specific relations between TRB and other enclosures. However, among the few South Scandinavian sites that remained unclassified with regard to their topographic location, one enclosure is of interest to the current investigation. As mentioned before (chapters 6.1 and 10.1), the Gammeltoft Odde site is found on a very shallow elevation on what might have been (in the Neolithic) a small island (or the end of a very elongated and narrow peninsula) which stretched either into a lake or fjord. The only comparison within South Scandinavia comes from the Ballegård enclosure in Djursland.

It is possibly no coincidence that the Haddenham site in Cambridgeshire (which contains one of the best parallels to the entrance construction of the Gammeltoft Odde enclosure) is situated in a comparable setting: it lies very few metres above sea level in a rather flat terrain surrounded by wetlands (Evans 1988, 127). This setting is often en-

countered in South Britain, in which region at least one periodically flooded enclosure site (Etton) is presently known (Oswald et al. 2001, 91 ff.). Comparable settings also seem to have been common in Central Europe, where this phenomenon has not yet received the attention it deserves (Knoche 2013, 21f.). However, as mentioned earlier, the best parallel to the specific topographic setting of the Gammeltoft Odde enclosure is known from the northern French coast (Lillemer in northern Brittany – Laporte et. al. 2007). Thus, it is likely that information relayed through the near-coastal communication network at the fringes of the North Sea and the Channel can account for the choice of Gammeltoft Odde for a building site.

As apparent from Fig. 116, the vast majority of enclosures in South Britain have closed circuits of segmented ditches, while the Continental dataset shows a more equal distribution between closed and partial ditch circuits, albeit with a majority of closed ones (data for the British sites: Oswald et al. 2001, for the Continental sites: Geschwinde/

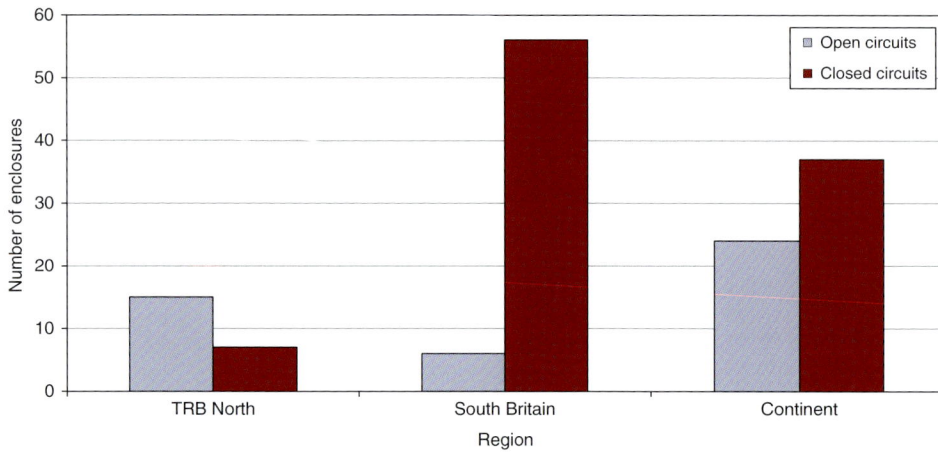

Fig. 116 | *A comparison of the relative numbers of enclosures with open and closed ditch circuits in the TRB North Group distribution area with those in southern Britain (data from Oswald et al. 2001) as well as those in Central Europe (data from Geschwinde & Raetzel-Fabian 2009).*

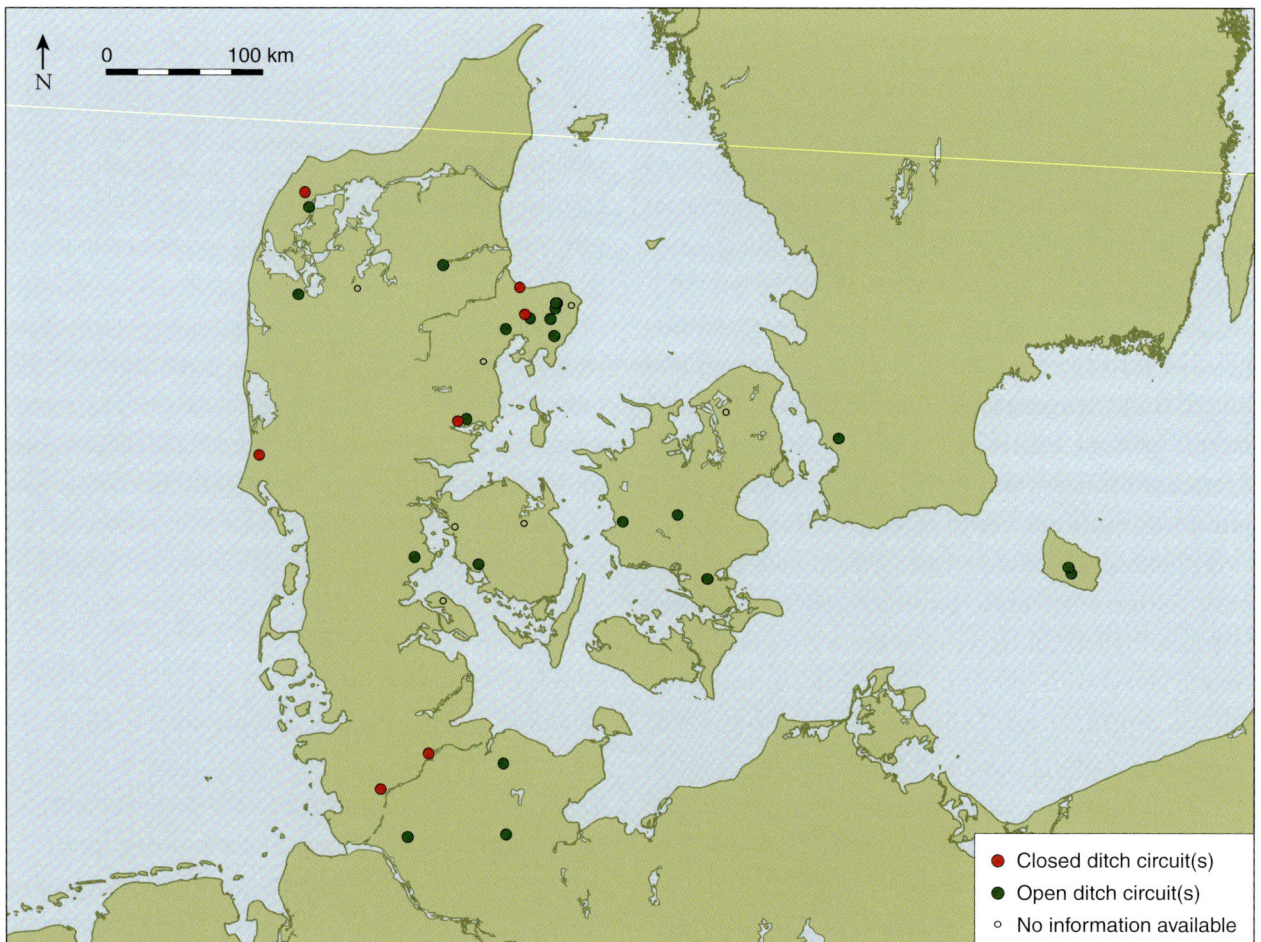

Fig. 117 | *The distribution of enclosures with open or closed ditch circuits in South Scandinavia. At present, enclosures with closed ditch circuits are only known from the western part of this region.*

Raetzel-Fabian (2009, 219 ff. Abb. 161)). As apparent from Geschwinde and Raetzel-Fabian's table, there are regional differences within the Continental dataset. For example, all but one site from the north of France certainly (or probably) belong to their "Umfassungstype 1", which describes enclosures marked by partial circuits. If this region is examined in isolation, it resembles South Scandinavia, while the remainder of the Continent resembles Britain.

The Gammeltoft Odde enclosure is one of only seven TRB North Group sites for which closed ditch circuits have been proven (or are likely). The other six include Blakbjerg (Boas 2001), Büdelsdorf (Hage in press), Albersdorf Dieksknöll (Dibbern 2012), Liselund (Westphal 2000), (possibly) Store Brokhøj (Madsen, B./Fiedel 1987) and Bjerggård (latest plan in T. Madsen, unpublished). In seven other cases, the type of ditch circuit (closed or partial) is unknown. However, enclosures for which partial ditch circuits have been demonstrated (or are likely) represent the largest group by far (25 cases).

Thus, the Gammeltoft Odde enclosure belongs to a group of enclosures that is rare in Scandinavia and dominant in southern Britain. Whether this can be viewed as an indication of contact with Britain cannot be demonstrated with the same degree of probability as was possible for several of the other cases described above. Enclosures with closed ditch circuits are known from locations outside the west coast of Jutland. However, all

sites which are presently known are indeed from Jutland, and thus the western part of South Scandinavia (Fig. 117).

Fig. 118 gives an overview of the size of South Scandinavian enclosures in comparison to their counterparts from Britain and Continental Europe. The size classes defined by Raetzel-Fabian (1999) were used to produce the chart. Consequently, the enclosures have been defined as small (below 2 ha), medium (between 2 and 10 ha), large (10-20 ha) and very large (more than 20 ha). The data for Britain were taken from Oswald et al. 2001. Those for Central Europe were taken from Geschwinde/Raetzel-Fabian (2009, 219 ff. Abb. 161).

In both Britain and South Scandinavia, it appears that small- or medium-sized enclosures make up the largest part of all known sites by far, while the enclosures in Central and Western Europe (excluding the British Isles) have a completely different size distribution. In those parts of Europe, small enclosures are almost unknown and medium-sized ones make up less than one third of the total sample. The dominant group in Central and Western Europe (except the British Isles) were the large enclosures. The very large, monumental sites (which are very rare in Scandinavia) also appear in quantity. When Scandinavia is juxtaposed with Britain, it appears that there was a tendency for slightly larger enclosures in the former region as expressed in the higher frequency of medium-sized compared to small sites (the mirror image of British frequencies).

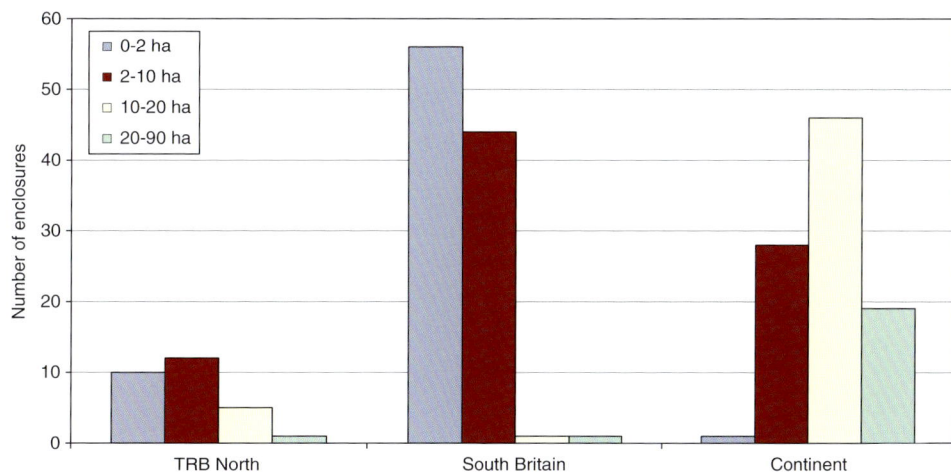

Fig. 118 | *Comparison of the size of enclosures within the TRB North Group distribution area (excluding Mecklenburg) with those from south Britain and Western and Central Europe.*

Furthermore, large sites are known from Scandinavia in some number, whereas they are almost unknown in Britain.

In summary, it can be stated that Scandinavian enclosures appear to be comparatively closely related to their British counterparts with regards to size, while Central European examples clearly diverge (especially from those in Britain). This finding is in agreement with the fact that numerous examples of clear relations in enclosure architecture details between British and Scandinavian sites and present but rarer examples of architectural links between Scandinavian and Central European enclosures could be described in the previous chapters.

Observations regarding specific architectural details are confirmed by the observation of the particular geographic locations of the South Scandinavian enclosures; they are predominantly found in sub-regions of South Scandinavia that are geographically close to Central and Western European regions from which the same architectural details are known. Unfortunately, it is not possible to confirm the size-related affinities of South Scandinavian enclosures to British sites by comparable geographical observations, as the amount of size-related data is insufficient at present to allow for detailed comparisons on a sub-regional scale. Therefore, it is impossible to conclusively determine whether the size-distribution of South Scandinavian enclosures indicates that they are more closely related to British than to Central European sites, or whether such observations actually reflect a genuine Scandinavian development. In the future (i.e. when more data about the size of enclosures in different parts of South Scandinavia becomes available), it may be possible to recognize regional trends.

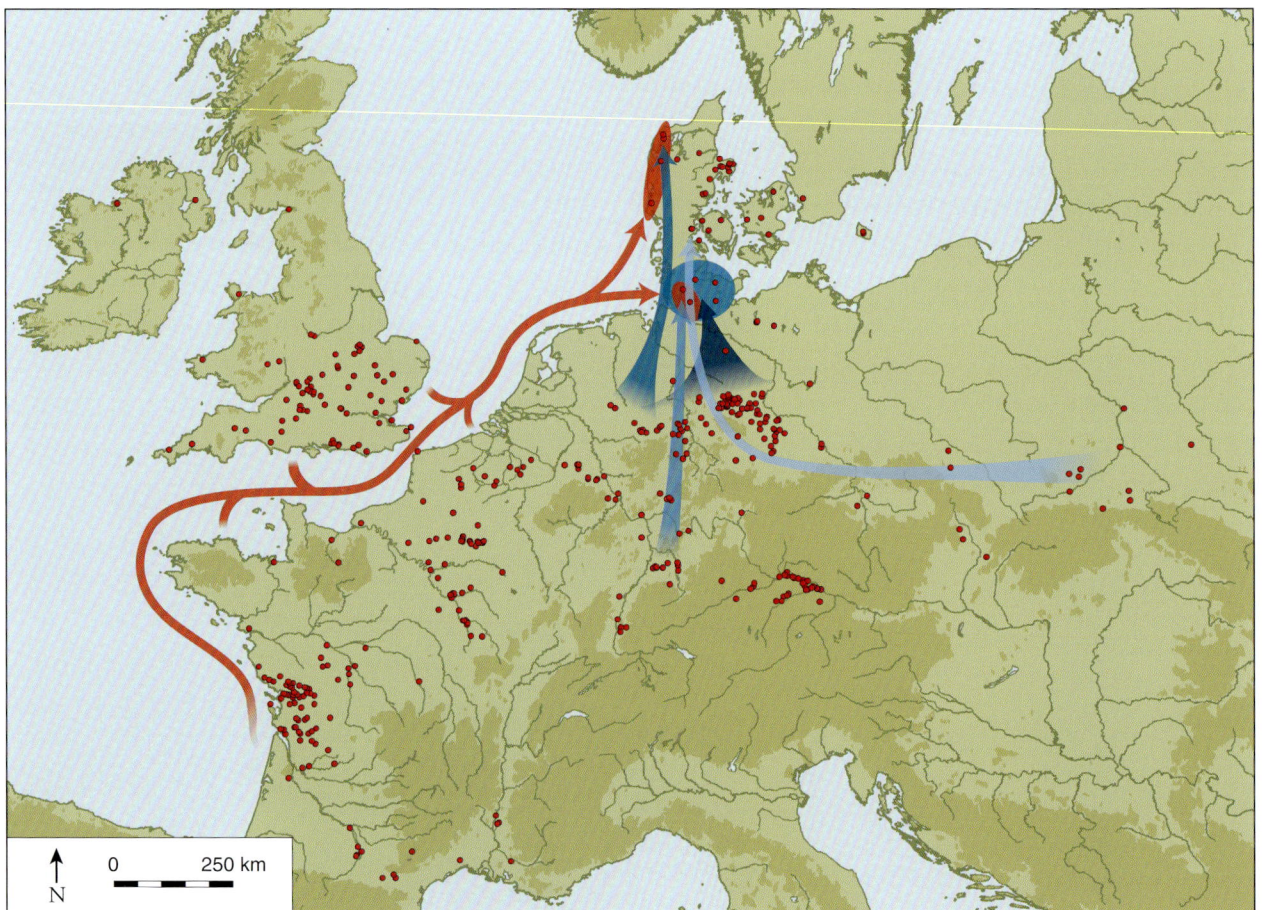

Fig. 119 | *Enclosures in the distributional periphery of the TRB North Group show distinct relations to enclosures in neighbouring as well in regions located further afield. The map reflects both near-coastal and overland contact networks.*

10.2.9 Discussion

The comparison of TRB North Group enclosure traits (i.e. the number of partial segmented ditch circuits, the spacing between them, the size of the enclosures, entrance constructions, ditch design) with those from southern Britain and Western and Central Europe allows for a number of conclusions to be drawn. It can be stated that it is, in fact, possible to identify both general and specific traits with clear regional distribution patterns in a number of South Scandinavian enclosures. The sites for which typical Western European traits could be identified are all located close to the west coast of Jutland. In several cases, only very few European counterparts could be picked out. When viewed in isolation, these observations must be taken with a grain of salt, especially when considering the large number of enclosures in almost all regions of Europe for which insufficient information was available. However, in the case of Western European elements, a concurrent distribution pattern could be demonstrated. Many individual traits could be detected in central western France, southern Britain, the Continental area adjacent to the Channel (northern France, Belgium) and on the west coast of Jutland. This distribution pattern clearly indicates the existence of a communication network stretching along the Atlantic fringe and the southern North Sea coast. Specific traits from a Central European architectural tradition could, furthermore, be detected in enclosures in the southernmost part of South Scandinavia as well as on the west coast of Jutland (Fig. 119).

These observations suggest the presence of two different areas of enclosure construction within the TRB North Group: a periphery zone and a core area. In the periphery zone, enclosures show specific architectural elements related to enclosures in both Western and Central Europe. This zone includes the western and southern parts of Jutland. Western elements dominate along the west coast of Jutland, whereas southern, Continental elements come to the fore in southern Jutland (as could be expected from the respective geographical proximities of the two regions). However, Central European elements have also been identified in

northwest Jutland. Another instance of such influence was detected at the Sarup I enclosure on the island of Funen (see below, chapter 10.4.1.2). This would be outside the 'periphery zone' defined here. Future investigations should show whether or not these Central European elements were truly predominant in the western and southwestern parts of South Scandinavia, as is suggested by the present evidence. It should also be considered whether some resemblances between South Scandinavian enclosures and those outside the area might be due to indirect contact between different groups linked up in a communication network while other resemblances could reflect the immigration of especially Central European groups.

The specific traits characterising the enclosures of the periphery zone are lacking in what could be called the core zone of South Scandinavian enclosure construction (which includes all of Denmark except western and southern Jutland – excepting Sarup). Enclosures in this area seem to reflect a more genuine Scandinavian construction style dominated by medium to large enclosures on promontories delimited by a maximum of two partial circuits of segmented ditches, wetlands, rivers or more or less steep slopes. Although they do exist, enclosures showing these traits outside South Scandinavia appear to be comparatively rare.

The size distribution of the enclosures in South Scandinavia indicates that they belong to a Western European (perhaps even specifically British) tradition more than to a Central European one, irrespective of location.

Two or three different diffusion mechanisms of specific architectural traditions appear to have been at work. The first is of very large scale, probably of long duration and of a very general character. This mechanism resulted in the inclusion of the South Scandinavian causewayed enclosures in a broad cultural Western European tradition which also affected other aspects of Neolithic life in Scandinavia.

The second type of diffusion mechanism worked specifically between neighbouring groups. This does not necessarily mean that it was operative only over comparatively short distances;

the nearest enclosure-building neighbours were often several hundred kilometres away. Furthermore, several of these neighbour-connecting mechanisms could have been linked in what one might describe as 'chains', enabling the passage of specific information over considerable distances. Just as was the case with the first mechanism described here, elements other than those specifically linked to enclosure architecture may well have been relayed in this way. Megalithic graves are a possible example. The main difference to the first mechanism is that it was only effective at the western and southwest periphery of South Scandinavia (see the discussion above).

However, it is possible that the first and second mechanisms are, in fact, the same. The apparent difference in the geographical distribution of elements relayed by these diverse means may thus be explained by the different powers of penetration of the various information types (which may have been determined by the intensity of the contacts which engendered them in the first place). This could explain why all Scandinavian enclosures can be ascribed to a general Western European building tradition, while several specific Western European architectural elements (which were certainly bound to specific beliefs) were only taken up in a restricted area close to the nearest external contact responsible for the distribution of that specific information.

There remains, however, at least one other diffusion mechanism which was at work at causewayed enclosures. Through this last, specific information could be relayed over very large distances, irrespective of cultural borders and/or periphery and core zones within South Scandinavia. Another peculiar characteristic of this mechanism (which was bound to long-distance routes and may (or may not) have been connected to long-range personal mobility) is the fact that the information passed on by this mechanism was only effective in the immediate surroundings of said long-distance routes. Such a mechanism could explain the presence of Central European elements as far north as at Vilsund and is described in more detail in a later chapter (10.4).

The starting point for the investigation of the European context of the South Scandinavian enclosures was the question whether the appearance of these monuments in the TRB North Group distribution area was due to an impulse from abroad, or whether it was based on internal social developments. The discussion of architectural links can point to various possible regions of origin for such an impulse. However, this alone of course cannot solve the problem outlined here. The fact that specific elements deriving from specific regions can be identified in specific TRB enclosures can be explained in a variety of different ways. Either this was the result of an impulse from specific regions, or TRB groups deliberately chose to incorporate specific elements from regions with which they had close contact at a given time. Of special interest in this regard are the west coast enclosures of Vilsund and Albersdorf Dieksknöll, because they clearly re-combine elements of both Western and Central European origin. While it may seem logical to interpret this as an indication that some internal development caused enclosure construction, the possibility that an impulse from one of the regions jump-started construction and that elements from the other region were incorporated in the creation of a genuine, local enclosure type cannot be excluded. In the present case, this almost certainly would imply an impulse from Central Europe and the inclusion of Western European elements. Both enclosures (again, Vilsund and Albersdorf Dieksknöll) are located near the west coast of Jutland. As has been argued, a communication network along the North Sea, Channel and Atlantic coastlines can be demonstrated within this region. Specific Western European enclosure elements may well have been known (and could be included in enclosure construction at Vilsund and Albersdorf Dieksknöll) due to this contact network. However, there is nothing that could indicate the existence of comparable contacts with Central Europe at these two sites.

The existence of a periphery zone with clear links to neighbouring regions as well as a core area with enclosures constructed in a more genuine Scandinavian style is also worthy of interest with regard to this current question. However, it too could be interpreted in several different ways: Enclosure building could have started due to external influences in the periphery zone, spreading into the core area. In this case, dates should reveal that the oldest enclosures were built in the periphery zone. But enclosure building could also have started due to internal developments which occurred concomitantly in both the periphery and the core zone. The reflection of specific enclosure building traditions from neighbouring regions in the periphery zone could simply be the knock-on effects of communication networks connecting with other enclosure-building groups.

It is apparent that information concerning the chronology of the construction of the enclosures is needed before further light can be shed on this area. The information provided by the discussion of the different individual architectural elements is not sufficient in this regard, although it does demonstrate that most architectural elements encountered in Scandinavian enclosures were known in other parts of Europe (either earlier or contemporaneously). At the very least, the elements that are known to have been present earlier in other regions must be regarded as foreign imports. The same is probably true for the elements which appeared contemporaneously in South Scandinavia and other parts of Europe. These could have either been invented in the TRB North Group (and then spread from there), or resulted from social interaction between TRB groups and other Neolithic people outside Scandinavia, thereby appearing in several areas at the same time. However, these scenarios are rather unlikely. One must recall that in many of the cases discussed above, no precise construction date was known for TRB enclosures. The earliest known construction dates for any enclosure in South Scandinavia were, therefore, used for chronological comparisons. It is unlikely, however, that these early datings apply in all cases. In most instances, the elements in question probably appeared earlier outside of the TRB distribution area. Furthermore, if some of these elements resulted from the interaction of specific groups, it could be argued that the outcome of this innovative process was closely related to this specific interaction/situation. In such a case, one cannot expect that the solutions reached would have been attractive for other groups living further away. However, the distribution maps for the elements in question show that they were widely distributed throughout the various communication networks.

The datings of TRB enclosures as discussed thus far cannot indicate whether the initiative to introduce enclosures (with specific architectural elements) in South Scandinavia was taken locally, or whether it was triggered by some external development. Therefore, general enclosure construction chronology in Europe is discussed below in an attempt to cast light on this important issue.

10.3 Aspects of enclosure chronology

The role and importance of Neolithic groups in other parts of Europe to the introduction of causewayed enclosures in South Scandinavia can be investigated not only by looking at the architecture of these monuments, but also by identifying their place in the overall development of European enclosure building practices. It is to this end, therefore, that the following contrasts Scandinavian enclosures with a large body of comparable monuments within the area stretching between the Atlantic coast and eastern Poland. Naturally, it follows that a precondition for this task is knowledge of local enclosure chronologies. The following discussion will therefore begin with that subject before segueing into a European perspective of the chronology problem overall.

10.3.1 Scandinavian enclosure chronology

In general, the state of research concerning enclosure chronology in South Scandinavia is poor. ^{14}C datings are only available for 13 of the 39 known sites (Tab. 12). However, it is only in a scant three (possibly four) of these 13 cases that those dates can be related to said enclosure's construction. In other words, radiometric datings for the construction of causewayed enclosures in South Scandinavia are available for only 8-10% of known

Enclo-sure	Lab code	Sample material	Sample age (years)	Age bp	Sample error	cal BC 1-sigma	cal BC 2-sigma	Context	Source
Rastorf	KIA-34019	charcoal	unknown	4690	30	3518-3377	3627-3371	ditch	Steffens 2009
Büdelsdorf	GrN-6420	charcoal	unknown	4505	60	3341-3104	3484-3013	fenced pit	Hage in press
	GrN-6422	charcoal	unknown	4080	60	2852-2498	2871-2476	ditch	Hage in press
	KI-424	charcoal	unknown	4620	130	3627-3310	3647-2941	fenced pit	Hage in press
	KI-465	charcoal	unknown	4680	70	3622-3370	3640-3341	fenced pit	Hage in press
	KI-470	charcoal	unknown	4460	100	3339-3020	3489-2900	fireplace	Hage in press
	KI-488	charcoal	unknown	4200	70	2894-2678	2917-2579	ditch	Hage in press
	KI-497	charcoal	unknown	4370	110	3321-2889	3365-2680	fireplace	Hage in press
Albersdorf Dieksknöll	KIA-42587	hazelnut	1	4850	24	3655-3637	3695-3539	ditch	Dibbern 2012/Dibbern personal communication
	KIA-42600	charcoal, alder or hazel	> 2 cm diam.	4752	30	3632-3520	3637-3382	ditch	Dibbern 2012/Dibbern personal communication
	KIA-42585	charcoal, alder	2-3 cm diam	4766	31	3634-3524	3640-3384	ditch	Dibbern 2012/Dibbern personal communication
	KIA-42586	charcoal, ilex	> 2 cm diam.	4670	24	3513-3373	3519-3370	ditch	Dibbern 2012/Dibbern personal communication
	KIA-42601	charcoal, wil-low or populus	> 2 cm diam.	4155	28	2869-2676	2877-2632	ditch	Dibbern 2012/Dibbern personal communication
	KIA-42602	charcoal, hormbream or cherry	< 2 cm diam.	4166	29	2874-2680	2880-2634	ditch	Dibbern 2012/Dibbern personal communication
Starup Lange-landsvej	AAR-12005	charcoal, birch	< 25	4847	46	3695-3537	3711-3522	palisade	Lützau-Pedersen/Witte 2012; Lützau Pedersen personal communication
	AAR-12006	charcoal, oak	< 50	4816	42	3650-3532	3695-3519	palisade	Lützau-Pedersen/Witte 2012; Lützau Pedersen personal communication
	AAR-12007	charcoal, hazel	< 25	4580	42	3493-3127	3499- 3265	ditch	Lützau-Pedersen/Witte 2012; Lützau Pedersen personal communication
	AAR-12011	charcoal, oak	< 25	4637	41	3500-3362	3621-3348	ditch	Lützau-Pedersen/Witte 2012; Lützau Pedersen personal communication
	AAR-13797	charcoal, oak	< 30	4595	56	3500-3125	3518-3102	ditch	Lützau-Pedersen/Witte 2012; Lützau Pedersen personal communication
	AAR-13799	chacoal, birch	< 40	4850	30	3691-3543	3702-3536	ditch	Lützau-Pedersen/Witte 2012; Lützau Pedersen personal communication
	AAR-13800	charcoal, hazel	< 10	4767	34	3635-3524	3640-3383	ditch	Lützau-Pedersen/Witte 2012; Lützau Pedersen personal communication
	AAR-13801	charcoal, hazel	< 15	4734	28	3630-3384	3634-3378	ditch	Lützau-Pedersen/Witte 2012; Lützau Pedersen personal communication
	AAR-13802	charcoal, hazel	< 15	4694	47	3621-3375	3631-3368	ditch	Lützau-Pedersen/Witte 2012; Lützau Pedersen personal communication
	AAR-13806	charcoal, oak	< 50	4945	56	3772-3660	3936-3639	ditch	Lützau-Pedersen/Witte 2012; Lützau Pedersen personal communication
Stävie 4:1	St-6003	charcoal	unknown	4055	90	2850-2474	2881-2348	pit (oven) in interior	Larsson 1992
	St-6000	unknown	unknown	3930	90	2567-2290	2836-2140	pit in interior	Larsson 1992
	Ua-26016	food residue	unknown	4360	85	3262-2891	3345-2780	unknown	Andersson 2003
Sarup I	K-2628	cereal grains	1	4580	70	3498-3111	3620-3031	pit in interior	Andersen, N.H. 1981
	K-2629	wood	unknown	4690	90	3628-3369	3655-3116	palisade	Madsen/Petersen 1984
	K-2630	wood	unknown	4600	90	3517-3116	3631-3030	palisade	Madsen/Petersen 1984
	K-2631	wood	unknown	4620	90	3623-3124	3634-3094	palisade	Madsen/Petersen 1984
	K-2632	wood	unknown	4760	90	3640-3381	3706-3360	palisade	Madsen/Petersen 1984
	AAR-15368	cereal grains	1	4476	23	3326-3097	3336-3030	pit in interior	Kanstrup et al. in press
	AAR-15771	cereal grains	1	4500	30	3336-3105	3347-3097	pit in interior	Kanstrup et al. in press
	AAR-15772	cereal grains	1	4471	60	3334-3030	3355-2935	pit in interior	Kanstrup et al. in press
	AAR-15773	cereal grains	1	4548	30	3363-3125	3367-3104	pit in interior	Kanstrup et al. in press
	AAR-15367	cereal grains	1	4543	30	3361-3122	3365-3104	pit in interior	Kanstrup et al. in press

Enclo-sure	Lab code	Sample material	Sample age (years)	Age bp	Sample error	cal BC 1-sigma	cal BC 2-sigma	Context	Source
Sarup II	K-2767	unknown	unknown	4480	90	3340-3030	3486-2913	unknown	Andersen, N.H. 1981
	K-2910	cereal grains	1	4400	90	3315-2908	3345-2892	unknown	Andersen, N.H. 1981
	K-2766	animal bone	< 10	4340	90	3262-2879	3341-2699	unknown	Andersen, N.H. 1981
Toftum	K-2978	oyster shell	unknown	4500	85	3353-3092	3492-2921	ditch	Madsen/Petersen 1984; Madsen personal communication
	K-2979	cardium shell	unknown	4620	70	3519-3139	3630-3102	ditch	Madsen/Petersen 1984; Madsen personal communication
	K-2980	oyster shell	unknown	4520	85	3361-3097	3498-2927	ditch	Madsen/Petersen 1984; Madsen personal communication
	K-2981	oyster shell	unknown	4690	70	3626-3372	3638-3354	ditch	Madsen/Petersen 1984; Madsen personal communication
	K-2982	oyster shell	unknown	4550	90	3488-3098	3617-2936	ditch	Madsen/Petersen 1984; Madsen personal communication
	K-2983	oyster shell	unknown	4590	90	3511-3106	3631-3025	ditch	Madsen/Petersen 1984; Madsen personal communication
	K-2984	oyster shell	unknown	4530	85	3364-3098	3507-2928	ditch	Madsen/Petersen 1984; Madsen personal communication
	K-2985	charcoal	unknown	4500	85	3353-3092	3492-2921	ditch	Madsen/Petersen 1984; Madsen personal communication
	K-2986	charcoal	unknown	4690	90	3628-3369	3655-3116	ditch	Madsen/Petersen 1984; Madsen personal communication
	K-2987	charcoal	unknown	4500	85	3353-3092	3492-2921	ditch	Madsen/Petersen 1984; Madsen personal communication
	K-2988	charcoal	unknown	4730	90	3634-3377	3702-3198	ditch	Madsen/Petersen 1984; Madsen personal communication
Blakbjerg	AAR-16555	animal bone	< 10	4361	31	3011-2918	3086-2904	ditch	this volume
	AAR-16556	animal bone	< 10	4363	29	3011-2919	3085-2906	ditch	this volume
	AAR-16557	animal bone	< 10	4129	26	2858-2631	2870-2583	ditch	this volume
Kains-bakke	K-3686	marine shells	unknown	4180	80	2887-2638	2918-2497	pit in interior	Wincentz Rasmussen 1986
	K-3687	marine shells	unknown	4150	80	2874-2633	2901-2494	pit in interior	Wincentz Rasmussen 1986
	K-3719	animal bone	unknown	4140	85	2872-2624	2898-2491	pit in interior	Wincentz Rasmussen 1986
	K-3929	marine shells	unknown	4050	85	2849-2472	2879-2348	pit in interior	Wincentz Rasmussen 1986
	K-3930	marine shells	unknown	4070	85	2854-2490	2888-2355	pit in interior	Wincentz Rasmussen 1986
	K-3931	marine shells	unknown	4070	85	2854-2490	2888-2355	pit in interior	Wincentz Rasmussen 1986
	K-3932	marine shells	unknown	3970	85	2616-2309	2856-2205	pit in interior	Wincentz Rasmussen 1986
	K-3933	marine shells	unknown	4030	85	2848-2464	2873-2343	pit in interior	Wincentz Rasmussen 1986
	K-3935	marine shells	unknown	3950	90	2573-2299	2852-2149	pit in interior	Wincentz Rasmussen 1986
	K-3936	marine shells	unknown	4040	75	2837-2470	2873-2350	pit in interior	Wincentz Rasmussen 1986
	K-4462	animal bone	< 20	4070	85	2854-2490	2888-2355	pit/ditch	Wincentz Rasmussen 1986
	K-4463	animal bone	< 20	4150	70	2873-2635	2895-2500	pit/ditch	Wincentz Rasmussen 1986
	K-4464	animal bone	< 20	4310	80	3090-2873	3227-2668	pit/ditch	Wincentz Rasmussen 1986
	K-4465	animal bone	< 20	4190	80	2891-2640	2926-2496	pit/ditch	Wincentz Rasmussen 1986
	K-4467	animal bone	< 20	4180	85	2888-2636	2924-2491	pit/ditch	Wincentz Rasmussen 1986
Lønt	AAR-15369	cereal grains	1	4498	23	3334-3105	3341-3098	cultural layer	Kanstrup et al. in press
Liselund	AAR-7205	cereal grain	1	4688	49	3619-3374	3631-3365	pit in interior	unpublished; J. Westphal, pers. comm.
Gammel-toft Odde	AAR-17438	hazelnut	1	4339	29	3311-3020	3330-2931	ditch	unpublished; S. Troldtoft Andresen, pers. comm.
	AAR-17444	birch bark/ wood	< 3	4702	35	3623-3378	3632-3371	ditch	unpublished; S. Troldtoft Andresen, pers. comm.

Tab. 12 | ^{14}C-dates for TRB North Group enclosures. Only the dates for the sites of Albersdorf Dieksknöll, Starup Langelandsvej and Sarup I can be related to the time of enclosure construction.

sites. In addition to the generally poor state of excavation and publication, the acidic soils of the region are at least partly to blame for this situation. Bone preservation is poor and soil samples (which could later have been searched for datable material such as charred grain or charcoal) were generally not taken. Furthermore, as was already stated above, the lack of characteristic artefacts in the deepest layers in the ditches is a typical trait not only of the South Scandinavian, but also of British and Western as well as Central European enclosures. Therefore, a reliable date for the time of construction can rarely be established by archaeological dating. Nonetheless, the following discusses all available evidence.

10.3.1.1 ^{14}C-dated enclosures

Precise information on the context and nature of the samples from enclosures that have been dated by ^{14}C is not always available. Therefore, it is not even possible to always decide whether the published datings were made from samples retrieved in the enclosure elements (palisades or ditches), or whether the dated samples were found in features in the sites' interiors.

As far as can be judged, all three datings from the Swedish Stävie enclosure were made on samples from pits/ovens in the interior. Therefore, these dates cannot determine the site's time of construction. The original publication (Larsson, L. 1982) claimed a late TRB/PWC date due to the lack of any finds which pre-dated the early third millennium BC. However, it was soon realised that the ditch segments were not completely excavated (Madsen, T. 1988, 319; Andersson 2003, 139). Furthermore, as the architecture of this site was very much like that of the typical TRB enclosures constructed around the EN-MN transition, it is likely that the Stävie enclosure was constructed at that time (see L. Larsson 2012, 118 for a detailed analysis). Therefore, the available ^{14}C-dates almost certainly reflect an episode of secondary use rather than the construction period of the site. The latter remains unknown.

A single date made on cereal grains from Lønt is described as having originated from a "dark

cultural layer" (Kanstrup et al. in press, appendix A) and, therefore, probably does not date to the time of enclosure construction. A comparable situation occurs with the Liselund enclosure from which a hitherto unpublished ^{14}C-date (on cereal grain found as part of a large deposition in a pit in the interior of the site) has kindly been provided by J. Westphal.

The precise context of the datings from the Sarup II enclosure is not specified in the publications of N.H. Andersen (1981; 1997). However, it appears that none of the three datings available relate directly to the ditches or palisades of this site. This appears to be the case for at least a portion of the datings from the remaining eight enclosures which have been radiocarbon dated. However, in only three of these eight cases is it possible to relate the available measurements to construction time features with a sufficient degree of certainty. These three sites include Albersdorf Dieksknöll, Starup Langelandsvej and Sarup I.

The sequential calibration of a series of six ^{14}C-samples from a section through a ditch from Albersdorf Dieksknöll allows the oldest phase to be dated to (or slightly earlier than) around 3650 BC (Dibbern 2011; 2012, 272 ff. Abb. 3). This makes Albersdorf Dieksknöll the oldest presently known causewayed enclosure of the TRB North Group. However, the data for the Starup Langelandsvej site indicate that this enclosure was constructed at almost the same time (Lützau-Pedersen/Witte 2012, 83 ff.). For this site, ten dates are available: eight from samples retrieved from ditch segments and two from the palisade. All were made from charcoal with sample ages lower than 50 years (in most cases lower than 25). Due to the complex depositional history of the ditch sediments, the time of construction can best be determined by datings from the palisade. Because of the complex interwoven design of ditches and palisade at Starup Langelandsvej (Fig. 89), both were almost certainly constructed at the same time. The pooled average of the two palisade datings is 4830 ± 31 bp or 3693-3526 BC cal (2σ), probably 3653-3537 BC cal (1σ). Thus, the enclosure appears to have been built around 3600 BC.

The last site for which the time of construction can be determined by the ^{14}C-datings which are currently available is Sarup I. The ten available dates belong to two series, one of which was made during excavation in 1980 (Madsen/Petersen 1984, 117 note 53). The second is of very recent date (Kanstrup et al. in press, appendix A). These new data were all made on cereal grains from pits located in the interior of the enclosure and are, therefore, not suited for establishing its construction date. One of the five older dates was also sourced from cereals from the interior, while the remaining four were made on preserved wood from the palisade. Just as was the case at Starup Langelandsvej, the palisade and ditches of the Sarup I enclosure are closely interwoven and are doubtless contemporaneous. By dating the palisade, the enclosure construction can, therefore, be established. The combined average of the palisade datings is 4668 ± 45 bp or 3628-3360 BC cal (2σ), probably 3516-3371 BC cal (1σ). The dates point to a probable construction date in the 35th century BC. However, the age of the samples is unknown; therefore, a slightly younger date (34th century BC) cannot be excluded. This date harmonizes with the Fuchsberg Group (EN II) date which had already been established from the archaeological material.

Four samples from four different layers taken from a ditch stratigraphy from Gammeltoft Odde were submitted for ^{14}C-dating. These yet-to-be published results were kindly put at my disposal by S. Troldtoft Andresen. Two of the samples were very small; the laboratory declared their dates to be unreliable. These results have been omitted from Tab. 12. The older of the remaining two dates was made from birch bark found preserved near the bottom of the ditch. While this layer may represent the earliest deposits, one cannot exclude the possibility that its presence was the result of recutting. Unfortunately, the calibrated result (2σ) does not allow for the potential construction time to be pinpointed exactly, suggesting rather a large interval spanning the late 37th to the early 34th century BC. Due to the plateau in the calibration curve, the time interval obtained by calibrating with a likelihood of 1σ is essentially the same.

For the Rastorf site, a single date points to the time around the 35th century BC (Steffens 2009, 77 Tab. 19). However, as was clearly stated by Steffens, the sample on which this date was made came from a secondary recut. Therefore, it does not date the construction of the enclosure.

Eleven ^{14}C-dates were published by Madsen & Petersen (1984, 117 note 53) for Toftum. Although the sample material used was described (marine shells and bones) the stratigraphical context in which they were found was not. However, it is apparent from the publications of the site (Madsen, T. 1978a; 1978b; 1988, 311ff.; unpublished) that, although shell layers were found in the ditches, they were not located at their bottoms. The datings made from shell samples, thus, cannot determine the enclosure's time of construction. Furthermore, the dated bones come from a context very close to the shell layers, as they would not have been preserved in the acidic soil should they have been located elsewhere. The dates made on bones (which are more or less identical to those made on the shells), therefore, can also not be used to date the construction of the site. The combined average of all eleven dates is 4602 ± 25 bp, or 3500-3340 BC cal (2σ), probably 3490-3360 BC cal (1σ). The 35th or early 34th century BC can, therefore, be identified as a terminus ante quem for the construction of the Toftum enclosure. Unfortunately, the bottom layers in the ditches did not contain any material that could have been subjected to archaeological dating (Madsen, T. unpublished).

Several ^{14}C-dates are also available for the Kainsbakke enclosure, more precisely for one pit in a straight row (A47)(see chapter 3)(Wincentz Rasmussen 1984, 98 note 5). However, these dates exclusively relate to a secondary phase of site use. All are very young (calibrated around 2900-2700 BC) and date huge PWC deposits (layer 3 in Wincentz Rasmussen 1984, 85 Fig. 5). Numerous stratigraphically older layers (layers 4-8) were poor in artefacts and hence have not been radiometrically dated. Therefore, the available ^{14}C-dates cannot date the time of Kainsbakke enclosure's construction.

Recently, Hage (in press) published seven ^{14}C-dates for the Büdelsdorf enclosure. All of these dates were made in the early 1970s. Unfortunately, a portion of the lot had large sample errors. All were made on bulk charcoal of unknown (almost certainly rather high) sample age. Only two of the dates relate to the ditch. However, both of these indicate secondary use phases during the Single Grave Culture period. The features dated from the interior of the site include large fenced wattle and daub pits parallel to the course of the ditches. The datings of these pits demonstrate that the construction of the enclosure was completed during EN II at the latest.

Lastly, it is important to mention the Blakbjerg enclosure in Djursland. Three cattle bones from well defined, undisturbed layers reflecting the repeated deposition and recutting of a ditch segment were submitted by the author for AMS-dating, thanks to a grant from Dronning Margrethe II's Archaeological Foundation. These samples date the three use phases of the enclosure identified by Torfing (2011; 2013). The oldest of these was represented by a vessel found on the bottom of the ditch and can typologically be dated to the transition between the early and late parts of the Early Neolithic (the EN I-EN II transition). The second phase belongs typologically to the late Early Neolithic (EN II) and the third to the earliest Middle Neolithic (MN A Ia). The results of the three AMS measurements, however, are unexplainably young, even to the point of contradicting the stratigraphy. Therefore, they cannot be used to date the construction of this causewayed enclosure.

10.3.1.2 Archaeologically dated enclosures

Due to the poor state of publication, more or less reliable archaeological datings of the construction of causewayed enclosures can be established in only a few cases. While an archaeological date has been given in the cursory publications of many sites, the stratigraphical position of the material on which these dates were based is rarely evident. The exceptions include seven different sites.

One of these is Bjerggård in east Jutland. As clearly stated by T. Madsen (1988, 310), Fuchsberg pottery was found on the bottom of at least one of the ditch segments, dating the construction of this monument to the late Early Neolithic (EN II), probably in the 35th or 34th century BC.

A construction in the late Early Neolithic (Virum Group) and thus in the 35th or 34th century BC can also be established for the Markildegård enclosure, where numerous characteristic vessels were found on the bottom of ditch segments (Østergård Sørensen 1995b).

The literature reports that a third enclosure was built during this phase – 35th or 34th century BC. This is the Vasagård east enclosure on the island of Bornholm. Finds from the bottom of ditch segments at Vasagård have been attributed to the time in question. However, they have not been published (Kaul et al. 2002, 122).

The Vilsund enclosure (see chapter 10.2.7) can probably be added to the list of late Early Neolithic enclosures (as indicated by the late Volling style funnel beaker recovered from one of the postholes of the peculiar post/bank construction).

Somewhat more uncertain is the situation regarding the Sigersted III enclosure, for which very little information has been published. The sparse information relevant for dating (from an online database) has been referenced by Klatt (2009, 123 f.) and points to the transition between Early and Middle Neolithic, i.e. around the 34th century BC.

The excavator dates the Sarup II enclosure to MN A Ib based on finds from the ditches (which appear to have been found at their very bottoms) (Andersen, N.H. 1997, 74 Fig. 94). Based on ^{14}C-dates for MN A Ib from other sites together with the datings from the site itself, it is possible to estimate construction around 3200 BC.

Finally, the Blakbjerg enclosure can be dated to the EN I – EN II transition by a funnel beaker found on the bottom of the ditch (Torfing 2011). The vessel shape corresponds to E. Koch's (1998) type III, which is dated to between 3800 and 3500 BC. It is decorated by bundles of short hanging lines at the transitional space between belly and shoulder. A comparable decoration is known from a type III beaker from Øgårde in Zealand's Aamose bog (Koch, E. 1998, pl. 56.102). The decoration of this vessel has been executed by incision, while the Blakbjerg vessel is decorated by twisted cord impressions. This decorating technique appears with EN II around 3500 BC. The Blakbjerg vessel can, therefore, most likely be dated to the EN I - EN II transition in the late 36th or early 35th century BC.

10.3.1.3 Enclosure-related sites

A number of the pits from the Lystrup Kildevang I site have been dated by means of ¹⁴C. These datings' average (4935 ± 29 bp – Skousen 2008, 169) indicates an age between 3773 and 3653 BC (2σ), probably 3758-3658 BC (1σ). These are the oldest of all available dates for any causewayed enclosure or related site in South Scandinavia. It appears thus that the first (failed ?) attempts to build something that resembled a causewayed enclosure in the region could have occurred in the second half of the 38th century BC.

The Aalstrup site (Madsen, T. 2009) may well represent another early attempt at enclosure construction. No ¹⁴C-datings are available from Aalstrup. However, the shards found inside the ditch segments belong to the EN I Volling Group and can be dated to between 3800 and 3500 BC. The site may well be just as old as Lystrup Kildevang I.

Unfortunately, no ¹⁴C-datings were available from the classic location at Troldebjerg. Nevertheless, Troldebjerg is the type site of the earliest Middle Neolithic (MN A Ia). The enclosure-like palisade found at the site probably dates to that period (i.e. around 3300 BC).

The chronology of the Triwalk-site in Mecklenburg has recently been discussed on the basis of typological and stratigraphical information as well as 11 ¹⁴C-dates (Müller, J./Staude 2012). The results of this study indicate that construction started in the 35th century BC.

The last site to be discussed is Sarup Gamle Skole (Andersen, N.H. 2009). While no ¹⁴C-dates are available for the ditch segments which were excavated, a vessel found at the bottom of one of them indicates construction in the late Early Neolithic (35th/34th century BC). The row of ditches runs exactly parallel to a fenced grave construction for which N. H. Andersen reports ¹⁴C-dates pointing to the later part of EN I (2009, 31). The possible relation between both might indicate that the ditches belong to the earliest part of the possible age range.

10.3.1.4 Summary and discussion

The construction dates of Scandinavian causewayed enclosures can only be established for ten out of 39 sites. Only three of these were dated by means of ¹⁴C, while the ages of the remaining seven were established based on archaeological material from the bottom of ditch segments. At present, it appears that enclosure building started in the 37th century BC and continued until approximately the 33rd century BC. Evidence from the related Kildevang I site might indicate a slightly earlier start of the building sequence in the second half of the 38th century BC. From the available archaeological evidence, it appears unlikely that this timeframe will change much when/if ¹⁴C-datings become available for more enclosures. However, the Kainsbakke site could indicate enclosure construction in the early 3rd millennium.

The evidence indicates that the majority of sites were constructed in the 35th and 34th century BC. However, too few enclosures have been dated (only ca. 25% of all sites known at present) for these data to be taken uncritically at face value. The fact that archaeological datings within this timeframe have been given in the literature for almost all of the remaining sites must not be overestimated, as illustrated by the investigations of Geschwinde & Raetzel-Fabian (2009, 165ff.) in northern central Europe. Geschwinde & Raetzel-Fabian made small-scale excavations to collect samples for ¹⁴C-dates from the bottom layers of ditches that were typically very poor in (or were totally devoid of) characteristic artefact material, just as they are in South Scandinavia. In consequence, several enclosures whose construction archaeologists estimated in the Bernburg Culture (due to characteristic artefacts found in the upper parts of their ditches) were found to actually date to the late Michelsberg Culture (several centuries earlier). It must be expected that a number of Scandinavian enclosures would also date to earlier periods, should ¹⁴C-measurements be done.

No certain statements can be made regarding the question of whether enclosures began to be built throughout South Scandinavia at approximately the same time or whether the first monuments of this type were constructed in the periphery zone. The oldest enclosure known at present (Albersdorf Dieksknöll) is located in the southern periphery zone. However, the site of Starup Langelandsvej (which is almost as old as Albersdorf Dieksknöll) is not. Furthermore, the Lystrup Kildevang I site (older than both of these two sites, which might also be indicative of the first attempts to construct an enclosure) is located in the core zone (in eastern Jutland). Considerably more enclosures have to be dated by series of ^{14}C-datings before the discipline can establish whether or not the picture as it stands at present is a true reflection of historical reality. Of special importance in this regard would be the dating of enclosures from the western periphery of the west coast of Jutland (outside the zone which overlaps with the southern periphery), none of which have yet been dated. Ongoing work with the pottery excavated in the ditches of one of these sites – Liselund in Thy – might well hint an early construction date (the later part of TN I) for this enclosure (T. Danborg Torfing, personal comment).

To sum up, one must conclude, therefore, that the datings of causewayed enclosures which are presently known do not conclusively indicate whether or not enclosure construction in Southern Scandinavia was initiated from the outside. Therefore, the available evidence will be viewed in a European context below.

10.3.2. European enclosure chronology

The start of causewayed enclosure construction in South Scandinavia in the 37th or possibly even the (late) 38th century BC is of particular interest. This date is strikingly similar to the high precision dates which have recently been established for causewayed enclosures in the British Isles (Whittle et al. 2011a). In Britain, enclosure construction appears to have begun in the late 38th century BC, culminating in the 37th century BC (when the vast majority of the ca. 40 monuments dated were built). Construction ended altogether in the 36th century BC. The only exception to this rule is the Magheraboy site in Ireland which had

a particularly early construction date in the 40th or 39th century BC.

Given the similarity between the start dates of British and Scandinavian enclosure construction and the architectural links between enclosures in both regions as well as with Continental sites, a proper investigation of causewayed enclosure chronology in Europe seems necessary. Several comparable studies have already been published in recent years (Raetzel-Fabian 1999; Meyer/Raetzel-Fabian 2006; Geschwinde/Raetzel-Fabian 2009, 185ff; Müller, J. 2010, 254; Whittle et al. 2011b). However, none of these had access to the dating evidence for the Scandinavian sites discussed above and only one (Whittle et al. 2011b) addresses the entire distribution area of causewayed enclosures. However, due to qualitative differences between the dates obtained by exhaustive Bayesian modelling in their study of the British Isles and those available by a "visual inspection of ^{14}C-dates" for Continental sites, Whittle et al. were somewhat cautious in drawing any far-reaching conclusions. However, as will be demonstrated below, it is well worth considering the Continental evidence in combination with that from Britain in spite of the indisputable differences in precision present between the two datasets.

While a short summary of the earliest development of causewayed enclosures in Europe is provided, a detailed investigation will only be conducted for the sites that were constructed during the period between 4400 and 3200 BC. Furthermore, Cerny Culture enclosures in northern France (ca. 4700-4400 BC) have also been added to the investigation. Geographically, the area between the Atlantic and the eastern borders of Poland has been covered. In the easternmost parts of Poland, it appears as if only very few causewayed enclosures were constructed which resemble the type encountered in Scandinavia. The comparatively few sites which date to the late Lengyel and early Funnel Beaker Culture from within this region have been added, nevertheless, as (in one case, at least) very specific architectural traits known from Denmark have local parallels (i.e. the clavicle-type ditches from Starup Langelandsvej, see chapter

10.2.2). The selection of sites was the same as that completed above for architectural comparisons between South Scandinavia and the remainder of Europe (see appendix).

The earliest enclosures with constructional similarities to the causewayed enclosures of South Scandinavia were built as early as ca. 5300 BC in Central Europe's Linear Pottery Culture. It was at Rosheim in Alsace that archaeologists first realised that the long stretches of continuous ditches probably never existed as such, but were likely created piecemeal over time by an amalgamation of shorter ditch segments (Jeunesse 1996; Jeunesse/Lefranc 1999). Between 5300 and 4900 BC, causewayed enclosures with this trait were built in the Linear Pottery groups from the Upper Rhine Valley, the Paris Basin, Belgium and the Rhineland as well as the central parts of Europe (Jeunesse 2011). However, the number of these sites is rather limited.

In what would correspond to Central Europe's Mittelneolithikum (ca. 4900-4400 BC), comparable enclosures continued to be built in this area while also extending into parts of the Danube Valley in Bavaria, Austria and southeast Poland (Jeunesse 2011, 50 Fig. 15). Of special interest are the six known enclosures from the Cerny Culture in the Paris Basin (ca. 4700-4400 BC) as well as one site in the Loire (Fig. 120). These sites' chronologies, construction details and locations seem to comprise the roots of an enclosure-building boom between ca. 4400 and 4000 BC (Jeunesse 2011, 51ff.). South Scandinavian enclosures apparently belong to the same building tradition and, therefore, can be ultimately traced back to enclosure development in the Cerny Culture.

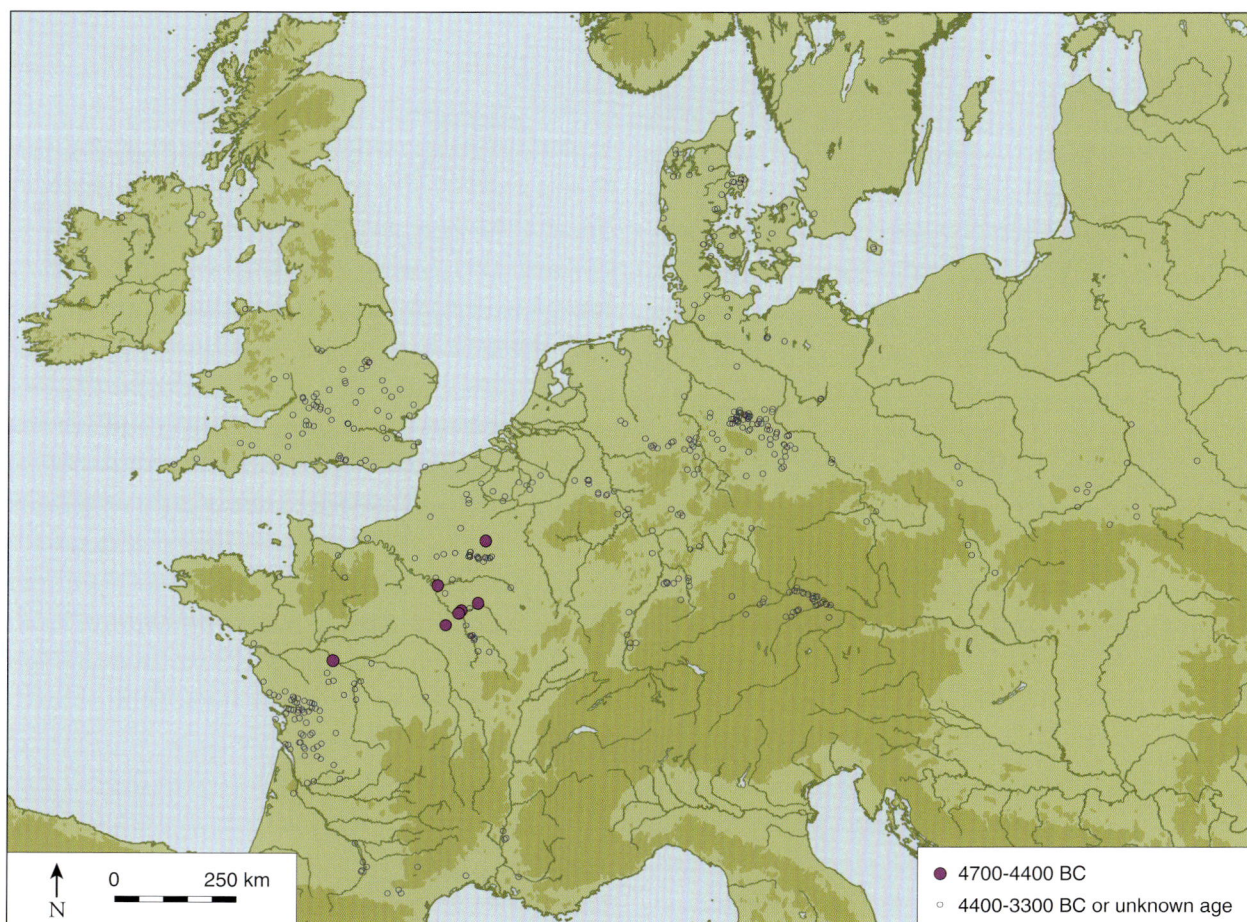

Fig. 120 | *The seven known enclosures of the Cerny Culture in northern France (ca. 4700-4400 BC) probably constitute the origin of the building tradition that led to the construction of the first enclosures in South Scandinavia approximately 1000 years later.*

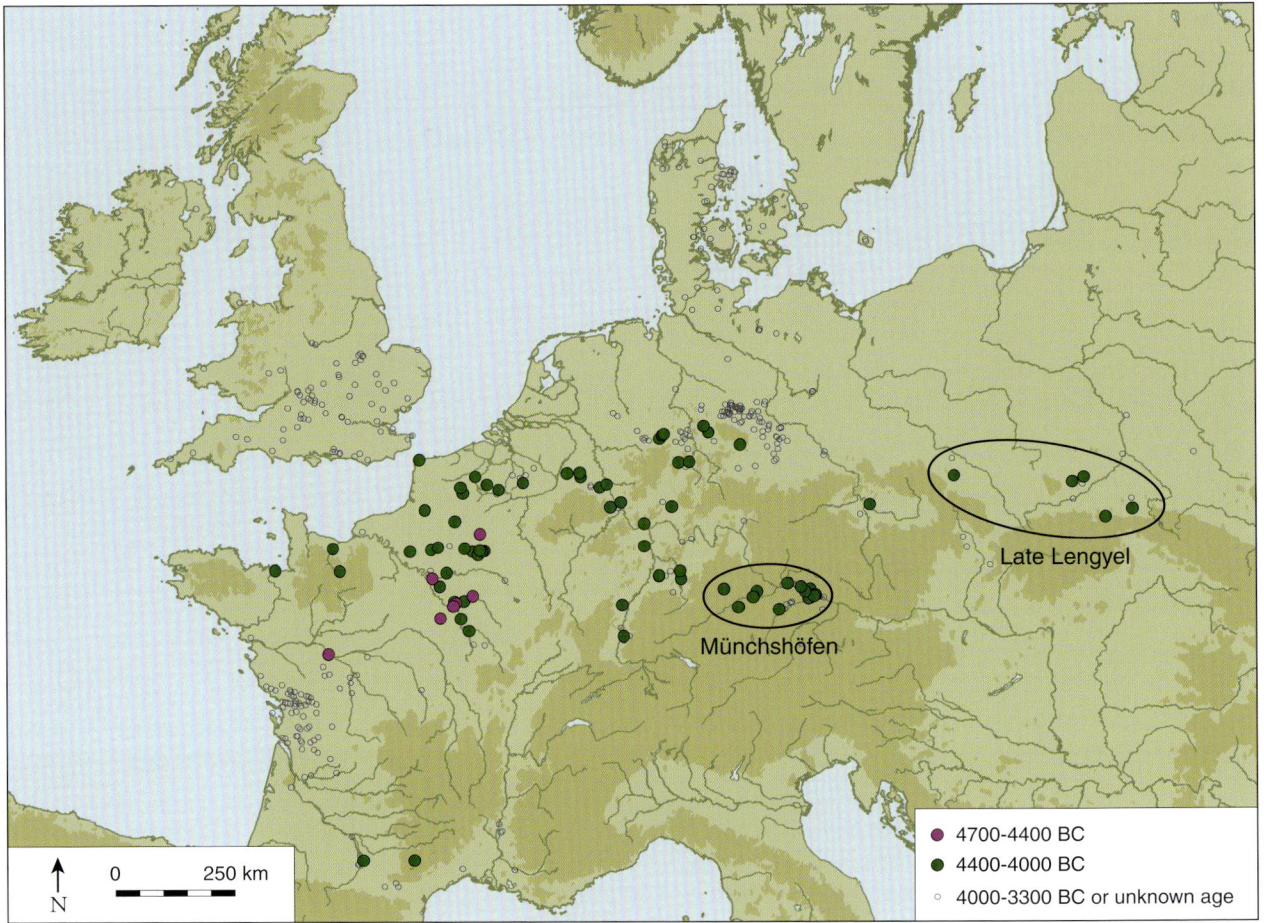

Fig. 121 | *Between 4400 and 4000 BC, a considerable number of Western European-like causewayed enclosures were constructed in an area stretching from France to Germany. In at least one instance, this even extended as far as Bohemia. Although they were constructed differently, contemporaneous enclosures of the Münchshöfen and late Lengyel Culture are included on the map.*

10.3.2.1 Enclosures from 4400 to 4000 BC

The time horizon between 4400 and 4000 BC includes the formative stage of the Michelsberg Culture (Jeunesse et al. 2004), the older Michelsberg Culture (MK I and MK II) and the older phases of related groups in France and Belgium (Noyen, Chasséen septentrional and méridional and Spiere). The number of enclosures from this time period within the Paris Basin is considerable (even despite the fact that they cannot all be precisely dated). The cultural dynamics which developed in this region led to the construction of comparable sites in bordering regions in the east – especially the Rhine Valley and areas on both sides of the upper Weser River as well as its tributaries (the Werra and Fulda rivers)(Fig. 121). Geschwinde and Raetzel-Fabian (2009, 185ff.)

describe the cultural history of this horizon in detail. They also point to the Michelsberg enclosure at Urbach in Thuringia (Walter et al. 2007, 258ff.) south of the Harz Mountains as the easternmost of the enclosures constructed in the course of the cultural development rooted in the Paris Basin. However, as evidenced by the enclosure discovered at Kly in central Bohemia (Gojda et al. 2002), the Michelsberg influence reached even farther to the (south-) east in the late 5th millennium BC. The Kly enclosure was dated to MK II by a type 2 tulip beaker discovered at the base of one of the site's two ditches.

In the last decade, a number of comparable Chasséen Culture enclosures were discovered in southwest France (Gandelin 2011, 170ff.; Vaquer 2011; Convertini 2012). As was already noted by

Jeunesse (2011, 62) and Vaquer (2011, 242), these enclosures may well have been borrowed from contemporary cultures of the Paris Basin, just as were Michelsberg and Spiere sites in Belgium and Germany. Only very few of the Chasséen méridional enclosures can be precisely dated to one of the phases distinguished here. In general, the enclosures which exclusively consisted of palisades (which were not included in this survey) appear to be the oldest. These are followed by causewayed enclosures both with and without palisades between the late 5th and mid 4th millennium BC (Vaquer 2011, 242).

It is also possible that the first enclosures in central western France (close to the Atlantic coast approximately between the mouths of the Loire and Garonne rivers) were built at the end of the horizon between 4400 and 4000 BC. The dating evidence available for the earliest sites in this region (e.g. Sandun: Letterlé et al. 1990; Périgny "Quatre Chevaliers": Soler 2010; Montagan I: Cassen 1987; Loups: Burnez 1996) is still rather poor. At present, no conclusive evidence points to such an early date. Therefore, the sites in question have been attributed to the next chronological horizon (4000-3750 BC).

In summary, it can be concluded that a core high-density area of causewayed enclosures existed in a region which stretched from the eastern borders of the Seine to the Harz Mountains, (with a single outlier in Bohemia) in the chronological horizon between ca. 4400 and 4000 BC. The Paris Basin in northern France was probably the origin of the impulses which led to intensive enclosure construction in the Spiere Group and the Michelsberg Culture in the wake of the latter's eastward expansion. A comparable (if possibly much weaker) development in southwest France's Chasséen méridional probably also derived from northern France. As argued recently by Knoche (2013), this phenomenon could be connected to the development of a new, mobile type of Neolithic economy based on cattle herding and transhumance.

In Fig. 121, two further groups of enclosures from the time in question have been added. These include the comparatively numerous sites of the Münchshöfen Culture in the Bavarian Danube Val-

ley as well as a few late Lengyel sites in southern and southeastern Poland. These enclosures resemble western European causewayed enclosures but diverge, for example, in terms of the lesser frequency of the interruptions of the ditches as well as the occasional rectangular shape of their outlines. These divergent traits can be traced back (at least in part) to local predecessors that either do not belong to the causewayed enclosure tradition as described by Jeunesse (2011), or do so only to a minor degree (Meyer/Raetzel-Fabian 2006, 10ff.). The enclosures in question have been added to the map because it was possible in some cases to point out specific structures that had matches with Scandinavian sites. The same is true for enclosures from these areas in the following time horizons: Jordanów Culture sites in Poland and the Czech Republic, southeastern TRB and Lublin-Volhynian Culture sites in Poland between 4000 and 3750 BC and Altheim Culture sites and enclosures belonging to the southern or southeastern TRB groups in the Czech Republic and Poland between 3750 and 3500 BC.

10.3.2.2 Enclosures from 4000-3750 BC

Fig. 122 depicts a map of enclosure sites including the enclosures which were built between ca. 4000 and 3750 BC as well as earlier sites. It is important to note that only enclosures built on new locations were considered; all instances in which activity continued at existing enclosures (see discussion of this point below) were discounted.

In France and Belgium, enclosures built during the chronological horizon under discussion belong to later phases of the different regional groups of the Chasséen Culture, the later phase of the Noyen and Spiere Group as well as to Michelsberg Culture phase MK III. The subsequent Michelsberg Culture phase (MK IV) probably existed during both this horizon as well as the one which followed (see Knoche 2008 for a detailed discussion of the absolute dating). The few sites that were possibly constructed in MK IV were mapped under the following horizon (between 3750 and 3500 BC). The map discussed here (4000-3750 BC) also includes MK III enclosures from Germany. Furthermore, the Jordanów Culture, Lublin-Volhynian Culture as well as an early phase of the southeastern TRB in the Czech Republic and Poland were included.

Between 4000 and 3750 BC, the area in which causewayed enclosures were constructed was enlarged in two directions: westwards and northwards. In the west, the Atlantic coast was probably reached in central western France at the very beginning of this phase (see discussion above). At Magheraboy in Ireland, the first enclosure in the British Isles appears to have been constructed during this time horizon (Cooney et al. 2011, 574ff.). This enclosure is of particular interest, because it appears to be earlier than all other enclosures in Britain, despite both its remote location and the fact that enclosure construction generally appears to have started in southern Britain and then spread to the northwest (Bayliss et al. 2011, 694 Fig. 14.16). Accordingly, one would then expect the Magheraboy enclosure to have been one of the latest rather than earliest enclosures in Britain.

In terms of this study, the appearance of an early enclosure in Ireland (should the dating be confirmed rather than the result of some kind of unrecognized error) is of special interest. As described earlier, causewayed enclosures only appear to have been built in areas that saw Neolithic settlement some time prior to enclosure construction. In southern Britain and South Scandinavia, as much as ca. 300 years passed between the introduction of the Neolithic and the construction of enclosures. Another comparable case from Westphalia is discussed below. Thus, the Magheraboy enclosure could indicate that some kind of

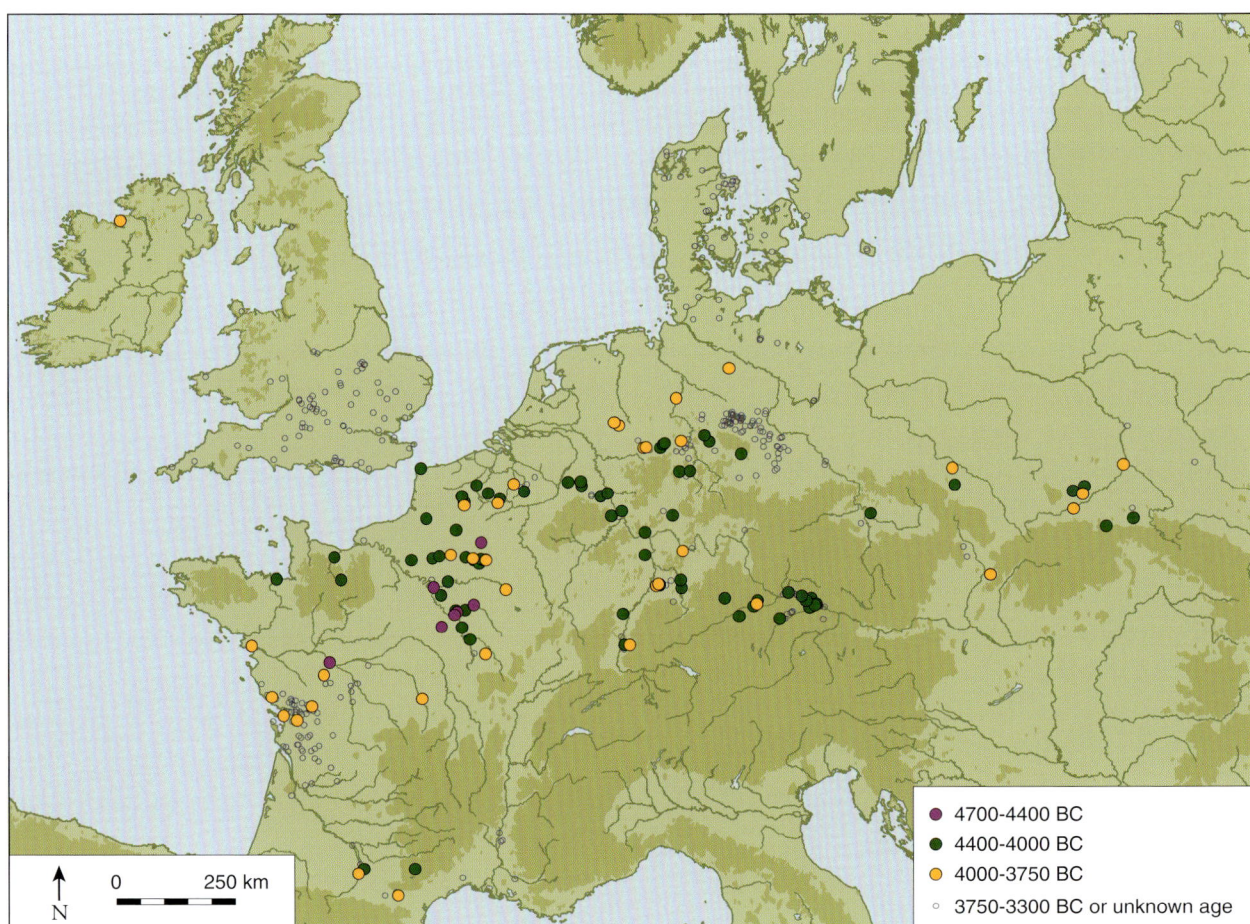

Fig. 122 | *In the time horizon between 4000 and 3750 BC, enclosure building activity decreased compared to the preceding time horizon. Nevertheless, the area in which enclosures were built was extended to the north and west.*

very early neolithisation had occurred in the area. Such a neolithisation would not fit the course of events as described by Bayliss et al. (2011), who argue that Neolithic practice was introduced into Britain from the Continent in a single event in the late 41st century BC. The earliest appearances of the Neolithic in Britain have been recorded in the southeastern British areas which lay closest to the European mainland. Indeed, it is from this region that neolithisation spread north and northwest (Bayliss et al. 2011, 839 Fig. 14.177). Sheridan (2010), on the other hand, argues for a different (more complicated) history of neolithisation in the British Isles. According to her, there were several waves of colonisation by farmers who left different parts of northern France and sailed to various parts of Britain. Sheridan suggests that this development also touched parts of Ireland and likely began as early as ca. 4300 BC. Again, if confirmed, the construction of a causewayed enclosure at Magheraboy as early as in the 40th or 39th century BC could support this view. However, Magheraboy is situated in a part of Ireland which Sheridan did not include in her early neolithisation model. Therefore, many questions remain unresolved.

With regard to the relation between (earlier) Neolithic settlement and enclosure construction, a closer look at the part of northern central Germany that saw an enlargement in its area of enclosure construction is of interest. As is apparent from Fig. 122, a string of enclosures appears to have been built in the early fourth millennium BC between Nottuln-Uphoven in western Westphalia (Knoche 2008) and Walmstorf in the Lüneburg area (Richter, P.B. 2002). All of the sites are located north of the loess belt in areas dominated by sandy soils. Evidence for Neolithic settlement in these areas prior to enclosure construction in the MK III horizon is sparse (Knoche 2008, 121ff.). However, it does exist. The best-known indications are certainly the finds of Bischheim and Bischheim-related pottery at the Hüde I site at Lake Dümmer in northwestern Germany (Kampffmeyer 1983). It can be added that a single pit with finds of the (early) Bischheim Group was discovered at the enclosure site of Nottuln-Uphoven itself (Knoche

2008, 33). Aside from predominantly single finds of heavy stone stools (shoelast axes), these two inventories are the best indications of Neolithic settlement in the area prior to the MK III horizon (compare Knoche 2008, 120 Abb. 5.6 and 134 Abb. 5.12). It appears, therefore, that neolithisation also preceded the earliest construction of causewayed enclosures by several hundred years in Westphalia and Lower Saxony.

10.3.2.3 Enclosures from 3750-3500 BC

During the next chronological horizon – here defined as the time between ca. 3750 and 3500 BC – the first enclosures in South Scandinavia were constructed (Fig. 123). As described above, the same is true for the British Isles with the notable exception of the Irish Magheraboy enclosure. Before discussing the evidence for enclosure building between 3750 and 3500 BC (as apparent from Fig. 123) in detail, it is necessary to make a few introductory remarks regarding the dating and cultural attribution of the sites mapped.

In the British Isles, only enclosures the construction of which has been dated by ^{14}C-analysis to the period between 3750 and 3500 BC were attributed to the chronological horizon in question. Taking into account the scarcity of sites that were dated either earlier (1) or later (0) by the same method, it is very likely that the vast majority of enclosures for which no ^{14}C-analyses are available also belong to the same time period. Nevertheless, these sites have been marked as undated in Fig. 123. Due to the work of Whittle et al. (2011a), it is possible to state that most of the enclosures that are shown as belonging to the chronological horizon between 3750 and 3500 BC were constructed in the 37th century BC and were thus built during a restricted part of the time span under consideration. However, no other region in Europe comes even close with regard to the precision of dating achieved for sites in the British Isles. Therefore, a somewhat wider chronological horizon (3750-3500 BC) was used for the analyses conducted here.

Southern Britain is not the only region which witnessed an enclosure construction boom at the time in question. In the Matignons ancien

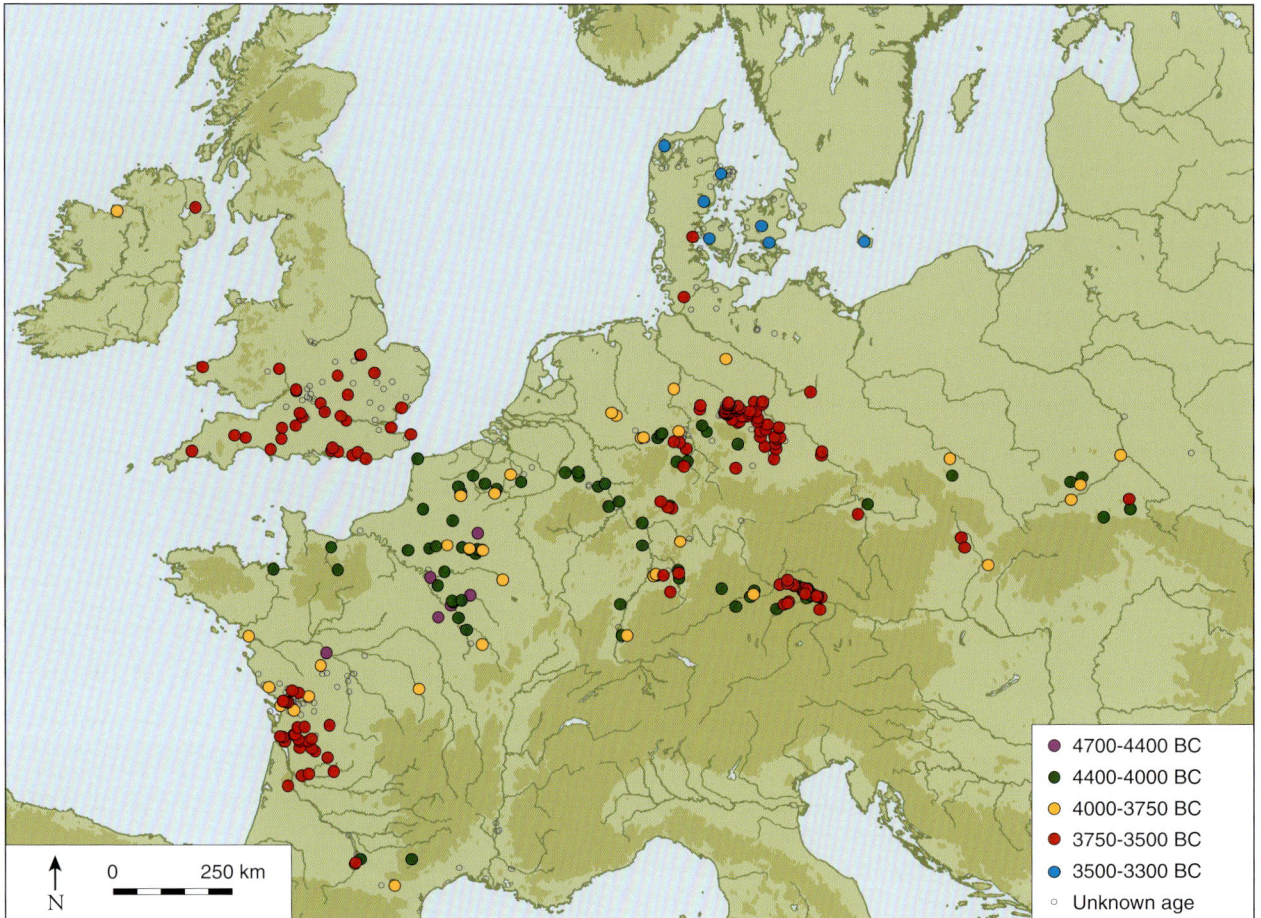

Fig. 123 | *An enclosure building boom is observable between 3750 and 3500 BC in many parts of Europe. The first enclosures in South Scandinavia were also constructed during this period.*

Culture in central western France, a comparable phenomenon took place between 3750 and 3500 BC. The dating of Matignons ancien enclosures, however, is almost completely reliant on a ceramic analysis (both typological and technological), as few ^{14}C-analyses from enclosures are available. Interestingly, Ard's (2011) study (used for the selection of sites) convincingly singled out the enclosures that belong to the Néolithique récent I (namely, the period which has been brought into question here). These enclosures represent only a minor subset of the very large number of sites known from that area. Nevertheless, those that might belong to the horizon discussed here (but which cannot be precisely dated) have been added to the map as 'undated'. The selection is based on information published by Cassen (1987) and Kerdivel (2009).

The third region in which a massive construction of new enclosures is evident is that located between eastern Westphalia/northern Hessia and the Elbe River. At least one site ca. 100 km to the east of the Elbe in Potsdam (Beran/Hensel 2004; Beran 2009) also belongs to this horizon and indicates that the development stretched further east than is immediately apparent from Fig. 123. The few known enclosures in Mecklenburg-Vorpommern (Zietlitz, Ruthen, Plate 3, Plate 14 – see Klatt 2009, catalogue) may also belong to this horizon. However, their relational dating is uncertain; they could also be somewhat earlier or later.

Many of the enclosures mapped in northern Hessia, eastern Westphalia and southern Lower Saxony have been dated by [14]C. Examples include Calden (Raetzel-Fabian 2000), Warburg-Rimbeck (Knoche 2003) and a number of sites in the Braunschweig area of Lower Saxony (Geschwinde & Raetzel-Fabian 2009). Others (as well as most of the sites in Saxony-Anhalt) can be dated typologically, as was convincingly argued by Geschwinde & Raetzel-Fabian (2009, 207ff., Zeithorizont B). As wrote Geschwinde and Raetzel-Fabian, there is a slight possibility that a few of the sites might have been built in the preceding horizon (particularly during its final period). However, even should this have been the case, there would still have been a massive wave of enclosure construction in the region between 3750 and 3500 BC.

The enclosures in the western part of the area covered by Geschwinde and Raetzel-Fabian belong to the final phases of the Michelsberg Culture (possibly MK IV but overwhelmingly MK V), while those in the eastern parts can be attributed to the Baalberge Group of the TRB Culture (see Geschwinde/Raetzel-Fabian 2009, 202 ff. for a detailed discussion of the border between these regions).

The fourth region in which a massive wave of enclosure construction can be observed between 3750 and 3500 BC is in the Bavarian Danube Valley. The sites mapped here all belong to the Altheim Culture and diverge clearly in type from the enclosures discussed thus far by their generally very small size and their consistently rectangular or trapezoid shape (Matuschik 1991, 37ff.; Meyer & Raetzel-Fabian 2006, 32ff.). It is possible that a few of the sites were constructed just before 3750 BC. Should this have been the case, it is probable that only very few sites would have been concerned. The numerous enclosures from the subsequent Chamer Culture have not been mapped. Most (if not all) of these can be dated to after 3200 BC; they are thus irrelevant to the developments which took place in South Scandinavia.

Very few new enclosures appear to have been built to the east of the regions discussed so far between 3750 and 3500 BC. Those sites depicted belong to the Baalberge Group in Bohemia and Moravia as well as the southeastern TRB in Poland. A very low level of enclosure building can also be observed in those parts of France, Belgium and Germany in which enclosures had already been built. This is especially true in the region west of the Rhine Valley.

Finally, in South Scandinavia, the first enclosures were built between 3750 and 3500 BC. Only proper causewayed enclosures which could be ascribed to the time horizon in question by means of ^{14}C datings were mapped; the possible "proto-enclosures" discussed above were omitted. Furthermore, the few enclosures that can be dated at present to 3500 – 3200 BC have been indicated as such, while the remainder is depicted as undated.

The lack of newly built enclosures in the former core area of enclosure construction in northern France, Belgium and the westernmost parts of Germany is as remarkable as is the building boom in the regions described above. Not a single new enclosure appears to have been built in the Michelsberg distribution area between the Rhine and the Seine. However, east of the Rhine, things appear to have been different. A considerable number of new enclosures were built in an area stretching from the Neckar Valley in southwest Germany over the southern and northern parts of Hessia towards Westphalia at the western periphery of the "boom-zone" to the east in Lower Saxony and Saxony-Anhalt. These sites form a strikingly linear distribution pattern (Fig. 124) to which this text will return below.

10.3.2.4 Enclosures from 3500-3200 BC

With regard to the (assumed) date of most enclosures in the TRB North Group, sites belonging to the subsequent time horizon (3500-3200 BC) were added to the map in Fig. 123. With regards to this map, one must recall that a large number of enclosures in the central western parts of France were omitted from the selection. Dating enclosures in this region in the absence of large numbers of ^{14}C-datings relied heavily on typological ceramic investigations; for this reason, it is not possible to differentiate between sites that were constructed between 3500 and 3200 BC and those that were constructed between 3200 and 2900 BC. Therefore, enclosure construction certainly continued in the region immediately after 3500 BC. However, it is impossible to quantify this activity at present.

Apart from the central western parts of France and South Scandinavia, Central Europe was alone in possibly being witness to some enclosure construction activity from 3500-3200 BC. However, less than a handful of Salzmünde Culture sites could theoretically belong to the time in question. Due to the reasons given in chapter 10.2 these sites were excluded from the map (Fig. 123).

10.4 Enclosure construction 3750-3500 BC and European corridors of (ritual) communication

In several areas, the development of enclosure building between 3750 and 3500 BC distinguished itself from that of preceding and succeeding times. One of these points was in the intensity of its construction activity (Fig. 125). Seventy-three new enclosures were registered between 4400 and 4000 BC. In the next horizon (4000-3750

BC), this number was reduced to 35. If the number of new enclosures per century within these two chronological horizons are calculated, 18.25 enclosures/century were constructed during the early period, while only 14 enclosures/century were built during the second. As the vast majority of enclosures from the early horizon belong to its second half, the slowing down of enclosure construction after 4000 BC was probably much more dramatic than reflected by the averages calculated for the entire periods.

In the time horizon between 3750 and 3500 BC, no less than 145 new enclosures were registered – more than four times as many as in the preceding horizon of equal length (58 enclosures/century). In practice, the number of newly built enclosures in this time horizon was certainly considerably high-

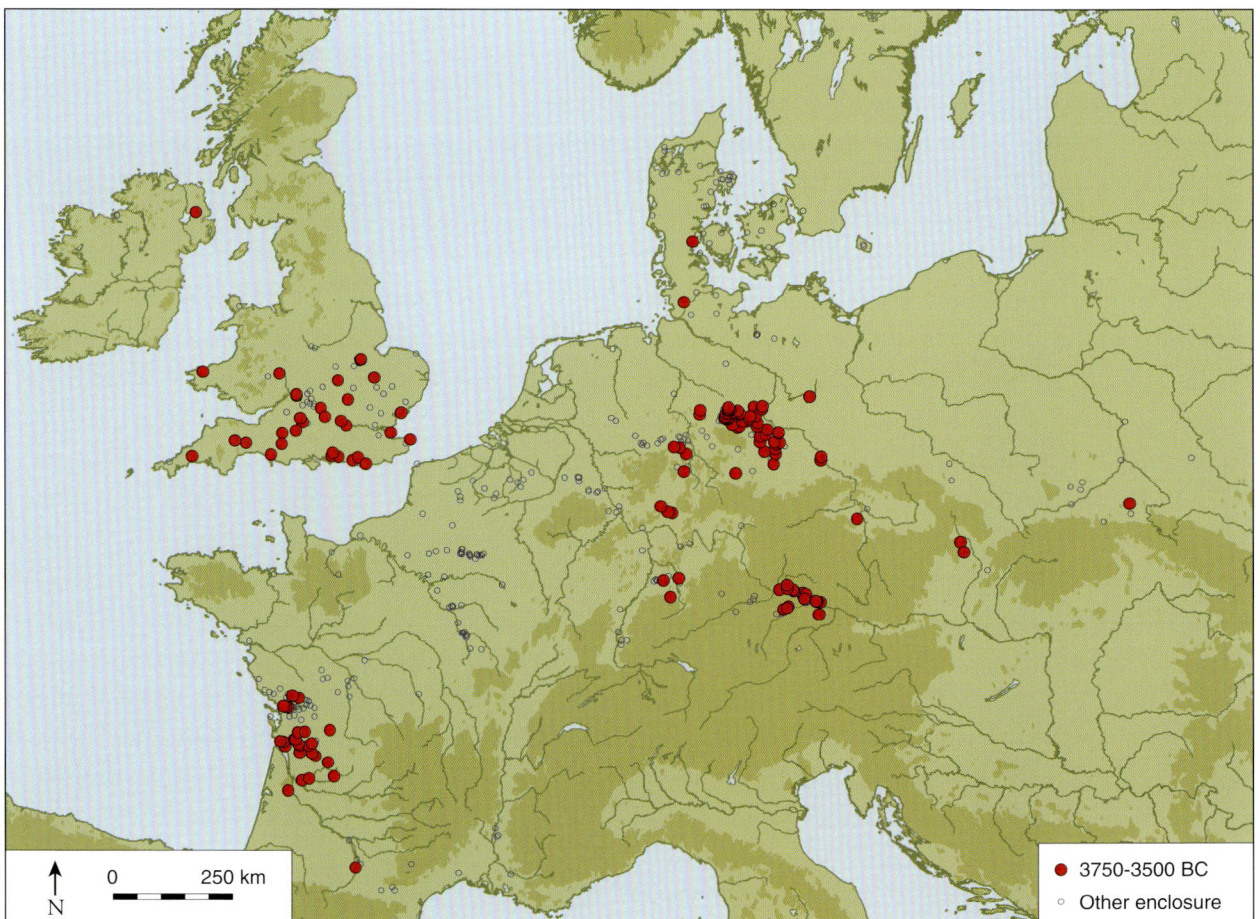

Fig. 124 | *When viewed in isolation, the particular distribution pattern of enclosures built between 3750 and 3500 BC shows four pronounced regional concentrations and a peculiar linear distribution pattern in the area of present day Germany.*

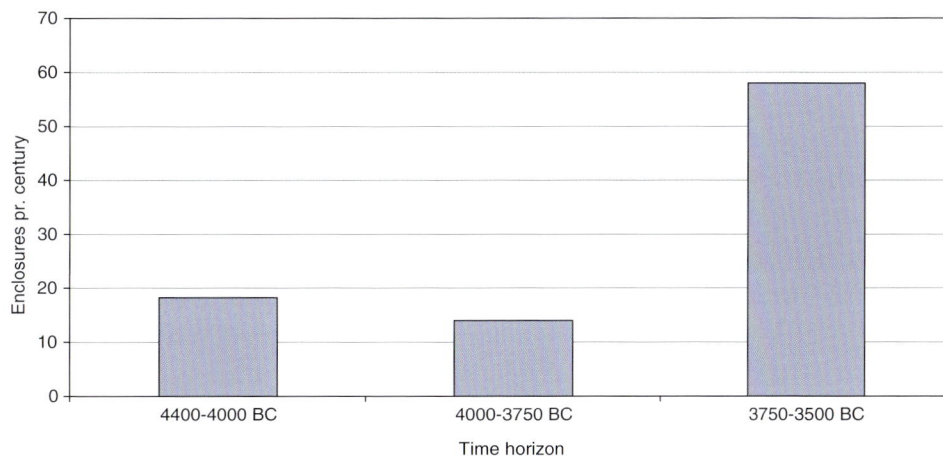

er. For example, 34 British sites have been counted as "not dated" because they were not part of Whittle et al.'s (2011a) dating programme. As argued above, these sites almost certainly all belong to the horizon in question here.

Albeit on a much smaller, regional basis, comparable observations were made by Raetzel-Fabian (1999, 93f.) and Knoche (2008, 150f.). Knoche (2008, 151) writes that the reduction of enclosure-activity in Michelsberg III (horizon 4000-3750 BC) is not only apparent in the scarcity of newly constructed sites, but also in the discontinued use of the enclosures which already existed.

Another point in which the chronological horizon between 3750 and 3500 BC differs from preceding times is in the location in which enclosures were built. The overwhelming majority of these were constructed at the extreme periphery (or even completely outside) the area which had earlier witnessed enclosure construction (Fig. 123). The latter is true for south Britain and South Scandinavia. Central western France, by contrast, saw only very few of these monuments prior to the 38th/37th century BC. No enclosures from the time horizons preceding 3750-3500 BC are known from areas north and east of the Harz Mountains. However, in this region, several enclosures (although not of the causewayed type) were built much earlier (during the Linear Pottery Culture in the 6th millennium BC)(Meyer/Raetzel-Fabian 2006, 8 Fig. 2).

The frequency of newly established enclosures in the core area of comparatively intensive enclosure construction between 4400-4000 BC changed in the subsequent time horizon. Between 3750-3500 BC, there were only few new enclosures. In fact, these figures were even lower than those counted in the preceding horizon (4000-3750 BC). Nevertheless, there are two remarkable exceptions to this observation. In the Bavarian Danube Valley, large amounts of Altheim enclosures were built in the same region in which abundant enclosure construction had taken place between 4400 and 4000 BC by the Münchshöfen Culture. The second exception is the narrow corridor which stretches northwards from the Neckar Valley. As mentioned above, this region had considerable numbers of enclosures which were constructed during early and middle Michelsberg Culture times. In fact, the region forming this corridor was the only area that witnessed considerable enclosure construction activity throughout the three major chronological horizons defined here.

When viewed together, the distribution of all enclosures built between 4400 and 3200 BC (Fig. 123) shows a clear and surprisingly dramatic picture, especially concerning the period from 3750-3500 BC. After having been comparatively stable geographically for 600-700 hundred years, the second half of the 38th to the 36th century BC witnessed a sudden enlargement of the area in which enclosures were built. The regions touched by this development were located to the west, northwest, north and northeast of the former distribution areas of enclosures.

Despite differences in quality and the precision of the dating between the various regions, there can hardly be any doubt that the pattern described above is the reflection of a true historical development. Furthermore, it is hard to imagine that the construction of numerous enclosures in geographically separate regions with vastly differing cultural backgrounds should have happened at the same time coincidentally. It could be argued that southern Britain and South Scandinavia could have seen comparable social developments following contemporaneous neolithisation a few centuries earlier. Thus, it is plausible that Early Neolithic societies in both regions reached some kind of internal breaking point of social tension, causing them to take over the enclosure concept at approximately the same time. But other regions – most notably the Bavarian Danube Valley and the corridor stretching northwards from the Neckar Valley and also the region north and east of the Harz Mountains – had a completely different cultural development, beginning the neolithisation process some 1500 years earlier. Still, exactly the same sequence appears to have happened there. There is, therefore, only one logical explanation for the pattern: the enclosure building boom observed at the time in question was not the result of local developments, but must rather have been triggered by some central event in the European Neolithic. What happened, therefore, bears striking resemblance to the process of neolithisation, at least in southern Britain and South Scandinavia, but possibly also in other regions of Europe, like the north alpine forelands (Klassen in press). One aspect of this similarity is the fact that events happened at approximately the same time in regions of Europe that were both diverse and separate. Moreover, while the results of these events were related within the individual regions, right from the start they nonetheless showed a distinct local identity.

This can easily be demonstrated by a look at enclosure design in the four main regions of enclosure construction (Fig. 126). In central western France, very complex enclosures appeared with few ditch interruptions, enclosed space divisions and especially distinct, pincer-like entrance constructions. In Britain, typical constructions from the same period were comparatively small and were

almost round enclosures; they often had wide ditch spacing. In northern central Germany on the other hand, very large, monumental enclosures were typical, often with very specific site plans (including a façade). Bavarian Altheim Culture enclosures, by contrast, were very small and had a distinct sub-rectangular shape. In all regions, the enclosure concept was certainly known prior to the beginnings of intense construction in the 38th century BC. What happened at this time was, thus, not the introduction of a completely new cultural habit, but rather the activation of an idea that had been passively present for centuries.

The observation of this enclosure building boom in the 38th to 36th centuries BC raises some important questions. What happened in the European Neolithic at this time that could cause populations with vastly differing cultural backgrounds to construct large numbers of enclosures in an area which stretched from the French Atlantic coast to the River Elbe and from the northern parts of Ireland to the Bavarian Danube Valley? Is it possible to point to a particular region from whence the events were triggered? If so, how did the impulse reach to extend across all affected regions? Why were only some parts of the total distribution area of enclosures affected while others were not? What does this tell us with regard to the function of causewayed enclosures? Was enclosure construction the only change that happened at this time? If not, did change only affect regions with newly built enclosures, or did it also have consequences in intermediate areas as well?

Obviously, the first of these questions is the most important. However, it is also the most difficult to answer. If a solution could be found, it would also be much easier to answer the questions which followed. Until now, only a single theory has been proposed which could possibly present a veritable answer to the question(s) raised. In a recent article, Gronenborn (2007) argued that a climatic crisis (traceable by various means) affected Neolithic populations. This caused a food crisis and thereby triggered increased violence. Gronenborn interprets causewayed enclosures (at least those of the Michelsberg Culture in the southwest of Germany)

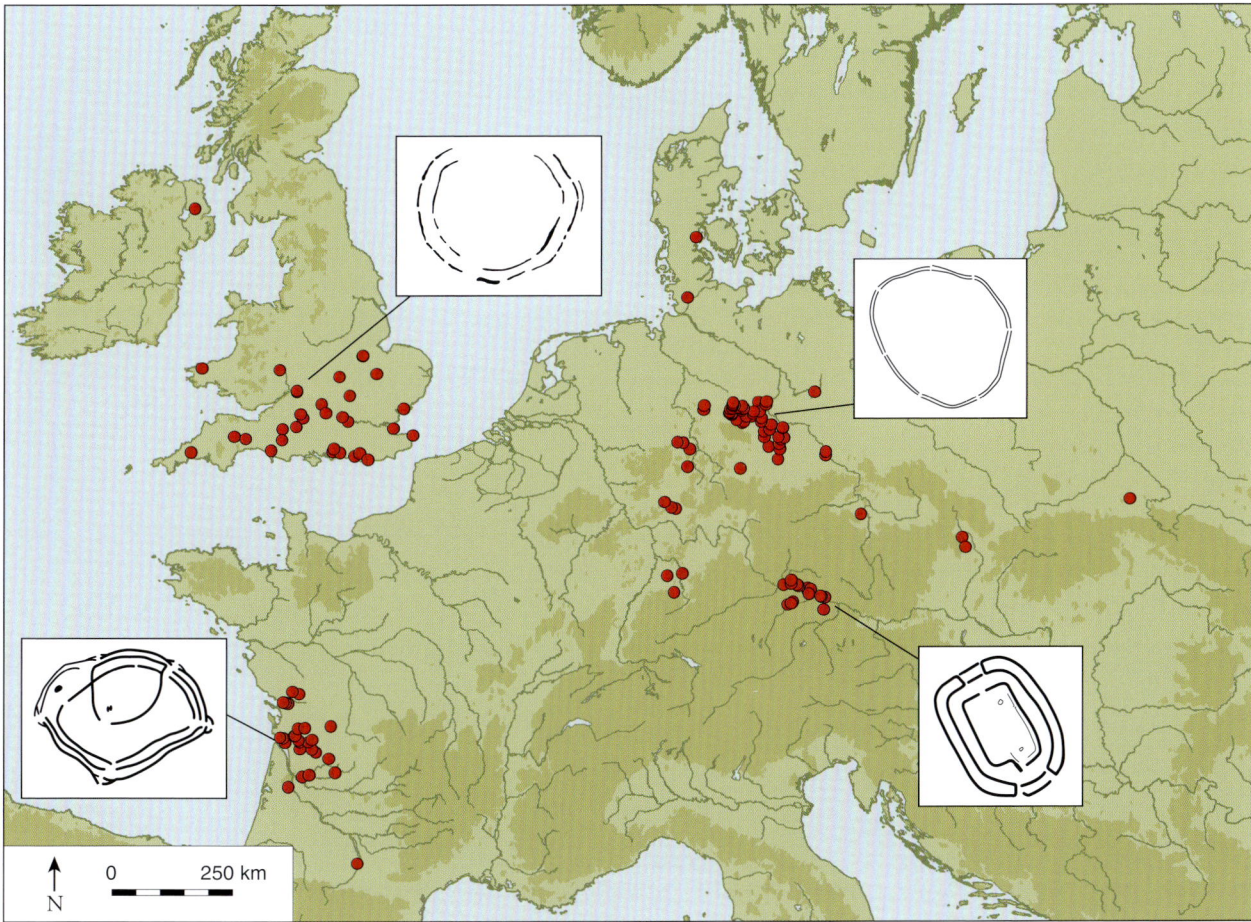

Fig. 126 | *Despite being contemporaneous and having the same initiating impulse, the enclosures that were built between 3750 and 3500 BC in the four main regions of activity are characterised by distinct local architectural identities from the very beginning.*

as defended settlements with increased depositions of humans that died a violent death (either in armed conflict or as the result of ritual torture).

Could Gronenborn's observations explain enclosure construction in many seemingly independent regions of Europe? Gronenborn interprets the causewayed enclosures of the Michelsberg Culture as defensive sites. This interpretation is, however, difficult to maintain as among others Jeunesse (2011) has recently argued in his review of this type of monument in European prehistory. Strong arguments against such an interpretation are also presented by Knoche (2013) in his recent work on the relation between an economy based on transhumance, routes and enclosures. It can be added that no settlement traces contemporaneous with enclosure construction are known from any

Scandinavian site. Enclosures clearly had a ritual function at the time of their construction. The same must be true for most (if not all) causewayed enclosures in other regions, given the striking similarities in construction and use between the different places. This does not necessarily contradict Gronenborn, however. Increased ritual activity can also be used as a means of resolving conflict and tension (e.g. Madsen, T. 1988).

However, other observations render the climatic crisis an unlikely catalyst for the enclosure building boom. As Knoche (2008, 140) pointed out, it is by no means certain that climatic change (which affected Neolithic economy in the northern forelands of the Alps) would necessarily have had the same effect in other parts of Europe. Furthermore, even for the north alpine region, whether increased precipitation and lower temperatures would have truly been problematic for the groups thereby affected is debatable (Stauch/Banghard 2002, 380 f.). Investigations of faunal assemblages from alpine pile-dwellings demonstrate that the hunting of deer in particular increased as a flexible response to what would likely have been a reduced cereal harvest (e.g. Schibler 2010).

The climatic crisis can also be ruled out as a primary cause of the enclosure construction boom, due to the precise dating of British enclosures. Whittle et al. (2011a) demonstrated that enclosure construction started in the later 38th century BC. Dendrochronology in the north alpine foreland, by contrast, evidences increased hunting as response to climatic change which did not begin before ca. 3660 BC. Thus, intensive enclosure construction began before climatic deterioration. Therefore, the latter changes cannot have caused the phenomenon under discussion here. Furthermore, as Whittle et al. (2011b, 883ff.) argued, there was a first boom of enclosure construction in the second half of the 5th millennium BC, which cannot have been related to a climatic crisis. Finally, it should be noted that climatic change was unlikely to have caused enclosure construction in some regions and not in others. At the very least, the linear distribution pattern of newly built enclosures between the Neckar Valley in southwest Germany and Westphalia renders any climatic explanation unlikely.

Climatic events would have provided a convincing reason for which considerable parts of Europe were affected by the enclosure construction boom at the same time. However, as argued above, things appear to have been much more complicated. Rather than addressing the events in the 38th to 36th century BC which triggered an enclosure building boom, the following attempts to first answer some of the subsequent questions which arose in relation to this fascinating topic. In this way, archaeological investigation can move forward from a position of strength. By examining the other occurrences and trends which were in existence, it is possible to gather additional clues.

Perhaps the most promising means of tackling these questions is by attempting to uncover how an 'impulse' that activated enclosure construction in different parts of Europe was transmitted (and from where). Optimism in this regard is based on the fact that answers to these questions can most likely be found in the enclosures themselves. Therefore, it is possible that they exist within the body of data that has already been compiled.

The geographical distribution of enclosures between 3750 and 3500 BC is the starting point for the investigations which follow. As previously mentioned, two different patterns are identifiable: isolated, regional concentrations of many enclosures at the periphery of the European enclosure construction area in its entirety and a linear pattern leading from southern to northern Germany.

The first pattern gives the impression of an "explosion". Its shape could potentially point to a region somewhere between the various regional enclosure concentrations (which was the site at which the event that triggered construction happened or, alternatively, the place from which enclosure construction itself was transmitted). The linear distribution of a number of enclosures in Germany, on the other hand, could reflect a kind of corridor through which the impulse could have been transmitted which caused the development in the northern periphery of the core area. The region from which the incentive to construct enclosures could potentially have been emitted would thus be situated either in the north or south of the total distribution area. In this regard, it is worth noting that most of registered enclosures were constructed in the north and northwest portion of the total distribution area. Indeed, the Altheim enclosures in the Bavarian Danube Valley (as well as those making up the linear pattern from the Neckar Valley) are the only ones present within regions that had previously seen enclosure construction. It could, thus, be argued that these parts of the former core area were affected more heavily by whatever happened than the other parts. This argument supports the placement of the source region of the impulse in the south of the total distribution area (i.e. somewhere in the northern alpine foreland between Bavaria and the Rhine).

At this point, it is important to clearly distinguish between two regions: the one in which the events that triggered enclosure construction actually took place and the region from whence this impulse was distributed to all the areas that in consequence witnessed enclosure building booms. The above considerations may indicate that southern central Europe was most heavily affected by whatever caused the development in question, and that it was from there that an impulse was transmitted to other enclosure construction areas. However, this cannot be conflated with the centre of events. It could equally be imagined that this centre was situated (far) outside the area under consideration in a region which had no enclosure construction tradition. Given its heavy impact on the Altheim Culture, this region could be situated east (or southeast) of Bavaria.

The following investigates whether or not it is possible to identify an area in southern central Europe which could be connected to enclosure building areas in central western France, Britain and northern central Germany. One part of this investigation queries if and how the start of enclosure building in the TRB North Group related to overall development. Whether or not an area in south Germany was the origin of the impulse (or whether it only served as a transmitter) is another point of interest that is discussed secondarily.

10.4.1 Southern central Europe and South Scandinavia

The southern end of the linear distribution of enclosures built between 3750 and 3500 BC lies in the Neckar River Valley (Fig. 124). The southernmost registered site is Leonberg "Silberberg" (Seidel 2009), but the enclosure of Heilbronn-Klingenberg "Schlossberg" (Seidel 2008) and the probable enclosure site of Zaisenhausen "Hard" (Lehmann 1992) are situated close by. A further three clusters (consisting of two to three enclosures each) are aligned on a north-south axis. It is interesting to note that two contemporary South Scandinavian enclosures (Albersdorf Dieksknöll and Starup Langelandsvej) would be situated along this same

axis, should it be prolonged from the two northernmost enclosure sites: Betheln "Beusterburg" (Tackenberg 1951) and Rössing (Linke 1989; Geschwinde/Raetzel-Fabian 2009) in Lower Saxony. As is demonstrated below, this is no coincidence. It is most likely a reflection of a corridor of privileged information exchange (of which at least one important part was directly related to causewayed enclosures and their ritual functions).

As was demonstrated above in the discussion of several South Scandinavian enclosures, the investigation of specific architectural traits is a suitable method for detecting links between enclosures in different regions. This argument is followed somewhat further here, with a special emphasis on entrance constructions. Entrance constructions have generally been observed only in a few cases within the TRB North group's distribution area. While this may be due (at least in part) to insufficiencies in the state of exploration and the publication of known sites, a deficient state of research alone is an unlikely cause for the pattern observed. Indeed, the much larger dataset represented by the Central European enclosures is much the same. In point of fact, Meyer & Raetzel-Fabian (2006, 24) posited that, in many cases, erosion was at fault for the total destruction of potential traces of such constructions. Indeed, this seems a likely explanation, at least for lighter constructions. However, some entrance constructions appear to have been very solid. On occasion, these were dug even deeper than the ditches by which the enclosures were formed. Aside the one at Gammeltoft Odde (chapter 10.2.6), a few other examples are known from the TRB North Group. At Albersdorf Dieksknöll, an oblong pit (which most likely served as the foundation for some variety of massive, potentially tent-shaped wooden construction) was found in the middle of a causeway. It was oriented at right angle to the course of the ditches (Fig. 104). Here again, its depth was greater than that of the ditches. The two posts inserted into this pit have already been discussed (chapter 10.2.6). Therefore, the following observations concentrate on the transverse pit itself. Furthermore, fenced entrance passageways have been excavated at Sarup I and Büdelsdorf. At Sarup I, an additional trans-

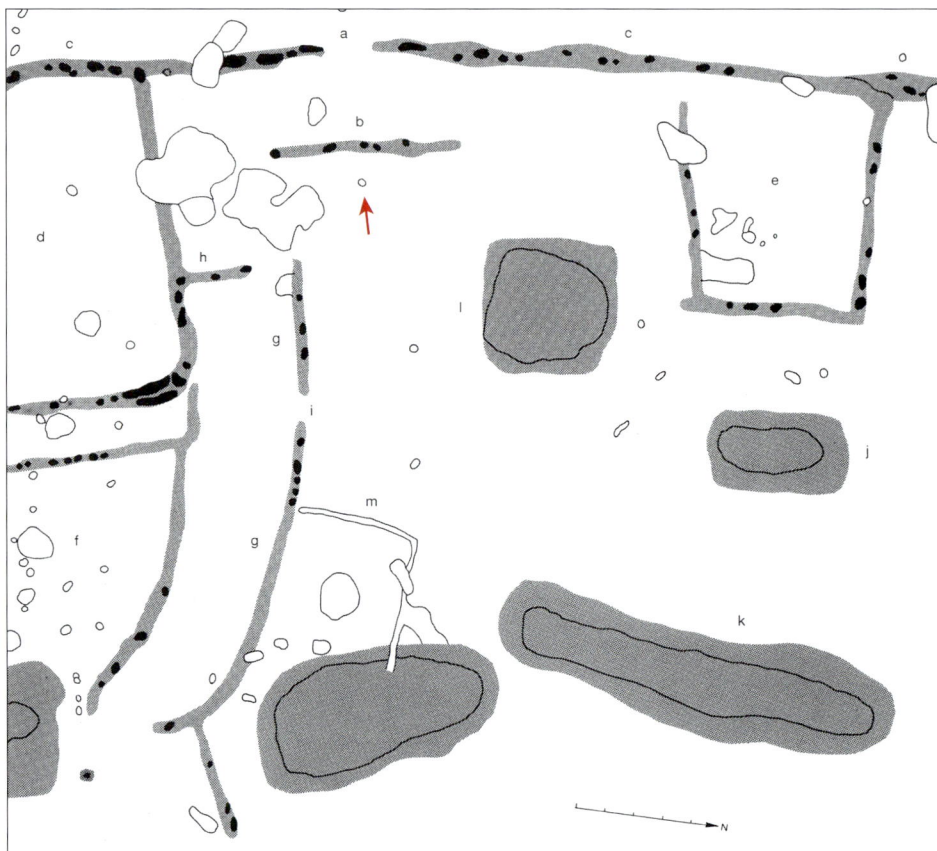

Fig. 127 | *The only entrance to the Sarup I enclosure consisted of a narrow opening in the palisade. A fenced entrance passageway as well as a screen in front of the opening were also found (from Andersen, N.H. 1997, arrow added).*

verse screen was found in front of the only entrance through the palisade (Fig. 127). Although the transverse screen remains the primarily focus here, other entrance structures are also briefly discussed.

It is germane to investigate the spatial distribution of parallel constructions, as it is unlikely to be influenced by regional or local differences in the degree of erosion (and/or secondary factors) due to the depth of the foundations. Furthermore, under the right conditions, both the transverse pits and even the screens are visible from the air. This is the case at Albersdorf Dieksknöll (transverse pits: Arnold 1997, 21 and 23 Abb. 5) as well as at Müsleringen (screen – see below). Many of the Continental sites that are known only from aerial survey can, therefore, be included in analysis (which considerably adds to the reliability of the resultant distribution patterns).

The following section engages only with very close parallels to these specific structures. For example, a number of variations of transverse screens are known, both in isolation and as part of much more complex constructions. Both versions are present at Sarup I. However, this investigation restricts itself to the simple isolated screen (Fig. 127), as this is much more easily compared with other structures than complex buildings' multiple (and varied) details. With regard to the transverse pits in causeways, only constructions which are nearly identical to that at Albersdorf Dieksknöll are described here. Related structures (such as two or three parallel pits) are not included. It might be argued that the slightly divergent elements known from a number of sites in many parts of Europe merely reflect multiple phase versions of the Scandinavian examples. Alternatively, the latter may have been much more complex (conceivably reduced by erosion to their present form). Interestingly, the latter point is not substantiated by the excavation results from Sarup, for example (at which site even quite delicate structures were preserved). Furthermore, the mapping of parallels to the Nordic structures results (at least in part) in very specific distribution patterns that can be confirmed by other observations.

10.4.1.1 Transverse pits on causeways

As stated above, a transverse pit was observed on a causeway at the Albersdorf Dieksknöll enclosure in northern Germany (Fig. 104; Dibbern 2011; 2012). Comparable single, transverse, oblong pits bisecting entrances are known from the start of enclosure construction in Central Europe in the 6th millennium BC (Linear Pottery Culture) onwards (Meyer/Raetzel-Fabian 2006, 4), albeit only in comparatively few cases. In the 6th millennium BC, these entrance constructions were present in the Bavarian Danube Valley as well as in North Rhine-Westphalia. In the Bavarian Danube Valley, the tradition of building these kinds of entrances can also be traced from the (early) 5th millennium (Künzig-Unternberg: Petrasch 1990, 471) through to the first half of the 4th millennium BC (Altheim site of Bad Abbach-Alkofen: Fig. 128; Petrasch 1986). In southwest Germany, at least two (but probably three) Michelsberg sites within a narrow region stand out, as they have the same kind of entrance construction. The Bruchsal "Aue" (Reiter 2005) and the Ilsfeld "Ebene" (Seidel 2008) enclosures both date to the older part of the Michelsberg Culture (MK II, late 5th millennium BC). Excavators are somewhat uncertain of the feature excavated at Ilsfeld "Ebene", as it could only be documented below an existing ditch. This unusual situation was interpreted as the reflection of the removal of a former entrance with transverse pit in a second building phase of the enclosure (Seidel 2008, 82). The last of the three enclosures with transverse pit on a causeway – Heilbronn-Klingenberg "Schlossberg" (Seidel 2008) – demonstrates that the specific building tradition was maintained in the region until the 37th century BC (the date of the feature at Albersdorf Dieksknöll).

This survey included only the pits placed between two ditches in the middle of a causeway. Slightly related structures are known from the late Münchshöfen ("Fazies Wallerfing") enclosure of Bergheim in Bavaria. At that enclosure, two narrow transverse pits were placed next to each other on a causeway (although this was done between two ditch circuits)(Meixner 2001, 20 Fig. 11).

Due to the small number of sites known from the late 5th and first half of the 4th millennium BC with deep transverse pits in enclosure entrances, it is dif-

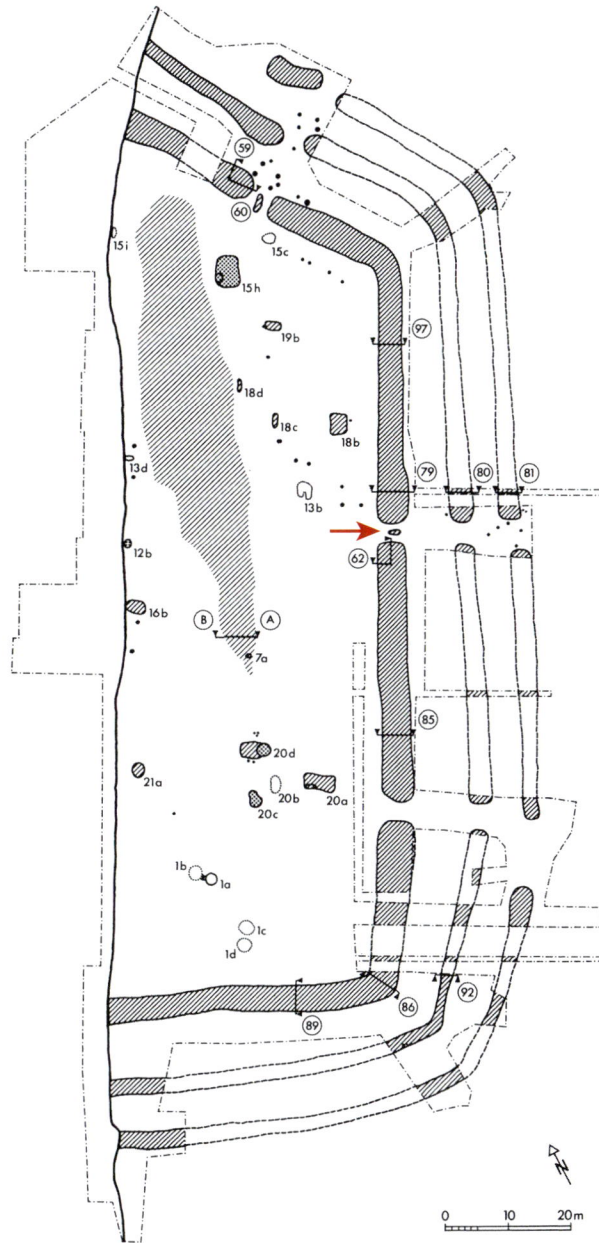

Fig. 128 | *An entrance construction consisting of a transverse pit at the Altheim Culture Bad Abbach-Alkofen enclosure in Bavaria constitutes a good parallel to the transverse pit observed at the TRB enclosure of Albersdorf Dieksknöll (from Petrasch 1986, arrow added).*

ficult to interpret the distribution pattern they represent (Fig. 129). Nonetheless, as mentioned above, one must assume that this distribution is not influenced by differentials in the degree of preservation. Moreover, the number of enclosures investigated between south Germany and Albersdorf Dieksknöll

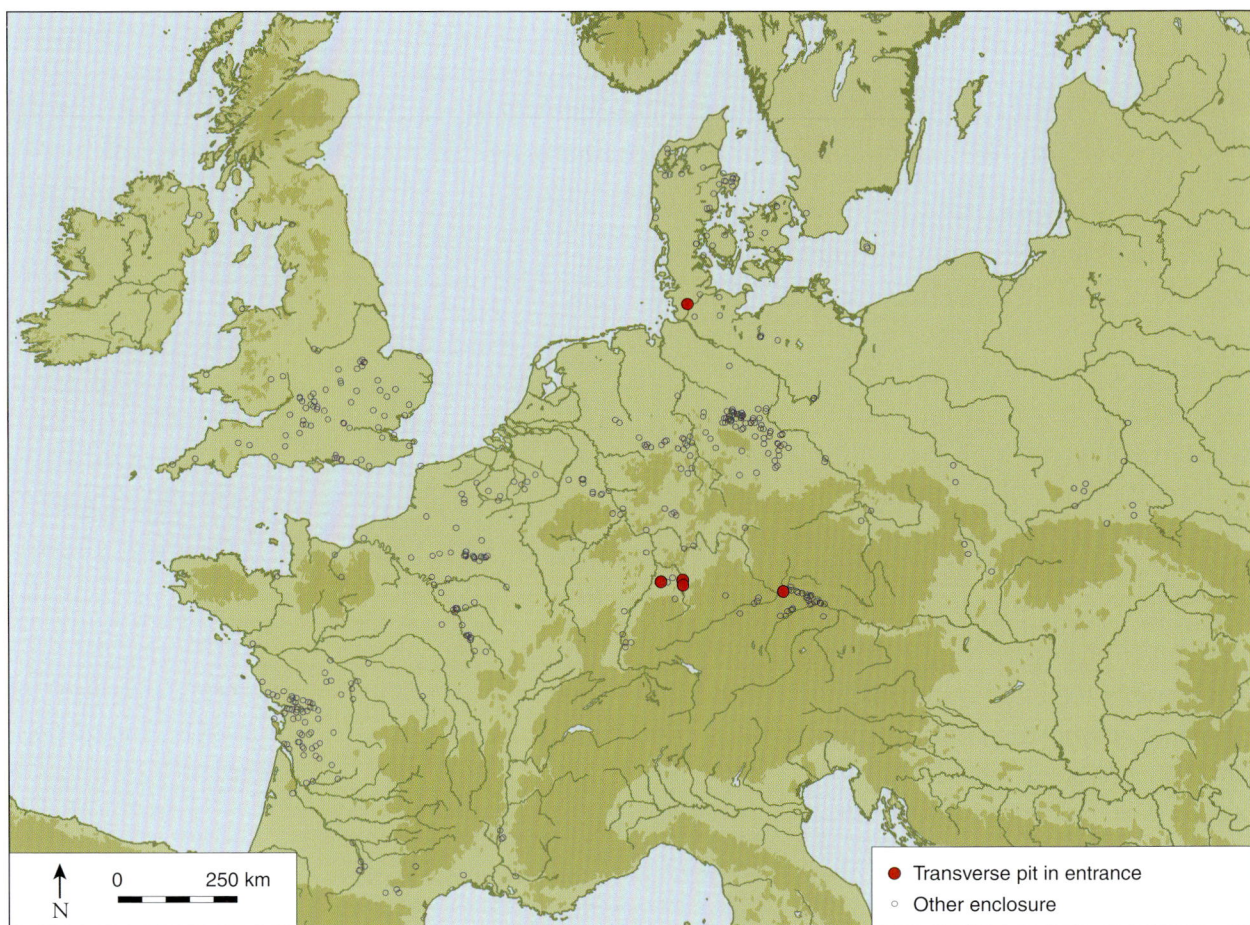

Fig. 129 | *The European distribution of transverse pits as entrance constructions in enclosures from the later 5th and first half of the 4th millennium BC. For references to individual sites, see the text.*

is considerable; the structures in question are large enough to be visible in aerial photos (such as is the case at Albersdorf Dieksknöll itself). While it is always difficult to formulate an argument based on the presence of absence, it can be cautiously assumed that some kind of comparatively direct relation existed between Schleswig-Holstein and the Neckar Valley. The distribution of transverse pits in causeways demonstrates a privileged system of information exchange. In this way, it is feasible to posit that enclosures between the northern and southern extremities of the linear distribution sharing the 3750-3500 BC construction window had a direct relationship.

Furthermore, this band not only connected the Neckar Valley to South Scandinavia, but also said sites to the concentration of contemporaneous enclosures in the Bavarian Danube Valley (e.g. the

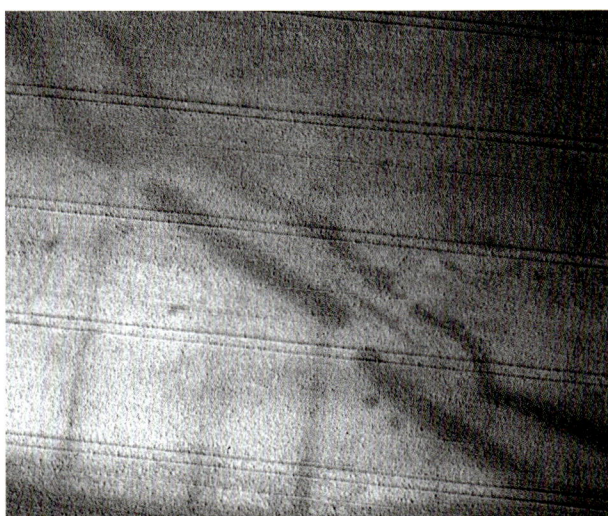

Fig. 130 | *An entrance construction consisting of a transverse screen is visible from the air at the enclosure of Müsleringen in Lower Saxony, northern Germany (from Freese 2010).*

Altheim site of Bad Abbach-Alkofen). This observation supports the idea that the creation of these monuments was part of the same specific historical process. It should be added that the connection between the Bavarian Danube Valley and the Neckar Valley region is already apparent from the distribution of enclosures built between 4400 and 4000 BC (Fig. 121). The historical developments in the 3750-3500 BC horizon are, thus, likely to have been based on information exchange along an established long-distance route.

10.4.1.2 Entrance screens

A transverse screen is present between the palisade and the rows of segmented ditches at Sarup I (it was placed slightly in front of the only opening/ entrance in the palisade)(Fig. 127). The same type of entrance screen is known elsewhere, albeit only at the Bergheim enclosure in Hesse (Raetzel-Fabian 1988, 90 Fig. 123a), Müsleringen along the Weser River (Fig. 130; Freese 2010, 4f. Fig. 2; Ramminger 2012) and (possibly) at Neckarsulm-Obereisesheim "Hetzenberg" (Seidel 2008, 18 Abb. 7). Müsleringen lies between the TRB North Group distribution area and that of the Michelsberg Culture to the south. This site is presently under investigation; recent finds indicate that it should be ascribed to the early 4th millennium BC in the Early Neolithic of northwestern Germany (Knoche 2013, 171). At Neckarsulm-Obereisesheim Hetzenberg, two entrance screens were observed (Seidel 2008, 33ff.). One example certainly represents a variant of the Sarup screen, although it has a minor gap in the middle (see the following discussion on 'split screens'). The second, interestingly, demonstrated a bipartite division only in the lower parts of the foundation trench (it remained uninterrupted in the upper parts). It appears, thus, that the gap between the two halves of the screen was somehow filled, although possibly in a different manner than is apparent from proper Sarup-type screens. The Hetzenberg site was included in the mapping of Sarup screens, nonetheless (Fig. 131).

A slightly different (but related) screen was found at the Orsett enclosure in southern Britain (Hedges/Buckley 1978, 238 Fig. 14). It deviated from the

examples referred to above in that it was curved. Moreover, not only was it asymmetrically placed in relation to the entrance, but it was also situated off-center inside of the palisade. The screens that were found at Sarup and Müsleringen, lay between a segmented ditch and the palisade. At Bergheim, it was placed between two segmented ditches. The screen at Neckarsulm-Obereiseisheim "Hetzenberg" was found on the inside of three segmented ditches. Therefore, while they were certainly generally related, the screen at Orsett cannot be directly compared with the Continental evidence.

The distribution of Sarup type screens in front of causewayed enclosure entrances has a linear pattern leading from the Neckar Valley in southwest Germany up to Denmark (Fig. 131). This exactly mirrors the one observed for some of the enclosures built in the 3750 to 3500 BC time horizon. Therefore, the distribution of Sarup-type screens confirms that the distribution of enclosures built from 3750-3500 BC reflects historical reality, as was suspected, due to the distribution of transverse pits on causeways.

It is of interest to note the age of known Sarup-type screen constructions; Neckarsulm-Obereiseisheim "Hetzenberg" (Seidel 2008, 37 ff.) and Bergheim (Geschwinde/Raetzel-Fabian 2009, 219 Abb. 161) both belong to the older Michelsberg Culture and date to ca. 4000 BC (or slightly earlier). Müsleringen probably belongs to the early fourth millennium BC, while Sarup I was probably built in the 35th or 34th century BC.

It appears that the Sarup type entrance screens were specifically used only in enclosures situated in a narrow corridor leading almost strictly from the Neckar Valley in southern central Europe to Denmark. This corridor must reflect one or, indeed, perhaps several parallel roads to which specific beliefs were tied. It appears to be a parallel for the examples referred to above within Denmark (e.g. stone heap grave roads, see chapter 9.3.4), albeit on a much larger scale. It is remarkable that for at least half a millennium, the same specific ideas concerning the way in which an enclosure entrance should be constructed were exclusively bound to this south-north corridor. At present, it appears that the specific knowledge regarding this feature was passed on orally over tens of generations and was used in practice only on very rare occasions. Indeed, many generations may have passed between individual construction events. Transverse pits in causeways may well be another specific feature bound to this corridor, which might well eventually demonstrate that the existence of the corridor within the TRB North Group distribution area is older than suggested by the construction date of the Sarup enclosure. In fact, at least theoretically, the corridor could indeed be much older, having become the medium of the transmission of specific ritual knowledge after it was first established. Knoche (2013) has recently suggested that Central European roads owed their existence to a mobile economy based on cattle herding, and that this raison d'être could have extended into South Scandinavia around 4000 BC. Therefore, argued Knoche (2013), the particular meaning and use of roads could have moved northwards as part of the neolithisation process in South Scandinavia. This idea could also explain why South Scandinavian causewayed enclosures were only built in regions which were also the focus of very early Neolithic settlement. These earliest routes could have been associated with ancestral immigrants. However, some observations cast doubt on the applicability of this idea with regard to the emergence of causewayed enclosures. Firstly, the earliest Neolithic assemblages from South Scandinavia (which reflect Michelsberg types quite strongly and may, thus, testify to the immigration of Michelsberg herders (Klassen in press; Sørensen/Karg in press)) are located at significant distances from the coastline.

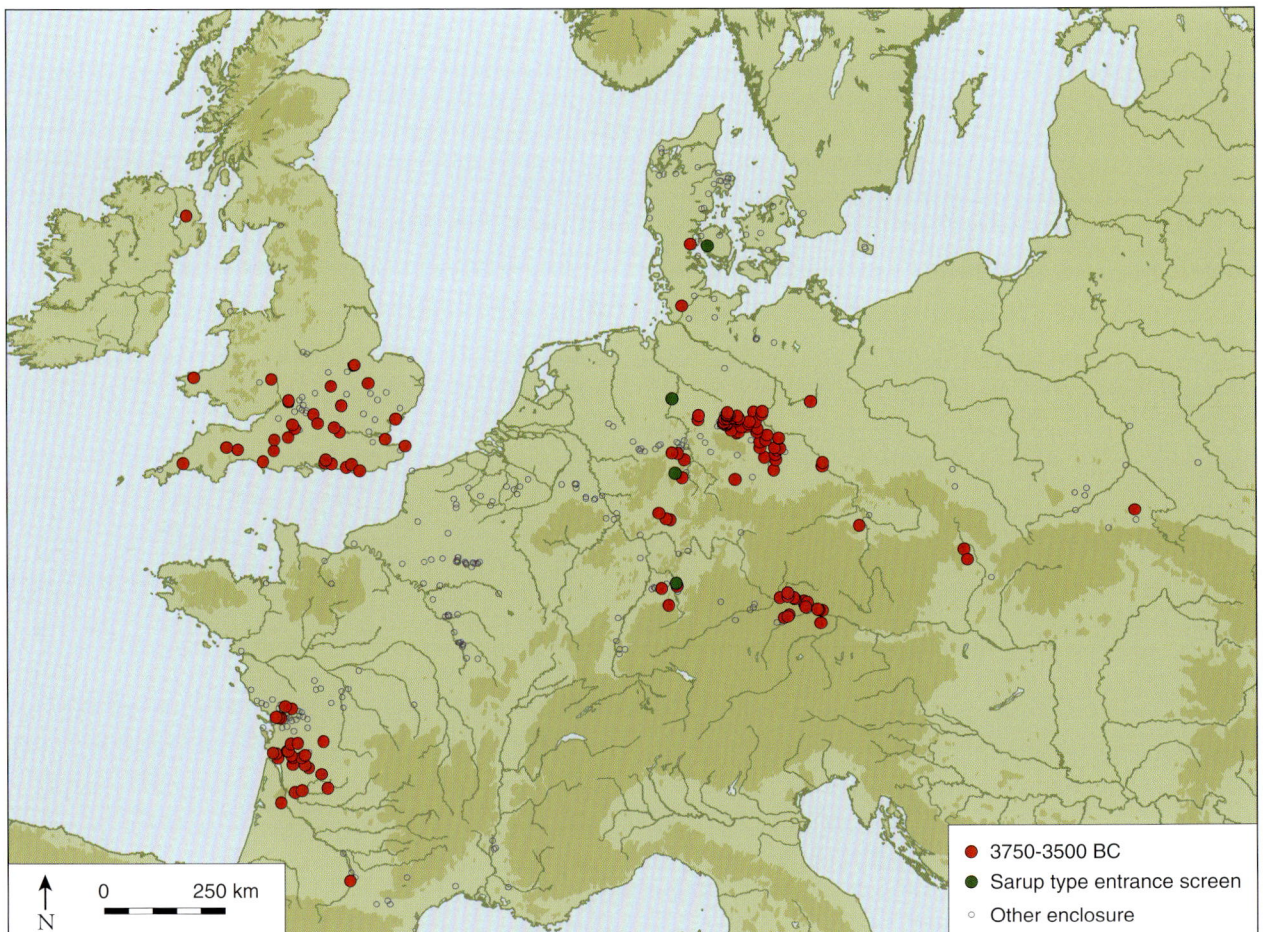

Fig. 131 | *The distribution of enclosure entrance constructions in the shape of simple screens shows the same linear distribution pattern between the Neckar Valley in southwest Germany and South Scandinavia as that observed for a group of enclosures built between 3750 and 3500 BC.*

Therefore, they were situated outside the area in which enclosures were later built. Although the precise use of coastal fishing and catching sites seems to have changed compared to Ertebølle times (Andersen, S.H. 1995; Johansen 2006), the economy of the earliest TRB societies in the near-coastal areas shows a distinctive continuation of Late Mesolithic traditions with regards to the importance placed on fishing and marine hunting. There is nothing to suggest that cattle herding would have been crucially important to such societies. Moreover, there would be no need for herd movements along transhumance routes due to abundant natural grazing grounds present along the extremely long South Scandinavian coastlines (chapter 9.3.4). At present, therefore, it must be concluded that there is no evidence to connect immigrating Michelsberg herders/herder societies to those South Scandinavian routes along which causewayed enclosures were subsequently constructed. Of course, this does not exclude the possibility that other inland routes originated due processes as that proposed by Knoche.

The date at which the routes along which causewayed enclosures were built could thus well be identical to that of the earliest enclosures – probably the 38th or 37th century BC. It can't be excluded either, however, that these routes were created at the time of neolithisation a few centuries earlier due to a process that is unknown at present.

10.4.1.3 Other entrance structures

Although they cannot contribute to the question of links between Scandinavian enclosures and the Neckar Valley in southern Germany, a few other examples are mentioned in order to bring to a close this treatment of Scandinavian entrance structures. Entrances in the form of gateways made of minor posts leading to palisade openings have been found at Büdelsdorf (Hage in press), Sarup I (Andersen, N.H. 1997, 42 Fig. 40a) and Sarup II (Andersen, N.H. 1997, 66 Fig. 79)(Fig. 127). Comparable structures at Albersdorf Dieksknöll appear to be linked directly to the palisade (Arnold 1997, 23 Fig. 5). This type of entrance structure might well have been present at other enclosures and yet remain invis-

ible to excavators due to the erosion of the shallow postholes. From a wider European context, these structures are known from a comparably large number of sites across a large swathe of Europe stretching from England to Slovakia (see Oswald 2001, 52f. for British and Meyer/Raetzel-Fabian 2006 for Continental examples). Thus, entrance gateways are geographically very widespread, which does not allow for any conclusions to be drawn regarding the origin of this trait in the enclosures from South Scandinavia.

At Sarup I, a transverse screen was integrated in the gateway leading to the entrance. This feature can be compared to the "bastions" found at the Michelsberg enclosures in Urmitz on the Rhine, Calden in Hesse (Raetzel-Fabian 2000, 46ff.) and Großfahner in Thuringia (Barthel 1984; Raetzel-Fabian 2003). While not as frequent as the simple gateways, these constructions thus also show a rather dispersed distribution, which does not allow for further conclusions to be drawn at present.

10.4.1.4 Fenced rectangular annexes

Small fenced annexes of rectangular or slightly rhomboid shape adjacent to palisades have been found at the causewayed enclosures of Sarup I (Andersen, N.H. 1997, 34ff.) and Sarup II (Andersen, N.H. 1997, 66ff.) as well as at Starup Langelandsvej (Fig. 89). The results of magnetometer measurements at Assenbakke in Djursland may reflect further examples (Klassen/Klein, this volume). Comparable structures are known from Büdelsdorf (see Andersen, N.H. 1997, 274 for a discussion of the slightly diverging evidence from this site). At Sarup II, small ditch segments were found inside some of these fenced areas; at Sarup I, fenced annexes were found between ditch segments. At Starup Langelandsvej, ditch segments followed a curved course around the fenced annexes.

Just as was the case with the fenced gateways leading to the entrances, as we know from N.H. Andersen's compilation (1997, 292), comparable structures are known from a number of sites of very diverse age from large parts of Europe. Nevertheless, it should be noted that no example is known from the well-explored British enclosures.

N.H. Andersen (1997, 160) has already emphasized the fenced annex found at Sandomierz in southeastern Poland (Fig. 89) as a particularly close parallel to the evidence from Sarup I. The similarity between this Polish construction and Danish finds some 950 km away appears even stronger today, as the Sandomierz enclosure shows a curved ditch segment around the fenced annex and an opening almost identical to those observed at Starup Langelandsvej (see chapter 10.2.2). Nevertheless, the geographically and chronologically isolated position of this single Polish parallel makes it difficult to draw any further conclusions.

10.4.1.5 Further links

In addition to the entrance constructions discussed above, at least three categories of finds allow links between southern central Europe and South Scandinavia to be clearly demonstrated at the time in question. At least a portion of these finds were made in causewayed enclosures, which makes them especially interesting for this investigation.

Tetraploid naked wheat
*(*Triticum durum/turgidum*)*
The presence of tetraploid naked wheat was recently demonstrated by impressions of threshing debris in a clay disk at the Albersdorf Dieksknöll enclosure as well as by macrofossils from the Frydenlund settlement (unpublished excavation by N.H. Andersen) in the Sarup area in Denmark (Kierleis/Fischer in press; Kierleis, personal communication). This type of cereal is called "Pfahlbau-Weizen" or "pale dwelling wheat" in the older literature, although more recent publications sometimes refer to it as "macaroni wheat". It is thought to have originated in the Mediterranean and to have spread to Central Europe in the mid 5th millennium BC (Jacomet/Schlichterle 1984; Maier 1996; Maier 1998; Herbig 2009, 1283). Its main distribution in Central Europe is located in the western part of the north alpine area, where it has been found in numerous settlements (especially pile-dwellings) in southwest Germany and Switzerland (Jacomet 2007; Herbig 2009). The Michelsberg enclosure site of Heilbronn-Klingenberg "Schloss-

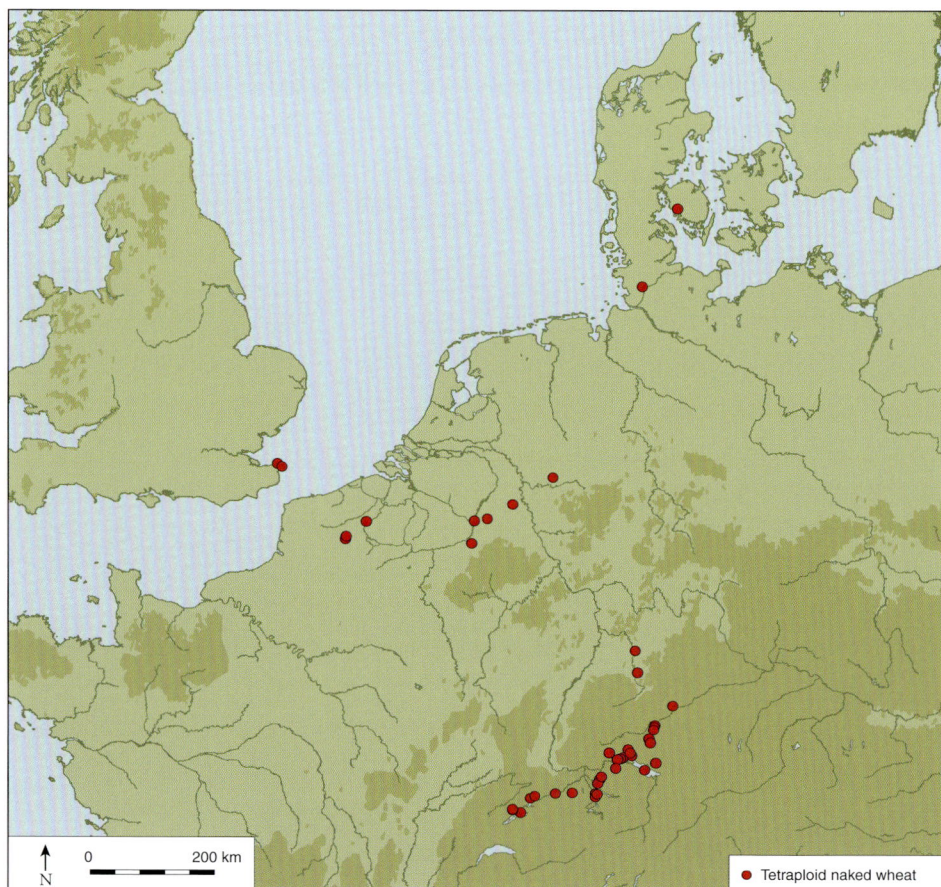

Fig. 132 | *The distribution of tetraploid naked wheat finds north of the Alps between ca. 4500 and 3500 BC.*

berg" in the Neckar Valley has also produced evidence for the cultivation of tetraploid naked wheat (Stika 1996). Recently, the same type of cereal was found in Dutch Michelsberg Culture contexts (Bakels 2003) as well as those from the Bischheim Group of the German Rhineland (Arora/Zerl 2004), the Spiere Group in Belgium and adjoining parts of France (Bostyn et al. 2012, 558; Vanmontfort et al. 2004), the British Early Neolithic (Kierleis/Fischer in press with reference to unpublished paper by W. Carruthers) as well as in a Rössen site in Westphalia (Brink-Kloke/Meurers-Balke 2003). Fig. 132 shows the distribution of the find places which date before ca. 3300 BC. Finds from western and southern Europe (Italy, southern France, Spain and Portugal) were not included in the map.

As it is not possible to identify the cereal type in question on the basis of conventional grain investigations alone, it may well have been much more common than has hitherto been believed. It must also be added that plant macrofossils have been investigated at comparatively few Michelsberg sites (Schamuhn/Meurers-Balke 2008). Tetraploid naked wheat, thus, may have been more common in this culture than has hitherto been thought. However, given the sum of archaeological knowledge, it is reasonable to assume that the cultivation of the tetraploid naked wheat at Albersdorf Dieksknöll and Frydenlund had its origins in the Michelsberg Culture in the Neckar Valley in southwest Germany, as both regions appear to have been intimately linked (as demonstrated by the aforementioned enclosure entrance constructions). Thus, tetraploid naked wheat probably constitutes an example of a commodity that was not directly related to causewayed enclosures. However, according to the finds noted in several enclosures, it may well have been distributed along the same corridor that linked the Neckar Valley to South Scandinavia. Therefore, it is important to note that this corridor probably served purposes which were not ritual in nature. Moreover, this information intimates that a commodity such as a specific type of cereal was not subject to the same strict regulations as those which apparently restricted specific enclosure construction traits to a single corridor.

This pattern is suggested by the fact that tetraploid naked wheat has been identified in enclosures in the Netherlands, Belgium and France which were obviously not situated along the South Scandinavian- Neckar Valley corridor. This text returns to this observation below.

Copper finds
One of the most obvious links between South Scandinavia and southern central Europe are copper finds made of a specific type of arsenical copper (Fig. 133) which is known as Mondsee copper (Matuschik 1998). The following treats with both Mondsee copper as well as Riesebusch copper

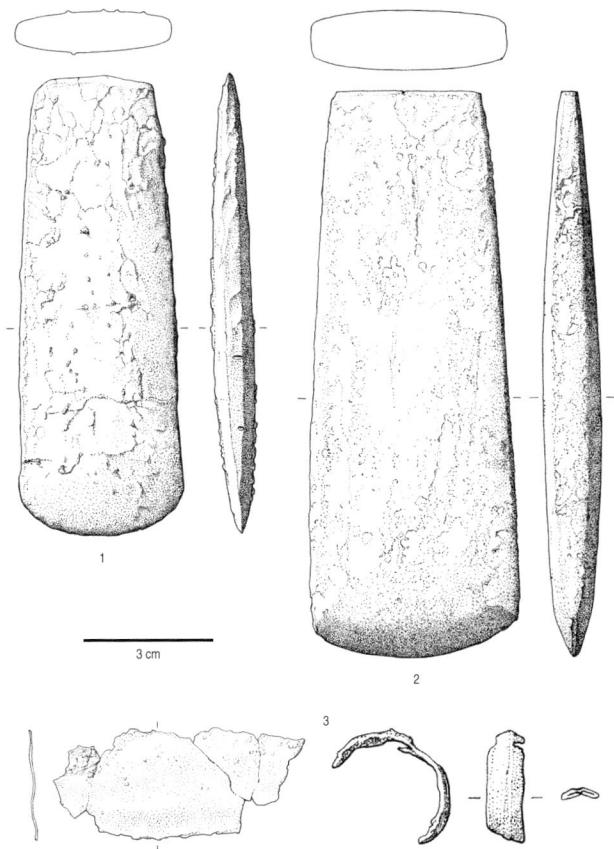

3 cm

Fig. 133 | *The inventory of Early Neolithic copper finds in South Scandinavia is dominated by copper flat axes. Most of these are single finds, but a few depositions have also been recovered. Copper trinkets (rings, spirals, discs, sheets) are known from a few graves and depositions as well. All finds depicted here are from Djursland. 1 Egens, 2 Agri, 3 Konens Høj (from Klassen 2000).*

(Klassen 2000; Klassen/Stürup 2001). The latter is a variant of Mondsee copper and appears to come from the same source but deviates slightly in its chemical composition. Mondsee copper is completely dominant among the abundant copper finds from the north alpine forelands between the 38th and 33rd century BC. Within the north alpine foreland region, the metal is known from numerous single finds as well as from the pile-dwellings of the Mondsee Group and the Altheim-, Pfyn and Cortaillod Cultures. Abundant traces of metalworking – especially crucibles – have been recovered from these settlements (e.g. Schlichterle/Rottländer 1982). The largest concentration of crucibles is known from the pile-dwellings of the Mondsee Group in the area around Salzburg, Austria. Abundant copper ores are known from the same area. This has led many researchers to suspect that the metal actually originated in the eastern Alps (e.g. Matuschik 1998; Klassen 2000). However, the latest scientific investigations seem to negate this conclusion. Instead, they suggest that Mondsee copper originated from another region which has yet to be identified, probably further to the east/southeast (E. Pernicka, personal communication).

Artefacts made of Mondsee copper are also present in large quantities in South Scandinavia (Klassen 2000). In fact, the amount of metal (in weight) present there is much larger than that in the entire north alpine region and all areas in between put together. Even though the origin of this metal can no longer be located in the Alps, there is no doubt regarding the fact that it is via the north alpine region that it reached South Scandinavia. Most of it was re-melted and cast into new forms (in the north, copper flat axes were particularly common). These axes show clear typological links to those known from southern Germany and Austria, nevertheless. Furthermore, several items appear to not have been remelted in Scandinavia. These original objects can be identified as imports from the Mondsee Group and (first of all) from the Pfyn Culture in southwest Germany and eastern Switzerland (Klassen 2000).

The import of metal from the latter region is also clearly apparent from a total distribution map

(Fig. 134) previously published (e.g. Klassen/Stürup 2001; Klassen et al. 2007). For the current study, a renewed investigation was made into the distribution of Mondsee copper between the Alps and South Scandinavia. Apart from an increased density of finds in the eastern parts of Germany, the distribution pattern remains the same. Many analyses of north alpine finds still are unpublished; therefore, the mapping for this region was based on the map published by Matuschik (1998, 239 Abb. 235) with only very few additions and removals.

The map in Fig. 134 clearly shows the large number of finds in the north alpine forelands and in South Scandinavia as well as a minor concentration in northern central Germany between the Elbe and Harz. It is also apparent that metal was exchanged throughout the Upper Rhine Valley and from there through Hesse and Lower Saxony towards the Baltic Sea. Finds from Lower Saxony are shown on the map in a different colour because they have not yet been analysed. Therefore, they cannot be allocated as proven examples of Mondsee copper. However, the items in question (all are copper flat axes: Laux 2000, nr. 1, 3, 9-11) can be conclusively dated to the time horizon in question (ca. 3800-3300 BC) by means of typology. In this study, they are assumed to consist of Mondsee copper as this metal was the dominant copper type (to the exclusion of all others) during this time period in the region stretching between the Alps and South Scandinavia. The finds seem to indicate a possible division of the exchange route into two parts: one leading north along the Weser River and another leading north from the concentration of Mondsee copper artefacts in the Baalberge Group distribution area in Saxony-Anhalt.

It is also worth noting that the route of metal artefacts between the north alpine pile-dwelling area south of the Danube and the Upper Rhine Valley apparently did not follow the course of the Rhine from the find-rich shores of Lake Constance. Instead, several finds indicate that the metal might have been exchanged from Upper Swabia across the Swabian Alps towards the Neckar Valley and from there further west to the Upper Rhine Valley. Thus, the starting point of the enclosure corridor in

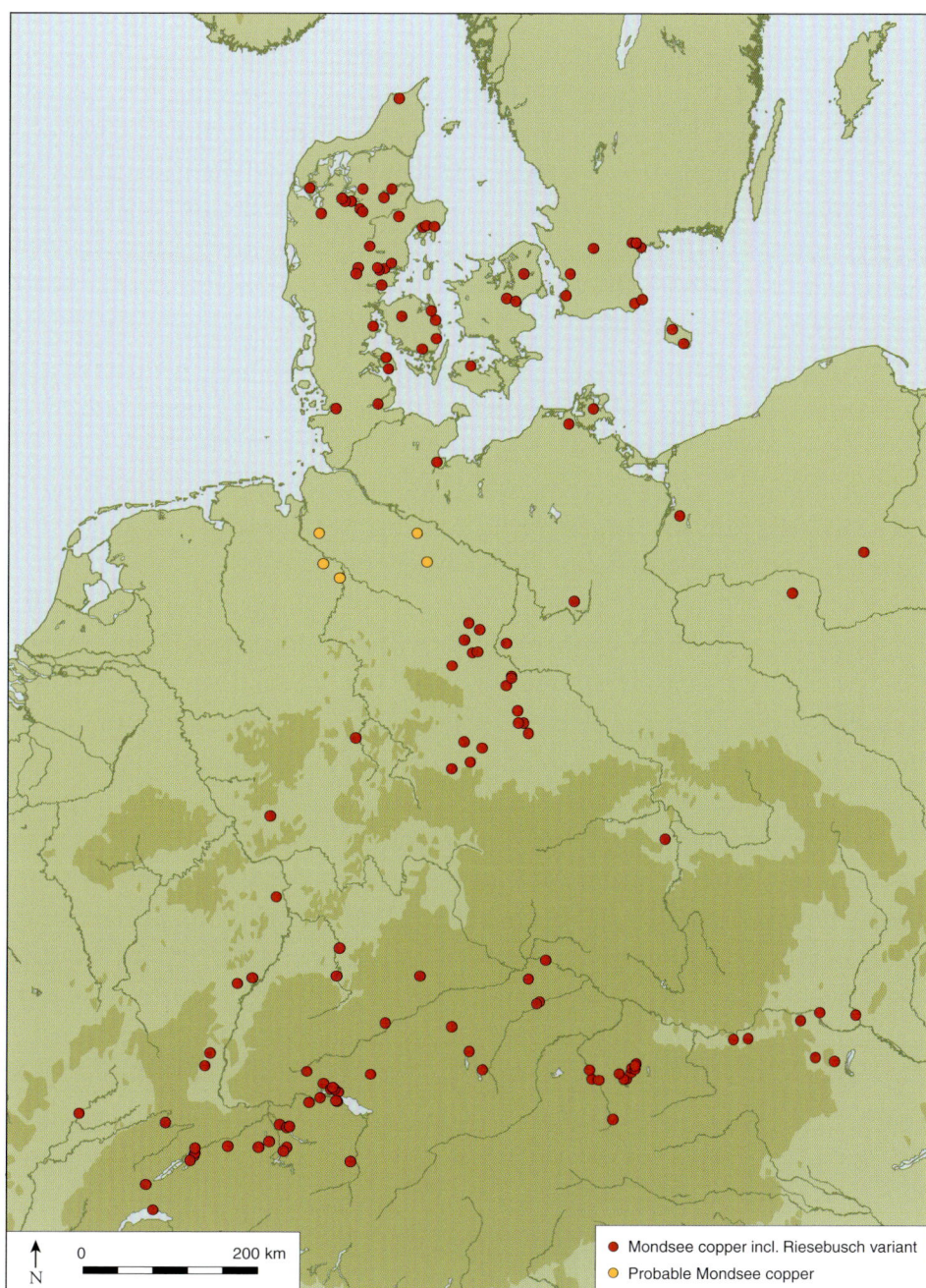

Fig. 134 | *A distribution map of Mondsee copper (including the Riesebusch variant) demonstrates the exchange route between the north Alpine area and South Scandinavia. A number of copper flat axes from Lower Saxony in northern Germany have been added to the map (in spite of missing analyses) because they can be typologically dated to the time in question. Mondsee copper was the dominant metal type in this part of Europe between the 38th and 33rd centuries BC. Therefore, the axes under discussion almost certainly also consist of this copper. The total amount of Mondsee copper known from South Scandinavia surpasses that in the remainder of Europe (which would be indicative of an intense exchange from the north Alpine region). Apart from the Neckar Valley and Kraichgau regions in southwest Germany, the copper exchange route seemed to have avoided the late Michelsberg Culture distribution area.*

the Neckar Valley described above played a role in copper exchange. In fact, one of the enclosure sites there (Heilbronn-Klingenberg "Schlossberg": Seidel 2008, 311) has yielded both crucibles attesting to the pyro-metallurgical working of copper and copper finds. According to Seidel (2008, 312), these items might be slightly older than the enclosure's construction and may belong to a Michelsberg Culture pre-enclosure settlement on the same site.

The copper finds from Heilbronn-Klingenberg "Schlossberg" are remarkable. In addition to further copper items from two other enclosures and one settlement (Seidel 2008, 313f.; finds are not analysed) from the neighbouring Kraichgau region, they represent the only known Michelsberg Culture metal finds. Within the entirety of the Michelsberg Culture's large distribution area, southwestern Germany must, therefore, have been of special significance. This is also apparent from the comparison of the linear distribution pattern of enclosures and specific types of entrance construction as well as Mondsee copper exchange routes. In the southern half of Germany, both clearly deviate. Indeed, it is apparent that, apart from the Neckar Valley and the Kraichgau region, copper exchange routes avoided the Michelsberg Culture distribution area. This is not only apparent from the fact that exchange took place through the Upper Rhine Valley (which at the time in question belonged to the Munzingen B and not the Michelsberg distribution area) rather than along the long-distance route that obviously existed between the enclosures which formed the linear distribution pattern. It is also intriguing to note the concentration of Mondsee copper finds in the Baalberge Group distribution area in Saxony-Anhalt. This concentration coincides with the area's concentration of enclosures built between 3750 and 3500 BC. However, the enclosures are also found further west, in the distribution area of the late Michelsberg Culture. In that location, however, not a single metal find was made. Moreover, the western border of the copper distribution spread almost exactly coincides with the border between the Baalberg and late Michelsberg Cultures as described by Geschwinde & Raetzel-Fabian (2009, 204 Abb. 153).

The Michelsberg Culture distribution area between the northern end of the Upper Rhine Valley and the Harz Mountains is practically devoid of Mondsee copper finds. Only a single object (a triangular copper flat axe from Hertingshausen near Kassel) has been mapped for this area. However, the metal analysis for this object is very old and of dubious quality. Furthermore, the axe belongs to a typological group of flat axes that generally consists of metals which are both of different origins and of greater age (Klassen et al. 2011, 18). Therefore, it is likely that not a single Mondsee copper find is known from the area in question, although it is obvious that the metal must have passed the region on its way from the Upper Rhine Valley to the distribution area of the Baalberge Group as well as further north to South Scandinavia. Together with the other aspects described above, this remarkable finding underlines the 'metal-rejectant' character of the Michelsberg Culture as well as the special status of the Neckar Valley and the Kraichgau in this regard. This can hardly be explained other way than by the presence of a special significance assigned to metal and metal working incompatible with the social or religious beliefs of those groups which used Michelsberg pottery.

The distribution of Mondsee copper demonstrates that any impulses that could have caused enclosure building would have reached South Scandinavia on two partly different paths, both of which involved the Neckar Valley and Kraichgau region. While the relationship between enclosure building and the path demonstrated based on the distribution of enclosures and specific entrance structures is obvious, the existence of a relationship between metal exchange and enclosures is unsure. In this regard, however, it is important to note the context of metalworking during this time (Fig. 135). As described above, the vast majority of the abundant finds of crucibles and metal droplets that testify to the casting of copper in the north alpine region were found in pile-dwellings. Another category of sites – hilltop settlements – has also frequently delivered metalworking evidence, especially in the eastern and central parts of the north alpine forelands. South of the Danube, the Altheim Culture site at Altheim is the only enclosure which produced evidence for metalworking (Driehaus 1960). However, outside the area in which pile dwellings were used (i.e. north of the Danube) it is important to note that, with a single exception, (a hilltop settlement of the southeastern TRB in Cmielów in Poland: Krzak 1963), all remaining evidence for metalworking in the period 3800-3300 BC comes from enclosures. The late Michelsberg site of Heilbronn-Klingenberg "Schlossberg" has already has been mentioned. Other examples include the Bohemian Baalberge enclosure at Makotřasy (Pleslová-Štiková 1985), the Moravian TRB enclosure at Laškov (Podborsky et al. 1993) and the southeastern TRB site of Gródek (Kowalcyk 1957). Großobringen southeast of the Harz has to be mentioned (Müller, D.W. 1988) as the last known enclosure with traces of metalworking, although this site belongs to the Bernburg Culture and, thus, is slightly younger (ca. 3000 BC).

It appears thus that metalworking north of the Danube was almost exclusively bound to enclosures. It is, therefore, possible to imagine that enclosure-related ideas could have been exchanged with metal artefacts from the north alpine foothills to South Scandinavia.

Ceramic typology
Obvious resemblances between some Early Neolithic Funnel Beaker vessel types in South Scandinavia and those of the Munzingen Culture in the Upper Rhine Valley have been described on several occasions (see Klassen 2004, 169 ff; Knoche 2008, 171 with note 933). The present author did not initially accept these similarities as signs of contact, interpreting them rather as the results of parallel developments in several parts of Europe. However, Knoche convincingly argued in favour of contact on the basis of a much more detailed analysis of inventories located between the Munzingen Culture distribution area in the

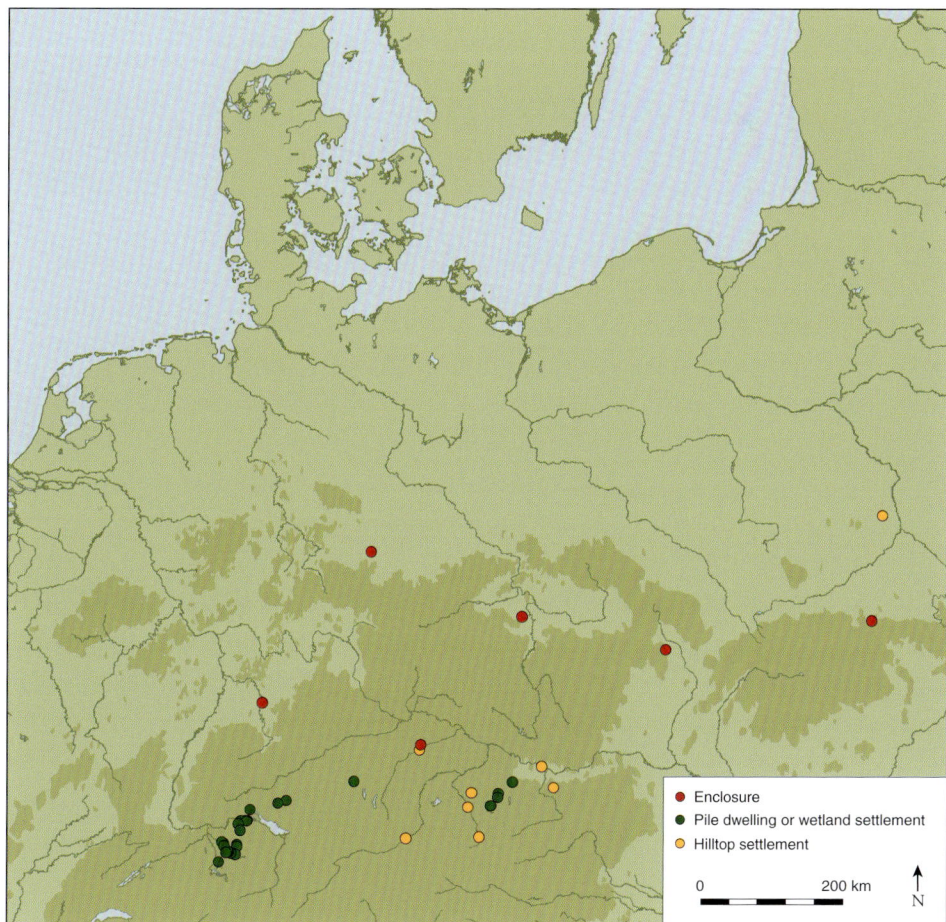

Fig. 135 | *Finds of crucibles and other proofs of copper metallurgy in groups belonging to the wider TRB Culture as well as to contemporaneous groups in the north Alpine forelands. In the latter region, most crucibles have been discovered in pile dwellings, while others are from hilltop settlements. A single find is known from an enclosure (at Altheim in Bavaria). Further to the north, copper working clearly appears to have been bound to enclosures (data from Klassen 2000).*

Upper Rhine Valley and South Scandinavia. It appears, thus, that strong influences on South Scandinavia from the southwestern parts of Central Europe can indeed be identified in vessel forms and decoration techniques. Munzingen-inspired pottery appeared in South Scandinavia in the second phase of the Oxie Group (Koch beaker type 1) around 3800 BC. The metal exchange route described above (which followed the Munzingen (B) group distribution area in the Upper Rhine Valley) indicates that the appearance of Munzingen-like ceramic vessels in South Scandinavia and the import of copper from the north alpine region might have been two closely related processes.

10.4.1.6 Summary and conclusion

In summary, it can be stated that a massive amount of evidence supports contact between South Scandinavia and both southern central Europe in general and the Neckar Valley and Kraichgau regions in particular from 3750 to 3500 BC. Part of this evidence is directly related to enclosures; the linear distribution of sites from this time horizon and the distribution of two specific kinds of entrance constructions (i.e. transverse pits in causeways and Sarup-type screens). Other elements (tetraploid naked wheat, copper finds and ceramic vessel types) also demonstrate the presence of intense communication and exchange which appears to have followed routes which diverged at least in part. Through the almost-exclusive appearance of metalworking traits in enclosures north of the Danube, these elements can also be linked to enclosures (at least in part). Therefore, there can be no doubt that the construction of causewayed enclosures in South Scandinavia could have been initiated through an impulse that originated (or, more likely, was relayed) from the Neckar Valley/ Kraichgau region.

The investigation of both the distribution of transverse pits in causeways as well as that of copper finds further links the Bavarian Altheim Culture distribution area (in which an enclosure building boom was present between 3750 and 3500 BC) to exactly the same part of southwest Germany.

The construction boom in Bavaria could, therefore, have been caused by an impulse from southwest Germany. Alternatively, an impulse originating in the Altheim distribution area (or further east) could have been passed on to the Neckar Valley and Kraichgau region from whence it could have reached South Scandinavia.

10.4.2 Southern central Europe and northern central Germany

The influences exerted by the Munzingen Culture described in the preceding chapter also acted on the distribution area of enclosures in the northern part of Central Europe between eastern Westphalia and the Elbe River. At least this is true for the western part of the region (the late Michelsberg Culture distribution area). Knoche (2008, 172 ff.) has described the strong influence of the north alpine forelands on this region in detail. This includes the distribution of different types of Bavarian flint – especially the Baiersdorf-Plattenhornstein – and the construction of rectangular or trapeze-shaped pit-dwellings (both of which originated from the Altheim Culture). Even several causewayed enclosures demonstrate design principles that may have originated in the Altheim Culture (Knoche 2008, 173).

It can be concluded that multiple relations can be demonstrated between the north alpine forelands and the 3750-3500 BC high density area of enclosures in northern central Germany. It appears that influences from both the Upper Rhine Valley and the Bavarian Altheim Culture were present, while connections with the Neckar and Kraichgau regions are indetectable. As previously described, it is possible that the Mondsee copper finds in the eastern part of the area passed through that very region. However, it is equally possible that they were exchanged more directly between Bavaria and Saxony-Anhalt along the Naab Valley towards Franconia and then across the Franconian Forest towards the Saale Valley. Thus far, no finds have been recovered from this area. However, this might be a reflection of the fact that the metal could simply have been passed on towards the north. Thus, it is possible that an impulse that could have led to intense enclosure construction activity north and east of the Harz Mountains reached that region directly from the Bavarian Altheim Culture.

10.4.3 Southern central Europe and southern England

In order to evaluate potential contacts between the Neckar Valley/Kraichgau region and southern England, it is necessary to return to the investigation of enclosures with very large ditch circuit spacing (chapter 10.2.3). The main distribution of this architectural trait is in southern Britain. However, it is also known from central western France as well as from the Mølbjerg I enclosure in northwestern Jutland (Fig. 94). As described above, all three regions appear to be linked by a maritime communication network along the fringes of the Atlantic, the Channel and the North Sea. One of the French sites (Echiré "Les Loups") probably belongs to the early 4th millennium BC and, therefore, appears to be slightly older than the other French, British and certainly also the Danish enclosures. However, this does not necessarily mean that this enclosure design principle was invented near the French Atlantic coast, nor that it spread from there.

Apart from the sites already described, two other Continental enclosures were constructed according to the same principles: Leonberg "Silberberg" (Seidel 2009) in the Neckar region and Heerlen-Schelsberg in the Netherlands (Schreurs/Brounen 1998; Schreurs 2005). When looking at the total distribution map of all enclosures, it is apparent that both of these could be classed as members of a group of enclosures arranged in a linear distribution pattern that stretched from the Neckar/Kraichgau region to the northern parts of the Upper Rhine Valley and along the Middle Rhine through the German Rhineland, the Dutch province of Limburg and Belgium towards the northern French coast (see Fig. 121, sites dated 4400-4000 BC). Of the enclosures which formed this linear pattern, only some at the southern end in the Neckar Valley/ Kraichgau region were built between 3750-3500 BC. All others are older (sometimes considerably so). This is also true for Heerlen-Schelsberg with its wide ditch circuit spacing (which belongs to the MK I/II phases of the Michelsberg Culture in the later 5th millennium BC). At present, this is the oldest known site with wide ditch spacing. However, as discussed by Seidel (2009), the construction of Leonberg "Silberberg" may (at least in part) date to the Bischheim Group, making this enclosure possibly even older than Heerlen-Schelsberg. It can be concluded that the architectural concept of wide ditch circuit spacing was probably invented somewhere along a linear distribution pattern of enclosures stretching from southwestern Germany to the Channel. Thus, it is entirely possible that it reached southern Britain from the centre of the Continent along the described linear distribution pattern (which probably reflects a long-distance corridor comparable to that identified between the same southwest German region and Denmark). While all the enclosures along the route were constructed before the onset of enclosure building in Britain, many of them remained in use for considerable spans of time, including the first half of the 4th millennium BC.

While wide ditch circuit spacing is the only constructional trait that can be followed from the Neckar valley/Kraichgau region across the Channel to southern Britain, at least two other elements confirm the identification of the linear arrangement of enclosures between these regions as a reflection of a long-distance route.

The first of these is an entrance construction closely related to the Sarup-type screen described above. The construction in question consists of a screen which has a narrow gap in the middle. For this reason, it is henceforth referred to as a 'split-screen' (Fig. 136). Such screens are known from two enclosures in the Neckar Valley/Kraichgau region: Neckarsulm-Obereisesheim "Hetzenberg" (Koch, R. 1971, 52 Abb. 1; Koch, R. 2005, 15 Abb. 8; Seidel 2008, 18 Abb. 7) and Leonberg "Silberberg" (Seidel 2009, 32 Abb. 4). The Michelsberg enclosure of Heerlen-Schelsberg in the Netherlands (Schreurs 2005, 311 Fig. 5f) is the only other site outside the region at which this split-screen entrance construction has been identified (Fig. 137). The comparatively large geographical gap between southwest German

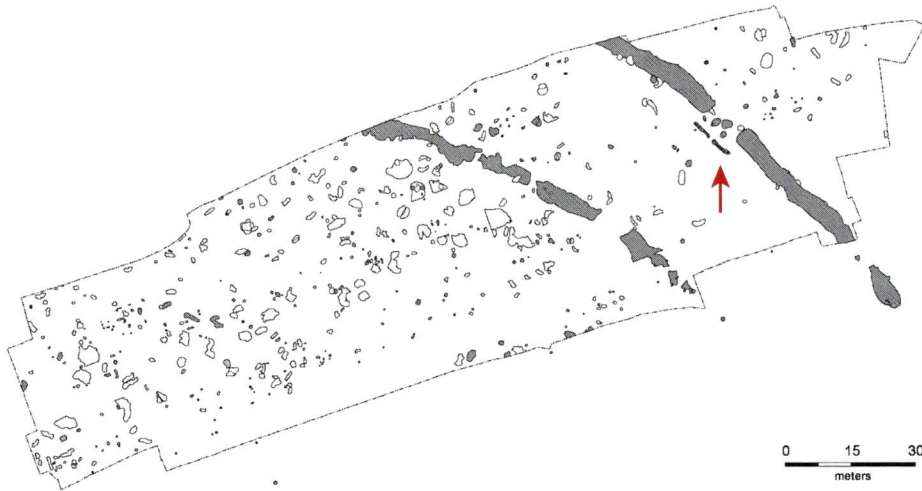

Fig. 136 | *Split-screen in front of an entrance to the Michelsberg enclosure at Heerlen-Schelsberg in the Netherlands (from Schreurs 2005, arrow added).*

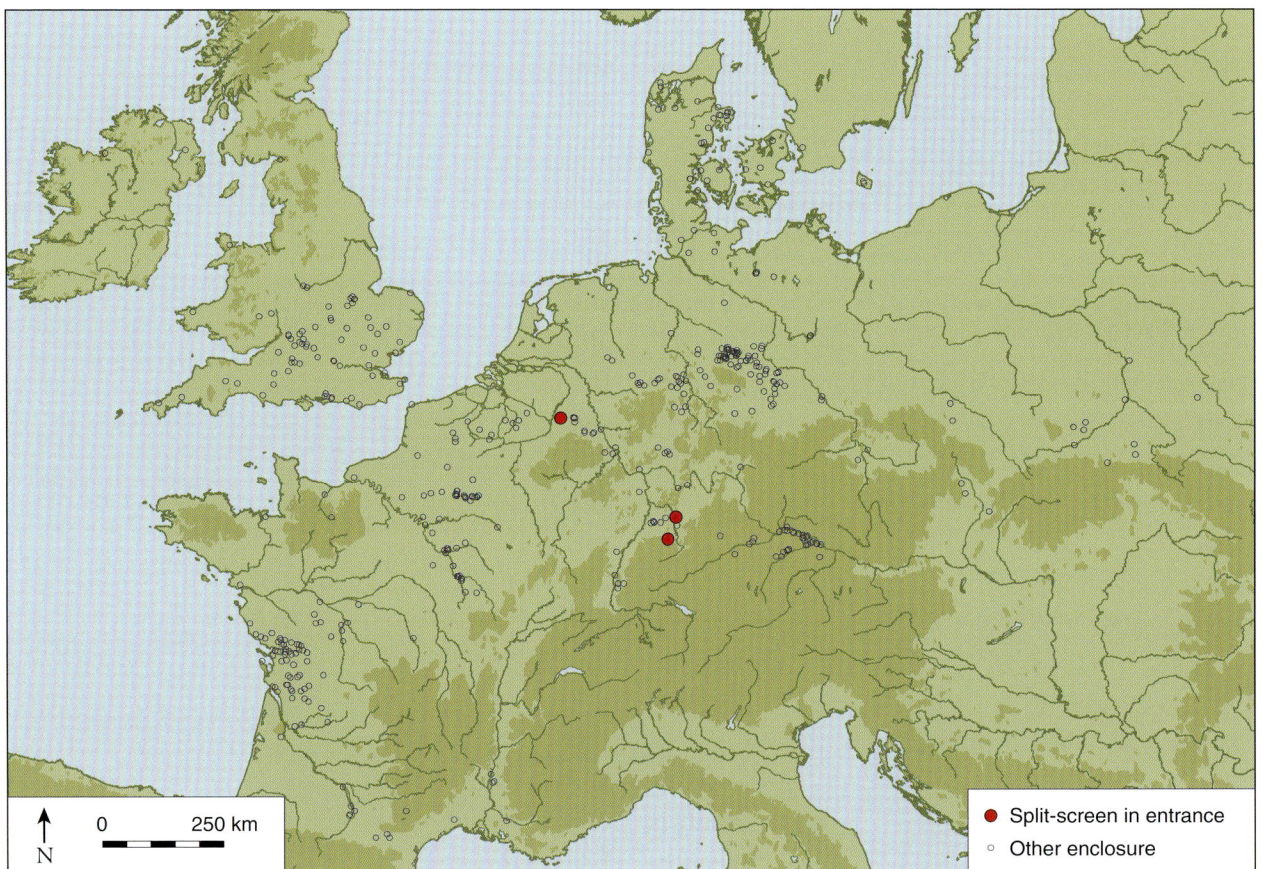

Fig. 137 | *The European distribution of split-screens in front of enclosure entrances. This construction appears to have been used only in enclosures situated in a corridor/at a long-distance route leading from southwest Germany to the Channel.*

and Dutch occurrences is reminiscent of even more extreme observations regarding the distribution of transverse pits in causeways (Fig. 129) and does not contradict the idea of related occurrences. In this regard, it is worth noting that some of the same en-

closures (Leonberg "Silberberg" and Heerlen-Schelsberg) are characterised by both wide ditch circuit spacing and by the presence of split-screens in front of entrances (an observation that clearly supports the idea of intense communication along a long-distance route). It should also be noted that wide ditch spacing and split-screens appear to be elements that appear exclusively in the enclosures which lie along this route. This is a structural parallel to the route which led from the Neckar Valley/Kraichgau region towards South Scandinavia (which was also associated with the exclusive appearance of a specific architectural trait: the Sarup-type entrance screen).

The second element indicating a long-distance route between the Neckar Valley/Kraichgau region and the Channel following the linear distribution of enclosures is the distribution of tetraploid naked wheat finds, which have already been discussed. These finds were not exclusively bound to enclosures, although tetraploid naked wheat has been found in a number of them. Fig. 138 shows the distribution of these enclosures. It appears that this type of cereal was exchanged not only from the north alpine region along a long-distance route towards Denmark as described above, but also along the route towards the Channel. This is evident from finds in the enclosures of Heilbronn-Klingenberg "Schlossberg" (Stika 1996), Heerlen-Schelsberg (Bakels 2003), Spiere "De Hel" (Vanmontfort et al. 2004) and Carvin "La Gare de l'Eau" (Bostyn et al. 2012).

Recently reported, the first finds of tetraploid naked wheat from southeast Britain (Kierleis/Fischer in press) were made in ordinary pits rather than in causewayed enclosures. Therefore, these finds were not added to the map Fig. 138. However, there is little doubt that the exchange of tetraploid naked wheat towards Britain must have been related to the route under discussion.

Apart from wide ditch circuit spacing, the different width of the ditches in the individual circuits is a typical element of British enclosures (see chapter 10.2.4 with Figs. 96 and 97). It should, therefore, be noted that also this element can possibly be derived from Continental building traditions bound to at least one enclosure located on the route leading from the Neckar Valley/Kraichgau region to the Channel. As was already discussed, this trait has been observed at the Belgian Michelsberg enclosure of Thieusies "Ferme de l'Hosté" (Vermeersch/Walter 1975; 1978; 1980), where it was, unfortunately, impossible to date. It is also a possibility,

therefore, that this Continental enclosure reflects an inspiration which came from southern Britain (and not the other way around). However, as far as it was possible to establish the time of construction, all known enclosures on the route leading from southwest Germany to the Channel were constructed before the onset of British enclosure construction. It is likely, therefore, that the same rule applies to the Thieusies site. For this reason, the diverging width of the individual ditch circuits within individual enclosures in Britain is likely to be an element derived from the Continent, probably through a connection to the long-distance route which led to southern Germany.

In summary, it can be concluded that multiple strings of evidence indicate the existence of a long-distance route between the Neckar Valley/Kraichgau region in southwest Germany and the northern French coast along the Channel. Enclosures were constructed prior to the 38th century BC along this route. Indeed, several specific constructional traits appear exclusively in enclosures along this route. It is, thus, a structural parallel to the route which was demonstrated between the same south German region and Denmark. The available evidence also indicates that several specific architectural traits typical for southern British causewayed enclosures appear for the first time in enclosures along the route in question. Thus, they must be assumed to have been transmitted across the Channel from the Continent. Even though they were built before British enclosures, it seems that the Continental sites were still in active use in the 38th to 36th century BC. In the light of this evidence, one must conclude that enclosure construction in Britain could very well have started due to impulses transmitted along a long-distance route from the Neckar/Kraichgau region.

10.4.4 Southern central Europe and central western France

It has been possible to demonstrate contacts between southwest Germany and the enclosure building regions in Britain, Bavaria, northern central Germany and South Scandinavia. Furthermore, it

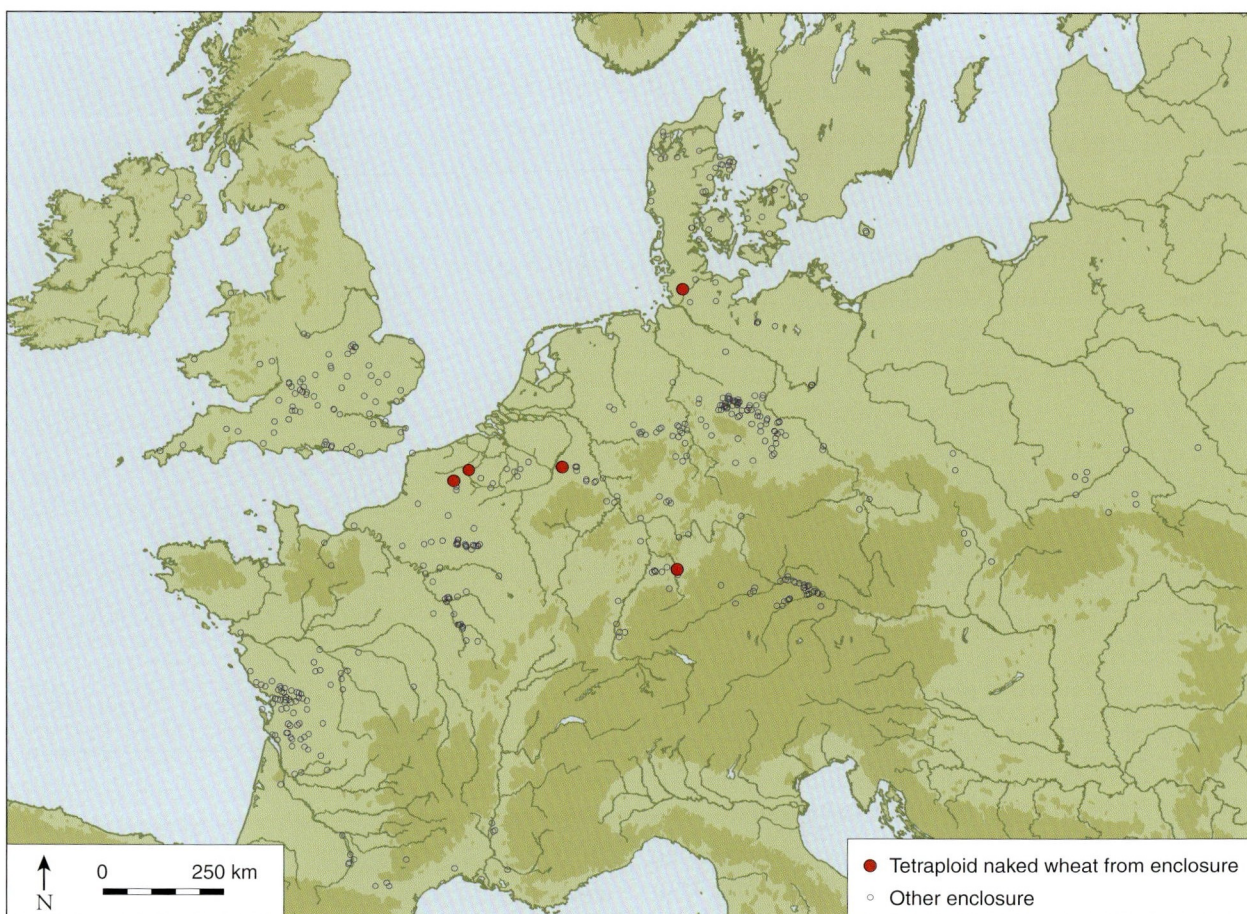

Fig. 138 | *The European distribution of enclosures with tetraploid naked wheat finds.*

was also possible to show that these were directly related (among others) to causewayed enclosures in all cases. However, this is not possible for the last region that saw an enclosure building boom between 3750 and 3500 BC: central western France. Almost no enclosures were built in the region between southwest Germany and the area between the mouths of the Loire and Garonne rivers in western France. Moreover, no artefacts that could have been exchanged between both regions have been identified. It is possible, therefore, that the immense increase in enclosure construction in central western France (which was certainly somehow related to comparable developments in other parts of Europe) cannot be directly related to southern central Europe. An alternative explanation could be provided by the communication network that has been demonstrated along the Atlantic fringe, the Channel and the North Sea. Western French

enclosures, thus, could be closely connected to those in southern Britain not only architecturally, but also genetically. However, this is only one possible explanation. There are some clues concerning influences reaching the French Atlantic coast from southern central Europe at the time in question, although these are not directly related to enclosures.

Knoche wrote that the dynamics of Neolithic groups in the north alpine forelands (including southwest Germany) were clearly felt in those areas west of the Rhine. The appearance of flat-based pottery types in this area (which can generally be characterised by the use of round-based pottery) was doubtless due to these influences (Knoche 2008, 172). With regard to the present investigation, therefore, it is of interest to note that these flat-based pottery forms in the 38th/37th century BC did not only appear in Burgundy and the Paris Basin, but also as far west as the Matignons ancien

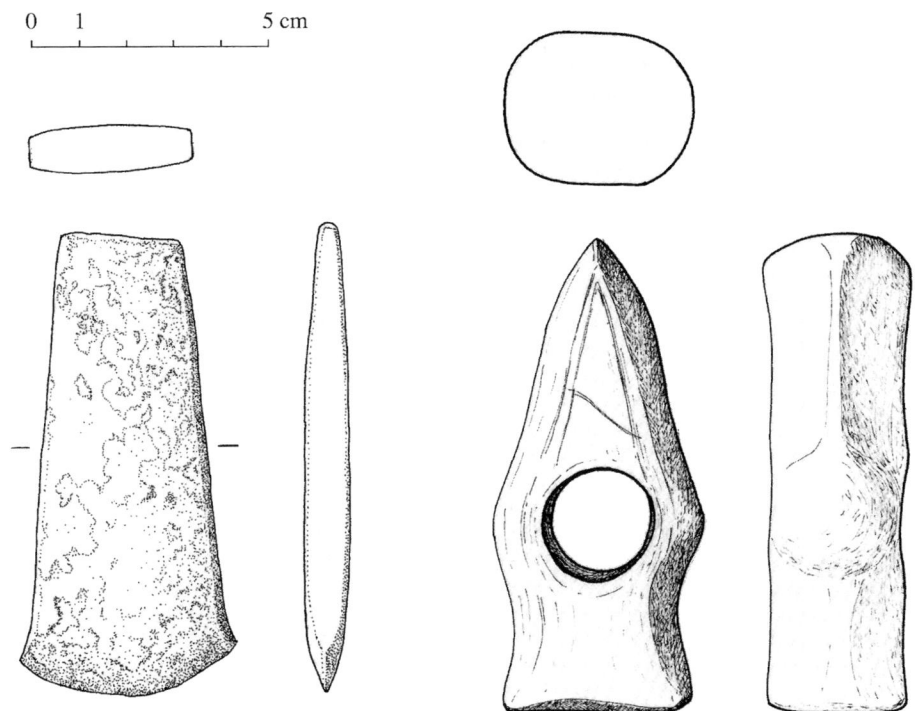

Fig. 139 | *Copper flat axe from Pont-de-Roide (Doubs, France) and flat hammer axe of serpentine from Héricourt (Haut-Sâone, France). These artefacts testify to relations between southern central Germany and areas west at the time of major enclosure construction between 3750 and 3500 BC (from Klassen et al. 2007).*

Group distribution area in central western France (Vendée, Charente-Maritime; see Ard 2011). The numerous enclosures constructed in the area between 3750 and 3500 BC belong to this very group. While some enclosures had been built in the area from around 4000 BC onwards, the enclosure building boom in the 38th/37th century BC can, thus, be chronologically linked to the appearance of influences from the northern alpine forelands (including southern central Germany).

Exactly how these influences reached so far west has yet to be established. At present, it is possible to follow them to the distribution area of the Néolithique moyen Bourgignon, where Knoche (2008, 172) noted flat-based pottery in the younger phases. Imports from the Pfyn Culture – a few copper flat axes as well as stone flat hammer axes (Fig. 139) – can also be demonstrated for this area, reaching the Saône River in the west (Klassen et al. 2007, 119, Fig. 14). Both hammer axes and copper flat axes (in addition to the one from Pont-de-Roide published in Klassen et al. 2007, an unpublished find from Mantoche at the Saône River has been recovered) indicate that the Pfyn Culture played a key role in this respect in the area around the west-

ern part of Lake Constance. Whether these objects were passed on through the Upper Rhine Valley (as indicated by the distribution of the hammer axes (Klassen et al. 2007, 119 Fig. 14)) or through western Switzerland (as indicated by the general distribution area of Mondsee copper)(comp. Fig. 134) is not yet clear. However, the ideas regarding flat-based pottery that obviously followed these objects speak in favour of the Upper Rhine Valley, as does the distribution of copper flat axes of the types in question (Klassen et al. 2007, 107 Fig. 6).

It can be concluded that it is not presently possible to demonstrate enclosure-related links between southern central Europe and central western France. It is possible, however, to demonstrate that influences from Central Europe reached the Matignons ancien Group at the Atlantic coast during precisely the period 3750-3500 BC. Thus, the situation is somehow related to that observed in northern central Germany. For the latter area, no direct, enclosure-related links to southern central Europe could be demonstrated. However, this was possible on a general level with regard to two cultural groups in this area: the Altheim Culture and the Munzingen Group (Knoche 2008). Both of these were intimately linked to the Pfyn Culture in the area around Lake Constance (Altheim via the intermediate Pfyn-Altheim Group – Mainberger 1988; with regard to the Munzingen Culture see Jeunesse 1989 and Seidel 2008, 318ff.). This suggests that central western France was subject to the same potential information flow as were the other regions under investigation. Exactly how the contacts between southern Germany and the region at the French Atlantic coast worked in practice remains to be established. It is possible (even likely) that the two regions were connected by a long-distance route. Nevertheless, it is not possible at present to demonstrate the existence of such a route due to the reasons given above.

10.4.5 Other long-distance routes

It is necessary to emphasize the fact that the reconstruction of long-distance routes with relation to causewayed enclosures between southern central Europe and different regions as described above makes no claims of completeness. On the contrary,

as was convincingly demonstrated by Geschwinde/ Raetzel-Fabian (2009) and Knoche (2013), other routes of comparable importance must have existed during the time in question. However, this study took its point of departure in South Scandinavia; the parameters by which the routes were investigated were chosen accordingly. The important east-west routes described by Geschwinde/ Raetzel-Fabian and Knoche cannot be revealed by these analyses. However, these most certainly can be detected by means of the investigation of different traits. Although such an investigation is beyond the scope of this study, it does represent an important task for future research. The investigations conducted here have revealed the existence of important crossroads in the Neckar Valley/Kraichgau region in present day southwest Germany (see below). Other regions of comparable importance certainly existed, e.g. where the north-south route between southwest Germany and Denmark crossed the east-west routes reconstructed by Geschwinde/Raetzel-Fabian and Knoche (i.e. the region around Paderborn in eastern Westphalia).

11 Conclusion: Long-distance routes, enclosures and South Scandinavia

Long-distance routes through large parts of Neolithic Western and Central Europe did exist, at least from the late 5th millennium onwards (Fig. 140). However, the investigation of the actual age, geographical extent and the mechanisms behind the creation of these routes was not the topic of this study (but see Knoche 2013 for an excellent and in-depth study in this regard). Nonetheless, it appears that some of these routes were prolonged as new regions at the western and northern fringes of Europe were incorporated into the Neolithic world. The purpose and function of said routes was almost certainly diverse. However, as far as is evident from this study, ritual functions were one major aspect of at least some of these roads/tracks and waterways. Exchange was certainly also an important aspect, at least for a portion of them. As exemplified by the copper finds discussed above, this exchange may very well have also had a ritual aspect. This is evident from the fact that some exchange goods appear to have passed along stretches of these routes without being taken up and used by the people who lived along them. An alternative explanation for these phenomena would be the presence of the long-distance movement of individuals or bigger groups of people along roads/tracks and waterways. While this certainly appears possible or even likely, it cannot be demonstrated by the investigations carried out in this study.

At least some trans-European routes had individual ritual connotations, as evidenced by specific elements of ritual practice that were only carried out along specific, individual transport corridors. In some cases at least, these elements of ritual practice were apparently activated only for short periods of time. However, knowledge of these elements was kept alive for hundreds of years. Said knowledge was eventually reactivated in instances of route extensions, as evident from the spatio-temporal distribution of certain elements of enclosure architecture (especially entrance constructions).

In the 38th to 36th centuries BC, an impulse released by either a single dramatic event or, more likely, by strong cultural and social change somewhere in Europe was transmitted through and along these routes towards the western, northwestern and northern periphery of Neolithic Europe. Once it arrived, these impulses activated ritual practices bound to causewayed enclosures. In consequence, causewayed enclosures were constructed in large numbers. The area of present day southwest Germany played a key role in this process, as many of the long-distance routes in question met there in an area which stretched from the southern parts of the Upper Rhine Valley to Lake Constance and the Neckar Valley and Kraichgau region.

The events of the 38th to 36th centuries BC had very different effect on enclosures along these long-distance routes. For example, no enclosure building can be traced along the zone which lead from the Neckar Valley/Kraichgau region over

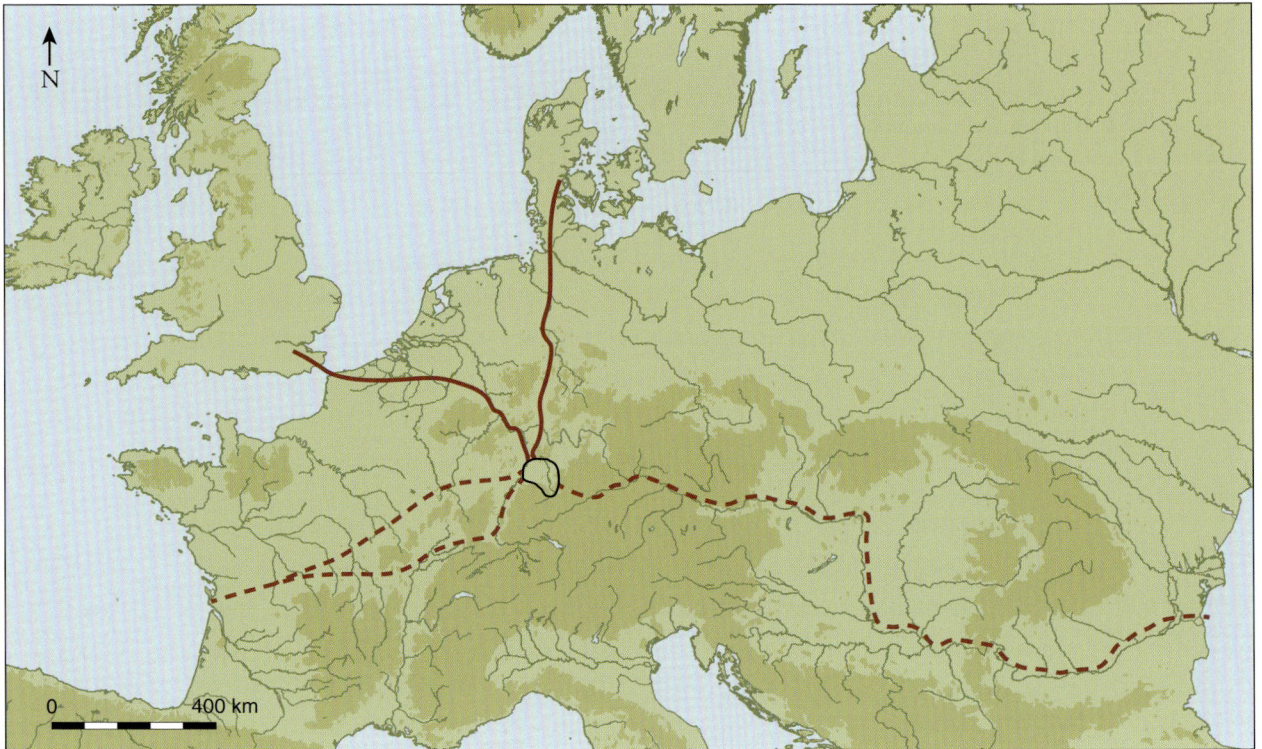

Fig. 140 | *In the late 5th and early 4th millennium BC, long-distance routes connected the Neckar Valley and Kraichgau region in southern central Europe to South Scandinavia and the British Isles. They likely also extended to Bavaria (and further on to the Black Sea) and the French Atlantic coast. In the case of the British Isles and South Scandinavia, the direct relation of these routes to enclosures could be demonstrated with certainty. It is likely that the routes towards western France and Bavaria also played a decisive role in the local development of enclosure construction in the time between 3750 and 3500 BC.*

the Upper and Middle Rhine Valley, the German Rhineland, the southern parts of the Netherlands, Belgium and northern France and across the Channel to southern Britain, despite the fact that the impulse that led to intensive enclosure construction in Britain was probably exclusively relayed along this route. By contrast, enclosure construction was present only in a narrow zone along the route leading from the same starting point towards Denmark, in spite of the fact that the surrounding areas were part of the same archaeological culture's distribution area.

In several regions (especially at the end of the trans-European routes along the periphery of Neolithic Europe) and (in at least two cases) also in Central European regions, intensive enclosure construction in the 38th to 36th century BC did not initially appear to have been linked to roads/

tracks and waterways, considering the numerous enclosures which were built in many parts of the landscape. However, as demonstrated by Geschwinde & Raetzel-Fabian (2009) and Knoche (2013), this distribution pattern is probably the result of a single prehistoric communication and exchange route having branched out in multiple paths. Furthermore, different types of enclosures were constructed at the same time. It is one specific of these types (the largest, monumental one with a specific site design) that was demonstrably related to long-distance routes (Geschwinde/Raetzel-Fabian 2009).

Enclosures were only built along these specific, ritually important long-distance routes several hundred years after the neolithisation of the regions through which they led. They were constructed at regular intervals which corresponded to approximately one hour's travel (either by walking or paddling). Naturally defined border situations were chosen as building locations. However, the fact that the same distance between enclosures can be observed in areas with completely different cultural and natural background indicates that these locations were not necessarily associated with the territorial borders between groups. Knoche (2013) recently noted that enclosures in Westphalia were likewise constructed in natural border situations. He connected these situations with shifts in the natural environment, suggesting that the placement of the enclosures was a reflection of different cattle pasturing opportunities related to the different types of landscape. While this may be true for the enclosures Knoche investigated, it does not apply to South Scandinavia, where changes in the landscape are far more gradual. Therefore, it seems more likely that the association between routes, border regions and ritual sites is due to the general ritual connotations of such locations which are apparent in anthropological data (Rudebeck 2002, 172ff.). Furthermore, one should not forget that enclosures were built at very short, regular distances from each other. Indeed, this rule probably also applied to Westphalia, where a number of sites on the routes Knoche investigated have yet have to be discovered (Knoche 2013). For this region as well, it is difficult, therefore, to imagine that a shift in grazing potential would have been associated with such short and regular distances.

As discussed earlier (chapter 9.3.4), observations regarding not only the short, regular inter-enclosure distance, but also those related to the inclusion of waterways in the system of communication and exchange as well as those related to the very infrequent activities in the enclosure ditches bring some of Geschwinde & Raetzel-Fabian's (2009) and Knoche's (2013) ideas into question. However, it is important to note that these doubts only concern the intimate relation between the function and background of causewayed enclosures on one side and that of cattle herding on the other side. Ideas regarding the origin of Central European routes and the emergence of a new type of economy based

on mobile cattle herding in Central Europe's Jungneolithikum are convincing and represent an important contribution to our general understanding of the period in question.

Southern central Europe and especially the Neckar Valley/Kraichgau region appear to have played a key role in the network of (ritual) long-distance routes through Central and Western Europe. This is probably due to the fact that this region is situated at the juncture of Western and (south) Eastern European long-distance routes. Such junctures or crossroads can generally be demonstrated to be ritually significant areas (Rudebeck 2002). The region is linked to southeastern Europe and the Black Sea by means of a short crossing of the Swabian Alps, Upper Swabia and the Danube Valley. The Neckar could also be a means of connecting to Western and Northwestern Europe by means of the Rhine to which it is a tributary.

The key role of the Neckar Valley and Kraichgau area as border region is underlined by the fact that that zone was the only area in which copper artefacts were in use in the otherwise metal 'phobic' Michelsberg Culture. In one case (the Heilbronn-Klingenberg "Schlossberg" site) archaeologists uncovered proof that this extended even to metallurgical activity itself. Apart from the metal, the cross-cultural importance of the site is underlined by a range of elements (both imports and local adoptions) that would otherwise belong to the circle of pile-dwelling cultures to the south. These include the Pfyn and Pfyn-Altheim Cultures which themselves had eastern roots (Schlichterle 1998, 173ff.; Seidel 2008, 326ff.; 2010; Matuschik 2010, 119).

However, several lines of evidence indicate that southwest Germany was not the origin of the impulse that led to massive enclosure building along the western and northwestern peripheries of Europe. It seems, rather, that this area functioned as the transmitter of an impulse which originated further to the east. The most important of these bodies of proof involves the fact that enclosure building activities in the 38th to 36th century BC had an intensity gradient which ranged from east to west. The Altheim Culture distribution area in the east appears to have been the most heavily affected. It is the only region in which abundant and widespread construction activity took place and which had also witnessed massive enclosure construction in the late 5th millennium BC (Münchshöfen enclosures). Intensive enclosure building took place further to the west along the long-distance route from the Neckar Valley/ Kraichgau region towards South Scandinavia. However, said intensive construction was limited to a narrow corridor around and along the long-distance route through which that impulse was transmitted to Scandinavia. Even further afield along the Rhine and points west, the impulse simply passed on to southern Britain without triggering enclosure building along the route by which it travelled. The establishment of Neolithic cultures in Western Europe were not affected, while comparatively new Neolithic societies in central western France, southern Britain and (possibly) in South Scandinavia as well reacted strongly to the information passed on through the network of long-distance routes. The fact that massive

enclosure building went on in northern central Germany may well have to do with close contacts with the Altheim Culture in that area.

The assumed role played by the metal-friendly Pfyn Culture in the transmission of the impulse that led to enclosure building in central western France combined with the correlation of enclosure building with the spread of copper and metallurgical activities are further arguments which support the presence of an impulse from the east. The dynamics of the different cultural groups in southern central Europe – from Munzingen in the west to Altheim in the east, which exerted heavy influence on groups north of the Danube and up to South Scandinavia as described in detail by Knoche (2008, 129ff.) – can probably be understood as another reflection of massive eastern/southeastern influences on southern central Europe. At least, this is indicated by the fact that there were elements of clearly eastern origin (like flat-based pottery) that spread rapidly and replaced "western" round-based vessels even in the area around the Lower Rhine. The distribution of Mondsee

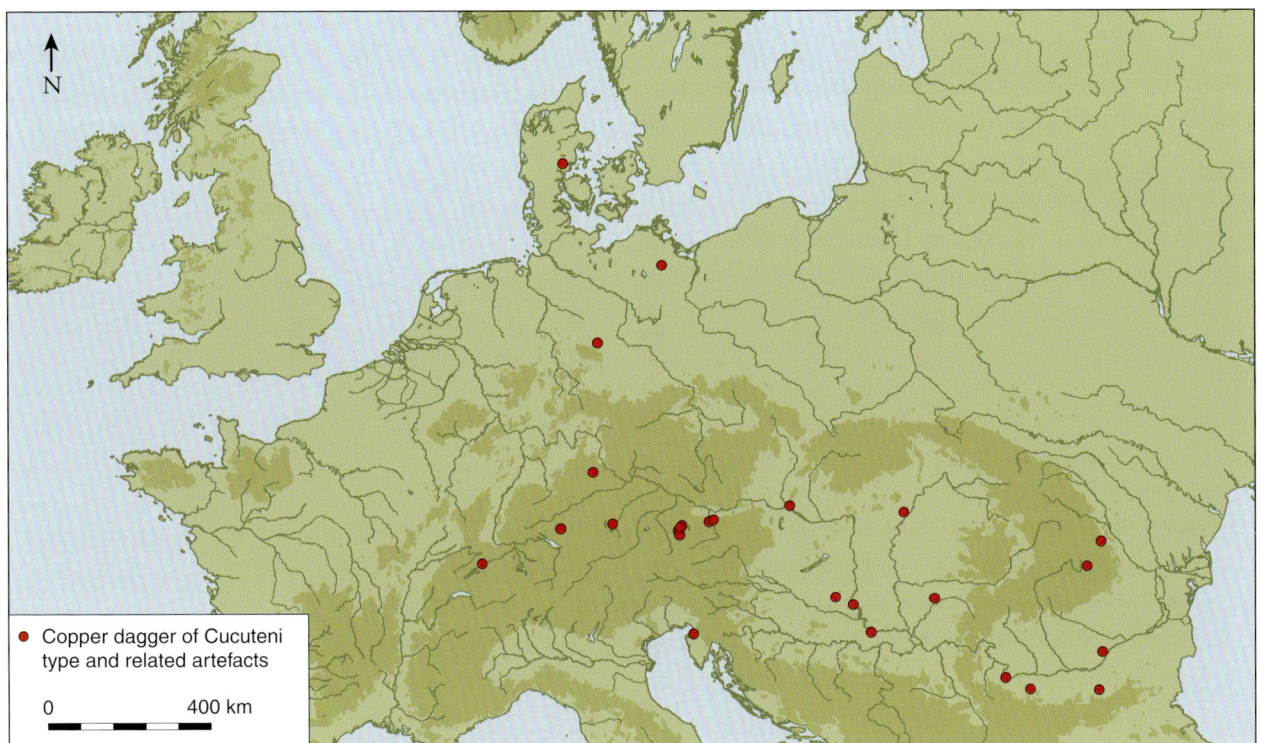

Fig. 141 | *The distribution of Cucuteni type copper daggers and related artefacts relates the western Pontic region to Central and Northern Europe (data from Matuschik 1998 with additions).*

copper finds tells the same story. The chemical composition of this metal type is – as described earlier by Schubert (1981) and Matuschik (1998) – identical to that of contemporaneous arsenical copper known from Southeast Europe. Given the present state of knowledge, it is likely that both groups of metal are, in fact, identical and have the same Southeast European origin. The distribution of Cucuteni type copper daggers (including the Mondsee variant (see Matuschik 1998)) which consist of this material link the west Pontic area to southern central Europe and the enclosure-building zones of northern central Europe and South Scandinavia (Fig. 141).

It seems, then, that radical social and economic changes in the Black Sea region (evident in the contemporaneous formation of the gigantic, planned settlements of the Tripolye Culture with sizes of up to 400 ha and up to 2700 houses in present day Ukraine (Videjko 1995)) could have caused enclosure building as far away as western France, Britain and South Scandinavia. The appearance of round tumuli in the Baalberge Culture in the heart of Europe during this time may indeed be a reflection of the dynamics of the Pontic region. Mondsee copper, metal smelting and a Cucuteni type copper dagger all arrived ca. 3738 BC (Billamboz 1998) at the Pfyn-Altheim settlement of Bad Waldsee-Reute "Schorrenried" in Upper Swabia (which had links to the Neckar Valley region). This date exactly matches the beginnings of the enclosure building boom in different regions of Western and Central Europe as evidenced by the available chronology. The Reute date is the oldest presently known for Mondsee copper artefacts.

The example listed above of the possible influence that a region as far east as the Black Sea could have had on southern Germany is intended only as illustrations of the potential long-distance mechanisms which could have caused enclosure building in Western, Northwestern, Northern and Central Europe in the 38th to 36th centuries BC. Although these influences may very well have been the catalyst(s) for subsequent events, this causality cannot be conclusively demonstrated here. The events that triggered enclosure building may well

have been located somewhere else, perhaps closer to Central Europe. However, as argued above, it is likely that the region in question should be sought to the east of the Bavarian Altheim Culture's distribution area.

T. Madsen (1988), N.H. Andersen (1997) and D. Raetzel-Fabian (1999, 95) concluded that the construction of enclosures could be understood as a reaction to cultural change independent of their actual function. This was obviously the case in large parts of France, Belgium and the westernmost parts of Germany, where the intensive enclosure building activity in the second half of the 5th millennium BC can be clearly related to the cultural dynamics of the Paris Basin (and probably with the development of an economy with an emphasis on cattle herding, as described by Knoche (2013)). This began with the formation of the Cerny Culture and reached its apogee with the rapid spread of the Michelsberg Culture towards the Rhine and beyond (e.g. Schier 1993; Jeunesse 1998; Jeunesse et al. 2004). With regard to South Scandinavia, there was a strong correlation between phases of enclosure construction and phases of cultural change, as was recently emphasized by L. Larsson (2012, 119f.). Indeed, even the presence of two enclosure construction phases (the second being related to the palisade enclosures of the early 3rd millennium which have not been dealt with here) can be identified in relation to two distinct phases of cultural change. The present study adds a nuance to this pattern; the trigger for cultural change (and thus enclosure building) may, in some cases, have been located at a great distance from the place at which construction activity actually took place. The impulse that emerged from cultural change in one region could be funnelled into narrow corridors associated with long-distance routes and be effective at a distance from its source with (apparently) unaffected areas in between.

This observation is also relevant with regard to the explanatory models of T. Madsen (1988) and N.H. Andersen (2011, 153) who emphasized a relation between economic change and enclosure construction. Indeed, while this correlation seems to have existed in South Scandinavia, it was not necessarily present in the manner that Madsen and Andersen had assumed (i.e. economic change was not an entirely local development). As indicated by the strong influence of the younger Munzingen Culture on the Oxie Group and the presence of tetraploid naked wheat (which both appear to have been contemporaneous with the construction of the first enclosures), it is clear that economic change and enclosure construction may well be two branches of the same developmental flow which itself may have been rooted in an area distant from Scandinavia.

In terms of the function of these enclosures, Raetzel-Fabian's (1999) observations can be somewhat refined on the basis of the survey of large parts of Western and Central Europe conducted in this study. Despite the fact that, from the very beginning, the overall architecture of those enclosures built in different regions of Europe in the 38th to 36th century BC reflected local identities, there were rather clear and specific similarities linked to the function of those enclosures (i.e. inter-enclosure distance, the re-cutting of ditches, the deposition of human bones, etc.). Indeed, this suggests that, whatever the region in which they were located, enclosures had the same overall primary function. However, as was apparent in the South Scandinavian case, secondary functions of divergent local or regional character were probably at play in many parts of Europe.

The primary function of enclosures in Western and Central Europe clearly had to do with the performance of rituals related to cultural change. It is possible that the integration or rejection of impulses related to cultural change in local communities was negotiated at these sites. This change could have been of social, economic or ritual character. The frequent acts of violence observed in enclosures were possibly directly linked to these activities and may, therefore, have been a reflection of conservative groups opposing the integration of novelties.

The standardization of inter-enclosure distances along long-distance routes is intriguing. The presence of such regulated distances contradicts the idea that enclosures functioned as central sites

in territories belonging to individual groups. It is likely that they relate to a specific function of the route, which, according to the evidence from the enclosures, must be assumed to reside in the ritual domain. Travelling along such a route (and encountering an enclosure once per every hour of travel) could have been a spiritual experience, which might possibly be compared to a pilgrimage with regular stations of worship. However, this is not the most convincing interpretation. The complex entrance structures present at many enclosures could also be considered to have been a kind of obstacle. It appears that anything that entered the enclosure from the route was viewed as potentially dangerous. Such foreign entities, it seems, were thought of as things which should be carefully controlled before they were eventually released through the performance of safety-ensuring rituals. The remains of humans and animals frequently encountered in such locations may indicate that it was not always possible to remove such dangers without deadly force. The enclosed space could thus possibly be understood as a kind of temporary quarantine station; when open, the ditches prevented the enclosed dangerous elements from affecting their surroundings. Knoche (2013) has recently presented similar ideas ("Bannkreis").

The location of South Scandinavian enclosures at naturally defined borders may relate to the perception of different parts of the landscape as individual, wild and/or dangerous entities. Anthropological data suggest that passage through such border locations was considered to be ritually safe (Helms 1988; 1993, 224f.). As ritual sites, enclosures may have played an important role in ensuring this safety. Stretches of roadway (or even entire routes) may have been thought to be important by Neolithic groups residing at considerable distances. Thus, people from distant places may have participated in the construction of enclosures. The above-mentioned examples of Stonehenge and Herxheim certainly indicate the feasibility of such a scenario. This could also explain how it was possible to construct such large and very labour-intensive enclosures at the short spatial intervals that have been recorded (see chapter 9.3.5.6).

Naturally, these considerations lead one to contemplate the nature of the traffic which traversed these routes. As demonstrated above, the routes were hardly intended to serve exclusively ritual functions; potential everyday commodities like cereals were obviously distributed along them without the limitations apparent from the mapping of ritual structures. The same almost certainly was true with regard to cattle, even though the inclusion of rivers and firths indicate that this was not the case everywhere. Did long-distance travel take place along these routes? If so, was it ritual specialists (among others) who travelled? Were enclosures and the re-cutting events which took place at them reactions to (or against) the movement of larger groups of people along the selfsame routes? Was ritually-related traffic conducted at enclosures and/or restricted to processions of local people? No answers can be given at present. However, it appears that enclosure construction and subsequent use (re-cutting) were exceptional events that occurred (on average) only on a generational scale. This does not exclude the use of the sites for other functions at the same time or in between human action within (or involving) the ditches.

From the mapping of different constructional traits and the investigation of enclosure chronology, it is apparent that the first South Scandinavian enclosures were constructed in the course of a developmental flow that affected large parts of Western and Central Europe. The introduction of enclosures in the area, therefore, cannot be related to local social and economic developments, as was proposed by T. Madsen (1988). However, the available dating evidence for South Scandinavia is too limited to allow for an accurate evaluation of the extent of this development. It may have been restricted to a select few sites along a single long-distance route from southern Germany. However, it may also have been much more comprehensive than is apparent from the evidence gathered thus far. Nonetheless, local factors appear to have played an important role in further developments (as indicated by the relative abundance of enclosures built after 3500 BC and before 3200 BC). At that point in time, enclosure construction either ceased completely and was substituted by the creation of other types of monuments (e.g. Britain), or was considerably reduced (e.g. central Germany, Bavaria). Only western central France appears to have witnessed continued intensive enclosure construction activity comparable to that in South Scandinavia. Another clearly local element was the transformation of many (but certainly not all) enclosure sites into apparently regular settlements. This tended to take place following their initial ritual use (which may or may not have continued, either within (or as part of) an otherwise domestic framework.

It is of interest to compare the development of enclosures in South Scandinavia to the intensity of forest felling and the import of copper. If the present picture of few enclosures in the later part of the EN I from ca. 3750 BC onwards and a clear intensification of enclosure building in the EN II around 3500 BC is correct, then it is evident that it had a clear correlation with the amount of Mondsee copper imported (Klassen 2000, 236 Fig. 111) and the intensity of human impact on the environment (e.g. Madsen, T. 1990; Dörfler et al. 2012). Furholt (2011b) recently interpreted this general development as the transition between a "Virtual Neolithic" and a "Practiced Neolithic". According to Furholt, during the Virtual Neolithic phase, all elements of the "Neolithic package" were present in South Scandinavia. However, they were only used on a limited scale that did not effectively change social reality and human identities. However, the latter was the case in the "Practiced Neolithic" after 3500 BC. According to the present state of knowledge, the chronological border between both phases should be pushed back to the 38th/37th century BC, as both the construction of enclosures and megalithic graves (Andersson/Wallebom 2013a; 2013b; Eriksen/Andersen in press) apparently began at that point in time. Furthermore, the start of monument building – an important parameter within Furholt's definition – appears to have been linked to the first appearance of pottery decorated with incised or impressed vertical fringes/grooves on the belly. Pottery decoration is another of the elements Furholt used in his definition; the vertical fringes/grooves represent what he believes is a "passive drift style" without importance for the social reality of the contemporaneous groups. Only locally developed, complex decorations (such as the Fuchsberg style) should have played this role.

While some adjustments to the chronology and content of Furholt's definitions are necessary (i.e. the "Practiced Neolithic" should start around 3800 BC with the construction of earthen long barrows and the use of Volling/Svaleklint/Svenstorp pottery with highly complex decorative patterns), his general understanding of the Early Neolithic makes sense. While there may be regional variations within South Scandinavia, it is interesting to note that the southwestern parts of the region show the first appearance of enclosure construction. In turn, this can be linked to the first appearance of pottery decorated with vertical shallow grooves or incised fringes (Witte/Lützau Pedersen 2012, 82; Dibbern 2012, 292, Taf. 1.2/3). This decorative pattern probably originated in Southeast Europe in the 37th century BC. Thereafter, it spread rapidly into the region stretching from the western parts of the Black Sea (the mouth of the Danube) to South Scandinavia, possibly even to southern Britain (Furholt 2009, 236). Thus, it is possible that this decorative motif, arsenical copper and the impulse that triggered enclosure construction in many parts of Western and Central Europe have a common origin. A recent (and much older) 14C-date for the pottery decoration in question from a shard from Bebensee LA 76 in northern Germany (Hartz 2011, 266) does not contradict the chronology proposed here; this completely isolated date was taken from food residue on a shard found on a fishing site along the shores of a lake. It is possible, therefore, that this date is affected by a freshwater reservoir effect, as are other food residue dates from other sites which were found along the Trave River (Fischer/Heinemeier 2003).

The interpretational model presented here views enclosures as ordered sections of linear paths through the landscape rather than as centres in group territories. The latter assumption emerged in Scandinavian archaeology 30 years ago and has gradually developed into a widely-acknowledged 'fact' that is in need of revision.

As argued above, enclosures appear to have been constructed in naturally defined border positions. Whether or not these positions were identical (at least in some cases) to the borders of group territories cannot be determined here. However, taking into account the general picture of Early Neolithic settlement as described by T. Madsen (1982) and Johansen (2006), this does not seem to be particularly likely. It is by no means sure that there were territories other than those claimed by the (obviously highly mobile) single farmsteads (probably much smaller than the typical ca. 5 km between two enclosure sites) or those possibly claimed by much larger, ethnical groups (probably much larger than the typical ca. 5 km between enclosures). It is, however, noteworthy that many enclosure sites developed into ever larger, probably increasingly-stable settlements over the course of the later parts of the TRB Culture. The rich finds typically found on the surface of such settlements were one of the criteria in Madsen's (1988) predictive approach, which resulted in the proposition of enclosure sites at ca. 8-10 km from each other (which estimate is twice the typical inter-enclosure distance recorded here). This is of particular interest because a distance of ca. 5 km (one hour's walk) is typically the distance from the village to the furthest fields in societies which practice shifting cultivation (Carlstein 1980, 147ff.), as was the case in the TRB Culture (Madsen, T. 1990). Therefore, although there appears to have been a relation between (some) enclosures and group territories, this was not present at the time of enclosure construction. It seems that approximately every second enclosure site developed into a settlement placed centrally in a territory that stretched ca. 5 km (or one hour's walk) to naturally defined border situations on both sites. Whether the ritual structures found at these border situations were still in use or not at the time in question is not presently known. It is entirely possible that ritual activities in the ditches ceased on sites that developed into settlements, but continued on the sites that were situated at the borders of later TRB territories. If so, the character and function of these rituals may well have changed to reflect

a possible functional shift. However, the opposite situation is also possible, and would probably also have involved an evolution in ritual practices.

As suspected in the predictive modelling approach and confirmed through the survey of the European evidence in combination with (somewhat standardised) inter-enclosure distances, the relation between Neolithic routes and enclosures offers great possibilities for the future detection of causewayed enclosures in South Scandinavia and beyond. If some sites are already known within a specific region and if it can be established that said sites might have been situated along the same Neolithic route, then the sites which should lie in between should be comparatively easy to predict. One important aspect of this method is to determine whether the routes in question were water- or land based. The relation between many known enclosures and historically known main roads is of particular importance in this regard. The numerous enclosures in the Djursland region are mainly linked to water-based routes. If these enclosures are taken out of the equation, correlations between historically known main roads and enclosures are even stronger. Thus, these roads can be used as a starting point in future predictive studies. For example, both the Hygind and Sarup enclosures on the southwestern part of the island of Funen are related to the same historical road that followed the portion of the coast which lay between them (Fig. 44). Future discoveries of enclosures along this route are likely, and several suspected sites have already been identified (M. Runge and N.H. Andersen, pers. communication).

12 Summary

· ·

Since their first discovery, causewayed enclosures have engaged both scholarly interest and imagination, both within South Scandinavia and in the rest of Europe. Excluding immediate 'common sense' interpretations, few other prehistoric constructions have witnessed such lively discourse, especially of such long duration. However, since the early 1980s, the debate in South Scandinavia has been primarily concerned with comparatively minor details; almost all researchers seem to agree that the Scandinavian enclosures served as central sites within a specific territory. Ritual and social functions are the favored interpretations, while other possibilities (like military or economical functions) have only rarely been proposed within recent research history.

The current Scandinavian view of these enigmatic sites has been formed by the thorough investigation of a single site (the Sarup enclosure) by N.H. Andersen and by T. Madsen's regional study in east Jutland. The focus of the latter emphasized the settlement systems of whole regions rather than the specific rituals conducted at individual sites. It is, therefore, of crucial importance to our general understanding of early TRB societies. Over the course of his study, Madsen was the first scholar to attempt to predict the location of undiscovered enclosures, as knowledge of all existing sites within a given region is a precondition for any thorough understanding of the spatial and social organization of Scandinavian farming societies in the second half of the 4th millennium BC.

This study represents an attempt to develop and test a new methodology for predicting the location of causewayed enclosures in South Scandinavia. To this end, the Djursland Peninsula in eastern Jutland (Denmark) was chosen as the area of concentration. In a secondary step, the results obtained for this region were compared to those obtained by Madsen. This comparison highlighted the subsequent necessity to view South Scandinavian enclosures in a wider European context. It is to this very subject that the final chapters of this book are devoted.

Djursland was chosen as the principle area of investigation for the present study due to a number of different factors. Of these, the most important include accessibility and the high number of known enclosures in the region. The latter enable the identification of the regionally-valid criteria that were used 5500 years ago in the choosing of enclosure construction locations.

Djursland Peninsula juts out into the Kattegat from the east coast of Jutland (Denmark) just north of Aarhus (Denmark's second largest town). Djursland measures approximately 50 km from north to south as well as from east to west. For various reasons, several parts of the region have been excluded from the investigation area. The total amount of area investigated measured just over 1000 km².

Today, the peninsula is roughly rectangular in shape (apart from several sub-peninsulas in the south) and constitutes a single landmass. However, in the Neolithic, Djursland looked very different. Over the intervening millennia, the landscape was transformed by isostatic and eustatic movements. At the time of interest for this study (in the early Subboreal) it was an archipelago. A large fjord (Kolindsund) penetrated the centre of the peninsula from east to west, splitting the landmass into a number of islands. Additional minor fjords further added to the complexity of the coastline. The area north of Kolindsund was dominated by a large island. The terrain (mostly situated between 40 and 60 m a.s.l.) was made up of a rolling moraine plateau with shifting sandy and loamy soils. Immediately south of Kolindsund, a completely flat, narrow band of very poor sandy and gravelly soils was followed by an undulating moraine landscape, at least some parts of which were made up of heavy soils. The latter sub region was not included as part of the investigation area.

Principally due to the work of N.A. Boas, a large number of causewayed enclosures are already known in Djursland. Nine certain and several possible sites can be listed. Almost all of these are located close to the northern coast of Kolindsund, where they appear to be situated like beads on a necklace. To this, one site (Lystrup Kildevang I) has to be added, which shows many of the characteristics of classical causewayed enclosures but lacks the typical segmented ditches. This site was classified as an enclosure-related site. Unfortunately, the current state of research into the many enclosures or related sites in Djursland is poor, due mostly to the fact that only minor excavations have taken place. Furthermore, publications are restricted to a few preliminary papers. Many of the sites also remain completely unpublished.

The Djursland sites can be compared to a further 29 known causewayed enclosures within the distribution area of the TRB North Group. Lacking a geographical term to describe the entirety of the region in question (Schleswig-Holstein in northern Germany, Denmark and southern Sweden), 'South Scandinavia' is used henceforth, regardless of the fact that northern Germany is not formally classified as being part of Scandinavia. The few known enclosures from Mecklenburg-Vorpom-

mern and Brandenburg in northern Germany have not been counted among the TRB North Group enclosures. In South Scandinavia, aside from the 38 proper sites, a total of five enclosure-related sites can be listed.

The basics of any attempt to predict the location of causewayed enclosures in South Scandinavia were established by T. Madsen in a number of papers published between 1979 and 1988. He identified some of the most crucial factors at play during the ancient choice of construction sites and used them in his own attempts to point out all existing enclosures in his investigation area. These criteria include the location of the enclosures predominantly on promontories surrounded by water in the form of rivers, wet areas or fjords, the proximity to concentrations of megalithic graves, the preference for well-drained soils, the abundance of finds from different TRB periods and a size that is much larger than that of typical contemporaneous settlements.

Recently, S. Klatt presented a new approach to predicting the location of causewayed enclosures. This approach was entirely based on Madsen's criteria. However, contrary to his work, Klatt's study was computer-based and employed GIS methods. In this way, Klatt's study resembles the present approach. However, Klatt's approach also differs in some important regards to that employed within this work. Klatt calculated probability grids for each of the parameters he employed (distance to water, proximity to megalithic graves, density of megalithic graves in the surroundings, topography) and then combined the values of the individual grids via multiplication to obtain a final result. Unfortunately, this approach is flawed, not only by a lack of source criticism regarding the megalithic graves, but also by problems with defining a promontory within the GIS system.

Within this study, all hitherto employed predictive criteria have been subjected to a critical evaluation by analyzing the 32 Danish enclosures which are presently known in detail. Thus, it can be stated that all of the criteria originally identified by Madsen are still valid. However, none of them can be certainly relied upon as a means of pointing out enclosure locations. Most of these sites are located on promontories. However, this is not true for all of them. Almost all are bordered by rivers, wetlands or fjords, but a few (those located on hilltops) are not. Almost all are found on very well-drained soils. However, a select group were constructed on clayey ground. In many cases, considerable numbers of megalithic graves have been found very close to known enclosures. However, in several cases, this is not the case. It is not possible to state whether this is due to an actual lack of megaliths at the sites in question, or whether megaliths were once present, but have since been destroyed. Large numbers of finds covering a large area are often present on enclosure sites. By contrast, there are also some cases in which sites are almost devoid of finds.

Three new predictive parameters were identified over the course of this study. Many of the known enclosures in Djursland appear to be spaced at regular distances of on average 4-6 km to each other. The same distances are found in other parts of South Scandinavia and – most importantly – in many other parts of Europe (Germany, France, and England). Inter-enclosure distance thus not only is well-suited to use as a predictive parameter for locating new enclosures, but also apparently contains information on the function of these monuments on a European scale. In two cases, causewayed enclosures in South Scandinavia were uncovered during the excavation of Viking Age or Early Medieval fortifications. The survey demonstrates that Neolithic enclosures often are located in proximity to fortifications from early historical times. In fact, there is a relationship between the location of the two structures from vastly different time periods in approximately one out of every three cases, making the nearby presence of such fortifications a suitable predictive parameter. The most important of all predictive parameters employed in the investigation, however, is the proximity to a (reconstructed) prehistoric road or path. As demonstrated by the survey of Danish enclosures, it was more specifically the crossing of rivers by the roads/paths that appear to have guided the choice of Neolithic enclosure location. Comparable observations have

been made in Central Europe, where only historically-known roads were employed in the studies. The investigation of Danish sites demonstrates that a distinct relation between old main roads (from a late 18th century map) and causewayed enclosures also exists in South Scandinavia.

The first step of the predictive process targeted promontory type enclosures. The analysis of known Danish enclosures demonstrates that the majority of the promontories used for enclosure construction were either located near the confluence of two rivers or at points where rivers flowed into fjords. This observation is of great importance for the GIS-approach, as it bypasses the problem of defining a promontory in a GIS-based query. Rather than searching for promontories themselves, water-defined promontory borders were sought in their stead. Both river confluences and river mouths are easily defined as point datasets and have the additional advantage of combining the topography criterion with the proximity to water criterion.

Prior to this step, the course of the coastline at the time of enclosure construction (ca. 3500 BC) was reconstructed in order to obtain the precise locations of river mouths. Approximately 1200 km of prehistoric roads and tracks in Djursland were reconstructed for this study by using lines formed by Neolithic and Bronze Age barrows across the surrounding landscape. River crossings could subsequently be easily defined as point datasets by combining the reconstructed prehistoric roads/paths dataset with that established for freshwater streams.

The analysis of known Danish enclosures has demonstrated that river crossings by prehistoric roads or paths were almost always located at a distance of 800 m or less from enclosures. In the approach employed here, all river confluences or river mouths that were located less than 800 m from one of the reconstructed river crossings were consequently selected as potential enclosure locations. Based on the inter-enclosure distance location parameter as well as other predictive parameters, further sites were highlighted amidst those derived by the first step by looking for well-suited topographic locations on hilltops or in river loops, etc.

After an initial process of evaluating these potential sites on the ground via site visits and by the other predictive criteria, no less than 121 remained to be tested for the actual presence of an enclosure. In general, trial excavation, field survey, aerial survey and geophysical survey all are suitable methods for this step of the predictive process. However, trial excavation could not be employed in the present study, both due to the high costs involved as well as the refusal of land access by many landowners. An evaluation of extant aerial photographs led only to the discovery of few suspicious features, of which none clearly indicated the presence of a classical causewayed enclosure. A total of 48 sites could be subjected to field survey (or were surveyed by others). This resulted in the discovery of certain or probable TRB finds on no less than two thirds of their number. It appears, thus, that the method developed here is generally suitable to the location of TRB sites. However, the number of new sites identified is so large that these cannot possibly all represent causewayed enclosures.

The resources to implement a geophysical survey of a total of 20 locations were made available by the Danish Agency for Culture (KUS). The selection of those sites included in this geophysical survey was based on the results of the field survey. Furthermore, some were selected in order to answer specific questions (either with regard to the investigation area or with regard to the value of specific predictive parameters). In general, sites in non-coastal settings were prioritized, as the vast majority of known enclosures have been found close to the Neolithic coastline. One important objective with the geophysical survey, therefore, was to test whether or not this distribution was a true reflection of prehistoric reality.

Geophysical survey was carried out by a team from Kiel University in February 2012 using a magnetometer and ground penetrating radar. As far as was possible, both techniques were employed. Unfortunately, the heterogenic South Scandinavian soils (which often contain large amounts of magnetic stones like granite) imply that geophysical survey is not an easy way to detect prehistoric structures. Moreover, research has shown that en-

closure ditches are not always detectable by magnetometer survey. This was demonstrated by the same team within work done on two TRB enclosures in northern Germany. This problem (which is due to the lack of magnetic contrast between Neolithic ditches and their fill) was confirmed by tests completed on a site within the investigation area at which the presence of a Neolithic ditch was known. Nonetheless, survey of the remaining 19 sites revealed one certain and three probable or possible enclosure. In the case of the three probable or possible sites, the identification of the anomalies detected (thought to represent the remains of enclosure ditches and palisades) is in need of verification by trial excavation. At present, it is impossible to exclude the possibility that these anomalies are caused by geological rather than man-made features. A certain enclosure was detected on Assenbakke Hill, just east of the small town of Hornslet at a distance of 3 km from the former coastline. The site offered optimum survey conditions, as the subsoil there consists of pure meltwater sand. Furthermore, it had not been ploughed for approximately two decades. Two parallel rows of ditches (ca. 5 m wide and 1 m deep) were found cutting a marked promontory located at the confluence of two rivers. One of these rows was apparently not segmented and demonstrates never-before-seen U-shaped extensions. The second row is segmented and is characterized by massive deposits of material with magnetic properties (probably pottery or burned wattle and daub). It is possible that the anomalies detected do not represent a regular enclosure ditch, but rather a row of large oven constructions resembling those found at the Büdelsdorf enclosure in northern Germany. Further features detected by magnetometer survey at Assenbakke include fenced compartments of a total size of ca. 60 by 40 meters which lay just in front of the ditches. The possible remains of a round barrow, other grave constructions as well as an Early or early Middle Neolithic house were also detected.

Despite uncertainties regarding several of the results of the geophysical survey, the approach was generally successful and resulted in the discovery of one or more additional causewayed enclosures within the Djursland region. An evaluation of the individual predictive parameters shows that, besides the basic river-crossing/prehistoric road or path parameter, vicinity to an important historic road, a specific topography, proximity to water in the form of a river confluence or river outlet, the presence of depositions of selected artefacts, the typical inter-enclosure distance of approximately 4-6 km (in combination with other parameters) and a specific pattern of surface finds are the best-suited criteria to employment within a predictive modelling approach designed to find causewayed enclosures. On the other side of the spectrum is the vicinity to megalithic graves criterion, which did not prove to be effective at all.

In regard to the different test methods, it must be stated that neither aerial survey nor geophysical survey were completely reliable tools when used within the soil and climate conditions typical of South Scandinavia. With regards to geophysical survey, it is important not to rely on a single survey technique, but always (as far as possible) to use different (but complimentary) methods. The four certain, probable or possible enclosures found in the course of this study number among the sites that were judged to be among the most promising based on the results of the field survey alone, thereby demonstrating the effectiveness of this simple test method.

The results of the present study demonstrate that the presence of causewayed enclosures located at a distance from the Neolithic coastline must be reckoned with, at least in Djursland. The four potential enclosures found are all located between 1.8 and 3.3 km from the nearest fjord or bay. It is possible that the same inter-enclosure distance rule as that which applies to near-coastal sites applies to the location of these inland sites. However, due to the uncertain status of several of these sites, this cannot yet be confirmed.

At the present state of research, ten certain, four probable and seven possible enclosures can be listed for Djursland alone, although the latter group may include enclosure-related sites instead of proper causewayed enclosures. Four certain enclosure-related sites are presently known in the area.

Examination of the relation between all identified certain, probable or possible enclosures or enclosure-related sites from Djursland and the contemporary coastline demonstrates that no site was located more than 3.5 km from the shore. Upon closer inspection, a slightly bi-modal distribution is apparent. One group of enclosures/related sites was located very close to the coastline (less than 500 m away), while a second group was predominantly found approximately 3 km away. In fact, an almost identical distribution was found for all known enclosures from Denmark and southern Sweden. Only a single enclosure (Sigersted III on the island of Zealand) was located more than 4 km away from the coastline. It can be stated, therefore, that causewayed enclosures can generally only be expected in near-coastal locations, while they rarely appear to have been constructed in the interior. The data for the entirety of Denmark and south Sweden also indicate that the data presently available for Djursland may very well be representative of the Neolithic situation, despite the fact that many unconfirmed sites were included in the analysis.

In the next step, the relation between enclosures/enclosure-related sites and Mesolithic/Neolithic settlements was investigated in Djursland in general. While the settlements of the late Mesolithic Ertebølle Culture are primarily found directly on the contemporary coastline (with rare exceptions), a slight enlargement of the settled area can be observed in the first part of the Early Neolithic (EN I, ca. 4000-3500 BC). Sites from this phase appear to be located within a zone which stretched 3-4 km inland from the coast. In the following phase of the late Early/early Middle Neolithic (EN II – MN A I, ca. 3500-3200/3100 BC), settlement spread much further inland, as judged from the distribution of contemporary megalithic graves. It can be concluded, therefore, that the distribution of causewayed enclosures and related sites in Djursland is comparable to that of settlements in EN I. However, it differs greatly from that in EN II/MN A I. This result is most surprising, as enclosures are generally believed to have been constructed in the latter phase. There are three possible explanations for this observation.

The first is that the distribution pattern available at present is inaccurate. It would suggest that enclosures are indeed present in the interior of the country, but have not yet been found. Based on the investigation of all known enclosures in Denmark and South Sweden, even if it cannot be completely ruled out, this explanation appears unlikely. In this regard, it is important to note that the only enclosure ever found at distance from the coast (Sigersted III) was located in a region where settlement was also present within EN I. This site thus confirms the relationship between enclosures and settlements in the preceding phase of the Neolithic (EN I).

The second possible explanation for this spatial distribution is that knowledge of enclosure chronology is inaccurate, that the sites in question were actually built earlier than was hitherto believed (i.e. in EN I). In fact, enclosure construction in late EN I was recently demonstrated for two sites in the southern parts of the TRB North Group distribution area. However, there is still ample evidence for building activity in subsequent periods (i.e. EN II/MN A I). Thus, it is possible that enclosure construction in Djursland started in (late) EN I. However, it is unlikely that all of the numerous sites were constructed at this early date. Therefore, the second possible explanation for the observed distribution of enclosures does not appear likely.

This leaves only one explanation for the distribution pattern observed here. Causewayed enclosures were obviously related to the earliest Neolithic (EN I) societies and the areas settled thereby. Therefore, enclosure construction was limited to the coastal zone, despite the fact that large parts of the interior were settled during the same period in which enclosures were constructed. This indicates that groups settling the interior might have participated in the construction and use of coastal sites. In some way, the newly settled areas in the interior were ill-suited to enclosure construction. The same observation generally applies to the earliest Neolithic settlements in England and South Scandinavia. There can be no doubt that these earliest Neolithic settlers knew of the enclosures constructed by the Michelsberg Culture as well as related groups in Belgium, Germany and northern France. Nonetheless, enclosure construction did not begin with neolithisation. Rather, it started approximately 300 years thereafter. Regions which had only recently succumbed to the neolithisation trend thus appeared to have been unsuited to enclosure construction. The theory in which (relatively) distant groups used (and probably also constructed) enclosures is corroborated by evidence from the European Neolithic, as demonstrated by Stonehenge and the Linear Pottery Culture enclosure of Herxheim in Germany.

The restriction of causewayed enclosures to the coastal zone might have had to do with the long-distance routes to which they related. There are several prominent examples from South Scandinavia (the Döserygg site in Scania and the somewhat later routes marked by the presence of stone heap graves in northwest Jutland) demonstrating that specific routes (as well as the process of travelling on them) might have had ritual importance.

This interpretation obviously conflicts with the model of the emergence and function of enclosures as proposed by T. Madsen for east Jutland. Madsen believed that enclosures were central sites that were constructed by the dispersed population of a given region in order to solve conflict and avoid violence. The model was clearly inspired by the work of C. Renfrew in England, who had proposed a comparable model a decade prior. However, British archaeologists no longer believe that enclosures were located in the centre of some prehistoric territory. A fresh look at the Danish evidence also garners doubts concerning this assumption, as enclosure sites appear to be identical to naturally-defined borders in the landscape. This was also confirmed by the frequent co-appearance of fortifications from the Viking Age/ or Medieval period (which were constructed in border situations important for controlling travel). The surprising congruence between Neolithic sites and sites of later military importance can thus probably be explained by a related reading of the landscape.

An alternative to the east Jutland model would suggest that causewayed enclosures were built at regular intervals (approximately 4-6 km) which corresponded to an hour's walk or water trans-

port. They are located in naturally defined border situations, which were, however, not necessarily identical to borders between group territories. The territories appear to be too small to support this. Furthermore, it appears unlikely that very diverse Neolithic groups in different parts of Western and Central Europe should have had exactly the same regularized territory size. People from an area much larger than the ca. 5 km between two neighbouring enclosures participated in the construction and use of individual monuments. These were constructed along land or water routes with specific ritual significance, which was possibly related to an ancestor cult. Apart from ritual functions, enclosures seem to have fulfilled some of the social functions previously bound to large coastal fishing sites.

One important aspect of T. Madsen's east Jutland model is the assumption that enclosure construction in South Scandinavia started exclusively as the response to a local social need. Taking into account the large number of surprising similarities between South Scandinavian enclosures and those in different parts of Europe, this assumption is not convincing and was investigated in detail within the confines of this study. Enclosure architecture and chronology were employed to this end. The architectural analysis demonstrated the marked influence of the British enclosure tradition on South Scandinavian enclosures located close to the west coast of Jutland. Several typical British traits (like wide ditch circuit spacing, differing widths of the individual ditch circuits in multi-circuit enclosures, enclosures with two possible variants of an egg-shaped plan and entrance constructions consisting of two massive posts on a causeway) did appear in South Scandinavia, but only in enclosures located in proximity to the North Sea. They are absent from the remainder of Scandinavia. Enclosures with three or more (partial) ditch circuits have only been observed in the southern parts of the distribution area of TRB North Group enclosures and probably indicate a distinct relation to a group of enclosures in northern central Germany. The completely straight course of a framed turf wall that represents the enclosing constructional element of

the Vilsund enclosure in northwestern Jutland can best be compared with parallels from a restricted region of Westphalia, Germany. Finally, the peculiar ditch design (clavicle-shaped ditches bordering rectangular annexes to a palisade) of the Starup Langelandsvej enclosure finds a distinctive parallel only at Sandomierz in southeast Poland. In every case in which distinct parallels could be identified, it could be stated that the foreign enclosures were either definitively older or possibly contemporary to those from Scandinavia. Therefore, it is likely that the architecture of the Scandinavian sites in question reflects the inclusion of foreign ideas. Based on these observations, a core zone of enclosure construction in the eastern parts of South Scandinavia with monuments built in a genuine, Scandinavian style is discernable from a periphery zone in which the enclosures showed a marked influence from neighbouring regions. In some cases, different foreign traditions seem to have been combined in enclosures along the west coast of Jutland. Some visible western European influences can be traced to southern England. However, some sites showing the same traits also are known from central western France and the northern French and Belgian coast. These observations seem to reflect a communication network along the fringes of the Atlantic, the Channel and the North Sea.

Observations regarding architectural similarities between South Scandinavian enclosures and comparable sites abroad do not allow pinpointing the cause of enclosure construction in the distribution area of the TRB North Group. This construction could have been triggered by an impulse from abroad. Alternatively, construction could have started as a result of internal change in TRB North Group society. In this latter case, observed architectural similarities to enclosures abroad would only reflect an inspiration unrelated to the cause of enclosure construction.

A closer look at the chronology of enclosures in South Scandinavia reveals a very deficient state of research. ^{14}C-dates are only available from 13 of a total of 39 known enclosures. Moreover, it is only in three cases these dates can be related to the time of the enclosures' construction. In a

further five cases, the available information is sufficient to establish the time of construction based on artefact typology. At present, therefore, it is possible to date the construction of only ca. 20% of all known enclosures.

The available data indicate that causewayed enclosure construction in South Scandinavia started in the 37th or possibly 38th centuries BC and continued until the 33rd century BC, with a single possible outlier in the early 3rd millennium. This information was subsequently compared to that available for more than 400 related sites from Western, Central and (to a minor degree) Southeastern Europe.

The concept of the causewayed enclosure appears to have been invented in the Linear Pottery Culture of Central Europe in the second half of the 6th millennium BC, but the roots of the development leading to the construction of the Scandinavian enclosures can be found in the Cerny Culture in northern France in the mid 5th millennium BC. From there, enclosure construction spread rapidly to the east and reached Bohemia around 4000 BC. After 4000 BC, the frequency of enclosure construction declined. However, in the second half of the 38th and especially in the 37th centuries BC, an enclosure construction boom affected central western France, the British Isles (especially southern England), northern central Germany as well the Bavarian Danube Valley. At the same time, enclosure construction in the former core activity area in northern France, Belgium and western Germany almost completely ceased. Exceptions include a number of enclosures which can be found in a linear corridor stretching from the Neckar River Valley in southwest Germany towards northern Germany. The earliest enclosures in South Scandinavia also belong to this horizon and the two sites that can be dated accordingly with a degree of certainty (Albersdorf Dieksknöll and Starup Langelandsvej) are situated exactly on a hypothetical prolongation of the described linear corridor in Germany.

The distribution map of enclosures built between 3750 and 3500 BC clearly shows an interrelated development in many spatially isolated parts of Europe. This can only be understood as the ac-

tivation of knowledge which must have been passively present by means of some central impulse. Obviously, South Scandinavia was also touched by this impulse (which caused the beginnings of enclosure construction). It appears, thus, that this process must be related to exterior events and cannot be explained by internal social developments in TRB society.

An attempt was made to identify how and from where the identified central impulse was relayed. For this purpose, the distribution of specific constructional details concerning enclosure entrances was investigated. This resulted in the identification of corridors to which individual constructional elements were exclusively bound. For example, a certain type of screen blocking the direct line of sight into enclosures is known only from a scant few enclosures, all of which are located in the same linear corridor that connects the Neckar Valley to South Scandinavia. The enclosures are probably all located beside the same long-distance route, which must have had a special ritual significance. This corridor indicates the existence of a strong connection between southwestern Germany and Scandinavia. The latter is confirmed by the distribution pattern of several other elements (including copper finds and tetraploid naked wheat). Another long-distance route could be identified between the Neckar Valley and the Channel coast in northern France. Furthermore, the Neckar Valley also seems to have had connections to the Bavarian Danube Valley, northern central Germany and (potentially) central western France. The impulse that led to the enclosure building boom between 3750 and 3500 BC, therefore, appears to have been relayed from the Neckar Valley. However, the event(s) that caused the impulse more likely occurred further to the east, probably somewhere in Southeastern Europe. The latter region is linked to southern Germany by the Danube. It is not possible at present to identify the precise origin and nature of these event(s).

In conclusion, it can be stated that causewayed enclosures (or at least a subset of causewayed enclosures) were constructed at regular intervals (of approximately one hour's travel) along trans-Euro-

pean long-distance routes that met in the Neckar Valley in southwest Germany. While they were certainly also used for profane activities, these routes had distinct and individual ritual connotations. Groups may have travelled considerable distances to participate in the construction of enclosures along these routes. Information that caused parallel events in many spatially separated parts of Europe could have been relayed quickly along these lines of transport, exchange and communication. Travelling along them and encountering an enclosure after every hour's worth of travel could have been a spiritual experience. The complex entrance structures present at many enclosures often seemed similar to obstacles. It appears that anything that entered the enclosure from the route was viewed as potentially dangerous and had to be carefully controlled before it was eventually released. These persons, animals and/or objects were likely processed by means of the performance of rituals that would ensure safety. The frequent remains of humans and animals may indicate that it was not always possible to remove the aspects of danger without bloodshed. The enclosed space could, thus, possibly be understood as a kind of temporal quarantine station in which, when open, the ditches prevented the dangerous elements they enclosed from affecting their surroundings. Enclosures in South Scandinavia must be envisaged as having been constructed along those routes with special ritual connotation. These connotations were obviously restricted to routes established during the very first phases of Neolithic settlement and thereby explain why enclosures are only found in regions that were settled prior to the start of enclosure construction.

13 References

· ·

Amtmann/Schwellnus 1989
G. Amtmann/W. Schwellnus, Neue jungsteinzeitliche Erdwerke im Rheinland. Archäologie im Rheinland 1989, 34-37.

Andersen, A.H. 1987
A.H. Andersen, Skævinge Boldbaner. Arkæologiske Udgravninger i Danmark 1986 (København 1987), Nr. 16.

Andersen, H.H. 1961
H. H. Andersen, Køkkenmøddingen ved Mejlgård. KUML 1960, 26-35.

Andersen, N.H. 1974
N.H. Andersen, En befæstet, yngre stenalderboplads i Sarup. Foreløbig meddelelse. Fynske Minder 1974, 71-88.

Andersen, N.H. 1975a
N.H. Andersen, Sarup, et befæstet neolitisk anlæg på Sydvestfyn. Kuml 1973-74, 109-120.

Andersen, N.H. 1975b
N.H. Andersen, Die neolithische Befestigungsanlage in Sarup auf Südfünen. Archäologisches Korrespondenzblatt 5, 1975, 11-14.

Andersen, N.H. 1976
N.H. Andersen, Sarup, keramikgruber fra to bebyggelsesfaser. KUML 1976, 11-46.

Andersen, N.H. 1981
N.H. Andersen, Sarup. Befæstede neolitiske anlæg og deres baggrund. KUML 1980, 63-97.

Andersen, N.H. 1982
N.H. Andersen, A Neolithic Causewayed camp at Trelleborg near Slagelse, West Zealand. Journal of Danish Archaeology 1, 1982, 31-33.

Andersen, N.H. 1987
N.H. Andersen, Hygind. Arkæologiske Udgravninger i Danmark 1986 (København 1987), nr. 149.

Andersen, N.H. 1988
N.H. Andersen, Hygind. Arkæologiske Udgravninger i Danmark 1987 (København 1988), nr. 120.

Andersen, N.H. 1989
N.H. Andersen, Hygind. Arkæologiske Udgravninger i Danmark 1988 (København 1989), nr. 126.

Andersen, N.H. 1993
N.H. Andersen, Tragtbægerkulturens store samlingspladser. In: St. Hvass/B. Storgaard (ed.), Da Klinger I Muld. 25 års arkæologi i Danmark (Århus 1985), 100-103.

Andersen, N.H. 1997
N.H. Andersen, The Sarup Enclosures. Sarup vol. 1. Jutland Archaeological Society Publications XXXIII:1 (Højbjerg 1997).

Andersen, N.H. 1999a
N.H. Andersen, Saruppladsen. Tekst. Sarup vol. 2. Jysk Arkæologisk Selskabs Skrifter 33:2 (Højbjerg 1999).

Andersen, N.H. 1999b
N.H. Andersen, Saruppladsen. Katalog. Sarup vol. 3. Jysk Arkæologisk Selskabs Skrifter 33:3 (Højbjerg 1999).

Andersen, N.H. 2000
N.H. Andersen, Kult og ritualer I den ældre bondestenalder. KUML 2000, 13-57.

Andersen, N.H. 2009
N.H. Andersen, Sarupområdet på Sydvestfyn I slutningen af 4. årtusinde f.Kr. In: A. Schülke (red.), Plads og rum i tragtbægerkulturen. Bidrag fra Arbejdsmødet på Nationalmuseet, 22. september 2005. Nordiske Fortidsminder Serie C Bind 6 (København 2009), 25-44.

Andersen, N.H. 2011
N.H. Andersen, Causewayed enclosures and megalithic monuments as media for shaping Neolithic identities. In: M. Furholt/F. Lüth/J. Müller (eds.), Megaliths and

Identities. Early Monuments and Neolithic Societies from the Atlantic to the Baltic (Bonn 2011), 143-154.

Andersen, S.H. 1975
S.H. Andersen, Ringkloster. En jysk indlandsboplads med Ertebølle-Kultur. KUML 1973/74, 11-108.

Andersen, S.H. 1986
S.H. Andersen, De forhistoriske tider på Aggersborgegnen. In: F. Nørgaard/E. Roesdahl/R. Skovmand (eds.), Aggersborg Gennem 1000 År. Fra Vikingeborg Til Slægtsgård (Herning 1986), 29-52.

Andersen, S.H. 1991
S.H. Andersen, Norsminde. A Køkkenmødding with Late Mesolithic and Early Neolithic Occupation. Journal of Danish Archaeology 8, 1989, 13-40.

Andersen, S.H. 1993
S.H. Andersen, Bjørnsholm. A Stratified Køkkenmødding on the Central Limfjord, North Jutland. Journal of Danish Archaeology 10, 1991, 59-96.

Andersen, S.H. 1995
S.H. Andersen, Kystbebyggelse i senmesolitikum og tidligneolitikum. I: Bebyggelsesarkæologi. Prioroteringsmøde, Moesgård, d. 3. oktober 1994. Det Arkæologiske Nævn og SHF's forskningsprogram "Bebyggelse og Kulturlandskab" (København 1995), 12-24.

Andersen, S.H. 1998
S.H. Andersen, Ringkloster. Ertebølle trappers and wild boar hunters in eastern Jutland. A Survey. Journal of Danish Archaeology 12, 1994-95, 13-59.

Andersen, S.H. 2008
S.H. Andersen, The Mesolithic-Neolithic transition in Western Denmark seen from a kitchen midden perspective. A survey. In: Between Foraging And Farming. An Extended Broad Spectrum Of Papers Presented To Leendert Louwe Kooijmans. Analecta Praehistorica Leidensia 40, 2008, 67-74.

Andersen, S.H. in preparation
S.H. Andersen, Ertebølle Fishers and Hunters in Djursland. Museum East Jutland Publications, in preparation.

Andersen, S.T. 1998
S.T. Andersen, Pollen analytical investigations of barrows from the Funnel Beaker and Single Grave Cultures in the Vroue area, West Jutland, Denmark. Journal of Danish Archaeology 12, 1994-95, 107-132.

Andersson 2003
M. Andersson, Skapa plats i landskapet. Tidig- och mellanneolitiska samhällen utmed två västskånska dalgångar (Lund 2003).

Andersson/Nilsson 2009a
M. Andersson/B. Nilsson, Håslöv 13:1. UV Syd Rapport 2009:10, Forundersökning 2008 (Lund 2009).

Andersson/Nilsson 2009b
M. Andersson/B. Nilsson, Döserygg och Skegriedösarna. Megalitgravarna på Söderslätt i ny belysning. Ale 2009:4, 1-15.

Andersson/Wallebom 2013a
M. Andersson/B. Wallebom, Döserygg and the Skegrie Dolmens. New Light on the Megalithic Graves in southwest Scania, southern Sweden. In: J.A. Bakker/S.B.C. Bloo/M.K. Dütting (eds.), From Funeral Monuments to Household Pottery. Current advances in Funnel Beaker (TRB/TBK) research. Proceedings of the Borger Meetings 2009, The Netherlands. BAR International Series 2474 (Oxford 2013), 121-134.

Andersson/Wallebom 2013b
M. Andersson/B. Wallebom, Döserygg and Skegrie. Megalithic centres in south-west Scania, southern Sweden. In: D. Fontijn/A.J. Louwen/S. Van Der Vaart/K. Wentink (eds.), Beyond barrows. Current Research on the Structuration and Perception of the Neolithic Landscape through Monuments (Leiden 2013), 115-139.

Andresen et al. 2008
J. Andresen/R. Birch Iversen/P. Jensen, On the War-path: Terrestrial Military Organisation in Prehistoric Denmark. In: A. Posluschny/I. Herzog/K. Lambers (eds.), Computer Applications and Quantitative Methods in Archaeology: Layers of perception. Advanced technological means to illuminate our past (Bonn 2008), 1-8.

Aner 1963
E. Aner, Die Stellung der Dolmen Schleswig-Holsteins in der nordischen Megalithkultur. Offa 20, 1963, 9-38.

Anthony 1990
D.W. Anthony, Migration in Archaeology: The Baby and the Bathwater. American Anthropologist 92-4, 1990, 895-914.

Ard 2011
V. Ard, Traditions céramiques au Néolithique récent et final dans le Centre-Ouest dea la France (3700-2200 avant J.C.) : filiations et interactions entre groupes culturels. PhD thesis, Université Paris Ouest nanterre La Défense (Nanterre 2011).

Arnold 1992
V. Arnold, Aus der Luft gegriffen: Jungsteinzeitliches Erdwerk auf dem Dieksknöll bei Albersdorf, Kreis Dithmarschen. Archäologische Nachrichten aus Schleswig-Holstein 3, 1992, 32-33.

Arnold 1993
V. Arnold, Frühneolithisches Grabenwerk auf dem Dieksknöll in Albersdorf, Kreis Dithmarschen. Archäologie in Schleswig 3, 1993, 5-12.

Arnold 1994
V. Arnold, Erste Untersuchungsergebnisse im steinzeitlichen Erd- und Grabenwerk auf dem Dieksknöll bei Albersdorf. Dithmarschen 1994-3, 49-53.

Arnold 1997
V. Arnold, Das jungsteinzeitliche Erd- oder Grabenwerk auf dem Dieksknöll bei Albersdorf – erste Untersuchungsergebnisse. In: V. Arnold (Hrsg.), Wall und Graben. Befestigung von der Steinzeit bis ins Mittelalter in Schleswig und Holstein (Schleswig 1997), 14-25.

Arnold 2000
V. Arnold, Neolithisches Erdwerk "Dieksknöll". Archäologie in Deutschland 2000-3, 48.

Arora/Zerl 2004
S.K. Arora/T. Zerl, Bischheimer Siedlungen – archäobotanische Ergebnisse und ein fraglicher Perlenfund. Archäologie im Rheinland 2003, 48-50.

Bakels 2003
C. Bakels, Die neolithischen Weizenarten des südlimburgischen Lößgebiets in den Niederlanden. In: J. Eckert/U. Eisenhauer/A. Zimmermann (Hrsg.), Archäologische Perspektiven. Analysen und Interpretationen im Wandel. Festschrift für Jens Lüning zum 65. Geburtstag. Internationale Archäologie – Studia honoraria Band 20 (Rahden/Westf. 2003), 225-232.

Bakker 1976
J.A. Bakker, On the Possibility of Reconstructing Roads from the TRB Period. Berichten van de Rijksdienst voor het Oudheidkundig Bodemonderzoek 26, 1976, 63-91.

Bakker/Knoche 2003
J.A. Bakker/B. Knoche, Erdwerke, Grabmonumente, Wegeplanung. Archäologie in Deutschland 2003/4, 22-25.

Barthel 1984
S. Barthel, Latènesiedlung von Großfahner, Kr. Erfurt. Alt-Thüringen 20, 1984, 81-139.

Bauch 1991
W. Bauch, Erdwerk und Megalithgräber der Trichterbecherkultur von Büdelsdorf, Kr. Rendsburg-Eckernförde. Archäologie in Schleswig 1, 1991, 13-15.

Bauch 1993
W. Bauch, Ein neolithisches Erdwerk in Schleswig-Holstein. Archäologie in Deutschland 1993, 6-9.

Bayliss et al. 2011
A. Bayliss/F. Healy/A. Whittle/G. Cooney, Chapter 14: Neolithic narratives: British and Irish enclosures in their timespans. In: Whittle et al. 2011a, 682-847.

Beck 2013
M. R. Beck, Højensvej 7 – en tidligneolitisk langhøj med flere faser. Aarbøger for Nordisk Oldkyndighed og Historie 2011-2012, 33-117.

Becker 1947
C.J. Becker, Mosefundne Lerkar Fra Yngre Stenalder. Studier Over Tragtbægerkulturen I Danmark. Aarbøger for Nordisk Oldkyndighed og Historie 1947, 1-318.

Behrends 1998a
R.-H. Behrends, Ein Weg aus der Jungsteinzeit nachgewiesen? Archäologische Nachrichten aus Baden 58, 1998, 3-7.

Behrends 1998b
R.H. Behrends, Neue Forschungen zur Michelsberger Kultur im Kraichgau. In: J. Biel/H. Schlichterle/A. Zeeb (Hrsg.), Die Michelsberger Kultur und ihre Randgebiete. Probleme der Entstehung, Chronologie und des Siedlungswesens. Kolloquium Hemmenhofen 21.-23. Februar 1997. Materialhefte zur Archäologie Baden-Württembergs 43 (Stuttgart 1998), 115-119.

Beran 2009
J. Beran, Landschaft der Trichterbecherkultur in Brandenburg: Ausgrabungen 1998 bis 2007. In: H.-J.Beier/E. Claßen/ Th. Doppler/B. Ramminger (Hrsg.),Varia neolithica VI. Neolithische Monumente und neolithische Gesellschaften (Langenweißbach 2009),123-131.

Beran 2010
J. Beran, Noch ein Grabenwerk der Trichterbecherkultur? Neolithische Grab- und Siedlungsbefunde in der Potsdamer Holzmarktstraße. Archäologie in Berlin und Brandenburg 2009, 3-7.

Beran/Hensel 2004
J. Beran/N. Hensel, Streitaxt im Ringgraben. Eine Anlage der Trichterbecherkultur in Potsdam. Archäologie in Berlin und Brandenburg 2003, 48-49.

Beran/Hensel 2007
J. Beran/N. Hensel, Steinzeit unter dem Schloß. Grabenanlagen, Siedlungen und Gräber der Jungsteinzeit in Potsdams Stadtmitte. Archäologie in Berlin und Brandenburg 2006, 30-35.

Beranek 2007
R. Beranek, Frühgeschichtliche Fernwege im Kreis Storman und im Raum Lübeck. Jahrbuch Kreis Storman 2007, 34-83.

Berghausen/Faßbinder 2004
K. Berghausen/J. Faßbinder, Neuentdeckung bei der Messdatenpflege: Ein neolithisches Erdwerk bei Berghofen. Das Archäologische Jahr in Bayern 2004, 30-33.

Billamboz 1998
A. Billamboz, Dendrochronologische Untersuchungen in der Moorsiedlung Reute-Schorrenried/Bad Waldsee. In: Mainberger 1998, 361-384.

Birkedahl 1988
P. Birkedahl, Lokes Hede. Arkæologiske Udgravninger i Danmark 1987 (København 1988), nr. 299.

Birkedahl 1995
P. Birkedahl, Stenaldertræf på Lokes Hede. In: J. Hertz (Hrsg.), 5000 år under motorvejen (København 1995), 30-31.

Bjørn/Hingst 1973
A. Bjørn/H. Hingst, Back- und Töpferöfen der jüngeren Steinzeit aus Schleswig-Holstein. Die Heimat 80, 1973, 108-110.

Blanchet/Martinez 1988
J.-C. Blanchet/R. Martinez, Les Camps Néolithiques Chasséens dans le nord-ouest du Bassin Parisien. In: C. Burgess/P. Topping/C. Mordant/M. Maddison (eds.), Enclosures and defences in the Neolithic of Western Europe vol. 1 (Oxford 1988), 149-165.

Boas 2001
N.A. Boas, Blakbjerg. En befæstet plads fra tragt-bægerkulturen i yngre stenalder ca. 3500 f.Kr. In: En by og dens mennesker. Marie Magdalene før og nu (Ryomgård 2001), 4-8.

Boelicke 1977
U. Boelicke, Das neolithische Erdwerk Urmitz. Acta Praehistorica et Archaeologica 7/8, 1976/77, 73-121.

Bostyn et al. 2012
F. Bostyn/N. Layol/M.-F. Dietsch-Sellami/Ph. Feray/J. Lantoine, Une occupation singulière du Néolithique moyen II à Courrières (Pas-de-Calais). Bulletin de la Société Préhistorique Française 109-3, 2012, 547-567.

Boureux 1982
M. Boureux, La prospection aérienne de la vallée de l'Aisne. Revue archéologique de Picardie, Numéro special 1, 1982, 21-42.

Braasch 2002
O. Braasch, Aerial survey and Neolithic Enclosures in Central Europe. In: G. Varndell/P. Topping (eds.), Enclosures in Neolithic Europe (Oxford 2002), 63-68.

Brandt 1998
J. Brandt, Zietlitz, Ldkr. Parchim. Jahrbuch Bodendenkmalpflege in Mecklenburg 45, 1997 (1998), 472-473.

Brandt 2000
J. Brandt, Plate, Ldkr. Parchim. Jahrbuch Bodendenkmalpflege in Mecklenburg 47, 1999 (2000), 551.

Brink-Kloke/Meurers-Balke 2003
H. Brink-Kloke/J. Meurers-Balke, Siedlungen und Gräber am Oespeler Bach (Dortmund) – eine Kulturlandschaft im Wandel der Zeiten. Germania 81, 2003, 47-146.

Brozio 2011
J.P. Brozio, Von Siedlungen und Grabenwerken der Trichterbecher-Gemeinschaften. Archäologie in Deutschland 2011-2, 24-25.

Brøndsted 1962
J. Brøndsted, Bronzezeit in Dänemark. Nordische Vorzeit band 2 (Neumünster 1962).

Burmeister 2011
S. Burmeister, Innovationswege – Wege der Kommunikation. Erkenntnisprobleme am Beispiel des Wagens im 4. Jt. v.Chr. In: Sozialarchäologische Perspektiven: Gesellschaftlicher Wandel 5000-1500 v.Chr. zwischen Kaukasus und Atlantik. Internationale Konferenz in Kiel 15.-18. Oktober 2007. Archäologie in Eurasien 24 (Berlin 2011), 211-240.

Burnez 1996
C. Burnez, Le site de Loups à Echiré – Deux Sèvres. Édition Musée du Tumulus de Bougon (Niort 1996).

Bødker Enghoff 2011
I. Bødker Enghoff, Regionality and biotope exploitation in Danish Ertebølle and adjoining periods. Scientia Danica. Series B, Biologica vol. 1 (Copenhagen 2011).

Carlstein 1980
T. Carlstein, Time Resources, Society and Ecology: On the capacity for Human Interaction on Space and Time. Part 1: Preindustrial Societies. Meddelanden från Lunds Universitets Geografiska Institution Avhandlingar LXXXVIII (Lund 1980).

Case 1956
H. Case, The Neolithic causewayed camp at Abingdon, Berks. The Antiquaries Journal 36-1, 1956, 11-30.

Cassen 1987
S. Cassen, Le Centre-Ouest de la France au IVème millénaire av. J.C. BAR International Series 342 (Oxford 1987).

Cassen/Boujot 1990
S. Cassen/Ch. Boujot, Grabenumfriedungen im Frankreich des 5. bis 3. Jahrtausends v.u.Z. Jahresschrift für Mitteldeutsche Vorgeschichte 73, 1990, 455-468.

Cassen/Scarre 1997
S. Cassen/Ch. Scarre (eds.), Les enceintes néolithiques de a Mastine et Pied-Lizet (17). Fouilles archéologiques et études paléo-environnementales dans le marais Poitevin (1984-1988)(Chauvigny 1997).

Chmielewski 2008
T. Chmielewski, Remarks on relative and absolute chronology of early and middle Eneolithic in the area of south-east Poland and west Ukraine. Przegląd Archeologiczny 56, 2008, 41-100.

Cichy et al. 2011
E. Cichy/K. Schierhold/M. Baales, Untersuchung eines Grabenkopfes am neolithischen Erdwerk von Bad Sassendorf. Archäologie in Westfalen-Lippe 2010, 39-41.

Constantin et al. 2009
Cl. Constantin/L. Demarez/C. Bakels/I. Deramaix/L. Hachem/A. Salavert, L'enceinte Michelsberg de Blicquy – La Couture du Couvent. Anthropologica et Paehistorica 120, 2009, 151-202.

Convertini 2012

F. Convertini, Mid- late Neolithic Enclosures in the South of France. In : A. Gibson (ed.), Enclosing the Neolithic. Recent studies in Britain and Europe. BAR International Series 2440 (Oxford 2012), 125-145.

Cooney et al. 2011

G. Cooney/A. Bayliss/F. Healy/A. Whittle/E. Danaker/L. Cagney/J. Mallory/J. Smyth/Th. Kador/M. O'Sullivan, Chapter 12: Ireland. In: Whittle et al. 2011a, 562-669.

Curwen 1938

E.C. Curwen, The early development of agriculture in Britain. Proceedings of the Prehistoric Society 4, 1938, 27-51.

Delor et al. 1988

J.P. Delor/J.P. Jacob/A. Heurtaux/H. Leredde/C. Pellet, Inventaire des Encenites Néolithiques de la Vallée de l'Yonne Répérées par Prospection Aerienne. In.: C. Burgess/P. Topping/C. Mordant/M. Maddison (eds.), Enclosures and defences in the Neolithic of Western Europe vol. 1 (Oxford 1988), 227-229.

Demarez/Constantin 1986

L. Demarez/C. Constantin, L'Enceinte Michelsberg de Blicquy (La Couture du Covent)(Hainaut). Fouilles 1985. Notae Paehistoricae 1986, 43.50.

Dibbern 2011

H. Dibbern, Das Albersdorfer Erdwerk und seine Nutzungsgeschichte. Archäologische Nachrichten aus Schleswig-Holstein 2011, 30-32.

Dibbern 2012

H. Dibbern, Das Albersdorfer Grabenwerk – eine mehrphasige Anlage mit ritueller Funktion. In: Hinz/Müller 2012, 271-295.

Dibbern/Hage 2010

H. Dibbern/F. Hage, Erdwerk und Megalithgräber in der Region Alberstorf – ein Vorbericht zu den Grabungskampagnen am Dieksknöll und Brutkamp. Archäologische Nachrichten aus Schleswig-Holstein 2010, 34-37.

Dobat 2013

A.M. Dobat, Kongens Borge – Rapport over undersøgelserne 2007-2010. Jysk Arkæologisk Selskabs Skrifter 76 (Højbjerg 2013).

Dörfler et al. 2012

W. Dörfler/I. Feeser/C. van den Bogaard/S. Dreibrodt/ H. Erlenkeuser/A. Kleinmann/J. Merkt/J. Wiethold, A high quality annually laminated sequence from lake Belau, Northern Germany: Revised chronology and its implications for palynological and tephrochronological studies. The Holocene 22 (12), 2012, 1413-1426.

Driehaus 1960

J. Driehaus, Die Altheimer Gruppe und das Jungneolithikum in Mitteleuropa (Mainz 1960).

Dubois 1999

J. Dubpis, Archéologie aérienne en Touraine (France). Revue archéologique de Picardie, Numéro special 17, 1999, 359-366.

Dubouloz et al. 1988

J. Dubouloz/M. Lebolloch/M. Illet, Middle Neolithic Enclosures in the Aisne Valley. In.: C. Burgess/P. Topping/C. Mordant/M. Maddison (eds.), Enclosures and defences in the Neolithic of Western Europe vol. 1 (Oxford 1988), 209-226.

Dubouloz et al. 1991

J. Dubouloz/D. Mordant/M. Prestreau, Les enceintes « néolithiques » du Bassin Parisien. In : A. Beeching/D. Binder/J.-Cl. Blanchet/Cl. Constantin/J. Dubouloz/R. martinez/D. Mordant/P.-P. Thevenot/J. Vaquer (eds,), Identité du Chasséen. Actes du Colloque International de Nemours, 17-18-19 mai 1989. Mémoirs du Musée de Préhistoire d'Ile de France no. 4 (Nemours 1991), 211-229.

Ebbesen 1979

K. Ebbesen, Stordyssen i Vedsted. Studier over tragtbægerkulturen i Sønderjylland. Arkæologiske Studier VI (København 1979).

Ebbesen 1985

K. Ebbesen, Fortidsminderegistrering i Danmark (København 1985).

Ebbesen 1994

K. Ebbesen, Simple, tidligneolitiske grave. Aarbøger for Nordisk Oldkyndighed og Historie 1992, 47-83.

Eckert 1987

J. Eckert, Ein mittel- und jungneolithischer Siedlungsplatz bei Nottuln, Kreis Coesfeld. Bericht über die Ausgrabungen 1983-1984. Ausgrabungen und Funde in Westfalen-Lippe 4, 1986, 39-63.

Eckert 1990

J. Eckert, Überlegungen zu Bauweise und Funktion Michelsberger Erdwerke im Rheinland. Jahresschrift für mitteldeutsche Vorgeschichte 73, 1990, 399-414.

Engelhardt 1995

B. Engelhardt, Ein neolithisches Erdwerk bei Ringkam. Das Archäologische Jahr in Bayern 1995, 34-37.

Engelhardt 2006

B. Engelhardt, Ein neuer Typ eines Münchshofener Grabenwerks in Oberhinkofen. Das Archäologische Jahr in Bayern 2006, 25-28.

Eriksen 1984

P. Eriksen, Det neolitiske bopladskompleks ved Fannerup. KUML 1984, 9-76.

Eriksen/Madsen 1984

P. Eriksen/T. Madsen, Hanstedgård. A Settlement Site from the Funnel Beaker Culture. Journal of Danish Archaeology 3, 1984, 62-82.

Eriksen/Olesen 2002
P. Eriksen/L.H. Olesen, Fortiden set fra himlen. Luft-fotoarkæologi i Vestjylland (Holstebro 2002).

Eriksen/Andersen in press
P. Eriksen/N.H. Andersen, Dysserne – vor ældste arkitektur I sten. Jutland Archaeological Society Publications, in press.

Evans 1988
Ch. Evans, Excavations at Haddenham, Cambridgeshire: A „Planned" Enclosure and its Regional Affinities". In: C. Burgess/P. Topping/C. Mordant/M. Maddison (eds.), Enclosures and defences in the Neolithic of Western Europe vol. 1 (Oxford 1988), 127-147.

Fiedel 2006
R. Fiedel, Kendte og ukendte gravhøje i Hørning sogn. Årbog Kulturhistorisk Museum Randers 2006, 27-48.

Fiedel/Berg Nielsen 1989
R. Fiedel/Berg Nielsen, Bopladser og en grav, yngre stenalder. Arkæologiske Fund 1987-88, Kulturhistorisk Museum Randers, 55.

Fischer/Gotfredsen 2006
A. Fischer, A.B. Gotfredsen, Da landbruget kom til Nordvestsjælland – tidligt tamkvæg i Åmosen. Fra Nordvestsjælland. Årbog for kulturhistorien i Nordvestsjælland 2005-6, 35-54.

Fischer/Heinemeier 2003
A. Fischer/J. Heinemeier, Freshwater Reservoir effect in ^{14}C-dates of food residue on pottery. Radiocarbon 45-3, 2003, 449-466.

Freese 2010
H.-D. Freese, Ein neolithisches Erdwerk an der Weser nahe Stolzenau im Landkreis Nienburg (Weser). Nachrichten aus Niedersachsens Urgeschichte 79, 2010, 3-9.

Fritsch et al. 2010
B. Fritsch/M. Furholt/M. Hinz/L. Lorenz/H. Nelson/G. Schafferer/S. Schiesberg/K.-G. Sjögren, Dichtezentren und lokale Gruppierungen – Eine Karte zu den Großsteingräbern Mittel- und Nordeuropas. Journal of Neolithic Archaeology 2010 (online publication).

Furholt 2009
M. Furholt, Die nördlichen Badener Keramikstile im Kontext des mitteleuropäischen Spätneolithikums (3650-2900 v.Chr.). Studien zur Archäologie in Osteuropa Band 3 (Bonn 2009).

Furholt 2011a
M. Furholt, Entstehung der frühen Einzelgräber – Was geschah vor 4800 Jahren? Archäologie in Deutschland 2011-2, 30-31.

Furholt 2011b
M. Furholt, A Virtual and a Practiced Neolithic? Material Culture Symbolism, Monumentality and Identities

in the Western Baltic Region. In: M. Furholt/F. Lüth/J. Müller (eds.), Megaliths and Identities. Early Monuments and Neolithic Societies from the Atlantic to the Baltic (Bonn 2011), 107-120.

Gandelin 2011
M. Gandelin, Les enceintes chasséennes de Villeneuve-Tolosane et de Cugnaux dans leur contexte du Néolithique moyen européen. Archives d'Ecologie Préhistorique (Toulouse 2011).

Geschwinde/Raetzel-Fabian 2009
M. Geschwinde/D. Raetzel-Fabian, EWBSL. Eine Fallstudie zu den jungneolithischen Erdwerken am Nordrand der Mittelgebirge. Beiträge zur Archäologie in Niedersachsen Band 14 (Rahden 2009).

Ghesquière et al. 2011
E. Ghesquière/D. Giazzon/C. Marcigny, L'Enceinte Néolithique Moyen de Goulet « Le Mont » (Orne) dans son Contexte Environnemental. Revue Archéologique de Picardie, Numéro special 28 (2011), 183-205.

Giersing 2004
T. Giersing, Et mellemneolitisk palisadeanlæg ved Helgeshøj, Østsjælland. Aarbøger for Nordisk Oldkyndighed og Historie 2001, 7-34.

Gietzelt 2000
M. Gietzelt (Hrsg.), Geschichte Dithmarschens (Heide 2000).

Glob 1949
P.V. Glob, Barkær – Danmarks ældste landsby. Nationalmuseets Arbejdsmark 1949, 5-16.

Glørstad/Sundström in press
H. Glørstad/L. Sundström, Hamremoen – an Enclosure for the Hunter-Gatherers? Offa, in press.

Gojda et al. 2002
M. Gojda/D. Dreslerová/P. Foster/R. Křivánek/M. Kuna/S. Vencl/M. Zapotocký, Das Erdwerk Kly in Mittelböhmen. Auswertung der nichtdestruktiven Methoden zur Erkenntnis eines Siedlungsareal Types. Archéologické Rozhledy LIV, 2002, 371-430.

Gorka/Faßbinder 2007
T. Gorka/J. Faßbinder, Münchshöfen oder Michelsberg? Ein jungneolithisches Grabenwerk bei Riedling. Das Archäologische Jahr in Bayern 2007, 17-20.

Gronenborn 2007
D. Gronenborn, Climate Change and Socio-Political Crises: Some Cases from Neolithic Central Europe. In: T. Pollard/I. Banks (eds.), War and Sacrifice. Studies in the Archaeology of Conflict (Leiden/Boston 2007), 13-32.

Gronenborn 2010
D. Gronenborn, Eliten, Prestigegüter, Repräsentationsgräber. Eine Spurensuche nach politischen Organisationsformen. In: C. Lichter (ed.), Jungsteinzeit im

Umbruch. Die "Michelsberger Kultur" und Mitteleuropa vor 6000 Jahren. Katalog zur Ausstellung im Badischen Landesmuseum Schloss Karlsruhe 20.11.2010 - 15.5.2011, 243-249.

Grünewald 2013
Ch. Grünewald, Schöne Aussichten an der Lippe. Archäologie in Deutschland 2013-2, 51.

Guldin 2011
A. Guldin, Eine Straße erzählt Geschichte(n)…Ein neu entdecktes Erdwerk der Jungsteinzeit im Trassenbereich der geplanten Autobahn A 20 bei Bad Segeberg. Archäologische Nachrichten aus Schleswig-Holstein 2011, 33-35.

Hage 2014
F. Hage, Neue Untersuchungen eines altbekannten Platzes. Das jungsteinzeitliche Grabenwerk von Büdelsdorf. Marschenrat zur Förderung der Forschung im Küstengebiet der Nordsee. Nachrichten 51.

Hage in press
F. Hage, Das trichterbecherzeitliche Grabenwerk von Büdelsdorf LA 1. In: Proceedings of the conference „Salzmünde – Regel oder Ausnahme?" Halle/Saale, 18.-20. Oktober 2012.

Hartz 2011
S. Hartz, From pointed bottom to round and flat bottom – tracking early pottery from Schleswig-Holstein. Berichte der Römisch-Germanischen Kommission 89, 2008, 241-276.

Haßmann 2000
H. Haßmann, Die Steinartefakte aus der befestigten neolithischen Siedlung von Büdelsdorf, Kreis Rendsburg-Eckernförde. Universitätsforschungen zur prähistorischen Archäologie Band 62 (Bonn 2000).

Hedges/Buckley 1978
J. Hedges/D. Buckley, Excavations at a Neolithic Causewayed Enclosure, Orsett, Essex, 1975. Proceedings of the Prehistoric Society 44, 1978, 219-308.

Heinrich 1999
D. Heinrich, Die Tierknochen des frühneolithischen Wohnplatzes Wangels LA 505. Ein Vorbericht. Offa 54/55, 1997-98, 43-48.

Helms 1988
M. Helms, Ulysses's Sail. An Ethnographic Odyssey of Power, Knowledge, and Geographical Distance (Princeton 1988).

Helms 1993
M. Helms, Craft and the Kingly Ideal. Art, Trade and Power (Austin 1993).

Herbich/Tunia 2009
T. Herbig/K. Tunia, Geophysical survey of large Neolithic structures in loess regions. The case of Slonowice. Archaeologia Polski 54-1, 2009, 13-35.

Herbig 2009
Ch. Herbig, Recent archaeobotanical investigations into the range and abundance of Neolithic crop plants in settlements around Lake Constance and in Upper Swabia (southwest Germany) in relation to cultural influences. Journal of Archaeological Science 36, 2009, 1277-1285.

Hernek 1988
R. Hernek, Den spetsnackiga yxan av flinta. Fornvännen 83, 1988, 216-223.

Hingst 1971a
H. Hingst, Eine befestigte jungsteinzeitliche Siedlung in Büdelsdorf, Kreis Rendsburg-Eckernförde. Offa 28, 1971, 90-93.

Hingst 1971b
H. Hingst, Ein befestigtes Dorf aus der Jungsteinzeit in Büdelsdorf. Archäologisches Korrespondenzblatt 1, 1971, 191-194.

Hingst 1973
H. Hingst, Eine befestigte jungsteinzeitliche Siedlung in Büdelsdorf, Kreis Rendsburg-Eckernförde. Offa 30, 1973, 228-229.

Hingst 1974
H. Hingst, Die steinzeitliche Siedlung. Offa 31, 1974, 137-139.

Hingst 1981
H. Hingst, Büdelsdorf. Reallexikon der Germanischen Altertumskunde Band 4 (Berlin 1981), 91-95.

Hinz/Müller 2012
M. Hinz/J. Müller (eds.), Siedlung, Grabenwerk, Grosssteingrab. Studien zu Gesellschaft, Wirtschaft und Umwelt der Trichterbechergruppen im nördlichen Mitteleuropa. Schwerpunktprogramm 1400. Frühe Monumentalität und soziale Differenzierung Band 2 (Bonn 2012).

Hinz et al. 2012
M. Hinz/I. Feeser/ K.-G. Sjögren, J. Müller, Demography and the intensity of cultural activities: an evaluation of Funnel Beaker Societies (4200-2800 BC). Journal of Archaeological Schience 39, 2012, 3331-3340.

Hock 1989
H.-P. Hock, Die Besiedlung des mittelrheinischen Bekkens im Neolithikum. Dissertation Universität Mainz (Mainz 1989).

Hoika 1986
J. Hoika, Die Besiedlung des Oldenburger Grabens für Besiedlung und Verkehr im Neolithikum. Offa 43, 1986, 185-208.

Hoika 1987
J. Hoika, Das Mittelneolithikum zur Zeit der Trichterbecherkultur in Nordostholstein. Untersuchungen zu Archäologie und Landschaftsgeschichte mit einem Exkurs zu den Ausgrabungen am Flintholm im Bundsø auf Alsen (Neumünster 1987).

Holst et al. 2001
M.K. Holst/H. Breuning-Madsen/M. Rasmussen, The South Scandinavian barrows with well preserved oak-log coffins. Antiquity vol. 75, 2001, 126-136.

Hougaard Rasmussen 1989
G.Hougaard Rasmussen, Ballegård. Arkæologiske Udgravninger i Danmark 1988 (København 1989), Nr. 307.

Hubert 1971
F. Hubert, Neue Ausgrabungen im Michelsberger Erdwerk in Boitsfort (Belgien). Germania 49, 1971, 214-218.

INRAP 2009
Archéologie en Bourgogne.Cinquante-quatre sciècles d'occupation humaineau bord de l'Yonne, á Passy et á Véron (Yonne). Publications INRAP, 2009.

Jacomet 2007
St. Jacomet, Neolithic plant economies in the northern Alpine Foreland from 5500-3500 BC cal. In: S. Colledge/J. Conolly (eds.), The Origins and Spread of Domestic Plants in Southwest Asia and Europe (Walnut Creek 2007), 221-258.

Jacomet/Schlichterle 1984
St. Jacomet/H. Schlichterle, Der kleine Pfahlbauweizen Oswald Heer's – Neue Untersuchungen zur Morphologie neolithischer Nacktweizen-Ähren. In: W. van Zeist/W.A. Casparie (eds.), Plants and Ancient Man. Studies in palaeoethnobotany (Rotterdam/Boston 1984), 153-176.

Jacobsen 1984
J.A. Jacobsen, A Contribution to the Evaluation of Archaeological Field-Surveying. Journal of Danish Archaeology 3, 1984, 187-198.

Jantzen 2005
D. Jantzen, Töpferei und Feuerkult – Vom Leben auf der Anhöhe bei Triwalk, Lkr. Nordwestmecklenburg. In: Th. Terberger (Hrsg.), Die Autobahn A20 – Norddeutschlands längste Ausgrabung. Archäologische Forschungen auf der Trasse zwischen Lübeck und Stettin. Archäologie in Mecklenburg-Vorpommern 4 (Schwerin 2005), 33-36.

Jensen/Nikolaisen 1989
N.M. Jensen/E. Nikolaisen, Åsum Enggård. Arkæologiske Udgravninger I Danmark 1988 (København 1989), Nr. 136.

Jensen/Nikolaisen 1990
N.M. Jensen/E. Nikolaisen, NAU 88. De arkæologiske resultater. In: NAU 88. HARJA: Arkæologisk Forening, December 1990 (Odense), 7-27.

Jessen 1920
A. Jessen, Stenalderhavets udbredelse i det nordlige Jylland. Med 1 Kort og an English summary of the contents. Danmarks Geologiske Undersøgelse, II. Række, Hæfte 35 (København 1920).

Jeunesse 1989
Ch. Jeunesse, La Culture De Munzingen Dans Le Cadre Du «Jungneolithikum» Du Sud-Ouest De L'Europe Centrale D'Après Les Découvertes Recentes Des Sites Alsaciens De Didenheim (Haut-Rhin) Et Geispolsheim (Bas-Rhin). Cahiers de L'Association pour la Promotion de la Recherche Archéologique en Alsace 5, 1989, 155-184.

Jeunesse 1996
Ch. Jeunesse, Les enceintes á fossés interrompus du Néolithique danubien ancien et moyen et leurs relations avec le Néolithique récent. Archäologisches Korrespondenzblatt 26, 1996, 251-261.

Jeunesse 1998
Ch. Jeunesse, Pour une origine occidentale de la culture de Michelsberg? In J. Biel/H. Schlichterle/M. Strobel/A. Zeeb (Hrsg.), Die Michelsberger Kultur und ihre Randgebiete – Probleme der Entstehung, Chronologie und des Siedlungswesens. Kolloqium Hemmenhofen 21.-23.2. 1997. Materialhefte Zur Archäologie In Baden-Württemberg 43 (Stuttgart 1998), 29-45.

Jeunesse 2010
Ch. Jeunesse, Die Michelsberger Kultur. Eine Kultur ohne Friedhöhe. In: C. Lichter (ed.), Jungsteinzeit im Umbruch. Die "Michelsberger Kultur" und Mitteleuropa vor 6000 Jahren. Katalog zur Ausstellung im Badischen Landesmuseum Schloss Karlsruhe 20.11.2010 - 15.5.2011,90-95.

Jeunesse 2011
Ch. Jeunesse, Enceintes à fossé discontinu et enceintes à pseudo-fossé dans le néolithique d'Europe centrale et occidentale. In : A. Denaire/ Ch. Jeunesse/Ph. Lefranc (éd.), Nécropoles et enceintes danubiennes du Ve millénaire dans le Nord-est de la France et le Sud-Ouest de l'Allemagne. Actes de la table ronde internationale de Strasbourg organisée par l'UMR 7044 (CNRS et Université de Strasbourg). Maison Interuniversitaire des Sciences de l'Homme-Alsace (MISHA), 2 juin 2010 (Strasbourg 2011), 31-71.

Jeunesse/Lefranc 1999
Ch. Jeunesse/Ph. Lefranc, Rosheim « Saint-Odile » (Bas-Rhin), un habitat Rubané avec fossé d'enceinte – Première partie : les structures et la céramique. Cahiers de l'Association pour la Promotion de la Recherche Archéologique en Alsace 15, 1999, 1-111.

Jeunesse et al. 2004
Ch. Jeunesse/Ph. Lefranc/A. Denaire, Groupe de Bischheim, origine du Michelsberg, genèse du groupe d'Entzheim. La transition entre le Néolithique moyen et le Néolithique récent dans les régions rhénanes. Cahiers de l'Association pour la Promotion de la Recherche Archéologique en Alsace 18/19, 2002/2003 (Zimmersheim 2004).

Johannsen/Laursen 2010
N. Johannsen/S. Laursen, Routes and Wheeled Transport in Late 4th – Early 3rd Millennium Funerary Customs of the Jutland Peninsula: Regional Evidence and European Context. Prähistorische Zeitschrift 85, 2010, 16-58.

Johansen 2006
K.L. Johansen, Settlement and Land Use at the Mesolithic-Neolithic Transition in Southern Scandinavia. Journal of Danish Archaeology 14, 2006, 201-223.

Johansen et al. 2004
K.L. Johansen/S.T. Laursen/M.K. Holst, Spatial patterns of social organization in the Early Bronze Age of South Scandinavia. Journal of Anthropological Archaeology 23, 2004, 33-55.

Joussaume 1988
R. Joussaume, Analyse structurale de la triple enceinte de fosses interropus á Champ-Durand, Nieuil-sur-l-Autize, Vendée. In: C. Burgess/P. Topping/C. Mordant/M. Maddison (eds.), Enclosures and defences in the Neolithic of Western Europe vol. 2 (Oxford 1988), 275-299.

Jørgensen, E. 1983
E. Jørgensen, Høje og hegnet næs. Skalk 1983-5, 3-8.

Jørgensen 1993
E. Jørgensen, Jyske stendyngegrave. In: S. Hvass/B. Storgaard (eds.), Da klinger I Muld…25 års arkæologi i Danmark (København/Århus 1993), 112-113.

Jørgensen, E. 1995
E. Jørgensen, Abschnittseinhegung und Grabhügel bei Lønt. In: V. Arnold (Hrsg.), Wall und Graben. Befestigung von der Steinzeit bis ins Mittelalter in Schleswig und Holstein (Schleswig 1995), 7-13.

Jørgensen, E. 2000
E. Jørgensen, Yngre Stenalder. In: P. Ethelberg/E. Jørgensen/D. Meier/D. Robinson, Det Sønderjyske landbrugs Historie. Sten- og Bronzealder. Skrifter udgivet af Historisk samfund for Sønderjylland Nr. 81 (Haderslev 2000), 63-133.

Jørgensen, G. 1977
G. Jørgensen, Et kornfund fra Sarup. Bidrag til belysning af tragtbægerkulturens agerbrug. KUML 1976, 47-64.

Jørgensen, G. 1982
G. Jørgensen, Korn fra Sarup. Med nogle bemærkninger om agerbruget i yngre stenalder i Danmark. KUML 1981, 221-231.

Kadrow 2011
S. Kadrow, Confrontation or social strategies? Danubian fortified settlements and the Funnel Beaker monuments in SE Poland. In: M. Furholt/F. Lüth/J. Müller (eds.), Megaliths and Identities. Early Monuments and Neolithic Societies from the Atlantic to the Baltic (Bonn 2011), 185-198.

Kampffmeyer 1983
U. Kampffmeyer, Der neolithische Siedlungsplatz Hüde I am Dümmer. In: Frühe Bauernkulturen in Niedersachsen. Linienbandkeramik, Stichbandkeramik und Rössener Kultur (Oldenburg 1983), 119-134.

Kannegaard Nielsen 1989
E. Kannegaard Nielsen, Nederst. Arkæologiske Udgravninger i Danmark 1988, 144-146.

Kannegaard Nielsen 1991
E. Kannegaard Nielsen, Nederst. Arkæologiske Udgravninger i Danmark 1990 (København 1991), 145-146.

Kannegaard Nielsen/Brinch Petersen 1993
E. Kannegaard Nielsen/E. Brinch Petersen, Burials, people and dogs. In: St. Hvass/B. Storgaard (ed.), Digging into the Past. 25 Years Of Danish Archaeology (Århus 1993), 76-80.

Kanstrup et al. in press
M. Kanstrup/M.K. Holst/P.M. Jensen/I.K. Thomsen/B.T. Christensen, Searching for long-term trends in prehistoric manuring practice. $\Delta^{15}N$ analyses of charred cereal grains from the 4th to the 1st millennium BC. Journal of Archaeological Science, in press.

Kaul 1988
F. Kaul, Neolitiske gravanlæg på Onsved Mark, Horns Herred, Sjælland. Aarbøger 1987, 27-83.

Kaul et al. 2002
F. Kaul/F.O. Nielsen/P.O. Nielsen, Våsagård og Rispebjerg. To indhegnede bopladser fra yngre stenalder på Bornholm. Nationalmuseets Arbejdsmark 2002, 119-138.

Kellner-Depner 2011
C. Kellner-Depner, 389 Beinum Fst. 9, Gde. Stadt Salzgitter, Kfst., ehem. Teg.Bez. BS. Nachrichten aus Niedersachsens Urgeschichte Beiheft 14, 2011, 198.

Kerdivel 2009
G. Kerdivel, Occupation de l'espace et gestion des ressources à l'interface entre massifs primaires et bassins secondaires et tertiaires : l'exemple du Massif armoricain et des ses marges au Néolithique. PhD thesis, Université de Rennes 1 (Rennes 2009).

Kierleis/Fischer in press,
W. Kierleis/E. Fischer, Neolithic cultivation of tetraploid free threshing wheat in Denmark and Northern Germany: implications for crop diversity and societal dynamics of the Funnel Beaker Culture. Vegetation History and Archaeobotany, in press.

Kjærum 1955
P. Kjærum, Tempelhus fra Stenalder. Kuml 1955, 7-35.

Kjærum 1957
P. Kjærum, Storstensgrave ved Tustrup. Kuml 1957, 9-23.

Kjærum 1967
P. Kjærum, Mortuary Houses and Funeral Rites in Denmark. Antiquity 41, 1967, 190-196.

Klassen 1999
L. Klassen, The debate on the Mesolithic-Neolithic transition in the western Baltic: A central European perspective. Journal of Danish Archaeology 13, 1996-97,171-178.

Klassen 2000
L. Klassen, Frühes Kupfer im Norden. Untersuchungen zu Chronologie, Herkunft und Bedeutung der Kupferfunde der Nordgruppe der Trichterbecherkultur (Højbjerg 2000).

Klassen 2004
L. Klassen, Jade und Kupfer. Untersuchungen zum Neolithisierungsprozess im westlichen Ostseeraum unter besonderer Berücksichtigung der Kulturentwicklung Europas 5500-3500 BC. Jutland Archaeological Society Publications Vol. 47 (Højbjerg 2004).

Klassen in press
L. Klassen, Neolithisation and introduction of causewayed enclosures. Two structurally related processes. In: J. Thomas/M. Larsson/J. Debert (eds.), In Dialogue. Tradition and Interaction at the Mesolithic-Neolithic Transition, in press.

Klassen/Stürup 2001
L. Klassen/S. Stürup, Decoding the Riesebusch-copper: Lead-Isotope Analysis applied to Early Neolithic Copper Finds from South Scandinavia. Prähistorische Zeitschrift 76-1, 2001, 55-73.

Klassen et al. 2007
L. Klassen/P. Pétrequin/H. Grut, Haches plates en cuivre dansk le Jura français. Transferts à longue distance de biens socialement valorisés pendant les IVe et IIe millénaires. Bulletin de la Société Préhistorique Française 104, 2007, 101-124.

Klassen et al. 2011
L. Klassen/M. Dobeš/P. Pétrequin, Dreieckige Kupferflachbeile aus Mitteldeutschland und Böhmen. Zum kulturgeschichtlichen Hintergrund einer bemerkenswerten Fundgruppe. Alt-Thüringen 41, 2008/9 (2011), 7-35.

Klatt 2009
S. Klatt, Die neolithischen Einhegungen im westlichen Ostseeraum. Forschungsstand und Forschungsperspektiven. In: Th. Therberger (Hrsg.), Neue Forschungen zum Neolithikum im Ostseeraum. Archäologie und Geschichte im Ostseeraum 5 (Rahden 2009), 7-134.

Knoche 2003
B. Knoche, Das jungsteinzeitliche Erdwerk von Rimbeck bei Warburg, Kreis Höxter. Frühe Burgen in Westfalen 20 (Münster 2003).

Knoche 2008
B. Knoche, Die Erdwerke von Soest (Kreis Soest) und Nottuln-Uphoven (Kreis Coesfeld). Studien zum Jungneolithikum in Westfalen. Münstersche Beiträge zur Ur- und Frühgeschichte Band 3 (Münster 2008).

Knoche 2013
B. Knoche, Rite, Routen, Rinder – Das jungneolithische Erdwerk von Soest im Wegenetz eines extensiven Viehwirtschaftssystems. In: W. Melzer (ed.), Soester Beiträge zur Archäologie 13 (Soest 2013), 119-274.

Knudsen/Hertz 1993
S.A. Knudsen/E. Hertz, Bækbølling I. Arkæologiske Udgravninger i Danmark 1992, nr. 362.

Koch, E. 1998
E. Koch, Neolithic Bog Pots from Zealand, Møn, Lolland and Falster. Nordiske Fortidsminder Serie B Volume 16 (København 1998).

Koch, R. 1971
R. Koch, Zwei Erdwerke der Michelsberger Kultur aus dem Kreis Heilbronn. Fundberichte aus Schwaben N.F. 19, 1971, 51-67.

Koch, R. 2005
R. Koch, Das Erdwerk der Michelsberger Kultur auf dem Hetzenberg bei Heilbronn-Neckargartach. Teil I – Funde und Befunde. Forschungen und Berichte zur Vor- und Frühgeschichte in Baden-Württemberg band 3,I (Stuttgart 2005).

Kowalcyk 1957
J. Kowalcyk, Sprawodzdanie z badán osady kultury pucharów lejkowatych w Gródku Nadbużnym, pow. Hrubieszów. Wiadomości Archeologicne 24, 1957, 300-306.

Kowalewska-Marszałek 1990
H. Kowalewska-Marszałek, Sandomierz – Wzgorze Zawichojskie. Beispiel einer neolithischen befestigten Anlage in Südostpolen. Jahrbuch für Mitteldeutsche Vorgeschichte 73, 1990, 237-248.

Kowalewska-Marszałek 2007
H. Kowalewska-Marszałek, The „Lengyel-Polgár" settlement in the Sandomierz Upland. Micro-Regional Studies. In: J.K. Kozłowski/P. Raczky (eds.), The Lengyel-Polgár and related cultures in the middle/late Neolithic in Central Europe (Kraków 2007), 431-448.

Kristensen 1989
I.K. Kristensen, Storgård IV. An early Neolithic Long barrow near Fjelsø, North Jutland. Journal of Danish Archaeology 8, 1989, 72-87.

Kristensen 2009
I.K. Kristensen, Kogegruber – i klynge eller på rad og række. Kuml 2008, 9-56.

Krzak 1963
Z. Krzak, Report on the excavations on the Hill Ga-wroniec-Palya at Cmielów, District of Opatów, in 1961. Sprawodzdania Archeologicne 15, 1963, 65-83.

Kühn 1989
H.J. Kühn, Esesfeld. In: Reallexikon zur Germanischen Altertumskunde Bd. 7 (Berlin 1989), 567-571.

Laporte et al. 2007
L. Laporte/ J.-N. Guyodo/C. Bizien-Jaglin/V. Bernard/F. Bertin/S. Blanchet/M.-F. Dietsch-Sellami/V. Guitton/A.-L. Hamon/G. Hamon/Q. Lemouland/A. Lucquin/A. Noslier/L. Quesnel, Nouvelles découvertes en milieu humide autour de l'habitat ceinturé du Néolithique moyen à Lillemer (Ille-et-Vilaine, France). In: M. Besse (dir.), Sociétés néolithiques. Des faits archéologiques aux fonctionnements socio-économiques. Actes du 27e colloque interrégional sur le Néolithique (Neuchâtel, 1 et 2 octobre 2005). Cahiers d'archéologie romande 108 (Lausanne 2007), 341-349.

Larsson, L. 1982
L. Larsson, A causewayed enclosure and a site with Valby pottery at Stävie, Western Scania. Meddelanden från Lunds Universitets Historiska Museet 4, 1982, 65-114.

Larsson, L. 1989
L. Larsson, Brandoffer. Der frühneolithische Fundplatz Svartskylle im südlichen Schonen, Schweden. Acta Archaeologica 59, 143-153.

Larsson, L. 2012
L. Larsson, Mid Neolithic Enclosures in Southern Scandinavia. In: A. Gibson (ed.), Enclosing the Neolithic. Recent studies in Britain and Europe. BAR International Series 2440 (Oxford 2012), 109-123.

Larsson, M. 1984
M. Larsson, Tidigneolitikum I Sydvästskåne. Kronologi och bosätningsmönster. Acta Arch. Lundensia Series in 4 N 17 (Bonn/Lund 1984).

Laux 2000
F. Laux, Die Äxte und Beile in Niedersachsen I (Flach-, Randleisten- und Absatzbeile). Prähistorische Bronze-funde Abt. IX Band 23 (Stuttgart 2000).

Le Bolloch 1984
M. Le Bolloch, La Culture de Michelsberg dans la Vallée de l'Aisne. Revue Archéologique de Picardie No. 1-2, 1984, 133-145.

Lehmann 1992
B. Lehmann, Zaisenhausen (Ldkr. Karlsruhe). Fundbe-richte aus Baden-Württemberg 17/2, 1992, 34-35.

Lehmphul 2009
R. Lehmphul, Grab-Gruben-Grabenwerk. Ein mehrperi-odiger Fundplatz bei Rathsdorf, Lkr. Märkisch-Oderland. Archäologie in Berlin und Brandenburg 2008, 40-43.

Letterlé et al. 1990
F. Letterlé/D. Le Gouestre/N. Le Meur, Le site d'habitat ceinturée du Néolithique moyen armoricain de Sandun à Guérande (Loire-Atlantique). Essai d'analyse des structures. In : D. Cahen M. Otte (eds.), Rubané et car-dial. ERAUL 39 (Liège 1990), 299-313.

Linke 1989
F.-A. Linke, Ein neues neolithisches Erdwerk im Land-kreis Hildesheim. Berichte zur Denkmalpflege in Nie-dersachsen 9-3, 1989, 157-159).

Liversage 1992
D. Liversage, Barkær. Long Barrows and Settlements. Arkæologiske Studier IX (København 1992).

Lodewijckx et al. 2005
M. Lodewijckx/B. Vanmomtfort/R. Pelegrin, Een mid-denneolithisch aardwerk op de Hermansheuvel te Assent (Vlaams-Brabant). Notae Praehistoricae 25, 2005, 175-177.

Lornsen 1987
D. Lornsen, Ein karolingischer Stützpunkt im Norden. Archäologie in Deutschland 1987-1, 36-39.

Lübke 1999
H. Lübke, Die dicken Flintspitzen aus Schleswig-Hol-stein. Ein Beitrag zu Typologie und Chronologie eines Großgerätetyps der Trichterbecherkultur. Offa 54/55, 1997/98, 49-95.

Lück et al. 1999
E. Lück/M. Eisenreich/G. Wetzel, Geophysikalische Erkundung der Grabenanlage von Dyrotz, Landkreis Havelland. Archäologie in Berlin und Brandenburg 1998 (1999), 25-28.

Lütjens/Wiethold 1999
I. Lütjens/J. Wiethold, Vegetationsgeschichtliche und archäologische Untersuchungen zur Besiedlung des Bornhöveder Seengebietes und seines Umfeldes im Neolithikum. Archäologische Nachrichten aus Schleswig-Holstein 9/10, 1998/1999, 30-67.

Lützau Pedersen 2010
S. Lützau Pedersen, Skår af en helhed...In: H. Lyngstrøm (ed.), Brudstykker af en helhed. Specialer i forhistorisk arkæologi 2008 og 2009 fra Københavns Universitet (København 2010), 41-51.

Lützau Pedersen/Witte 2012
S. Lützau Pedersen/F. Witte, Langelandsvej i Starup – en ceremoniel samlingsplads fra bondestenalderen. In: S.Å. Karup/L.S. Madsen/B.V. Rønne (eds.), Langs Fjord og dam. Lokalhistorie omkring Haderslev (Haderslev 2012), 77-88.

Madsen, A.P. 1888
A.P. Madsen, Undersøgelse af Kjøkkenmøddingen ved Mejlgaard i 1888. Aarbøger for Nordisk Oldkyndighed og Historie 1888, 299-309.

Madsen, B. 1984
B. Madsen, Flint Axe Manufacture in the Neolithic: Experiments with Grinding and Polishing Thin-Butted Flint Axes. Journal of Danish Archaeology 3, 1984, 47-62.

Madsen, B./Nielsen 1977
B. Madsen/P.O. Nielsen, To tidlig-neolitiske jordgrave. Antikvariske Studier 1, 1977, 27-34.

Madsen, B./Fiedel 1988
B. Madsen/R. Fiedel, Pottery manufacture at a Neolithic Causewayed Enclosure near Hevringholm. Journal of Danish Archaeology 6, 1987, 78-86.

Madsen, M. 2010
M. Madsen, Tidligneolitikum på Sjælland – afgrænsningen af den første agrare bebyggelse. In: H. Lyngstrøm (ed.), Brudstykker af en helhed. Specialer i forhistorisk arkæologi 2008 og 2009 fra Københavns Universitet (København 2010), 9-18.

Madsen, T. 1975
T. Madsen, Tidlig neolitiske anlæg ved Tolstrup. KUML 1973/74, 121-154.

Madsen, T. 1978a
T. Madsen, Toftum ved Horsens, et befæstet anlæg tilhørende tragtbægerkulturen. Kuml 1977, 161-184.

Madsen, T. 1978b
T. Madsen, Toftum – Ein neues neolithisches Erdwerk bei Horsens, Ostjütland (Dänemark). Archäologisches Korrespondenzblatt 8, 1978, 1-7.

Madsen, T. 1979
T. Madsen, Earthen Long barrows and Timber Structures: Aspects of the Early Neolithic Mortuary Practice in Denmark. Proceedings of the Prehistoric Society 45, 1979, 301-320.

Madsen, T. 1982
T. Madsen, Settlement Systems of Early Agricultural Societies in east Jutland, Denmark. A Regional Study of Change. Journal of Anthropological Archaeology 1982-1, 197-236.

Madsen, T. 1988
T. Madsen, Causewayed Enclosures in South Scandinavia. In.: C. Burgess/P. Topping/C. Mordant/M. Maddison (eds.), Enclosures and defences in the Neolithic of Western Europe vol. 2 (Oxford 1988), 301-336.

Madsen, T. 1990
T. Madsen, Changing patterns of land use in the TRB culture of South Scandinavia. In: D. Jankowska (ed.), Die Trichterbecherkultur. Neue Forschungen und Hypothesen, Teil I (Poznań 1990), 27-41.

Madsen, T. 2009
T. Madsen, Aalstrup – en boplads og systemgravsanlæg ved Horsens Fjord. In: A. Schülke (red.), Plads og rum i tragtbægerkulturen. Bidrag fra Arbejdsmødet på Nationalmuseet, 22. september 2005. Nordiske Fortidsminder Serie C Bind 6 (København 2009), 105-138.

Madsen, T. unpubl.
T. Madsen, Systemgravsanlæg fra yngre stenalder ved Horsens Fjord. Unpublished manuscript.

Madsen, T./Jensen 1982
T. Madsen/H.J. Jensen, Settlement and land use in Early Neolithic Denmark. Analecta Praehistorica Leidensia 15, 1982, 64-86.

Madsen, T./Petersen 1984
T. Madsen/J.E. Petersen, Tidligneolitiske Anlæg Ved Mosegården. Regionale og kronologiske forskelle i tidligneolitikum. Kuml 1982-83, 61-120.

Mahnkopf 2004
G. Mahnkopf, Ein Erdwerk der Münchshöfener Kultur in Langenreichen. Das Archäologische Jahr in Bayern 2004, 25-27.

Maier 1996
U. Maier, Morphological studies of free-threshing wheat ears from a Neolithic site in southwest Germany, and the history of the naked wheats. Vegetation History and Archaeobotany 5, 1996, 39-55.

Maier 1998
U. Maier, Der Nacktweizen aus den neolithischen Ufersiedlungen des nördlichen Alpenvorlandes und seine Bedeutung für unser Bild von der Neolithisierung Mitteleuropas. Archäologisches Korrespondenzblatt 28, 1998, 205-218.

Mainberger 1988
M. Mainberger, Das Moordorf von Reute. Archäologische Untersuchungen in der jungneolithischen Siedlung Reute-Schorrenried (Staufen 1998).

Malmer 2002
M.P. Malmer, The Neolithic of South Sweden. TRB, GRK, and STR (Stockholm 2002).

Manceau 2011
L. Manceau, La céramique Néolithique moyen II de l'enceinte de Lauwin-Planque (Nord): approche technologique et morphologique. In: F. Bostyn/E. Martial/I. Praud (eds.), Le Néolithique du nord de la France dans son contexte européen. Habitat et économie aux 4e et 3e millénaires avant notre ère. Actes du 29e Colloque interrégional sur le Néolithique, Villeneuve d'Ascq, 2-3 octobre 2009. Revue Archéologique de Picardie, No spécial 28, 2011, 421-436.

Martens/Nielsen 1996
J. Martens/P.O. Nielsen, Sigersted III. Arkæologiske Udgravninger i Danmark 1995, Nr. 82.

Martinez 1982

R. Martinez, L'enceinte néolithique du "Cul Froid" à Boury-en-Vexin (Oise). Premièrs résultats. Revue archéologique de Picardie, 1-2, 1982, 3-6.

Martinez/Blanchet 1988

R. Martinez/J.-C- Blanchet, Les Chamos néolithiques chasséennes dans le Nord-Ouest du Bassin parisien. In: C. Burgess/P. Topping/C. Mordant/M. Maddison (eds.), Enclosures and defences in the Neolithic of Western Europe vol. 1 (Oxford 1988), 149-165.

Mathiassen et al. 1942

Th. Mathiassen/M. Degerbøl/J. Troels-Smith, Dyrholmen. En Stenalder Boplads Paa Djursland (København 1942).

Mathiassen 1944

Th. Mathiassen, The Stone-Age Settlement at Trelleborg. Acta Archaeologica 15, 1944, 77-98.

Matuschik 1991

I. Matuschik, Grabenwerke des Spätneolithikums in Süddeutschland. Fundberichte aus Baden-Württemberg 16, 1991, 27-55.

Matuschik 1998

I. Matuschik, Kupferfunde und Metallurgie-Belege, zugleich ein Beitrag zur Geschichte der kupferzeitlichen Dolche Mittel-, Ost- und Südosteuropas. In: Mainberger 1988, 207-261.

Matuschik 2010

I. Matuschik, Michelsberg am Bodensee. In: C. Lichter (ed.), Jungsteinzeit im Umbruch. Die "Michelsberger Kultur" und Mitteleuropa vor 6000 Jahren. Katalog zur Ausstellung im Badischen Landesmuseum Schloss Karlsruhe 20.11.2010 – 15.5.2011, 116-120.

McLaren 2000

F.S. McLaren, Revising the wheat crops of Neolithic Britain. In: A.S. Fairbairn (ed.), Plants in Neolithic Britain and beyond. Neolithic Studies Group Seminar Papers 5 (Oxford 2000), 91-100.

Meixner 2001

D. Meixner, Das Erdwerk der jüngeren Münchshöfener Kultur von Bergheim, Landkreis Neuburg-Schrobenhausen, Oberbayern. Das archäologische Jahr in Bayern 2001, 20-22.

Meller/Schunke 2013

H. Meller/T. Schunke, Die Ahnen schützen den heiligen Ort – Belege für Kopf- und Schädelkult in Salzmünde. In: H. Meller (ed.) 3300 BC. Mysteriöse Steinzeittote und ihre Welt (Halle/Saale 2013), 349-361.

Mertz 1924

E.L. Mertz, Oversigt over sen- og postglaciale Niveauforandringer i Danmark. Danmarks Geologiske Undersøgelse, II. Række Hæfte 41 (København 1924).

Meyer/Raetzel-Fabian 2006

M. Meyer/D. Raetzel-Fabian, Neolithishe Grabenwerke in Mitteleuropa. Ein Überblick. Journal of Neolithic Archaeology 2006 (online publication).

Midgley 2008

M. Midgley, The Megaliths of Northern Europe (London/New York 2008).

Mikkelsen 1989

M. Mikkelsen, Kappelhage. Arkæologiske Udgravninger i Danmark 1988 (København 1989), nr. 164.

Mischka 2011

D. Mischka, The Neolithic burial sequence at Flintbek LA 3, north Germany, and its cart tracks: a precise chronology. Antiquity 85, 2011, 742-758.

Monchablon et al. 2011

C. Monchablon/M. Baillieu/M. Bouchet/A. Goutelard/I. Praud, L'enceinte néolithique moyen II de Carvin « La Gare D'Eau » (Pas-de-Calais). Présentation préliminaire. In: F. Bostyn/E. Martial/I. Praud (eds.), Le Néolithique du nord de la France dans son contexte européen. Habitat et économie aux 4ᵉ et 3ᵉ millénaires avant notre ère. Actes du 29ᵉ Colloque interrégional sur le Néolithique, Villeneuve d'Ascq, 2-3 octobre 2009. Revue Archéologique de Picardie, No spécial 28, 2011, 407-419.

Mordant 1997

D. Mordant, Le complexe des Réaudins à Balloy : enceinte et nécropole monumentale. In : C. Constantin/D. Mordant/D. Simonin (éd.), La culture de Cerny. Nouvelle économie, nouvelle société au Néolithique. Actes du colloque international de Nemours, 9-11 mai 1994 (Nemours 1997), 449-479.

Mordant/Mordant 1988

C. Mordant/D. Mordant, Les Enceintes Néolithiques de la Haute-Vallée de la Seine. In: C. Burgess/P. Topping/C. Mordant/M. Maddison (eds.), Enclosures and defences in the Neolithic of Western Europe vol. 1 (Oxford 1988), 231-254.

Müller, D.W. 1988

D.W. Müller, Kupferführende Kulturen im Neolithikum der DDR. Congresso Internazionale L'Età Del Rame In Europa, Viareggio 1987. Rassegna Di Archeologia 7, 1988, 157-174.

Müller, J. 2001

J. Müller. Soziochronologische Studien zum Jung- und Spätneolithikum im Mittelelbe-Saale-Gebiet (4100-2700 v.Chr.). Vorgeschichtliche Forschungen band 21 (Rahden/Westd. 2001).

Müller, J. 2010

J. Müller, Dorfanlagen und Siedlungssysteme. Die europäische Perspektive: Südosteuropa und Mitteleuropa. In: C. Lichter (ed.), Jungsteinzeit im Umbruch. Die

"Michelsberger Kultur" und Mitteleuropa vor 6000 Jahren. Katalog zur Ausstellung im Badischen Landesmuseum Schloss Karlsruhe 20.11.2010 – 15.5.2011, 250-257.

Müller, J. 2011
J. Müller, Megaliths And Funnel Beakers. Societies In Change 4100-2700 BC (Amsterdam 2011).

Müller, J./Staude 2012
J. Müller/K. Staude, Typologien, Vertikalstratigraphien und absolutchronologische Daten: Zur Chronologie des nordwestmecklenburgischen Trichterbecherfundplatzes Triwalk. In: Hinz/Müller 2012, 35-59.

Müller, S. 1897
S. Müller, Vor Oldtid (København 1897).

Müller, S. 1904
S. Müller, Vej og Bygd I Sten- og Bronzealderen. Aarbøger for Nordisk Oldkyndighed og Historie 1904, 1-64.

Neergaard 1900
C. Neergaard, Affaldsdyngen ved Ørum Aa. In: Madsen, A.P./Müller, S./Neergaard, C./Petersen, C.G.J./Rostrup, E, Steenstrup, K.J.V/Winge, H., Affaldsdynger Fra Stenalderen I Danmark Undersøgte For Nationalmuseet (Paris/Kjøbenhavn/Leipzig 1900), 135-144.

Nielsen, H. 1988
H. Nielsen, An early Neolithic Pottery Deposition at Ellerødgård I, Southern Zealand. Journal of Danish Archaeology 6, 1987, 63-77.

Nielsen, J./Bech 1989
J. Nielsen/J.H. Bech, Vilsund. Arkæologiske Udgravninger i Danmark 1988, nr. 165.

Nielsen, P.O. 1977
P.O. Nielsen, Die Flintbeile Der Frühen Trichterbecherkultur In Dänemark. Acta Archaeologica 48, 1977, 61-138.

Nielsen, P.O. 1985
P.O. Nielsen, De første bønder. Nye fund fra den tidligste Tragtbægerkultur ved Sigersted. Aarbøger 1984, 96-126.

Nielsen, P.O. 1993
P.O. Nielsen, Bosættelsen. In: St. Hvass & B. Storgaard (eds.), Da Klinger I Muld… 25 års arkæologi i Danmark (Københvan/Århus 1993), 92-95.

Nielsen, P.O. 1998
P.O. Nielsen, Sigersted III. Arkæologiske Udgravninger I Danmark 1997, nr. 121.

Nielsen, P.O. 1999
P.O. Nielsen, Sigersted III. Arkæologiske Udgravninger i Danmark 1998, nr. 144.

Nielsen, P.O. 2000
P.O. Nielsen, Sigersted III. Arkæologiske Udgravninger I Danmark 1999, nr. 129.

Nielsen, P.O. 2004
P.O. Nielsen, Causewayed Camps, palisade enclosures and central settlements of the Middle Neolithic in Denmark. Jonas 14, 2004, 19-33.

Nielsen, S. 1999
S. Nielsen, The Domestic Mode of Production and Beyond. An archaeological inquiry into urban trends in Denmark, Iceland and Predynastic Egypt. Nordiske Fortidsminder Serie B Volume 18 (København 1999).

Nilsson/Nilsson 2003
M.-L. Nilsson/L. Nilsson, Et källspring i Saxtorp. In: M. Svensson (ed.), I det Neolitiska rummet. Skånska spår – arkeologi längs Västkustbanan (Lund 2003), 242-295.

Nobis 1983
G. Nobis, Wild- und Haustierknochen des Fundplatzes Siggeneben-Süd. In: J. Meurers-Balke, Siggeneben-Süd. Ein Fundplatz der frühen Trichterbecherkultur an der holsteinischen Ostseeküste. Offa Bücher Band 50 (Neumünster 1983), 115-118.

Noe-Nygaard 1995
N. Noe-Nygaard, Ecological, sedimentary, and geochemical evolution of the late-glacial to postglacial Åmose lacustrine basin, Denmark. Fossils & Strata 37, 1995, 1-436.

Noe-Nygaard et al. 2005
N. Noe-Nygaard/T.D. Price/S.U. Hede, Diet of aurochs and early cattle in southern Scandinavia: evidence from ^{15}N and ^{13}C stable isotopes. Journal of Archaeological Science 32, 2005, 855-871.

Nösler et al. 2011
D. Nösler/A. Kramer/H. Jöns/K. Gerken/F. Bittmann, Aktuelle Forschungen zur Besiedlung und Landnutzung zur Zeit der Trichterbecher- und Einzelgrabkultur in Nordwestdeutschland – ein Vorbericht zum DFG-SPP „Monumentalität". Nachrichten aus Niedersachsens Urgeschichte 80, 2011, 23-45.

Odgaard 1985
B.V. Odgaard, Kulturlandskabets historie i Vestjylland. Foreløbige resultater af nye pollenanalytiske undersøgelser. Antikvariske Studier 7, 48-59.

Odgaard 1986
B.V. Odgaard, Enkeltgravskulturens miljø i Vestjylland belyst gennem pollendiagrammer. In: Ch. Adamsen/K. Ebbesen (red.), Stridsøksetid i Sydskandinavien. Arkæologiske Skrifter 1 (København 1986), 194-195.

Odgaard/Rostholm 1988
B.V. Odgaard/H. Rostholm, A Single Grave Barrow at Harreskov, Jutland. Excavation and Pollen Analysis of a Fossil Soil. Journal of Danish Archaeology 6, 1987, 87-100.

Ödman 2002
    A. Ödman, Borgeby – Mer Än 1000 År. Del 1, Borgebys Historia (2002).

Olesen 1994
    L.H. Olesen, Når man ser det hele lidt fra oven – arkæologi fra luften. Holstebro Museums Årsskrift 1993, 19-34.

Olsen/Schmidt 1977
    O. Olsen/H. Schmidt, Fyrkat. En jysk vikingeborg. I. Borgen og Bebyggelsen. Nordiske Fortidsminder Serie B Bind 3 (København 1977).

Oswald et al. 2001
    A. Oswald/C. Dyer/M. Barber, The creation of monuments. Neolithic causewayed enclosures in the British Isles (London 2001).

Panloups/Praud 2011
    E. Panloups/Y. Praud, L'éperon barré du Néolithique moyen II: Premiers résultats de la fouille du Mont d'Hubert á escalles (Pas-de-Calais). In: Journées archéologiques de la Région Nord-Pas-de-Calais, 13 et 14 octobre 2011, Arras. Résumés des Communications, 19-20.

Parker Pearson 2012
    M. Parker Pearson, Stonehenge : exploring the greatest Stone Age mystery (London 2012).

Petrasch 1986
    J. Petrasch, Das Altheimer Erdwerk bei Alkofen, Ge. Bad Abbach, Lkr. Kehlheim. Berichte der Bayerischen Bodendenkmalpflege 26/27, 1986, 33-80.

Petrasch 1990
    J. Petrasch, Mittelneolithische Kreisgrabenanlagen in Mitteleuropa. Berichte der Römisch-Germanischen Kommission 71, 1990-1, 407-564.

Pleslová-Štiková 1985
    E. Pleslová-Štiková, Makotřasy: A TRB site in Bohemia. Fontes Arch. Pragenses Vol. 17 (Pragae 1985).

Podborský et al. 1993
    V. Podborský et al., Praveké Dejiny Moravy. Vlastivedna Moravské Zem A Lid, Nováda Svazek 3 (Brno 1993).

Raetzel-Fabian 1988
    D. Raetzel-Fabian, Die ersten Bauern. Jungsteinzeit in Nordhessen. Vor- und Frühgeschichte im Hessischen Landesmuseum in Kassel 2 (Kassel 1988).

Raetzel-Fabian 1999
    D. Raetzel-Fabian, Der umhegte Raum – Funktionale Aspekte jungneolithischer Monumental-Erdwerke. Jahresschrift für Mitteldeutsche Vorgeschichte 81, 1999, 87-117.

Raetzel-Fabian 2000
    D. Raetzel-Fabian, Calden. Erdwerk und Bestattungsplätze des Jungneolithikums. Architektur – Ritual – Chronologie. Universitätsforschungen zur Prähistorischen Archäologie 70 (Bonn 2000).

Raetzel-Fabian 2002
    D. Raetzel-Fabian, Monumentality and Communication. Neolithic Enclosures and Long Distance Tracks in West Central Europe. www.jungsteinsite.de, article from January 5th, 2002.

Raetzel-Fabian 2003
    D. Raetzel-Fabian, Eine neue Parallele zu den Einbauten im spätmichelsbergzeitlichen Erdwerk von Calden, Kreis Kassel www.jungsteinsite.de, article from July 15th, 2003.

Rakovsky 1990
    I. Rakovsky, Zur Problematik der äneolithischen Höhensiedlungen in Mähren. Jahresschrift für mitteldeutsche Vorgeschichte 73, 1990, 149-157.

Ramminger 2012
    B. Ramminger, Mahlstein auf Grabensohle. Archäologie in Deutschland 2012-2, 50.

Rassmann 2011
    C. Rassmann, Identities overseas? The long barrows in Denmark and Britain. In: M. Furholt/F. Lüth/J. Müller (eds.), Megaliths and Identities. Early Monuments and Neolithic Societies from the Atlantic to the Baltic (Bonn 2011), 167-176.

Rasmussen/Skousen 2012
    U. Rasmussen/H. Skousen, Rituals at Springs during the Early Neolithic in Scandinavia. Non-monumental behaviour in a Time of Megalith Tombs and Causewayed Enclosures. In: M. Furholt/M. Hinz/D. Mischla (eds.), "As Time Goes By?" Monumentality, Landscapes and the Temporal Perspective. Universitätsforschungen zur Prähistorischen Archäologie Band 206 (Bonn 212), 145-158.

Ravn 2005
    M. Ravn, Fjordbønder. Skalk 2005-2, 5-12.

Ravn 2011
    M.Ravn, The early Neolithic Volling site of Kildevang – its chronology and intra-spatial organisation. Berichte der Römisch-Germanischen Kommission 89, 2008, 135-163.

Reiter 2005
    S. Reiter, Die beiden Michelsberger Anlagen von Bruchsal „Aue" und „Scheelkopf": Zwei ungleiche Nachbarn. Materialhefte zur Archäologie in Baden-Württemberg Heft 65 (Stuttgart 2005).

Remmel 2002
    H. Remmel, Ein Sperr-Riegel in der Lewitzwanne. Sensationelle Entdeckung von Erdwerken der Jungsteinzeit bei Plate. Mecklenburg-Magazin 48, 2002, 21.

Renfrew 1973
    C. Renfrew, Monuments, Mobilisation and Social Organisation in Neolithic Wessex. In: C. Renfrew (ed.), The Explanation of Cultural Change: models in prehistory (London 1973), 539-558.

Richter, J. 1987a
J. Richter, Brown Bear (Ursus arctos) from Kainsbakke, East Jutland. Journal of Danish Archaeology 5, 1986, 125-134.

Richter, J. 1987b
J. Richter, Evidence for the natural deposition of fish in the middle neolithic site, Kainsbakke, Djursland. Journal of Danish Archaeology 5, 1986, 116-124.

Richter, J. 1989
J. Richter, Animal husbandry in a Danish pitted ware culture site. In: E. Iregren/R. Liljekvist (red.), Fauna-historiska studier tillägnade Johannes Lepiksaar (Lund 1989), 43-56.

Richter, P.B. 2002
P.B. Richter, Das neolithische Erdwerk von Walmstorf, Ldkr. Uelzen. Studien zur Besiedlungsgeschichte der Trichterbecherkultur im Ilmenautal. Veröffentlichungen der urgeschichtlichen Sammlungen des Landesmuseums zu Hannover Band 49 (Oldenburg 2002).

Rinne/Müller 2012
C. Rinne/J. Müller, Grabenwerk und Großsteingräber in einer Grenzregion. Erste Ergebnisse des Projektes Haldensleben-Hundisburg. In: Hinz/Müller 2012, 347-375.

Rosenberg 2006
A. Rosenberg, Ullerødgård. Bygherrerapport NFHA2424 (Hillerød 2006).

Rudebeck 2002
E. Rudebeck, Vägen som rituell arena. In: K. Jennbert/A. Andrén/C.Raudvere (eds.), Plats och praxis. Studier av nordisk förkristen ritual. Vägar till Midgård 2 (Lund 2002), 167-200.

Rück 2012
O. Rück, Die baalbergezeitliche Kreisgrabenanlage Belleben I (Salzlandkreis, Sachsen-Anhalt). Die Ausgrabungen 2009 bis 2011 – Vorbericht und erste Ergebnisse. In: Hinz/Müller 2012, 389-409.

Sahlström 1935
K.E. Sahlström, Väglederna inom den västgötska gångriftsbygden. Västergötlands Fornminnesförenings Tidskrift 4, 9, 1935.

Scarre 2001
C. Scarre, Enclosures and related structures in Brittany and western France. In: T. Darvill/J. Thomas (eds.), Neolithic Enclosures in Atlantic North-West Europe (oxford 2001), 24-42.

Schack Pedersen/Strand Petersen 1997
St.A. Schack Pedersen/K. Strand Petersen, Djurslands Geologi (København 1997).

Schamuhn/Meurers-Balke 2008
S. Schamuhn/J. Meurers-Balke, Verkohlte Früchte aus dem Michelsberger Grabenwerk in der Soester Altstadt. In: Knoche 2008, 255-258.

Schibler 2010
J. Schibler, Crisis? What crisis? Die Nahrungskrise im 37. Jahrhundert und ihre Bewältigung. In: C. Lichter (ed.), Jungsteinzeit im Umbruch. Die "Michelsberger Kultur" und Mitteleuropa vor 6000 Jahren. Katalog zur Ausstellung im Badischen Landesmuseum Schloss Karlsruhe 20.11.2010 – 15.5.2011, 173-178.

Schier 1993
W. Schier, Das westliche Mitteleuropa an der Wende vom 5. zum 4. Jahrtausend: Kulturwandel durch Kulturkontakt? In: A. Lang/H. Parzinger/H. Küster (Hrsg.), Kulturen zwischen Ost und West. Festschrift G. Kossack (Berlin 1993), 19-60.

Schierhold et al. 2012
K. Schierhold/R. Gleser/M. Baales, Zur Genese und Struktur der hessisch-westfälischen Megalithik. In: Hinz/Müller 2012, 411-429.

Schlicht 1962
E. Schlicht, Von alten Verkehrswegen: die Hünengräberstraße des Hümmlings. Jahrbuch des Emsländischen Heimatvereins 9, 1962, 74-85.

Schlicht 1968
E. Schlicht, Die Funde aus dem Megalithgrab 2 von Emmeln, Kreis Meppen. Studien zur Keramik der Trichterbecherkultur im Gebiet zwischen Weser und Zuidersee. Göttinger Schriften zur Vor- und Frühgeschichte 9 (Neumünster 1968).

Schlichterle 1998
H. Schlichterle, Was macht Michelsberg in den Ufersiedlungen des Bodensees? In: J. Biel/H. Schlichterle/A. Zeeb (Hrsg.), Die Michelsberger Kultur und ihre Randgebiete. Probleme der Entstehung, Chronologie und des Siedlungswesens. Kolloquium Hemmenhofen 21.-23. Februar 1997. Materialhefte zur Archäologie Baden-Württembergs 43 (Stuttgart 1998),169-175.

Schlichterle/Rottländer 1982
H. Schlichterle/R. Rottländer, Gußtiegel der Pfyner Kultur in Südwestdeutschland. Fundberichte aus Baden-Württemberg 7, 1982, 59-71.

Schou Jørgensen 1977
M. Schou Jørgensen, Risby-vejene.Veje over Risby Å fra stenalder til Vikingetid. Nationalmuseets Arbejdsmark 1977, 42-51.

Schreurs 2005
J. Schreurs, Het Midden-Neolithicum In Zuid-Nederland. In: J. Deeben/E. Drenth/A.-F van Oorsouw/L. Verhart (eds.), De Steentijd Van Nederland. Tweede druk. Archeologie 11/12, 301-332.

Schreurs/Brounen 1998
J. Schreurs & F. Brounen, Resten van én Michelsberg aardwerk op de Schelsberg te Heerleen. Een voorlopig bericht. Archeologie in Limburg 76, 1998, 21-32.

Schubert 1981
E. Schubert, Zur Frage der Arsenlegierungen in der Kupfer- und Frühbronzezeit Südosteuropas. In: H. Lorenz (Hrsg.), Studien zur Bronzezeit. Festschrift W.A. von Brunn (Mainz 1981), 447-459.

Schülke 2009
A. Schülke, Tragtbægerkulturens landskabsrum: udtryk og ramme for social kommunikation. Et studie over Nordvestsjælland. In: A. Schülke (red.), Plads og rum i tragtbægerkulturen. Bidrag fra Arbejdsmødet på Nationalmuseet, 22. september 2005. Nordiske Fortidsminder Serie C Bind 6 (København 2009), 67-87.

Schwarz 2003
R. Schwarz, Pilotstudien. Zwölf Jahre Luftbildarchäologie in Sachsen-Anhalt (Halle 2003).

Sehested 1884
N.F.B. Sehested, Nogle Meddelelser om Kjøkkenmøddingen ved Mejlgaard (København 1884).

Seidel 2008
U. Seidel, Die Michelsberger Erdwerke im Raum Heilbronn, Band 1. Materialhefte Zur Archäologie Baden-Württembergs 81/1 (Stuttgart 2008).

Seidel 2009
U. Seidel, Die jungneolithische Abschnittsbefestigung von Leonberg "Silberberg", Kr. Böblingen. Fundberichte aus Baden-Württemberg 30, 2009, 29-63.

Seidel 2010
U. Seidel, Lehmbrüste, Tierbestattungen und Tonäxte – Kein „Kultareal" im Michelsberger Erdwerk von Heilbronn-Klingenberg. In: I. Matuschik/Ch. Strahm (Hrsg.), Vernetzungen. Festschrift für Helmut Schlichterle (Freiburg 2010), 165-178.

Sheridan 2010
A. Sheridan, The Neolithisation of Britain and Ireland: the Big Picture. In: B. Finlayson G. Warren (ed.), Landscapes in Transition (Oxford 2010), 89-105.

Siegmund 1993
F. Siegmund, Das jungneolithische Erdwerk am Northeimer Kiessee. Ein Vorbericht über die Ausgrabung 1992. Nachrichten aus Niedersachsens Urgeschichte 62, 1993, 19-56.

Skousen 2008
H. Skousen, Arkæologi I Lange Baner. Undersøgelser forud for anlæggelsen af motorvejen nord om Århus 1998-2007 (Højbjerg 2008).

Skaarup 1985
J. Skaarup, Yngre Stenalder på Øerne syd for Fyn. Meddelelser fra Langelands Museum (Rudkøbing 1985).

Skaarup 1993
J. Skaarup, Megalitgrave. In: St. Hvass/B. Storgaard (ed.), Da Klinger I Muld. 25 års arkæologi i Danmark (Århus 1985), 104-109.

Soler 2010
L. Soler, L'enceinte du Néolithique moyen des Quatre Chevaliers à Périgny, Charente-Maritime. L'Archéothéma 10, sept.-oct. 2010, 47.

Sparrevohn 2009
L.R. Sparrevohn, Omkring en å. Tragtbægerkulturens særlige steder. In: A. Schülke (red.), Plads og rum i tragtbægerkulturen. Bidrag fra Arbejdsmødet på Nationalmuseet, 22. september 2005. Nordiske Fortidsminder Serie C Bind 6 (København 2009), 45-65.

Stauch/Banghard 2002
E. Stauch/K. Banghard, Das ganz normale Michelsberg. Neues zur jungneolithischen Siedlungsgeschichte zwischen Rhein und Neckar. In: P. Ettel/R. Friedrich/W. Schier (Hrsg.), Interdisziplinäre Beiträge zur Siedlungsarchäologie. Gedenkschrift für Walter Janssen. Internationale Archäologie, Studia Honoraria 17 (Rahden/Westfalen 2002), 369-390.

Steffens 2009
J. Steffens, Die neolithischen Fundplätze von Rastorf, Kr. Plön. Eine Fallstudie zur Trichterbecherkultur im nördlichen Mitteleuropa am Beispiel eines Siedlungsraums. Universitätsforschungen zur Prähistorischen Archäologie Band 170 (Bonn 2009).

Stika 1996
H.-P. Stika, Vorgeschichtliche Pflanzenreste aus Heilbronn-Klingenberg. Archäobotanische Untersuchungen zum Michelsberger Erdwerk auf dem Schloßberg (Bandkeramik, Michelsberger Kultur, Späthallstatt/Frühlatène). Materialhefte zur Archäologie in Baden-Württemberg 34 (Stuttgart 1996).

Stürup 1965
B. Stürup, En ny jordgrav fra tidligneolitisk tid. KUML 1965, 13-22.

Svane 1984
S. Svane, Danske Helligkilder og Lægedomskilder (København 1984).

Svensson 2002
M. Svensson, Palisade Enclosures – The Second Generation of Enclosed Sites in the Neolithic of Northern Europe. In: A.A. Gibson (ed.), Behind wooden walls: Neolithic Palisaded Enclosures in Europe (Oxford 2002), 28-58.

Sylvest/Sylvest 1960
B. Sylvest/I. Sylvest, Årpgårdfundet. KUML 1960, 9-25.

Sørensen/Karg in press
L. Sørensen/S. Karg, The expansion of agrarian societies towards the north – new evidence for agriculture during the Mesolithic/Neolithic transition in South Scandinavia. Journal of Archaeological Science, in press (online: http://dx.doi.org/10.1016/j.jas.2012.08.042)

Tackenberg 1951

K. Tackenberg, Die Beusterburg. Ein jungsteinzeitliches Erdwerk in Niedersachsen (Hildesheim 1951).

Thomas 1991

J. Thomas, Rethinking the Neolithic (Cambridge 1991).

Thorpe 1996

I.J. Thorpe, The Origins of Agriculture in Europe (London/New York 1996).

Torfing 2011

T. D. Torfing, Overgangen fra Tidlig- til Mellemneolitikum på Djursland. En analyse af keramik og stil på udvalgte lokaliteter. Unpublished Master-Thesis, University of Århus (Højbjerg 2011).

Torfing 2013

T.D. Torfing, The Network of Style. An analytic study of style and pottery from two causewayed enclosures. Journal of Neolithic Archaeology 15, 2013, 64–87 [doi 10.12766/jna.2013.5].

Troels-Smith 1942

J. Troels-Smith, Geologisk datering af Dyrholm-Fundet. In: Th. Mathiassen/M. Degerbøl/J. Troels-Smith, Dyrholmen. En Stenalderboplads Paa Djursland. Det Kongelige Danske Videnskabernes Selskab. Arkæologisk-Kunsthistoriske Studier, Bind I, Nr. 1 (Købehavn 1942), 137-212.

Troldtoft Andresen 2013

S. Troldtoft Andresen, Gammeltoft Odde – en kultisk samlingsplads ved Filsø fra bondestenalderen. Opdatering – Årbog for Varde By og Omegn & Ringkøbing-Skjern Museum 2012, 202-210.

Uenze 1981

H.-P. Uenze, Die endneolithische befestigte Siedlung von Dobl, Ldkr. Rosenheim. Bayerische Vorgeschichtsblätter 46, 1-37.

Ungerath/Cziesla 2007

O. Ungerath/E. Cziesla, Grabenwerk, Bestattung und Siedlung. Befunde unterschiedlicher Zeitstellung bei Dyrotz, Lkr. Havelland. In: Archäologie in Berlin und Brandenburg 2006, 37-40.

Uzarowicz-Chmielewska 1991

A. Uzarowicz-Chmielewska, Stryczowice, Site 1. A Funnel Beaker Settlement. In: D. Jankowska (ed.), Die Trichterbecherkultur. Neue Forschungen und Hypothesen. Material des Internationalen Symposiums Dymaczewo, 20-24 September 1988, Teil II (Poznań 1991), 155-158.

Vanmontfort et al. 2004

B. Vanmontfort/A.-J. Geerts/Ch. Casseyas/C. Bakels/Ch. Buyclens/F. Damblon/R. Langohr/W. Van Neer/P.M. Vermeersch, De Hel in de tweede helft van het 5de millenium v.Chr. Een midden-Neolitische enclosure te Spiere (prov. West-Vlaanderen). Archeologie in Vlaandern VIII, 2001/2002 (2004), 9-77.

Vaquer 2011

J. Vaquer, Les enceintes à fossés du Néolithique, du Chalcolithique et du Bronze ancien dans la zone nord pyrénéenne. Revista d'Arqueologia de Ponent 21, 2011, 233-252.

Vedsted 1986

J. Vedsted, Fortidsminder og kulturlandskab: en kildekritisk analyse af tragtbægerkulturens fundmateriale fra Norddjursland (Ebeltoft 1986).

Vermeersch/Walter 1975

P.M. Vermeersch/R. Walter, Le site néolithique à Thieusies. Archaeologica Belgica 177, 1975, 9-13.

Vermeersch/Walter 1978

P.M. Vermeersch/R. Walter, Die Palisadengräben des Michelsberger Fundplatzes in Thieusies (Belgien). Archäologisches Korrespondenzblatt 8, 1978, 169-176.

Vermeersch/Walter 1980

P.M. Vermeersch/R. Walter, Thieusies, Ferme de l'Hosté, site Michelsberg, I. Archaeologica Belgica 230, 1980.

Videjko 1995

M. Videjko, Großsiedlungen der Tripol'e Kultur in der Ukraine. Eurasia Antiqua 1, 1995, 45-80.

Wallbrecht 2000

A. Wallbrecht, Die Höhensiedlung der Michelsberger Kultur auf dem Salzberg bei Höckelheim, Stadt und Landkreis Northeim, und der westeuropäische Flint östlich der Weser. Vorlage und Diskussion der Funde unter Berücksichtigung der älteren und jüngeren Kulturhorizonte. Veröffentlichungen der Urgeschichtlichen Sammlungen des Landesmuseums zu Hannover 48 (Oldenburg 2000).

Walter et al. 2007

D. Walter/S. Birkenbeil/T. Schüler/M. Seidel/R.-J. Priloff, Mittelneolithische Funde aus dem Einzugsgebiet der Goldenen Aue im südlichen Harzvorland. In: Terra praehistorica. Festschrift für Klaus-Dieter Jäger. Neue Ausgrabungen und Forschungen in Thüringen, Sonderband 2007. Beiträge zur Ur- und Frühgeschichte Mitteleuropas 48 (Langenweißbach 2007), 253-268.

Westphal 2000

J. Westphal, Liselund. In: St. Hvass & Det Arkæologiske Nævn (Hrsg.), Vor skjulte kulturarv. Arkæologien under overfladen. Til Hendes Majestæt Dronning Margrethe II, 16. april 2000 (Esbjerg 2000), 50-51.

Wetzel 2000

G. Wetzel, Burgwall und Grabenanlage von Berge. Neolithische und slawische Grabenanlage von Dyrotz. In: Führer zu archäologischen Denkmälern in Deutschland 37. Potsdam, Brandenburg und das Havelland (Stuttgart 2000), 156-159.

Whittle et al. 2011a
A. Whittle/F. Healy/A. Bayliss, Gathering Time. Dating the Early Neolithic Enclosures of Southern Britain and Ireland. 2 vol. (Oxford 2011).

Whittle et al. 2011b
A. Whittle/A. Bayliss/F. Healy, Chapter 15: Gathering time: the social dynamics of change. In: Whittle et al. 2011a, 848-914.

Wilhelmi 1977
K. Wilhelmi, West-Westfalen zwischen Michelsberger und Trichterbecherkultur. Archäologisches Korrespondenzblatt 7, 1977, 9-21.

Willms 1982
Ch. Willms, Zwei Fundplätze der Michelsberger Kultur aus dem westlichen Münsterland, gleichzeitig ein Beitrag zum neolithischen Silexhandel in Mitteleuropa. Münstersche Beiträge zur Ur- und Frühgeschichte 12 (Hildesheim 1982).

Willroth 1986
K.-H. Willroth, Landwege auf der cimbrischen Halbinsel aus der Sicht der Archäologie. Siedlungsforschung 4, 1986, 9-44.

Wincentz Rasmussen 1984
L. Wincentz Rasmussen, Kainsbakke A47: A Settlement Structure from the Pitted Ware Culture. Journal of Danish Archaeology 3, 1984, 83-98.

Wincentz Rasmussen 1986
L. Wincentz Rasmussen, Nye C14 dateringer for grubekeramisk kultur i Danmark. In: Ch. Adamsen/K. Ebbesen (eds.), Stridsøksetid i Sydskandinavien. Arkæologiske Skrifter 1 (København 1986), 211-212.

Wincentz Rasmussen 1994
L. Wincentz Rasmussen, Ballegård. Arkæologiske Udgravninger i Danmark 1993 (København 1994), Nr. 341.

Wincentz Rasmussen 2000
L. Wincentz Rasmussen, Kainsbakke. Arkæologiske Udgravninger i Danmark 1999 (København 2000), Nr. 399.

Wincentz Rasmussen 2002
L. Wincentz Rasmussen, Ginnerup. Arkæologiske Udgravninger i Danmark 2001 (København 2002), Nr. 394.

Wincentz Rasmussen 2011
L. Wincentz Rasmussen, Stormandsgård på Nordbakken. Museum Østjylland Årbog 2011, 18-23.

Wincentz Rasmussen/Boas 1982
L. Wincentz Rasmussen/N.A. Boas, Kainsbakke og Kirial Bro. To bopladser fra den grubekeramiske kultur ved Grenå. Antikvariske Studier 5, 1982, 104-114.

Wincentz Rasmussen/Richter 1991
L. Wincentz Rasmussen/J. Richter, Kainsbakke. En kystboplads fra yngre stenalder. Aspects of the palaeoecology of neolithic man (Grenå 1991).

Wincentz Rasmussen/Harder 2003
L. Wincentz Rasmussen/M.J. Harder, Galgebakken. Arkæologiske udgravninger i Danmark 2002 (København 2003), Nr. 356.

Woll 2003
B. Woll, Das Totenritual der frühen Nordischen Trichterbecherkultur. Saarbrücker Beiträge zur Altertumskunde 76 (Bonn 2003).

Zápotocký 1992
M. Zápotocký, Streitäxte des mitteleuropäischen Äneolithikums. Quellen und Forschungen zur prähistorischen und provinzialrömischen Archäologie Band 6 (Weinheim 1992).

Zeeb-Lanz 2010
A. Zeeb-Lanz, Die bandkeramische Grubenanlage von Herxheim (Südpfalz) – ein überörtlicher Ritualort und sein Umfeld. In: I. Matuschik/Ch. Strahm (Hrsg.), Vernetzungen. Festschrift für Helmut Schlichterle (Freiburg 2010), 63-73.

Zeeb-Lanz 2012
A. Zeeb-Lanz, Das „Isotopen-Netzwerk" stellt sich vor: Bericht vom Workshop am 6. Februar 2010 in Speyer. Archäologisches Nachrichtenblatt 17-2, 2012, 165-174.

Zeeberg 2000
P. Zeeberg (transl.), Gesta Danorum – Saxos Danmarks historie (Københvan 2000).

Zich 1993
B. Zich, Die Ausgrabung chronisch gefährdeter Hügelgräber der Stein- und Bronzezeit in Flintbek, Kreis Rendsburg-Eckernförde. Ein Vorbericht. Offa 49/50, 1993, 13-51.

Østergård Sørensen 1995a
P.Østergård Sørensen, Markildegård – mødested gennem årtusinder. In: J. Hertz (Hrsg.), 5000 år under motorvejen (København 1995), 32-33.

Østergård Sørensen 1995b
P. Østergård Sørensen, Markildegård. En tidligneolitisk samlingsplads. Kulturhistoriske Studier 1, 1995, 13-45.

Østergård Sørensen/Boas 2002
P. Østergård Sørensen/N.A. Boas, Kainsbakke II. Arkæologiske Udgravninger i Danmark 2001 (København 2002), Nr. 395.

Appendix

· ·

European enclosures that were selected for comparison to the TRB North Group sites. Most of these sites have been previously compiled in regional inventories (to which references are given, when available).

Enclosure	Country	Reference
Lugasson "Roquefort"(Gironde)	France	Ard 2011
Villegouge "Roanne" (Gironde)	France	Ard 2011
Abzac "Petreau" (Gironde)	France	Ard 2011
Saint-Léon-sur-L'Isle "Fontaine de la Demoiselle" (Dordogne)	France	Ard 2011
Bouteilles-Saint-Sebastien "Chez Nicou" (Dordogne)	France	Ard 2011
Brie-sous-Barbezieux "Chez Joly" (Charente)	France	Ard 2011
Saint-Germain-de-Lusignan "La Coterelle" (Charente-Maritime)	France	Ard 2011
Barbezieux "Font Rase" (Charente)	France	Ard 2011
Barzan "La Garde" (Charente-Maritime)	France	Ard 2011
Biron "Réjolles" (Charente-Maritime)	France	Ard 2011
Juillac-le-Coq "Les Matignions" (Charente)	France	Ard 2011
Bougneau "Pont d'Usson" (Charente-Maritime)	France	Ard 2011
Semussac "Chez-Reine" (Charente-Maritime)	France	Ard 2011
Saint-Georges-de-Didonne/ Médis "Boubes, le Marais de Belmont" (Charente-Maritime)	France	Ard 2011
Mainxe "Montagant" (Charente)	France	Ard 2011
Thénac "Peu-Richard" (Charente-Maritime)	France	Ard 2011
Préguillac "Le Tailis/Les Arnoux" (Charente-Maritime)	France	Ard 2011
Mérignac "Cluseaux" (Charente)	France	Kerdivel 2009
Courcoury "Les Orgeries" (Charente-Maritime)	France	Ard 2011
Taillebourg "Domaine de la Brossadières" (Charente-Maritime)	France	Kerdivel 2009
Authon-Ebéon "Le Chemin Saint-Jean Le Grand Lopin" (Charente)	France	Ard 2011
Blanzac-les-Matha "Fief Contenu" (Charente-Maritime)	France	Kerdivel 2009

Enclosure	Country	Reference
Chenommet "Bellevue Les Grands Champs" (Charente)	France	Ard 2011
La Brée-les-Bains "Pointe des Boulassiers" (Charente-Maritime)	France	Kerdivel 2009
Lozay "Tablier" (Charente-Maritime)	France	Kerdivel 2009
Landrais "Le Gué Charreau/ Le Marais Chaban" (Charente-Maritime)	France	Kerdivel 2009
Surgères "Le Cornet" (Charente-Maritime)	France	Kerdivel 2009
Brioux-sur-Boutonne "Virollet" (Deux-Sèvres)	France	Kerdivel 2009
Benon "Fontaine Miraculeuse" (Charente-Maritime)	France	Kerdivel 2009
Prin-Deyrancon "Terre de Claigne" (Deux-Sèvres)	France	Kerdivel 2009
Nuaillé-d'Aunis "Le Mastine" (Charente-Maritime)	France	Kerdivel 2009
Longèves "Langle" (Charente-Maritime)	France	Kerdivel 2009
Villedoux "Le Rocher" (Charente-Maritime)	France	Ard 2011
Courcon d'Aunis "Les Pieds de Cresse" (Charente-Maritime)	France	Kerdivel 2009
Frontenay-Rohan-Rohan "Champ Fiard" (Deux-Sèvres)	France	Kerdivel 2009
Saint-Hilaire-la-Palud "Bîmes ou de Prairie de Saint-Hilaire" (Deux-Sèvres)	France	Kerdivel 2009
Thorigné "Les Forgettes" (Deux-Sèvres)	France	Kerdivel 2009
Marans "La Grande Bastille" (Charente-Maritime)	France	Kerdivel 2009
Vouillé "Pommeraie" (Deux-Sèvres)	France	Kerdivel 2009
Vouillé "Champs Rouges" (Deux-Sèvres)	France	Kerdivel 2009
Niort "La Rousille" (Deux-Sèvres)	France	Kerdivel 2009

Enclosure	Country	Reference
Vix "La Maison de la Chaume" (Vendée)	France	Kerdivel 2009
Gué de Velluire "Le Haut du Tertre" (Vendée)	France	Kerdivel 2009
Echiré "Les Loups" (Deux-Sèvres)	France	Kerdivel 2009
Chaillé-les-Marais "Rue des Venelles" (Vendée)	France	Kerdivel 2009
Saint-Maxire "Parc" (Deux-Sèvres)	France	Kerdivel 2009
Saint-Maxire "Haut de la Croisette" (Deux-Sèvres)	France	Kerdivel 2009
Saint-Maxire "Tourniotte" (Deux-Sèvres)	France	Kerdivel 2009
Villiers-en-Plaine "Bellevue ou Les Sablières" (Deux-Sèvres)	France	Kerdivel 2009
Nieul-sur-L'Autise "Champ-Durand" (Vendée)	France	Ard 2011
Saint-Benoit-sur-Mer "Les Groix" (Vendée)	France	Kerdivel 2009
Le Langon "La Caboge" (Vendée)	France	Kerdivel 2009
Auzay "Les Châtelliers du Vieil-Auzay" (Vendée)	France	Ard 2011
Talmont-Saint-Hilaire "Les Vioillières" (Vendée)	France	Kerdivel 2009
Mouzeil-Saint-Martin "Le Pijouet" (Vendée)	France	Kerdivel 2009
Mareuil-sur-Lay-Dissais "L'Ouche du Fort" (Vendée)	France	Kerdivel 2009
Chauvigny "Le Plan Saint-Pierre" (Vienne)	France	Kerdivel 2009
Migné-Auxances "Le Temps-Perdu" (Vienne)	France	Kerdivel 2009
Landevielle "La Gaubretière 2" (Vendée)	France	Kerdivel 2009
Availles-en-Chatellerault "Les Pieces du Port-à-Chillou" (Vienne)	France	Kerdivel 2009
Bruère-Allichamps (Cher)	France	Cassen/Boujot 1990
Airvault "Les Fourneaux" (Deux-Sèvres)	France	Kerdivel 2009
Marnes "Le Chafaud" (Deux-Sèvres	France	Kerdivel 2009
Leugny "Les Grandes Varennes" (Vienne)	France	Kerdivel 2009
Thouars "Fertevault" (Deux-Sèvres)	France	Kerdivel 2009
Sandun (Loire-Atlantique)	France	Scarre 2001
Gravon (Seine-et-Marne)	France	Jeunesse et al. 2004
Chatenay-sur-Seine (Seine-et-Marne)	France	Jeunesse et al. 2004
Périgny	France	Jeunesse 2011
Villeneuve-Tolosane (Haute-Garonne)	France	Gandelin 2011
Cugnaux (Haute-Garonne)	France	Gandelin 2011
Pezens "La Poste Vielle" (Aude)	France	Gandelin 2011
Saint-Michel-du-Touch à Toulouse (Haute-Garonne)	France	Vaquer 2011
Seilh "Chateau Percin" (Haute-Garonne)	France	Vaquer 2011
Carcassonne "Camp d'Auriac" (Aude)	France	Vaquer 2011
Castelferrus "Saint Genes" (Tarn-et-Garonne)	France	Vaquer 2011
Ventenac-Carbardès (Aude)	France	Vaquer 2011
Casetlnau-le-Lez (Hérault)	France	Vaquer 2011
Saint-Vigor-d'Ymonville (Seine-Maritime)	France	Jeunesse 2011

Enclosure	Country	Reference
Noyers (Yonne)	France	Jeunesse 2011
Sermoise (Aisne)	France	Dubouloz et al. 1988
Couvrelles (Aisne)	France	Dubouloz et al. 1988
Grisy (Seine-et-Marne)	France	Jeunesse et al. 2004
Goulet (Orne)	France	Kerdivel 2009
Saint-Martin-de-Fontenay "Diguet" (Calvados)	France	Jeunesse 2011
Villers-Carbonnel (Somme)	France	http://www.inrap.fr
L'Etoile (Somme)	France	Jeunesse et al. 2004
Corbehem (Pas-de-Calais)	France	Seidel 2008
Crécy-sur-Serre (Aisne)	France	Jeunesse 2011
Cuiry-lès-Chaudardes (Aisne)	France	Dubouloz et al. 1988
Pernant "Le Roc Poitier" (Aisne)	France	Le Bolloch 1984
Pernant "Le Chemin de la Voyette" (Aisne)	France	Le Bolloch 1984
Vézaponin "La Ferme Saint Léger" (Aisne)	France	Le Bolloch 1984
Épagny "Montagne de Rots" (Aisne)	France	Le Bolloch 1984
Mouy "Camp Barbet" (Oise)	France	Martinez/Blanchet 1988
Égligny (Seine-et-Marne)	France	Mordant/Mordant 1988
Marolles-sur-Seine (Seine-et-Marne)	France	Mordant/Mordant 1988
Saint-Denis-lès-Sens (Yonne)	France	Delor et al. 1988
Champlay (Yonne)	France	Delor et al. 1988
Migennes (Yonne)	France	Delor et al. 1988
Charmoy (Yonne)	France	Delor et al. 1988
Beaumont (Yonne)	France	Delor et al. 1988
Gurgy (Yonne)	France	Delor et al. 1988
Cravant (Yonne)	France	Delor et al. 1988
Chemilly-sur-Yonne (Yonne)	France	Delor et al. 1988
Ciry-Salsogne (Aisne)	France	Dubouloz et al. 1988
Lauwin-Planque (Nord)	France	Manceau 2011
Carvin (Pas-de-Calais)	France	Monchablon et al. 2011
Fontenoy "Les Quatres Ages" (Aisne)	France	Le Bolloch 1984
Fontenoy "La Tuillerie" (Aisne)	France	Le Bolloch 1984
Ambleny "La Vierzaine" (Aisne)	France	Boureux 1982
Boury-en-Vexin (Oise)	France	Martinez 1982
Bazoches-sur-Vesles (Aisne)	France	Seidel 2008
Catenoy (Oise)	France	Cassen/Boujot 1990
Concevreux (Aisne)	France	Seidel 2008
Maizy-sur-Aisne (Aisne)	France	Seidel 2008
Missy-sur-Aisne (Aisne)	France	Seidel 2008
Bourg-et-Comin (Aisne)	France	Dubouloz et al. 1988
Osly-Courtil (Aisne)	France	Jeunesse et al. 2004
Pontavert (Aisne)	France	Seidel 2008
Compiègne (Oise)	France	Cassen/Boujot 1990
Noyen (Seine-et-Marne)	France	Jeunesse et al. 2004
Mairy (Ardennes)	France	Seidel 2008
Vignely (Seine-et-Marne)	France	Jeunesse et al. 2004
Cigogné (Indre-et-Loire)	France	Dubois 1999
Passy-Veron (Yonne)	France	INRAP 2009
Épineau-Les-Voves (Yonne)	France	INRAP 2009
Villers-en-Prayères (Aisne)	France	Boureux 1982
Balloy (Seine-et-Marne)	France	Jeunesse 2011
Barbuise "Courtavant" (Aube)	France	Jeunesse 2011
Maisons-Alfort (Val-de-Marne)	France	Jeunesse 2011
Fontenay-sur-Loing (Loiret)	France	Jeunesse 2011
Villeneuve-la Guyard (Yonne)	France	Jeunesse 2011
Antran (Vienne)	France	Kerdivel 2009

Enclosure	Country	Reference
Escalles "Mont d'Hubert" (Pas-du-Calais)	France	Panloups/Praud 2011
Distré "Les Murailles 2" (Maine-et-Loire)	France	Kerdivel 2009
Le Bernard "La Prée Noire" (Vendée)	France	Kerdivel 2009
Châteneuf-du-Rhone "La Roberte" (Drôme)	France	Convertini 2012
Clansayes 2 (Drôme)	France	Convertini 2012
Saint-Paul-Trois-Château "Les Moulais" (Drôme)	France	Convertini 2012
Vernègues "L'Héritière II" (Bouches-du-Rhône)	France	Convertini 2012
Cavanac "La Farguette" (Aude)	France	Convertini 2012
Lillemer (Ille-et-Vilaine)	France	Laporte et al. 2007
Schlatt "Schlatter Berg"	Germany	Seidel 2008
Munzingen	Germany	Seidel 2008
Opfingen	Germany	Seidel 2008
Sasbach "Limberg"	Germany	Seidel 2008
Buchhofen-Nindorf	Germany	Matuschik 1991
Holtzheim	Germany	Seidel 2008
Ergolding	Germany	Matuschik 1991
Essenbach-Altheim	Germany	Matuschik 1991
Essenbach-Koislhof	Germany	Matuschik 1991
Künzing-Bruck	Germany	Matuschik 1991
Kothingeichendorf	Germany	Matuschik 1991
Osterhofen-Linzing	Germany	Matuschik 1991
Osterhofen-Neu-Wisseling	Germany	Matuschik 1991
Oberschneiding	Germany	Matuschik 1991
Leonberg "Silberg"	Germany	Seidel 2009
Irlbach "Am Auwald"	Germany	Seidel 2008
Aiterhofen-Ödmühle	Germany	Matuschik 1991
Goldburghausen "Goldberg"	Germany	Seidel 2008
Mötzing-Haimbuch	Germany	Matuschik 1991
Riekofen	Germany	Matuschik 1991
Bad Abbach-Alkofen	Germany	Matuschik 1991
Köfering	Germany	Matuschik 1991
Regensburg-Barbing	Germany	Matuschik 1991
Ilsfeld "Ebene"	Germany	Seidel 2008
Untergrombach "Michelsberg"	Germany	Seidel 2008
Bruchsal-Heidelsheim "Altenberg"	Germany	Seidel 2008
Zaisenhausen "Hard"	Germany	Seidel 2008
Bruchsal-Heidelsheim "Aue"	Germany	Seidel 2008
Bruchsal-Auberg "Scheelkopf"	Germany	Seidel 2008
Heilbronn-Klingenberg "Schlossberg"	Germany	Seidel 2008
Ittlingen "Dattenberg"	Germany	Seidel 2008
Neckarsulm-Obereisesheim "Hetzenberg"	Germany	Seidel 2008
Monsheim II	Germany	Seidel 2008
Bügstadter Berg	Germany	Seidel 2008
Markt Kreuzwertheim	Germany	Seidel 2008
Wiesbaden-Schierstein	Germany	Seidel 2008
Uttershausen	Germany	Geschwinde/Raetzel-Fabian 2009
Staffelstein	Germany	Seidel 2008
Glauberg	Germany	Seidel 2008
Mayen	Germany	Seidel 2008
Florstadt-Leidhecken	Germany	Seidel 2008
Ranstadt-Dauernheim	Germany	Seidel 2008
Urmitz	Germany	Seidel 2008
Butzbach-Griedel "Galgenberg"	Germany	Seidel 2008
Miel	Germany	Seidel 2008
Hundisburg-Olbetal	Germany	Rinne/Müller 2012

Enclosure	Country	Reference
Bonn "Venusberg"	Germany	Seidel 2008
Inden 9	Germany	Seidel 2008
Lich-Steinstrass	Germany	Seidel 2008
Koslar 10	Germany	Seidel 2008
Jülich	Germany	Seidel 2008
Großfahner	Germany	Geschwinde/Raetzel-Fabian 2009
Krautheim	Germany	Meyer/Raetzel-Fabian 2006
Bergheim (Schwalm-Eder-Kreis)	Germany	Seidel 2008
Eulau	Germany	Müller 2001
Felsberg-Wolfershausen	Germany	Seidel 2008
Uichteritz	Germany	Geschwinde/Raetzel-Fabian 2009
Mehltheuer	Germany	Geschwinde/Raetzel-Fabian 2009
Krumpa	Germany	Müller 2001
Riesa	Germany	Geschwinde/Raetzel-Fabian 2009
Wallendorf "Hutberg"	Germany	Seidel 2008
Calden	Germany	Seidel 2008
Schraplau	Germany	Geschwinde/Raetzel-Fabian 2009
Halle-Dölauer Heide	Germany	Meyer/Raetzel-Fabian 2006
Urbach	Germany	Geschwinde/Raetzel-Fabian 2009
Warburg-Daseburg	Germany	Knoche 2008
Kyna	Germany	Geschwinde/Raetzel-Fabian 2009
Warburg-Rimbeck	Germany	Knoche 2008
Anröchte-Mellrich	Germany	Knoche 2008
Seulingen	Germany	Geschwinde/Raetzel-Fabian 2009
Müllingsen	Germany	pers. comm. B. Knoche
Oppin	Germany	Geschwinde/Raetzel-Fabian 2009
Soest "Burgtheaterplatz"	Germany	Seidel 2008
Borgentreich-Bühne "Rothenbreite"	Germany	Knoche 2008
Büren-Brenken	Germany	Seidel 2008
Quetzölsdorf	Germany	Geschwinde/Raetzel-Fabian 2009
Bad Sassendorf	Germany	Cichy et al. 2011
Petersberg	Germany	Geschwinde/Raetzel-Fabian 2009
Siersleben	Germany	Geschwinde/Raetzel-Fabian 2009
Krosigk	Germany	Müller 2001
Borgentreich-Borgholz	Germany	Knoche 2008
Bad Karlshafen-Helmarshausen	Germany	Knoche 2008
Salzkotten-Oberntudorf	Germany	Seidel 2008
Bernburg	Germany	Geschwinde/Raetzel-Fabian 2009
Odendorf	Germany	Geschwinde/Raetzel-Fabian 2009
Sinzenich	Germany	Geschwinde/Raetzel-Fabian 2009
Zülpich	Germany	Geschwinde/Raetzel-Fabian 2009
Borchen-Kirchborchen	Germany	Knoche 2008
Brakel-Erkeln	Germany	Knoche 2008
Freckleben	Germany	Geschwinde/Raetzel-Fabian 2009
Northeim "Kiessee"	Germany	Seidel 2008
Brakel "Hellenberg"	Germany	Knoche 2008

Enclosure	Country	Reference
Radisleben	Germany	Müller 2001
Kustrena	Germany	Geschwinde/Raetzel-Fabian 2009
Boffzen	Germany	Knoche 2008
Merzien	Germany	Müller 2001
Lausigk	Germany	Geschwinde/Raetzel-Fabian 2009
Scheuder	Germany	Geschwinde/Raetzel-Fabian 2009
Einbeck "Kühner Höhe"	Germany	Seidel 2008
Altenburg	Germany	Geschwinde/Raetzel-Fabian 2009
Derenburg	Germany	Geschwinde/Raetzel-Fabian 2009
Löderburg	Germany	Müller 2001
Mahndorf	Germany	Geschwinde/Raetzel-Fabian 2009
Gr. Börnecke	Germany	Geschwinde/Raetzel-Fabian 2009
Wasserleben	Germany	Geschwinde/Raetzel-Fabian 2009
Wolmirsleben	Germany	Geschwinde/Raetzel-Fabian 2009
Nottuln-Uphoven	Germany	Seidel 2008
Krottorf	Germany	Geschwinde/Raetzel-Fabian 2009
Eilenstedt	Germany	Geschwinde/Raetzel-Fabian 2009
Alikendorf	Germany	Müller 2001
Klein Döhren "Fst. 1"	Germany	Geschwinde/Raetzel-Fabian 2009
Ostharingen	Germany	Geschwinde/Raetzel-Fabian 2009
Hornburg "Tempelhof 2"	Germany	Geschwinde/Raetzel-Fabian 2009
Oschersleben	Germany	Geschwinde/Raetzel-Fabian 2009
Hornburg "Tempelhof"	Germany	Geschwinde/Raetzel-Fabian 2009
Hornburg "Über der Landwehr"	Germany	Geschwinde/Raetzel-Fabian 2009
Werlaburgdorf "Lietfeld"	Germany	Geschwinde/Raetzel-Fabian 2009
Winnigstedt "Schmiedeberg"	Germany	Geschwinde/Raetzel-Fabian 2009
Wanzleben	Germany	Geschwinde/Raetzel-Fabian 2009
Börßum "Spitzberg"	Germany	Geschwinde/Raetzel-Fabian 2009
Heiningen	Germany	Geschwinde/Raetzel-Fabian 2009
Jerxheim "Mittelbreite"	Germany	Geschwinde/Raetzel-Fabian 2009
Beinum	Germany	Kellner-Depner 2011
Altbrandsleben	Germany	Geschwinde/Raetzel-Fabian 2009
Klein Flöthe	Germany	Geschwinde/Raetzel-Fabian 2009
Jerxheim "Fst. 6"	Germany	Geschwinde/Raetzel-Fabian 2009
Betheln "Beusterburg"	Germany	Seidel 2008
Hordorf	Germany	Müller 2001
Ohrum	Germany	Geschwinde/Raetzel-Fabian 2009
Hoiersdorf "Hoppenburg"	Germany	Geschwinde/Raetzel-Fabian 2009
Hoiersdorf "Blauer Berg"	Germany	Geschwinde/Raetzel-Fabian 2009

Enclosure	Country	Reference
Wittmar "Lappenberg"	Germany	Geschwinde/Raetzel-Fabian 2009
Wobeck "Hasenberg"	Germany	Geschwinde/Raetzel-Fabian 2009
Groß Dahlum	Germany	Geschwinde/Raetzel-Fabian 2009
Schöningen "Steinkuhle"	Germany	Geschwinde/Raetzel-Fabian 2009
Eitzum "Auf dem Rottland"	Germany	Geschwinde/Raetzel-Fabian 2009
Sambleben "Schimmelberg"	Germany	Geschwinde/Raetzel-Fabian 2009
Warberg	Germany	Geschwinde/Raetzel-Fabian 2009
Hachum	Germany	Geschwinde/Raetzel-Fabian 2009
Rössing	Germany	Geschwinde/Raetzel-Fabian 2009
Groß Vahlberg	Germany	Geschwinde/Raetzel-Fabian 2009
Niedersickte-Dormorgen "Fst. 2"	Germany	Geschwinde/Raetzel-Fabian 2009
Barleben	Germany	Geschwinde/Raetzel-Fabian 2009
Niedersickte-Dormorgen	Germany	Geschwinde/Raetzel-Fabian 2009
Rüningen "Dornenhai"	Germany	Geschwinde/Raetzel-Fabian 2009
Niedersickte-Dormorgen "U Fst"	Germany	Geschwinde/Raetzel-Fabian 2009
Wolmirstedt	Germany	Geschwinde/Raetzel-Fabian 2009
Müsleringen	Germany	Freese 2010
Walmstorf	Germany	Richter 2002
Ruthen	Germany	Klatt 2009
Plate 14	Germany	Klatt 2009
Plate 3	Germany	Klatt 2009
Zietlitz	Germany	Klatt 2009
Esesfeld	Germany	Klatt 2009
Bad Segeberg	Germany	Guldin 2011
Albersdorf-Dieksknöll	Germany	Dibbern 2012
Rastorf	Germany	Klatt 2009
Büdelsdorf	Germany	Klatt 2009
Osterwick	Germany	Knoche 2008
Oberhinkofen	Germany	Engelhardt 2006
Aholming Tabertshausen	Germany	Meyer/Raetzel-Fabian 2006
Buxheim	Germany	Meyer/Raetzel-Fabian 2006
Landau a.d. Isar I	Germany	Meyer/Raetzel-Fabian 2006
Landau a.d. isar II	Germany	Meyer/Raetzel-Fabian 2006
Murr	Germany	Meyer/Raetzel-Fabian 2006
Oberpöring-Niederpöring	Germany	Meyer/Raetzel-Fabian 2006
Altdorf	Germany	Meyer/Raetzel-Fabian 2006
Ergolding-Kopfham "Galgenberg"	Germany	Meyer/Raetzel-Fabian 2006
Straßkirchen	Germany	Meyer/Raetzel-Fabian 2006
Trieching	Germany	Meyer/Raetzel-Fabian 2006
Kobern-Gondorf	Germany	Meyer/Raetzel-Fabian 2006

Enclosure	Country	Reference
Riedling	Germany	Gorka/Faßbinder 2007
Langenreichen	Germany	Mahnkopf 2004
Feldkirchen	Germany	Jeunesse 2011
Berghofen	Germany	Berghausen/ Faßbinder 2004
Bergheim (Kr. Neuburg-Schrobenhausen)	Germany	Meixner 2001
Atting-Rinkam	Germany	Engelhardt 1995
Potsdam 3 "Schloss"	Germany	Beran/Hensel 2004
Potsdam 14 "Holzmarktstraße"	Germany	Beran 2010
Ahlen-Dolberg	Germany	Grünewald 2013
Bundsø	Denmark	Klatt 2009
Vasagård øst	Denmark	Klatt 2009
Vasagård vest	Denmark	Klatt 2009
Markildegård	Denmark	Klatt 2009
Sarup I	Denmark	Klatt 2009
Sarup II	Denmark	Klatt 2009
Lønt	Denmark	Klatt 2009
Starup Langelandsvej	Denmark	Lützau Pedersen/ Witte 2012
Hygind	Denmark	Klatt 2009
Åsum Enggård	Denmark	Klatt 2009
Trelleborg	Denmark	Klatt 2009
Sigersted III	Denmark	Klatt 2009
Bjerggård	Denmark	Klatt 2009
Toftum	Denmark	Klatt 2009
Skævinge Boldbaner	Denmark	Klatt 2009
Voldbæk	Denmark	Klatt 2009
Fuglslev	Denmark	Boas 2001
Galgebakke	Denmark	Klatt 2009
Ballebakke	Denmark	Klatt 2009
Ginnerup	Denmark	Klatt 2009
Kainsbakke	Denmark	Klatt 2009
Assenbakke	Denmark	this volume
Blakbjerg	Denmark	Klatt 2009
Grenå	Denmark	Boas 2001
Skærvad	Denmark	Boas 2001
Mølbjerg I	Denmark	Klatt 2009
Mølbjerg II	Denmark	pers. comm. L. Helles Olesen
Liselund	Denmark	Klatt 2009
Gammeltoft Odde	Denmark	Troldtoft Andresen 2013
Søby Møllegård	Denmark	Klatt 2009
Store Brokhøj	Denmark	Klatt 2009
Lokes Hede	Denmark	Klatt 2009
Vilsund	Denmark	Klatt 2009/ this volume
Springfiled Lyons	Great Britain	Oswald et al. 2001
Dorstone Hill	Great Britain	Oswald et al. 2001
Southmore Grove	Great Britain	Oswald et al. 2001
Crofton	Great Britain	Oswald et al. 2001
Dorney	Great Britain	Oswald et al. 2001
Magheraboy	Ireland	Whittle et al. 2011a
Donegore	Ireland	Whittle et al. 2011a
Green Howe	Great Britain	Whittle et al. 2011a
Southwick	Great Britain	Whittle et al. 2011a
Upton	Great Britain	Whittle et al. 2011a
Etton	Great Britain	Whittle et al. 2011a
Uffington	Great Britain	Whittle et al. 2011a
Northborough	Great Britain	Whittle et al. 2011a
Barholm	Great Britain	Whittle et al. 2011a
Alrewas	Great Britain	Whittle et al. 2011a

Enclosure	Country	Reference
Mavesyn Ridware	Great Britain	Whittle et al. 2011a
Roughton	Great Britain	Whittle et al. 2011a
Haddenham	Great Britain	Whittle et al. 2011a
Husbands Bosworth	Great Britain	Whittle et al. 2011a
Fornham All Saints	Great Britain	Whittle et al. 2011a
Dallington	Great Britain	Whittle et al. 2011a
Briar Hill	Great Britain	Whittle et al. 2011a
Great Wilbraham	Great Britain	Whittle et al. 2011a
Hill Croft Field	Great Britain	Whittle et al. 2011a
Cardington	Great Britain	Whittle et al. 2011a
Kedington	Great Britain	Whittle et al. 2011a
Broadwell	Great Britain	Whittle et al. 2011a
Banc Du	Great Britain	Whittle et al. 2011a
Hembury	Great Britain	Whittle et al. 2011a
Raddon	Great Britain	Whittle et al. 2011a
Whitehawk	Great Britain	Whittle et al. 2011a
Barkhale	Great Britain	Whittle et al. 2011a
Carn Brea	Great Britain	Whittle et al. 2011a
Lodge Farm	Great Britain	Whittle et al. 2011a
Burford	Great Britain	Whittle et al. 2011a
Sawbridgeworth	Great Britain	Whittle et al. 2011a
Peak Camp	Great Britain	Whittle et al. 2011a
Crickley Hill	Great Britain	Whittle et al. 2011a
Abingdon	Great Britain	Whittle et al. 2011a
Down Ampney	Great Britain	Whittle et al. 2011a
Buckland	Great Britain	Whittle et al. 2011a
The Trundle	Great Britain	Whittle et al. 2011a
Bury Hill	Great Britain	Whittle et al. 2011a
Halnaker Hill	Great Britain	Whittle et al. 2011a
Offham Hill	Great Britain	Whittle et al. 2011a
Langford	Great Britain	Whittle et al. 2011a
Aston Cote	Great Britain	Whittle et al. 2011a
Banbury	Great Britain	Whittle et al. 2011a
Freston	Great Britain	Whittle et al. 2011a
Maiden Bower	Great Britain	Whittle et al. 2011a
Salmonsbury	Great Britain	Whittle et al. 2011a
Eastleach	Great Britain	Whittle et al. 2011a
Gatehampton Farm	Great Britain	Whittle et al. 2011a
Chalk Hill	Great Britain	Whittle et al. 2011a
Burham	Great Britain	Whittle et al. 2011a
Rybury	Great Britain	Whittle et al. 2011a
Knap Hill	Great Britain	Whittle et al. 2011a
Kingsborough 1	Great Britain	Whittle et al. 2011a
Kingsborough 2	Great Britain	Whittle et al. 2011a
Staines	Great Britain	Whittle et al. 2011a
Windmill Hill	Great Britain	Whittle et al. 2011a
West Kington	Great Britain	Whittle et al. 2011a
Eton Wick	Great Britain	Whittle et al. 2011a
Orsett	Great Britain	Whittle et al. 2011a
Eastry	Great Britain	Whittle et al. 2011a
Robin Hood's Ball	Great Britain	Whittle et al. 2011a
Whitesheet Hill	Great Britain	Whittle et al. 2011a
Hambledon Hill	Great Britain	Whittle et al. 2011a
Court Hill	Great Britain	Whittle et al. 2011a
Combe Hill	Great Britain	Whittle et al. 2011a
Maiden Castle	Great Britain	Whittle et al. 2011a
Helman Tor	Great Britain	Whittle et al. 2011a
Bryn Celli Wen	Great Britain	Oswald et al. 2001
Sandomierz	Poland	Kowaleswka-Marszalek 1990
Grodek Nadbuzny	Poland	Kadrow 2011
Bronocice	Poland	Kadrow 2011

Enclosure	Country	Reference
Stryczowice	Poland	Uzarowicz-Chmielewska 1991
Zlota Grozdisko I	Poland	Kowaleswka-Marszalek 1990
Slonowice	Poland	Herbich/Tunia 2009
Podleze	Poland	Jeunesse 2011
Zaracyca	Poland	Andersen 1997
Tyniec Maly	Poland	Kowaleswka-Marszalek 1990
Strzyzow	Poland	Kadrow 2011
Zimno	Poland	Kadrow 2011
Las Stocki	Poland	Kadrow 2011
Stävie	Sweden	Klatt 2009
Makotrasy	Czech Republic	Pleslova-Stikova 1985
Kly	Czech Republic	Gojda et al. 2002

Enclosure	Country	Reference
Uhersky-Brod-Kyckov	Czech Republic	Rakovsky 1990
Laskov-Rmiz	Czech Republic	Rakovsky 1990
Otaslavice-Obrava Noha	Czech Republic	Rakovsky 1990
Heerlen "Schelsberg"	Netherlands	Schreuers 2005
Petit Spiennes	Belgium	Seidel 2008
Blicquy	Belgium	Seidel 2008
Chaumont-Gistoux	Belgium	Seidel 2008
Spiere "de Hel"	Belgium	Seidel 2008
Assent "Hermansheuvel"	Belgium	Lodewijckx 2005
Ottenbourg	Belgium	Seidel 2008
Boitsfort-Etangs	Belgium	Seidel 2008
Opvelp	Belgium	Seidel 2008
Thieusies	Belgium	Seidel 2008

Part II

Geophysical survey of potential Neolithic enclosure sites in Djursland

By Lutz Klassen & Christina Klein

1 Introduction

· ·

The present research project attempted to develop a predictive model for the location of causewayed enclosures within the TRB Culture in Djursland (Klassen, this volume). Given that testing the outcome of this model was essential, we used geophysical survey to this purpose (see Klassen, this volume, chapter 7.3, for a detailed discussion of testing methods). Thanks to a grant from the Danish Agency for Culture (KUS), geomagnetic and ground penetrating radar (GPR) measurements were conducted by the Archaeo-Geophysics department of the Institute of Geosciences, Christian-Albrechts-University Kiel at 20 locations in February of 2012 (Fig. 1). The team consisted of C. Klein, E. Erkul, H. Stümpel, A. Ismail, J. Herrford, K. Olbert, A. Fediuk and D. Rose. The following text provides an account of the choice of investigative techniques as well as the results of the campaign.

While trial excavation would certainly have been the best method for testing a given location for the presence of Neolithic enclosures, it was not feasible here (due to cost concerns, the duration of excavation projects and the requisite land access permissions, etc.). In fact, when asked for permission to conduct geophysical measurements, almost all land owners pointed out that they would not allow excavations on their land. Therefore, very few (if any) sites could have been tested by means of trial excavation. Furthermore, while it was possible to conduct geophysi-

cal measurements on 20 sites over a four week period, it would have taken considerably more time to investigate the same number of sites by trial excavation. Naturally, this would also have resulted in higher costs.

The disadvantage of geophysical survey as compared to classical excavation, (especially in the heterogenic quaternary soils of South Scandinavia) lies in the difficulties in producing results which have the same degree of certainty. Geomagnetic surveys on two known north German enclosure sites (Büdelsdorf and Albersdorf Dieksknöll) by S. Lorra (1996) and the University of Kiel (unpublished) failed to produce any evidence for the ditches which were known to be present at both sites. The simple reason for this negative result is the lack of magnetic contrast between the natural surroundings and the fill of the ditches. Said ditches appear to have been regularly and deliberately backfilled with the same material that had previously been excavated from them. While it is still reasonable to assume that, under certain circumstances, geomagnetic survey would be able to detect the ditch segments of a Neolithic enclosure (e.g. when the ditches had been marked by glacial boulders/sealed with stone packing, when quantities of organic matter or fired clay/ceramics had been deposited in them or when they stood open long enough for a layer of humus to have formed inside), it is impossible to know in advance if these conditions were present at a po-

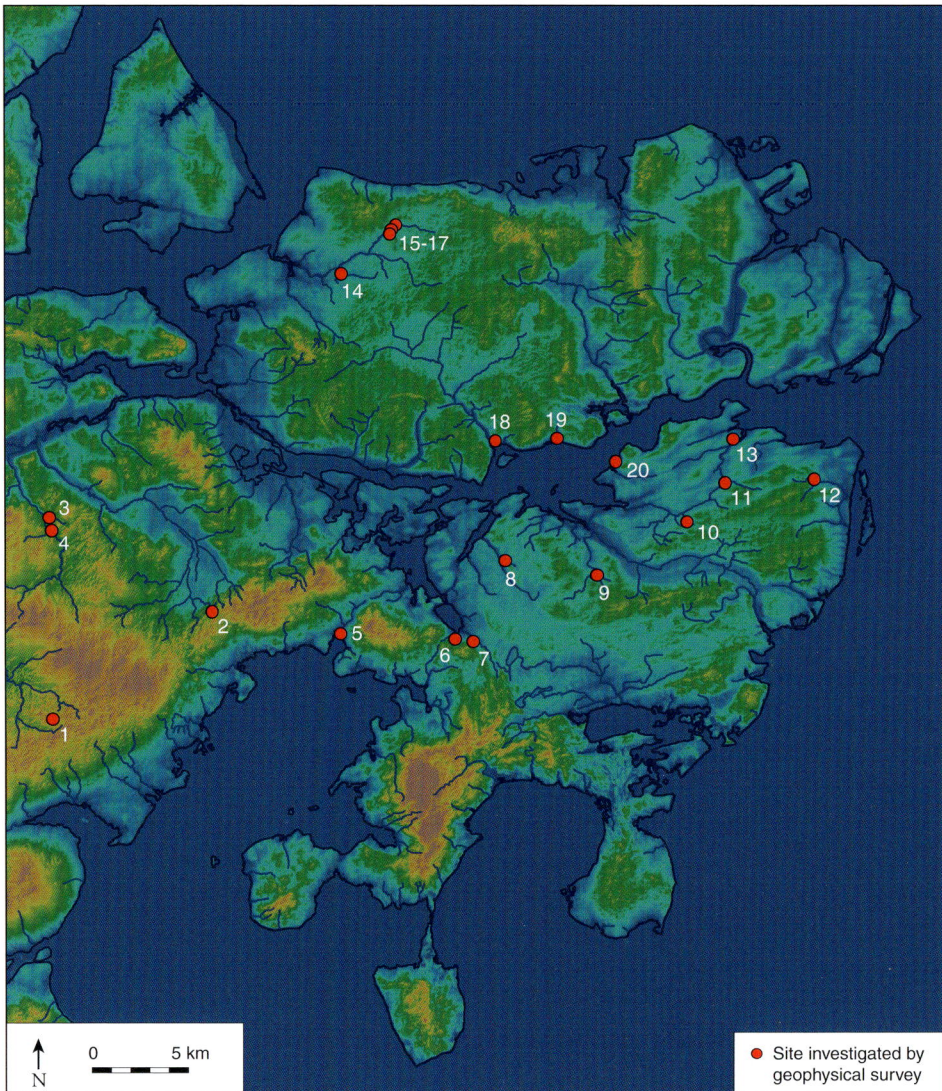

Fig. 1 | *The geographical distribution of the 20 sites on which geophysical survey was conducted in February, 2012. An approximate reconstruction of Djursland's coastline around 3500 BC was used as the background map. 1: 24 Todbjerg Møllebakke; 2: 58 Assenbakke; 3: 70 Skader N; 4: 70 Skader SØ; 5: 1 Følle Vig; 6: 3 Korup Sø; 7: Taastrup Kolindvej; 8: 79 Mårup N; 9: 28 Næsdrup Høj; 10: 53 Trustrup II; 11: 55 Fladstrup S; 12: 63 Høbjerg V; 13: 11 Revn I; 14: 31 Nielstrup I; 15: 41 Tustrup I; 16: 41 Tustrup II; 17: 41 Tustrup III; 18: 7 Vejvad Bro; 19: 8 Pognæs I; 20: 10 Søby I.*

tential enclosure site. Furthermore, even if these conditions were present, this was not necessarily true for all ditch segments in a (partial) circuit. Should this be the case, geomagnetic survey has the potential to reveal some ditch segments (or at least parts of some ditch segments). However, it is possible that the evidence would not be clear enough to recognize the anomalies as parts of (partial) enclosure ditch circuits. Furthermore, depending on the local geography, it is possible that the geological features recorded in geophysical measurements might be confused with enclosure ditches (Mennenga et al. 2013).

Therefore, ground penetrating radar (GPR) was chosen as the main investigation technique for the survey. GPR has several desirable advantages

within the context under investigation here. Obviously, one of the chief among these is the fact that this technique is able to detect disturbances in the natural layering of the soil directly. Thus, contrary to geomagnetics, its functionality is not necessarily dependant on the presence of deviant material in the ditch segments. Furthermore, this technique records profiles that provide information on the vertical extent of the features under investigation. Naturally, this is desirable when looking for ditches whose dimensions are roughly known. Nevertheless, GPR also has its disadvantages. Compared to geomagnetics, the area that can be covered/investigated within a given amount of time is much smaller, making the technique much more expensive in practice, effec-

Fig. 2 | *Geophysical techniques used in the present project. A) Geomagnetic survey with handcart and GPS-tracking, B) Two-channel ground penetrating radar (GPR) with GPS tracking dragged on a tractor-pulled sledge. Photos: Christina Klein.*

tively reducing the investigation area that can be covered for the same amount of money. Furthermore, the data handling involved is much more complicated as well as time consuming (which further augments costs). Another disadvantage is the complexity of the results. While an archaeologist with limited experience will be able to read geomagnetic plans to a certain degree, the same does not apply for GPR-produced profiles. Finally, pulling GPR antennas over the ground (either by hand or by a tractor) is much more harmful to crops than the light handcart needed for geomagnetic survey. In planted fields, therefore, GPR can only be used under certain weather circumstances (frozen earth, preferably with snow cover). Even then, some fields will be inaccessible due to the type of crop present.

The general ability of GPR to detect the ditch segments of a causewayed enclosure within the distribution area of the TRB North Group (and thus on soils roughly comparable to those encountered in Djursland) was proven by geophysicists from the University of Kiel at the Albersdorf Dieksknöll enclosure (unpublished). The same department conducted the geophysical survey in Djursland.

The GPR measures vertical profiles from which horizontal area renderings can be interpolated. These horizontal representations can be produced

for different depths (time slices) and are more accurate with decreased profile spacing. In the current case, comparatively wide spacing between the profiles was chosen because the sought-after structures (ditch segments) have a considerable size. This was accomplished by means of having a small tractor drag two-channel measuring equipment at 1 m intervals. (Fig. 2). The distance between the individual profiles thus was ca. 0.5 m. In two cases (in which the areas to be investigated were harvested corn fields), these distances were increased to approximately 1 m, due to the fact that the GPR antenna could not be dragged over the desiccated corn stalks.

Antennas with different frequencies were used for the two channels. The lower frequency 200 MHZ antenna had a larger penetration depth than the higher frequency 400 MHz antenna (which has a higher resolution in the upper soil horizon). As it was, it happened that the 200 MHz antenna produced results that were more easily interpreted. Therefore, in almost all cases, the following account of the measurement results refers to measurements with this latter antenna.

Due to the reasons described above, GPR was chosen as the main investigation technique. Nevertheless, geomagnetics were also used wherever possible to produce additional information. GPR could not be used due to the crops present on one site and parts of another. In these cases, geomagnetic investigation was the only survey method applied.

In total, measurements were conducted on 20 sites under mostly favourable weather conditions (dry, very cold, light snow cover). Of these 20 sites, 19 were investigated by GPR and 11 by geomagnetics. Ten of the sites were surveyed using both techniques. The surveyed area was considerable; it totalled 22.88 ha for geomagnetics and 11.96 ha for the GPR. The numbering of the sites follows Klassen's study (this volume).

2 Results of the geophysical survey

Taastrup Kolindvej, Feldballe Parish

Previous archaeological investigations had produced evidence for the presence of a potential Neolithic enclosure ditch segment at the Taastrup Kolindvej site in central Djursland. In a narrow trench dug in the course of road construction work, a ditch profile ca. 5 m wide and up to ca. 1.5 m deep was observed below the modern field surface. A flint axe fragment was found at the bottom of this ditch, while a large, almost metre-sized boulder was recorded higher up. Unfortunately, this ditch could not be properly recorded, due to the collapse of the profile. The available information is due, therefore, to the account given by excavator E. Kannegaard Nielsen from East Jutland Museum.

Thus, the presence of a potential enclosure at this location was known in advance. Therefore, the site was not chosen in order to test the predictive model, but rather to test the feasibility of geomagnetics and GPR under local soil conditions. The area on which the survey was conducted measured 1.0 ha (geomagnetics) and 0.21 ha (GPR measurements). It was placed in accordance with the available information from the previous excavation and was situated at a crossroads (Fig. 3).

The magnetogram of the site (Fig. 4) shows many anomalies. This is not unexpected, given local soil conditions (heterogenic quaternary soils including many stones with different magnetic properties). Most anomalies are probably caused by geological structures. However, a few may well be of human origin. This is true for a large and very dark positive anomaly of symmetrical round shape found close to the centre of the area (possibly a stone-built fireplace or pit containing pot boilers). Unfortunately, we cannot exclude the possibility that the anomaly was caused by a modern piece of metal. Some (possibly related) features are more difficult to recognize because they are situated in areas with many other (geological) anomalies. No (segmented) ditch is visible in the magnetogram. As is apparent from the GPR measurements (see below), one of the magnetic anomalies recognizable on the plan can indeed be related to a ditch. However, the anomaly

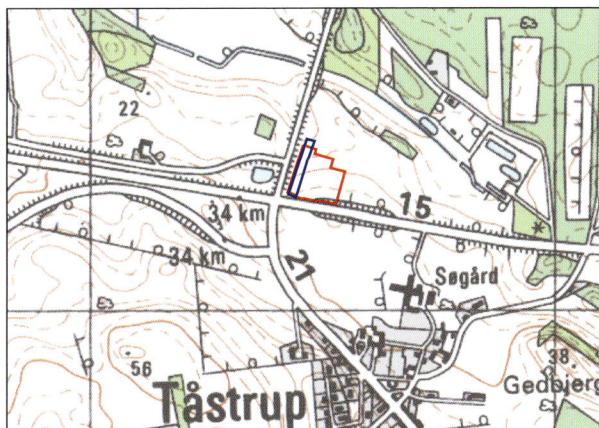

Fig. 3 | *Taastrup Kolindvej. The location of the areas investigated by geomagnetics (red) and GPR (blue). Map sheet 1315 II SV 1:25.000 (not to scale), © The Danish Geodata Agency.*

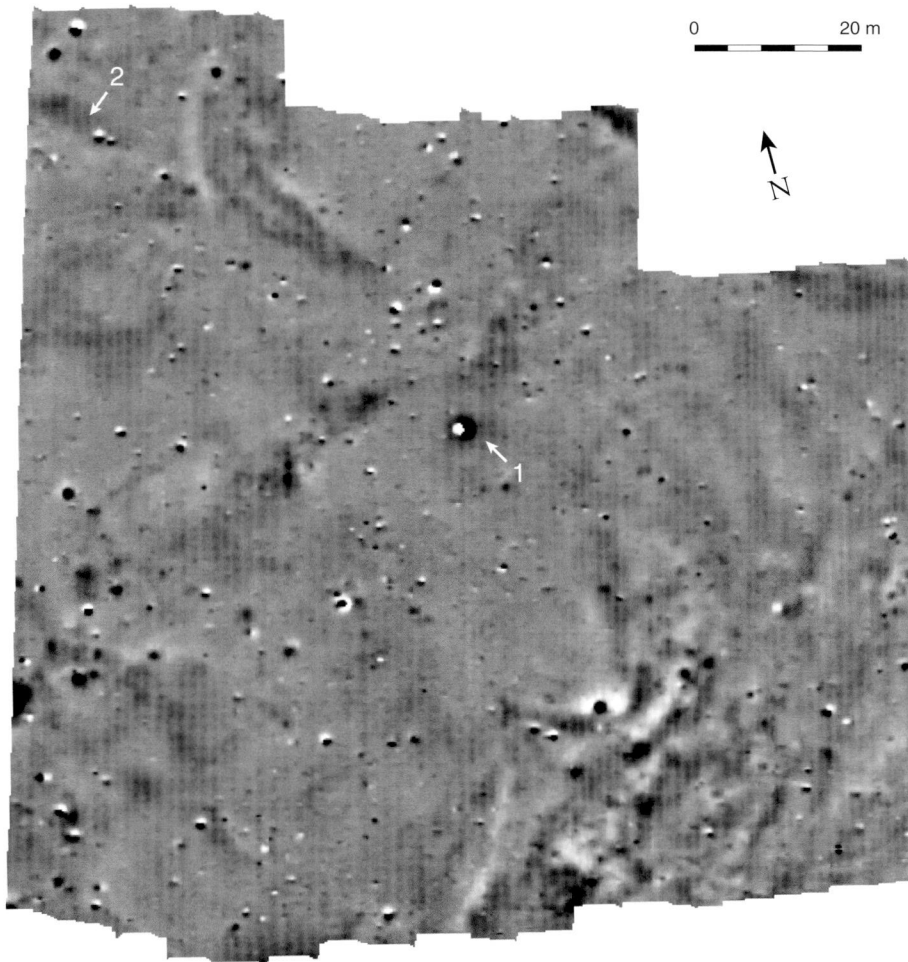

Fig. 4 | *Taastrup Kolindvej. The results of the geomagnetic survey (±12 nT). 1) Possible stone-set fireplace, 2) Positive anomaly related to the ditch structure. The remaining anomalies are probably of geological or modern origin. Archaeo-Geophysics, Institute of Geosciences, CAU Kiel.*

is not identifiable as such because it does not cover the entire course of the ditch. This finding clearly underlines methodological difficulties in using geomagnetics to detect Neolithic enclosures in South Scandinavian soils.

In the GPR measurement area rendering, a strikingly linear, very dark (radar-reflective) feature was immediately apparent in the northwest (Fig. 5). Nevertheless, this feature is only ca. 80 cm wide, and does not represent an enclosure ditch. As revealed by the radar profiles, this dark, reflective feature was caused by a row of large stones in a ditch (Fig. 6). The ditch is hardly visible in the area rendering measured by GPR. It is revealed only in some timeslices (depths) as a slightly irregular lighter coloured band ca. 5 m in width (Fig. 5). A look at individual radar profiles shows the ditch to be recognizable between ca. 50 and 150 cm below the present surface. It is ca. 5 m wide and has a rounded bottom.

The result of the geophysical measurements is in good accordance with the observations made during the excavation at the site. Due to GPR measurements, it is now possible to follow the ditch which was previously known only from a single profile 16 m to the southeast. Furthermore, it can be demonstrated that the large stone observed on excavation was not an exception; a row of comparable stones runs for almost the entire length of the ditch. As revealed by the geomagnetic measurements, none of these boulders appear to consist of any type of magnetic rock (i.e. granite); granite boulders of this size would cause strong positive anomalies.

Large stones in Neolithic enclosure ditches or related sites have previously been observed at Aalstrup (Madsen 2009), Markildegård (Sørensen 1995a; 1995b) and Toftum (Madsen, unpubl.) and have been interpreted as surface markers of the course of the re-filled ditches. The same could be the case at Taa-

Fig. 5 | *Taastrup Kolindvej. The area rendering of the GPR measurements (400 MHz antenna, time slice 20-24 ns) clearly shows a dark streak in the northern part of the area. Observations from previous archaeological investigations to the west (as well as radar profiles) allow this anomaly to be interpreted as a row of large stones in a ditch. The ditch itself is hardly visible and shows as a ca. 5 m wide band that is slightly lighter than its surroundings on both sides of the dark streak. Archaeo-Geophysics, Institute of Geosciences, CAU Kiel.*

strup Kolindvej. While the stones at Aalstrup and Markildegård possibly only marked the ends of individual ditch segments, almost the entire ditch at Taastrup Kolindvej appears to have been marked/covered. A comparably close stone spacing in a ditch was observed at the unpublished Fuglslev enclosure in Djursland (N.A. Boas, oral comm.).

The investigations at Taastrup Kolindvej are well-suited to demonstrating the potential of geophysical survey at Neolithic enclosure sites as well as the particular advantages of a combination of geomagnetics and ground penetrating radar. At the same time, these investigations also underscore the difficulties involved in demonstrating the presence of Neolithic enclosure ditch segments. As could be expected, geomagnetics failed in detecting the

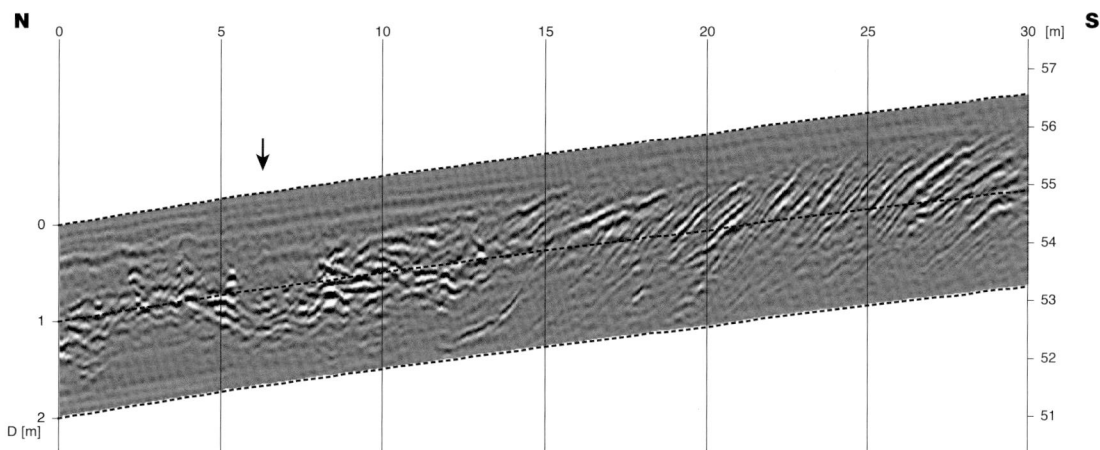

Fig. 6 | *Taastrup Kolindvej. The radar profile (recorded with a 400 MHz-antenna) shows a ca. 5 m wide, round bottomed ditch extending ca. 150 cm below the present day ground surface. A large stone in the ditch causes a strong reflection. Archaeo-Geophysics, Institute of Geosciences, CAU Kiel.*

ditch. Had it not been for the row of large boulders, the ditch may well have been overlooked entirely, as it is also hardly recognizable in the GPR area rendering. Only the detailed study of individual GPR profiles allowed for its identification as well as the establishment of its shape and dimensions.

Furthermore, due to the restricted size of the area under investigation, it is uncertain whether the ditch at Taastrup Kolindvej is in fact part of a Neolithic enclosure (see Klassen, this volume, chapter 3.10).

Because of the difficulties in identifying enclosure ditches present even via GPR measurements, the data for the remaining 19 sites were subjected to detailed scrutiny.

10 Søby I, Albøge Parish

At sites 3 Korup Sø and 10 Søby I, the circular structures visible in aerial photos from the 1970s were interpreted as potential reflections of Neolithic enclosures (see Klassen, this volume, chapter 7.3.3 Fig. 55 and 56). Unfortunately, geophysical measurements could not confirm this. Instead, the

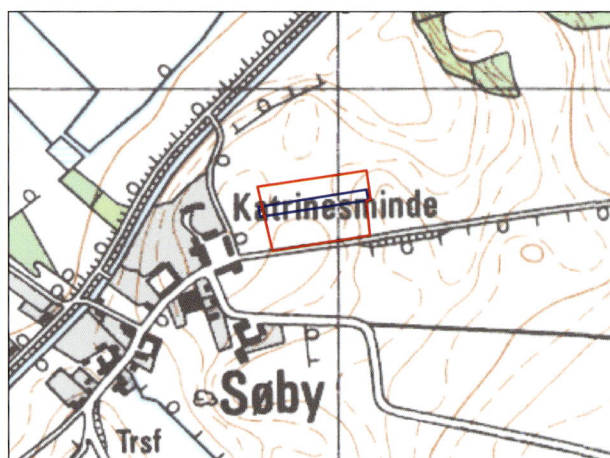

Fig. 7 | *10 Søby I. The location of the areas investigated by geomagnetics (red) and GPR (blue). Map sheet 1315 II NØ 1:25.000 (not to scale), © The Danish Geodata Agency.*

results revealed these unusual forms as the likely results of natural geological processes.

At 10 Søby I, an area measuring 1.8 ha was investigated with geomagnetics; 0.3 ha were examined by GPR. These investigation areas were laid out in accordance with the circular structure visible

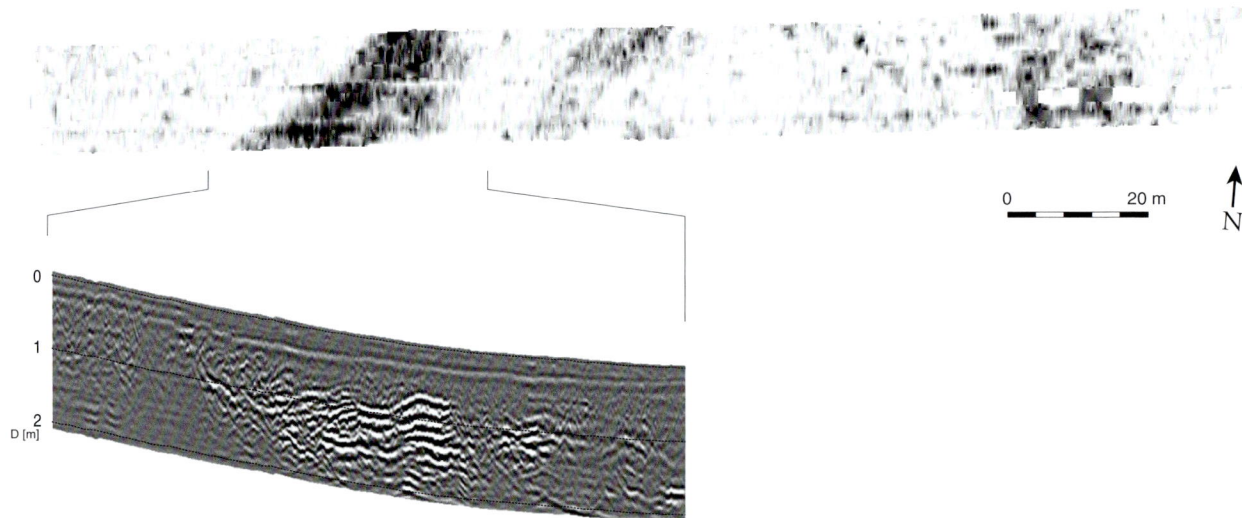

Fig. 8 | *10 Søby I. Results of the GPR measurements. A) In the area rendering (400 MHz antenna, time-slice 20-24 ns), the natural ditch structure is clearly visible as a dark, band-shaped feature running obliquely through the western part of the investigation area. B) The highly radar-reflective layers inside a ditch like-structure at depths below 1 m are clearly visible in the radar profiles recorded with the 400 MHz antenna. The structure appears much wider than 10 m in the profile because the latter was measured at oblique angle to the course of the ditch. Archaeo-Geophysics, Institute of Geosciences, CAU Kiel.*

Fig 9 | 10 Søby I. Re-
sults of the geomag-
netic survey (±6 nT).
Apart from some lost
pieces of metal, no
structures of certain
human origin can be
identified. Archaeo-
Geophysics, Institute of
Geosciences, CAU Kiel.

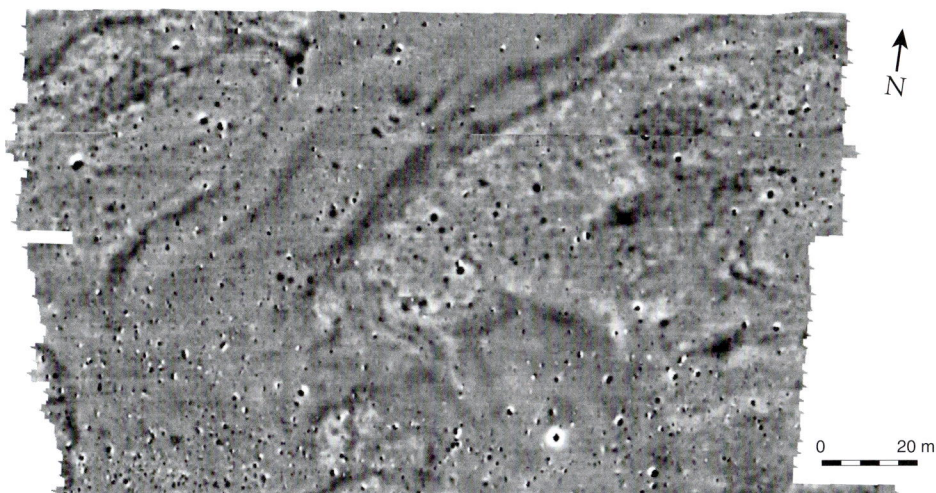

in aerial photos. Said circular structure apparently followed the edge of a natural depression (Fig. 7). GPR measurements demonstrated the existence of a ditch structure which led from the northeast towards the circular feature visible on the photo. The dimensions of this ditch structure (width ca. 12 m) are too large to reflect a Neolithic enclosure ditch. More likely, they reflect the site of an ancient water flow channel (Fig. 8). The geomagnetic measurements did not produce any evidence for any certain man-made structures, showing instead only geological features and vast amounts of strong positive anomalies from field stones/lost metal items (Fig. 9).

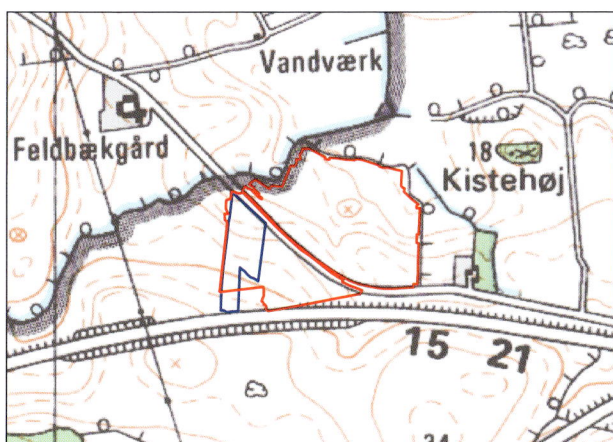

Fig. 10 | 3 Korup Sø. The location of the areas investigated by geomagnetics (red) and GPR (blue). Map sheet 1315 II NØ 1:25.000 (not to scale), © The Danish Geodata Agency.

3 Korup Sø, Bregnet Parish

At site 3 Korup Sø, the entire area (6 ha) covered by the circular structure visible on aerial photos was geomagnetically surveyed. The part of the area south of the road which bisects the space under investigation was examined by GPR (0.8 ha)(Fig. 10).

GPR measurements confirm the presence of irregular patches on the perimeter of the circle visible in the aerial photo (Fig. 11). The strong reflection is probably due to the high water content at these spots. The radar profiles suggest that they represent shallow depressions not more than 60-80 cm in depth (Fig. 12). Drilling in one of these depressions produced evidence of a series of very wet (natural) depositions.

The shallow wet depressions are barely visible in the geomagnetic plan (Fig. 13); they appear as rather homogenous zones bordered by areas with many positive anomalies that often form linear, approximately north-south oriented structures (themselves likely of geological origin). In the northern part of the area (north of the road), a circular geological structure can also be seen.

Nonetheless, several man-made structures are visible in the geomagnetic plan. A large angled linear structure appears in the centre of the area, positioned on a slight elevation in the terrain. The length of the sides of this structure (one of which appears to end at the modern day road) is almost 30 m. The shape of this feature very much

Fig. 11 | *3 Korup Sø. The area rendering of the GPR measurements (200 MHz antenna) clearly shows large radar-reflective patches near the surface which coincide with the dark patches seen on aerial photos. Archaeo-Geophysics, Institute of Geosciences, CAU Kiel.*

resembles that of a drainage system and it must, therefore, be assumed to be of rather recent date. The fact that this drainage should have been established on a natural elevation that offers good natural drainage is, nevertheless, somewhat odd. It may have something to do with a modern traffic accident in the area (causing large amounts of petrol to run into the field). As explained by the land owner, considerable digging was done afterwards in order to remove the petrol.

To the east of this probable drainage structure (on the opposite side of a channel-like depression created by water flow) a rather strong linear positive anomaly shows exactly the same orientation as one side of the angled drain. Just south of it are faint traces of a second angled structure comparable to the one further west. The strong anomaly is probably not due to any geological process, as it (as well as the possible drain located south of it) is oriented completely differently than the geological structures that are clearly identifiable. Therefore, both structures are probably contemporaneous (and thus of more or less modern age).

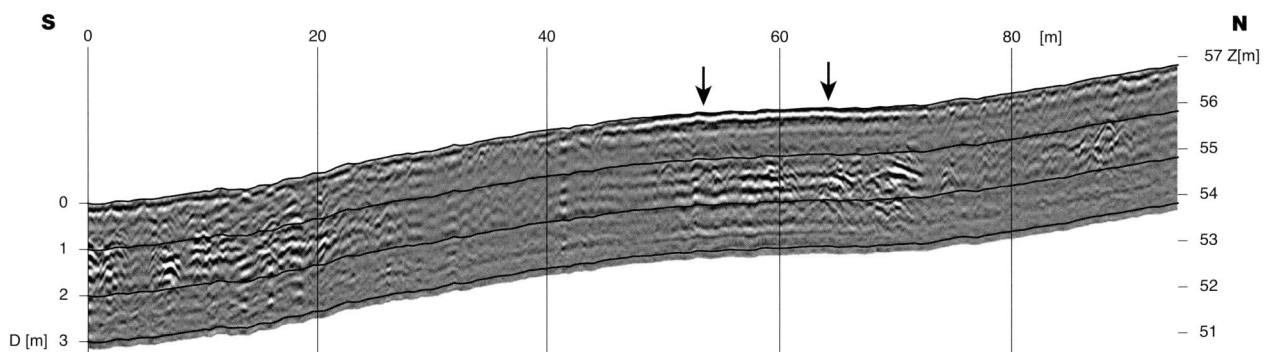

Fig. 12 | *3 Korup Sø. The radar profile through one of the dark patches visible in Fig. 11 reveals a shallow depression (not more than 60-80 cm deep) with very radar-reflective properties close to the surface which can be interpreted as a natural phenomenon. Archaeo-Geophysics, Institute of Geosciences, CAU Kiel.*

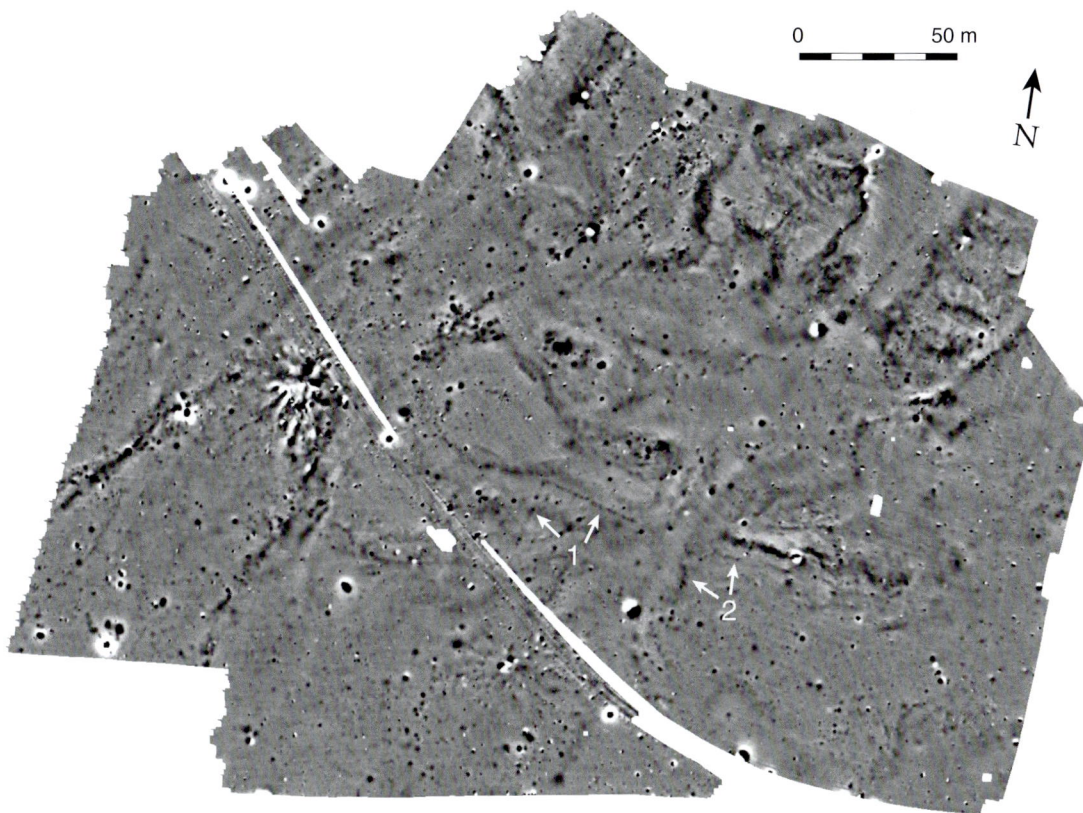

Fig. 13 | 3 Korup Sø. Results of the geomagnetic survey of the site (±12 nT). The angled linear structure in the centre of the area (1) and possibly a comparable (but much weaker) structure to the east (2) probably reflect a modern drain. A few of the dark anomalies may well be prehistoric pits, but the vast majority of features are of geological origin. North of the road dividing the investigation area, an arc-shaped geological structure can be identified which must be responsible for the ring-shaped structure visible in aerial photos. Archaeo-Geophysics, Institute of Geosciences, CAU Kiel.

31 Nielstrup I, Vivild Parish

Strong positive magnetic anomalies of particular symmetric, round shapes (which can most probably be interpreted as the result of stone-set fireplaces or fire-cracked stone dumps) have been identified at a number of sites. Of these, those found at sites 11 Revn I, 31 Nielstrup I and 1 Følle Vig are of special interest, because they can possibly date from the TRB Culture (see Klassen, this volume, chapter 7.3.2.2).

At site 31 Nielstrup I, the features under discussion were discovered in two clusters, both of which are located in a cleared, rectangular area surrounded by woods. This opening in the forest (as well as areas to the south, north and east) was investigated by geomagnetic survey. In total, said survey covered 2.0 ha. A further 0.3 ha were covered by GPR in two separate areas (Fig. 14).

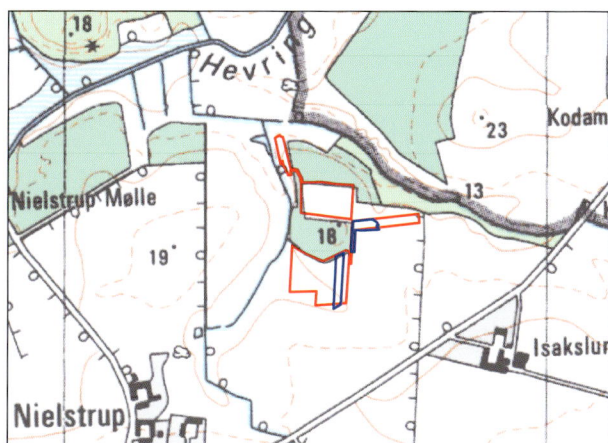

Fig. 14 | 31 Nielstrup I. The location of the areas investigated by geomagnetics (red) and GPR (blue). Map sheet 1315 I SV 1:25.000 (not to scale), © The Danish Geodata Agency.

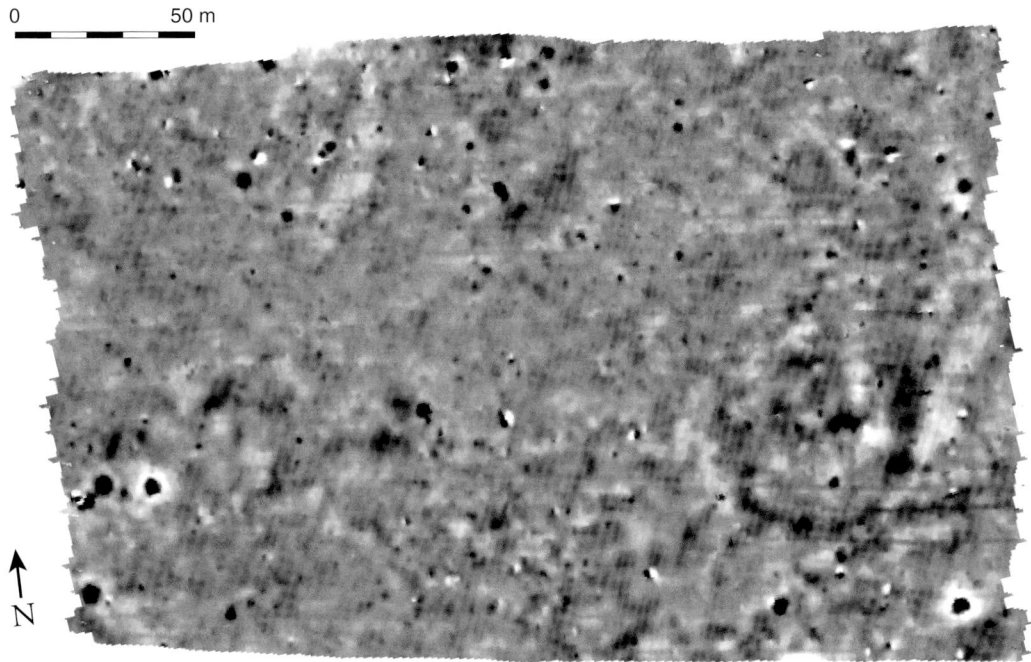

Fig. 15 | *31 Nielstrup I. Geomagnetic survey of the central investigation area (±6 nT) produced evidence for several strong and very symmetrical and round anomalies. According to previous archaeological investigations at the site, these are probably caused by stone-set fireplaces. Several other anomalies cannot be identified more precisely, but are possibly man-made structures that possibly date to the TRB Culture. Archaeo-Geophysics, Institute of Geosciences, CAU Kiel.*

The results of geomagnetic survey appear in Fig. 15. Most of the strong positive anomalies visible in the northern part of this area are probably due to the fireplaces/pits with fire-cracked stones that were uncovered by earlier excavations (but were often not properly excavated). Additional features (hitherto unregistered) are visible in the southwest corner. The anomalies in the southeast part are possibly identical to several fireplaces that have been recorded in earlier investigations.

Besides the strong anomalies probably due to stone-set fireplaces (or the occasional large natural boulder), a number of more diffuse, dark anomalies are seen throughout the entire area. They seem to concentrate especially in the southeast corner. These anomalies probably also represent Neolithic pits and other constructions (a few of which were found during fieldwork in the 1980s).

In the remaining areas of site 31 Nielstrup I surveyed with geomagnetics, several strong, round and symmetric positive anomalies are visible which probably also represent stone-set fireplaces (Fig.

16A-C). This is true for the somewhat disturbed northern area, the northernmost part of the southern area as well as the westernmost part of the eastern area. However, there were no traces of enclosure ditches in the geomagnetic plans.

Investigation by GPR demonstrated the presence of ditch structures to the east and south of the small forest on the site. However, these ditch-structures are much too large to have had anything to do with Neolithic enclosure ditches. Moreover, they are located on the lowest part of the terrain (Fig. 17). Therefore, they can be identified as geological structures (former water flow channels).

In summary, it can be stated that the evidence for stone-set fireplaces (or pits filled with fire-cracked stones) at site 31 Nielstrup I was enlarged by geophysical survey. A number of likely Neolithic structures of unknown nature were found. According to the GPR investigation, no enclosure ditches were present. While it is not impossible that such ditches could be hidden in unsurveyed

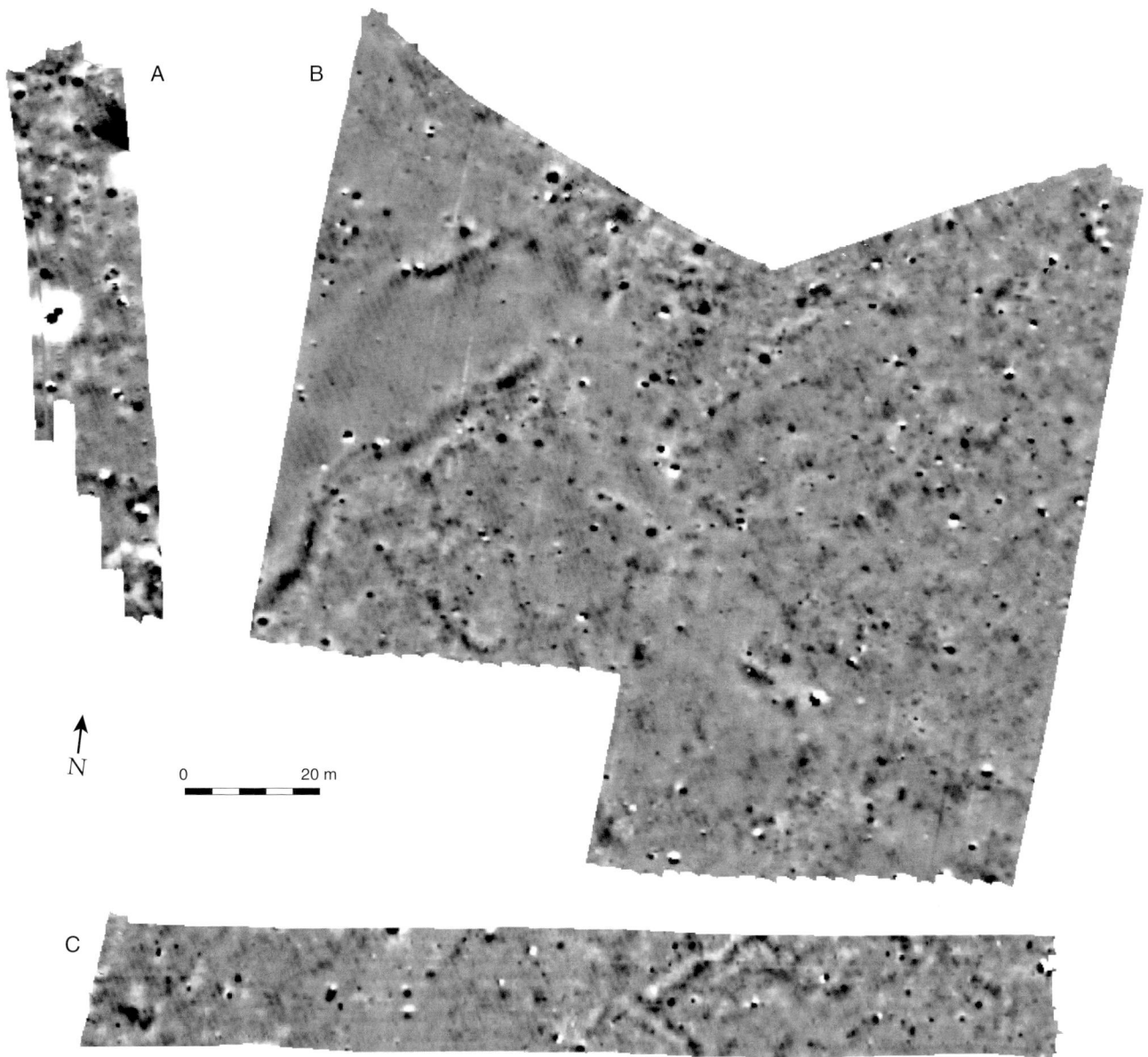

Fig. 16 | *31 Nielstrup I. Geomagnetic survey of different parts of the investigation area (±6 nT). Several probable stone-set fireplaces as well as other, probably man-made structures of unidentified nature can be recognized. A) northern part, B) southern part and C) eastern part. Archaeo-Geophysics, Institute of Geosciences, CAU Kiel.*

Fig. 17 | *31 Nielstrup I. GPR profile (200 MHz antenna) from the eastern investigation area showing a ca. 20 m wide natural ditch structure in the lowest part. Archaeo-Geophysics, Institute of Geosciences, CAU Kiel.*

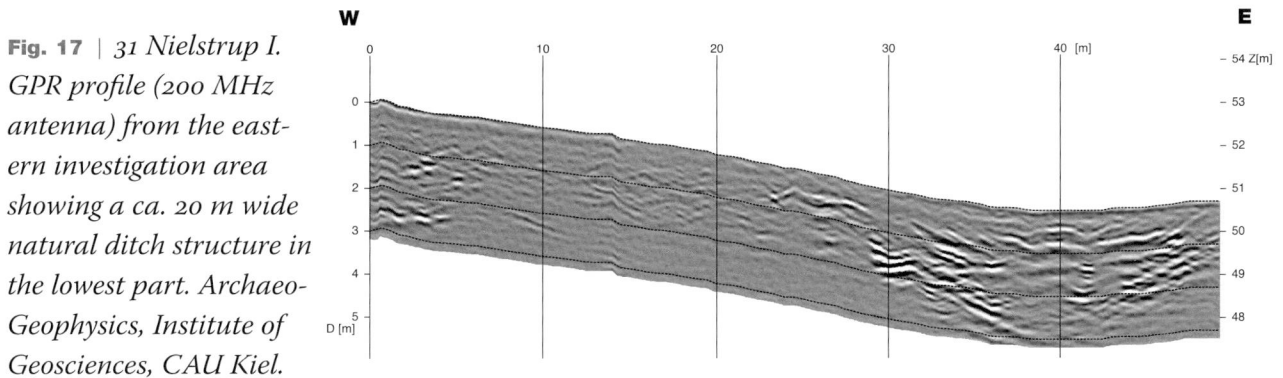

Results of the geophysical survey · 299

parts of the area (e.g. inside the woods), this does not seem very likely given the promontory's topography.

11 Revn I, Vejlby Parish

Geophysical investigation at site 11 Revn I was carried out with both geomagnetics and GPR. Geomagnetic survey covered two separate areas which were 250 and 300 m long and 50 and 35 m wide respectively. The combined area of both measured 2.4 ha. The area investigated by GPR was similar to the southern of the two geomagnetically surveyed areas, albeit somewhat longer (400 m). It measures 1.13 ha in size (Fig. 18).

In the Revn I geomagnetic plan, strong positive anomalies are apparent in a linear arrangement (Fig. 19). This is true especially for the northern part of the northern investigation area. However, several also appear in the northernmost part of the southern investigation area. The area with the highest frequency of these anomalies is identical to that with the highest density of Neolithic surface finds as well as with the area in which possible pits can be identified in aerial photos (Klassen, this volume, chapter 7.3.1 Fig. 57). As the surface finds belong almost exclusively to the TRB Culture, the same is probably true for the features which caused the anomalies (at least in some instances). Others may be caused by geo-

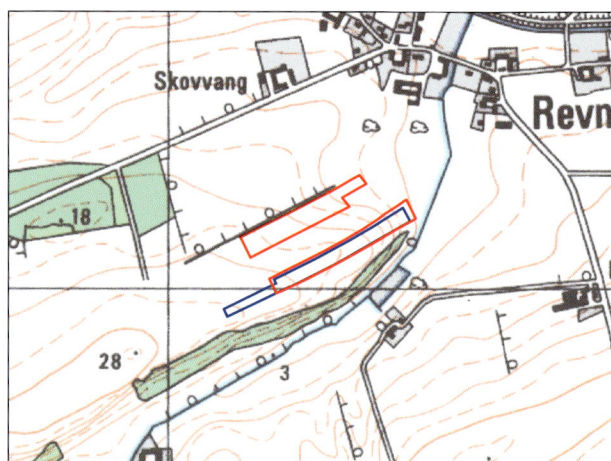

Fig. 18 | *11 Revn I. The location of the areas investigated by geomagnetics (red) and GPR (blue). Map sheet 1315 II NØ 1:25.000 (not to scale), © The Danish Geodata Agency.*

logical features. Without excavation, this cannot be confirmed at present. It is also unknown whether these anomalies were caused by stone set fireplaces or fire-cracked stones as at 31 Nielstrup I, or if they represent pits with depositions of other types of materials with magnetic properties (e.g. pottery).

The arrangement of pits in long lines is in fact known from the northern TRB. A 60 m long row consisting of 46 pits was excavated at Triwalk in northeast Germany. This row of pits was visible for a further 200 m in the geophysical survey re-

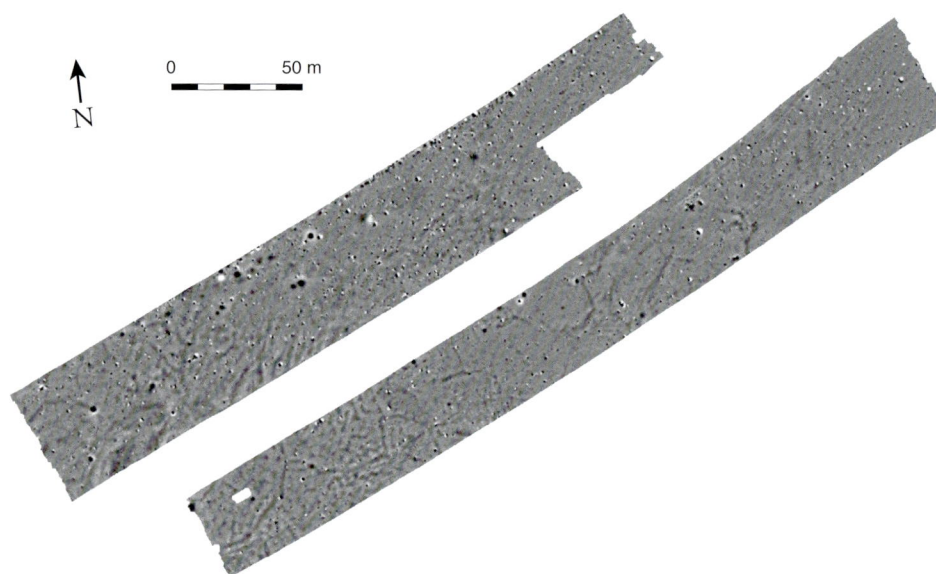

Fig. 19 | *11 Revn I. Results of the geomagnetic survey (±12 nT). Many strong, round anomalies probably representing stone-set fireplaces are visible, especially in the northern parts of the two investigation areas. Archaeo-Geophysics, Institute of Geosciences, CAU Kiel.*

sults (Müller/Staude 2012). The pits show traces of recutting comparable to that of ditches in causewayed enclosures. Therefore, Triwalk has been classified as an enclosure-related site (Klassen, this volume, chapter 4).

Triwalk appears thus to be the best potential parallel to 11 Revn I. No segmented ditches were found at Triwalk. The same is true for Revn I, where any anomalies/signals that could reflect such ditches are missing (both from the geomagnetic and GPR measurements). In summary, it can be concluded that geophysical survey produced potential evidence for the presence of an enclosure-related row of pits at site 11 Revn I. However, their presence must be confirmed through excavation.

1 Følle Vig, Bregnet Parish

At site 1 Følle Vig, two separate areas to the west and to the south of a minor forest were investigated by geomagnetics and GPR (Fig. 20). Both investigation areas are separated by a minor road. While the entirety of accessible area has been covered by geomagnetics (both sub areas combined yielded a total of 3.63 ha), an area measuring ca. 200 m in length and 30 m in width (0.57 ha) was measured with GPR in the northern sub area. In the southern part of site 1 Følle Vig, a 120 m long and 5-6 m wide zone oriented east to west (parallel to the road) and a ca. 60 m long and 30 m wide area at right angles to the latter were investigated by GPR. When combined, the areas total 0.29 ha.

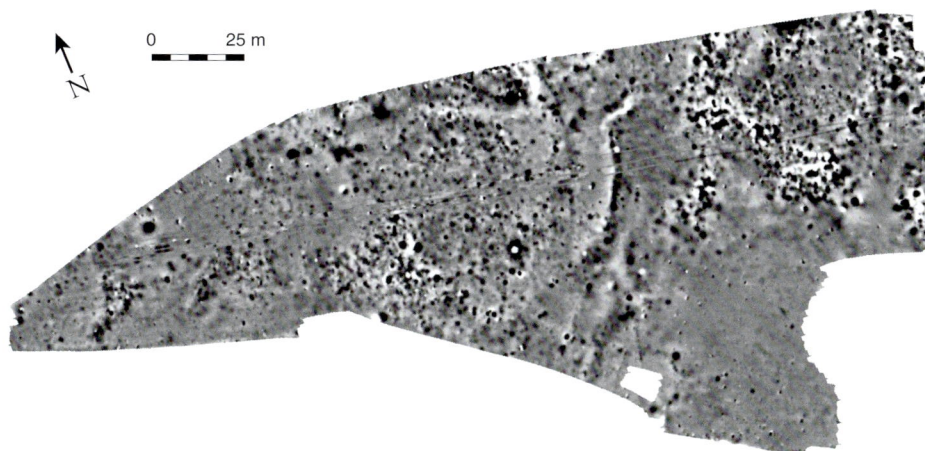

Fig. 20 | 1 Følle Vig. The location of the areas investigated by geomagnetics (red) and GPR (blue). Map sheet 1315 II SV 1:25.000 (not to scale), © The Danish Geodata Agency.

Geomagnetic survey revealed a number of round positive anomalies at the northern edge of the southern investigation area (Fig. 21). Just as at 31 Nielstrup I, these probably reflect stone set fireplaces. Several more of these may be hidden in other parts of the area (further south and east). However, they are more difficult to identify because they are situated in areas with many other strong anomalies (the results of geological structures/stone accumulations). Earlier trial excavations to the north and east of this part of the investigation area demonstrated the existence of stone-set fireplaces at the site. Unfortunately, these could not be dated (unpublished investigations by Ebeltoft Museum, j.nr. EBM 806). Contrary to the

Fig. 21 | 1 Følle Vig. Results of the geomagnetic survey of the southern investigation area (±12 nT). A number of characteristic anomalies close to the northern border are probably caused by stone-set fireplaces. Archaeo-Geophysics, Institute of Geosciences, CAU Kiel.

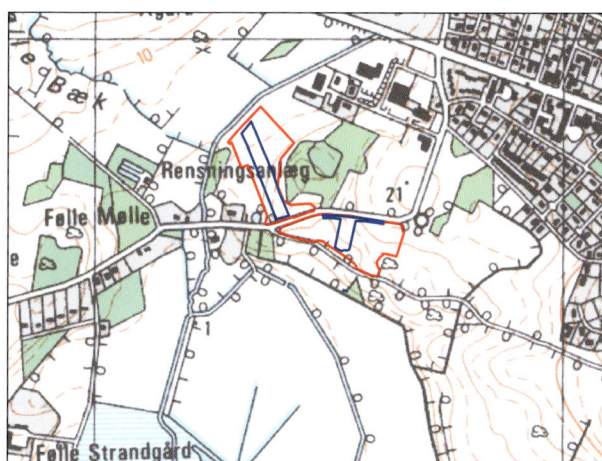

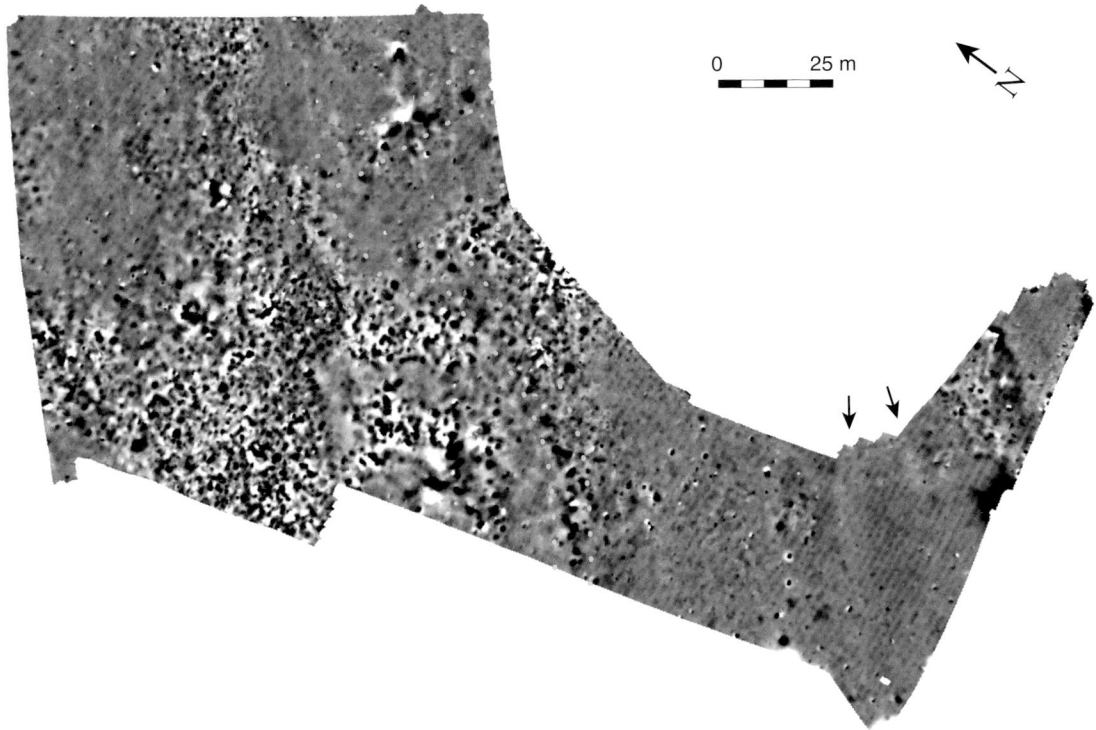

Fig. 22 | *1 Følle Vig. Results of the geomagnetic survey of the northern investigation area (±12 nT). Weak, parallel, band-shaped anomalies in the southern part of the investigation area are probably caused by geological structures in the subsoil; the linear feature consisting of many small, round anomalies probably reflects a man-made structure of unknown type and age. Archaeo-Geophysics, Institute of Geosciences, CAU Kiel.*

situation at 31 Nielstrup I (and, possibly, at 11 Revn I), there is, therefore, no information that might link these features to the TRB Culture. Although such a date cannot be excluded, the fireplaces more likely belong to the Younger Bronze Age.

There are no hints at the existence of ditch segments in the geomagnetic plan for this part of the investigation area. The same is true for GPR measurements.

In the southernmost part of the northern investigation area (just west of the large, very strong anomaly caused by a modern traffic sign at the road), the geomagnetic plan shows two weak, parallel band-shaped positive magnetic anomalies running southwest-northeast (Fig. 22). These structures are clearly visible as light stripes separated and bordered by dark stripes at depths of circa 2 m below the surface in the GPR area rendering (Fig. 23). The width of the white stripes measures ca. 6-7 m, which would match well with the expected widths of the ditches from a Neolithic enclosure. However, these

structures coincide with a topographical ridge in the area. While this does not necessarily mean that they do not represent Neolithic ditches (they may well have been placed in such a position), it could indicate that these anomalies have a geological origin. Radar profiles are useful in resolving this dilemma. They clearly show areas with weak radar reflective properties (marked by light areas in the area rendering) between oblique soil layers (Fig. 24). The width of these areas in the profiles is ca. 10 m (rather than 6-7 m) because of the fact that the profiles were measured at an oblique angle to the course of the band-shaped features. The oblique layers are part of several ditch-like structures (themselves revealed as geological features by their size: ca. 20-40 m in width)(Fig. 24). It can be concluded that the linear features visible in both geomagnetics and the GPR area rendering represent geological features.

A linear feature appears in the geomagnetic plan of the northern investigation area of site 1 Følle Vig (Fig. 22). It represents a slightly convex row 80

m in length which consists of point-shaped positive anomalies, running from southwest to northeast. At its northern end, a northwest-southeast rectangular linear feature measuring 40 by 25 m consists of the same type of positive anomalies. A geologic origin appears unlikely, given the shape of this feature. The single anomalies that make up the rows also appear to be slightly different from the numerous anomalies that are almost certainly caused by naturally-occurring stones in the underground. Furthermore, the course of the lines does not follow the topography. Therefore, this peculiar feature (for which there are no known parallels) probably represents a man-made construction. The positive magnetic anomalies from which it is formed may represent selected stones in a stone setting or postholes with or without supporting stones from a palisade construction. There are no hints whatsoever as to the dating of this structure. The area is grass-covered. The molehills revealed only insignificant flint debris, probably Neolithic in age.

Fig. 23 | *1 Følle Vig. The area rendering of the GPR measurements (200 MHz antenna, time slice 44-48 ns) of the northern investigation area (excerpt of the southernmost part of the investigation area) shows the band-shaped structures in the southern part which are also apparent from geomagnetic survey. Archaeo-Geophysics, Institute of Geosciences, CAU Kiel.*

79 Mårup N, Nødager Parish

Structures that might represent ditches of Neolithic enclosures were detected on four of the sites investigated by geomagnetic and/or GPR measurements (79 Mårup N, 58 Assenbakke, 53 Trustrup II and 55 Fladstrup S).

Site 79 Mårup N was investigated by GPR only. The investigation area was ca. 250 m long and 20

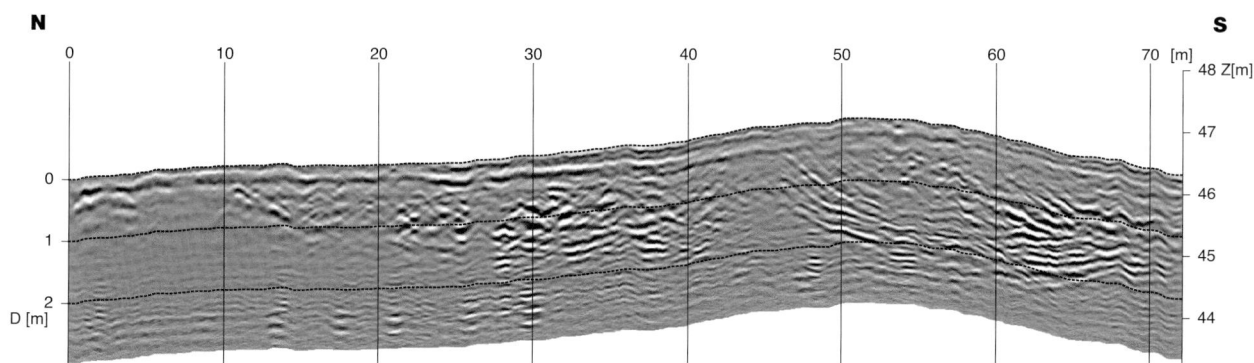

Fig. 24 | *1 Følle Vig. Excerpt of radar profile (200 MHz antenna) from the northern investigation area showing the geological structures responsible for the band-shaped anomalies depicted in Figs. 22-23. Archaeo-Geophysics, Institute of Geosciences, CAU Kiel.*

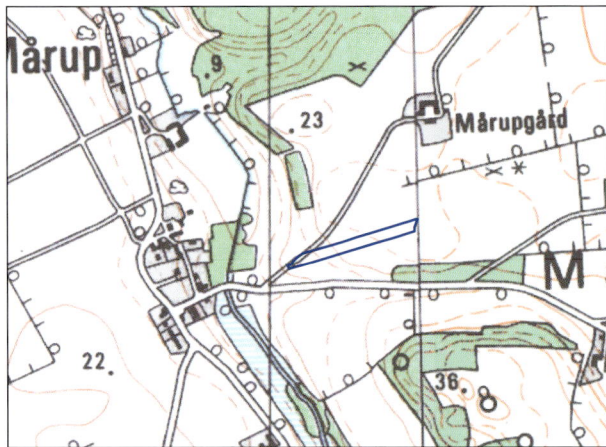

m wide and covered 0.51 ha. It was laid out in such a manner that it cut diagonally through a promontory formed by two minor rivers (Fig. 25).

A possible single enclosure ditch appears as a bright and somewhat diffuse linear feature in the GPR area rendering at ca. 210 m from the Mårup Å River to the west. It is best visible at depths of around 1-2 m and is oriented perpendicularly to the oblong measurement area (Fig. 26). The radar profiles show a V-shaped feature (ca. 2 m deep and up to 8-10 m wide) in the upper portion (Fig. 27). The width and oblique natural layers on the western flank also could indicate a geological feature. However, this feature might also have a man-made origin. TRB North Group enclosures ditch width has been recorded at measurements of up to 10 m (Guldin 2011). If confirmed as a Neolithic ditch, this would delimit an enclosure ranging in size between 3 and 4 ha. However, until this can be confirmed by trial excavations, site 79 Mårup N can only be classified as a possible enclosure site.

53 Trustrup II, Lyngby Parish

A comparable situation appears from site 53 Trustrup II. At Trustrup II, an east-west oriented area (ca. 17 x 210 m) and a north-south area (ca. 35 x 260 m) were investigated by GPR (Fig. 28). Both

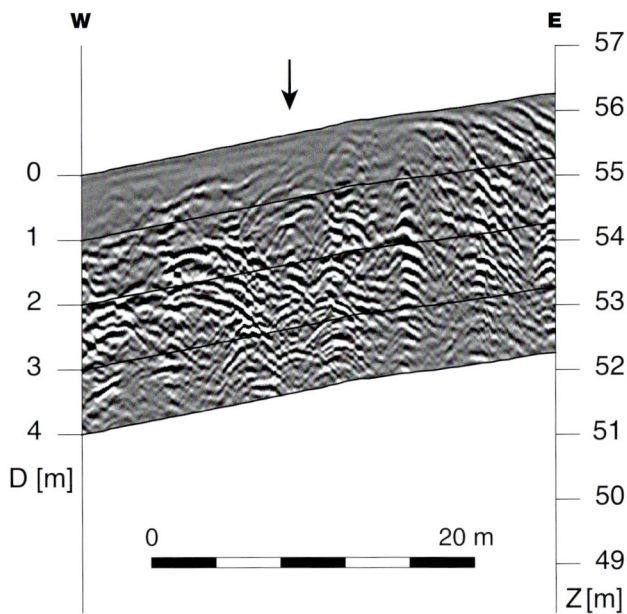

Fig. 27 | *79 Mårup N. Radar profile showing a possible Neolithic enclosure ditch. Archaeo-Geophysics, Institute of Geosciences, CAU Kiel.*

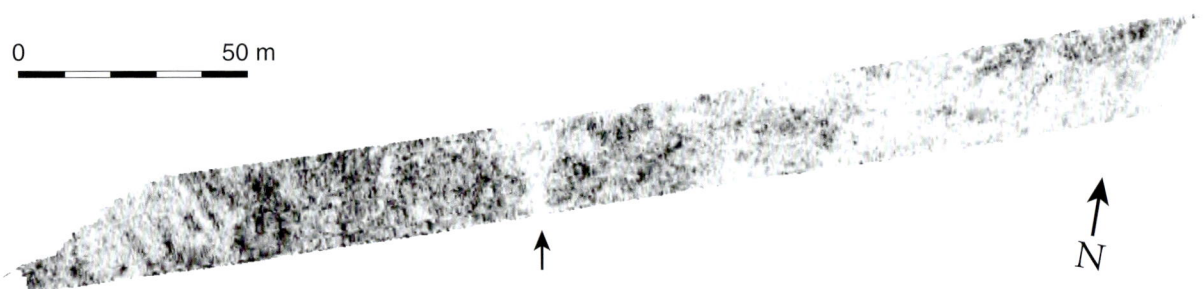

Fig. 26 | *79 Mårup N. The area rendering of the GPR measurements (200 MHz antenna, time slice 24-28 ns) shows a possible ditch segment of a Neolithic enclosure as a band-shaped light feature running across the measurement area. Archaeo-Geophysics, Institute of Geosciences, CAU Kiel.*

investigation areas were laid out in such a way that they ran from low-lying, wet areas to a hilltop, where they meet at a right angle. In total, the area covered measures 1.23 ha in size.

In the east-west oriented branch of the investigation area, a well-defined, linear, radar-reflective feature can be found close to the hilltop (Fig. 29). Said structure is oriented north-south and is, thus, perpendicular to this part of the investigation area. This linear feature possibly reappears in the north-south oriented branch of the investigation area ca. 50 m to the north of the meeting point of the two branches. It can be followed here for ca. 30 m along a curved, diagonal course before it takes a sharp turn and then runs almost precisely north-south for a further 40 m. Provided that it continues after

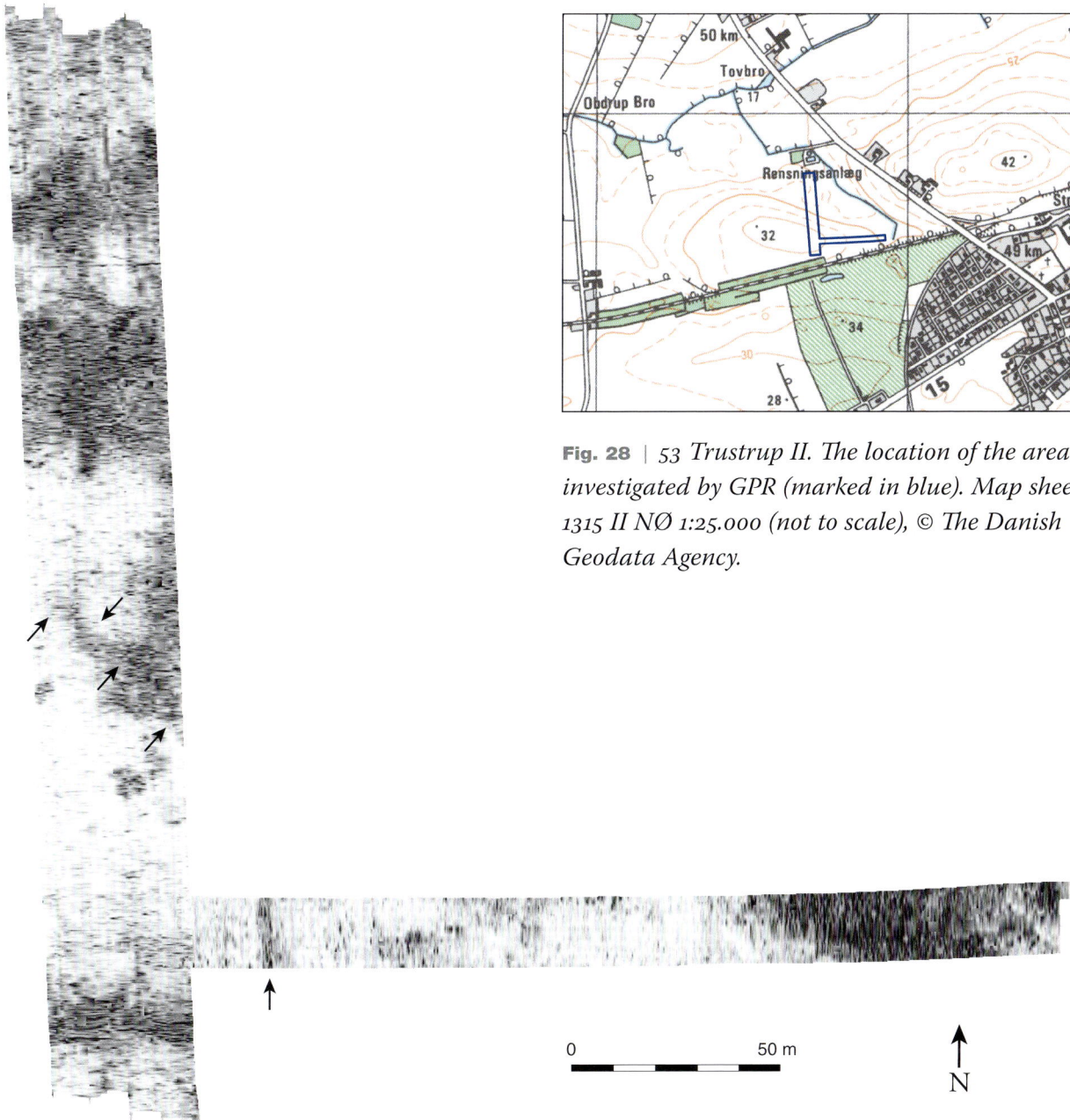

Fig. 28 | 53 *Trustrup II. The location of the area investigated by GPR (marked in blue). Map sheet 1315 II NØ 1:25.000 (not to scale), © The Danish Geodata Agency.*

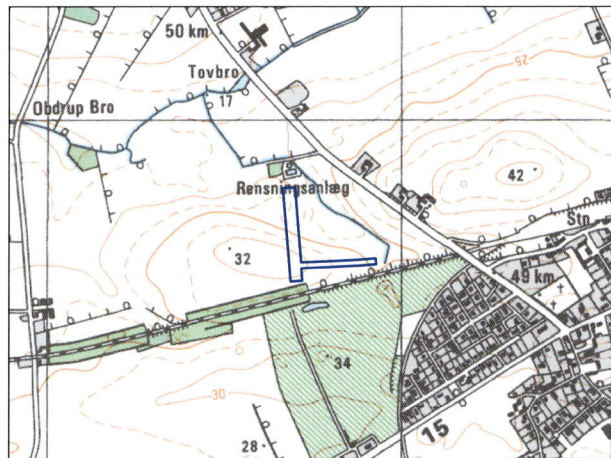

Fig. 29 | 53 *Trustrup II. In the area rendering of the GPR measurements (200 MHz antenna, depth layer 100-120 cm), linear, radar-dark features possibly belonging to the same ditch structure are seen in both parts of the angled investigation area. Archaeo-Geophysics, Institute of Geosciences, CAU Kiel.*

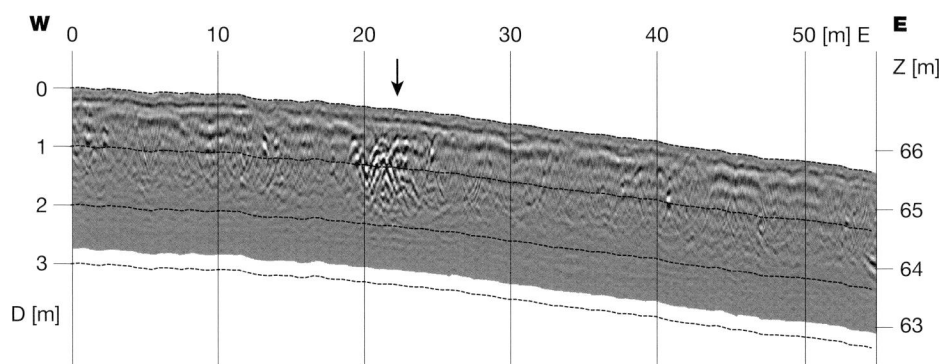

Fig. 30 | *53 Trustrup II. Radar profile (200 MHz antenna) of a possible Neolithic ditch with a width of up to 7 m at the surface and a depth of ca. 1.7 m. Archaeo-Geophysics, Institute of Geosciences, CAU Kiel.*

that point, the course of the feature cannot be followed, as it enters a very radar-reflective area. This last (completely linear) part of the course of the described radar anomaly should nevertheless be regarded with caution. It is oriented in exactly the same direction as were the GPR antenna readings. In the northernmost part of this branch of the investigation area, several comparable, completely linear features can be observed that share exactly the same orientation. These clearly give the impression of being measurement errors of some kind. Furthermore, their width is somewhat smaller than both that of the curved part of the anomaly and the linear anomaly in the second branch of the investigation area. Therefore, the linear, north-south part of the anomaly has been disregarded here.

Just north of the hill, at the northern end of the north-south branch of the investigation area lies a sewage treatment plant. Therefore, the remaining potential ditch structure was first interpreted as the possible reflection of a sewage line. However, it would be strange to find sewage pumped over a hill. Moreover, a control of the course of all sewage pipes around the hill showed that there were no pipes in the area which surrounds the radar feature discussed here. Therefore, this feature must represent either a geological phenomenon or a man-made structure of possible prehistoric age. In that case, abundant surface finds from both the TRB and the Late Neolithic provide a possible age for this structure. As no ditch constructions are known from the Late Neolithic, a TRB date and, thus, the presence of an enclosure would be the most obvious explanation.

The radar profiles show a structure ca. 4.5 m wide with highly radar-reflective layering below the plough horizon (ca. 1.75 m below the surface). This radar-reflective zone is flanked by oblique layers forming a V-shaped structure which measures ca. 2 m deep/7 m wide at the surface (Fig. 30). While this may well be a Neolithic enclosure ditch, the possibility that it represents a geological feature cannot be excluded. The possible interruption at the feature's sharp turn would be characteristic of an enclosure ditch. According to the apparent course of the possible ditch, if a Neolithic enclosure were present at the site, it would have been of the rare hilltop type and would have covered an area of ca. 2 ha. However, just as at site 79 Mårup N, a trial excavation is needed to determine whether the feature detected by GPR measurements is geological or man-made. Until then, site 53 Trustrup II can be regarded only as a possible Neolithic enclosure.

55 Fladstrup S, Homå Parish

At site 55 Fladstrup S, the tip of a pronounced promontory bordered by two confluent watercourses was examined by both geomagnetics and GPR (Fig. 31). The areas investigated measured 1.5 ha (geomagnetics) and 0.23 ha (GPR). The measurements with the latter technique were restricted to the northernmost parts of the area. Nevertheless, even this reduced area revealed some features which were obviously man-made. Unfortunately, field reconnaissance in the area subjected to geophysical survey could not be properly completed (the field was harvested but unploughed). That being said, the area immediately to the west delivered abundant TRB finds from one (or several) Middle Neolithic phases of the culture.

Geomagnetics revealed an area marked by geological structures as well as a (more or less) even spread of strong positive anomalies which most probably represent stones (Fig. 32). Several of these seem to be of considerable size. These observations match well with the farmer's account of having removed large boulders from the field. In the southernmost part of the area, there are considerably fewer geological structures and stones. These characteristics appear to be caused by the local geology, as there is an outcrop of loamy underground in an otherwise sandy field. Indeed, such sandy soil characterizes the area.

There are a few positive magnetic anomalies that either certainly or probably represent anthropogenic features. This is true for two com-

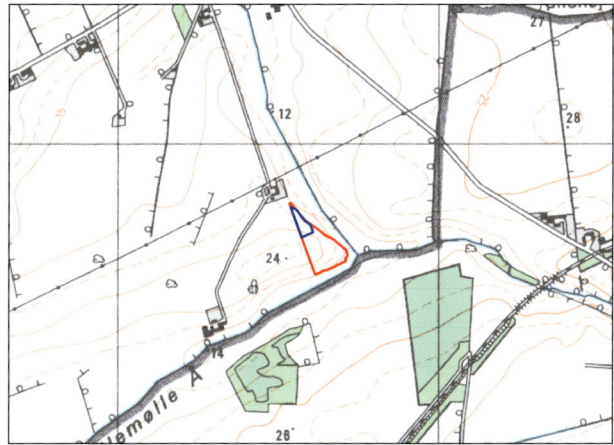

Fig. 31 | *55 Fladstrup S. The location of the areas investigated by geomagnetics (red) and GPR (blue). Map sheet 1315 II NØ 1:25.000 (not to scale), © The Danish Geodata Agency.*

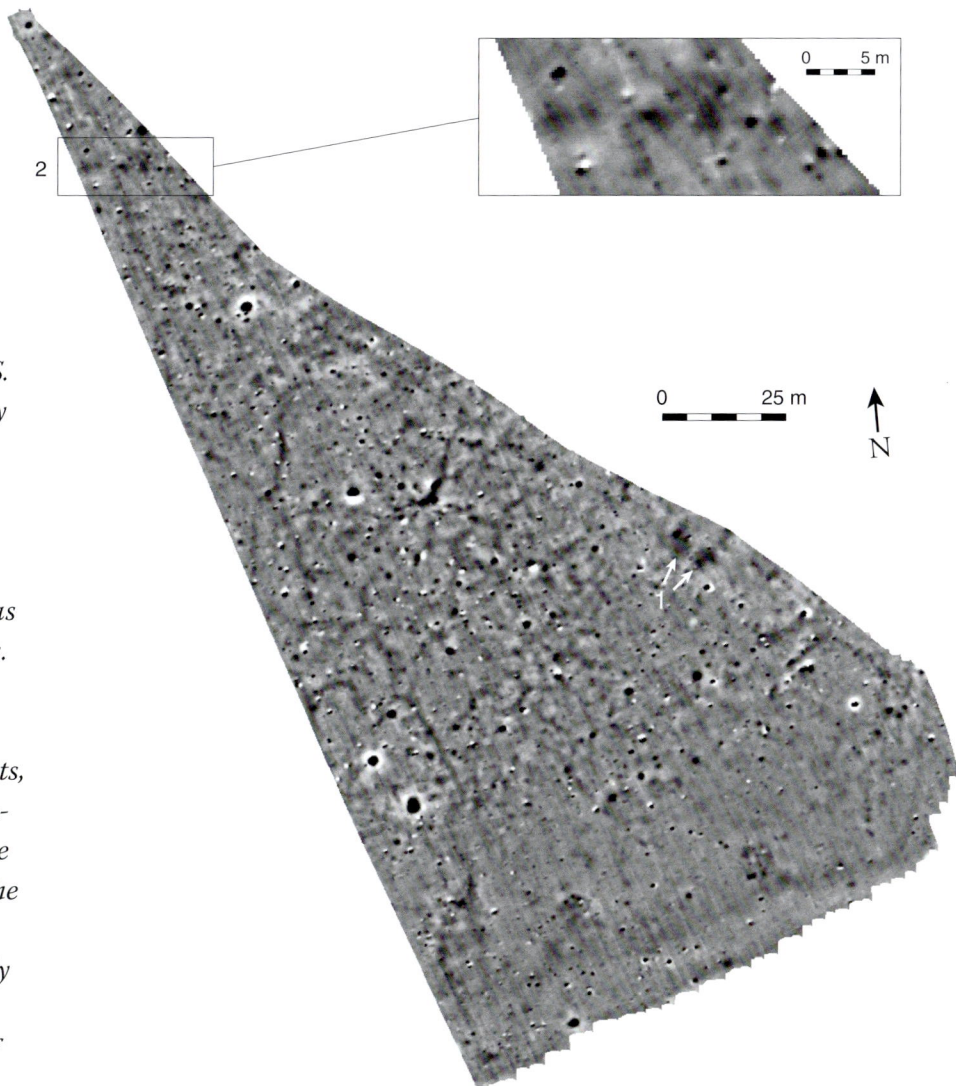

Fig. 32 | *55 Fladstrup S. The geomagnetic survey (±6 nT) shows an area marked by many positive anomalies caused by stones, possibly lost items of metal as well as by geological structures. Two somewhat diffuse anomalies (1) probably represent prehistoric pits, while a band of anomalies running through the northernmost part of the area (2) probably indicate a ditch with loosely spaced posts. Archaeo-Geophysics, Institute of Geosciences, CAU Kiel.*

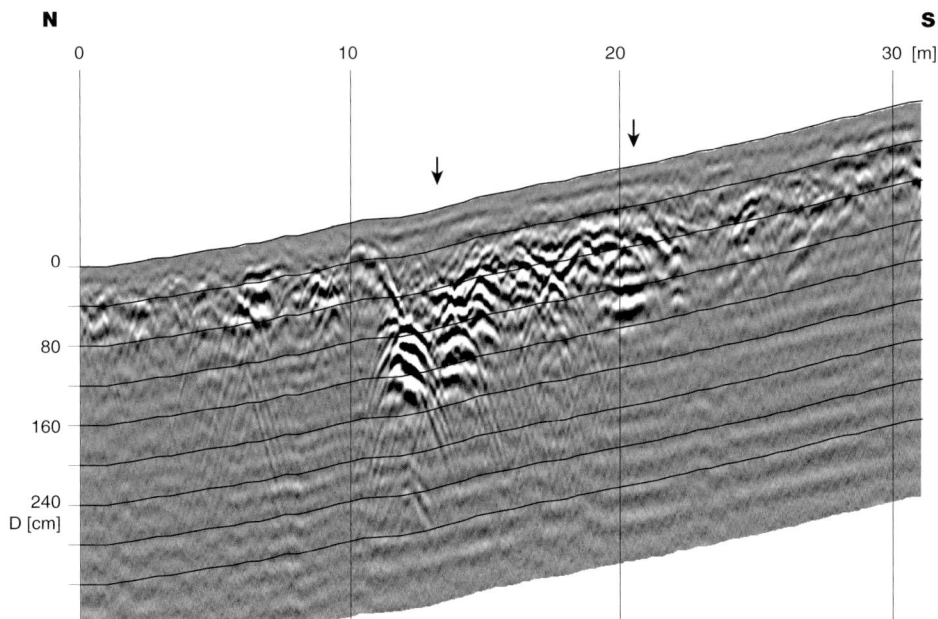

Fig. 33 | 55 *Fladstrup S. Radar profile (200 MHz antenna) showing a possible palisade trench and a deep pit/segment of a ditch with radar reflections indicating the presence of stones. Archaeo-Geophysics, Institute of Geosciences, CAU Kiel.*

paratively large, diffuse spots at the eastern edge of the investigation area (which possibly represent pits) as well as for a narrow band of anomalies that cut obliquely across the northernmost, narrow part of the investigation area. The anomalies forming this band are weaker than those that must be caused by stones in the field. It is likely, therefore, that they represent a row of pits with decayed organic matter inside. These features can potentially be interpreted as representing a palisade with loosely spaced posts. Compared to the palisade trench excavated at Sarup (Andersen 1997, 29ff.) the possible palisade at Fladstrup would have been less dense (i.e. the posts were spaced further apart). On the geomagnetic plan, the possible palisade ditch appears to have a width of ca. two metres. This would have been very wide, especially when compared to the 130 cm width observed at Sarup. However, the anomalies visible in a geomagnetic plan may be larger than the actual features causing them. In the present case, this suspicion is confirmed by radar profiles. Said profiles show a zone of highly radar reflective material measuring ca. 1.20 m wide and up to ca. 1.70 m deep (Fig. 33).

The investigation with GPR also revealed a number of anomalies which measured up to 2 m deep ca. 3-8 m north of the possible palisade (Fig. 33). These anomalies do not seem to constitute an un-interrupted ditch, as they are absent from several of the profiles. At the top, they measure 5-6 m in width. Strong parabola-shaped radar reflections indicate the presence of both large stones (in the northern part to the left) as well as smaller stones (in the western part to the right) within these anomalies. These reflections overlay the edges of the features, which makes it difficult to precisely describe its cross-section and depth.

A probable explanation for the observations described here is that of an interrupted ditch or a row of large pits. This is also apparent from the GPR area rendering (which shows part of the potential palisade trench as a row of dark spots)(Fig. 34). The most prominent of these spots is situated exactly where the potential ditch is interrupted and may thus represent some kind of entrance construction. Both the possible interrupted ditch and the possible palisade/row of loosely spaced posts appear as radar-reflective areas in the GPR area rendering. In case of the 'ditch', this is doubtless at least partly the result of the presence of stones. However, it may also be due to the presence of a higher water content than lies in the undisturbed natural surroundings. This same cause is likely to explain the dark appearance of the possible palisade.

The possible interrupted ditch is invisible in the geomagnetic plan. According to the farmer, dark spots appear in the field after ploughing in this area.

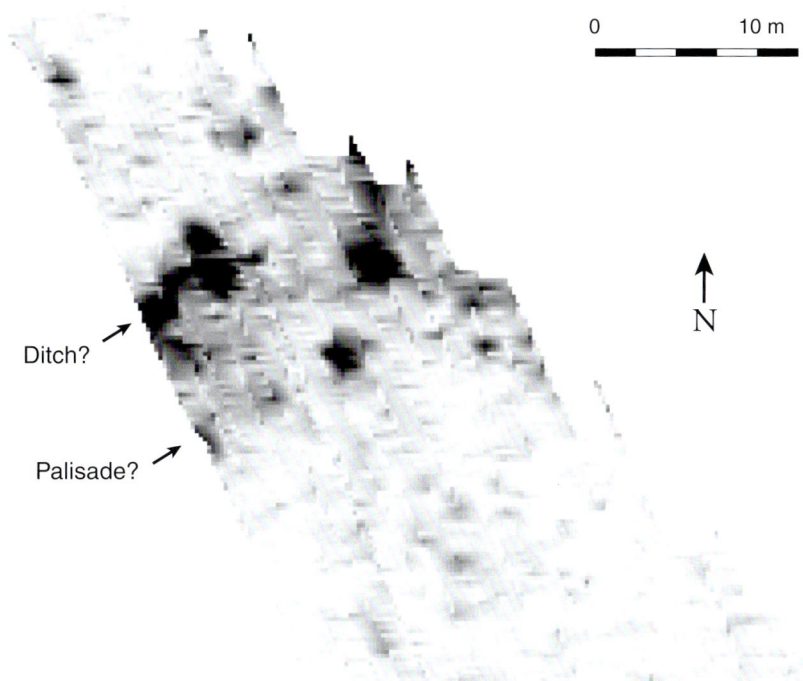

Fig. 34 | *55 Fladstrup S. Area rendering of the GPR measurements (200 MHz antenna, depth layer 40-45 ns) showing the course of a possible row of pits and possible palisade. Archaeo-Geophysics, Institute of Geosciences, CAU Kiel.*

Ditch?

Palisade?

0   10 m

N

In summary, it can be concluded that the geophysical measurements at 55 Fladstrup S revealed structures that can be interpreted as a palisade/row of loosely spaced posts and a row of deep pits or an interrupted ditch. The information on the dimensions and constituents of the features as well as the parallel arrangement of those features both correspond with observations of similar constructions/features from excavated causewayed enclosures. Even the positioning of these features matches; the potential palisade/row of loosely spaced posts is situated on the inside and the interrupted ditch at the outside of the potentially enclosed area. Therefore, there might well be a Neolithic enclosure on the promontory. If this is true, the site would have had a size of 3 ha (or more). However, as only a very short part of the possible ditch and palisade are covered by the geophysical measurements, trial excavation is necessary in order for these suspicions to be confirmed.

58 Assenbakke, Hornslet Parish

At site 58 Assenbakke, geophysical survey with both geomagnetics and GPR was conducted on a ridge-shaped hill bordered by two confluent watercourses (Fig. 35). The subsoil at this location consists of pure meltwater sand and is apparently without any naturally-occurring stones. This offered favourable conditions for geomagnetic measurements which were conducted on the entirety of accessible surfaces (i.e. those parts with a more or less horizontal surface that were not covered by trees or other impenetrable vegetation). The geomagnetically-investigated area measured 250 x 60 m. In total, the overall area represents 0.75 ha.

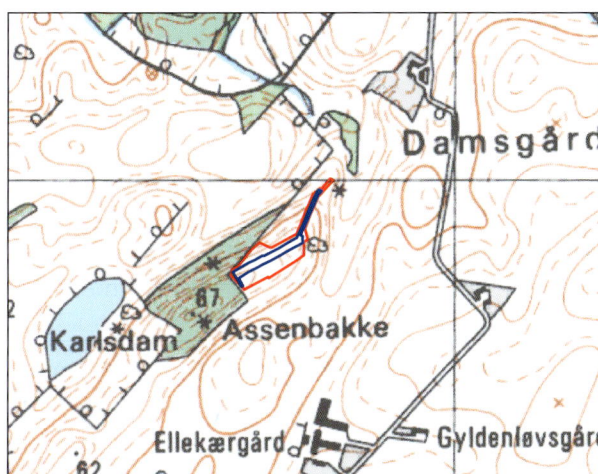

Fig. 35 | *58 Assenbakke. The location of the areas investigated by geomagnetics (red) and GPR (blue). Map sheet 1315 III SØ 1:25.000 (not to scale), © The Danish Geodata Agency.*

A

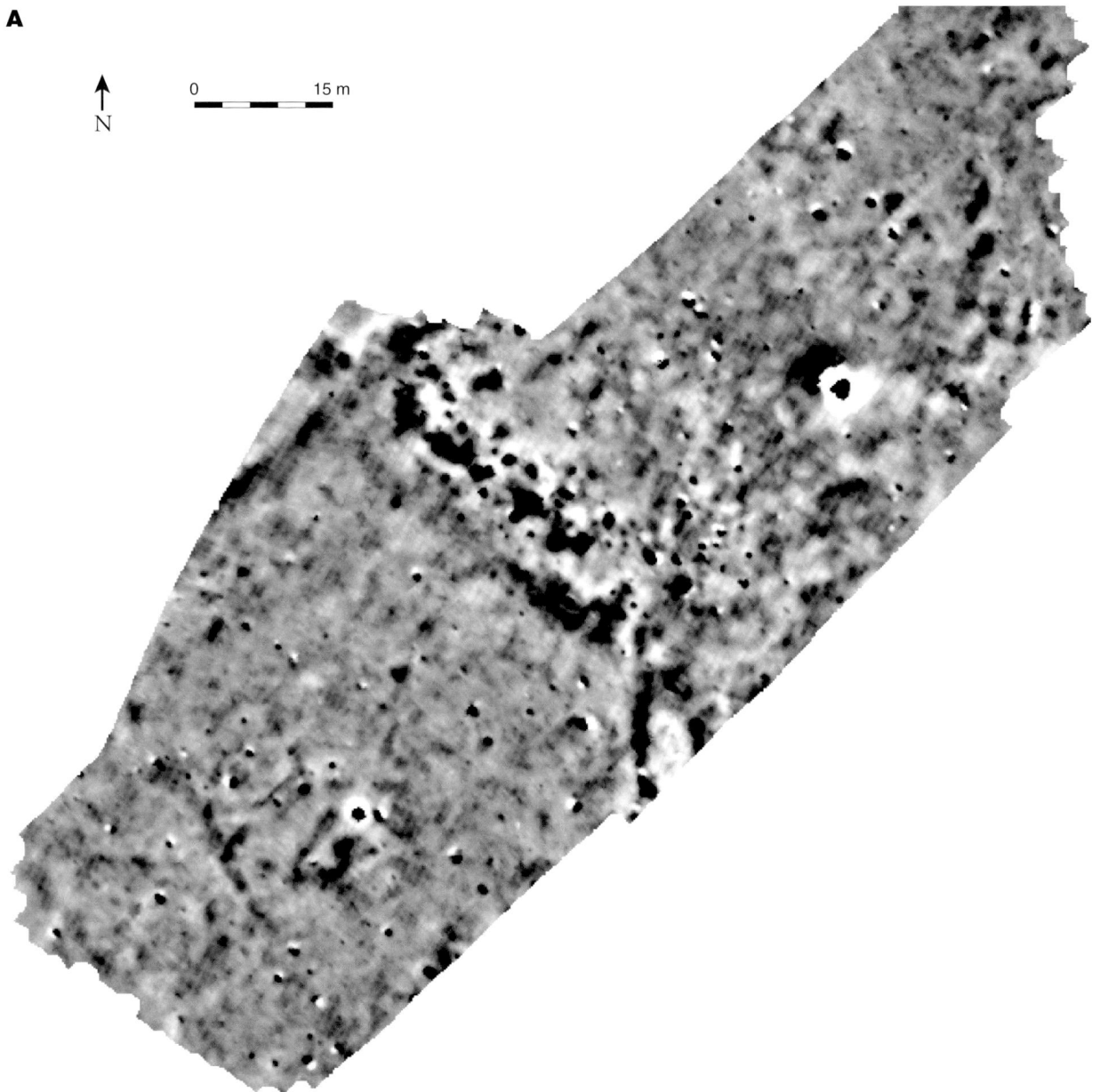

Fig. 36 | 58 Assenbakke. A) Geomagnetic survey plan (±6 nT) showing a wealth of different structures. B (Opposite page)) Interpretation of the different structures as discussed and illustrated below. Archaeo-Geophysics, Institute of Geosciences, CAU Kiel.

The outlay of the area covered by GPR measurements (0.25 ha) follows the topography of the site in a slightly angled course.

The results of the geomagnetic measurements are shown in Fig. 36 A/B and reveal a bewildering number of diverse structures in the western parts of the surveyed area.

The sharply delimited, very black anomalies with white auroras found on all other geophysically investigated sites in Djursland could be explained as the result of either naturally-occurring stones in the subsoil or as lost metal items (broken parts of harvesting implements etc.). In the case of Assenbakke, naturally-occurring stones can be excluded. According to the farmer who owns the land, the field on top of the hill has not been ploughed for many years (today the site is grass-covered, see Klassen (this volume), chapter 7.3.3.2 Fig. 63). Nonetheless, it is still possible that the most powerful anomalies are caused by pieces of metal. A comparison of the

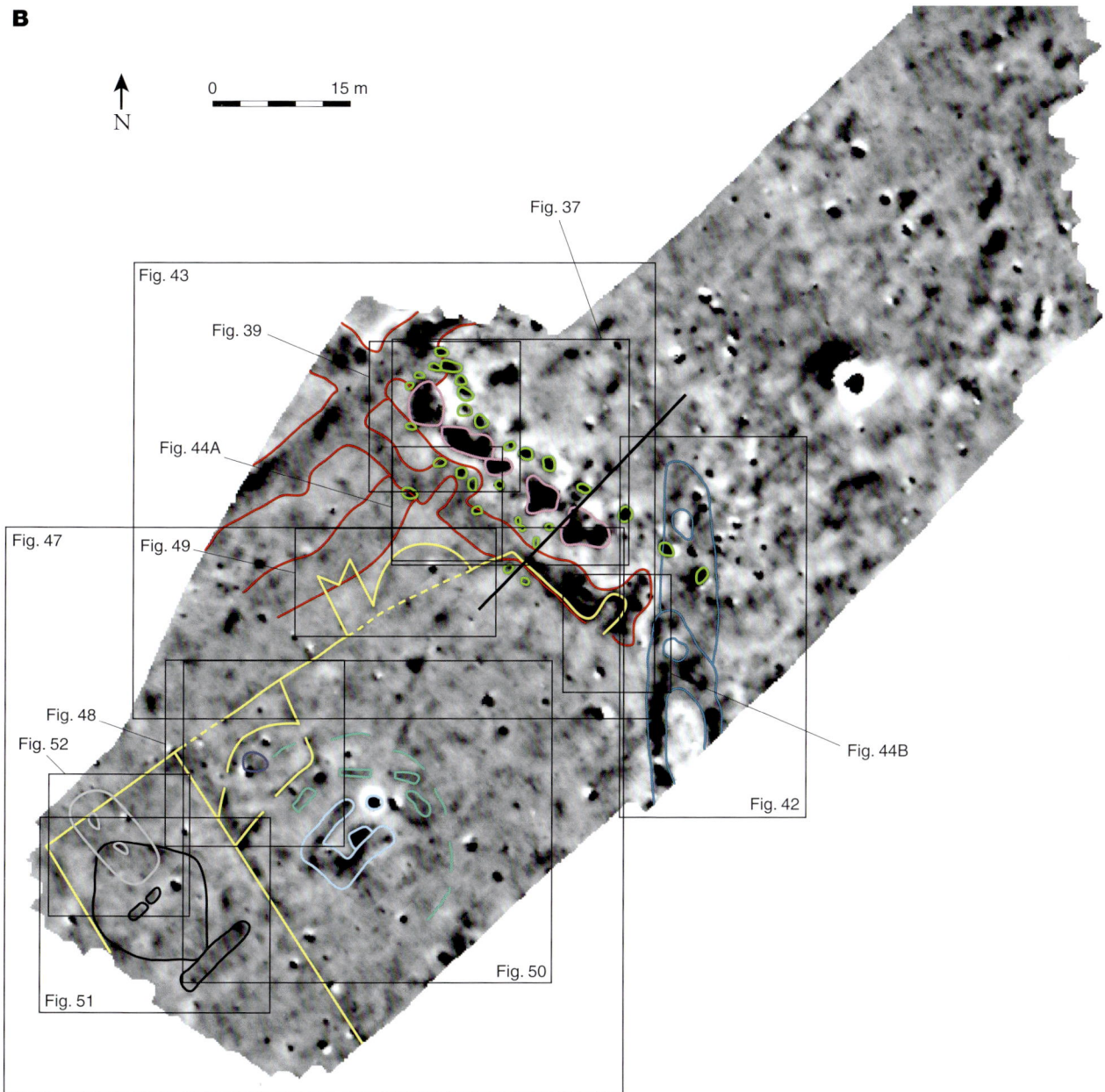

B

magnetometer measurements for different gradients reveals that all but the very largest of the anomalies appear much weaker at 12 nT than at 6nT or even 3 nT. Many lose their white aurora. This indicates that many of these anomalies could be caused by magnetic stones (such as granite) rather than by accidental loss (although the latter option cannot be excluded). Contrary to what was the case on the other investigated sites, these anomalies have, therefore, not been excluded before archaeological interpretation. Potential stones could have been brought to their present location by humans.

The most prominent of the recorded features is a band of strong positive anomalies that cuts across the measured area (the ridge). It is oriented nearly in a north-south direction with a slight deviation towards southeast-northwest. On closer inspection, this band of anomalies can be subdivided into a number of different features. The most prominent (i.e. darkest) of these can be described as a segmented band of irregularly shaped areas, some of which can be possibly subdivided (Fig. 37; marked in pink in Fig. 36 B). The individual segments of this band have lengths of between 5 and 8 m and widths between 2 and 4 m. The total length of the band measures ca. 28 m. Several GPR profiles across this band of anomalies reveal a ditch or pit-structure which measures approximately 1 m deep near to the dark magnetic anomalies (Fig. 38). However, this structure is apparently missing on the two neighbouring profiles measured. It appears, therefore, to be segmented rather than continuous. As only a restricted number of profiles have been measured (covering a ca. 13 m wide zone), it is not possible to precisely reconstruct individual ditch segments or pits. The cross-section of the features appears somewhat irregular in at least one profile. This might be the result of asymmetrical recutting.

These ditch segments or pits measured up to ca. 6 m at the surface in the GPR profiles and are thus somewhat wider than the magnetic anomalies. The latter must represent material with magnetic properties deposited in the segmented ditch or the pits. As the magnetic anomalies show more segments than can be identified in the GPR profiles,

the depositions in question appear to be uneven.

To the east, the segmented ditch or row of pits is bordered by a row of (approximately) circular dark anomalies of restricted size (marked in light green in Fig. 36 B, partly visible in Fig. 37). The row stretches some 40 m and thus protrudes over the segmented ditch anomalies both in the north (ca. 2 m) and in the south (ca. 10 m). This may well indicate that the segmented ditch/pit structure is longer than is apparent from the magnetometer measurements. Part of it may well be invisible due to the lack of magnetic material deposits in its northern- and southernmost parts.

Anomalies comparable to those appearing in a row on the eastern side of the segmented ditch are also found on its western side, where they do not form a continuous line (but rather appear in groups). In the 12nT magnetogram, these anomalies apparently enclose the two northernmost dark band anomalies, apart from a gap which appears on the western side of the southern anomaly (Fig. 39). This fits well with the lack of a ditch/pit structure found in the GPR profiles, as the gap is situated immediately to the south of the southernmost of the two magnetic anomalies (marked in pink) encircled by the row of small anomalies (light green).

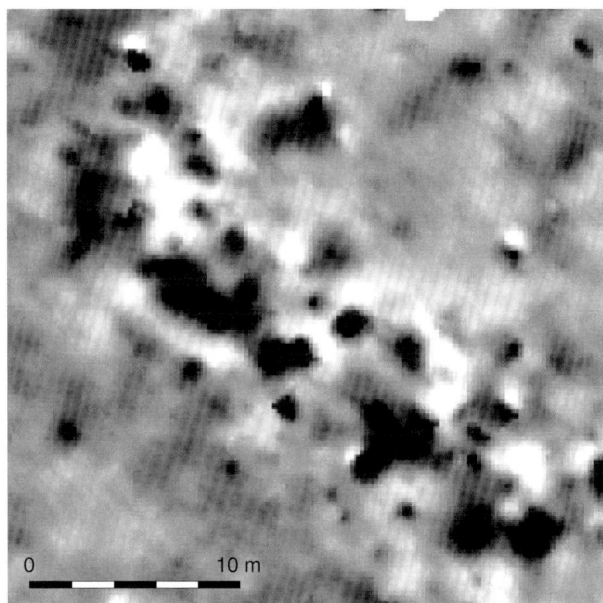

Fig. 37 | 58 Assenbakke. Magnetogram (±6 nT) with band-shaped row of dark anomalies stretching across the northern part of Assenbakke Hill. Some of the anomalies can apparently be subdivided. Archaeo-Geophysics, Institute of Geosciences, CAU Kiel.

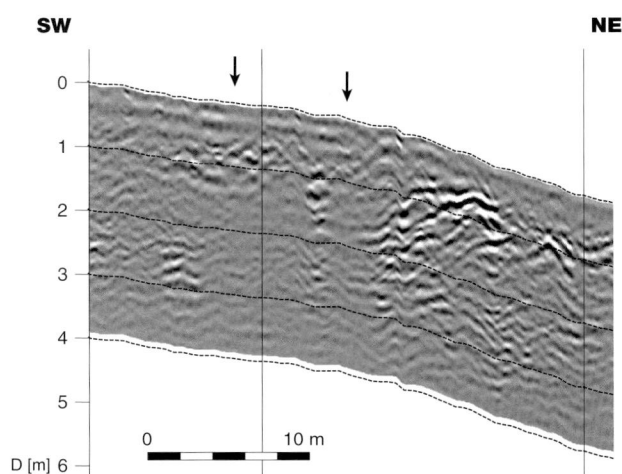

Fig. 38 | 58 Assenbakke. Radar-profile (200 MHz antenna) showing V-shaped ditch-structures in the area of the segmented band of dark magnetic anomalies (Fig. 37) as well as under the somewhat lighter, parallel band to the west of it. Archaeo-Geophysics, Institute of Geosciences, CAU Kiel.

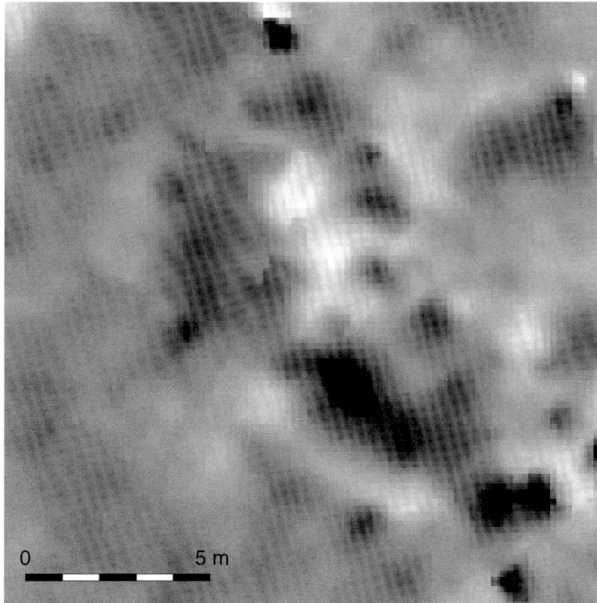

Fig. 39 | *58 Assenbakke. Detail of the magnetogram (±12 nT) of the northernmost anomaly forming the described segmented band of anomalies which shows a row of small, round anomalies surrounding them and an apparent gap to the southwest. The anomalies probably represent postholes. Archaeo-Geophysics, Institute of Geosciences, CAU Kiel.*

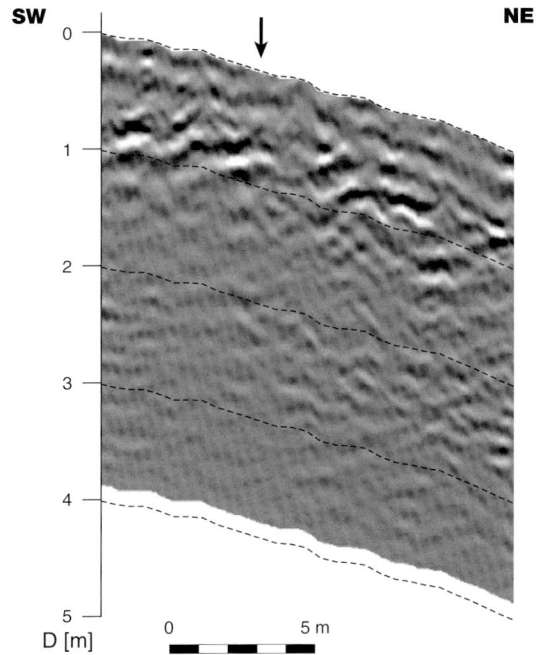

Fig. 40 | *58 Assenbakke. Radar profile (200 MHz antenna) of one of the small, round anomalies found to the east of the suspected row of ditch segments or pits and partly surrounding them. The profile indicates that these anomalies can be interpreted as postholes. Archaeo-Geophysics, Institute of Geosciences, CAU Kiel.*

In one case, a GPR profile was measured just across one of the small, approximately circular anomalies. From this profile, it is apparent that it reaches down into the ground for ca. 60 cm (Fig. 40). These anomalies should most probably be interpreted as postholes. Their moderate depth either indicates erosion or that the posts did not extend very high above ground (1-1.5 m ?). The comparatively strong magnetic anomalies caused by these features probably cannot be explained by the decomposition of organic material (wooden posts) alone. Possible explanations include the presence of stones used to hold the posts in fixed positions (comparable examples were excavated at Sarup: Andersen 1997, 83 Fig. 116) and the alteration of iron-based minerals in the earth through fire (the burning of posts).

Structures comparable to those from Assenbakke (Fig. 41) are known from several causewayed enclosures (or related structures): Sarup II (Andersen 1997, 67 Fig. 80 and 69 Fig. 83), Büdelsdorf (Hingst 1971, 192 Abb. 1) and possibly Kainsbakke (unpublished; information kindly provided by Lisbeth W. Rasmussen). Pits/ditch segments surrounded by posts have been exca-

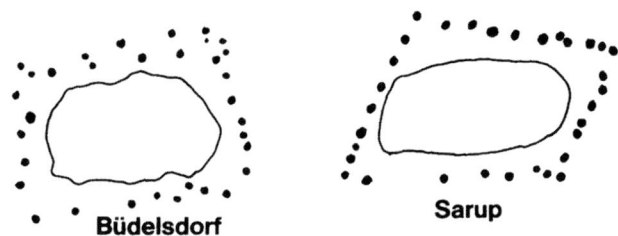

Fig. 41 | *The fenced ditch segment at the Sarup enclosure as well as the fenced oven structure at the Büdelsdorf enclosure represent probable parallels to some structures observed in the geomagnetic measurements at site 58 Assenbakke (from Madsen 1988).*

vated in both Sarup and Büdelsdorf. However, while the structures at Sarup can be interpreted as fenced ditch segments, Hage (in press) has recently presented strong evidence at Büdelsdorf

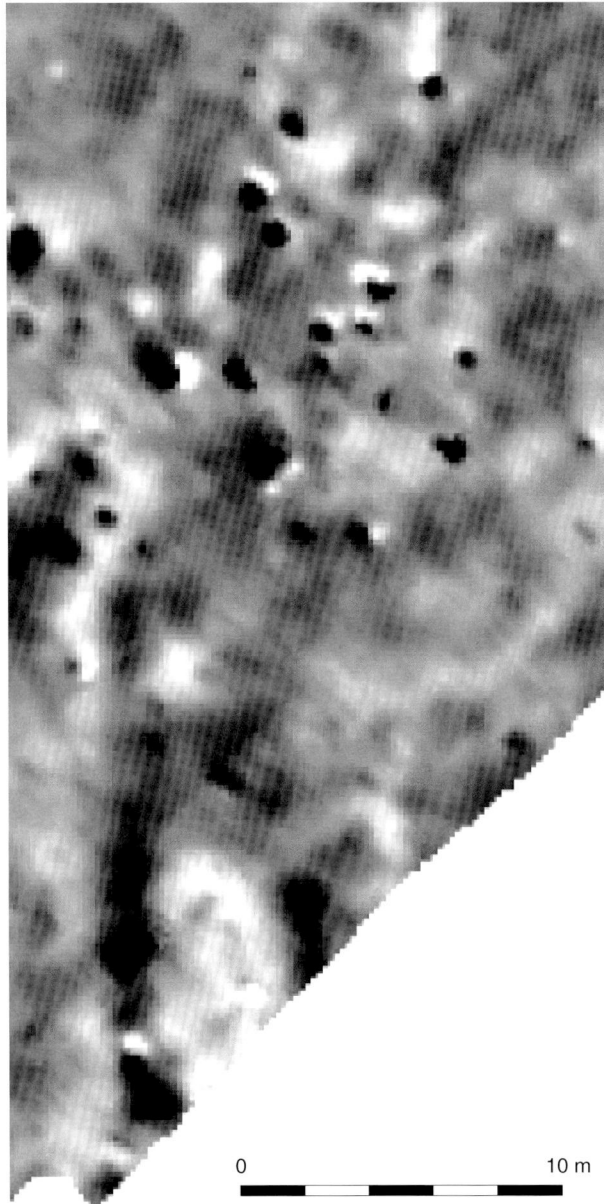

Fig. 42 | *58 Assenbakke. In the magnetogram (±6 nT), an approximately north-south oriented band-shaped anomaly consisting of a darker southern and weaker northern part is identifiable. Both taper at the ends into a pointed shape and include depositions of less magnetic material (which appears light in colour). This anomaly possibly also represents some kind of ditch structure. Archaeo-Geophysics, Institute of Geosciences, CAU Kiel.*

for the allocation of these features as ovens, most likely used for the production of pottery.

Without excavation it is not possible to decide which function the features at Assenbakke might have fulfilled. However, the striking parallels between Assenbakke and Büdelsdorf in particular (the individual pits as well as the fenced areas have comparable dimensions) are of interest with regard to interpreting the strong magnetic anomalies. These might well be caused by the remains of a wattle and daub construction, as was the case at Büdelsdorf (Hage in press), or by massive depositions of (mis-) fired pottery, as is known from the Store Brokhøj enclosure in Djursland (Madsen/Fiedel 1988).

At Büdelsdorf, the ovens are arranged in a row that runs parallel to the innermost ditch circuit on its inner side (see Klassen (this volume), Fig. 86). The same could have been the case at Assenbakke. This is apparent from another band-shaped feature in the magnetogram (Fig. 42; marked in blue in Fig. 36 B). The structure in question stretches over a length of 36 m from the border of the investigation area in the south in a southwest-northeast direction, where it ends in a pointed shape. The width is ca. 7.5 m in the south, tapering to ca. 6 m in the north. There appears to be a subdivision at the approximate midpoint of the ditch in which the southern part appears much darker and clearer than the northern part. The division between both sections follows an oblique course in relation to the direction of the feature and thus gives the southern part a pointed shape comparable to that of the northern part. Bright internal features are discernible close to the pointed ends of both sub-sections. In the southernmost segment an additional, marked feature of this type of considerable size (ca. 9 x 4 m) can be observed. The smaller, bright features close to the pointed ends of the two sub-sections are somehow reminiscent of ditch A3063 from Sarup I, at the end of which a block of soil was left untouched (Andersen 1997, 44 Fig. 44).

The negative anomalies (light parts) must be caused by the presence of a material that is less magnetic than the naturally occurring sand. It may be sand with different magnetic properties dug up from deeper layers in the hill. However, taking into account this comparatively strong contrast with the natural surroundings, it may also be external, low magnetic material deposited on the site. The most likely material would be chalk (in the form of either marine shells or travertine). The deposition of shells in enclosure ditches has been observed in no less than seven of the partly excavated sites in Djursland (St. Brokhøj, Blakbjerg, Ballegård, Galgebakken, Ginnerup, Skærvad and Kainsbakke), all of which are situated either directly along the coast or much closer to it than the Assenbakke site. The latter is 3 km away from the shore of Kalø Vig Bay, while the maximum distance to the sea for the seven sites listed above is ca. 800 m (Store Brokhøj). If it was the white colour that was decisive for the deposition of marine shells in the ditches (and not the shell material itself), this may have been substituted by travertine. There are several springs on the side and at the foot of Assenbakke Hill. One of these was worshipped as a sacred spring until the 19th century (Svane 1984, 216 no. 2045[2]). Whether or not travertine could actually have been extracted from these springs in the Neolithic is unknown.

Although somewhat weaker, the fact that negative magnetic anomalies are also visible around the dark anomalies (indicating the segmented ditch) as well as around the postholes described above could indicate that they are caused by dug up, low-magnetic subsoil. Alternatively, it could be assumed that external material was deposited in both the segmented ditch and in the band-shaped structure described here. While neither potential possibility is easily brought to the fore, both indicate that the 36 m long, pointed structure discussed here must also represent some form of ditch. Unfortunately, no GPR profiles are available from that area to corroborate this interpretation.

Finally, it should be noted that at least two of the features interpreted as postholes from a fence-like structure are located within the northern subpart of the band-shaped structure described above. This may indicate a difference in the ages

of the two structures represented by the different magnetic anomalies.

The most complex band-shaped feature in the geomagnetic measurements is the one running parallel to the segmented ditch at its western side (Fig. 43; marked in red in Fig. 36 B). It appears as a 4-4.5 m wide, slightly darkened stripe in the geomagnetic plan. From the previously-described structure (blue in Fig. 36 B) in the south towards the border of the measurement area in the north, it can be followed over a length of almost 50 m. Some disturbances in the band-shaped feature discussed above (blue) can indicate that it continued for another 10 m further south, but was either cut off by the construction of the feature marked in blue in a later phase or vice versa.

In the northern part, the band-shaped structure (marked in red) is cross-shaped, with an arm running at right angles to the part described above. This transverse section can be followed for ca. 35 m within the geophysically investigated zone and also appears to continue beyond its borders.

This complex, band-shaped structure is also identifiable as a ditch by means of GPR profiles, with dimensions comparable to those of the segmented ditch. Although no certain segmentation can be identified in the GPR profiles, it may have been present in some areas at least (as indicated by patches of stronger anomalies, especially in the approximately east-west running part for which no GPR profiles are available). These anomalies may well represent an older segmented ditch system that was transformed into a large continuous ditch in a later stage. Such a process has been observed at the Sarup I enclosure. At Sarup I, ditch segments reaching lengths of more than 100 m have been proved to have been present in earlier phases as much smaller individual segments (Andersen 1997, 25 Fig. 16 and 46 Fig. 46).

Two peculiar strictly rectangular and U-shaped protrusions of comparable dimensions (ca. 4.5 x 3-3.5 m) can be seen on the western side of the north-south arm of the ditch at a distance of 22 m (Fig. 44A/B). The width of the sides of these features appears to be 1-1.5 m, and (at least in the case of the northernmost of the two) some postholes

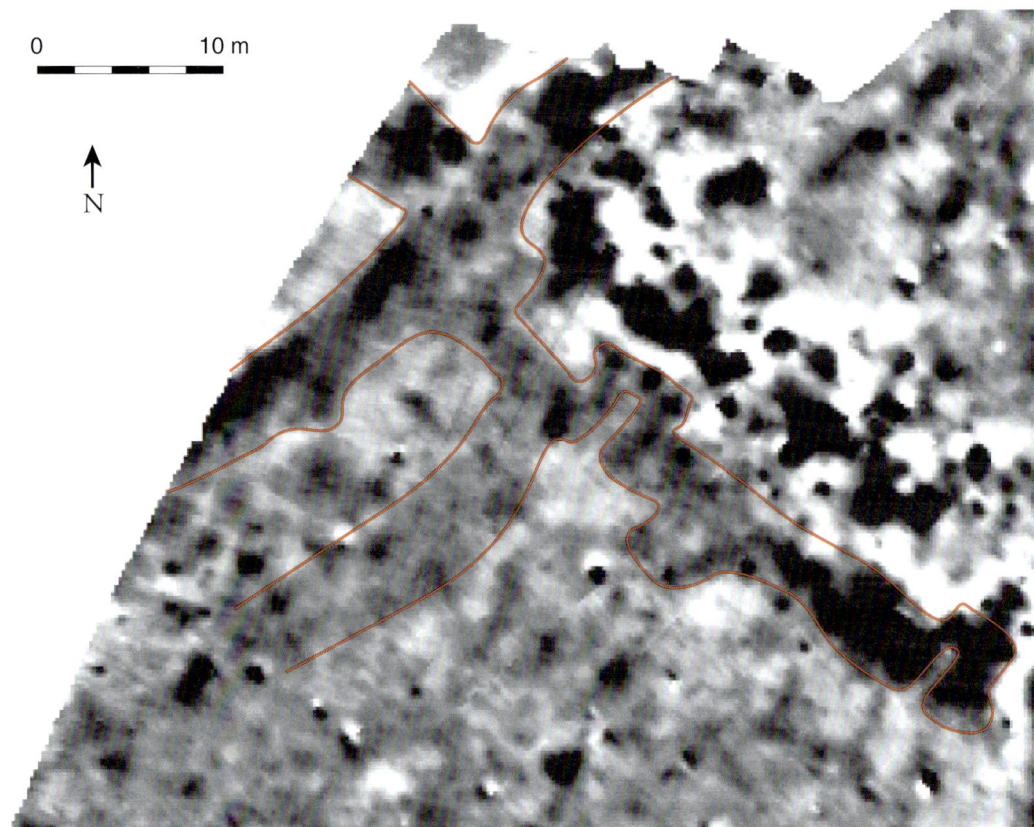

Fig. 43 | *58 Assenbakke. In this version of the magnetogram (±3 nT), a complex band-shaped anomaly is clearly seen parallel to and to the west of the segmented ditch or row of pits. In the northern part of the area, a somewhat darker branch lies at a right angle. A much weaker, comparable feature runs on its southern side. According to GPR profiles available for a minor section, this anomaly probably reflects a continuous ditch 4 – 4.5 m wide and up to 1 m deep. Depositions of different materials (as shown by said materials' magnetic properties) inside this ditch structure are identifiable. Archaeo-Geophysics, Institute of Geosciences, CAU Kiel.*

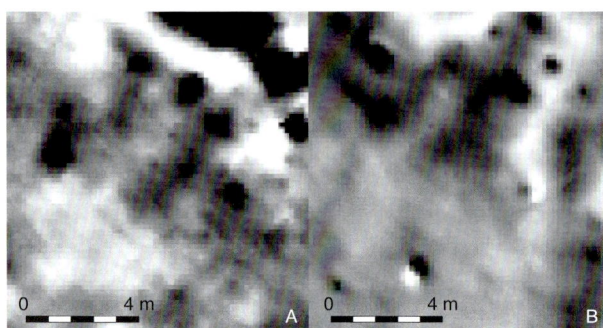

Fig. 44 | *58 Assenbakke. Rectangular, U-shaped features integrated in the continuous ditch structure. A) Northern structure (±3 nT), B) Southern structure (±6 nT). As apparent from several dark, round anomalies, posts seem to have been part of the northern structure. Archaeo-Geophysics, Institute of Geosciences, CAU Kiel.*

appear to be associated with it. Unfortunately, no GPR profiles are available for any of these structures. Therefore, their precise character cannot be established.

The features are reminiscent of the rectangular fenced areas that are known from the Sarup I palisade (Andersen 1997, 35 Fig. 28) as well as that from Starup Langelandsvej (Lützau-Pedersen 2010, 43; Lützau Pedersen/Witte 2012) enclosures. However, the Assenbakke structures are presumably associated with a ditch and not a palisade. Furthermore, they are completely open at one side, whereas the fenced areas referred to above are either completely (or almost completely) closed. Contrary to the two comparative examples, the sides of the Assenbakke features are rather wide and possibly constitute foundation trenches. They might be indicative of the presence of some kind of entrance to the enclosed area. However, this does not appear very likely, as there appears to be only a single opening in one narrow side, while such an opening appears to be missing in the opposite side. If these U-shaped structures should represent some kind of passageway into the enclosure, these narrow sides should have an opening. Furthermore, in case of the northern of the two structures, a dark anomaly representing a ditch segment (or large pit) is located directly opposite to the U-shaped structure. Passing through the latter would, therefore, have led into a ditch or pit and not into the enclosed area via a causeway.

There are two other groups of Neolithic constructions that resemble the rectangular U-shaped Assenbakke structures more closely, but which are not associated with ditch structures (as is apparently the case at Assenbakke). These features are the Early Neolithic graves of the Troelstrup-type (Fig. 45) as defined by Madsen (1979, 309) and a variant of the early Middle Neolithic mortuary house (Fig. 46).

Troelstrup-type graves have a rectangular horseshoe shape with one open side. The walls of these features were built of stone, wood or a combination of both. They were settled in foundation trenches. Some of these features can be rather small with side-lengths of only ca. 2-3 m, such as was the case at Strynø (Skaarup 1985, 337 Fig. 391) or Stengade 1 (Kaul 1988, 69 Fig. 45). However, there are also larger examples which completely agree with the Assenbakke features in both size and shape, such as at Lindegården (Liversage 1981; 1983, 8 Fig. 3). The best parallel appears to be a find from the Rustrup long barrow in Central Jutland (Fig. 45). It differs, however, in having a posthole in the middle of the open side. This posthole likely represents the remains of a roof-bearing post.

The second group of rectangular Neolithic U-shaped features that resemble the structures observed at Assenbakke are a few early Middle Neolithic mortuary houses with one open gable (Fig. 46). These represent a rare subgroup (only three known examples) of all mortuary houses.

Two of the finds (Søndermølle III and Herrup XLIII in Sevel Parish) are from northwest Jutland (Becker 1996), but are either much (Søndermølle III) or somewhat (Herrup XLIII) smaller than the constructions at Assenbakke. The third find is from Tustrup in Djursland (Kjærum 1955; 1967) and is a bit larger than the features under discussion. All three mortuary houses either show a posthole (Søndermølle III; Herrup XLIII) or a large stone (Tustrup) in the entrance area, which served as roof-bearing elements. No such constructions are visible in the geomagnetic plans of the Assenbakke site. While it is possible that postholes may have been present but remained invisible to the geophysical measurements, this does not seem likely.

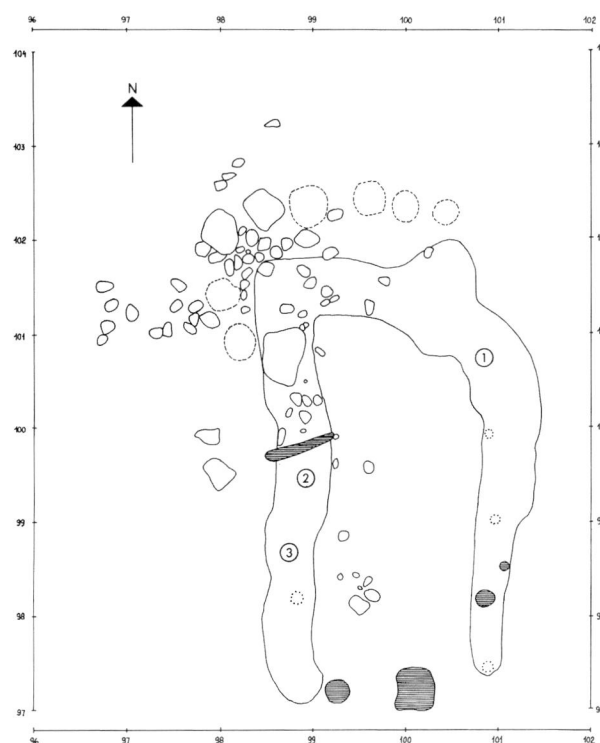

Fig. 45 | *Grave of Troelstrup-type from the Early Neolithic long barrow at Rustrup, central Jutland (from Fischer 1976). The U-shaped structure has dimensions comparable to those of the two features depicted in Fig. 44 and represents the foundation trench for a grave chamber built of wood or a combination of wood and stones. Note the posthole in the middle of the open side of the chamber (which probably once held a roof-bearing post).*

In summary, it can be concluded that no convincing parallels can be found to the two rectangular horseshoe-shaped features apparently integrated into the ditch running across Assenbakke Hill. The resemblance to the Troelstrup-type of Early Neolithic graves (and to some Middle Neolithic mortuary houses) is, however, rather strong. Therefore, it is possible that the structures observed represent mortuary constructions of some kind.

There appears to be another branch to the ditch (marked in red in Fig. 36 B) in the geomagnetic plan with the highest contrast (Fig. 43). This seems to run parallel to the east-west orientated branch, ca. 7-8 m to the south. In the latter area, the branch can be followed for a distance of ca. 22 m from the north-south branch of the ditch to a dark anomaly that possibly represents some kind of pit. The branch seems to have the same dimensions as the cross-shaped ditch-structure. However, no radar profiles are available by which to illustrate its depth.

To the west of the north-south running ditch structure and to the south of the last described feature, a number of different (mostly rather weak)

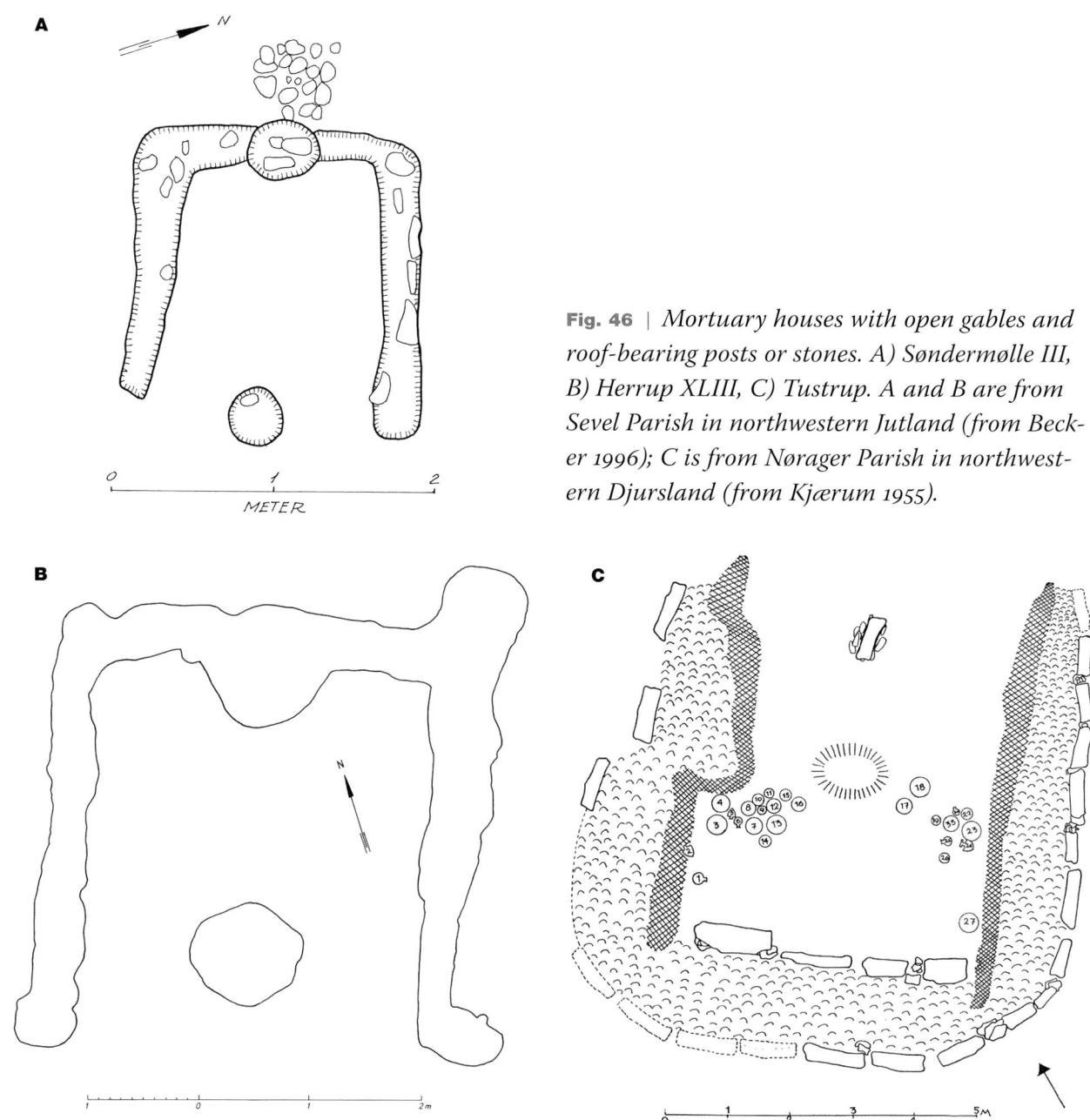

Fig. 46 | *Mortuary houses with open gables and roof-bearing posts or stones. A) Søndermølle III, B) Herrup XLIII, C) Tustrup. A and B are from Sevel Parish in northwestern Jutland (from Becker 1996); C is from Nørager Parish in northwestern Djursland (from Kjærum 1955).*

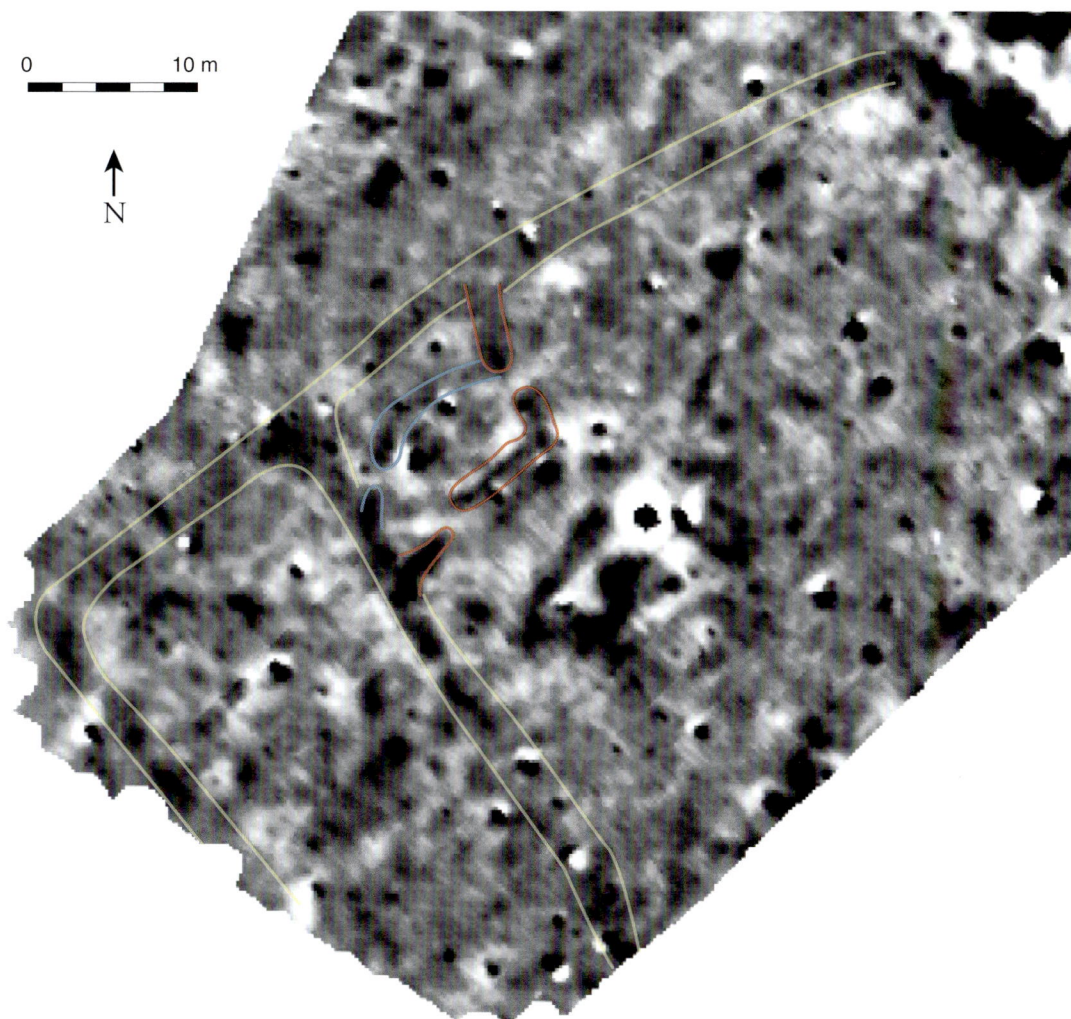

Fig. 47 | *58 Assenbakke. Narrow, linear and only slightly darkened anomalies in the magnetogram (±3nT) probably represent the foundation trenches for some kind of fence or palisade. A large, subdivided rectangular feature (marked in yellow), a parallelogram-shaped compartment (marked in red) and (inside the latter) an arc-shaped feature (marked in blue) can be identified. Parts of the course of these anomalies – especially the northern part – are very weak and difficult to detect. Some of the interruptions of the anomaly probably represent entrances to the fenced areas. Archaeo-Geophysics, Institute of Geosciences, CAU Kiel.*

structures can be identified. These can be divided into two groups, one of which appears to consist of narrow band-shaped structures that can possibly be identified as foundation trenches for some kind of fence or palisade (marked in yellow in Fig. 36 B). At least, this is suggested by the ca. 80-100 cm width of the possible trenches. A few GPR profiles cross this feature which (in some cases at least) appear to extent ca. 50-60 cm into the ground.

Two different sets of these possible fence foundation trenches are identifiable. The most important of these is marked in yellow in Fig. 36 B and is

enlarged in Fig. 47 (yellow markings). It is a rectangular feature measuring 60 x 36 m and is oriented parallel to both the double ditch system in the east and to the two transverse arms of one of the ditch structures to the north. The structure may be even larger and continue to the southwest (outside the investigation area, as this part of Assenbakke Hill is covered by woods).

The area enclosed by the rectangular feature has been further subdivided by a potential fence/palisade that separates a ca. 17 m wide area in the westernmost part from a ca. 43 m wide zone in the eastern part. Furthermore, a parallelogram-shaped area (ca. 11.5 x 9.5 m) has been separated from the northwest corner of the eastern of the two rectangular areas (marked in red in Fig. 47). Inside this distinctive 'room' (which appears to have entrances to the east and to the south) another subdivision by a (possibly interrupted) curved feature is visible (blue markings in Fig. 36 B). In the southernmost of the two compartments defined by the latter structure, a circular anomaly (ca. 2 m in diameter) with a darkened perimeter probably represents a pit (Fig. 48). A strong magnetic anomaly at the southern part of this pit could be caused by a stone, burnt wattle and daub and/or by pottery. Unfortunately, modern metal debris cannot be excluded from the list of possibilities. No convincing parallels to these structures have hitherto been noted in South Scandinavian archaeological literature.

An M-shaped structure (ca. 4.5 by 5 m) is attached to the northern side of the probable fence/palisade (marked in yellow in Fig. 36 B). From there, it stretches to one of the branches of the probable ditch-structure (marked in red in Fig. 36B), which it might have cut (Fig. 49, marked in red). The fence/palisade (marked in yellow in Fig. 36 B), or at least the M-shaped enclosure on its northern side, therefore, appear to be younger than at least one of the branches of the complex ditch structure (marked in red in Fig. 36 B).

Immediately to the east of the M-shaped structure, a semi-circular feature (which could also represent a foundation trench for a fence or palisade) encloses an area measuring ca. 10 x 4.5 m (Fig. 49, marked in black).

Although no parallels to the peculiar M-shaped structure are known, it somehow resembles the rectangular, fenced annexes from the sites of Sarup I and Starup Langelandsvej mentioned above. The semi-circular feature has a possible parallel in a fenced annex at Sarup I, which consists of two parallel fences and an opening (Andersen 1997, 39 Fig. 36).

A number of features can be identified in the eastern of the two large compartments defined by the possible fence/palisade (marked in yellow in Fig. 36 B). The most prominent of these is yet another

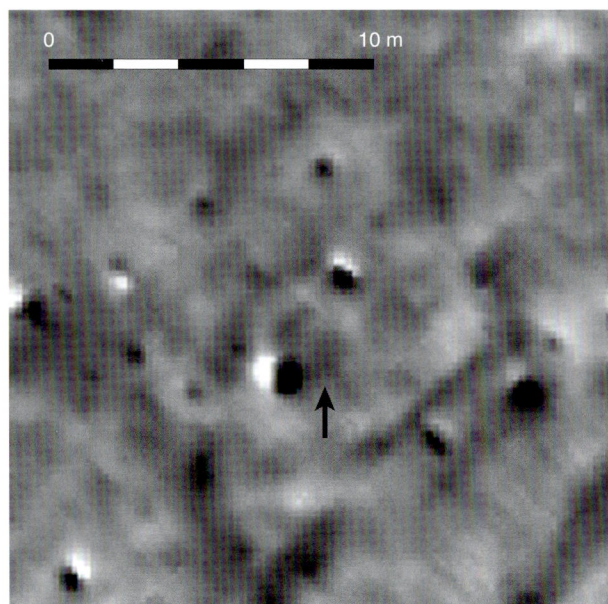

Fig. 48 | *58 Assenbakke. Enlargement of the parallelogram-shaped fenced area (±6 nT magnetogram). A circular anomaly with dark perimeter probably represents a pit (ca. 2 m diameter) inside the southern of the two compartments created by an arc-shaped fence. Archaeo-Geophysics, Institute of Geosciences, CAU Kiel.*

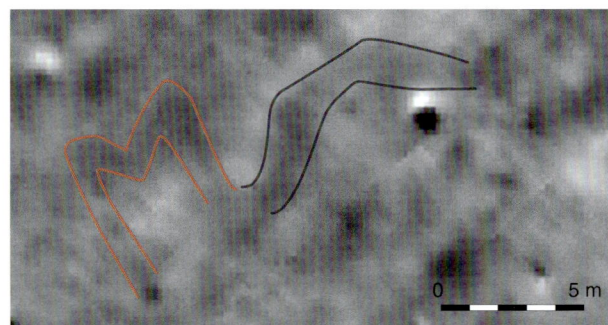

Fig. 49 | *58 Assenbakke. Magnetogram (±6 nT) showing an M-shaped and a crescent-shaped annex probably attached to the northern part of a fence (marked in yellow in Fig. 36 B). Archaeo-Geophysics, Institute of Geosciences, CAU Kiel.*

rectangular U- or horseshoe-shaped structure. The feature measures 7 x 4 m and has a slightly asymmetrical outline (Fig. 50, red marking). It is oriented southwest-northeast with opening in the northeast. Inside this structure (and situated directly at its southeastern side) is a particularly dark magnetic anomaly of semi-circular shape measuring ca. 2.5 x 1.5 m (marked in orange in Fig. 50). The comparatively strong anomaly suggests the presence of larger amounts of magnetic material and might indicate that the feature causing the anomaly is somewhat smaller than the measurements given here.

This structure has a striking resemblance to the Tustrup mortuary house referred to above (Fig. 46 C). Both are of an almost identical size (ca. 25-30 square m), although the Assenbakke structure is slightly longer and less wide (7 x 4 m) than the Tustrup mortuary house (5 x 6 m). Both have one open side (gable) and both show one irregular side (wall). At Tustrup, this irregularity was a niche (ca. 2 x 1m) which covered a stone-filled pit of unknown function. Furthermore, at Tustrup, a large, dressed stone (supposed to have been at least 1.6 m high and assumed to have had some function as roof-bearing element) is positioned exactly in the middle of the open gable. At Assenbakke, a very powerful positive magnetic anomaly is seen in a comparable location just outside the U-shaped structure. The magnetic signal is most likely to be caused by a modern piece of metal, but a long, vertically oriented stone of a highly magnetic type of rock cannot be completely ruled out without further investigation. It is thus possible, (although not likely), that the U-shaped structure

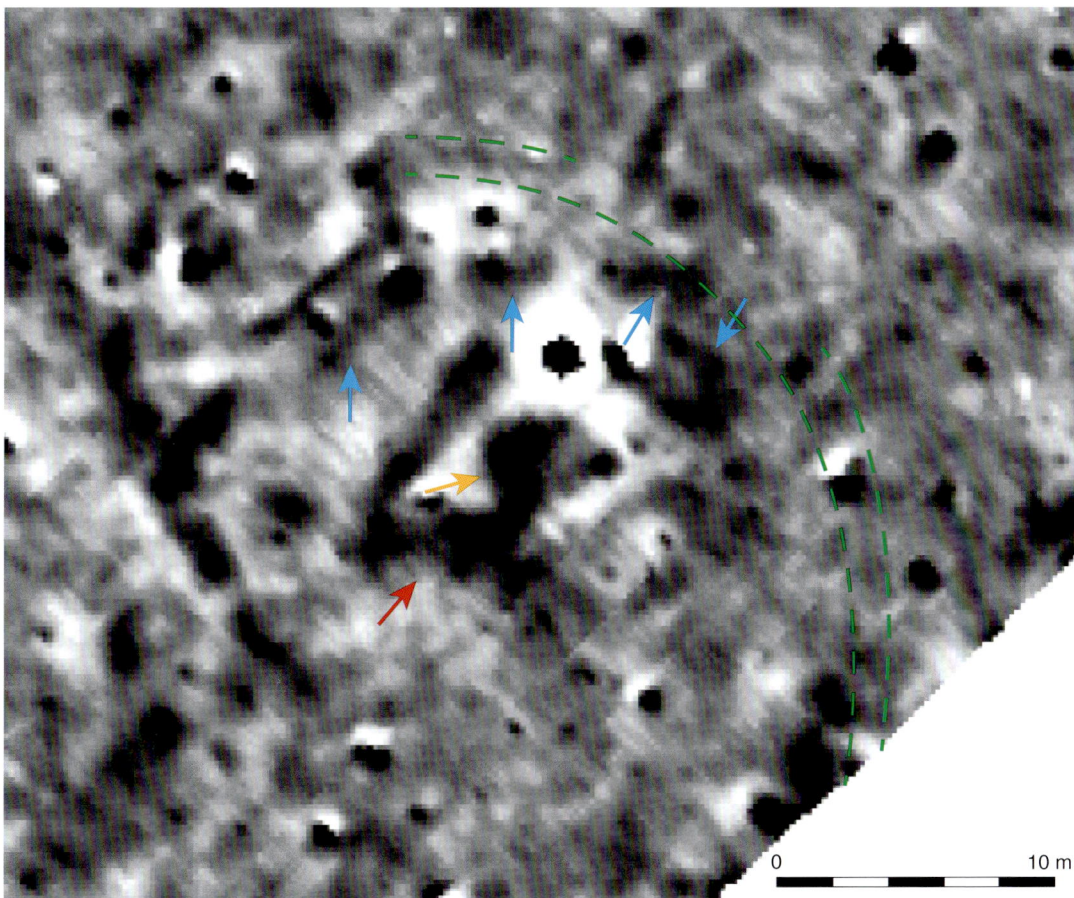

Fig. 50 | 58 Assenbakke. Magnetogram (±3 nT) showing a slightly asymmetrical, rectangular, U-shaped structure (marked in red) with an extension on the interior of one side (marked in orange). This structure might represent a mortuary construction related to Troelstrup graves and mortuary houses. Note the very strong anomaly in front of the open side of this construction. This might be due to a very large stone that might have been part of the construction. Furthermore, possible traces of secondary burials (marked in blue) and the outer limit of a possible round barrow (green) have also been indicated. Archaeo-Geophysics, Institute of Geosciences, CAU Kiel.

at Assenbakke and the mortuary house excavated at Tustrup share even more characteristics than those discussed above.

Several other features seem to be related to the rectangular U-shaped structure. Three rectangular, oblong anomalies with lengths ranging between 2.5-3 m and widths of ca. 80-90 cm are seen spaced at 2 to 3 m intervals on the northern and north-western side of the U-shaped feature (Fig. 50, blue markings). These features appear to be oriented tangentially on a circular course ca. 15 m in diameter which encircles the U-shaped structure.

There are two possible interpretations for these structures. The first possibility is that the anomalies are due to some kind of kerb structure which delimited a barrow. Possibilities include rectangular pits in which magnetic materials were deposited or the traces of wooden kerbs/removed and dressed kerbstones. However, none of these have ever been observed at a TRB round barrow. Furthermore, if a kerb structure had been present, this would normally be expected to have surrounded the barrow rather than having been present in groups only, as was the case at Assenbakke.

It is more likely, therefore, that the tangential anomalies represent secondary burials dug into the foot of an existing barrow. Their size is completely in line with such an interpretation. Unfortunately, it is not possible to date these probable secondary burials without excavation, as this kind of burial was practised from the later parts of the Neolithic until the younger Iron Age. A good example was excavated only 20 km west of Assenbakke at Refshøjgård (Klassen 2005, 20 Fig. 3), in which a number of graves were placed tangentially in a Single Grave barrow in the Younger Roman Iron Age. Like at Assenbakke, they appear in groups of one to three graves.

It should be remarked that the primary burial in the Refshøjgård mound (which dates to the earliest Single Grave Culture around 2800 BC) was made up of a wooden cist that was supported by a U-shaped stone setting closed by large stones in the open end. The Assenbakke structure could, therefore, also date from the Single Grave Culture. However, there are some lines of evidence which are against this interpretation. One of these is the fact that no finds from the earliest Single Grave Culture are known from the region surrounding Assenbakke. In fact, the Refshøjgård barrow is the easternmost of all of the graves which are known in Jutland from the earliest Single Grave Culture (Klassen 2005, 43 Fig. 16). Another argument against a Single Grave Culture date is the size of the Assenbakke structure; it is far bigger than that of any Single Grave Culture structure of the shape in question. Furthermore, the 'niche' observed inside of one arm of the U-shaped feature has no parallels in Single Grave Culture burials.

In summary, it can be concluded that the U-shaped structure discussed here most likely dates to the TRB Culture. However, a later date cannot be excluded without excavation.

Traces of a round barrow (in which secondary burials would have taken place, as suits the features observed) are in fact visible at Assenbakke in the geomagnetic survey. They reveal themselves as a circular feature with a ca. 21 m diameter with the U-shaped structure at its centre (Fig. 50, green markings). This circle is partially delimited to the north by a narrow but distinctive curved anomaly. However, it is generally revealed by slight differences in colour (the interior is lighter than the exterior) or as a diffuse, light band.

It should be mentioned that a round barrow is listed in the parish register only 120 metres to the southwest (register number 141104-2). This demonstrates that round barrows were indeed erected on Assenbakke Hill. As this only partly preserved barrow from the parish register is not dated, there is unfortunately no demonstrable relation between it and the construction revealed by geophysical measurements.

The 21 m diameter barrow on Assenbakke Hill does not necessarily date to the same time as the U-shaped structure at its centre; an extant, smaller barrow could have been enlarged at need with secondary burials. Nevertheless, the presence of the probable secondary burials suggests that the U-shaped structure was located inside a round barrow. It appears unlikely that a barrow was erected over a free standing structure (mortuary house) in order to place burials in tangential positions at its periphery.

The interpretation of the round structure(s) as being indicative of a (multiphase) grave mound whose central structure dates to the TRB Culture indicates that the U-shaped structure represents some kind of grave construction rather than a mortuary house, as would be suggested by similarities with the Tustrup find. Obviously, the construction is closely related (or possibly even identical) to the Troelstrup-type graves known from Early Neolithic long barrows. As was already indicated by Becker (1996, 332ff.), there seems to have been a distinct relation between the Troelstrup graves and the mortuary houses which appear to have had identical constructions (at least in part). For example, the Troelstrup grave inside the Rustrup long barrow (Fig. 45) has a posthole in the middle of the open gable. Its construction appears, therefore, to be identical to that of the three mortuary houses from Tustrup, Søndermølle III and Herrup XLIII (Fig. 46). Furthermore, many Troelstrup-type graves demonstrate constructions involving stones. The earliest such grave from Hejring (Madsen 1979, 303ff.) includes a stone which measures 1.4 m in size. This is a good parallel, then, to the construction of the mortuary house at Tustrup. The Hejring grave is dated to the late Early Neolithic (or possibly to the Early to Middle Neolithic transition), while according to the abundant ceramics found inside, the Tustrup mortuary house dates to MN A I (Kjærum 1955). It appears possible, therefore, for a development of the U-shaped construction to be described. This began with Troelstrup-type graves in long barrows in the first part of the Early Neolithic (EN I). These continued to be built throughout the late part of the Early Neolithic (EN II). In this phase, very large stones appear to have been integrated in the construction itself. In the beginning of the Middle Neolithic, the U-shaped constructions were no longer integrated into grave mounds, but were instead erected as separate buildings (mortuary houses). As such, they were associated with mounds holding megalithic graves, such as was the case at Tustrup.

The observation of a U-shaped structure very similar to Troelstrup graves as well as a possible TRB mortuary house inside a round barrow is of particular interest. If the Assenbakke structure really belongs to the TRB Culture (which seems likely), it is possible to precisely date it. The construction of round barrows debuted in the late Early Neolithic (EN II), which would suggest that the structure under discussion has an early date indeed. Troelstrup graves have hitherto been described only in terms of their relationship to long barrows. Inclusion in a round barrow as well as the fact that a very large stone was possibly part of the construction confirm the idea of a late Troelstrup type grave, which can probably be dated to the Early to Middle Neolithic transition or to the earliest Middle Neolithic (MN A Ia), given that U-shaped structures from MN A Ib onwards no longer appear to have been integrated in grave mounds (after MN A Ib, they were constructed as free-standing mortuary houses instead). The presumed Assenbakke grave should, therefore, be approximately contemporaneous with the causewayed enclosure 30 m to the east, as indicated by the fence/palisade (yellow on Fig. 36 B) which both encloses the grave and concomitantly shows a distinct relation to the continuous ditch in front of the segmented ditch or row of large pits. Furthermore, it is of interest to note that this fence appears to be an integrated part of the construction of the southernmost of the two U-shaped structures associated with the continuous ditch (Fig. 44 A/B). This observation indicates that the U-shaped structures might also have a distinct link with rituals related to death and burial.

A number of very weak anomalies (straight and curved linear) can be observed in the area between the possible TRB grave structure inside a grave mound and the continuous ditch. However, these appear so faint that it is not possible to decide whether they were caused by humans or geological or biological activities.

Additionally, a number of structures can be observed in the westernmost of the two large compartments delimited by the possible fence/palisade (marked in yellow in Fig. 36 B). These consist of two distinct, rectangular anomalies (marked in black in Fig. 36 B) which appear to be related to each other, as they share the same southwest-northeast orientation. The southernmost of the two is the largest (it measures ca. 9 x 2 m). The northern measures 4 x 1 m und is interrupted in the middle. This latter structure appears to be situated in the centre of a rhombic structure measuring ca. 16 x 12 m. The pointed southern end of this structure ends exactly in the middle of the longer of the two rectangular features, thereby indicating the suspected relation between the two (Fig. 51).

No parallels to this peculiar construction are known. Nevertheless, two observations indicate that it might represent some kind of burial structure. The first is the fact that it is located inside the western-most of the two potential large fenced/palisaded compartments. This is an obvious parallel to the probable round barrow which was situated inside the other compartment. Furthermore, the larger of the two rectangular features is oriented exactly identically to the probable U-shaped grave construction inside the round barrow. Moreover, it shows a precise alignment with its northern side. Both, therefore, must be assumed to be more or less contemporaneous (which would allow the western structure to be

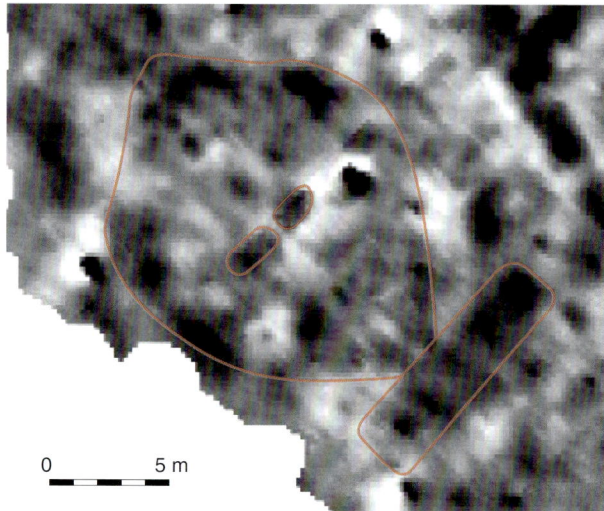

Fig. 51 | *58 Assenbakke. ±3 nT magnetogram showing two parallel, oblong rectangular features of different size and an almond-shaped row of anomalies. The smaller of the two oblong anomalies is interrupted in the middle and is situated in the centre of the pointed oval structure, while the pointed end of this structure ends exactly at the larger of the rectangular features. Archaeo-Geophysics, Institute of Geosciences, CAU Kiel.*

dated to the Early to Middle Neolithic transition). The alignment of the two structures possibly also indicates that the possible fence/palisade (marked in yellow in Fig. 36 B) was built after the construction of the two tombs, as the alignment would be difficult to achieve without inter-visibility.

Very distinct rows of anomalies are observable (which likely represent the presence of posts)(Fig. 52; grey marking on Fig 36 B) in the northwest corner of the area which was investigated geo-magnetically. These shape a ca. 11 m long and 5 m wide rectangular feature with rounded ends. Except in the southeast, where there is a gap, the anomalies show very close spacing. Two somewhat larger, stronger, oblong rectangular anomalies are oriented longitudinally on the central, longitudi-nal axis through the rectangular feature delimited by the probable postholes. The southernmost of these rectangular anomalies is difficult to recog-nize because it disturbs/is disturbed by one of the anomalies making up the possible grave structure described above (Fig. 51).

There cannot be much doubt that this structure reflects a house. Its architecture shows pronounced similarities to those of excavated Early Neolithic houses (see e.g. Steffens 2009, 41 Abb. 19 for a com-pilation of house plans from that period). In shape and dimensions it is almost identical to the late Early Neolithic house from Strandby Skovgrave in the Sarup area (Fig. 53; Andersen 1997, 92 Fig. 123). The roof-bearing posts in this and other Early Neolithic houses are not spaced regularly along the central axis, but appear clustered in pairs. While no roof bearing posts can be identified in the geo-physical measurements at Assenbakke, they are probably hidden inside the two larger anomalies found on the structure's central axis.

The house type is so specific in construction that the Assenbakke house can be dated to the Early Ne-olithic or possibly earliest Middle Neolithic. Such a date may also be indicated by its orientation, which is parallel to that of the enclosure ditches/pits. As the house overlays both the possible fence/palisade (marked in yellow in Fig. 36 B) and the probable grave construction (marked in black in the same illustration), both cannot have been functional for long periods of time. Furthermore, the grave in question probably did not include a barrow, as this would have hindered house construction.

Many more anomalies which are seemingly identical or almost identical to those that can be interpreted as wall posts in the house described here, can be identified on the geomagnetic plan. Some of these seem to form oblong structures with parallel sides and, therefore, could also very well represent the remains of houses. However, as these anomalies are spaced less densely than those in the house structure (and because no features resembling roof-bearing posts appear in these possible structures), they will not be discussed further here.

All structures which have been described hitherto are located to the southwest of the ditches/row of pits running across the hill and are, thus, located outside the enclosed area. Inside the enclosure, groups of pits of an unknown purpose (dark anomalies) can be recognized, as can several linear features. The latter may well be of modern date (remains of furrows from the last ploughing). The most obvious feature is a large (ca. 2.5 m diameter) round and comparatively strong positive anomaly that might represent a prehistoric pit. However, the strongest of all anomalies (which might well be caused by a piece of metal) lay just beside this structure. It might, therefore, be a modern disturbance. On the other hand, size and shape align very well with the round pit detected within the fenced area to the front of the enclosure (Fig. 48).

The area inside the enclosure generally appears darker and more mottled than the area outside. Of course, this might be coincidence (or, indeed, be explained by geological conditions). However, no additional evidence supports these conclusions. Another explanation (which would probably be more likely) would depend upon the existence of a cultural layer formed by ritual and/or settlement activities on the site. This would cover those structures which were potentially present, thereby rendering them invisible. A proper field survey was not possible due to grass cover. However, a few items were collected from molehills (Klassen, this volume, Fig. 58.8/9). These include a fragmented (and partly burnt) blade, two thumbnail-sized fragments of undecorated wall

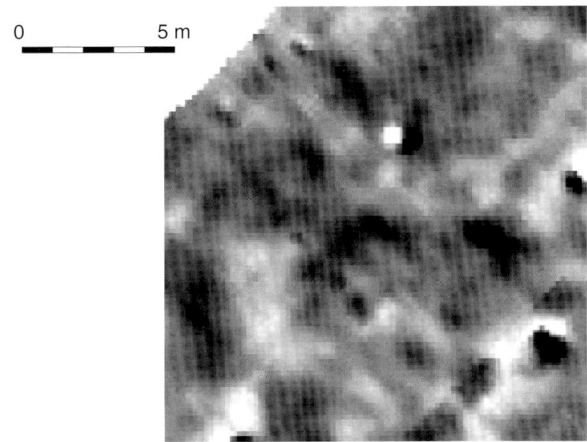

Fig. 52 | *58 Assenbakke. ±3 nT magnetogram showing wall posts as well as larger anomalies probably including the roof-bearing post of an Early Neolithic or early Middle Neolithic house (compare Fig. 36B). Archaeo-Geophysics, Institute of Geosciences, CAU Kiel.*

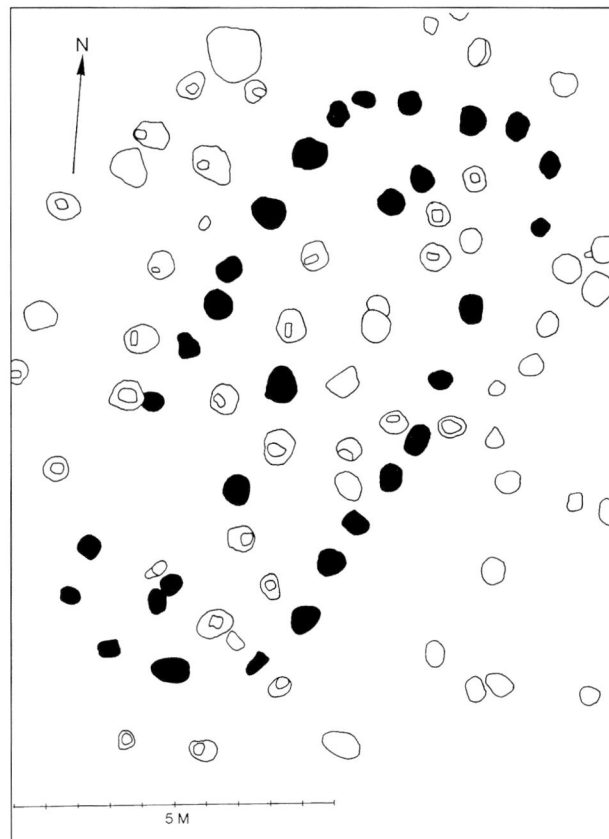

Fig. 53 | *Late Early Neolithic house from Strandby Skovgrave in the Sarup area which shows remarkable similarities to the construction visible in Fig. 52 (from Andersen 1997).*

shards as well as a flake, which B. Madsen (personal comment) believed was related to the production of a thick-butted flint axe. N.H. Andersen (personal comment) suggests that these shards are typical of the Middle Neolithic phase of the TRB in colour, fabric and consistency. While these shards could date to MN A I (and thus a phase in which causewayed enclosures were still constructed), axe production debris must postdate enclosure construction, thereby indicating later activities at the site. This can be understood as a hint towards the possible presence of a cultural layer inside the enclosed area.

The distance from the ditch/pit structure to the confluence of the two rivers that delimit the hill in the east is ca. 300 m. Geomagnetic survey has been carried out in the entire accessible area, which is very limited in size due to the topography of the hill. The entire area covered by geomagnetics measured ca. 250 m in length (of which ca. 190 m lay within the enclosure). However, the width of this zone varied greatly. The geophysically-surveyed area of the 110 m farthest away from the ditches and closest to the river confluence measured a scant 10 m or less across (not depicted in Fig. 36). It is very difficult to recognize patterns in such a narrow area, should they even be present. All that can be stated, therefore, is that a number of very strong anomalies are visible in the measurements from this part of the enclosure. However, whether they represent prehistoric, modern or geologic features cannot be decided. The lowest part of the promontory has an extremely uneven surface and lies close to the river confluence, where it is unfortunately covered by shrubbery. This area might have been destroyed by sand pitting and has not been surveyed geophysically. Older, local accounts describe the discovery of stone tools at Assenbakke which have since disappeared (Carlsen 1977, 19). It is possible that this description refers to the tip of the promontory at the river confluence, but this cannot be verified.

58 Assenbakke: Conclusion

Due to favourable conditions (homogenous meltwater sandy subsoil with very few stones), the geophysical measurements at site 58 Assenbakke

have provided a wealth of evidence that is clear enough, at least in some parts, to be interpreted without excavation. It can be stated that a causewayed enclosure with either two parallel ditches (one continuous and one segmented) or one continuous ditch and a parallel row of pits is present on the hill. Further structures (i.e. ditches, fences, palisades, pits, a round barrow with a possible Troelstrup-type central chamber, another possible tomb of hitherto unknown type without a barrow and one longhouse) have been identified with some probability. From these observations, it is clear that these structures belong to multiple phases (some of which can be dated to the Early and Middle Neolithic transition around 3300 BC). The intimate combination of an enclosure ditch with fences encircling different types of tombs outside the enclosed area is unique and has never been previously observed. It confirms, however, the widely-held belief that ritual activities conducted at TRB causewayed enclosures were at least partly connected to death and burial.

Remaining sites

Geophysical survey at the remaining 10 sites (7 Vejvad Bro, 8 Pognæs I, 24 Todbjerg Bakke, 28 Næsdrup, 41 Tustrup I-III, 63 Højbjerg V, 70 Skader N and 70 Skader SØ) did not produce any evidence for Neolithic enclosure ditches or other structures that can certainly be dated to the time of causewayed enclosures. There is evidence for destroyed barrows with at least partly preserved tombs at 70 Skader N and possibly also 70 Skader SØ, settlement pits at 24 Todbjerg Bakke and fireplaces/pits with pot boilers at 41 Tustrup II and 70 Skader SØ. According to their size and topographical position, the barrows can probably be dated to the Bronze Age (or possibly even to the Single Grave Culture), while the other structures cannot be dated. Sites 7 Vejvad Bro, 8 Pognæs I, 41 Tustrup III and 63 Højbjerg V were only investigated by GPR. Due to the distance between the profiles measured, minor structures such as those referred to for the other sites are unlikely to be discovered.

3 Evaluation

· ·

The discovery of one certain (58 Assenbakke), one probable (55 Fladstrup S) and two possible (53 Trustrup II, 79 Mårup N) Neolithic enclosures in course of the geophysical survey demonstrates that the method chosen for the campaign is generally effective. However, the investigation of a total of 20 different sites with very divergent types of soil and a total of three different methods (GPR, geomagnetics and then both techniques combined) has also demonstrated that using geophysics instead of conventional archaeological excavation is far from an easy method of finding the sites in question.

While it is possible to cover relatively large areas within a given amount of time and to obtain a result from said measurements which is comparatively easy to interpret within a short turnaround time, geomagnetics alone are not well suited to either detecting or exploring causewayed enclosures in South Scandinavia. There are two reasons for this. In the first instance, the generally highly heterogenic quarternary soils include large amounts of stones with magnetic properties and rarely produce any clear plan of the (often much fainter) anomalies due to prehistoric activity. Therefore, it is hardly a coincidence that the only case in which geomagnetics produced comparatively convincing evidence for the existence of a segmented ditch was at site 58 Assenbakke. Of all 20 locations investigated, this was the only one that was situated on a rather homogenous soil substrate (meltwater sand) without any naturally occurring disruptive elements like magnetic stones. For the second, there is abundant archaeological evidence

from excavated causewayed enclosures that the excavated ditches were (in many cases) quickly backfilled with the material originally excavated from them. As a result, no magnetic contrast exists between the infill of the ditches and the natural surroundings, rendering the ditches practically invisible to geomagnetic survey. In the actual campaign, this could be demonstrated at the site of Taastrup Kolindvej, at which an attempt to produce evidence for a known ditch was not successful. Another example includes site 55 Fladstrup S, where traces of a possible palisade trench were detected by geomagnetic survey, while a possible segmented ditch (or a row of large pits running parallel to the trench) remained invisible. They were only revealed by GPR. The fact that a row of segmented ditches or pits could be detected at site 58 Assenbakke is due only to the abundant amounts of material with magnetic properties (possibly large amounts of burnt clay or pottery) that were deposited in the ditches. According to the evidence from excavated enclosures, this was certainly not the case for all monuments of the type in question. It is likely that Assenbakke is an exception in this regard; enclosures with no or very few finds in the ditches are known (e.g. Starup Langelandsvej (Lützau Pedersen 2010; Lützau Pedersen/Witte 2012) or Esesfeld (Lornsen 1987; Kühn 1989)). At the same time, finds or stone packings in others showed distributions which were very uneven.

Ground penetrating radar was chosen as the main investigation technique for the current project because of the limitations of geomagnetics for detecting Neolithic enclosure ditches in South Scandinavian soils. The detection of certain, probable or possible ditches on four locations demonstrates that, in general, this technique is well suited for this purpose. However, things are not always as straightforward as would be ideal. Compared to geomagnetics, GPR is a very slow and complex technique that allows only comparatively small areas to be covered in a given amount of time. Therefore, in many cases, GPR is employed as a means of gleaning more data about structures whose presence is already known. When looking for causewayed enclosures (which in South Scandinavia have an enormous size range, measuring somewhere between ca. 1 and possibly more than 20 ha), it is necessary to investigate in comparatively long "slices" in order to be sure that any eventual monuments will be covered. In this project, these standard operating procedures led to the investigation of areas which were over 400 m long. In turn, this caused the survey team to restrict the widths of the investigation areas and to increase the spacing between individual radar profiles to comparatively large values. Unfortunately, both of these restrictions decreased the possibility of enclosure detection. Interpreting the results from width-restricted areas is almost always difficult. Moreover, large profile spacing can cause problems in interpolation when producing area renderings. However, the latter represent the easiest means of detecting enclosure ditches by far. Examining individual profiles is painstaking and time-consuming work, which furthermore demands an expertise which only very few archaeologists possess.

In the current project, the certain or possible enclosure ditches that were discovered were either completely invisible in the area renderings of the GPR measurements or were hardly detectable. At the Albersdorf Dieksknöll enclosure (unpublished investigations), GPR led to much better results. At the moment, the reasons for this difference remain unknown. However, the large profile spacing and potentially more heterogeneous soils and ditch fillings count among the most likely explanations.

In this project, the combination of geomagnetics and GPR proved the most successful method. Radar profiles provide an idea of the vertical ex-

tent of anomalies detected with geomagnetics, thereby enabling an evaluation of whether or not they might represent the sought-after ditches. Furthermore, as already described above for site 55 Fladstrup S, both techniques complement each other insofar as it is possible to detect different structures with different techniques (i.e. a palisade (even under the given soil conditions) versus the ditches).

As demonstrated by the results for site 1 Følle Vig, matters can be extremely complex, even if a combination of both techniques is used. Here, both geomagnetics and the area rendering of the GPR measurements produced evidence for the presence of two parallel structures exactly the size of Neolithic enclosure ditches. Only the close scrutiny of the individual radar profiles allowed for the structures to be identified as the result of geological processes.

In summary, it can be concluded that the detection of causewayed enclosures with geophysical prospection under South Scandinavian soil conditions is generally possible. However, a combination of geomagnetics and GPR measurements in comparatively large areas and with comparatively close spacing between individual radar profiles is necessary to ensure that enclosures are not overlooked. Furthermore, scrutiny of the individual radar profiles is necessary, as ditches may be invisible in GPR measurement area renderings. However, the results come from a process which is demanding in terms of both time and resources. While trial excavations may, therefore, seem the better alternative, this is not necessarily the case. Potential enclosure ditches may be recognized rather easily after the removal of topsoil. However, the documentation of profiles is necessary to corroborate the initial interpretation. This can also prove demanding with regard to both time and resources. Finally, if farmers are unwilling to allow archaeological excavation in their fields (a situation which was encountered several times over the course of this project), then, in many cases, geophysical survey may be the only way to move forward. Therefore, it is hoped that the experience gathered by this project may be used to the advantage of future explorations.

4 References

· ·

Andersen 1997
   N.H. Andersen, The Sarup Enclosures. Sarup vol. 1.
   Jutland Archaeological Society Publications XXXIII:1
   (Højbjerg 1997).

Becker 1996
   C.J. Becker, Tragtbægerkulturens mellemneolitiske
   kulthuse. In: K. Fabricius/C.J. Becker (eds.), Stendyngegrave og Kulthuse. Studier over Tragtbægerkulturen i
   Nord- og Vestjylland. Arkæologiske Studier XI (København 1996), 277-342.

Carlsen 1977
   S. Sloth Carlsen, Hornslet by og sogn (Hornslet 1977).

Fischer 1976
   Ch. Fischer, Tidlig-Neolitiske Anlæg Ved Rustrup. Kuml
   1975, 29-71.

Guldin 2011
   A. Guldin, Eine Straße erzählt Geschichte(n)...Ein neu
   entdecktes Erdwerk der Jungsteinzeit im Trassenbereich der geplanten Autobahn A 20 bei Bad Segeberg.
   Archäologische Nachrichten aus Schleswig-Holstein
   2011, 33-35.

F. Hage, Das trichterbecherzeitliche Grabenwerk von
   Büdelsdorf LA 1. In: Proceedings of the conference
   "Salzmünde – Regel oder Ausnahme?" Halle/Saale, 18.-
   20. Oktober 2012.

Hingst 1971
   H. Hingst, Ein befestigtes Dorf aus der Jungsteinzeit in
   Büdelsdorf. Archäologisches Korrespondenzblatt 1, 1971,
   191-194.

Kaul 1988
   F. Kaul, Neolitiske gravanlæg på Onsved Mark, Horns
   Herred, Sjælland. Aarbøger 1987, 27-83.

Kjærum 1955
   P. Kjærum, Tempelhus fra Stenalder. Kuml 1955, 7-35.

Kjærum 1967
   P. Kjærum, Mortuary Houses and Funeral Rites in Denmark. Antiquity 41, 1967, 190-196.

Klassen 2005
   L. Klassen, Refshøjgård. Et bemærkelsesværdigt grav-
   fund fra enkeltgravskulturen. KUML 2005, 17-59.

Kühn 1989
   H.J. Kühn, Esesfeld. In: Reallexikon zur Germanischen
   Altertumskunde Bd. 7 (Berlin 1989), 567-571.

Liversage 1981
   D. Liversage, Neolithic Monuments at Lindebjerg,
   Northwest Zealand. Acta Archaeologica 51, 1980, 85-152.

Liversage 1983
   D. Liversage, Træbyggede grave fra den ældste
   bondestenalder. Nationalmuseets Arbejdsmark 1983,
   5-16.

Lornsen 1987
   D. Lornsen, Ein karolingischer Stützpunkt im Norden.
   Archäologie in Deutschland 1987-1, 36-39.

Lorra 1996
   S. Lorra, Geophysikalische Prospektion und Model-
   lierung archäologischer Fundplätze in Schleswig-Holstein (Bonn 1996).

Lützau Pedersen 2010
   S. Lützau Pedersen, Skår af en helhed...In: H. Lyngstrøm
   (ed.), Brudstykker af en helhed. Specialer i forhistorisk
   arkæologi 2008 og 2009 fra Københavns Universitet
   (København 2010), 41-51.

Lützau Pedersen/Witte 2012
   S. Lützau Pedersen/F. Witte, Langelandsvej i Starup –
   en ceremoniel samlingsplads fra bondestenalderen. In:
   S.Å. Karup/L.S. Madsen/B.V. Rønne (eds.), Langs Fjord
   og dam. Lokalhistorie omkring Haderslev (Haderslev
   2012), 77-88.

Madsen/Fiedel 1988

B. Madsen/R. Fiedel, Pottery manufacture at a Neolithic Causewayed Enclosure near Hevringholm. Journal of Danish Archaeology 6, 1987, 78-86.

Madsen 1979

T. Madsen, Earthern Long barrows and Timber Structures: Aspects of the Early Neolithic Mortuary Practice in Denmark. Proceedings of the Prehistoric Society 45, 1979, 301-320.

Madsen 1988

T. Madsen, Causewayed Enclosures in South Scandinavia. In.: C. Burgess/P. Topping/C. Mordant/M. Maddison (eds.), Enclosures and defences in the Neolithic of Western Europe vol. 2 (Oxford 1988), 301-336.

Madsen 2009

T. Madsen, Aalstrup – en boplads og systemgravsanlæg ved Horsens Fjord. In: A. Schülke (red.), Plads og rum i tragtbægerkulturen. Bidrag fra Arbejdsmødet på Nationalmuseet, 22. september 2005. Nordiske Fortidsminder Serie C Bind 6 (København 2009), 105-138.

Madsen unpubl.

T. Madsen, Systemgravsanlæg fra yngre stenalder ved Horsens Fjord. Unpublished manuscript.

M. Mennenga/ M. Karle/ I. Brandt/ A.Kramer/ H. Jöns, Neolithisches Erdwerk oder Gelifluktionsloben? Archäologische und geowissenschaftliche Forschungen an einem geomagnetischen Befund aus Holzhausen, Ldkr. Oldenburg. Journal of Neolithic Archaeology 15, 2013, 1-11 [doi 10.12766/jna.2013.001].

Müller/Staude 2012

J. Müller/K. Staude, Typologien, Vertikalstratigraphien und absolutchronologische Daten: Zur Chronologie des nordwestmecklenburgischen Trichterbecherfundplatzes Triwalk. In: M. Hinz/J. Müller (eds.), Siedlung, Grabenwerk, Grosssteingrab. Studien zu Gesellschaft, Wirtschaft und Umwelt der Trichterbechergruppen im nördlichen Mitteleuropa. Schwerpunktprogramm 1400. Frühe Monumentalität und soziale Differenzierung Band 2 (Bonn 2012), 35-59.

Skaarup 1985

J. Skaarup, Yngre Stenalder på Øerne syd for Fyn. Meddelelser fra Langelands Museum (Rudkøbing 1985).

Steffens 2009

J. Steffens, Die neolithischen Fundplätze von Rastorf, Kr. Plön. Eine Fallstudie zur Trichterbecherkultur im nördlichen Mitteleuropa am Beispiel eines Siedlungsraums. Universitätsforschungen zur Prähistorischen Archäologie Band 170 (Bonn 2009).

Svane 1984

S. Svane, Danske Helligkilder og Lægedomskilder (København 1984).

Sørensen 1995a

P.Ø. Sørensen, Markildegård – mødested gennem årtusinder. In: J. Hertz (Hrsg.), 5000 år under motorvejen (København 1995), 32-33.

Sørensen 1995b

P.Ø. Sørensen, Markildegård. En tidligneolitisk samlingsplads. Kulturhistoriske Studier 1, 1995, 13-45.